Rev. JACOB E. MALLMANN

DEED OF JOHN BOOTH TO CAPT. NATHANIEL SYLVESTER.

This Indenture made the eight Day of May in the yeare one thousand Six hundred fiftie and six betweene John Booth late of Shelter Island formerly called Menhansack gent of the one part and Captaine Nathaniell Silvister of the same of the other part Witnesseth that whereas James ffaret Esqr Deputie for the Right honoble Willm Earle of starling was by purchase from Unkenchie Sachem of pammanuck & the said Menhansack possest of Menhansack aforesaid beinge a member of Long Island called pammanack as aforesaid or lying nere unto the same as by a deede of bargaine & sale from the said sachem Reference being thereunto had more largely doth and may appeare; And whereas the said James ffarrest by deede under hand & seale bearing date the eighteenth of May one Thousand Six hundred ffortie & one for the considerations therein expressed conveyed unto Stephen Goodyeare of Newhaven Merchant, his heires & assignes for ever the aforesaid Iland of Menhansack wth all the Rivers woods uplands meadowes harbours & creeks & all other the apptening rights liberties & conveniences what soever there unto in any wise belonginge & appertaynnge wth all that right title & interest wch the said Willm Earle of Starlinge his heires or assigns or the said James florrett & his heires or assignes then did or at any time from thenceforth should clayme or demand together wth the aforesaid originall grant as by the last mencned & recited grant relacon thereunto beinge had more fully may appeare. And whereas alsoe the said Stephen Goodyeare by his bill of sale from Robert Carmand did stand seised of one Island comonly called by the name of Roberts Iland scituate lyinge neere Menhansack Island aforesaid hee the said Robert carmeand haveinge formerly purchased the same of Iyonancam Sachem of pammanack aforesaid.

The said Stephen Goodyeare by his deede poll bearinge Date the Nynth day of June one Thousand six hundred fiftie & one for the consideracons therein expressed did sell convey & make over all his estate right title & interest of in & to both the said Ilands together wth all rights liberties ymunities & priviledges belonging or in any wise appurteininge to them or either of them & theire & either of theire appurtunce unto Captaine Thomas Middleton Thomas Rous Constant Silvister gents, & the said Nathaniell Silvister and theire heires & assignes for ever as by the last mencloned grant more fully may Appeare and whereas Yoko Sachem of the said Menhansack formerly called Unkenchie Actoncocween Captaine Yowoconogus Sonquoequahisick some of his cheife men by their deede beareinge Date the seaven & twentieth Day of December one Thousand six hundred fiiftie & two for such consideracon as therein is expressed Did alien assigne bargaine & sell unto the said Thomas Middleton Thomas Rous Constant Silvister & Nathaniell Silvister & their heires & assignes for ever All that their Ilands of Ahaquazuwamuck otherwise called Menhansack with all the rivers woods uplands medows harbours & creeks with all other apptennep rights liberties [Book 2, page 48.] and conveniences whatsoever thereunto in any wise belonginge & appurteyninge as by the same deede last mentioned may appeare. And whereas the said Thomas Middleton for valuable consideracon purchased of the said Thomas Rous all his fowerth part in & throughout bothe the said Ilands & ioynt stock thereuppon for & to the use of the abovesaid John Booth & his heires & Assigns for ever by virtue whereof hee the said John Booth became legally possest of the same, hee the said John Booth for & in consideracon of the some of Seaven hundred poundes sterlinge before the sealeinge & delivir here of in hand payd by the said Nathaniell Silvister to the said John Booth to full satisfaction accordinge to agreement in that behalfe hath granted bargained & sold & by these puts Doth fully & absolutely grant bargaine & sell unto the said Nathaniell Silvister & his heires & assignes All his estate right tytle interest clayme & Demand whatsoever of in & to one intire fowerth part of the said Ilands soe bargained & sold as abovesaid & all the Dwellinge houses barne outhouses ffences Orchard yards gardens earable land meadows marches, harbours creeks woods underwoods comons & comon of pasture proffitts priviledges ymunities advantages & easemts wth theire & every of theire appurtennces & stock of cattle in & upon the said Menhansack thence called Shelter Iland as abovesaid in as large & ample manner to all intents & [Book 2, page 48.] purpose as hee said John Booth mought or ought to heave inioyed the same as if these p'nts had not beene thereof had or made To have & to hold the said intire fowerth part if both the said Ilands stock of cattle & all other thabove granted premises with theire & every of theire appurennes unto the said Nathaniell Silvister his heires & assignes To the only proper use & behoofe of him the said Nathaniell Silvister & of his heires and assignes for ever. And he the said John Booth for himselfe his heires executors administrators & for every of them doth covenant promise grant & agree to & wth the said Nathaniell Silvister his heires & assignes & to & with every of them by these p'nts in manner & form followinge That is to say That hee the said John Booth his heires executors & administrators shall & will warrant all & singuler the prmises above spesified wth theire & every of theire apptenntnes unto the said Nathaniell Silvister his heires & assignes against him the said John Booth & his heires & assignes & all & every other person & persons whotsoever now haveinge or weh at any time hereafter shall or may have or clayme any lawfull estate right tytle or interest by from or under him them or any of them his heires or any of their estate or tytle. And finally that hee the said John Booth & his heires & assignes shall & will at any time hereafter within the space of Seaven yeares next ensuinge the Date hereof att the proper cost & charge of him the said Nathaniell Silvister his heires & assignes Requiring further assurance ratifie & confirme such legall conveyance under his or their hands & seales when provided and Demanded as aforesaid beinge comprised within the warrantie herein specified. In witness whereof the parties first above named have hereunto interchangeable sett theire hands & seales the Day and yeare first above written.

JOHN BOOTH.

Sealed subscribed and Delivered
in the prsence of

GILES SILVISTER   DAVID GARDINER
THOMAS MAPS   GEORGE V. MILLER his marke.

HISTORICAL PAPERS

ON

SHELTER ISLAND

AND ITS

PRESBYTERIAN CHURCH

WITH

GENEALOGICAL TABLES

OF THE DESCENDANTS OF

BRINLEY SYLVESTER, SAMUEL HOPKINS, JOEL AND JOHN BOWDITCH, SAMUEL HUDSON, JOHN HAVENS, GEORGE HAVENS, JONATHAN HAVENS, JOSEPH HAVENS, HENRY HAVENS, NOAH TUTHILL, THOMAS CONKLING, ABRAHAM PARKER, DANIEL BROWN, SYLVESTER L'HOMMEDIEU, REV. DANIEL AND LUCRETIA HALL, SYLVESTER AND E. SARAH DERING, JONATHAN AND ABIGAIL DOUG- LASS, EPHRAIM AND MEHITABLE KING, MARY MAYO, EUNICE CASE, ESTHER CASE, LODOWICK HAVENS, ELIZABETH HA- VENS, ABIGAIL SAW- YER AND ANNA BOISSEAU.

BY THE

REV. JACOB E. MALLMANN

PASTOR PRESBYTERIAN CHURCH, SHELTER ISLAND. N. Y.

Reprinted by the
SHELTER ISLAND PUBLIC LIBRARY
Commemorating Its 100th Anniversary
1885 — 1985

List of Illustrations.

Frontispiece.

DEDICATED

TO

THE PEOPLE

OF

THE PLACE AND CHURCH

WHOSE HISTORY IS HEREIN SET FORTH

WITH

THE ESTEEM AND AFFECTION

OF

THE AUTHOR.

SYNOPSIS OF CHAPTERS.

CHAPTER I.

A precious duty. The occasion of it. The benefit derived from it. Shelter Island and its Presbyterian Church. Re-dedication. Its suggestion. How past and present are linked together. Quotation from Rev. Dr. McKenzie. A pleasant study. Attractive personalities. A desire. Our earliest historical reference. Year of 1637. A memorable year. "Paumanach." The land of tribute. The Indians of Shelter Island. The mission of Waiandance. Shelter Island's great Sachem. A celebrated Indian Quartette. An important grant of land to the Earl of Stirling. His commissioner. A wise selection. "Mr. Farrett's Island." First disposal of Shelter Island. The purchaser. His relation to the New Haven colony. Seeks to have the Island bought by that colony. Is unsuccessful. Continues as owner for ten years. 1651. The purchase of Shelter Island. A strange payment. How the English revolution under Cromwell led to the settlement of Shelter Island. The Puritan Exodus. The early struggle between the English and the Dutch for supremacy in the New World, and its outcome. Sketches of the company of four Englishmen who purchased the Island from Mr. Goodyear. Our original settler and his bride. Their eventful journey. A disputed title. Its settlement. An interesting paper. An apparent discrepancy. How explained. Withdrawal of the Indians from Shelter Island. Strange dogs. Death of Manhansett's Grand Sachem. The burial of Shelter Island's great Chief. (Whooping Boys Hollow.) Cockenoe, a noted Manhansett Indian.

CHAPTER II.

Nathaniel Sylvester's visit to England. Its pleasant purpose. Date of his marriage. Return to America. Who were in the party. The first landing place. Resuming the journey. "The Golden Parrot." Coming of slaves to Shelter Island. Founding of the first white settlement. Its growth. Anxious parents. A surprising thing. Shelter Island the refuge of the oppressed. Whittier, the poet's, tribute. George Fox's visit. An interesting retraction. "Cotjewaminick." "Manhansick Ahaquazuwamuck." Its meaning. The origin of Shelter Island's name. Tracing the various owners of Shelter Island. The English expedition of 1664. Conquest of the New Netherlands. Gov. Nicoll's grant to Nathaniel Sylvester of manorial rights. The consideration. Another change in Colonial Government. The exaction of the Dutch. Some State papers. Nathaniel Sylvester now sole owner. His large family. A romantic courtship. Death of Mr. Sylvester. Another important advent. The coming of the Nicoll family to Shelter Island. Troublous times. A respectable inheritance. William Nicoll the first, or Speaker Nicoll. A noble career. Sketch of his life. Some delightful coincidences. Governor Cornbury's detestable act. Persecution of two Presbyterian Clergymen. Their acquital. Notable and praiseworthy services.

CHAPTER III.

George Havens' purchase. Its position. His ancestors. His family. An abstract. A pleasant surprise. The growth of the community. Twenty men of great importance. What they did. What moved them. Shelter Island's first Town Meeting. The original Town officers. Biographical sketches of our Town Fathers. A recapitulation. First effort toward erecting a "Meeting House." An ancient subscription paper. When was the first church erected on Shelter Island? What historians say. The probable year. The style of architecture. Its suggestion. Who preached in it. A sketch of his life. His relation to Brinley Sylvester. His relation to the community. An important paper. Its high sense of responsibility. Its author. First meeting of Presbytery on Shel-

purpose in it. A smiling Providence. The very man. The first formal call to the pastorate. Mr. Lord accepts. The beginning of a brilliant ministry. A happy occasion. A lofty motive. God's seal upon it. The most remarkable revival as yet. Another one. Still another more powerful than the others. Mr. Lord's sacred enthronement in the hearts of his people. A privilege. His tragic death. Its awful gloom upon the community. Widefelt sorrow. "Those dear children—have they been hurt!" "The Lord have mercy, I am going." A solemn and memorable day in August, 1861. Rev. Dr. Whitaker's high tribute. Mr. Lord's charming personality. Unusual powers. His remarkable services in Boston. Rev. Mr. Jones's conversion. A bright gem in his crown. The church enlarged. Belfry added. Mr. Lord's family.

CHAPTER VII.

Other ambassadors of the Most High. Mr. Lord's successor. Rev. Charles H. Holloway. His coming to Shelter Island. Installed as pastor. Length of service. A man of marked literary ability. Building the present parsonage. Various homes of the clergy who resided on Shelter Island. The first parsonage owned by the Society. Mr. Holloway's successor. Coming of the Rev. Thomas Harries. Unanimously called as pastor. Dully installed. Various clergy assisting at installation. Mr. Harries' long term of service. An able and efficient servant. Ministry blessed with revival power. Number of persons who united with the Church during ministry. Memory greatly cherished. Forced to resign through ill health. Resolutions of the Church concerning his services. Moved to Brooklyn. Date of death. Place of birth. His early life. Called to the ministry. Various fields of labor. A preacher of righteousness for fifty years. Succeeded by the Rev. Dr. A. P. Bissell. Date of coming. Relation to the Society. His ministry favored with a blessed quickening. A scholarly man. The receiver of various degrees from American and European institutions. Place of birth. Course of study. Varied labors. His present honorable position. Dr. Bissell followed by the Rev. Benjamin F. Parliman. Term of service on Shelter Island. Blessed with a remarkable revival. Largest in gathering in the history of the Church. A memorable occasion. Two consecrated young souls. Their holy zeal. An untimely death, but not in vain. Another speedy death. Bro. Parliman's ministry. Conspicuous also for the erection of our cozy chapel. His place of birth and present charge. His successor, the author. Unanimously called as pastor. Installation services and those who took part. His place of birth. Parentage. Early life. Called from a mercantile life into the gospel ministry. Course of preparation. Graduation and ordination. First service in the ministry. Second service as pastor of the Newtown Presbyterian Church. His great privilege. Called to Shelter Island. His saintly mother. A tribute of love and an ardent wish. Representatives of the Church in the gospel ministry. Those who are living. Rev. Charles E. Havens and Rev. Nelson B. Chester. Sketches of their earnest and useful careers. Our noble roll of Ruling Elders. Short biographies of each of those who have passed to their eternal reward. Other noted worthy members of the Church and congregation. Conclusion. Poem, "Hallowed Echoes."

INTRODUCTION.

As an introduction to this volume, permit these few words concerning its origin. In July, 1896, feeling the need of renovating our church building, a meeting was called to consider the best means for raising the required funds.

Two means were decided upon, namely, the holding of a lawn festival and the circulation of a subscription paper among the members and friends of the church. These were immediately put into execution, with the happy result that we were able to completely renovate the interior of our main audience room by the third Sunday of the following March, at a cost of about fifteen hundred dollars, all of which was paid for, with a small balance besides, which was turned to missionary purposes. With gratitude to God for His favor upon our work, we felt the need of rededicating our renovated building to His service, and prepared accordingly a series of services to begin with Sunday, March 21st, and to continue through the week until and including the following Sunday. On the morning of the first Sunday the renovated building was rededicated, the rededicatory sermon being preached by the Rev. Arthur P. Newman, pastor of the Presbyterian Church of Bridgehampton, L. I. We turned to him for this important service not only because he is an able Presbyter and beloved, but because he is a successor in the pastorate of the Bridgehampton Church of the Rev. Dr. Aaron Woolworth, who preached the first dedicatory sermon when the present building was completed in 1817. Brother Newman's text was the same as Dr. Woolworth's, namely, Ps. 123:6, "The Lord hath done great things for us, whereof we are glad." It was an inspiring discourse, and cheered us on in our renewed endeavor. For the evening service of that Sunday we prepared a historical paper, and it was that effort which has led us on to the present result of this volume. We found so much that was interesting and valuable in our research that we were able but to touch the beginning of things on this island in our first paper. We continued our research and presented another installment on the 4th of April following. Again we resumed our study. With increasing delight we found our effort growing both in interest and in proportions. As we came to the time when Shelter Island was fully organized into a town by the election of town officials, and so met the names of the twenty men who were the founders of our town, we felt, in view of so much that is creditable and delightful in the history of this place, and of their undying connection with it, that their names were worthy of a more permanent form than had yet been given to them. Thus one thing led on to another until now behold what we have endeavored to do—write a series of historical papers on Shelter Island and its Presbyterian Church, with genealogical tables of most of the founders of the town and church. We say "behold" for the reason that it was something which we least intended to do when we started out in the preparation of an historical paper, to be read in connection with the rededication of our church. We feel that such an effort, had we known it at the beginning, would have made us hesitate to the degree of great reluctance, if not to entire refusal. It is only through the uniform kindness which we have received from one and another that we have been able to accomplish this. Among the many who have thus cheered us on and aided us greatly are the following to whom this public courtesy is due, namely, Rev. Epher Whitaker, D. D., and N. Hubbard Cleveland, of Southold, L. I.; Richard C. Fosdick, of St. Paul, Minn.; Miss Katherine E. Havens, of Stamford, Conn.; Mrs. M. S. D. Lawrence, of Quiogue, L. I.; the Misses Horsfords, of Cambridge, Mass.; Mrs. Daniel Hudson, and Byron Griffing, of Shelter Island; Mrs. Sophar Woodhull, of Laurel, L. I.; Mrs. Stuart Terry, of Peconic, L. I.; Miss Elizabeth M. Brown, of New London, Conn.; Mrs. Mabel L. Huntington, of Rome, N. Y.; Mrs. Emma H. Thomson, of New York city; William Wallace Tooker, of Sag Harbor, L. I.; Rufus King, of Yonkers, N. Y., and George R. Howell, archivist of the State Library, Albany, N. Y.

To them as well as to all who have in any way encouraged and assisted the author he extends most hearty and lasting thanks.

And now the volume is to go forth into the hands of the public. What is sought by its issue is simply this: to help fix in memory and in history the things it records as having occurred upon this beautiful island.

Faithfully yours,

Shelter Island, N. Y.
March 15, 1899.

J. E. MALLMANN.

ERRATA.

Page 42, line 38, for *George and Mary Havens of Fisher's Island* substitute *Jonathan and Hannah (Brown) Havens.*

Page 43, line 40, omit *daughter of Jonathan and Eliza Brown, and grand-daughter of the first Nathaniel Sylvester.*

Page 80, in table and wherever subsequently the name *Doughlass* is so spelt; it should be *Douglass.*

Page 127, line 16, for *Edward* read *Edgar.*

Page 136, line 18, for *Annable* read *Annabal.*

SHELTER ISLAND
AND ITS PRESBYTERIAN CHURCH.

CHAPTER I.

"Remember the former things of old."
—PROPHET ISAIAH.

THESE words enjoin upon us a precious duty, the duty of retro-
spection, of calling up the past. It therefore has to do with
history. In complying then with this charge, "Remember the former things of old," we shall endeavor to set before you that part of
the past which bears upon the history of this fair isle of the sea, and of
this honored Church of God. In other words, I am moved to give
you an historical paper; the subject of which is, "Shelter Island
and its Presbyterian Church." I am moved to do this, because the
occasion of this morning, namely, the rededication of this renovated
building to the service and glory of God, gives a fitting opportunity
to do what our text exhorts us to do, that is, take a glance backward
and "remember the former things of old." For such an event em-
phasizes the past; is in itself a reminder of former days. A rededication suggests a first or former dedication. It thus turns the mind
backward, and the mind once thus turned, seems to take delight in
travelling over the whole line of sequence and antecedents. Besides this, as I remarked in my opening sentence, the duty enjoined
in our text is a most precious duty, precious not only in the sense of
being valuable, a truth in itself sufficient to incite one's powers to
such a duty, but precious in the sense of exciting within us peculiar
affections and encouragements; in showing us how vitally the present is connected with the past; the present being but the outgrowth
of the past, as the man is but the outgrowth or development of the
boy. By this study we shall see, that the opportunities of to-day
are the flowers of the buds of yesterday. That without a past there
could never have been a present, much less a future, all of which is
precious, doubly precious, since as Dr. McKenzie says in his introduction to Dr. Byington's recent work on "The Puritan," "no study
is more essential than that which makes us wise in our past that we

may be prudent in our future." By the help of our God, I want to aid you in catching this thread of development; this sequence and consequence in the history of this beautiful island with which the life of our church is so closely interwoven. I can say, that to me it has been both a pleasant and a profitable study. It has excited within me those peculiar affections and encouragements already referred to. I have been thrilled by the many things of interest, the hallowed memories, sacred associations, attractive personalities, etc., connected with this garden spot of earth. And as I was thus affected, I understood, at least in part, why a beautiful daughter of this island and church, should have been moved to write the sweet poem, "My Native Isle," that Mrs. Mary Gardiner Horsford did. The subject is worthy of every line of it. I too have wished that the feelings which have come to me, while pursuing my present purpose, might have been voiced and versed through a poet's skill. This much will do for an introduction.

Let me now proceed to give you what I have been able to gather together from one source and another. The earliest reference bearing upon this island that has come under my notice bears the date of 1637. That, my hearers, is just two hundred and sixty years ago. It is a memorable year in the history of our country. Memorable for the conquest that the New England settlers achieved under the leadership of Capt. John Mason and Capt. John Underhill over the fierce tribe of Indians known as the "Pequoits," who had so long harassed and terrorized them. But in that year, goaded on to extreme measures by the murders that the Pequoits had committed, those early settlers rose up in their might and exterminated that tribe of savages by the aid of fire, sword and gun. It is in connection with that very work of conquest on the hills of Mystic, Conn., that this first reference touching our island is made. Before mentioning it, however, it will help us in our understanding of it, to know that the Pequoits were the most powerful tribe of Indians east of the Hudson River. Their chief sachem, according to Goodkin's History, "held dominion over divers petty Sagamores, who were chiefs of the tribes on Long Island, over the Mohegans, and over the Sagamores of Quinipiac, yea, over all the people that dwelt on the Connecticut River, and over some of the most southerly inhabitants of the Nipmuck country about Quinebaug." Hence the tribes on Long Island, including Shelter Island, were subject to the Pequoits; and acknowledged it, by paying them tribute. Indeed, the earliest name of the eastern end of Long Island was "Paumanack," meaning land of tribute. Immediately upon the conquest of the Pequoits in 1637, the Indians that dwelt upon Shelter Island, together with those of Long Island, sent representatives to the Englishmen of New England, desiring to be considered their friends and subjects by the payment of a tribute to them. Winthrop, who was Governor of the Massachusetts colony at the time, says in his journal, that upon the reduction of the Pequoits by the English in 1637, "Sachems from Long Island came voluntarily and brought a tribute to us of twenty fathom of wampum each of them." This is also established by the following statement, made by Lion Gardiner, who afterwards became the owner of Gardiner's Island, but who at this time was commander of the fort at Saybrook, Conn. He says: "Three days after the fight with the Pequoits, came Waiandance to me, to see if we were angry with all Indians. I answered, No; but only with such as killed Englishmen. Then he inquired if he (Gardiner) would trade with them, that is the Indians, adding, 'I will go to my brother, for he is the great Sachem of Long Island, and if we may have peace, and trade with you, we will give you tribute as we did to the Pequoits.' Now, the brother of Waiandance, of whom he speaks as the 'great Sachem of Long Island,' was 'Yovowan,' the Sachem of the tribe of Indians who lived on this Island; and who were known as the Manhasset tribe of Indians. Yovowan's name appears upon the deed of Gardiner's Island, dated 1639. He was also called 'Yenicoe,' 'Yennicok,' or 'Yennicott,' and 'Youco,' or 'Yocow.' "

This then, is our starting point, and, as a starting point, it will serve our purpose very well, since it tells us a number of things. First of all it tells us who dwelt here, prior to the advent of the white man; not only to the shores of Shelter Island, but, you might say, to the whole of Long Island; for not a settlement had yet been made on the whole of Long Island save at its most westerly extremity, that of Brooklyn—that information being the familiar one of the red man. It tells us, too, what was the relation of the tribe of Shelter Island Indians to the other tribes of Long Island; namely, that of chief. And it further tells us what was the disposition of these Indians towards the English: namely, to have been a peaceable and friendly one. Besides this, I have been able to gather the following, concerning the Indians who lived in this region at that time; by which I mean all the territory east of an imaginary line

running across Long Island at Riverhead. This territory was possessed by four tribes of Indians, the first of which was the "Man-
hansetts," of this island, whose Sachem was called "Yoco." The
second was the "Montauks," living on the southern strip of Long
Island, east of Easthampton, and whose Sachem was called "Waiandance." The third was the "Shinnecocks," living in the region of
Canoe Place and eastward to perhaps Easthampton, the Sachem of
which was called, at this time, "Witaneymen" or "Weenaganim."
The fourth tribe was the "Corchaugs," who possessed the whole of
the northern strip of Long Island now comprised in the townships
of Southold and Riverhead, whose Sachem was called "Momoweta."

The Sachems or chiefs of these four tribes were brothers, the
oldest of them being "Yoco," the Shelter Island Sachem. He was
the Grand Sachem, and was called "the Sachem of Paumanack,"
meaning "the land of tribute" or "contributing," as the eastern end
of Long Island was termed; derived, as we have seen, from the fact
that the Indians in this region paid tribute, first to the Pequoits
and afterwards to the English of New England; Indian names, be
it remembered, being invariably descriptive of locality and char-
acteristics. Our Yoco, however, was not only Grand Sachem of
these four tribes, but over all the tribes of Long Island, at least as
far west as Hempstead. He thus had ten or fifteen Sachems under
him to whom his word was law; the four Sachems of the tribes in
this region having taken under their protection all the other tribes as
far west as the Rockaways in Hempstead town. This protectorship
was agreed upon and confirmed May 29, 1645, by Rockouw, the
great Sachem of Cotsjewaninck (Ahaquazuwamminck). See Colonial History of New York, Vol. XIV., p. 60, and Plymouth Colonial Records, Vol. IX., p. 18. Our Indian Chief Yoco was the
principal party in making the various conveyances of land to the
English, in the eastern half of Long Island, as the deeds of those
early days will show. It was from him that Lion Gardiner purchased Gardiner's Island, May 3, 1639. In the deed of conveyance
his name is given as "Yovowan" and his wife's as "Aswaw."

But we must return again to our starting point in the year of
1637, for that year is of importance to us, not only as bearing the
first reference to this island, but as the year in which the Earl of
Sterling, having acquired the whole of Long Island and its adjacent
islands, through a grant from the English colony of Plymouth, given
upon request of King Charles the First, commissioned one James

Farrett to be his agent in disposing of this territory, for which service he was given the privilege of selecting as his own ten thousand of the best acres of the whole domain. With this commission bearing date of April 20, 1637, a copy of which can be seen in the Town Clerk's office of Southampton, Mr. Farrett sailed early in 1638. Upon his arrival in the new world he examined the whole of the territory covered by his master's patent; and, as one has well said, "with unerring judgment chose Shelter Island together with its little neighbor, Robbins Island, as his portion," according to the terms of his commission. By virtue of this choice and grant our island was first known among the English as "Mr. Farrett's Island." It is thus referred to in the deed of Southampton drawn up in 1639 or '40, which can be seen in the Southampton Town Clerk's office and is known as "Mr. Farrett's patent." Mr. Farrett, however, did not make this island his home, but simply selected it for his own commercial purposes. He soon disposed of it to a Mr. Stephen Goodyear, a merchant of high standing in the New Haven Colony, who bought it in the early part of 1641, and who shortly after the purchase became Deputy Governor of the New Haven Colony. Some three or four months after purchasing it, Mr. Goodyear sought to dispose of this island to the New Haven Company, as the following entry, bearing date of August 30, 1641, will show, namely: "Mr. Goodyear propounded his purchase of Mr. Farrett's Island to the town, but it was not accepted." Not being able to dispose of the island, it continued in his possession for ten years, or until 1651, when he sold it to a company of four gentlemen by the names of Thomas Middleton, Thomas Rouse, Nathaniel Sylvester and Constant Sylvester. The amount that these gentlemen paid to Mr. Goodyear for Shelter Island was "sixteen hundred pounds of good merchantable muscovado sugar," or a cash equivalent of from fifty to one hundred dollars.

As the years during which Mr. Goodyear remained the owner of this island are memorable ones in the history of England, the mother country, and the memorable events of that decade bear directly on the settlement of this island by at least one of the four gentlemen who purchased it in 1651, we will tarry a moment to dwell upon this period. As you know, it is the period taken up by the English revolution under Oliver Cromwell, that political upheaval which dethroned King Charles the First and his son and successor, King Charles the Second. It is the period of the Long Parliament. It is also the period of the Westminster Assembly, that ecclesiastical body which formulated our Confession of Faith and Catechism. It is the period in which Puritanism and Presbyterianism, after a whole century of oppression, came to the top, and Prelacy and Episcopalianism went to the bottom. Because of this change in public affairs, the exodus of Independants and Puritans which had been going on for upward of twenty years, ceased. So far as the Puritans were concerned, it had lasted twelve years, during which some thirty thousand of these God-fearing men had come to America's shores. Now, however, the King had been checked in his persecution. A struggle for supremacy between the King and Parliament had arisen. He endeavored to dissolve his Parliament, but was thwarted and driven into exile; afterwards taken prisoner, tried, condemned and beheaded in 1649. Oliver Cromwell was victorious. The royalists were crushed; and in turn they now sought out an asylum where they might take refuge. Hearing of the success of the Pilgrims and Puritans in this land, they turned their attention to this new world, and so they, like the Pilgrims and Puritans before them, took refuge in America. "Had there been no Oliver Cromwell," says one writer concerning our island, "Had there been no Oliver Cromwell, Shelter Island would have had a very different, and doubtless much more prosaic history," for it was that overthrow of the King by Oliver Cromwell that led the first settlers upon this island to leave England and come to America's shores. You can see then how the events of those years in England influenced the history of Shelter Island.

Then, too, the events that happened on this side of the Atlantic during those years are important to us. For here, too, there was a struggle for supremacy, between the Dutch who had settled about the Hudson River, and the English who had settled in New England. Both nations contended that Long Island with its adjacent islands belonged to them, and sought to take possession. But as both could not possess it, they at last agreed to divide it between them; the Dutch to take the western half and the English the eastern half; the dividing line to extend across the island from the western boundary of Oyster Bay straight to the ocean. This agreement was signed September 19, 1650, and was sent to England and Holland for ratification. England, however, refused to recognize the claim of the Dutch, and the result was a war, in which the Dutch were badly defeated. Such was the condition of things when Mr.

Goodyear disposed of this island to the four gentlemen already named. This shows us that the causes which led to the settlement of this island were altogether different from those which led to the settlement of New England.

Concerning the four gentlemen who purchased this island, I have been able to gain the following: they were all engaged in the West India sugar industry, perhaps partners in the business. This doubtless accounts for the purchase price of the island being sixteen hundred pounds of good merchantable muscovado sugar, a commodity which Mr. Goodyear, being a merchant, could easily dispose of. As Mr. Thomas Middleton is mentioned first, he may have been the oldest. He is spoken of as Captain. Mr. Middleton did not make the island his home. The second of the four gentlemen, Mr. Thomas Rouse, is said to have hailed from the neighborhood of Southwold, England, from whence he went to Barbadoes, where he became a wealthy sugar planter and united with the Quakers. The remaining two of the company, Nathaniel and Constant Sylvester, were brothers, the sons of Giles Sylvester, of England. They too had gone to the Barbadoes, and there engaged in the sugar business. Before going, however, to Barbadoes, they emigrated with their father to Holland, where the elder Sylvester passed away. This fact coupled with others to be mentioned would indicate that the Sylvesters were not in sympathy with the Established Church. Upon the death of the father in Holland, the family, consisting of the widow, four sons, Nathaniel, Constant, Giles and Joshua, and two daughters, moved to Barbadoes, where Nathaniel and Constant at least became prominent merchants, the latter being in time a member of the Governor's Council, and remaining there until his death in 1671. A fifth son, Peter, remained in London.

Nathaniel Sylvester soon changed his place of abode to Shelter Island, being the only one of the four to do so. He was followed later on by two of his brothers, Giles and Joshua, Giles remaining but a few years, after which he returned to England, where he married and died, while Joshua, after living with his brother a few years moved to Southold. I am told that the name of the vessel in which Nathaniel Sylvester came from the West Indies to Shelter Island was the "Golden Parrot." This was in the year 1652, the year after the purchase of the island from Mr. Goodyear, hence the date of the first white settlement on Shelter Island.

Upon coming here to live Nathaniel Sylvester brought with

him a young lady in the person of Grissel Brinley, whom he had lately married. This young lady was the daughter of Thomas Brinley, Esq., of Datchett, in County Bucks, the parish so well known to the million of readers of Shakespeare's play, "The Merry Wives of Windsor." Her father was auditor under Charles the First and Charles the Second, also keeper of the accounts of the dower of Henrietta Maria, positions implying great friendship of the royal family. In the middle aisle of the church at Datchett, near Windsor, lies a tombstone after English fashion bearing this inscription: "Thomas Brinley, Esq., Auditor General of the Revenues of King Charles I and II. Born in the city of Exon, married Anna Wade of Pettsworth in Sussex, by whom he had five sons and seven daughters. He was born in 1591, died 1661. One of his daughters married Nathaniel Sylvester, Esq. Francis, one of his sons, accepted a grant of land for his father's services and went to Newport, R. I." Because of his friendly offices to the king Mr. Brinley's estate was confiscated and a warrant issued for his arrest. He managed, however, to escape to the continent, where he was obliged to live in exile until the death of Oliver Cromwell and the return of Charles the Second to England, when he also returned and died shortly after. During his exile his family had been scattered, his daughter Grissel, at the early age of sixteen, having married Nathaniel Sylvester in 1652. Upon their marriage the young couple went to America, touching on their way at Barbadoes, where they were handsomely entertained at the home of Mr. Constant Sylvester. After leaving Barbadoes, and while nearing the coast of New England, they were shipwrecked, losing much of their goods which they had brought with them for their new home on this island. It was indeed an eventful journey, a brave undertaking for the young wife of sixteen. At last they reached this place and began to lay the foundation of a family career that may well be the pride of every Shelter Islander.

They were not long on the island before the Indians disputed their title and made complaint to the Commissioners of the United Colonies of New England assembled at Hartford. One of their number, called Checkanoe, appearing before that body on the 2d of September, 1652, to enter a protest, as the following record will show: "Whereas we were informed by Checkanoe, an Indian of Menhansick Island, on behalf of the Indian inhabitants of said island, that they are disturbed in their possession by Captain Mid-

dleton and his agents, upon pretense of a purchase from Mr. Goodyear, of New Haven, who bought the same of one Mr. Forrett, a
Scotchman, and by vertue thereof, the said Indians are threatened
to be forced off the said island, and to seek an habitation where they
can get it; the said Indians deny that they sold the said island to
the said Forrett, and that the said Forrett was a poor man, not able
to purchase it, but the said Indians gave to said Forrett some part
of the said island, and marked it out by some trees; yet never that
themselves be deprived of their habitation there, and therefore they
desired that the Commissioners (they being their tributaries) to
see they have justice in the premises, the Commissioners therefore,
in regard the said Mr. Goodyear is not present, and at their court,
to hear the complaint of the said Indians, and to satisfy the said
Indians if they can, if not to certify the Commissioners at the
next meeting, the truth of the promises, that some further order
may be taken therein as shall be meet." As a result of this protest
Capt. Middleton and his associates had to purchase Shelter Island
a second time from the Indians, the deed of which second purchase
appears among the records of Easthampton bearing date of Dec.
27th, 1652. Also a confirmatory paper of this second purchase is on
file among the Southold Town records, and reads as follows:

"Wee whose names are here underneath subscribed doe hereby
testify and declare that Yokee, formerly Sachem of Manhansick
Ahaquatawamock, now called Shelter Island, did on the three
and twentieth of March, 1652, give full Possession unto Capt. Nathaniel Silvester and Ensigne John Booth of the aforesaid island
of Ahaquatawamock, with all that was belonging to the same. And
hee the said Yokee, delivered unto the aforesaid Captaine Nathaniel
Silvester and Ensign John Booth one turfe and twige in their hands
according to the usual custome of England; after which delivery and
full possession given, the said Yokee with all his Indians that were
formerly belonging to said island of Ahaquatawamock did freely
and willingly depart the aforesaid island, leaving the aforesaid Captaine Nathaniel Silvester and Ensigne Booth in full possession of
the same. Unto which we Witness our hands the date as above
being the 23d of March, 1652.

> "JOHN HERBERT of Southold.
> "CAPT. ROBERT SEELEY of New Haven.
> "DANIEL LANE of New London.
> "GILES SILVESTER."

From the date of this paper it would seem that this transaction took place early in the year of 1652, prior even to the protest lodged with the Commissioners at Hartford, in consequence of which this second purchase from the Indians had to be made. But we need to remember that at that time the year began either after the 10th or with the 25th of March and not on the 1st of January. This made the first part of March to belong to the old year and the latter part to the new year. Hence the date of the above paper, being before the 25th of March, namely, the 23d of March, it belonged to the old year as indicated, 1652, though according to our method it would be 1653. We do not know what was the purchase price of this second sale, but with this sale the Indians agreed among other things to put away all their dogs; these dogs, it may be interesting to know, are believed to have been young wolves which the Indians had caught and trained to do them service, but which in spite of their training continued to be very ravenous, a frequent source of annoyance to the white settlers.

You will notice that in the confirmatory paper just read, it is stated that shortly after the second conveyance the Indians left this Island. If so, they dispersed among the Montauks, Shinnecocks and Corchaugs. Perhaps they scattered because of their Sachem's death, for Yoco, their chief, and the supreme chief of all the Long Island Indians, passed away to the happy hunting grounds in 1653. At least, such is the opinion of certain writers. In the Chronicles of East Hampton, by the late David Gardiner, there is an interesting account of the funeral of our noted Chief Yoco, which reads as follows: "His remains were transported for burial from Shelter Island to Montaukett, where was the burying ground of the Indians. In removing the body, the bearers rested the bier by the side of the road leading from Sag Harbour to Easthampton, near the third mile stone, where a small excavation was made to designate the spot. From that time to the present, more than 190 years, this memorial has remained, as fresh, seemingly, as if but lately made. Neither leaf nor stone, nor any other thing, has been suffered to remain in it. The Montauk tribe, though reduced to a beggarly number of some ten or fifteen drunken and degraded beings, have retained to this day the memory of the event, and no one individual of them now passes the spot in his wanderings without removing whatever may have fallen into it. The place is to them holy ground, and the exhibition of this pious act does honor to the finest feelings of the human heart. The excavation is about 12 inches in depth and 18 inches in diameter, in the form of a mortar." As late as 1845 the Rev. N. S. Prime, author of "An Ecclesiastical History of Long Island," being acquainted with the foregoing fact, examined the place anew and found it in its original form and freshness as above described. When the turnpike between Sag Harbor and Easthampton was laid out about 1860, the spot was plowed up and the sacred memorial of over two hundred years' standing was obliterated. One of Sag Harbor's respected citizens told me this past week, while speaking of this matter, that she remembered very well the very spot, and had seen with her own eyes the reverence that was paid to it by the Indians. She spoke of an Indian in particular, known in Sag Harbor as Stephen Pharaoh, or Talkhouse, who would get down by that spot whenever he passed and clean it out reverently, following the custom of his forefathers. This Indian died in 1882. That spot was known as "Whooping Boys' Hollow," so called because the Indians who bore the body of Yoco gave a parting whoop as they resumed their funeral march.

Before leaving the aborigines of this place, so interesting in their history, I wish to call your attention to another member of the Manhansett tribe, brother-in-law to Yoco, the chief, an Indian who played a most important part in the various transactions between the English and the Indians, acting as their interpreter and notary public. He has already been mentioned in this paper, for he was the representative of the Manhansett tribe before the commissioners at Hartford, when the protest was made, upon the strength of which Captain Nathaniel Silvester and his associates had to pay a second time for this island. He is there called "Checkanoe, an Indian of Manhansick Island." Just a year ago Mr. William Wallace Tooker, of Sag Harbor, issued a work entitled "John Eliot's First Indian Interpreter, Cockenoe-de-Long Island," an exceedingly interesting essay on this very Indian of Shelter Island. I have read and re-read this book with great interest, and believe with Mr. Tooker that this "Checkanoe, an Indian of Manhansick Island," was the young Indian who was so helpful to John Eliot, the great apostle to the Indians, both in acquiring the Indian language, in preaching to the Indians, and also in his translation of the Bible into the Algonquian tongue, which was the language of the Indians. I have not the time to dwell longer upon this unique character, who for nearly fifty years was such an important factor in the transactions of the early settlers with the Indians. His memory, however, is honored to this day, his name being given to an island in Long Island Sound, near the mouth of the Saugatuck river, in 1652, called "Cockenoe's Island," and is so designated at the present time on the Coast Survey Chart of the United States. It will pay you to read this book, which can be had from our Public Library. One thing, however, I wish to state, namely: This young Indian's literary ability is an evidence to me that God has made of one blood all nations that dwell upon the face of the earth. For just as soon as this Indian's mind was brought in contact with intellectual training, it readily grasped the knowledge that was sought to be conveyed and responded quickly to every intellectual touch, though it were but the mind of a heathen, offspring of a heathen ancestry that perhaps had never known literary characters. To me it was a surprising evidence of the truth that God is the Creator of us all and that we are all, white and red man, the offspring of a common parent.

CHAPTER II.

Our first installment of this historical paper closed with the burial of the great Manhansett chief Yoco and a reference to another celebrated Manhansett Indian named "Cockenoe." We now turn from the red man to the white man, from the aborigines to the original settlers of this island.

It is said that when Mr. Goodyear, Deputy Governor of New Haven, sold this island, in 1651, to Messrs. Middleton, Rouse and the Sylvester brothers, at least one of the four gentlemen, Captain Nathaniel Sylvester, was on the island or had visited it at the time of the purchase. This gentleman, as we have seen, decided to make the island his home. To that end, in due time, he shipped at least one cargo of building material, together with other articles, sending with these goods a force of workmen, who were to prepare a habitation for his coming. He had gone to England, and there early the next year, 1652, married Grissel Brinley, with whom he came to Shelter Island to make it his home. With them there came to America, Francis Brinley, brother of Mrs. Nathaniel Sylvester, who afterwards, according to the inscription on the slab in the aisle of the church at Dachette, received a grant of land in Rhode Island. There was also in the party another bride, sister of Francis Brinley and Mrs. Sylvester, namely, Anne Brinley, who had married Gov. William Coddington of Rhode Island, and finally besides these Giles Sylvester. These first touched at Barbadoes, from whence they sailed in the "Golden Parrot" for Shelter Island, arriving about the middle of 1652; that is, Captain Nathaniel Sylvester and his wife, Giles and Joshua Sylvester, Giles' name, as you will remember, appearing as one of the witnesses of the confirmatory paper of the second purchase of the island by Captain Nathaniel Sylvester and Ensign John Booth from the Indians. Giles is also mentioned in a letter written by Nathaniel Sylvester to Gov. John Winthrop of Connecticut, who lived at that time on Fisher's Island, bearing date of October 10, 1654. Joshua's name appears among the names of the early settlers of Southold in Dr. Whitaker's history of that place. Captain Nathaniel Sylvester brought with him, besides his wife and brothers, several servants and some slaves from Barbadoes. These, with what workmen were upon the island at their coming, constituted the first white settlement. In the course of time the settlement was increased by natural results, Mr. and Mrs. Sylvester becoming the parents of a large family of children, the first of which came upon earth about the middle of August, 1654, for in another letter to Mr. Winthrop, of Fisher's Island, bearing date of September 8, 1655, advice is sought in behalf of this baby, who had become ill, in these pathetic words: "Our grief is great to see the child lay in ye sad condition and here quite out of ye way of help."

Captain Nathaniel Sylvester became in time the owner of the whole island. We shall have occasion later on to trace this development in the ownership of our island. Thus far we have had occasion to mention, since the sale in 1651, in turn, the years of 1652, 1653, 1654, 1655. We now come to another interesting period. It is the period of the persecution of the Quakers in New England, beginning in 1656 and lasting till 1661. To us it is a surprising thing, that in this land of ours, persons should have been persecuted even unto death for their religious belief. Yet such is the truth. Persecuted, tortured, scourged and branded with hot irons. Among those who suffered thus was John Rouse, son of Thomas Rouse, one of the four gentlemen who bought this island from Mr. Goodyear. This John Rouse had his ears cut off for being a Quaker. Others were banished from the New England colonies upon pain of death if they returned. Such was the treatment that the New England settlers meted out to the Quakers. The adherents of this sect were looked upon then in about the same light as we look upon anarchists now. It was during these troublous times that this island became indeed a Shelter Island, as many of these persecuted Quakers found an asylum here and were succored by Captain Nathaniel Sylvester and his family.

Notably among those who found such shelter were Lawrence and Cassandra Southwick, an aged couple. After having been put into prison, starved and flogged, they were banished from New England with the threat that if they ever returned they would be put to death. The threat was not needed, for shortly after they had been received upon this island, they died and are believed to have been buried in the ancient graveyard now on the Horsford estate. The poet Whittier, you know, has immortalized this act of sheltering these refugees by making it the subject of one of his finest poems. Mary Dyer, who was hung upon Boston Commons, also received succor for a time on this island. Likewise William Leddra and Joseph Nicholson and wife. These, together with others, were here kindly treated and cared for, their wounds dressed and healed, and their spirits cheered and strengthened.

Besides these, others of this sect who came from England, notably John Taylor, of York, and William Robinson and George Fox, the great apostle of the Friends or Quakers, touched first at Shelter Island or in time tarried here.

James Bowden, in his "History of the Society of Friends," says that except this island and the colony of Rhode Island, there was not at this time a nook in the colonies of North America on which a Friend could land without exposing himself to severe suffering and the ship-master to a heavy penalty. The possession, therefore, of this island, he adds, by one who loved the truth was a providential circumstance peculiarly favorable to Friends at this juncture, and not to be viewed as one of mere chance.

From all this it has been claimed by one and another that Nathaniel Sylvester and his family were Quakers or Friends. Dr. Charles Evans, author of "Friends in the 17th Century," says that "he either became a Friend at the time he purchased the island, or he was convinced of the principles of the Friends soon after he obtained possession of it. Here the weary exiles, on account of religion, always found a home and a heart to receive, to succor and refresh them, so that the kindness and liberality of Nathaniel Sylvester were widely known and highly appreciated by Friends in America and Great Britain."

James Bowden in his work, to which reference has already been made, says of Nathaniel Sylvester that when he joined in religious professions with Friends, we are uninformed; but as early as the third month of 1659 he is referred to as one who had adopted our principles." This is also the opinion of his descendants, who live upon the estate to-day. Both Bowden and Evans think that these friendly acts of succor and refuge, which the proprietor of this island extended to the persecuted Quakers, gave to this island its present name of Shelter Island. As we shall have occasion to speak of the names given to this island at various times and their origin presently, we shall let this claim stand until then.

There is an interesting paper among the records of Southold, bearing date of the 28th of the eleventh month of 1657, the origin of which is perhaps connected with the persecution of the Quakers. This persecution led the writer to express himself rather strongly, which he afterwards regrets and retracts, as the paper will show.

It is signed by Giles Sylvester, and reads as follows: "Whereas, I am accused to say that all the ministers in New England were worse than witches, I owne I said soe, for which I am heartily sorrowfull, and owne to bee very inconsiderately spoken and to my folly and wickedness in it, and hope the Lord shall guide my wayes and words to be more circumspect and like to himselfe. Then the parties that heard them finding themselves grieved, I told them that I meane noe other than those that were formall and not spirituall, such was my meaning, though not expressed till exception was made; therefore, I say, as I sayed, it is very evill in me or in any man to say any such thing, for we ought not to speak evill of any man."

28th of the 11m., 1657.   GILES SYLVESTER.

Before leaving the Quakers it is worthy of record that George Fox, the founder of this sect, twice visited this island and was entertained by the Sylvesters. The Rev. Mr. Fox, in his journal of 1672, speaks of his visits to this island, and of his preaching to the Indians and the people, who were deeply impressed by what he said unto them.

And now let me refer briefly to the various names that have been given to this island. The first is Cotjewaminick, which appears upon a deed given to Sir Gardiner by Yoco, the Manhansick chief. It was also called by the Indians "Manhansick Ahaquashuwornock" or "Manhansick Ahaquazuwamuck," which is said to mean "at or about the island sheltered their fishing place," or "their sheltered fishing place at or about the island." The first English name which it bore was Mr. Farrett's Island or Farrett's Island. After Mr. Farrett sold the island to Mr. Goodyear, it was also known as Goodyear's Island, and when Mr. Goodyear disposed of it to the four English gentlemen, one of whom selected it as his dwelling place, namely, Captain Nathaniel Sylvester, it was known as Sylvester Island, appearing as such upon record as late as 1674. However, long before this, it was also called Shelter Island, and this, too, before the Quaker persecution began. Indeed, it is so called in the confirmatory paper, bearing date March 23, 1652, namely, "Wee whose names are here underneath subscribed do hereby testify and declare that Yokee, formerly Sachem of Menhansick Ahaquazuwamuck, now called Shelter Island." Hence Bowden and Evans are wrong in claiming that because of the friendly acts of succor and refuge which the proprietor of this island extended to the persecuted Quakers, the island received its present name of Shelter Island.

It received this name upon the coming of the Sylvesters in 1652, without doubt, suggested and determined by the meaning of the Indian name, Manhansick Ahaquatuwamock, a sheltered island or Shelter Island. It is a goodly name, and long may it be significant, not only of a popular watering place, but of friendliness, love of mankind, liberty of conscience, nobility of character, and every grace that should adorn a Christian and God-fearing community.

Let us now resume the tracing out of the various owners of this island. These have thus far been:

The Manhansett tribe of Indians;

King Charles I.;

Earl of Stirling;

James Farrett;

Stephen Goodyear, and

Messrs. Middleton, Rouse, Nathaniel and Constant Sylvester.

Now another name is introduced as part owner, namely, that of Ensign John Booth, who with Captain Sylvester made the purchase from the Indians in December, 1652. It may be that this John Booth simply represented Messrs. Middleton, Rouse and Constant Sylvester, as there is another paper on record bearing the date of 1656, which implies that Thomas Rouse was still the owner of one-fourth of the island, that paper being a release of his quarter of the island to Thomas Middleton for John Booth. John Booth thus, in 1656, takes the place of Thomas Rouse, and the owners are Middleton, Booth, Nathaniel and Constant Sylvester. This ownership continued for a while, when John Booth withdrew by selling his portion to Nathaniel Sylvester for 700 pounds sterling. Nathaniel Sylvester soon after conveyed a portion of this newly acquired quarter to his brother Constant. This happened September 12, 1662. It was now in the hands of Thomas Middleton, Nathaniel Sylvester and Constant Sylvester, and continued so until 1673, when Captain Nathaniel Sylvester became sole proprietor of the island, as will be shortly seen from documents bearing that date. Let us, however, return again to old England, for there certain things have happened since last we referred to her, that, like previous events, affected this island during these years of Captain Nathaniel Sylvester's residence upon it and in the progress of which he became sole proprietor. Our last reference to the mother country closed with Oliver Cromwell's decisive victory over the royalist forces, by which he became ruler of all England, assuming the title, not of King, but of Protector. He continued thus until his death in 1658. We also had occasion to state the rejection on the part of Cromwell for England, of the proposed division of Long Island, between the Dutch and the English, according to the proposed treaty agreed upon at Hartford, in 1650, between the Dutch and English colonists, which treaty was sent to Holland and England for ratification. In rejecting this treaty, the claims of the Dutch were entirely ignored, the reason given being in these words, "of not knowing of any plantations of the Netherlands there, save a small number upon Hudson's River." This, as was then stated, resulted in war, in which the English were the victors. While this war lasted, which was for about two years, there were troublous times for our early settlers here. Upon Cromwell's death, September 3, 1658, his eldest son, Richard, was proclaimed his successor. But he was not the success his father was at ruling, and so the people once more desired the restoration of kingly rule, inviting Charles II. to return and assume the crown, which he did on the 29th of May, 1660.

He immediately issued orders to the New England colonies to cease their persecution of the Quakers, having been kept informed, while in exile, of their suffering, through the writings of Mrs. Sylvester to her father, who was always near the King in his flight. On the 12th of March, 1663, King Charles II. gave to his brother, the Duke of York, an extensive grant of territory in the New World, which included the Dutch settlement of New Amsterdam and the whole of Long Island. Immediately upon receiving this patent, the Duke of York sought to take possession by constituting Colonel Richard Nicholls Deputy Governor of the Colony, and commissioning him to take possession of this territory. The following year, or in 1664, he sailed with a fleet of man-of-warsmen, and in due time appeared in New York harbor. He immediately issued a summons to surrender, which he enforced without bloodshed, and thus the English became possessors of New Amsterdam, now called New York in honor of the Duke of York, and the whole of Long Island, including the adjacent islands. This necessitated a confirmation in the title of this island, which the Sylvester brothers sought and received from Governor Nicolls. They also received from Governor Nicholls a perpetual exemption from taxes and other public burdens upon the payment of £150, "one-half of which was to be in beef and the other half in pork."

These papers read as follows, the latter, namely, the release, bearing the earlier date of the two, and therefore given first: "Richard Nicoll, Esqr., Govenor, under his Royall Highnesse, James, Duke Yorke and Albany, &c., of all his territorys in America: To all to whome these presents shall come; whereas Nathl. Sylvester, of Shelter Island, merchant for and on behalfe of himselfe and of his brother Constant Sylvester, off Barbadoes, Esqr., hath of his own voluntary free will and good affection to this government, advanct and paid towards ye the support and maintenance thereof, the sum of 150 lbs., the receipt whereof I doe hereby acknowledge. Now know yea, that by vertue of commission and authority given unto me, by his Royall Highnesse, James Duke of Yorke, I, for and in consideration of the aforesaid sum of 150 lbs., and for other good causes and considerations me thereunto moving, doe hereby grant unto ye said Nathaniel and Constant Sylvester, and to their heires and assignes forever. That ye said island called Shelter Island is, and forever hereafter shall be, by these presents discharged, exonerated and acquitted from all taxes and rates, either civill or millitary, and from all trayning, setting forth and keeping any soulders, horses, arms, troopers or other warlike provisions other than what they shall voluntarily doe, for the defence of their said island, and this government in cases of foreigne invasion or disturbance by the natives. Given under my hand and seale in James fforte ye 25th day of May, in ye year Anno Dom. 1666.   "RICH. NICOLL." (L. S.)

The confirmation is as follows: " A tract of land lying and being in a certain bite, bay, or arm of the sea, which runneth between the lands of Easthampton, Southampton and Southold, in the East Riding of Yorkshire, upon Long Island, heretofore purchased from the Indians by James fforett, agent to William, Earl of Stirling, and which hath since come by several deeds, conveyances and grants to the said Constant Sylvester, of the island of Barbadoes, Esq., and Nathaniel Sylvester, then inhabiting and residing in Shelter Island aforesaid, merchant; and which said manor and place of itself, and forever have, hold, and enjoy like and equal privileges and immunities with any other town, infranchised place or manor, within this government; but not to extend to the protecting any traitor, malefactor, fugitive or debtor, flying unto the said island, to the damage of any person, or the obstruction of the laws. The same to be held, as of his majesty, the King of England, in free and common soccage, and by fealty only, yielding and paying yearly one

lamb, upon the first day of May, if the same shall be demanded."
This paper bears the date of May 31, 1666.

You will notice, please, that in this document Governor Nicoll
places Shelter Island on the same footing with "any other town, infranchised place or manor within this government." Thus, as early
as 1666 Shelter Island was designated as a town, though not fully
organized as such by the selection of proper officers until 1730.

For a few years after this the island continued in the peaceful
ownership of the Sylvester brothers and Thomas Middleton. But
only for a few years. For in 1673, seven years later, the Dutch suddenly recaptured New York and all their lost territory. This involved another change in the government and proprietorship of
this island. Governor Colve, now being the ruler of Long Island
and its adjacent islands, by a formal act, dated April 28, 1673, declared Constant Sylvester and Thomas Middleton enemies of the
government and confiscated their ownership and interests in Shelter
Island. Constant Sylvester in the meantime had died, leaving his
portion to his heirs, while Thomas Middleton was in England. To
enforce this confiscation, several Dutch men-of-war appeared off
Shelter Island, with the following result as set forth in the colonial
documents of that day, written in Dutch, the translation of which,
as here given, being an exact copy of what is on record at the State
Capitol in Albany.

"Nathaniel Sylvester delivered in council an extract from his
Privileges. He was commanded to produce the original, which he
said he left home—on which the protocol being examined it was
ascertained that the Heirs of his Brother, late Constant Sylvester,
with one cos. Middleton, residing in England, were co-partners of
the Island, named Shelter Island—whose share must be confiscated in behalf of the State.

"To which the aforesaid Nathaniel Sylvester replys that a considerable sum of money was due to him by the aforesaid heirs of
Constant Sylvester—but after many discussions *pro* and *con* it was
finally agreed with the aforesaid Nathaniel Sylvester that he, in
compensation for the action of said heirs of Constant Sylvester and
Thomas Middel-towne—as for the confirmation of his Privileges—
shall pay to the Government the sum of five hundred pounds in provision of this country."

Following is the confiscation of Shelter Island and its transfer
to Nathaniel Sylvester:

"We, Cornelis Evertse, Jun., and Jacob Benckes, Comm., with our Military Counsil of the Navy, in the service of Their High and Mighty Lords, the States General of the United Netherlands, and His Serene Highness the Lord Prince of Orange, greeting—

"Be it known that we, in virtue of our commission of aforesaid High and Mighty Lords are authorised and qualified to make war with our men-of-war and confided soldiers against the King of England and France and their subjects—publick enemies of our State and to inflict them all possible damages by water as well as on land, and if possible to take and conquer their possessions, and when conquered to confiscate these in behalf of the High and Mighty Lords, the States General of the United Netherlands and His Serene Highness the Lord Prince of Orange, and further to dispose of these to their best advantage, so is it that we in virtue of aforesaid commission endeavored to execute it—for this end which by force of arms lawfully and brought under the submission of our Masters Fort James, now William Hendrick named, with the city of New-Yorke, now named New Orange, situated on the Island Manhattans, with all the lands, places and territories dependant from it, so as those were lately possessed by the subjects and in virtue of the commission of His Majesty of England, under the patronage of the Duke of Yorke, among which lands and territories is discovered a certain island known by the name of Shelter Island, situated to the east of Long Island, now in possession of Nathaniel Silvester—to whom however it belongs in part with heirs of Constant Sylvester and cos. Thomas Middletowne, residing in England, the Barbadoes, being subjects of his Majesty of England and of course open enemies of our Lords and Masters aforesaid, to whom in no manner can be permitted the liberty granted to all our good subjects who cheerfully submitted themselves under our obedience—but that in conformity to the laws and customs of all nations the goods and effects of our aforesaid enemies ought to be confiscated; therefore, we, in virtue of our aforesaid commission, confiscated in behalf of the aforesaid High and Mighty Lords, the State's General of the united Netherlands and his Serene Highness the Lord Prince of Orange, after mature deliberation with our military tribunal, all the right, property, title and pretention which the aforesaid heirs of Constant Sylvester and Thomas Middletowne, or any other individual of our lawful enemies may have in aforesaid island named Shelter Island. So as we now confiscate all their

interest and property in behalf of our Lords and Masters—never-
theless well understood that in this confiscation it is not in————
well expressly, after mature deliberation excluded the rights and
property of aforesaid Nathaniel Sylvester, either in regard to said
Island or his other real and personal property—goods, effects, fur-
niture, negros or whatever else within this government may belong
to him as lawful property—while his submission to the allegeaince
of our aforesaid Lords and Masters, Their High and Mighty Lords
the State's General of the united Netherlands and his Serene Highness the Lord Prince of Orange entitles him with all our other
good subjects to an equal protection with him.

"In Fort William Hendrick on 28 of Aug., 1673.

"This day Nathaniel Sylvester, agreeable to the agreement con-
cluded on yesterday, delivered his bond at the Secretary's office of
Secretary Bayard, on which the following transfer was made to him
and confirmed:

"The noble, valiant Military Tribunal in behalf of the High and
Mighty Lords, the States General of the united Netherlands and
His Serene Highness the Lord Prince of Orange—commanding the
Squadron now at anchor in Hudson's River, in New Netherlands—
greeting be it known: Whereas we in virtue of our commission by a
preceeding Act for sufficient motive confiscated in behalf of our
Master the lands, house, and goods, negros and effects of what nature
these might be, which belonged to the heirs of the late Constant
Sylvester and cos. Thomas Middleton, situated on Shelter Island,
to the east of Long Island, and being property belonging to subjects of England and publick enemies of our State, so is it, that we
have deemed it proper and resolved to confiscate said house, lands
with all the goods, negros, and effects belonging to enemies of our
State as aforesaid in behalf of our Lords and Masters and to sell
these to their advantage—so as we then in conformity with this
resolution agreed with Nathaniel Sylvester a partner of aforesaid
Shelter Isl. to whom the aforesaid interest, right and title of the
aforesaid heirs of Con. Sylvester and Thomas Middleton was sold
by us for the sum of five hundred Pound Sterling, payable in conformity to certain bond (obligation), declaring therefore to the
aforesaid Nathaniel Sylvester, his heirs and posterity in considera-
ting of the aforesaid sum to transfer and dedicate, so as we are doing
by this all the interest, right and title which the aforesaid heirs of

Constant Sylvester and Thomas Middleton might possess in aforesaid Island and its dependences as aforesaid, to be taken possession of, used and retained in full and lawful property by aforesaid Nathaniel Sylvester, his heirs and posterity—and further to act with it so as they might think proper or should wish to act with any other parts of the patrimonial land or effects with a further confirmation of all advantages, immunities and privileges, which have been granted and consented to the Island by the former Governor—as namely, execution of all taxes, either Politick or Military—the Custom House duties and recognition excepted—except that it might please their High and Mighty Lords the States General to resolve on any new general tax Item—That they shall not be amenable before any inferior Courts of Justice, but shall be prosecuted before the Chief Magistrate, and farther, that they shall not be obliged to attend any training, nor maintain any soldiers, neither to supply any necessaries of war—except what they voluntarily shall contribute for the defence of the aforesaid Island and Governor in a time of danger against any foreign invasion or troubles with the savages, all which aforesaid liberties and immunities annexed to the possession of aforesaid Island are by this again confirmed to the aforesaid Sylvester and his posterity—besides the liberty of conscience and all other privileges and immunities as shall be granted to all other subjects under this Government.

"Done fort William Hendrick,
29 Aug., 1673."

Nathaniel Sylvester has now become sole owner of Shelter Island. Shortly after the Dutch were again forced to surrender the Colony of New York to the English, but before doing so the Dutch Governor sent a ship with fifty soldiers to Shelter Island to collect the amount of the bond that Nathaniel Sylvester had given.

In his will, dated 1679, Mr. Sylvester tells how these soldiers landed on Shelter Island, surrounded his house and compelled him to pay this amount of five hundred pounds sterling. The Sylvesters have now lived twenty-two eventful years on this island and become the sole proprietors. During these years the Lord has prospered them materially, numerically and spiritually. The sugar trade has proved to be very lucrative, and the two earnest souls of Nathaniel and Grissel Sylvester have been blessed with eleven children, six sons and five daughters, named Giles, Nathaniel, Constant, Peter,

Benjamin, Joshua, Grissel, Patience, Eliza, Ann and Mercy. Two of the daughters, Grissel and Patience, are said to have been very handsome women. Both of them had very romantic court-ships, Grissel at first being engaged to a wealthy young English-man named Latimer Sampson, chief proprietor of what is now known on Long Island as Loyd's Neck. Mr. Sampson, being seized with consumption, died before their marriage, leaving all his possessions by will to his intended, Miss Grissel Sylvester. This was in 1674. Two years later she married James Loyd, of Boston, and became the progenitor of a distinguished line of descendants.

Patience Sylvester became the wife of Benjamin L'Hommedieu, an exiled Huguenot. Their meeting and courtship is so sweetly told by Mrs. Martha J. Lamb, in her article entitled, "The Manor of Shelter Island," that I shall make use of her language in telling it, namely: "The marriage of Patience Sylvester, the sister of Mrs. Lloyd, was also an exceptionally romantic affair. Among the exiled Huguenots of the period was Benjamin L'Hommedieu, who settled in Southold. There being no church on Shelter Island, the Syl-vester family were accustomed to attend Sabbath worship in Southold. One pleasant Sunday morning soon after his arrival, L'Hommedieu was attracted by an extremely novel object moving over the sparkling waters of the bay. As it came nearer he ob-served two remarkably handsome young women in a barge with a canopy over it, and six negro slaves rowing it. The vision haunted him. He went to church that morning, and despite Puritanical customs, permitted his eyes to remain open during prayers. The story is so like every other love story that it is hardly necessary to say that his French heart was hopelessly lost before the preacher had reached 'Amen' in his benediction. The sequel was a beautiful wedding, and Miss Patience Sylvester was henceforward Mrs. L'Hommedieu." She and her husband were likewise blessed with a remarkable progeny. The third daughter, Eliza, married Jona-than Brown, of this island. Of the sons three died without issue, leaving their inheritance of the island to Giles, the eldest son, so that in time Giles became the owner of four-fifths of the island, the other fifth being inherited by the second son, Nathaniel, who at this time lived in Newport, R. I. And now we come to the obituary note of Capt. Nathaniel Sylvester, the first white settler on the island, and whose relation to the memory and place is of such lasting interest to us. This truly good and noble soul passed away

ANCIENT BURIAL PLOT

in 1680. What we have been able to learn of him justifies the high eulogy that is chiselled into the stone erected to his memory by the Horsford's in the old cemetery upon their estate, and which reads as follows: "To Nathaniel Sylvester, First Resident proprietor of the Manor of Shelter Island, under Grant of Charles II, A. D. 1666. An Englishman intrepid. Loyal to Duty, Faithful to friendship, The soul of integrity and Honor, Hospitable to Worth and Culture, Sheltering ever the persecuted for conscience sake."

We turn now to another family, which likewise became prominent in the history of this island. I refer to the Nicoll - family. The date of this family's appearance in America is 1664, and the occasion and person through whom the family came to the New World was Matthias Nicoll, brother of Col. Richard Nicoll, commander of the expedition sent out by the Duke of York to take possession of New Amsterdam, Long Island and other territory. Upon the capture of New York and the assumption of the Governorship of the Colony by Col. Richard Nicoll, Matthias Nicoll was appointed by his brother, the Governor, secretary of the colony and member of the Governor's council. He was also appointed a judge of the Court of Sessions, and in 1672 became the first Mayor of New York. He was then a very prominent and influential citizen in the early history of this country. He died in the latter part of 1687. One son at least survived him, named William, who it is presumed by the historian Thompson, was born in England, and came over when a boy with his father in 1664, as in 1683 he was appointed the first Clerk of Queens County, which position he held until 1688. He was highly educated, choosing the profession of law, in which he became very prominent, being one of the ablest lawyers of the New York bar. Col. Richard Nicoll was succeeded in the Governorship by Col. Lovelace in 1667. Col. Lovelace's term was brought to a sudden end by the appearance of the Dutch and their retaking of New York in 1673. While under the Dutch rule Anthony Color was Governor. Then came the restoration again to English rule, bringing with it the appointment of Edmund Andros as Governor. He continued until 1683, when Col. Thomas Dougan was commissioned by the Duke of York to act as Governor. During the term of Gov. Dougan Charles II died in 1685. His brother, the Duke of York, succeeded him, taking the title of James II. He immediately revoked the powers which had been given to former governors to call assemblies in which the people were to have a voice in the government of the colonies, and determined that the governors should rule solely by his direction and instructions. All the colonies of New England now came under the King's power, including New York. And over all these Sir Edmund Andros was appointed ruler or Governor, with authority to appoint deputy or lieutenant governors in each colony. Under this power Sir Edmund Andros appointed Francis Nicholson Governor of New York. This order of things continued until April, 1689, when news having reached America that James II had been driven from the throne by the English, and that William and Mary had been proclaimed rulers of England, the people of Massachusetts arose against Andros, seized him, and after a period of confinement sent him to England. This happened at Boston. At New York the people likewise arose, led by one Jacob Leisler, who seized the fort and had himself proclaimed Governor under the pretence of holding the government for William and Mary until their properly authorized representative appeared and took command. This Leisler was an adventurer, seeking more his own personal ends than those of his superiors. William Nicoll therefore opposed him, and because of this opposition, he with others who had the courage and honesty to take such a stand, were put in prison. They remained in confinement until the arrival of Gov. Sloughter, in March, 1691, when they were released. Leisler was brought to trial, and William Nicoll, whom he had imprisoned, was appointed one of the King's councillors to conduct the prosecution. The result of the trial was a verdict of high treason, for which Leisler suffered death. Mr. Nicoll was subsequently appointed by Gov. Sloughter a member of the Governor's Council. Four years later, in 1695, he was sent to England by the Colonial Assembly on an important mission, for which service the Assembly allowed him $1,000. In 1698 he again suffered imprisonment for a short time at the hands of the Earl of Bellamont, who had been appointed Governor and who was of the same character as Leisler. In 1701 he was elected a member of the Colonial Assembly from this county, but not being a resident of the county he was not allowed to take his seat. He then moved into the county, taking up his residence at Islip, where he owned an immense tract of land of 9,000 acres. He was again elected to the Assembly in 1702, and continued a member of that body until his death in 1723. For the most of the time he was Speaker of the House, until failing health forced him to resign this high office in 1718. Altogether he served in the Assembly twenty-one years, and as Speaker for sixteen years. He was a mighty man; fearless, patriotic and able, enjoying in unbounded measure the confidence and esteem of the people.

In early life he married the daughter of Jeremias and Maria Van Rensselaer, of New York. He left a number of children, one of whom became as distinguished as himself. In 1695 William Nicoll bought of Giles Sylvester one-fourth of his estate, equal to one-fifth of the whole of Shelter Island. Upon the death of Giles Sylvester in 1704, who died without issue, Mr. Nicoll inherited from Mr. Sylvester another fourth of his estate, which made him owner of two-fifths of Shelter Island. It was thus that the Nicoll's became proprietors of Sachem's Neck, which has remained in the family until this day. Mr. William Nicoll was buried at Islip, and over his grave was placed a monumental tablet with this inscription: "Sacred to the memory of William Nicolls. Hospitality, charity and good will toward his fellow man, were the marked characters of his life; and a perfectly resigned submission to the will of his Creator distinguished the sincere Christian at the hour of death, which took place Nov. 20, 1723. Ae 64."

Now, my friends, I have pursued the history of this island thus far, and the career of this William Nicoll with peculiar delight. And that because of the coincidences and connections that exist between my former charge at Newtown and my present charge here on Shelter Island. Both communities had their birth in the same year, namely, 1652, and both were settled by Englishmen of Puritan principles. Both experienced the vicissitudes of the period thus far covered of a little more than fifty years. But that which above all binds the two together is the following, which is particularly pleasing to me. The same year in which William Nicoll took his seat in the Assembly and became Speaker of the House, namely, 1702, Lord Cornbury was appointed Governor of the Colony of New York. This appointment he received as a reward from His Majesty King William for espousing his cause in the overthrow of King James II. Now this Lord Cornbury was a man most obnoxious to the people, according to several historians. "His sense of justice," says Thompson, "was as weak as his bigotry was uncontrollable. Nor was there a Governor of New York so universally detested or so deserving of abhorrence." When he became Governor, being an Episcopalian, he endeavored to force Episcopacy upon the people, confiscating their church property, annulling their ordinances and otherwise by bigotry, despotism, injustice and insatiable avarice oppressed and aroused the people. Among the congregations that suffered most was the Presbyterian Church at Newtown, my former beloved charge.

He seized that church and took possession of it. At Jamaica he did a despicable thing in taking the parsonage of the Presbyterian minister, Mr. Hubbard, which Mr. Hubbard tendered him during an epidemic in the City of New York, Mr. Hubbard thereby putting himself to considerable trouble and inconvenience for the Governor's accommodation. In return for his kindness he, Cornbury, when leaving the place, delivered it into the hands of Episcopal parties, at the same time directing the sheriff to confiscate the parsonage land and church building. He then appointed Mr. Urquhart as rector of Jamaica, Newtown and Flushing, and at about the same time issued an order prohibiting other ministers from preaching within the bounds of his province without special license from himself, an entirely illegal and unwarrantable usurpation of the rights of the people, since the Duke of York had publicly decreed the right to every town of selecting its own minister. In these and many other ways this tyrannical Governor made the years of his rule a time of great trial. And here I quote from a previous historical discourse delivered at Newtown as follows: "Before this oppression Rev. Robert Breck had to flee. Others who followed him in preaching here (that is in Newtown) were put in prison. In 1707 Rev. John Hampton and the Rev. Francis Makemie, who were on their way to New England from the South, stopped at New York. Upon invitation of the people of Newtown these two Presbyterian clergymen visited the place to preach to them. What happened to them can best be stated from the records known as the "Narrative of Imprisonment," dated Jan. 23d, 1707. "The Rev. John Hampton, an itinerant minister, preached on Sunday, Jan. 20th, in the Presbyterian Church, Newtown, without having first procured a license from Gov. Cornbury, and also gave notice that Rev. Francis Makemie would officiate there on Wednesday. But Gov. Cornbury, anticipating them, had them both arrested as soon as they reached Newtown, by Thomas Carsdale, High Sheriff of Queens County, and Stephen Luff, Under Sheriff. They were kept as prisoners on parole at the houses of two of the neighbors that night. The next day they were led off in a sort of triumph to Jamaica, seven or eight miles out of the direct road, and there kept all day and night. On the 23d, at noon, they got to the Fort in New York. After vexation and delays they were tried for dissenting doctrines to the great disturbance of the Church by law established. The jury, however, acquitted them, but the Governor took his spite against them in imposing a long bill of costs upon them, £83 7s 6d, over four hundred dollars, which they had to pay before they were released. Livingston, writing shortly after this injustice, wrote: "If any want information concerning suffering of other dissenters, both in persons, estates and religious liberties, I recommend them to the body of inhabitants of Jamaica and Newtown."

And here let me say that it gives me unspeakable pleasure to be able to state to you that in the progress of preparing this historical review I have discovered who was by his able plea so largely instrumental in gaining the verdict of acquittal for Revs. Hampton and Makemie. That person was William Nicoll, to whom Giles Sylvester bequeathed such a large portion of Shelter Island. For this notable service I here publicly salute his descendants and invoke God's special blessing to rest upon them; and in blessing them may God likewise bless you all.

CHAPTER III.

The second section of our historical paper on Shelter Island and the Presbyterian Church closed with a courteous acknowledgment of the signal service which William Nicoll rendered, in espousing the cause of Revs. Makemie and Hampton against Lord Cornbury's persecution, and brought our review down to the year 1704, the year in which the said William Nicoll came by inheritance into possession of Sachem's Neck.

We now have cause to mention another family who about that time came upon this island, the members and descendants of which became very prominent in the life of this place, and of great service to our church. I refer to the Havens family. About 1698 Nathaniel Sylvester the 2d sold 1,000 acres to Geo. Havens. After disposing of this land the said Nathaniel Sylvester, having married Miss Margaret Hobert, daughter of Isaiah Hobert, of East Hampton, moved with his family to Newport, R. I., where he engaged in business as a merchant. The 1,000 acres which Mr. Havens bought of Mr. Sylvester covered all the central portion of the island, including the ground now belonging to our church. Though most of this purchase has passed into other hands, eighty-five acres still remain in the Havens family, being owned at present by Henry P. Havens, who is of the seventh generation in continuous possession, a direct descendant of the first George Havens. This George Havens was the son of William Havens, a Welshman, who came to America about the year 1635 and settled on Conanticut Island, near Newport, R. I. Upon making the foregoing purchase, Mr. George Havens moved to this island with his family, which consisted of himself, a wife and seven chidren, three sons and four daughters. Besides these children there was another son named George, who did not move with the family to Shelter Island, but continued to live in Rhode Island, as the following abstract of a deed indicates, namely: "For good and sufficient reasons I have and bear to my loving son, George Havens, of Kingstowne in ye Narrowgansett Country, have given to my said son George Havens —————— for ever, —————— if my said son George shall goe and live on said land hereinafter granted, that is too say two hundred and fifty acres of my farm on Shelter Island.

Dated Oct., in ye 13 year of his Majy's reigne, Anno Domini, 1701.   GEORGE HAVENS."

It is presumed that this son did not improve this offer, as his will is dated from Fisher's Island, Oct. 31, 1726. Mr. George Havens, Sr., continued to reside here until his death, in 1706.

While visiting the ancient burying ground of New London, Conn., this past summer, in search of certain epitaphs, I accidentally came upon the grave and tombstone of Mr. George Havens, the first Havens of Shelter Island. I had searched and inquired for it in all directions, but without success. One can therefore imagine the surprise and pleasure that was mine when the above discovery was made. The grave can be easily found by those interested, as it is marked by a small brown stone headstone, with the following inscription upon it: "George Havens, who deceased Feb. 25, 1706, ae 53 y'rs."

His wife survived him and married again a Mr. Thomas Terry, of Southold. She lived to the great age of 93, passing away in 1747, and was buried in the south church yard, where a suitable stone with clear inscription stands to her memory.

And thus the community continued to grow, both from natural increase and accretion, until in 1730, there were twenty men, most of them heads of families, residing on this island. Their names were as follows: William Nicoll, John Havens, Samuel Hudson, George Havens, Elisha Payne, Joel Bowditch, Abraham Parker, Edward Havens, Samuel Vail, Thomas Conkling, Edward Gilman, Brinley Sylvester, Jonathan Havens, Joseph Havens, Noah Tuthill, Sylvester L'Hommedieu, Henry Havens, Samuel Hopkins, John Bowditch, Daniel Brown.

These men organized Shelter Island into a municipality of its own, and are therefore the Founders of the Town of Shelter Island. Up to this date, 1730, our Island met with Southold in its Annual Town Meetings. J. Wickham Case, compiler of the Southold Town Records, says that in its earliest stages Shelter Island associated itself with Southold, so far as to recognize their books as the proper place for the record of deeds and valuable papers, and to meet (but not to vote) with them at their Annual Town Meeting. Shelter Island, however, as we have already seen, was placed on the same footing "as any other town, unfranchised place or manor within this government," as early as May, 1666, by Governor Nicoll. In 1683, when the Province and its dependencies was divided off into Shires and

Counties in response to an act bearing the date of 2d Nov., 1683, Shelter Island was again officially set off as a Township of Suffolk County. Still it was not fully organized into a town by the selection of town officers; perhaps because there were so few male inhabitants of full age living at that time on our Island. But in 1730 it was commanded by an act of the General Assembly of the Province of New York, dated 12th of July, 1729, to choose its first public officials. This act was entitled as follows: "To ascertain the allowance to the Representatives for the county of Suffolk and for other purposes therein mentioned." In the fourth clause of which we read: "And be it further enacted by the same authority that from and after the Publication of this act, it shall and may be lawful for the Inhabitants of Shelter Island, in the County of Suffolk, and they are hereby impowered and required, annually on the first Tuesday in the month of April, to elect and chuse among them two Asessors and a Collector, to assess and collect such Taxes as shall be now or hereafter laid or imposed on them, and a Constable and Supervisor for keeping the Peace and auditing their Public Accounts at the Time the County of Suffolk shall do, by virtue of this Act."

In response to that commandatory act of the Colonial Assembly, it met the following year for the first time in a Town meeting of its own, as the following record, the first that appears upon our Town records, will show: "Suffolk County, Precinct of Shelter Island, 7th April, 1730. At a meeting held at the said place and time, the inhabitants of this said precinct proceeded and chose according to an act of the Gen'l Assembly made in the Province of New York in the third year of the Reign of King George the Second over Great Britain, &c., as followeth, viz.:

WILLIAM NICOLL, Supervisor.
JOHN HAVENS, } Assessors.
SAMUEL HUDSON, }
EDWARD HAVENS, Collector.
EDWARD GILMAN, Constable."

I have deemed it important to fix if possible the antecedents of these twenty men, who were the founders of our town, and have devoted a great deal of labor to this matter, with the following results. We will begin with:

1. WILLIAM NICOLL, who was chosen to be the first Supervisor of the Town. He was the second son of William Nicoll, and

is known as William Nicoll the second, also in history as Speaker Nicoll. He was born in 1702, and graduated with his brother, Benjamin, from Yale College in 1724. Like his father, he was educated for the bar, and became an eminent lawyer, continuing his legal practice after taking up his residence on Sachem's Neck, somewhere about 1726. His father died in 1723 and bequeathed him all of his estate located on this island. He then removed to this island, where he became the representative or foremost man of the Town, serving as Supervisor for ten years. In 1739 he was elected to the Colonial Assembly, like his father before him, and continued to serve until his death, in 1768, a period of twenty-nine years, during the last nine of which he served as Speaker of the House. Thus our first Supervisor was a very distinguished man, an eminent statesman, reflecting no small honor upon Shelter Island, which continued to be his home until his death, which came to him suddenly at a house on the Hempstead Plains Dec. 3d, 1768, as he was returning from his public duties. Thompson says: "He was a man of sound and discriminating mind, bold and fearless as a politician, and an unwavering asserter of the rights and liberties of the colony. In all public acts as a legislator he was diligent and attentive to every duty devolving upon him." And Wood says in his history "that he resembled his father in his political sentiments, and was a decided friend of the rights of the colonies. He is supposed to have concurred in the addresses to the King, lords and commons, respectively, which were adopted by the Assembly in 1764 and 1765, and which he signed as their Speaker. These addresses abound with patriotic sentiments. In that of 1764 they say that 'It would be the basest vassalage to be taxed at the pleasure of a fellow subject." In that of 1765 they say that "An assumption of power by the British Parliament to tax the colonies, if asquiesced in or admitted, would make them mere tenants at will of his majesty's subjects in Britain."

This William Nicoll, dying without issue, left his estate on this island to a son of his brother Benjamin, also named William Nicoll, commonly called "Clerk Nicoll," because he served as County Clerk for twenty-six years, being the last Clerk of the County under the Colonial Government. He not only succeeded his uncle in the possession of the Nicoll estate on Shelter Island, but was also chosen to succeed him in the Assembly, and continued to serve in that body until it was dissolved in consequence of the Revolution. This is indeed a remarkable thing, that three William Nicolls should succeed each other, not only as the owners of that estate, but as representatives in the Assembly, the first William Nicoll serving twenty-one years, and as Speaker for sixteen years of the time; the second William Nicoll for twenty-nine years, and as Speaker for nine years of the time, and the third William Nicoll for nine years, or until the Colonial Assembly was dissolved. Truly Shelter Island can refer with pride to her first Supervisor.

2. JOHN HAVENS, one of the first two assessors of our Town, was the fourth son of George Havens and Eleanor Thurston, and married a lady whose given name was Sarah. He was elected Town Assessor in 1730, 1734, 1739 and 1744, and Overseer of the Poor in 1735, 1737 and 1743. In 1744 he moved to the Town of Brookhaven with his family, where he became an extensive land-owner and the progenitor of a large family. He died in 1750.

3. SAMUEL HUDSON, the second of the first two Assessors of our Town, was the son of Jonathan and Sarah Hudson. His parents came from Lyme, Conn., to Shelter Island. Samuel Hudson married Grissel L'Hommedieu, daughter of Benjamin and Patience L'Hommedieu, and granddaughter of the original settler of this island, Mr. Nathaniel Sylvester. Mr. Hudson served as County Clerk of Suffolk County from 1722 to 1730, and in 1746, with his brother Jonathan, joined Capt. James Fanning's company of volunteers and served in the expedition against Canada. He died Oct. 12th, 1781.

4. EDWARD HAVENS was the son of George and Mary Havens, of Fisher's Island. His father was the eldest son of the George Havens who purchased the 1,000 acres of Nathaniel Sylvester. Very little is known of this Edward Havens, save that he married Desire Terry in 1724. He was the first Collector of the Town. His name appears but once on the Town records, namely, in 1730.

5. EDWARD GILMAN. Of this person we know the least of all the twenty. Though we have searched in every direction, nothing has been found concerning him. The name "Gilman" does not appear in this region on any record save our own. The will of Joseph Moore, of Southampton, dated March 21, 1723, speaks of a daughter-in-law, "Sarah Gilman."

6. GEORGE HAVENS was the son of George and Mary Havens, of Fisher's Island, and brother to Edward Havens. He married Mary ———— and had a son named George, to whom,

with his mother, letters of administration were granted in 1734, the father and husband having died the previous year.

7. ELISHA PAYNE was the son of Cornelius and Constant (Havens) Payne. His father in 1698 bought 200 acres of land on this island from Giles Sylvester. At that time he lived on Gardiner's Island, as a husbandman. Upon becoming a landowner here he moved to this island, for in a bond of Giles Sylvester, dated 27th June, 1699, he is spoken of as a "yeoman of Shelter Island." Elisha Payne served the Town as Constable and Collector in 1740 and 1748 respectively. In 1748 he married Deliverance Tuthill, and died in 1761, leaving a widow and several children. (See census list of 1771.)

8. SYLVESTER L'HOMMEDIEU was the son of Benjamin and Patience L'Hommedieu, of Southold. He married Elizabeth More, and was the father of Samuel L'Hommedieu, a distinguished citizen of Sag Harbor, at one time a member of the Assembly. Sylvester L'Hommedieu served as Collector and Constable in 1732. He died March 9, 1788, and lies buried in the church yard at Southold, L. I.

9. HENRY HAVENS was the oldest son of John and Sarah Havens. My information is derived from the will of John Havens, of Brookhaven, in which he bequeathed to his oldest son Henry 370 acres of land on Shelter Island. The date of the will is 1749. This Henry Havens married Abigail Tuthill, sister of Noah Tuthill, one of the Town fathers. His father, John Havens, as has been already mentioned, moved to Brookhaven about the year 1745. Henry Havens was a town officer for over ten years.

10. THOMAS CONKLING was the son of John and Sarah (Horton) Conkling, of Southold, L. I., a descendant of one of the first settlers of that ancient town. In 1732 he married Rachel Moore, by whom he had five children. His youngest son, Benjamin, was the gentleman who at his death in 1826 bequeathed a large sum of money to our church. Thomas Conkling served the Town in the various positions as Assessor, Constable and Overseer of the Poor, from 1739 to 1761. He died in 1782 at the ripe age of eighty-seven.

11. JONATHAN HAVENS was the second son of George and Eleanor (Thurston) Havens, born at Jamestown, R. I., Feb. 22, 1681. Upon attaining his majority his father gave him 200 acres of his property on this island. In 1707 he married Hannah Brown, daughter of Jonathan and Eliza Sylvester Brown, and grand-

daughter of the fist Nathaniel Sylvester, by whom he had ten children.   He was an Assessor of the Town for twelve years, Overseer of the Poor two years, and Supervisor one year.   Mr. Havens died Aug. 5th, 1748, in the sixty-eighth year of his age, and lies buried in the south church-yard.

12. JOSEPH HAVENS was the son of Jonathan Havens and Hannah Brown.   According to his tombstone in the south churchyard he was born in 1714.   He was twice married.   His first wife was Madam Mary Watts, a lady of refinement.   She died in 1768. In 1769 he married Jemima Glover, by whom he had one son. Father, mother and son all passed away in a few years.   Mr. Havens was Constable and Collector of the Town in 1737.   He afterwards moved into the town of Southampton, from whence his will is dated.

13. NOAH TUTHILL was the third son of Deacon Daniel and Mehetable (Horton) Tuthill, born in Orient, L. I.   The Tuthills and the Hortons were among the first settlers of Southold, and their descendants are legion.   Noah Tuthill married a relation by the name of Hannah Tuthill.   Many of his descendants live among us to-day.   He was a Town officer for several years.   He died in 1766, and is supposed to have been buried in the family burying ground upon the Tuthill homestead in Orient.

14. JOEL BOWDITCH.   Who he was the son of or whence he came we cannot positively tell.   But it is presumed that he came to Shelter Island from the region of Sag Harbor.   A Joel Bowditch is mentioned by Judge Hedges in his "History of East Hampton" as a resident of that Town from 1704 to 1718.   In 1718 an Abigail Bowditch married Nathan Fordham, of Sag Harbor.   She had a grandchild named "Joel."   Joel Bowditch, the subject of this sketch, married Ruth ———— and had several children.   He was the progenitor of the Bowditch's who live among us, and served as Town officer for many years, or until his death, in 1746.

15. JOHN BOWDITCH.   What is said about Joel Bowditch applies equally as well to this man, as far as his parentage is concerned.   It is presumed that he was the son of Joel Bowditch.   We cannot tell whether he ever married; it is rather doubtful that he ever did.   His name appears but once among the Town officers, under date of 1738, when he was chosen Constable and Collector.

16. SAMUEL HOPKINS was the son of William and Rebecca Hopkins, of this place, a direct and close descendant of Stephen Hopkins and Giles Hopkins, two of the immortal Mayflower pil-

grims, being the great-grandson of the former and grandson of the latter. According to the inscription upon his tombstone at Miller's Place, Samuel Hopkins was born on Shelter Island about 1710. His father moved to Shelter Island about 1680, and in time became a man of considerable property. In an account book of William Hopkins, the following names appear between the dates of 1680 and 1710: Gideon Youngs 1681, Samuel King 1682, John Conklin 1682, Thomas Young 1685, John Tuthill 1685, Caleb Curtis 1688, John Marlin, Feb. 19, 1689, Thomas Torrey 1691, John Carter 1695, Samuel Glover 1696, James Rogers 1700, Edward Bonnet 1701, Jonathan Hains 1703, Cornelius Pain 1705, Indian Able, Indian Squaw, John Hobson, Jonathan Brown, Jacob Conklin, Jonathan Hudson, Lion Gardner, Henry Tuthill, Richard Brown, Rebecca Crook, William King, Walter Brown, Martha Collins, John Knowling, Thomas Russell, Mr. Emmons, Mary Young (widow). Samuel Hopkins was a carpenter and mason. From 1743 until 1756 he lived at Wading River. In 1757 he bought property at Millers Place and moved there, and made it his home until his death, in 1790. In 1733 he served this Town as Constable and Collector.

17. ABRAHAM PARKER. We cannot tell definitely who were the parents of Abraham Parker. He is said to have been born in Yorkshire, England. Several Parkers lived on this island prior to the organization of the Town. As early as 1698 a Nathaniel Parker appears as a witness on the deed of Giles Sylvester to Cornelius Payne. In 1701 a Daniel Parke appeared in the same capacity on the deed of George Havens to Jonathan his son. Abraham Parker married probably twice. His first wife was Sarah Hudson, daughter of Jonathan and Sarah Hudson. His second wife was Mary Hudson, the widow of Jonathan Hudson, who was brother to his first wife. He served as Collector and Constable in 1731, as Assessor in 1736, and as Overseer of the Poor in 1738 and 1742. He died in March, 1768.

18. DANIEL BROWN was the son of Daniel and Frances (Watson) Brown, born Nov. 15, 1710. His great-grandparents, Chad and Elizabeth Brown, came from England in the ship "Martin," which arrived at Boston in July, 1638. The same year they moved to Providence, R. I., where Chad Browne was one of the original proprietors of the Providence purchase. In 1642 he was ordained the first settled pastor of the Baptist church. The children of Chad and Elizabeth Brown were sons John, James, Jeremiah,

Judah or Chad, and Daniel. Their daughters were Mary, Deborah and Phebe. Jeremiah, the third son, was twice married, his second wife being Mary (Havens) Cook, widow of Thomas Cook and daughter of the first William Havens. His son Daniel, who married Frances Watson, was the father of the subject of this sketch. Like his grandfather, Jeremiah Browne, our Daniel Brown married twice, his second wife likewise being named Mary Havens, whom he married Dec. 21, 1735, and by whom he had a large family. He was Supervisor of this Town for twenty years. In 1747 he enlisted in the First Battalion (foot) under Capt. James Fanning, to go against Canada. In 1775 and '76, at the outbreak of the American Revolution, he was a member of the First, Second and Third Provincial Congresses. These and other items show him to have been a man of great importance in the community; one highly esteemed and greatly trusted by his fellow men.

19. SAMUEL VAIL was the son of John and Grace Vail, according to Moore's Index. His grandfather was also named John Vail, and was the first person by the name in this country, coming from Wales. In 1723 Samuel Vail married Hannah Petty. He was also in time a Town officer, serving as Constable and Collector in 1735 and as Overseer of the Poor in 1741. About this date he moved with his family to Orange County and settled in what is called the West Division of Goshen. Many of his descendants are living in that region at the present time. No genealogical record of the descendants of Samuel Vail has been attempted by the writer of this book, as a genealogy of the "Vail" family is in existence, gathered together by the late Mr. Alfred Vail. It is deposited in the New York Genealogical and Biographical Library, and can there be consulted by those interested.

20. BRINLEY SYLVESTER was the son of the second Nathaniel Sylvester and Margaret Hobert, of Easthampton, L. I., where he was born Nov. 28th, 1694. He married Mary Burroughs, daughter of Thomas Burroughs, of New York, at Southold, Dec. 2d, 1718, the Rev. Geo. Phillips officiating. He lived for awhile at Newport, R. I., whither his father had moved, upon disposing of 1,000 acres to George Havens, and engaged in business as a merchant. This left the father with comparatively little land on this island. His possessions, however, were vastly increased upon the death of his brother Giles, in 1704, who bequeathed to him of his estate an amount of land equal in extent to two-fifths of the

island. This, together with what he had retained, made him owner of about one-half of Shelter Island. Upon the death of his father, Brinley Sylvester, having inherited the large family estate on this island, moved from Rhode Island to this place, where he resided till his death in 1752. Upon coming to this island Brinley Sylvester set about improving the property. The original manor house he displaced by a more imposing mansion, built in 1733. It is said that when he was building this new house, which was the largest structure of its kind in the three counties of Long Island, it occasioned much talk among his puritan friends, and the raising of it was made a great affair for those days, Mrs. Brinley Sylvester coming from the west end of Long Island to see it. Much of the interior work, such as the cornices, panels, wainscoting, and the like, was executed in England, while that which was serviceable of the prior homestead, such as the doors, sashes, tiles, etc., were worked into the new building. That house is, as you know, still standing and well preserved, though now over a hundred and sixty years old, and in some of its parts spans the whole period of the settlement of this island, that is, two hundred and forty-five years. In it Brinley Sylvester lived like a lord, far exceeding all his predecessors in the grandeur of his living. He presided over his rich and extensive estate with great dignity, being a gentleman of polished manners, scholarly in his tastes and generous to a fault. For more than twenty years he held public office in this town, sometimes discharging the duties of several offices together. During this time he was also one of the Associate Justices of the Court of General Sessions. He likewise acted as Surrogate of the County, the will of John Gardiner, the third proprietor of Gardiner's Island, being admitted to probate before him on the 1st of August, 1738. As yet there being no church on the island, he with his family attended divine service at Southold, going all the way by water in a handsome barge rowed by four well matched negroes. Mrs. Sylvester, his wife, used to wear on such occasions a silk velvet mantle inwrought with gold, and sometimes the venerable clergyman, Mr. Youngs, would say, "I am afraid you are proud of your fine barge and rich dress, Mrs. Sylvester." "Oh, no, sir," she answered. "If there is anything I am proud of it is the fine linen I make." Mr. Brinley Sylvester kept a chaplain in his family in the person of the Rev. William Adams. His family consisted of himself, his wife and two daughters, named Mary and

Margaret. Mr. Sylvester was a man of ardent piety, a communicant of the church at Southold. He did much for religion on this island, as will be seen later on, and at his death left £100 sterling for the maintenance of religion on this island, the interest of which was to be expended in the support of a regular orthodox Presbyterian minister. His funeral was conducted by the Rev. William Throop, pastor of the Southold church, the sermon then delivered being afterwards printed in Boston. His body was at first buried in the Sylvester burying ground, and afterwards moved to the private cemetery in the rear of this church, where an appropriate monument is erected to his memory. In the death of this distinguished Christian gentleman the name of Sylvester became extinct on this island.

To recapitulate what I have now written of the founders of the Town. It will be seen that six of the twenty men bore the name of Havens. These, as one would suppose, were related to each other. Two of them were sons and the rest grandsons of George and Eleanor Havens. They were all born in America, and two of them on this island. To these six men several of the remainder of our Town fathers were also related through marriage, namely, Noah Tuthill, Elisha Payne, William Nicoll and Daniel Brown. Of the rest Abraham Parker, Samuel Hudson, Sylvester L'Hommedieu and Brinley Sylvester were related to each other, the last three being grandsons of our first settler, Nathaniel Sylvester. Then too it is thought that Joel and John Bowditch were father and son, while of the remainder Samuel Hopkins bore the proud distinction of being a direct and close descendant of the Mayflower Pilgrims. The ancestors of these men who were our Town fathers were English, Welsh, and in one instance French. All, except in one instance, as far as is known were born in this country, and a number of them on this island. They were sturdy men, men of intelligence, and not a few of them, men of renown. They were lovers of liberty, of virtue, of piety, ready to respond to their country's call, full of enterprise, industry and zeal; men who in every respect were worthy to be the founders of our Town. We do well to cherish their memory and imitate their virtues.

Thus far our history has been solely occupied with the settlement of this place and its development into a Town, a period covering eighty years or more. Now we come to the time when there first appeared something like a religious society on this island, and then only in the outward or material form of a meeting house or church

THE MANOR HOUSE

building. The absence of such a place of worship for these many years was not because the inhabitants lacked religious life and convictions, for, as Dr. Woolworth said in his dedicatory sermon, "From the beginning of the settlement of this island there were not wanting such individuals among its inhabitants as feared God, professed His name and manifested a commendable concern and zeal for His sacred cause. The population was, however, for a long time so inconsiderable that no exertions were made for the introduction of regular public worship among themselves. Those who were seriously disposed attended the churches in the vicinity of the island. This was the state of things until the early part of the last century, when a decent house of public worship was erected." And thus it was that the building of a sanctuary was so long delayed. Now, however, steps were taken towards the erection of a house of God, a place of worship. This was in 1732, as the following copy of a subscription paper will show:

"We whos names are hereunto subscribed haveing the Interests of Our Common Lord at heart and being willing to Contribute for the promoting and Incouraging the Cause and Interest of Religion upon Shelter Island, and Considering ye Small number of the Inhabitants do Covenant and promise to pay or Cause to be paid the Several Sums Affixed to our names to Brinley Sylvester or Order at or before the first day of January next ensuing the Date hereof, for the erecting, building and Compleating a Meeting house for the publick worship of Almighty God and not otherwise. In witness whereof we have Set to our names to Geather with ye Several Sums annexed this 19th Day of August Anno Dom., 1732."

	£	s.	d.
Benj. L'Hommedieu, Jr..		10	
Benj. Woolsey..........	2		
Benj.Youngs, Esq.......		10	
David Piersen...........		10	
Sam'l Huntting..........		5	
Abraham Hallsey........		6	
Francis Pelletrau........	1	8	
Hugh Gelston...........		15	
Theophilus Howell......	2	6	
Matthew Howell........		5	
Josiah Peirson..........		6	
Job Peirson		6	
Jonath. Whitehead......	1		
Js. Smith..............		15	
Mrs. Stilwell...........		14	
Edm. ——————		10	

	£	s.	d.
Edward Huntting.......		10	
Nath'l. Huntting........	2		
David Howell..........		2	
Elnathan White.........		4	
John Davies............		1	6
Theophilus Howell......		5	
Theophilus Peirson......		7	
Edward Howell.........		6	
Eleazer Miller	1	8	
Thomas Robinson.......		14	
Miss Steer.............		5	
Samuel Hutchinson, Esq.		12	
James Sell.............		3	10
Josiah Tapping.........		6	
John Meray............		10	
John Ledyard..........		12	

Morel Lester.............	10	Suton Grant 1	4
Alex. Munn.............	5	Plat. Smith.............	14
Mat. Burnes............	10	Ephraim Hopkins, Jr.,	
S. Whitehead...........	10	work................	13
Tho. Chatfield..........	10	Received of Dr. Howell..	5

How soon the purpose was accomplished it is hard to tell, since different dates by different writers have been given. Thompson, in the first edition of his "History of Long Island," says: "The first church was erected by the Presbyterians in 1733, the funds for defraying the expenses of which were collected upon the island and the adjacent towns." In his second edition, however, published some four years later than the first, greatly enlarged and far more correct, he changes the foregoing statement and makes it read thus: "The first meeting house was completed in 1743, and remained until 1816, when the present church was erected on the same site." He precedes this statement with another, which goes to show that the latter date is the correct one. That foregoing statement is to the effect that in 1742 Jonathan Havens, Jr., gave a half acre of ground near the middle of the island for the setting of a meeting house and for a burying ground, and the next year, in 1743, he associated with others in erecting a building for religious worship, and to accomplish their benevolent design contributions were solicited in the neighboring towns, and even in the cities of New York and Boston. Dr. Prime, who wrote an ecclesiastical history of Long Island, and which appeared two years later than Dr. Thompson's second edition, the purpose of which, as its title would imply, brought him into closer touch with church history here and elsewhere, for which reason we may believe it the more reliable in ecclesiastical matters, confirms in general the second date of Thompson. He says: "It is difficult to ascertain the exact date of the erection of the first house of worship, but it is supposed to have been somewhere near the middle of the last century." He further adds that it was built under the supervision of Brinley Sylvester, who was the principal proprietor of the island. All this goes to confirm the latter date of 1743 as the correct one, being nearer to the middle of the last century than 1733, and further, being the year following the one in which the donor of the land, Jonathan Havens, Jr., set apart his gift for the purpose of "setting a meeting house and for a burying ground. And since this is the date, I am inclined to believe that the effort set on foot in 1732 was accomplished in 1743. Perhaps the completion of the purpose was hastened toward the end by the great revival which spread over the eastern end of Long Island during the decade of 1740, for it is well known that a great religious awakening makes a community sensible of its religious needs, which most generally finds its expression in the erection of a sanctuary or in the renovation of the same.

Regarding that original meeting house of Shelter Island, built over one hundred and fifty years ago, there are still those living in our midst who remember it with affection. Its shape was quadrangle, with a quadrangle roof, by which is meant that its dimensions were the same on all four sides, and that its roof slanted upward and inward from all four sides, meeting in the center, the whole perhaps surmounted by a cupola. It has been described as "a small square building with four roofs meeting at a point." Some of its furnishings, such as the pulpit, sounding board, stairs and a few of its pews were brought from the Rutgers street church in New York. The building, according to Rev. Mr. Lord, was mainly owned by the proprietors of the island, who held the sole and exclusive right of the pews. It stood on this very spot where we now worship until the beginning of this present structure, when it was moved to the eastward, where the parsonage now stands, being there used while the new house of worship was being erected, after which it was again moved to the westward, near the middle of the lot opposite the grist mill, where it served the purpose of a sheepfold until time and decay had completed its destruction. Rev. Mr. Lord, in his historical sermon of 1856, speaks of it thus: "The place where it stood and its whole aspect rises up before me in vivid recollection. It was a house every way worthy of Goldsmith's Deserted Village, always abating its dimensions. It was old and of narrow accommodations. A quadrate building with a quadrate roof. It was at the time of its erection probably equal to the wants of the people, but at the time of which I am speaking the tooth of time had made such inroads upon it that it gave unmistakable evidence of decay. It had one semblance at least to the sanctuary of which the Psalmist speaks: 'In it the sparrow hath found an house, and the swallow a nest for herself, where she may lay her young.' Among the first ministers to officiate in the building was the Rev. William Adams, who occupied the position of chaplain to Mr. Brinley Sylvester and his family, having his home in the Manor House. Mr. Adams, at the time of his coming to this island, was a young man of twenty-seven years of age, the son of the Rev. Eliphalet Adams, of Connecticut, and a graduate of Yale in 1730. Upon graduation—I quote from the Annals of the American Pulpit—he became a tutor for two years, after which a preacher of more than sixty years. He was never married nor ordained, as he declared he would not be "encumbered either with a wife or a parish." He first preached in the North Parish of New London, now known as Montville, and later in North Groton, now called Ledyard, after the withdrawal of the Rev. Ebenezer Punderson. In 1735 he declined a unanimous call from the latter parish. In January, 1737, he began to preach in Guilford, and continued there until he came to this island, presumably in the latter part of that year, and here he continued until Mr. Brinley Sylvester's death in 1752. The next year, in October of 1753, his father died. He was then invited to supply the vacant pulpit of New London, which he did until February, 1756. In 1758 he began to preach at Orient, and continued there until 1760. In that year Mr. Thomas Dering, having moved with his family upon the estate of his wife, Mrs. Mary Sylvester Dering, he resumed his residence in the manor house as private chaplain, and continued in this relation until the breaking out of the Revolution, when Mr. Dering had to take refuge with his family within the American lines. Altogether he is said to have labored here for more than thirty years. He was here when the great evangelist Whitefield visited the island in 1764. His latter years were spent in New London, chiefly in social enjoyment and domestic repose. He frequently rambled into the country on visits to the farmers belonging to the parish, and always made it a point on such occasions to communicate more or less religious instruction. He was short and stout, wore a white wig and a cocked hat, and usually walked about the streets dressed in a black study gown. He was a respectable preacher, but in nowise eminent. He has left one sermon in printed form, preached on the day of Thanksgiving for the success of the British arms in the reduction of Montreal and the Conquest of Canada in 1760. He died September 25th, 1798, in the 88th year of his age.

While occupying the position of chaplain to the Sylvesters, Rev. Mr. Adams likewise fulfilled the duties of preacher and pastor to the community. This is established by the following paper, which is in substance a call to Mr. Adams extended by the citizens of this place to become their pastor:

"We the Inhabitance of Shelter Island in Suffolk County, In the
    Province of New York, by the providence of God being In-

capable of a Constant attendance upon ye Publick worship of
God in any of the neighboring Towns, and being sensable that
it is our Incumbent duty to do to the utmost of our power to
promote and advance ye Kingdom and Interests of our Lord
Jesus Christ, as well as the salvation of our own souls do therefore out of a sense of duty and for the Incouragement of a minister to preach the Gospel amongst us do promise and Ingage
every person for himselve to pay or cause to be paid the several
sums of New York money affixed to our respective names here
under written to Mr. William Adams to preach the Gospel on
Shelter Island as in such case is customary and that for the
space of one year, in witness whereof we have set our hand this
first Day of April Anno Dom., 1746:

For one Year.				Per Annum		
£	s.	d.		£	s.	d.
Joel Bowditch	2		Henry Havens	4		
Abraham Parker, Jr.	8		Joseph Havens		10	
Abraham Parker,	1		William Havens Hogneck,	1		
Elisha Pain	1	10	John Havens	1		
Samuel Case		12	William Havens	1		
Thomas Conkling	10		Noah Tuttell	2		

This paper, drawn up evidently by the same hand that drew up
the subscription paper of 1732, is in the handwriting of Mr. Brinley
Sylvester, so that both papers can be said to have had Mr. Sylvester
as their author. This call to the Rev. William Adams for his pastoral services bears the date of the first day of April, Anno Dom.
1746." The following April the Presbytery of Long Island met by
commission in this place, as the following extract of the Presbytery's
minutes will show:

"Shelter Island, April 21, 1747. Met according to the order
and appointment of Presbytery in the preceding session. Messrs.
Nathaniel Mather, Silvanus White and Samuel Buell, to communicate to each other the Sentiments and Dispositions of their particular Churches relative to Presbyterian Government as exhibited
in the Plan of our Covenanted Union. . . . . Upon representation
then made it appeared hopefull that most of the Churches on the
east end of Long Island would comply with and submit to Presbyterian Government."

On June 11, 1766, the Presbytery of Long Island held a most
important meeting on this island. It was for the express purpose
of ordaining a young man to the ministry of our Lord and Saviour
Jesus Christ. This is such an important event in the life of this

people that I embody entirely so much of Presbytery's minutes as apply to it, and which is as follows

"Met according to adjournment at Shelter Island, June 11th, 1766. Present, Messrs. Prime, Buell, Lewis, Barker, Brown, Tallmadge, Goldsmith, Paine and Rosse. Absent, Messrs. Mills, Reeve and Occam. Correspondents were the Rev. Messrs. Charles Jeffry, Smith and Abner Brush. Elder, James Reeve. Mr. Tallmadge moderator and Mr. Rosse chosen clerk.

"P. P. S. Q. S. Ordered that the minutes of the last Sederunt be read. Mr. Elam Potter exhibited to the Presbytery Three several sermons, composed from Texts of Scripture before given. And the Presbytery proceeded to further examination. Adjourned to to-morrow morning 8 o'clock.

"P. P. S. Q. S. Ordered the minutes of the last Sederunt be read. Referred the examination of Mr. Potter, and proceeded so far as to obtain satisfaction. Appointed his ordination at one o'clock, P. M. Attended in the following order—Mr. Lewis introduced the solemnity by prayer, Mr. Buell preached from James v: 20, Mr. Brown took the engagements of the Candidate and his profession of Faith as exhibited in our public standards of Orthodoxy; Mr. Smith prayed at the laying on of Hands, Mr. Tallmadge gave the right hand of Fellowship, and Mr. Prime the charge. Mr. Potter pointed out the Psalm and pronounced the blessing."

And thus on this island was one ordained to the gospel ministry. It must have been a memorable occasion, one that is worthy of a permanent place in the history of this island and church.

So far as I know this has been the only instance of ordination on our island. May it, however, not stand alone very long, but be followed by many others of the sons of this church, several of whom are now preaching the blessed gospel of the Son of God. In many respects the Rev. Elam Potter proved himself a workman skilled in his high office. The year after his ordination he went on an extended missionary tour southward, and on his return he became pastor of the Congregational Church in Enfield, Conn., from 1769 to April, 1776. In November, 1792, he was settled over the Presbyterian Church at Southold, where he remained until his death, in 1794. His remains were buried in the church-yard of that place, and over his grave was raised a brownstone slab bearing the following epitaph:

"Beneath this dust lie the remains of the Rev. Elam Potter,

a faithful good minister of Jesus Christ. He died Jany 5th, age 52, in the year 1794:

> Forbear to weep my loving friends,
> Death is the voice, Jehovah sends
> To call us to our home.
> Through these dark shades from pain redrest
> Is the right path to endless rest
> Where joys immortal bloom."

Mr. Potter was the son of Daniel Potter, and was born in East Haven, Conn., Jan. 1st, 1741-42. He graduated from Yale College in 1765. In a printed sermon of his, bearing date of Enfield, Sept. 12, 1777, there appears this closing note, in the form of an address: "To the whole land. My Countrymen and Brethren, I beseech you for the Lord's sake, put away the Negro Slavery; abhor all jesting with God's holy Word; submit to the glorious Immanuel, and let us honor Him, that we may be happy in His favour." May all who read these gracious words heed them so far as they apply to present conditions.

In the biographical sketch of the Rev. William Adams mention was made of Mr. Thomas Dering moving with his family to Shelter Island for the purpose of settling upon the estate which his wife had inherited from her father, Mr. Brinley Sylvester. In the coming of this Mr. Dering to this place there came a gentleman who proved himself indeed a worthy successor of the Sylvesters.

Through the kindness of Mrs. Mary S. D. Lawrence, a great-grand-daughter of Mr. Thomas Dering, I am able to give the following biographical sketch of his life:

"Mr. Thomas Dering was the son of Henry and Elizabeth Dering. He was born at Boston, Mass., May 16th, 1720, also the birthplace of his father, who was a merchant in that city. Thomas Dering was educated for a merchant, and upon the death of his father, which occurred in 1750, he, with his only brother, Henry, became the successor of his father until he removed to this island. On March 9th, 1756, he married Mary Sylvester at Newport, R. I., whither Mr. Brinley Sylvester had moved temporarily, for the education of his daughters. They were married by the Rev. Ezra Styles, afterwards President of Yale College. In the year 1760, and after the birth of three children, Mr. Dering moved with his family to this place, occupying the Sylvester mansion and grounds, which his wife had inherited upon the death of her father. He now began the life of a farmer, becoming successfully engaged in the pursuit of the various branches of agriculture. He was a man who loved the society of refined and religious people, one who counted it a privilege to entertain them. In return he enjoyed in an eminent degree the respect and esteem of a large circle of friends; especially was he favored with the friendship and correspondence of distinguished clergymen, as appears from letters still in the possession of his descendants. Among these were the following: Rev. George Whitefield, under whose preaching in Boston it is supposed he was first awakened to a saving knowledge of the truth; Rev. Charles Jeffry, of Brookhaven; Rev. Ebenezer Prime, of Huntington, whose first wife was a Sylvester; Rev. Dr. Samuel Buel, of East Hampton; Rev. James Brown and Rev. Dr. Aaron Woolworth, of Bridgehampton; Rev. Mr. Barker, of Aquebogue, with whom he placed his son Sylvester at the age of ten years for the study of Latin, and the Rev. Enoch Huntington, of Middletown, Conn., near whom Mr. Dering lived during the period of the Revolution while Shelter Island was in the possession of the British. Indeed, the large mansion he occupied seems ever to have been the welcome home and favorite resort of clergymen of various denominations, not only during his residence, but also during that of his father-in-law before him, and of his son Sylvester Dering after him. Having passed from the active duties of a merchant to the retirement of a farmer, he had ample time in which to cultivate the fellowship of his numerous friends, among whom, being a man of piety, he prized the most that of clergymen. Besides this he maintained a numerous correspondence with men in various parts, most of them being residents of Boston, which about this time was the cradle of Liberty. These kept him well informed concerning the events of the day, and through this touch with the movements towards liberty his mind became strongly biased towards Whig principles and the independence of the colonies. Among these correspondents was a lady named Miss Hepzibah Small, whose letters were most graphically written. At the breaking out of the difficulties between the colonies and the mother country, Mr. Dering took a decided stand for Liberty. In May, 1776, he was chosen a delegate to the New York Provincial Convention, which assembled at White Plains in July of that year, and which unanimously adopted the Declaration of Independence as passed by the Provincial Congress at Philadelphia, July 4th, 1776, whereupon the convention assumed the title of the Representatives of the State of

New York. In this body Mr. Dering served forty days, or until the British, by the battle of Long Island, obtained possession thereof, when he asked for leave of absence to look after his family and remove them to a place of security. He decided to remove to Middletown, Conn., whither he went in September, 1776, and the convention adjourned before he was able to return. Mr. Dering was also elected a member of the convention to form a constitution for the State of New York in 1777, which convention met at Fishkill. It is believed, however, that, owing to the state of his health he did not attend. He remained in Middletown, Conn., until the restoration of peace, in 1783, when he returned to his estate on this island. He had four children, three sons, Henry S., who died in infancy, Sylvester and Henry Packer, and one daughter, named Elizabeth. On his return to Shelter Island he found that great depredations had been committed upon his woodlands while the island was in the possession of the British. It is estimated that 3,300 cords of wood had been cut and taken away by the order of Lord Percy and Gen. Clinton for the use of the troops and ships stationed at Rhode Island under their command. For this damage no remuneration was ever made. With the active aid of his sons he again resumed the pursuits of agriculture, but was not destined long to enjoy the blessings by which he was surrounded, as a protracted illness caused by paralysis terminated his mortal existence Sept. 26th, 1785, in the 65th year of his age. His remains lie buried in the private cemetery in the rear of the church."

Among the clergymen whose acquaintance he enjoyed was the mighty evangelist Whitefield. This renowned preacher of righteousness is said to have made Mr. Dering's home his headquarters while visiting the eastern towns of Long Island, in 1764. During his stay upon the island he preached twice to its inhabitants, once in 'the meeting house and once in the grove near the manor house. He so enjoyed Mr. Dering's hospitality and his visit while here that he wrote him two letters so full of high regard and affection that I herewith give them to you as they appear in Prime's history. The first was written at Greenport, then known as Stirling:

"My Dear Sir: Stirling, Feb. 3, 1764, At night.
"What a winding world we live in! I have been a good way round, and now am come within sight of your house again. Yes-

terday the boat and all was just gone.   To-day, I trust, some have
felt themselves undone—one, upon the road, we overtook, sweetly,
sorely wounded.   Grace! Grace!   I am now come to wait for sailing.   Will you send a poor, but willing pilgrim, the promised sea-
provisions.   God feed you and yours with bread that cometh down
from heaven.   A thousand thanks for all favours.   Add to my obligation by continuing to pray for, my dear friend,

"Yours in the never-failing Jesus,
"G. W."

The next was written after his arrival in Boston, and is as follows:

Boston, May 2, 1764.

"And is Shelter Island become a Patmos?   It seems so by my
dear friend's letter.   Blessed be God!   Blessed be God!   What cannot a God in Christ do for His people.   All things well.   Though he
leads them seemingly in a round about, yet it is a right way.   Though
they pass through the fire, yet it does not consume—though
through deep, yea, very deep waters, yet it does not overwhelm, so
as to destroy them.   And all these are only earnests of good things
to come.   How many assurances, that we shall, at last, be carried
through the Jordan of death, and safely landed in the Canaan of
everlasting rest.   Surely he cannot be far from them now.   Such
frequent shocks that your earthly tabernacle and mine meet with,
must necessarily loosen the silver cords that hold them up.   What
then?   We have a house not made with hands—eternal—in the
heavens.

"Though we cannot join in singing, we can in repeating

'By Thee, we shall
Break thro' them all
And sing the song of Moses.'

"Methinks I hear you say Amen!   Hallelujah—and why?   Because His mercy endureth forever.   I could enlarge, but must away
to my throne.   It is but seldom I can climb so high.   But an
infinitely condescending Jesus vouchsafes to smile upon my feeble
labours, here and elsewhere.   Who knows but I may ere long come
your way.   Perhaps the cloud may point towards Patmos.   Mr.
Wright will be glad.   He is better and sends most cordial respects.
My poor prayers constantly wait upon your whole self, Mr. Adams
and your rising offspring.

"In sure and certain hope, if we never meet in this world, of a glorious resurrection to eternal life, in that which is to come, I subscribe myself, very dear sir

"Your truly affec. sympathizing friend, and willing servant, in our common never failing Lord,

                                        "G. WHITEFIELD."

Of all this, connected with that prince of preachers, Shelter Island may be justly proud. Here, again, Newtown, my former beloved charge, grasps hands with Shelter Island, as Newtown was likewise honored with the presence and preaching of this celebrated evangelist. There, like here, he preached in a neighboring grove, to an immense audience, that was deeply moved by his message. Among those who were then converted was a young man by the name of Peter Fish, who afterwards became pastor of that very church. Something akin to this was the conversion of Samuel L'Hommedieu, Esq., of Sag Harbor, when he was a young man, in connection with Whitefield's preaching on this island. He often spoke of this with delight, and also of his having assisted in making a raft that conveyed the evangelist with his horse and carriage from Southold to Shelter Island.

Before leaving Mr. Thomas Dering it is worthy of note that his family claims to be one of the oldest, if not the oldest, Saxon family extant, whose history can be traced in a direct line back to Ethelward, King of Diera.   Originally the Derings were powerful leaders or petty kings of Diera, in Saxony, whence one of them, a warrior, came to England, and settled first in Lydd, in Romney, Marsh, Kent. One of the more remote ancestors, Dering Miles, appears as a witness to a deed by which King Ethelwuff conveyed certain lands to a church at Rochester, A. D. 880.   The American branch of the Dering family came to this country through the person of Henry Dering, Esq., of Croscome, by Bumister, near Dorchester, in Dorsetshire, England, who was born in August, 1639, and came to Boston, New England, about 1660.

Among other possessions Mr. Dering owned a number of slaves, one of whom, by the name of Cato, was once caught in his wine cellar imbibing. Mr. Dering had him immediately brought before him for punishment, and, in order to make his punishment as effective as possible, both on the guilty one and the rest of the slaves, had them all summoned, with all the whites whom he had in his employ, in the large servants' kitchen.   Among the other slaves was one named Comus, who was remarkable for his keenness of intellect as well as for his immense stature, he being six feet and six inches tall.   While the sin and punishment of Cato was being discussed, this giant of a slave rose up and asked permission to plead for Cato, and having received permission from his master, proceeded as follows: "Massa, you have pigs and you have corn, 'spose them pigs get in and eat some of that corn.   The pigs are yours, and is not the corn yours just the same, if the pigs have eaten it?   Now Cato is yours and the cider he drank was yours before, and is it not still yours after he has drank it?   I do not see why Cato should be punished."   Mr. Dering rose and said: "Comus, thou reasoneth well. Cato, thou art discharged."

CHAPTER IV.

Through the kindness of Mrs. William Rysam Sleight, of Sag Harbor, I am able to give an exact copy of the original census list of Shelter Island, taken in 1771. It is an interesting and valuable addition to our work, showing the growth of the community since the organization of the Town in 1730. During these years the community has doubled in population. Its complexion has remained about the same. A few of the names registered in 1730 have disappeared and are not recorded in the list of 1771. These are Sylvester, Hudson, Tuthill, Vail, Hopkins and Gilman. In their place appear Dering, Sawyer, Case, King, Duval and Horton. The name of Havens is still vastly in the majority, as at the organization of the Town. Some names on the list of 1771 are identical with those of 1730. These are William Nicoll, Daniel Brown, Thomas Conkling, Joel Bowditch, Abraham Parker, Jonathan Havens, George Havens and Joseph Havens.

Only two of them, however, represent the same person, namely, Daniel Brown and Thomas Conkling. Forty years have now passed since the Town was fully organized, and with their passing have transported nearly all of the founders into eternity.

The census list of 1776 is also here given, being copied out of one of the volumes of Colonial Documents. It shows a slight change in the personnel of this community from the list of 1771.

To return once more to ecclesiastical matters. The first reference to religious matters in the records of the Town occurs in the minutes of 1771, under the following resolution: "It is voted that Messrs. William Nicoll and Nicoll Havens, inspect the accounts of those that have the care of the moneys left by Brinley Sylvester, Esq., towards the support of the Gospel on this island, and to make report next Town meeting."

As we have already seen, the Rev. Mr. Adams came to this island about 1737. He continued to reside here, with a short interregnum of two years, until the early part of the American Revolution, when he left with Mr. Dering, whose private chaplain he was, Mr. Dering feeling constrained for sake of safety to take refuge with his family within the American lines, and moved to Connecticut. The people on this island must then have enjoyed in some

HEADS OF FAMILIES.	WHITES.					BLACKS.				
	Males under 16	Males from 16 to 60	Males 60 and up	Females under 16	Females above 16	Males under 16	Males from 16 to 60	Males 60 and up	Females under 16	Females above 16
1. Jonathan Havens............			1	1	2	1	2	1	1	1
2. Thomas Dering.............	2	2		1	1	1	2			2
3. Daniel Brown.......	1	1	1		1	2				1
4. William Nicoll					1	2	1	1	2	2
5. William Havens.............	1	3		1	1					
6. James Sawyer.............	1	1	1	1	1					
7. Thomas Conkling...........		2	1		1					
8. Joel Bowditch........		2	1	1	1					
9. Nicoll Havens..............	1	1		2	1	1	1			1
10. Samuel Case................	1	3		2	2					
11. Abraham Parker.............	1	4		2	3					
12. Joseph L'Hommedieu.......	1	1		1	1					
13. Benjamin Sawyer	3	1		1	1					
14. Moses Sawyer..............	3	1		4	1					
15. Thomas Conkling, Jr........	4	1		1	1					
16. James Havens..............	5	2		1	1					
17. Abraham King.............	2	1			2					
18. Deliverance Pain	1	1		2	1					
19. Walter Havens.............	1	1		2	1					
20. John Duval		1			1					
21. George Duval	1	2		2	1					
22. Obadiah Havens............	1	1		1	3					1
23. Jonathan Havens, Jr........	1	1		1	1				1	
24. George Havens.............		1		1	1					
25. Samuel Case, Jr		1		1	1					
26. Joseph Havens...............	1	1			1					
27. Moses Horton..............	1	1		2	1					
	33	37	5	31	34	7	6	2	4	8
	Total Whites....140					Total Blacks.....27				

The above account of the number of the people on Shelter Island was taken the 18 day of February, 1771.   JONATHAN HAVENS, JR., Constable.

SUFFOLK COUNTY } *ss:* SHELTER ISLAND.

In compliance of a requisition to me from George Murison, Esq., High Sheriff of ye said County of Suffolk, as also in pursuance of a warrant to him from His Excellency, the Right Honorable John Earl, of Dunsmore, etc., I send the above as an exact account of all the inhabitants within my District, the heads of the families being included in the number of one hundred and forty Whites.

sense the labors and privileges of a resident preacher up to that time. The resolution of 1771 likewise gives evidence of religious interest. It then is hardly probable that such a religious dearth existed among them during the last century as has been pictured

HEADS OF FAMILIES.	WHITES.					NEGROES.	
	MALES.			FEMALES.		Males.	Females.
	Over 50	Over 16	Under 16	Over 16	Under 16		
Thomas Dering...............	1	2	1	2	1	4	1
Nichol Havens.................		1	1	5	4	8	6
Daniel Brown..................	1	1		1		1	1
William Nicoll.................		1	1	1		7	3
James Havens		2	4	1	3		
William Havens...............	1	2	1	1	1		
Thomas Conkling	1	1		1			
Obadiah Havens		4		3	3	1	1
Joel Bowditch.....	1	1		1			
Samuel Case...................	1		1	1			
Abraham Parker...............	1		1	2			
Benjamin Sawyer..............		3	3	2	2		
Moses Sawyer		1	2	2	2		
Samuel Case. Jr...............		1		1	3		
Phineas Parker		1	1	1	1		
Thomas Conkling, Jr...........		1	4	1	2		
Walter Havens............. ..		1	2	1	2		
John Bowditch		1	1	1	1		
Thomas Harlow................		1	1	1	1		
David Conkling................		1		1	1		
Noah Terry....................		1	2	1	1		
William Havens, Jr............		1	1	1	1		
William Brown.................		1		1			
Moses Horton..................	1		1	1	2		
Deliverance Pain..............			1	3			
George Daval..................	1			1			
John Daval.....	1			1			
	10	29	29	38	32	21	12

1776. Capt. Sam'l Case appeared before me, and made oath to the within list, that it contained a true and faithful account of the inhabitants of the Township of Shelter Island.
                                THOMAS DERING,
                                        Chairman Town Committee.

by some writers regarding Shelter Island. With a meeting house erected by the citizens of the place; with a resident clergyman in the home of one, who likewise was called by the community to be its pastor; with a fund or legacy of five hundred dollars (a considerable sum in those days), the interest of which was to help in the support of a regular orthodox Presbyterian minister; with the care and oversight of Long Island Presbytery, kindly bestowed in occasional supplies, of preachers in Presbyterial meetings and ordination; with a community largely made up of Pilgrim and Puritan descendants, visited by renowned preachers and mighty evangelists, and in constant touch with the religious communities of Southold, Easthampton, Bridgehampton and Southampton—it is more than probable that the people enjoyed the privileges of the gospel and the ordinances of God's house fully equal to their ability.　No doubt the Revolutionary war led to the suspension of the outward means of grace, as it drove some of the inhabitants, among them the more prominent, into exile.　And this brings us to a highly important period in the history of Shelter Island, the period of the Revolution. Some of the incidents that happened here have already been touched upon in the review of Mr. Thomas Dering's life.　But only some. For there were other patriots here who played an important part in that mighty struggle.　Indeed, Shelter Island was not behind any other place in its loyalty and devotion to the cause of liberty. Not only "not behind," but way ahead of many another community, as the paper here inserted fully proves.　This paper, which is a pledge to support the Colonies in resisting British oppression, was circulated upon Shelter Island shortly after the battle of Lexington, which was the signal for war with Great Britain.　It was signed with but one or perhaps two exceptions, by every man on Shelter Island.　What a record is this!　What a display of patriotism! Does it not lift the inhabitants of Shelter Island into the very front rank of noble citizens, ardent patriots and lovers of freedom? That paper is a crown of glory to Shelter Island that shall not fade away so long as history is true in its record and just in its meed of praise.　Let the present and future generations of this place enshrine it in undying affection, for what the Declaration of Independence is to the nation, this instrument is to Shelter Island, namely, its Magna Charta.

Besides Mr. Thomas Dering, who, as we have already seen, was a member of the Provincial Convention of New York that unanimously adopted the Declaration of Independence, upon which the Convention assumed the title of "The Representatives of the State of New York," besides Mr. Dering, Shelter Island was represented by Capt. James Havens, who kept a store in the house now occupied by his great grandson, Mr. Henry P. Havens, and known as "Hearts-Ease."　Still a third member was sent from here in the person of Capt. Daniel Brown, so that our little island furnished three members of the various Provisional Congresses that met in 1775 and 1776.　I doubt whether another community in all Suffolk County did as much.　As early as the summer of 1775, the British navy appeared in these waters, prowling around this island, to the number of thirteen ships of war, and during the progress of the war as many as twenty-one vessels lay at one time in Gardiner's Bay. That body of water became the rendezvous of the enemy's ships of war. The names of some of the vessels were as follows: The London, 120 guns; Grand Duke, 120 guns; Royal Oak, 100 guns; Bedford, 100 guns; Centurion, 80 Guns; Robust, 74 guns; Royal George, 74 guns, and the Culloden, 74 guns. Upon the disastrous result of the battle of Long Island to the American side, in August, 1776, the British took possession of the whole of Long Island, with its adjacent islands, and continued their sway of martial law throughout the war from 1776 to 1783.

During these years the inhabitants of Shelter Island suffered terribly for their loyalty to the cause of the Colonists. The officers of the enemy's vessels anchored in these waters would come ashore and compel the inhabitants to provide whatever they demanded. They forced every one at the point of the bayonet to swear allegiance to the king. Nothing was safe from the hands of the enemy, and not only from the enemy, but from some of their neighbors who were Tories.

Thompson in his history tells us that "the Tory inhabitants, whether natives or refugees (by which he means those who sympathized with the British) that the Tory inhabitants were the constant dread of those on the other side, who had anything to lose, or who had by their patriotism rendered themselves obnoxious to their despicable malice. Even the more inoffensive, who remained at home with their suffering families, were often harassed, and perpetually exposed to the predatory disposition of the worst men, and could hardly be said to have anything which they could call their own. In some instances the lives of peaceable citizens were sacrificed in the most unprovoked and wanton manner, disgraceful even to barbarians, because they would not discover their money and other valuables to the robbers. The property of those who had fled from their homes, and especially those engaged in the American service, was particularly the object of rapine, and in many instances the damages were immense. Woods and fences were lavishly used for fuel, and in any other way which served the purposes of those stationed in the neighborhood as well as for the garrisons of Brooklyn and New York."

During this time the administration of justice, according to historian Woods, was suspended and the British army became a sanctuary for crimes and robbery, the grossest offences being atoned for by enlistment therein. Those who had served in any wise in the cause of liberty had to fly into the American lines for safety, while those who remained at home were harassed and plundered of their property, the inhabitants of Suffolk County being perpetually exposed to the grossest insult and abuse. They had no property of a movable kind that they could, properly speaking, call their own; they were oftentimes deprived of the stock necessary to the management of their farms, and were deterred from endeavoring to produce more than a bare subsistence by the apprehension that a surplus would be wrested from them either by the military authority of the purveyor or the ruffian hand of the plunderer. The officers seized and occupied the best rooms in the houses of the inhabitants; they compelled them to furnish blankets and fuel for the soldiers, and hay and grain for their horses; they took away their cattle, sheep, hogs and poultry, and seized without ceremony and without any compensation whatever they desired to gratify their wants and wishes."

But these pecuniary losses were not the sorest trials that the inhabitants of Long Island endured under the tyranny of their oppressors. Besides these violations of the rights of person and property, the British officers did many acts of barbarity, for which there could be no apology. They made garrisons, storehouses or stables of the houses of public worship in several towns, and particularly of such as belonged to the Presbyterians. Among the Presbyterian churches that were thus pillaged was the one of Newtown, from which "they actually sawed off the steeple in derision, smashed its pews, tore off its siding and turned the sacred place into a prison, guard house, hospital and stable, and as a parting indignity demolished the whole."

The Presbyterian church of Islip was literally carried off by piecemeal to Jamaica to be used as barracks for the British soldiers. The church at Southold, our next of kin ecclesiastically, and the mother of this church, had no services in it during the whole eight years of the war. Its pastor, the Rev. John Storrs, went into the army as chaplain. Our Presbytery, the Presbytery of Long Island, could not gather during this time of trial, persecution and blood. One of its members, the Rev. Joshua Hart, languished for two years in the awful prison ships of the enemy anchored in the Wallabout of Brooklyn. All persons of importance in this region were driven into exile, only slaves and servants remained. Not even the farms could be tilled. From all this you can imagine the hardships that the people of this island had to endure during these eventful years.

As a sample of what they had to endure, I give you this extract bearing date of Sept. 15th, 1781: "On the evening of the 15th the British ransacked the house of Nicoll Havens on Shelter Island, took two fowling pieces, a silver hilted sword, a silver mounted hanger, some tea, &c. At Capt. James Havens' they took a watch, coat, fowling piece, &c. Then they went to widow Payne's, insulted the inmates of the house and threatened to burn it, made them produce a silver tankard, linen, a watch, a coat, and a fowling piece, &c." No wonder that at the close of the war, as the enemy's fleet departed, the people of this place assembled on the hills at Prospect and held a jubilee over their departure. One of the enemy's vessels, the Culloden, ran ashore on the east point of Fort Pond and became a total loss, the accident resulting from a blinding snowstorm that set in just as the squadron was rounding Gardiner's Point. Because of this, that point is designated as "Culloden's Point" on all charts to this day.

Dr. Woodworth, in his dedicatory sermon preached upon the dedication of the present church building, in 1817, speaking of this period, said: "The calamities and disastrous connections of the Revolutionary war were here experienced in great weight. The destruction of property, though great, was by no means the worst evil. The demoralizing effects were much more to be deplored. The public means of grace were suspended; the Sabbath of the Lord profaned, and that sense of God and the claims of serious religion, which rested but too lightly on the public mind, now seemed to be wholly erased. Vice in its various forms prevailed and failed not to produce its legitimate effects." Such in part were the vicissitudes of this people. But it was not in vain. The cause for which it had all been born, was not only worthy of it, but had gloriously triumphed.

At the close of the war the Legislature of New York passed on April 6th, 1784, a law governing the incorporation of religious societies, by the selection of a Board of Trustees, who should have charge of the temporalities and discharge such other duties as are therein stated. On that same day Shelter Island held its Town meeting, the first one after the war, and after selecting its officers, appointed a committee, consisting of Sylvester Dering and Jonathan N. Havens, to "inquire into and take charge of the monnies left by Brinley Sylvester, Esq., toward the support of the Gospel on Shelter Island and make report thereof to the Inhabitants of the Island." The next year a special meeting was called of the inhabitants of the Society of Shelter Island for the 26th of April, when the Church Society was duly organized, as the following record will show:

"These are to certify that a meeting of the Inhabitants of the Society of Shelter Island, held on the 26th day of April, 1785, legally named agreeable to a Law of this State to Enable all Religious Denominations to choose Trustees to take charge of their Temporalities, by the name and stile of Trustees of the Freeholders and Inhabitants of the Township of Shelter Island, the following Persons were chosen Trustees:

> JONATHAN N. HAVENS, ⎫
> SYLVESTER DERING, ⎬ Trustees.
> WILLIAM BOWDITCH, ⎭
>
> JAS. HAVENS, ⎫ Inspectors of the Election.
> JONATHAN N. HAVENS, ⎭

Suffolk County.

MEMORANDUM, that on this third day of May, 1785, personally appeared before me James Havens and Jonathan N. Havens, of Shelter Island, Inspectors of the Election, held at said Island on the 26th day of April, 1785, for the purpose of choosing Trustees to take charge of their temporalities, and acknowledged that Jonathan N. Havens, Sylvester Dering and William Bowditch were duly elected as Trustees for said Island, agreeably to this Certificate, and finding no material error therein do allow it to be recorded. THOS. YOUNGS, Judge.

Recorded this 18th day of June, 1785, in Suffolk County Register for recording the names of the persons elected to serve as Trustees for Religious Denominations in Lib. A, page 4. Per E. L'HOMMEDIEU, Clke.

The above is the first entry in the records of this society. After it comes another, which tells us the order in which the members of the Board served the society:

SUFFOLK COUNTY, ss. At a meeting of the Freeholders and Inhabitants of the Town of Shelter Island on the 25th Day of April, 1786, The Trustees of said Island provided according to the Law of this State Intitled ("an Act for Improving Religious Societies throughout this State") to draw Lots for their Numbers, which were as follows:

> William Bowditch, No. 1.
> Jonathan N. Havens, No. 2.
> Sylvester Dering, No. 3.

They then Proceeded to the choice of a Trustee in the place of the one that by Law then became vacant, when William Bowditch was re-chosen.

The first inventory made by the Trustees according to law was made the 16th of March, 1789, and is as follows:

AN INVENTORY OF ALL THE ESTATE, BOTH REAL AND PERSONAL, BELONGING TO THE CONGREGATION AND RELIGIOUS SOCIETY OF THE TOWN OF SHELTER ISLAND, TAKEN ON THE 16TH OF MARCH, 1789.

Real Estate.	PERSONAL ESTATE.				ANNUAL REVINEW.		
[None]	1 State Certificate of £50 : 0 : 0, payable January 1, 1790, bearing interest of 5 per cent. from January 1, 1785, and signed by GERARD BAUCKER, Treas.	50	....	....	......	....	....
	1 State Certificate of £28 : 0 : 9, payable January 1, 1790, bearing interest of 6 per cent. from January 1, 1785, and signed by GERARD BAUCKER, Treas.	28	....	9	......	....	....
	1 State Certificate for interest of £14 : 13 : 2, payable on the 1st of May, 1787, one-fourth part paid and signed GERARD BAUCKER, Treas.	10	19	11	......	...	....
	1 Bond against Jno. Franks of £58 : 3 : 3, bearing date the 25th of December, 1787.......	58	3	3	......	4	1	5
	1 Bond against Sylvester Dering of £19 : 10 : 8¼, bearing date January 1, 1789..............	19	10	8¼	......	1	3	5
	£	166	14	7¼		5	4	10

The society was now duly incorporated by the selection of these three men as trustees. One of them was the Supervisor of the Town; I refer to Jonathan N. Havens, a great-grandson of the first George Havens and a man of note; perhaps the greatest man native to this soil. He was the son of Nicoll Havens and Sarah Fosdick, his first wife, while Nicoll Havens was the son of Jonathan Havens and Catherine Nicoll. The subject of this sketch, Jonathan Nicoll Havens, thus bore the given name of his father and grandfather. He was born on the 18th of June, 1757. In 1773 he entered Yale College, at the age of sixteen, and graduated with honor in 1777. While in College he was president of the Linonian Society, from which it may be inferred that he was not inattentive to the uses of public speaking and composition. After graduating he returned to his home on this island, where he became partly engaged in agricultural pursuits. His principal occupation, however, was of a literary kind, the pursuit of the higher branches of learning. Several years were thus passed in retirement, seclusion and study. So engrossed was he at times in thought that he was unconscious of persons or things about him, as the following incident will show. A certain Major Jessup, of Southampton, a personal friend of Mr. Jonathan Nicoll Havens, while on a visit to Shelter Island one day, made a call on Mr. Havens, who saluted him as he entered the house, but immediately returned to his studies, forgetting altogether of his visitor, who after staying a long time departed without notice. On the day after he called again, in company with Mr. Sylvester Dering, and in conversation related the circumstance of his call on the day previous, upon which Mr. Havens assured him that he had felt unaware of his visit, so deeply had he been absorbed by the subject of his inquiry. Upon the death of his father, also a man of great prominence and highly esteemed, Jonathan N. Havens was chosen Clerk of the Town. This office his father had held from 1759, except during the period of the Revolution, to the time of his death, in 1783. His father also, with the office of Town Clerk, held the office of Supervisor for seven years before the beginning of the war, and at its close in the spring of the year in which he died, was again elected to both offices. Now the son, at a special meeting held Dec. 4th, 1783, is chosen to succeed his father as Town Clerk, and with this office begins a public career which gained for him a great name in the annals of his country. He continued to serve as Town Clerk until 1787, when he was chosen Supervisor, which office he discharged until 1793. In the meantime his ability had been spread abroad, so that in 1786 he was elected an Assemblyman from Suffolk County, to which office he was re-elected for ten consecutive years. In this body he became distinguished for his integrity and ability as a statesman. Among other important positions he was chairman of the committee which originated the law establishing public schools in the State of New York. Then, too, he was a member of the State Convention which met at Poughkeepsie on June 17, 1788, and adopted the Constitution of the United States. He was also elected a Justice of the Peace of the County of Suffolk in 1795. After his ten years of service in the Assembly of the State, he was chosen a United States Representative, being elected a member of the Fourth Congress, in which body he served until his death, in 1799, at the early age of 42. His death was a great shock to the community and to all who knew him. Thompson says: "He was not only a man of extraordinary abilities, but was distinguished likewise for industry and promptitude in everything which he undertook. The death of such a man at the age of 40 years (it should be 42) could not be otherwise felt than a subject of general regret with all who knew his worth." He was buried in the South churchyard, and over his remains was raised a tablet that bears this high eulogy: "Erected to the memory of Jonathan Nicoll Havens, Esq., Representative in the Congress of the United States. He was esteemed by a numerous acquaintance as a man of superior talent aud erudition, a philosopher, statesman and patriot, and died greatly lamented Oct. 25th, 1799, in the 42 yr. of his age." As Shelter Island can with pride point to her first supervisor, the Hon. William Nicoll, so can this religious corporation point with equal satisfaction to her first selected Trustee, the Hon. Jonathan Nicoll Havens.

Mr. Havens belonged to a distinguished family. One of his sisters, Esther Sarah Havens, married General Sylvester Dering, the second trustee, of whom we shall have occasion to speak later. Another sister, Mary Catherine, married the Hon. Ezra L'Hommedieu, also a noted statesman for more than thirty years, born in Southold, and considered by Dr. Epher Whitaker "the foremost of all the men who have lived all their life from birth to death in that noted town." A brother of Jonathan Nicoll Havens, named Rensselaer Havens, became a distinguished merchant, financier and patriot in New York City. He, with another gentleman, fitted out a vessel and presented it to the government during the war of 1812. While in Yale College Mr. Jonathan Nicoll Havens wrote the following letter, which is here given because of its interest in many ways, among them the parental respect it displays, the inconvenience of travel in those days, the use of the pillow case, etc., etc.

"New Haven, March 29th, 1774.
"Honored Sir:
"I take this opportunity by Mr. Hathoway to write you a few lines. By Cpt. Moses Sawyer, who came with him, I understand you are troubled with boils, for which am sorry, but am glad to hear the rest of the family are all well. I have not heard from you since my last, which I sent by Uncle Mumford when he was hear upon the

Assembly, which I suppose you have received afore this time. As the spring vacancy draws nigh, I begin to think of coming home, and I believe I shall want to bring home a pretty large bundle, as a good many of my shirts begin to wear out and some of my stockings, together with these I designed to have brought home, my cloath for a coat and some of my books which I make no use of, which I fear I shall not be able to perform, as having nothing but a pillow case which I was put to great difficulty with when I went home last, unless I had a pair of saddle-bags or some other conveniency, or could get a passage directly home in some boat, tho' I have not heard from you, whether you designed to send a boat on purpose. I should be glad to hear whether it is worth while to bring all the things home which I have mentioned or in what manner I shall act, and I remain with love to all, your loving and dutiful son,

"JONATH. N'LL. HAVENS."

The third trustee of the original board, Mr. William Bowditch, was born on this island about the year of 1751. He was the son of Joel Bowditch and Bethiah Case. His father was one of the twenty men who founded the Town in 1730.

Mr. Bowditch at the time of his selection as Trustee was Overseer of the Poor. He continued to serve the Town in various offices until 1794, when he was chosen Supervisor, which office he held for twenty years. Thus from 1784 to the time of his death, in 1820, he served the Town in almost every capacity, a period of thirty-six years. While as trustee he served this society from its incorporation, 1785, with the exception of three years, likewise until his death, a period of thirty-two years. He is best remembered as Squire Bowditch, and is considered by some to have been the moving spirit in the building of the present sanctuary.

That Board of Trustees has continued in existence down to the present time, and as it is characteristic of such Boards to continue in existence as long as the corporation which they represent continues to exist, and further, as this corporation gives every evidence of unending life, it is fair to assume that the Board will continue to exist until the end of time. Besides this, as the Rev. Mr. Harries said in his historical discourse, we may properly date the origin of this congregation from the time of the completion of the first meeting house, namely, in 1743. So that this assembly has existed by regular succession one hunderd and fifty-five years. You will notice that we are thus speaking of the existence of the religious assembly or congregation on this island, not the church, for as yet we have not reached the time when God in His Grace gathered together a body in which to dwell a sanctuary "made up of living stones."

At this date it is said there still lived quite a large number of Indians on the island. This conflicts somewhat with a previous statement that upon the purchase of the island from the Indians the latter left the island. Perhaps not all, but only a portion. However, what is here said is substantiated by good and sufficient evidence. The huts and wigwams of these remaining Indians formed quite a village on Sachem's Neck. In 1790 more than half of these were destroyed through fire, which broke out in one of them one morning, and spread to the rest, as they were pitched so near together. Some of the aborigines are remembered by those living and present with us at this time. The last of this race became the subject of a remarkable conversion, under the early ministry of the Rev. Daniel M. Lord, who speaks of her in particular in one of his sermons as follows:

"Of the fruits of this precious refreshing from the presence of the Lord twelve were gathered into the church at one communion season. Among these was one, the last of the aborigines who was born on Shelter Island. She had lived in ignorance and in the detriment of sin, without God and without hope in the world. More than fourscore years had made its deep furroughs on her brow. She had often sold herself to letchery and rum. It may be said for many, many years that no one cared for her soul. But God's time came, when all her race had been laid in the grave, and all those whom she had known in her youth were beneath the clods of the valley, then it was that God's word was spirit and life.

"The small amount of truth which she had heard, for she could not read in all her lifetime, had a resurrection. She was created anew in Christ Jesus unto good works, that she might walk in them. There are those present to-day (1856) who remember the bowed form but robust frame of Betty Tobs Caeser. They remember also the change that came over her. How she adjured the intoxicating cup and forsook her wicked ways and unrighteous thoughts and returned unto the Lord, who had mercy and abundantly pardoned. They saw the change and admired the grace that kindled in her heart

the flame of love to God and to man.   Not this alone, there are some
still lingering on these mortal shores who have listened to her voice
in prayer and have been constrained to feel that her lips were
touched with hallowed fire.   Nor can they forget the scene of the last
conflict of the dying Indian saint as visions of unutterable glory
burst upon her sight.   Each who witnessed that closing scene felt
for the Christian to die is gain.   Twenty-one years are past and yet
the vision of that hour stands out before me as the sun of yesterday.
Oh! death where is thy sting.   Oh! grave where is thy victory.
Thanks be to God who giveth us the victory through our Lord Jesus
Christ."

In looking over the first inventory of this religious corporation
we notice that no real estate is mentioned, though it is well known
that a church building existed on this island.   We are led to ask,
therefore, to whom did that building belong?   It belonged to certain freeholders on this island who were instrumental in its erection.
All its pews were under the control of certain families, who possessed the sole and exclusive right to the same.   In 1806 the parish
sought to increase the seating capacity of the original building, and
so they passed the following resolution: "Voted that the Pews occupied by Benjamin Nicoll, William Bowditch, Sylvester Dering, and
James Havens, be made narrower so as to make room for a Pew in
front of James Havenses pew and the next seat and another in
front of William Bowditches Pew and the next seat, and that the
Pews of Benjamin Nicoll, William Bowditch and Sylvester Dering,
and James Havens be moved back at the expense of the Parish, to
be paid by the Trustees out of the Public monies in their hands,
that any person wishing to build a pew in either of these places,
left for the purpose, may do it, by application to the Trustees on the
following conditions, to wit, that they build the pews at their expense, keeping an exact account thereof, to be delivered to the
Trustees, and that they, their heirs and assigns have use, &c., and occupy those pews untill called for by the Parish, when Parish shall pay
the person who built them, their Heirs and Assigns, the price the
Pews cost, after which they shall deliver them to the society."
In 1808 the Parish sought to get control of all the pews, as the following minutes of that date will show: "Voted that the Trustees consult the owners of Pews in the Meeting House, and know of them if
they will sell them, and at what price, and if all the owners of Pews
will sell, to call a Parish meeting that the Parish may determine to

purchase them or not." The purchase was never effected; and the whole system of ownership continued until the original building passed out of use because of decay.

Looking once more at that inventory, we see that the amount of personal property is given as £166 14s. 7¼d., or about $830. This shows that the legacy of Brinley Sylvester, amounting to £100, given in 1752, had increased to one and two-thirds of the original amount. It continued to grow so that the Trustees in the next inventory of 1793 reported it as about amounting to £188, or $940. The Society was thus in position to secure the preached Word, and did so by applying to the Presbytery of Long Island at its spring meeting, held at Southampton Apr. 21, 1789. The following item is to be found in the minutes of that date: "Mr. John Taylor, a candidate for the ministry from Connecticut, was appointed to preach at Sag Harbor and Shelter Island, they applying for supplies."

About this time Mr. Stephen Burroughs, author of "Memoirs of Stephen Burroughs," was engaged to teach school in this place. He speaks at some length in his "Memoirs" of his labors here as a school teacher, and mentions a number of citizens of that date with whom he lived and mingled.

Under date of Oct. 1st, 1795, we have the first reference in our Town records to the slaves that were on this island. According to the second census list there were thirty-three slaves on Shelter Island in 1776. These were owned as follows: five by Mr. Thomas Dering, fourteen by Mr. Nicoll Havens, two by Mr. Daniel Brown, ten by Mr. William Nicoll, and two by Mr. Obadiah Havens. Twenty-one of these were male and the balance were female negroes. At the close of the Revolution the chief principle in the bringing about of which was "that all men are created equal and that they are endowed by their Creator with certain inalienable rights, that among these are life, liberty and the pursuit of happiness," measures were taken to abolish the custom of slavery which had existed among the various colonies from their very inception. On February 22, 1788, the Legislature of New York passed an act for the manumitting of slaves within the Empire State. According to this act, slaves under the age of fifty years who were physically able to support themselves and thus not liable to become a charge upon the Town, could be given their freedom by their owners upon application to the overseers of the poor and justices of the peace of the county, subject to their approval. In accordance with this measure, on October 1, 1795, Mr. Sylvester Dering, Mr. Henry Dering and Mr. Nathaniel Gardiner applied for the privilege of manumitting a negro woman slave called "Matilda," of which they were the owners. These gentlemen being sons and son-in-law of Mr. Thomas Dering, deceased, had by inheritance come into possession of this slave, and now desired to give her her freedom. The privilege was granted, and Matilda was, according to the Town records, the first slave to gain her freedom on Shelter Island. In 1799 Rensselaer Havens sought the same privilege for one of his slaves, named "Dick," which was granted. The same year Samuel B. Nicoll released three of his slaves, who were father, mother and child, named respectively, Cade, Elizabeth and Armenie. In 1801 Desire Havens released a negro woman called "Fide." In 1806 Sylvester Dering did the same for one called "Violet," while in 1821 his widow released a slave called "London." Under date of June 1, 1804, Sylvester Dering makes affidavit to the birth of "Achilles, a male negro child born of a slave" belonging to him, and born the 10th day of February, 1804. These comprise all the references toward slaves and slavery as it existed on Shelter Island to be found in our Town records.

In 1794 it was voted "That one years Interest of the monies belonging to the Freeholders and Inhabitants of this Town for the support of the Gospel be appropriated by the Trustees for that purpose: and paid into the hands of Benjamin Nicoll, James Havens and Sylvester Dering, who are hereby appointed our Committee to procure a Person to Preach the Gospel in this place and to pay the same as they may agree, not exceeding the rate of four dollars for each Sabbath." The same year we find this curious entry in the Town records: "At a Special Town Meeting (held April 29th, 1794) called for the purpose of regulating the clam fishery, it was resolved that a tax of three pence, for every bushel of clams dug by non-inhabitants of the island, the proceeds of which save 20% was to be paid into the hands of the Religious Society for the purpose of supporting the gospel or maintaining a school on the said island as the freeholders and inhabitants of said island shall at their annual Town Meetings direct." The way they, however, disposed of this tax was to repeal it the next year; at the same time directing what revenue had been received from it should be placed in the hands of a School Committee consisting of William Bowditch and Ezekial Havens, to be disposed of by them for school purposes. The reso-

Rev. WHITEFIELD COWLES

AND THE
FLY-LEAF OF HIS MANUSCRIPT SERMON PREACHED IN THE ORIGINAL MEETING HOUSE
ON SHELTER ISLAND, N. Y., SUNDAY, AUGUST 21, 1798

lution passed by the society this year voting the interest of the monies in the hands of the Trustees to the securing of a preacher was repeated in 1795 and 1796.

From the treasurer's accounts we learn that in response to these resolutions the Rev. Whitfield Cowles preached on four Sabbaths in 1796, for which he received £4; and in 1797 the Rev. Jacob Cram preached one Sabbath, for which he was paid £1 4s. In 1798 the Rev. Whitfield Cowles preached again for the society twenty-four Sabbaths, for which he received £9 12s. The Rev. Jacob Cram was the son of Jonathan Cram, of Hampton Falls, N. H., born Oct. 12, 1762, a graduate of Dartmouth College, in 1782. After preaching here he became the pastor of the church in Orient. He died in Exeter, N. H., Dec. 21, 1833. The Rev. Whitfield Cowles was the son of Capt. Josiah Cowles, of Southington, Conn., born June 3, 1764. He graduated from Yale College in 1788, and in 1793 received the degree of A. M. The next year, 1794, he was ordained at East Granby, Conn. The same year he married one of Shelter Island's fair daughters, Miss Gloriana Havens. She died in 1802. The following year he married again, choosing for his second wife Miss Desire Brown, also of Shelter Island. Mr. Cowles' picture is given on the next page, together with a fac-simile of the fly leaf of one of his sermons preached in the meeting house on Shelter Island, Aug. 21st, 1798.

Besides the clergymen already mentioned there were others who are known to have occasionally preached here, among them being the Rev. Dr. Buell, pastor of the Easthampton Presbyterian Church from 1746 to 1798. In 1799 and 1800 Mr. John Rudd taught school on this island. While here he boarded with Gen. Sylvester Dering, who became strongly attached to him. He was a young man of good promise, and after leaving this place he opened a school in New York City, where he gained the good will of Bishop Moore, who instructed him in divinity, after which he became an Episcopalian minister, subsequently receiving the degree of D. D. and becoming the editor of a religious paper called the "Christian Messenger." The next year the Parish sought to gain a resident clergyman in the person of the Rev. Herman Daggett as preacher and teacher. Mr. Daggett had labored at Southampton for a number of years, leaving there in 1797 and going to Westhampton, where he labored until 1801. The action of the parish in seeking to gain the services of Mr. Daggett was the following: "Voted that the

Trustees be requested to make application to the Rev. Herman Daggett to come and reside with us as a preacher of the Gospel and a Teacher of our school for the term of ten years. Voted that we will give the Rev. Herman Daggett for Preaching to us on the Sabbath, and for Teaching our school during the time before mentioned, Three Hundred and fifty Dollars per annum, to be raised in the following manner:

"The Trustees annually to open a Subscription and present it to all the Inhabitants to sign what they will give for preaching each Sabbath for one year or during their residence on Shelter Island, the money raised by this Subscription together with the Annual Interest of our Public monies to be appropriated as far they will go towards the payment of Two Hundred Dollars of the before mentioned Salary—and in case the Subscription for the support of the Gospel and the Interest of the Public monies does not amount to the sum of two Hundred Dollars, it shall then be lawfull for the Trustees and they are hereby authorized and required to make up the deficiency out of any monies in their hands belonging to the Freeholders and Inhabitants of Shelter Island and given for the support of the Gospel—leaving the remaining part of the salary, viz., one hundred and Fifty Dollars to be raised by the Proprietors of the School—a true record of the votes.

(Seal)   "SYLVESTER DERING, Clk."

About the same time Mr. Daggett received this call or proposition, he also received a call from the church at Middletown, now known as Middle Island, whither he went and was installed Oct. 20th, 1801. There he remained until 1807 or 9, when he removed to Connecticut. Dr. Prime in his history speaks of him in the highest terms as "a man of sterling talents, respectable acquirements and peculiar excellence of character." What the parish did upon failing in their efforts to bring the Rev. Herman Daggett in their midst we cannot tell. In 1804 they made application again to the Presbytery of Long Island, with this result: "Supplies were requested for Shelter Island, and Messrs. Lyman Beecher, Joseph Hazzard, Daniel Hall and Zachariah Green were appointed for the purpose. Mr. Foster also offering to supply, it was agreed that he should take one Sabbath on Shelter Island." These men doubtless discharged their appointment. Among them are the names of two men who have left behind them an illustrious record, one, the Rev. Dr. Lyman

Beecher, as an able theologian and the father of a family noted for great preachers, among them the world-wide famous Henry Ward Beecher; the other, Zachariah Green, who is best known as an intense patriot during the Revolutionary War, though at the time of its commencement but sixteen years of age. Of another of these brethren, Daniel Hall, I shall have much to say presently. The following year, or 1805, the parish passed a resolution inviting the Rev. Benjamin Bell to preach to the inhabitants for one year, he to receive for his services three dollars per Sabbath. Mr. Bell responded to this call and preached for the society, as is seen from the treasurer's accounts. At the same meeting in which the parish invited the Rev. Mr. Bell, it was voted that "the Trustees repair the meeting house and pay for the same out of the Public monies in their hands for Religious purposes." That this was done the following entry will show: "To cash paid the Bills for shingling the Porch and repairing the Meeting House, £31.0.22." Another preacher who served during one Sabbath was the Rev. Mr. Boge.

About this time the Rev. Dr. Timothy Dwight, President of Yale College, made a visit to this island during one of his vacation trips through Long Island. His experiences, observations and impressions of these various journeys he fully describes in a series of volumes entitled "Travels in New England and New York." In one of these letters Dr. Dwight speaks very fully of his visit to Shelter Island. In those days the ferry ran from Stern's Point to the narrow neck of land just opposite on the northern arm of Long Island. The ferry was known as "Bushe's Ferry," so called because the owner's name was "Boisseau," which was pronounced "Busche." Not having the patronage in those days that the ferry enjoys now accounts for the poor or meagre accommodations that Dr. Dwight found, for he says: "We found the ferry had neither wharf nor ferry stairs on either side. The shore was a gradual slope. We were therefore obliged to ride to the boat, and with much difficulty to force our horses into it by leading them over the gunwhale."

Of the island itself, after describing its formation, soil products, etc., he says: "To the credit of the inhabitants, especially of the principal proprietors, it ought to be observed that they have customarily made considerable exertions to support schools and obtain the preaching of the gospel."

In 1806 the Rev. Daniel Hall, of Sag Harbor, where he had been pastor of the Presbyterian church for eight years, was asked to become the minister of the parish, according to the following record: "At a Parish Meeting held on Shelter Island at the Meeting House on the 5th of May, 1806, to consult about engaging the Reverend Daniel Hall to preach to us the ensuing year; and after examining the subscription for his support, Voted that the Trustees of the Freeholders and Inhabitants of Shelter Island invite the Rev'd Daniel Hall to preach to us for one year, and that they make the deficiency of the subscription up to three Dollars a Sabbath out of the Parish Monies." As that subscription list is in existence, and is of importance in many ways, I give it here as follows:

SUBSCRIPTION RECEIVED FOR MR. HALL, 1806.

	£	s.	d.		£	s.	d.
Bowditch, William	3	18	0	Carried over	29	13	8
Bowditch, John	1	6	0	Havens, Joseph, Sr	1	14	0
Bowditch, William, Jr	0	13	0	Havens, David	0	13	0
Bowditch, Samuel	0	8	8	Havens, Remington	0	13	0
Bousseau, John	0	8	0	Havens, Silvanus	0	13	0
Conklin, Benjamin	3	18	0	Hains, Henry	1	16	0
Case, Joseph	0	17	4	Harlow, Daniel	0	13	0
Case, Jacob	0	13	0	Harlow, Phebe	0	4	4
Doughlass, Jonathan	1	19	0	Mayo, Thomas	1	19	0
Dering, Sylvester	7	16	0	Nicoll, Benjamin	7	16	0
Havens, Obadiah	2	12	0	Pierson, Job	1	6	0
Havens, Ezekial	0	18	0	Reeve, Jonathan	0	8	0
Havens, Lodowick	0	17	4	Sawyer, Richard	0	13	0
Havens, Augustus	2	12	0	Tuthill, Thomas	0	17	4
Havens, Joseph, Jr	0	17	4	Havens, James, Jr	1	0	0
	29	13	8	Total,	49	9	4

Dollars............... 113.66½
Unmarked Contribution, 8.08½

$121.75

The Rev. Mr. Hall had just been released from his pastoral duties at Sag Harbor by the Presbytery upon his own request. He was the first settled pastor of that church, beginning his labors there in 1797 and continuing there until his removal to Shelter Island in 1806. Here he remained and served until his death in 1812. Mr. Hall has left an undying record behind him in the organization of this church, which he effected in 1808. In two years after his coming the condition of spiritual things had so far advanced as to make the organization of a church possible by the adoption, on Sept. 28th, 1808, of the following Confession of Faith and Church Covenant:

"Whereas it hath pleased God to favour us with the public administrations of his word, and considering the obligations that all are under, who have hope in the mercy of God through our Lord Jesus Christ, and desirous of the advancement and prosperity of his Kingdom, have severally agreed to the following articles of Faith and Covenant conformable to the order and discipline of the Presbyterian Church as established in the United States:

ARTICLES OF FAITH.

"We do profess and solemnly believe that there is only one living and true God subsisting in three persons, the Father, the Son, and the Holy Ghost.

"That the Scriptures of the Old and New Testaments is the Word of God, and the only infallible rule of Faith and practice.

"That the original state of mankind was that of purity and happiness; but through the disobedience of the first Adam, his whole posterity are fallen into a state of sin and misery, exposed to all the evils of the present state, and condemnation of the future.

"That God of his abundant mercy hath sent his Son to redeem and save that which was lost, and that all who truly believe in him are justified, saved and accepted of God, and continuing in the faith will have an open entrance into his Heavenly Kingdom.

"That God hath appointed a day in which he will judge the world in righteousness, by that man whom he hath ordained to be the Judge of quick and dead, that then the Lord Jesus Christ will admit the Righteous to the full enjoyment of his Heavenly Kingdom, and will sentence the wicked to everlasting punishment.

THE COVENANT.

"We do now as we humbly hope in divine mercy avouch the Lord to be our God, trusting alone for acceptance through the mediation of his dear Son, promising as God may enable us to walk in all the commandments and ordinances of the Lord, to have our hearts united to the people of God, to love and treat them as brethren, and in common with ourselves as members of the mistical body of Christ.

"We promise to submit ourselves to the government of the Church of Christ, and to this Church in particular, to walk towards each other in the fellowship of the Gospel and to seek in all things its spiritual peace and prosperity, so long as God in his providence shall continue our relation with them."

The following persons appeared, and after having heard the foregoing Articles of Faith and Covenant read, assented to them and requested their names inserted, viz.:

> Rev. Daniel Hall, Pastor.
> Lucretia Hall, his wife.
> Ephraim King.
> Mehitable King, his wife.
> Sylvester Dering and his wife
> E. Sarah Dering.
> Jonathan Doughlass and his wife
> Abigail Doughlass.
> Mary Mayo.
> Eunice Case.
> Anna Boisseau.
> Elizabeth Havens.
> Abigail Sawyer.
> Lodowick Havens.
> Esther Case.

To this body of believers the Sacrament of the Lord's Supper was administered by Mr. Hall on Sunday, October 16th, 1808. Though Congregational in form, it strongly leaned towards the Presbyterian fold from the very beginning, the preamble of its Confession mentioning that body as its model. Mr. Hall continued his connection with the Presbytery of Long Island until his death. That Presbytery had now for many years exercised a kindly oversight over the religious affairs of this island. As early as 1747 it had met by the good will of the inhabitants on this island by commission.

Again, in 1766, when it ordained the Rev. Elam Potter. It was repeatedly petitioned by the people of Shelter Island to appoint preachers to this place, which requests it cordially complied with, as has already been seen, and now in less than two years after the organization of the Church Presbytery holds its spring meeting upon Shelter Island under date of April 18th, 1810. The opening sermon of that session of Presbytery was preached by the Rev. Jonathan Huntting, at that time pastor of the church at Southold, and who was destined twenty years later to be the Stated Supply for a period of years to this very church. Rev. Mr. Hall continued his labors here with marked success until his death, which occurred Jan. 20, 1812, from tetanus, caused by the amputation of a cancerous foot. Dr. Prime, who was his successor in the pastorate of the Sag Harbor Presbyterian Church, speaks of him as having been a "remarkably affectionate preacher; a son of consolation rather than a Boanerges." His remains were buried in our south church-yard, and over his grave was raised a tablet bearing this inscription:

"Sacred to the Memory of
Rev. Daniel Hall,
Who died Jan. 20, 1812.
Ae 64.

"In all the various relations of life he lived like a Christian. As a husband and parent he was tender and affectionate. As a neighbor and friend, he was kind and benevolent. As a citizen he was truly patriotic, and as a minister of Jesus, he was faithful unto death."

Mr. Hall was born in New London, Conn., Sept. 19th, 1747. He was the son of Jonathan and Alice Hall. He left a widow, two sons, John and William, and three daughters, Sophronia, Lucretia and Mary.

Sophronia married Charles Doughlass, of Sag Harbor, and Lucretia married Capt. David Brown, of the same place. This doubtless led to Mrs. Hall's removal to Sag Harbor, where she died on Sept. 4th, 1825, aged 76, her remains being brought to this island for interment alongside those of her husband, where they now lie with a host of others awaiting the resurrection morn. All of the original members of this church have long since passed to their reward. The first person of that band of fifteen to be called away was Mrs. Mehitable King, wife of Ephraim King, who died in less than four months after the organization, namely, Feb. 2d, 1809, aged 73 years. The husband died July 8th, 1820. Their bodies were at first buried in the south church-yard, but afterwards removed to Sag Harbor.

The year following the organization of this church steps were taken at a special meeting of the parish, held the 6th of June, 1809, to procure a new meeting house, the trustees being then directed to pass a subscription paper among the people, with the condition that their subscriptions would not be binding unless at least one thousand dollars were subscribed. This effort, however, did not succeed. Perhaps because once more the national skies were growing dark by the appearance of a war cloud which did burst in storm upon the people, and once more Shelter Island became the butt of the enemy's abuse and destruction. For like in the war of the Revolution, another fleet of British warships made Gardiner's Bay their anchorage and headquarters. Among them were the Ramesis, Maidstone, Sylph Thunderer, Pantagenet and the brig Boxer. These blockaded the whole eastern coast, from Fisher's Island to Montauk, and sought to destroy the neighboring villages, sending off their barges by night and by day. Under the cover of darkness they made an assault upon Sag Harbor, setting fire to its wharfs, but were driven off by the soldiers stationed there, among whom were a number of men recruited from this island. The national forces sought to blow up the flagship of this squadron, which was the Ramesis, by the use of a torpedo sent down the sound from New York. The effort, however, failed, from the torpedo getting ashore a little to the northwest of Greenport. One of the British ships, the Sylph, was sent out to destroy it, and did so, after which it cruised around the eastern end of Long Island. While running around Montauk Point on Jan. 17th, 1815, she went ashore on the south side of Long Island and became a total wreck. Out of her crew of one hundred and twenty-one men only six were saved. Among the lost were the following officers: Captain George Dickens, commanding officer; Lieutenant George Butt, Lieutenant H. S. Marsham, Mr. James Still, surgeon; Mr. Thomas Atwell, master. Indirectly that torpedo did its work. The man who brought it down the Sound was named "Penny." He lived at Northwest in a lonely place. The British found him out and one night took him prisoner. He was transported to Halifax, where he was held a prisoner until the end of the war.

As in the Revolution so in the war of 1812, the enemy would come ashore on this island, day or night, and confiscate cattle, sheep, and whatever else they wanted. It was another season of trial and suffering to our fair isle. One night the enemy went ashore on Gull Island and threw the lamps of the lighthouse into the sea. But they paid dearly for this act of vandalism, as one of their barges ran ashore on Plum Island, resulting in its loss, together with several of its crew. Their bodies were found shortly after by others from the squadron and buried on the east side of that island. Over the grave of one was set a marker, upon which was inscribed the following epitaph:

"Safely at anchor here I lay
With several of our fleet,
And here will lie till I set sail
My Admiral Christ to meet."

Of course such wanton destruction of our beacon light had to be repaid in some way. So the Yankees bought an old square rigged vessel, and fixing a magazine in her hold, so connected that upon raising the hatches, it would explode, sailed her as near the fleet as they dared, and then under cover of darkness abandoned her. When the enemy noticed the vessel they put off in boats and brought her alongside of the fleet. Then a number of officers went aboard and started to raise the hatches, when the magazine exploded with terrific force, blowing the men into the sea to their destruction and the vessel to the bottom of the waters. The British were so incensed that they sent their barges up the Connecticut the next night and burned every vessel that they found as far up as Deep River.

Mr. Lodowick Havens, from whose personal record these facts have been culled, says the sound of that explosion was like an earthquake. The British sent an order ashore on this island for the people to immediately furnish a lot of provisions, but little heed at that time was given to it, as the people felt that the three companies of soldiers stationed at Sag Harbor were abundantly able to protect them. Every man, however, on the island, kept his gun and bayonet in the room where he slept, and carried it with him to meeting when there was one, which under such conditions was not often. When peace was again restored in 1814, the people once more assembled in jubilee, only this time instead of on Prospect Heights they met in the mansion of Gen. Sylvester Dering. It is not to be wondered at that in the presence of such a state of public affairs the attempt at procuring a new meeting house, set on foot in 1809, should have failed. The year following the restoration of peace, however, namely, 1815, the effort was renewed. Of this we shall speak later on.

A little more than two months after Mr. Hall's death, in 1812, this church took steps towards being fully organized according to

Presbyterian polity, with the view of being received into the Presbytery of Long Island. "At a meeting of the congregation of Shelter Island on Friday, March 27th, 1812, being a day of fasting and prayer, voted (the subject having previously been under consideration a suitable time) 'that it is their wish and desire that the church should be regularly organized with officers upon Presbyterian principles, and become regularly connected with the Presbytery of Long Island.' They also proceeded to the choice of three Elders and two deacons, and General Sylvester Dering, Jonathan Doughlass and Lodowick Havens were chosen Elders, and the two former Deacons. The above persons having declared their acceptance of this appointment were at the same time solemnly ordained according to the Directory."

They were ordained by the Rev. Aaron Woolworth, D. D., pastor of the Presbyterian Church of Bridgehampton, who by request attended and presided on that occasion. Upon being duly elected and installed into their sacred office these elders the next day, March 28th, made application to the Presbytery of Long Island, on behalf of the church, "to be received into that body agreeable to the above resolution."

Presbytery met that year at Huntington on April 9th, 1812, when the application was received and acted upon as follows: "A communication from the Church at Shelter Island was received containing a request that they might be received into connection with the Presbytery. The Presbytery having ascertained that the proceedings of that church were regular, resolved to grant their request, and they are thereby accordingly received." And since that time down to the present, a period of eighty-six years, this church has maintained its relation with that great branch of the Christian Church with dignity and honor.

Dr. Woolworth has left on record a personal account of Mr. Hall's ministry and the organization of this church, which is of such importance that it may well be added here: "Rev. Daniel Hall's ministry, though short, was connected with salutary effects. The public worship was well attended and the moral state of society much improved. Nor were individual instances of conviction and hopeful conversion wanting. By Mr. Hall's exertion a church was first formed which had before been supposed that the number of professors was so small as to render such an attempt inefficient. This may be considered as the dawn of that brighter day which has since opened upon you.   The standard of the cross was now in manner and form erected, and the King of Zion sanctioned it, by many unequivocal tokens of his approbation which have followed.   Some small additions were made to the church during Mr. Hall's ministry, and the little band walking in fellowship of the gospel were edified.

"His death, which took place in January, 1812, was considered as a severe rebuke of heaven, both by the church and congregation, by whom he was much esteemed and loved.   This mournful event it is believed was sanctified and made the means of leading Christians to a more feeling sense of their dependence upon God, and exciting them to greater steadfastness in prayer.   In the following spring the church was more completely organized by the choice and public consecration of elders, which from the smallness of its numbers had hitherto been delayed.   Well, my brethren, do you and I remember the solemnities of that day.   The sacrament of the Lord's Supper had just been administered, and after the ordination of the session they were publicly asked whether they would engage to maintain public worship on the Sabbath, when there should be no preaching, a thing which had never before been observed, to which under a deep and solemn sense of duty they consented on supposition that the people wished it.   The proposal was made to the congregation, who by a unanimous vote expressed their desire of this arrangement and engaged to countenance and encourage it.   Accordingly since that time the public worship has been uniformly kept up, and in general been well attended, and there is reason to believe the special blessing of God has accompanied it."

And now we have reached the time when our beloved church became fully organized as a Presbyterian church and in organic relation with the Presbytery of Long Island and the great Presbyterian Church of the United States of America.   Thus far our review has been largely devoted to the birth and life of this island as the charming abode of the white man.   We have gone into its civil history with increased delight, and would find pleasure in pursuing it down to the present time.   But that is not according to our purpose.   That purpose is to trace out the record of Shelter Island down to the organization of this Society, and from that point to confine the record to the Presbyterian church.   We have therefore reached the time when ecclesiastical and civil matters becoming distinct from each other, we must bid the latter an affectionate "good bye." We can say to the civil part of our research, that if we shall find the ecclesiastical as interesting, creditable, yea, glorious, we shall have lasting cause for thanksgiving to the Almighty, who shapes our ends, and in shaping them made those of the writer to run across this place, which when He formed He so lavishly beautified for the comfort, repose and rejuvenation of mankind.

CHAPTER V.

We will begin the ecclesiastical part of these historical papers with the erection of the present church building. Upon the close of the second war with Great Britain, in 1814, the effort begun in 1809 to procure a new meeting house, and which had been interrupted by the war, was once more taken up by the circulation of the following subscription paper, with its accompanying result:

"Shelter Island, September, 1815.

"Whereas the House of Public Worship on Shelter Island is too small comfortably to accommodate the Inhabitants, and so gone to decay as to render it very uncomfortable in wet and cold weather, and it being judged unfit to repair and enlarge, we the subscribers do agree to pay on demand the several sums affixed to our names, to the Trustees of the Freeholders and inhabitants of Shelter Island, as a donation towards building a new Meeting House, or place of Public Worship on said Island, and that as soon as the Trustees judge that a sufficient sum is subscribed and collected to commence the building, they shall call a meeting of the Society for the purpose of agreeing upon a place for the Building, and the choice of a Committee to purchase materials, and to contract with persons to build the same. The House to belong to the Society, and to be regulated by them agreeably to the laws of this State, in such case made and provided, and in case more money should be subscribed and collected than is necessary, the overplus to be added to the fund for the support of the Gospel on Shelter Island."

SUBSCRIBERS' NAMES.	PLACE OF ABODE.	AMOUNT.
Samuel Lord	Shelter Island,	$250.00 .
William Bowditch	" "	100.00
Sylvester Dering	" "	300.00
Benjamin Conklin	" "	200.00
Benjamin Glover	" "	25.00
Robert Harlow	" "	20.00
Jonathan Doughlass	" "	70.00
Obadiah Havens	" "	20.00
Phineas King	" "	50.00
Jeremiah King	" "	30.00
H. P. Dering	Sag Harbor,	80.00

SUBSCRIBERS' NAMES.	PLACE OF ABODE.	AMOUNT.
Thomas Mayo...........................	Shelter Island,	25.00
Henry Conklin	" "	20.00
Shadrach Conklin.......................	" "	20.00
Henry Hains............................	" "	10.00
Edward Cartwright, Jr..................	" "	5.00
Anderson Cartwright....................	" "	5.00
Comus, a blind Negro man..............	" "	2.50
Joseph C. Havens......................	" "	5.00
Abraham Crook.........................	" "	5.00
Samuel Bowditch.......................	" "	3.00
Josiah Mayo...........................	" "	4.00
Joseph Case...........................	" "	5.00
Diana R. Williams	" "	5.00
Jeremiah Case.........................	" "	3.00
Edward Cartwright.....................	" "	5.00
Sineus Conkling	" "	5.00
George W. Congdon....................	" "	5.00
	28 Subscribers....	$1277.50

An Account of Monies Subscribed by the Citizens of New York and Elsewhere, as a Donation Towards Building a Meeting House on Shelter Island.

SUBSCRIBERS' NAMES.	PLACE OF ABODE.	AMOUNT.
Henry Rutgers.........................	New York,	$100.00
Desire Havens	" "	150.00
Mary C. L'Hommedieu..................	" "	150.00
Rensselaer Havens.....................	" "	100.00
David Gelston.........................	" "	50.00
H. A. and J. G. Castor................	" "	50.00
Jone Kane.............................	" "	25.00
John Adams............................	" "	25.00
Philetus Havens.......................	" "	25.00
Gabriel Havens........................	" "	25.00
Nathaniel Richards....................	" "	25.00
Thomas H. Smith.......................	" "	25.00
Walter Bowne.........................	" "	25.00
Henry Eckford	" "	25.00
John Mowatt, Jr	" "	25.00
James Lovett..........................	" "	25.00
Edward H. Nicoll......................	" "	20.00
Edmund Smith..........................	" "	16.00
Abraham Riker.........................	" "	15.00
Najah Taylor..........................	" "	10.00
William Edgar	" "	10.00
Grover Wright.........................	" "	10.00
Eliphalit Williams....................	" "	10.00
A. H. Lawrence	" "	10.00
N. L. Griswold........................	" "	10.00
George Griswold.......................	" "	10.00

SUBSCRIBERS' NAMES.	PLACE OF ABODE.	AMOUNT.
John Grayham............................	New York,	10.00
Thomas Jenkins...........	" "	10.00
Jonathan Thompson........	" "	10.00
Matthew Bruin............................	" "	10.00
Libbius Loomis...........................	" "	10.00
John Smith Crary....	" "	10.00
Francis Thompson.......................	" "	10.00
Benjamin Strong...........................	" "	7.00
John B. Treadwell........................	" "	5.00
Philo L. Mills............................	" "	5.00
Daniel Oakley............................	" "	5.00
Peter Schermerhorn.....	" "	5.00
Mr. Desbrow.............................	" "	5.00
J. Boggs................................	" "	5.00
Amasa Jackson...........................	" "	5.00
William Lawrence........................	" "	5.00
Thomas R. Williams (a black)...............	" "	5.00
William Whitlock.........................	" "	5.00
Hubert V. Wagenen.	" "	2.00
John Taylor........	Albany,	40.00
Henry Huntington........................	Rome,	40.00
George Huntington.......................	"	20.00
Jno. L. Broome...........................	New York,	25.00
Charlotte Broome........................	" "	2.50
Garet N. Bleeker.........................	" "	3.00
John Connelly............................	Philadelphia,	10.00
Cash of four persons	"	15.00
David Dunham............................	New York,	20.00
James Mapes.............................	" "	5.00
Harry Landon............................	Southold,	25.00
Col. Benjamin Horton.....................	"	5.00
Gilbert Horton............................	"	5.00
Hannah Storr............................	Boston,	5.00
59 Subscribers, amount		$1320.50
28 " "		1277.50
87 " "		$2598.00

In less than three months from the date of the foregoing subscription paper all this had been gathered together. The Trustees, judging that a sufficient sum had been subscribed and collected to commence the building, gave public notice of a meeting of the society to be held in the school house on Friday, Dec. 8th, 1815, at 3 o'clock P. M. The meeting was held according to appointment, but that a more general attendance of the Society might be gained, adjourned without action for one week, or until Dec. 15th, at which time the Society, having made choice of William Bowditch as moderator and Sylvester Dering as clerk, passed the following resolutions: "Resolved, that the Meeting House to be erected shall be built on the Land where the old Meeting House now stands. Resolved, that Sylvester Dering, William Bowditch, Samuel Lord, Jonathan Doughlass and Henry Conklin be a committee to receive the monies subscribed for building said Meeting House from the hands of the Trustees, and to build the said Meeting House of such dimensions and materials as the Committee or a majority of them shall agree."

A few days after the subscription paper began to be circulated a violent storm swept over this island, something like a tornado, in those days called the "great September gale." This storm felled a large number of Shelter Island's most stately trees. Many of these belonged to Gen. Sylvester Dering, and these he generously donated to the Society for use in the proposed building. Out of them was hewn the massive timbers that form the enduring frame of our present building. "The stars," said the Rev. Mr. Harries, "the stars in their courses fought for them, and the fierce winds of heaven brought them the oaks of Bashan and the cedars of Lebanon." It is indeed an ill wind that blows nobody good. God encouraged the Society in its purpose to erect a new sanctuary for His praise in felling the necessary trees for its frame upon the estate of one whom He knew had His cause greatly at heart, and who would generously donate them for that purpose. The building committee having funds and material at hand went immediately to work, and in less than fifteen months the building was finished and ready for its furnishings. To do this an additional five hundred dollars was necessary, which the parish, at a meeting held March 14, 1817, unanimously authorized the trustees to borrow upon the note of the corporation.

During the year 1816, in which the building was under construction, a remarkable revival of religion was experienced on this island. Between forty and fifty persons were hopefully converted, or as the record notes it, "made to bow to the sceptre of Jesus." The origin of this work of grace began in the conversion of a husband and wife in the early part of the year 1815. These two persons were highly connected, and the marked change in their life greatly impressed the community with the power of religion. Soon a third person became seriously concerned about salvation and moved towards Christ. This deepened the impression upon the people and prepared the way for a monthly prayer meeting. This third person was a young woman whose conversion Dr. Woolworth speaks of as remarkable. The summer came, bringing an increased interest in public worship. The work of the Lord continued to spread and prosper through the fall to such a degree that by the time Christmas had arrived the people, instead of spending the evenings of that week in festivity and mirth, as they were wont to do, they spent them in prayer and other religious exercises, which "most of the young people attended, and the meetings were solemn and marked with animating tokens of divine presence. Things remained much in this state until February, 1816 (I am now quoting from Dr. Woolworth's dedicatory sermon, preached in 1817), when the spirit of the Lord was poured out as on the day of Pentecost. The work commenced in the school-house (then under the charge of Mr. Samuel Phillips, a young man of ardent piety, and who subsequently became editor and proprietor of the 'Republican Watchman'). The mind of one of the scholars was so deeply impressed as to constrain him to cry out and request the teacher to pray for him. This disclosure soon discovered that the minds of many others were the subjects of very special religious impressions. The usual exercises of the school the rest of the day were suspended and the time devoted to prayer, reading the Scriptures and religious conversation. Persons in the immediate neighborhood came in and were deeply affected with what they witnessed. The dismission of the school at night carried the news of the wonderful things which had taken place into most of the families on the island. Much the same scenes were renewed the next day at the school-house. Many came to see and hear and were convinced that what they saw and heard was indeed the work of God. Deep solemnity rested upon the minds of almost all the inhabitants. Religious meetings were at first attended every day or evening and thronged by multitudes anxiously inquiring, 'What shall we do to be saved?' The revival thus begun continued in great power for months. The occasional preaching of the Word, which was now frequently enjoyed, and other public religious exercises, were attended with surprising effects. While scarcely an individual in the whole limits of the congregation could be found indifferent and secure, great numbers were the subjects of deep and distressing convictions, under the influence of which they were led to affecting discoveries of their lost estate in themselves—the infinite evil of sin—the plague of their own hearts—their perishing need of an interest in Christ, and in order to this of being renewed by the power of divine grace in the spirit of their minds.

In this state of humiliation the mercy of God appeared for those who were brought out of darkness into marvellous light. The enmity of their hearts was slain, and their minds enlightened in the spiritual knowledge of God and divine things. The result of which was unfeigned submission and self-consecration to God, all issuing in repentance towards Him, faith in the Lord Jesus Christ and that composure, peace and joy of mind which these divine graces and that standing in the new covenant which they ensure, never fail to inspire. Though the experience of individuals in circumstantial things was very different, in essentials there was a remarkable sameness. All embraced and rejoiced in the gospel as a system of free grace in all its parts, intended to humble the creature and exalt the glorious Creator. In the course of this revival as many as fifty obtained hope of such a reconciliation to God. Among these were not a few of the stout-hearted, and such as were indeed far from righteousness. But in this day of the mighty power and sovereign grace of God, they were made willing and brought to bow as loyal subjects to the sceptre of the Prince of Peace. The additions made to the church were between forty and fifty, and the more immediate fruits of this work of grace were a great external reformation, both moral and religious—the prevalence of a spirit of brotherly love—and a great increase of knowledge as to the peculiar and appropriate doctrines of the gospel." It was indeed a wonderful work of grace. Oh that it might be repeated in our day! In April of that year, namely, 1816, the Rev. Stephen Tracy, a Congregational minister, renewed his labors on this island, having preached here the previous year. On May 5th, after divine service at a parish meeting, he was engaged to preach for six months from April 28th. He arrived in the midst of the great revival, and is accredited with accomplishing two very important matters for this church. "One was the gathering into the church of the fruits of the great revival of the winter of 1816, and the other was the building of this sanctuary." Rev. Stephen Tracy was born in Norwich, Conn., in the year 1749. He graduated from Princeton College in 1770. The same year he began his ministry at Peru, Mass., where he was ordained in 1772. Here he remained until 1775. Became pastor at Norwich (now Huntington), Mass., May 23, 1781, and remained there until January 1st, 1799. After that he labored as a home missionary until his death, in 1822.

Without doubt the results of that great awakening of 1816 had much to do with the erection and completion of the church building. True, it had been proposed and set on foot before the revival began, and considerable subscription and material had been gathered for it. Yet faint were the hopes, even by its best friends, that the project would be so soon accomplished, if accomplished at all. Such is the testimony of Dr. Woolworth. We need to remember that the community at this date was still a small one, numbering only between two and three hundred people, and that for them such an effort was indeed a great undertaking. But the coming of that gracious outpouring of the Holy Spirit united the hearts and hands of the people in their purpose and inspired them to success to the degree that in a little over a year from the time of starting the work was completed. It was considered by all a great achievement for this community, and has been so spoken of to me by some of the older persons in our midst.

The amount expended in the erection of that building was nearly four thousand dollars. And now that it is finished we turn our attention to its description and dedication. For information concerning these things I must rely on the historical discourses that the Rev. Mr. Harries delivered in 1871. Speaking of the edifice he says: "It was fifteen feet shorter than what it is to-day. On each side of the platform were four seats. In front of it was a platform about ten inches high, on the outer edge of which was a paneled breastwork elevated nearly four feet, with a small desk in the middle directly in front of the pulpit, for the use of the elders when reading and of the chorister when singing. This enclosure was called 'the altar'—as great a misnomer as to call Christ's ambassadors 'priests.' There were forty seats before the pulpit and four each side of it, making forty-eight. The first range on the south end, consisting of four seats, were reserved by the trustees for the colored people, and the next range for 'any white person.' The body pews were assessed at $2 each and the 'long side pews' at $3.50. They were rented on the 20th of June, at a meeting appointed for the purpose. The attendance was very large and the demand for seats pressing. The four reserved free for 'any white person' were consequently rented. All but two were sold at a premium, some of which were forty per cent. above the assessed value, the whole to be cancelled at the expiration of twelve months, but next year it was to be paid quarterly."

COPY OF THE FIRST PEW LIST.

AN ACCOUNT OF THE SALE OF THE PEWS IN THE MEETING HOUSE ON SHELTER ISLAND, JUNE 20, 1817, FOR ONE YEAR.

No. OF PEW	TO WHOM SOLD	$	cts.	No. OF PEW	TO WHOM SOLD	$	cts.
1	Henry Reeve............x	2		25	Sylvester Dering........x	3	
2	Samuel Bowditch......x	2		26	Edward Cartwright x	3	
3	Thomas Tuthill........x	2	30	27	Joseph H. Parker......x	3	25
4	Daniel Harley 1 17 x	2	35	28	Benjamin Nicoll.......x	3	85
5	Abraham Crook........x	2	90	29	Benjamin Nicoll.......x	4	25
6	John Champlin........x	3	05	30	Jacob Case............x	3	25
7	Anderson Cartwright...x	2	60	31	Abraham Crook x	3	
8	John Shearman........x	2	25	32	Esther Havens ¹·²⁵⁄²⁶....x	2	50
9	Elizabeth Havens......x	2	75	33	Henry P. Dering.......x	2	75
10	Phineas King..........x	3	12½	34	Libbeus Porter x	2	85
11	George Congdon.......x	3	65	35	Richd. F. Nicoll. x	3	
12	Samuel Lord..........x	4		36	Benjamin Glover......x	3	25
13	Samuel Lord..........x	3	50	37	Edward Cartwright, Jr..x	2	35
14	Benjamin Conklin......x	2	80	38	William Congdon and } Nancy Havens...... } .x	2	25
15	Joseph Case...........x	2	70				
16	Henry Hains..........x	2	65	39	George Havens........x	2	50
17	John Chester...... ...x	2	60	40	Gordon Havens........x	2	06
18	Lodowick Havens......x	2	55	41	William Bowditch......x	3	50
19	Jeremiah King.........x	2	30	42	William Bowditch......x	5	
20	Benjamin Nicoll.......x	2	20	43	Jonathan Doughlass....x	3	85
21	Justus Horton.........x	2	12½	44	Jonathan Reeve........x	3	75
22	Sineus Conklin........x	2	30	45	Caleb Loper...........x	4	25
23	Jeremiah Case.........x	2	30	46	Henry Conklin x	4	50
24	George Cartwright.....x	2	50	47	Abraham Sherril.......x	4	50
				48	Josiah Mayo...........x	3	75
		63	50			80	21
						63	50
					....Total....	143	71

ARTICLES OF VENDUE RESPECTING THE SALE OF THE PEWS IN THE MEETING HOUSE ON SHELTER ISLAND AGREED TO BY THE TRUSTEES, JUNE 20, 1817.

The sale of the Pews to be for one year. The Pews to be set up by any person at the price set on them by the Committee, and if no person will give any more, to be struck off to them, but any one has a right to bid and the highest bidder to have the Pew.

The money for which the Pews are sold is to be paid at the end of the year, and it is expected the money will be punctually paid to the Trustees without putting the Parish to the expense of collecting.   By order of the Trustees,

SYLVESTER DERING, Clerk.

"On the 17th of the following month, namely, the 17th of July, 1817, the building was dedicated. It requires no stretch of the imagination to conceive of its being filled to its utmost capacity. As you enter you behold 'a sea of faces' upturned to fix an excited eager gaze on the sage, ministerial veteran in the pulpit, Dr. Aaron Woolworth. To the left of him on the platform is the 'deacon's seat,' or more properly the 'elders'.' There are seated the five offi-

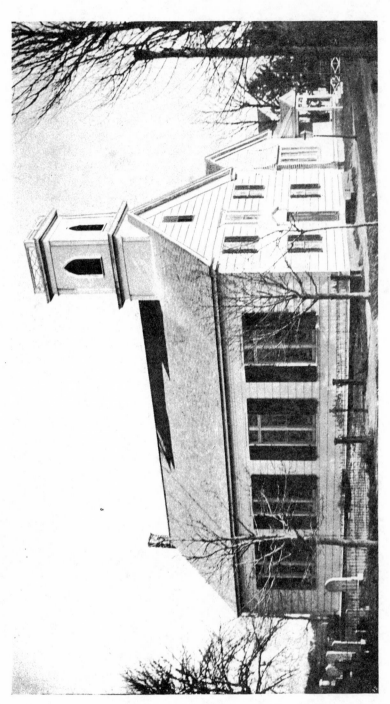

SHELTER ISLAND PRESBYTERIAN CHURCH

cers, viz.: Dering, Doughlass, Havens, Sherrill and Nicoll. The
preacher rises in the sacred desk. He is elevated eight feet above
the congregation, but he and they think it all right. It is significant of the exalted, heavenly nature of the minister and the office
he fills. He announces the hymn, and directly a venerable form
rises behind the little desk in front of the pulpit. It is the chorister.
His hymn book is before him. He announces the tune, strikes his
tuning fork on the desk, lifts it to his ear, and begins to sound a
note or two. The 'pitch' thus obtained, a volume of melodious
music fills the house. The dedication prayer is offered. Directly
the preacher reads from the 126th Psalm: 'The Lord hath done
great things for us whereof we are glad.' It is the text. The
sermon is a credit to the head and heart of its author and a fitting
tribute to the memorial occasion. That was a jubilee to this
people."

And with these lofty words the honored preacher of the occasion
consecrated the edifice "as an habitation of the God of Jacob,"
namely: "Be it henceforth dedicated to God as an house of prayer
in which His holy public worship in all its instituted branches shall
be celebrated; in which not only supplications and the sacrifices of
thanksgiving, repentance and prayer are to be offered up to the
God of all grace—but the adorable name of the King of Zion is to
be proclaimed in the preaching of the glorious gospel and the administration of the holy sacraments of the New Testament. May
the incomprehensible Jehovah, whose name is thus recorded in this
place, graciously condescend to take up His abode here, and liberally bestow upon His people the blessings of His grace and salvation, during not only the present but succeeding generations!"

While looking over some old church papers I came across the
manuscript of the following hymn, which was composed especially
for the service of dedication and sung at that time by the people.
The author's name I have been unable to discover, though much
inquiry has been made. It was certainly worthy of the writer and
the occasion:

> Be sacred this sequestered place,
>   These walls we consecrate to God,
> Who tho' He fills Heaven, Earth and space,
>   Yet makes His churches His abode.
> Within this House may sacred prayers
>   From contrite hearts, like incense, rise,
> And mental praise, with vocal airs,
>   Prelude the musick of the Skies.

Here free from passion, toil and strife,
 And every care that intervenes,
May mortals pass the bound of life
 To meditate on future scenes.

Here may the gospels, Heaven taught page,
 Be weekly opened and explained,
While blooming youth and hoary age
 Imbibe its truths with love unfeigned.

While conscience heaves repentant sighs,
 For sin against a Holy God,
May faith behold with raptured eyes
 Salvation in a Saviour's blood.

Long may this building be sustained,
 A temple for the God of love,
And children's children here be trained
 For glory in the World above.

And now the Society was fully equipped for work. Organized and officered, housed in a new and noble edifice, blessed with quickening power, it began anew its activity in the service of Almighty God.

The same month in which the church was dedicated the women of the Society, always ready and always willing, organized themselves into a missionary society known in those days as "Female Cent Societies." These societies were so called because each member pledged herself to give a penny a week towards the objects of the Society. The Society of the Shelter Island Presbyterian Church soon came into touch with other like societies, and shortly after its beginning received a congratulatory letter from the "Female Society of the Bridgehampton Presbyterian Church," of which the following is an extract: "To the Female Cent Society on Shelter Island: We have lately received the pleasing intelligence that a Female Cent Society was formed on Shelter Island. Permit us, dear sisters, to congratulate you on this auspicious event, and to assure you that we most cordially wish you success and prosperity. May your members be increased, your exertions encouraged, your graces invigorated, and every effort crowned with the divine benediction." This was gracefully responded to by Ann Willett Nicoll, secretary of the Shelter Island Society, as follows:

"The Cent Society of Shelter Island receive and acknowledge, with sentiments of grateful emotion, the united congratulations of the Female Cent Society of Bridgehampton. Permit us still to solicit the continuance of your friendship and interest in our behalf. Actuated by motives which encourage our hopes and stimulate our exertions, we look beyond the present to that period which may witness the happy effects of the united endeavor of our present infant Society. Were our means now equal to our wishes, how cheering would be our prospects. Still, we rejoice and desire to be thankful in being made the humble instruments of promoting the cause of Christ, and advancing the glory of our Heavenly Father, who constantly surrounds us by the smiles of eternal love, and every moment brings renewed expressions of His goodness and mercy. Notwithstanding our privileges and distinguished blessings, both temporal and spiritual, few have been our charities, small indeed have been our exertions in doing good. We desire to feel humble. May we all have contrition in contemplating these lamentable facts. We rejoice to hear of the general establishment of Cent Societies in our native land. We indulge the hope that they will still increase, that greater exertions will continue to be made for the extension of the Redeemer's Kingdom. How animating the reflection that the time is not far distant when the spirit of Christ will reign in every heart and all be united in the same glorious cause. It is a highly favored age in which we live. Even now the rays of the Sun of Righteousness are illuminating the remote corners of the earth, and subjects of the rich grace of God rapidly multiplying. How unceasing should be our praises, how expanded our gratitude, and may our benevolent efforts end only with existence. The Cent Society of Shelter Island was organized the 1st of July, 1817. It consists of 34 members. In behalf of this Society,

"ANN WILLETT NICOLL,

"Sec'y."

This church and community has always been highly favored with noble-hearted, whole-souled, spiritually-fervent consecrated women, of some of whom we shall have occasion to speak later on. We regret that the roll of that first Society and its list of officers cannot be here inscribed, but with great pleasure give the foregoing correspondence a place in our work.

For a period of eight years after the death of Rev. Daniel Hall

this church was without the services of a regularly installed pastor
or resident preacher.   Mr. Hall in his relations to this people was
looked upon as their pastor, though never installed as such by
proper authority.   Still that was his relation to them, and is so
recorded in the first book of records kept by the session, in which
he is twice spoken of as pastor, one of these being the notice
of his death, which is entered according to the following form:
"Rev'd Daniel Hall, our pastor, aged 64, Jan'y 20, 1812."   To
him therefore may be rightly attributed the honor of being the
first pastor of the Society now known as the Presbyterian Church
of Shelter Island, the organization of which he effected and which
stands as an enduring monument to his faithful and consecrated
labors.   During the eight years after his death the church was supplied with occasional preachers, some of whom served for several
months at a time, as in the case of Rev. Mr. Tracey.   Among these
were the pastors of the neighboring churches, Rev. Dr. Woolworth
of Bridgehampton, Rev. Ebenezer Phillips of Easthampton, Rev. J.
M. Babbit of Southampton, Rev. J. D. Gardiner of Sag Harbor,
Rev. Lathrop Thompson of Cutchogue.

One of these, who I cannot tell, perhaps the Rev. Mr. Tracy,
was small in stature though tall in intellect, for in a letter written by
a Shelter Island lady who had moved to Connecticut, from whence
she wrote to friends on this island, occurs this sentence: "Do you
keep that good little minister there yet?   I have not heard a better
sermon amongst all our ministers and preaching than he delivers."
And she had heard many in the Nutmeg State, having attended
several of what was known as "Association Days," when the ministers for a certain region would gather and hold several days of
continued preaching.   During a large portion of those eight years
the conditions of things on this island were greatly disturbed by
the war of 1812-15, as we have seen, and doubtless was the cause
of the delay in getting a resident preacher as successor to Mr. Hall.
Religious matters, however, were faithfully maintained by the elders
of the church, who had promised upon their ordination to maintain
public worship on the Sabbath when there should be no preaching.
And here a fitting opportunity presents itself of paying tribute
justly due to the memory of General Sylvester Dering, the first
elder chosen and ordained over this church.   A man whose life
was such a blessing to this place and people that he is rightly
esteemed, if not the best and noblest of all men who have lived on

Shelter Island, at least second to none in these qualities of mind and heart.

General Sylvester Dering was the second son of Thomas Dering and Mary Sylvester, and was born in Newport, R. I., Nov. 27th, 1758. He moved to this island with his parents when but two years old. And here he continued to live save during the period of the Revolution, until the day of his death, Oct. 8th, 1820, in consequence of a fall from his horse fourteen days previous. The Hon. Ebenezer Sage, of Sag Harbor, who was personally and intimately acquainted with Mr. Dering, wrote the following beautiful obituary upon his decease: "Died on the 8th inst. at his residence on Shelter Island, after an illness of fourteen days, in consequence of a fall from his horse, Gen'l Sylvester Dering, in the 62d year of his age.

"Few instances of mortality have stronger claims upon the sympathies of surviving relations, friends, society and country than that of this worthy man. He lived not for himself, his heart was formed for the exercise of all charities of this life. In all the relations he bore to society, he cheerfully and conscientiously discharged the duties of a husband, parent, brother, friend, neighbor and citizen. His children and grandchildren will never forget the paternal care and tenderness with which he watched over them from their childhood, and their surviving parent will mourn the remainder of her life the loss of a kind husband and her best friend. His extensive circle of relations and friends will, whenever they reflect upon the constancy of his love and attachment, not refuse to his memory the tribute of a tear. The inhabitants of the island on which he lived will never be guilty of the great ingratitude of forgetting the innumerable acts of kindness that they have for more than thirty years received from him as a neighbor, friend and counsellor; more especially the poor and fatherless, and those laboring under afflictions of either body or mind. Were they on beds of sickness, he administered to them as a physician; spread their pillows and watched over them as a nurse; consoling them as a friend; opening his purse to their wants and kneeling at their bedside and devoutly asking from the Great Physician relief for their sufferings and consolation beyond the power of human aid. Under his hospitable roof the friend and the stranger were equally welcome, and the poor never departed empty. It may be said that Providence for wise purposes has removed from among us a truly good man. The writer of this has known him nearly forty years, in all which time he has lived his neighbor and in habits of friendly intercourse, uninterrupted either by word or act, and does not believe he has said enough—not too much—nay, not enough until he has named the brightest gem in the character of his deceased friend. He was a Christian, and a Christian whose belief and professions were made abundantly manifest by his works. His heart at all times disposed to do good, was warmed and directed to the object by the divine precepts of the gospel of his Redeemer and holy influences of His Spirit. The church to which he belonged, and of which he was an elder and a deacon, will long mourn the loss of one of its brightest ornaments, and all who knew him will forget whatever imperfections they may have seen in his character and remember naught of all his life but the many amiable Christian and moral virtues. For to few can that divine benediction with more propriety be applied: 'Blessed are the dead that die in the Lord from henceforth; yea, saith the Spirit, that they may rest from their labors, and their works do follow them.' " Thompson in his history says: "With those who knew him best, we hazard nothing in saying that few better men ever lived. Benevolence and sympathy for the poor and afflicted were the tributes of his character, and as a public man he executed every trust confided to him with fidelity and honor. He was Supervisor of the Town many years, a Representative to the Assembly in 1804, and for some time a Major General of the militia." While Brigadier General he issued the following order:

Shelter Island, 16 May, 1809.

Brigade Orders:

The Brigadier General with peculiar pleasure communicates to the detachment from the brigade under his command the following General Orders:

General Orders:
Headquarters, N. Y., May 16, 1809.

The Commander in Chief agreeable to instructions from the President of 29 April last directs that the detachment of 14,389 of the Militia of this State required by General Order of Nov. 15, 1808, be no longer held in readiness for actual service, and in compliance with those instructions he with great pleasure avails himself of this occasion to present to those corps whose patriotism has induced them to volunteer their service, the approbation and thanks of the President of the United States.

THE COMMANDER IN CHIEF.

By order of the Commander in Chief, William Paulding, Adjt. Gen'l.

The Brigadier General orders the several Regiments of his Brigade to Parade for the Annual Review as follows:

Col. Rose's Regt. on the 9th of June next.
Col. Davis's Regt. on the 14th of June next.
Col. Conkling's Regt. on the 16th of June next.
Col. Young's Regt. on the 12th of June next.
Capt. Jermaine's Co. of Artillery on the 9th of June next.

By order of Brig. Gen'l. Sylvester Dering.

GILBERT HORTON,
Brigade Major.

Gen'l Sylvester Dering's remains were interred in the family plot in the rear of this church, and over them was placed a tablet bearing the following inscription:

Sacred
to
the memory of
GEN'L SYLVESTER DERING
Who departed this life
Oct. 8, 1820, aged 61 years.
He united a sound and active mind
With ardent and exemplary piety.
He lived not for himself,
But for the community around him,
He was a wise counsellor;
And faithful friend.
The prevailing disposition of his heart
Was sympathy for the distressed,
And corresponding efforts for their relief.
For a long course of years
He held various offices of trust,
In Church and State;
and died
Lamented, Honored, and Beloved.

Rev. Mr. Harries, speaking of Elder Dering, says among other things: "We owe him to-day for the existence of this sanctuary. But for his contributions and zealous efforts to collect funds, it could not have been erected. He ardently loved and unceasingly labored for the prosperity of Zion. His influence in the church and out of it was unbounded." And Rev. Mr. Lord also adds this tribute:

"General Dering was the son of a devotedly pious mother, one of the three godly women for whom it is said that Shelter Island was anciently distinguished. For many years previous to the organization of this church he seems to have been the only religious man who took an active part in the religious meetings. Indeed, without his presence and aid there were no religious meetings except some clergyman was present." And here we have occasion again to call your atttention to a very pleasing coincidence, namely, to the greatness that characterized the men who were the original occupants of the positions of trust to which they were severally chosen. Our first Supervisor, the Hon. William Nicoll, famed in the annals of Colonial New York; our first Trustee, the Hon. Jonathan N. Havens, equally famed in the annals of the Empire State and Nation; and now our first Elder, General Sylvester Dering, the noble-hearted, saintly patriot and Christian. All honor to these men who reflect so much glory upon community and church. How highly has God favored these in the bestowal of such great and noble citizens.

We can well imagine the grief of this community upon the death of such a man, the more so in view of the fact that just two months previous to a day another influential life had closed its career in their midst in the death of Squire William Bowditch. These two men were two of the original Trustees selected in 1785, and had continued in office together almost uninterruptedly for all these years. Now both had been removed by death, and sad indeed were the hearts of this people over the loss of two such helpful men. But their cup of bitterness was not yet full. Another potion was to be added six months later when the Rev. Aaron Woolworth, D. D., passed to his eternal reward. For this eminent servant of God had fostered this church ever since the death of the Rev. Daniel Hall. He had been their councillor and friend, he had ordained their elders, administered to them the blessed sacraments, rejoiced in their spiritual awakening, dedicated their house of God, and thus in many ways endeared himself unto them. He died after a brief illness in the full possession and exercise of all his powers, April 4th, 1821. Perhaps it was to this celebrated divine that the lady referred in her letter from Connecticut, for Dr. Prime in his history of Long Island speaks of Dr. Woolworth as follows: "Though of small stature, and by no means of prepossessing aspect, he was one of the most able, discriminating and pious divines that Long Island was ever blessed with." One of the early elders of this church, all of whom were ordained by Dr. Woolworth—three at the organization of the Society as a Presbyterian Church and two subsequently—one of these five elders, Richard Floyd Nicoll, soon after his ordination as an elder in 1816, began the study of theology with Dr. Woolworth, and was subsequently ordained a gospel minister by the Presbytery of Long Island, and in time became the preacher to this church for a short period. We shall have more to say of the Ruling Elders of this church later on. We now turn again to the condition of things prior to the death of Elder Sylvester Dering, or to the beginning of the year 1820. In the month of April of that year the Rev. William Evans was invited to fill the pulpit for four months, according to the following minute: "Parish Meeting, April 20, 1820. Voted unanimously to employ Mr. William Evans to preach the gospel to us, and that we will pay him four Dollars for every Sabbath he preaches for us or supplies the pulpit, he boarding himself. Voted that the trustees agree with Mr. Evans for four months—on the above terms and with this provision, that Mr. Evans be at liberty to take a voyage for his health when he shall choose, and if it is previous to the termination of four months, that he make up the time after his return." As no record of payment to the Rev. William Evans appears among the treasurer's accounts, it is thought that this effort proved futile, perhaps because of the ill health of Mr. Evans. Again the Society sought a preacher, this time in the person of one of their former elders, the Rev. Richard F. Nicoll, who in December of the same year, 1820, was unanimously invited to supply the pulpit for four months for five dollars per Sabbath. He responded to the invitation and supplied the pulpit during a brief period in the early part of the next year, 1821. The same year the Rev. Ezra Youngs, then a licentiate, was providentially led to this place and began about the middle of the year to preach to this people. He continued in this relation with slight intermissions from July, 1821, to the middle of the year 1828. This is established by the records of the parish meetings and the more tangible and convincing proof of the payments made to Mr. Youngs according to the treasurer's accounts. I mention these facts because this is an entirely different presentation of things concerning those early days from what has been said about them by other writers heretofore. During the seven years of Mr. Youngs' ministry in this place there were occasional supplies in the persons of Rev. Mr. Wickam for one Sabbath in 1821, Rev. Abraham Luce for one Sabbath in 1823, Rev. Mr. Moody for seven Sabbaths in 1825, Rev. David Wilson for nine Sabbaths in 1825, Rev. Mr. Moody again for one Sabbath in 1826, and the Rev. Daniel M. Lord in the fall of 1827, then a sophomore in college, employed here temporarily as teacher in the public school. A person still living with us remembers the subject of one of Mr. Moody's sermons, now preached over seventy-three years ago. It was this: "Building on sand." While laboring here the Rev. Mr. Youngs was received into the Presbytery of Long Island as licentiate on the 27th of August, 1823, and precisely five years later, after having assumed the duties of preacher to the Cutchogue Presbyterian Church, whither he went from here in the early part of 1828, was ordained to the gospel ministry, and there continued for nineteen years his relations to the Cutchogue church, after which he retired, but continued to live in the place until his death, August 25th, 1876, his funeral taking place on the 28th of that month, so that his admittance into Presbytery as a licentiate, his ordination to the gospel ministry and his burial all happened on the same day of the year. While serving as stated supply to this church he met her who was destined to become his wife, Miss Maria Nicoll, daughter of Samuel B. Nicoll, to whom he was married Oct. 4th, 1827, in the church, the first ceremony of that kind said to have been held in this sanctuary. His courtship was prosecuted somewhat under difficulties, not being acceptable to the parents of the young lady. One method resorted to in order to carry on their correspondence was for the bride-elect to get early to church and there slip into the Bible those epistles so dear to hearts engaged. These, upon opening the precious Book, would come into the hands of her intended. Mr. Youngs was a lineal descendant of Rev. John Youngs, first minister to the church at Southold. He was an able preacher, a graduate of Princeton University in 1815, having as his colleagues the Rev. Dr. Chas. Hodge, the renowned theologian; Gov. William Pennington, of New Jersey, and other distinguished men in Church and State. After his graduation he entered Andover

Theological Seminary, where he pursued a full course in Theology, and graduated in 1820 in a class of subsequent distinguished preachers and missionaries. He was licensed to preach by the Congregational Association of Andover. His subsequent advancement and ecclesiastical connections have already been dwelt upon. That he had some wit about him is shown by the following incident. In his day upon this island there was no bridge spanning Chase's Creek as there is to-day. Consequently those who wished to cross it would either ford it or row over it. Upon a certain occasion Mr. Youngs and Squire Chase had to cross the creek on the way to the latter's house. As they drew near to the water the squire proposed to the preacher that there was no need of him taking off his boots and wading through the water, remarking: "You just get on my back and I will carry you across." This being agreed to priest Youngs— the title by which the preachers were known in that day—priest Youngs mounted Squire Chase's back and thus they both crossed the stream. As Mr. Youngs dismounted from his friend's back he said: "Well, Squire, henceforth you can never say that you haven't been priest ridden." At another time, after marrying a loving couple, and being asked by the happy bridegroom what it cost, Mr. Youngs replied: "It is according to the kindness of the party." "Well," said the generous benedict, "which will you have, twenty-five cents or a load of sea weed?" "Give me," said Mr. Youngs, "the sea weed."

It was during the ministry of Rev. Mr. Youngs that this church inherited through the death of Mr. Benjamin Conkling, in 1826, a legacy of $8,000. Mr. Conkling was the youngest son of Thomas Conkling, one of our Town Fathers; a sea captain by occupation, in which profession he had amassed quite a fortune. After spending the major portion of his life plowing the seas he returned to his native place to spend the evening of his days among this people, during which he was a liberal supporter of this church, contributing fifty dollars annually towards its expenses, and upon his death, leaving no family, having never married, he bequeathed to this church the above-mentioned legacy, which, added to the legacy of Brinley Sylvester, that had grown to be about $1,000 at this date, made a total of $9,000. In 1834 the following inventory of property belonging to the Society was made, showing that it owned personal and real estate to the amount of $9,500, exclusive of the church lot and building.

INVENTORY OF ALL THE ESTATE BELONGING TO THE PRESBYTERIAN CHURCH AND
CONGREGATION OF SHELTER ISLAND, JUNE 1, 1834.

PERSONAL ESTATE.	$	cts.	ANNUAL REVENUE.	$	cts.
SYLVESTER DERING.—Note dated 26th August, 1813, for $1500. Part paid.			By order of the Court of Chancery there has been paid on these Notes and invested in Manhattan Co.'s Stock	561	86
SYLVESTER DERING.—Note dated 18th January, 1816, for $200. Part paid.					
The above Notes are in the Court of Chancery for settlement.					
Certificate for seventy-two shares Manhattan Stock...............	4234	50	Dividend........ ..	288	
JOSIAH DOUGHLASS. — Bond and Mortgage for $1400, dated 17th November 1826.................	1400		at 5 per cent	70	
JOSIAH DOUGHLASS.—Note for $400, dated 7th December, 1831........	400		at 5 per cent.......	20	
SAMUEL S. GARDINER. — Note for $300, dated 25th May, 1831. $40 paid on it.....................	260		at 5 per cent.......	13	
This Note is paid.					
Certificate for six shares Manhattan Stock	392	48	Dividend..........	24	
These above six shares of Manhattan Co.'s Stock were purchased with the money belonging to the Old Church Funds of Shelter Island.					
REAL ESTATE.					
One House and one Barn, ten acres Land, cost.....................	1550	90			

For one hundred and fifty years this community and church
have enjoyed the help of funds in maintaining the cause of religion
among them. Mr. Benjamin Conkling lived to be eighty-two years
old. He died Feb. 21, 1826, and was buried in the cemetery in
the rear of the church, where there stands a headstone with this
inscription upon it:

"In Memory of
Benjamin Conkling, who died Feb. 21, 1826, aged eighty-two.
It is but justice to the character of Mr. Conkling to say that he
was an obliging neighbor; in his habits industrious, in his dealings
honest. He liberally aided the cause of virtue and religion, and in
his last moments bequeathed a large proportion of his property to
the Presbyterian church and congregation of Shelter Island, for the
support of the gospel."

Close beside this stone and the grave of Mr. Benjamin Conkling is the grave of his brother, Shadrach Conkling, who died in January, 1827. It too has a headstone with a lengthy inscription upon it in singular contrast to that of Mr. Benjamin Conkling. It reads as follows:

"In Memory of
Shadrach Conkling, who died Jan. 23, 1827, aged eighty-eight. Mr. Conkling possessed a sound mind and excellent understanding, and was a firm patriot, a good neighbor, charitable and strictly moral. He owned, at the time of his decease, a large estate, which he bequeathed to his relations, who were all very poor, and among whom were seven orphan children. Posterity will decide upon the wisdom manifested in the disposition of the estates of these two brothers."

I do not intend to go into the merits of this proposition. One can, however, read very plainly between the lines of these epitaphs. Perhaps this significant fact will aid "posterity" in forming a correct opinion, namely, that while both men were wealthy bachelors, the latter contributed but twenty dollars to the erection of the present building, while the former gave two hundred dollars and yearly hired a pew, giving besides fifty dollars per annum to the support of the church. But we look in vain for Mr. Shadrach Conkling's name upon the pew lists of those ten years which are still in existence.

CHAPTER VI.

At the close of the Rev. Ezra Youngs' ministry, in 1828, during the last six months of which he preached here but a third of the time and two-thirds at Cutchogue, he was succeeded by the Rev. Jonathan Huntting. In September of that year the parish authorized the trustees "to make use of five hundred dollars of the Publick property to hire a Minister to Preach the Gospel unto us." Mr. Huntting had just ceased to be the pastor of the Southold church, his pastoral relation being dissolved on the 27th of August, 1828. To that church he had ministered more than twenty-two years, and now, at the age of fifty, in the very prime of his powers, God gave him to this flock as their shepherd and leader. He here continued to labor until the fall of 1832, a period of four years, during which his labors were blessed to a marked degree. He did not change his place of residence, however. That still remained at Southold, from whence he came weekly to minister unto this people. On June 19th, 1832, the parish sought to induce him to take up his abode on this island by passing the following resolution: "Voted that the Trustees be authorized to allow the Rev. Jonathan Huntting the sum of four hundred dollars a year for preaching for us provided he will come on the island and live." To this proposition he declined, but still continued to supply the pulpit, in response to the action of the parish, to the following 1st of July, when the trustees were instructed to "hire the Rev. Jonathan Huntting until they could procure another clergyman," presumably to come and live upon the island; and to this end they were at the same time directed "to write to procure a clergyman to preach for us on trial." Mr. Huntting was a man of marked ability and power; in life pure and transparent, in labors devoted and successful. His long pastorate at Southold is in itself a high testimonial to his excellency of character and acceptableness as a preacher, a workman that needed not to be ashamed, rightly dividing the word of truth. There are those living among us to-day who remember him with great esteem and warm affection. One good brother in the parish of Franklinville, whither Mr. Huntting went after ceasing to serve this people, in speaking of him to me said: "Mr. Huntting was a wonderful man, a powerful preacher. I can hear him pray now (nearly sixty years since the

time). He put his whole soul into it." The year after he was ordained at Southold, namely, the year 1808, he married Miss Julia
Sayre, of Easthampton, his own native place. How he met this most
estimable woman and proposed to her has been told to me by the
same brother, and will doubtless be as interesting to others as it was
to me, for which reason it will be here repeated. The story is as
follows: "While on his way to Presbytery, which met in that year
at Easthampton, Mr. Huntting passed through Franklinville on
horseback. It was the usual mode of travel in those days, and the
route from Southold to Easthampton was by way of Mattituck, Riverhead, Canoe Place, Southampton and so on to the place of desti-
nation. Reaching Franklinville, Mr. Huntting dismounted to pay
his respects to Mr. Seldon Herrick, who at the time was a widower.
Here Mr. Huntting met Miss Sayre, who happened to be at Mr.
Herrick's on a visit. As Mr. Huntting was about to resume his
journey, Miss Sayre and Mr. Herrick joined him, the lady intending
at the time to return to her home. And so they started off together,
Mr. Herrick and Miss Sayre in a carriage, and the dominy on his
horse. After they had gone some distance and were crossing the
sandy plains south southeast of Riverhead Mr. Herrick proposed a
change to Mr. Huntting, he to ride the preacher's horse and Mr.
Huntting to take his place in the carriage. This was readily agreed
to, so Mr. Herrick mounted the steed and Mr. Huntting placed himself alongside the fair and attractive damsel. Such close contact
had its effect, for before long their friendship ripened so fast that the
dominy proposed to Miss Sayre right then and there, and was accepted. By this time Mr. Herrick, having become tired of riding
on the dominy's horse, suggested to Mr. Huntting that they resume
their original positions, which was agreed to and effected. Now it
happened that Mr. Herrick, being a widower, was also in search of
another helpmeet, and thinking the present a good chance to get
one, broached the subject to Miss Sayre and proposed to her. To
his great astonishment and discouragement Miss Sayre responded
that while the dominy was in the carriage he had made a similar
proposal and had been accepted. They were married Sept. 20,
1808."

Mr. Huntting was born Feb. 13, 1778, graduated from Yale
College in 1804, returned to his native place and became an instructor in the academy in Easthampton, at the same time prose-
cuting the study of theology under the instruction of Rev. Dr.

Lyman Beecher, his pastor, and the Rev. Mr. Bogart, of Southampton. On the 10th of October, 1805, he was licensed to preach by the Presbytery of Long Island. As a licentiate he supplied the pulpit in Fishkill for five months in 1806. In June he began his labors at Southold, where he was ordained and installed as pastor the 20th of August, 1807. His subsequent labors have already been stated, except that he frequently supplied this pulpit after the close of his continued services in 1832. As for instance in 1834, when he preached for a month. Again in 1837 for a like period. Again in 1842, when he supplied for two months, and in 1843, when he ordained two of the members as elders in this church. During them all his home continued at Southold, where he died December 30th, 1850. Thirty persons united with this church during his ministry, most of them being the gracious fruits of a mighty revival that occurred during the last part of 1831 and the early part of 1832. During that revival they held seasons of services called "four days' meetings," when various members of the Presbytery would be present to assist the preacher in his revival efforts. In all one hundred and thirty-two persons had by this date united with the church since its organization in 1808. The next person to unite with this Society was Mr. John Bowers, who joined by letter Oct. 10th, 1833. He afterwards felt himself called to the gospel ministry, and in time became a Congregational pastor, being ordained at Wilbraham, Mass., on May 11, 1856. He supplied the pulpit at Agawam Falls for one year. After this he was called to St. Johnsbury, Vt., where he was installed as pastor over the Third Congregational Church Feb. 4th, 1858, and continued to reside there until his death, just five years later, on Feb. 4th, 1863.

Mr. Huntting was succeeded by the Rev. Daniel M. Lord, already known to this people, having taught school here during the winter of 1827-8, and at the same time supplying their pulpit and taking charge of the weekly prayer meeting. "That winter," says Mr. Lord in his historical discourse, "was memorable for two events, (1) for the burning of the school-house, with the loss of all the school-books, and (2) for a revival of religion, during which some fifteen or eighteen indulged the hope in the mercy of God. It was a work characterized by deep solemnity and pungent convictions for sin." At this time, as we have seen, Mr. Lord was a sophomore in Amherst College, with his eye set on the ministry. Upon completing his college course he entered Princeton Theological Seminary, where he pursued the study of theology for over two years. At a special meeting of the church, held Nov. 28th, 1832, the trustees were directed "to hire Mr. Daniel Lord to preach for us until the third Tuesday in June next, and that they allow Mr. Lord at the rate of four hundred Dollars a Year."

In his historical discourse Mr. Lord says: "In the fall of 1833, having been licensed to preach by the second Presbytery of Long Island, I visited this island and preached my first sermon in the schoolhouse, the church being closed while undergoing repairs. Mr. Huntting having declined to remove to this place, the good people, under the influence of that sermon, passing over all my early imperfections, and unmindful of the proverb that a prophet is not without honor save in his own country, gave me a unanimous invitation to preach to them for six months." During the winter and spring of that ministry the word was accompanied by the mighty power of God. The Lord revived his work. The church was quickened and sinners were saved. Of the fruits of this precious refreshing from the presence of the Lord twelve were gathered into the church at one communion season, among them being the last of the aborigines, upon whose remarkable conversion we have dwelt in a previous chapter. At the close of the six months he was cordially invited to preach to the people for a period of three years, a longer period than had yet been named in engaging the services of previous clergymen.

I am inclined to believe that the date of Mr. Lord's return to this people should be 1832 instead of 1833, and that for the following reasons. Mr. Huntting retired from the relation of stated supply to this people in the fall of 1832. In November of that year Mr. Lord was invited to preach "until the third Tuesday in June next." The following October, or to be precise, on Oct. 14th, 1833, at a special meeting of the parish the trustees were "authorized to hire Mr. Daniel Lord to preach for us three years, and to allow Mr. Lord the income of our stock." The same day the trustees held a meeting and "directed their Treasurer to settle with Mr. Lord and pay him what is due. Also to hire Mr. Lord for three years according to the Vote of the Society." What, however, confirms 1832 as the true date is this reference in Mr. Lord's own discourse, namely: "It was during my brief ministry that the session passed the following vote: 'Aug. 24, 1833, That it be required of members of this church to abstain from making use of ardent spirits as a beverage and to make the violation of this rule a matter of discipline.'"

Mr. Lord did not serve the three years period as invited to do by the parish in its meeting of Oct. 14, 1833, but continued only till the following May, 1834. In April of that year, after a searching examination in theology, experimental religion, philosophy, the sacred languages, polity of the church, etc., by Presbytery, then in session at Southampton, which he passed to the great credit of himself and the commendation of this court of our church, he was ordained April 16, 1834, to the exercise of all the rights of the gospel ministry as an evangelist. As Mr. Lord returned again to this charge after an absence of about fourteen years, we shall have occasion to speak of him again. Previous to his going away in 1834 his successor, the Rev. Randolph Campbell, at the time a member of the Theological Seminary at Princeton, was introduced to the people of this church and congregation. The introduction was mutually agreeable, and resulted in the following action by the church in its annual meeting held June 17, 1834, "Voted that the Trustees be authorized to hire Mr. Randolph Campbell two Years and alow him the use of the parsonage and four hundred dollars in money a Year to preach for us." "According to a Vote of Parish the Trustees hired Mr. Randolph Campbell to preach for us two Years beginning Last Sabbath in September, 1834." Mr. Campbell responded and continued to labor here until September, 1837, a period of three years. He proved to be an able minister of the New Testament. His ministry to this church was greatly blessed and owned of God in the conversion of many souls. Several revivals visited this people. On the 17th of January, 1836, twenty-five persons were received into church fellowship. These were followed by a number of others on two successive communion services. Many among us to-day remember Mr. Campbell with tenderest memories. The two oldest members of our church in point of connection, Mrs. Glorian (Cartwright) Preston and Mrs. Frances H. (Chester) Jennings, joined the church during Mr. Campbell's ministry, on Jan. 17, 1836, now over sixty-two years ago. Rev. Mr. Harries speaks of Mr. Campbell as being "modelled after the Scotch type of the Puritan character, a good scholar, an ardent Christian, rigidly adhering to the rule of duty prescribed in the Word of God, and a very able defender and expounder of its principles. He won and carried with him the hearts of his people, and even at this remote period his name is often mentioned with respect and love."

Shortly after his arrival in this place he married a lady from New Jersey. She, however, lived but a few months after their union, being stricken with death while in New York City in September, 1835, at the early age of twenty-five. He married a second and a third time, and at his death left several children.

Mr. Campbell was born at Piscataway, N. J., Dec. 31, 1809; graduated from Princeton College, now University, in 1829. He then became a tutor for three years, after which he entered Princeton Theological Seminary, from 1832 to 1834. Upon leaving the seminary he began his labors here. Like his immediate predecessor and fellow student at the seminary, he was ordained an evangelist by the Presbytery of Long Island April 30th, 1835, during his labors in this place.

He was called from this church to the church at Newburyport, Mass., the church which is noted all over the world as the final resting place of the remains of the great evangelist, the Rev. George Whitfield, these being deposited beneath the pulpit, where they have now reposed in the tranquil sleep of death for more than a hundred years. Mr. Campbell continued as pastor of that famous church for forty years, until 1877; then he went West to Nebraska for a short period, returning again to Massachusetts, in which State he continued to live until his death, which took place in Rowley, Mass., Aug. 9, 1886, at the age of seventy-six years.

Mr. Campbell was succeeded by the Rev. William Ingmire, who was unanimously invited to settle here as preacher of the gospel with the promise of four hundred and fifty dollars per annum and use of parsonage as payment for his services, this action being taken at a special meeting on July 15, 1838. Who had preached here during the nine months previous to this date, since the time of Mr. Campbell's departure, we cannot tell. That there were those who supplied during the months the records clearly imply. Mr. Ingmire continued to labor here for three years, but not with very encouraging results. His services were attended with more or less trial. It was a time of great financial depression, and the community felt it. Further, Mr. Ingmire was the successor of a brilliant man, and suffered by the comparison. During this time the funds of the church were in jeopardy. No interest was received, and the means of the church greatly crippled. "The commercial embarrassment of 1836-7 had well nigh dissipated the whole of the large sum given to the church by the late Mr. Conkling. At this distance of time, however," continues Mr. Lord, "we can readily perceive that God in his providence ordered that loss in great mercy to this people, for enough of these funds were saved to answer the purpose of the benevolent donor to secure the object he had in view, viz., the giving of the gospel to this church and congregation. Left without a minister and destitute in a measure of the means for the support of the gospel, the church was cast down but not destroyed." Its spiritual life was also very low, only two persons uniting with the church during the three years of Mr. Ingmire's ministry, which came to a close the second day of July, 1841. Again the parish sought the services of "the Rev. Jonathan Huntting to supply us with preaching occasionally, for which they (the trustees) was to pay him as they could get funds, allowing him 5 Dollars per Day and pay his ferryges." This was on July 11th, 1841.

In 1842 the Rev. Anson Sheldon supplied the pulpit for five Sundays in June and July. His services were so acceptable to the people that on August 1st, 1842, he was unanimously invited to labor among them for one year at a salary of $400 and the parsonage. He accepted the call for his services and continued to labor here until June, 1847, a period of five years. The church once more took on new life. The things ready to die were measurably strengthened, and the congregation, according to Mr. Harries, was in a better condition when Mr. Sheldon left the parish than it was when he began his labors here. A number of souls were converted during his ministry, fifteen of whom united with the church, two of whom still continue with us, namely, Mrs. Rosina Tuthill and Mrs. Maria Beebe. With these there were two young ladies who were sisters that united by letter. They were Mary L'H. and Phebe D. Gardiner, daughters of Samuel S. Gardiner and Catherine L'Hommedieu, and descendants of Nathaniel Sylvester, the original settler and last sole proprietor of Shelter Island. These ladies lived with their parents in the manor house. Both in time and turn married the late Prof. Eben Norton Horsford, Mary L'H. in 1847 and Phebe D. in 1860, Mary having died in 1855. Mrs. Phebe D. Horsford is still living as the widow of Prof. Horsford, who passed away the 1st of January, 1893. Mary L'H. (Gardiner) Horsford proved to be a distinguished member of this church, and deserves special mention here, being an exceptional woman both in piety and talent. Her religious life was far above the average. She seemed to live in another atmosphere. Her self control and spiritual repose was wonderful, so much so that one day her stepmother said to her: "Mary, haven't you any human nature?" "Yes," she replied, "it was born with me, but grace has subdued it." One can read that spirit of consecration and devotion in the following poem, of which she was the author, and which likewise testifies to her exceptionable literary ability:

1

My native isle! My native isle!
  Forever round thy sunny steep
The low waves curl, with sparkling
    foam,
  And solemn murmurs deep;
While o'er the surging waters blue
  The ceaseless breezes throng,
And in the grand old woods awake
  An everlasting song.

2

The sordid strife and petty cares
  That crowd the city's street,
The rush, the race, the storm of life,
  Upon thee never meet;
But quiet and contented hearts
  Their daily tasks fulfil,
And meet with simple hope and trust
  The coming good and ill.

3

The spireless church stands plain and
    brown,
  The winding road beside;
The green graves rise in silence near,
  With moss-grown tablets wide;
And early on the Sabbath morn,
  Along the flowery sod,
Unfettered souls, with humble prayer,
  Go up to worship God.

4

And dearer far than sculptured fame
  Is that gray church to me,
For in its shade my mother sleeps,
  Beneath the willow tree;
And often, when my heart is raised
  By sermon and by song,
Her friendly smile appears to me
  From the seraphic throng.

5

The sunset glow, the moonlit stream,
  Part of my being are;
The fairy flowers that bloom and die,
  The skies so clear and far;
The stars that circle Night's dark
    brow,
  The winds and waters free,
Each with a lesson all its own,
  Are monitors to me.

6

The systems in their endless march,
  Eternal truth proclaim;
The flowers God's love from day to
    day
  In gentlest accents name;
The skies for burdened hearts and
    faint
  A code of Faith prepare,
What tempest ever left the Heaven
  Without a blue spot there?

7

My native isle! my native isle!
  In summer climes I've strayed,
But better love thy pebbled beach
  And lonely forest glade,
Where low winds stir with fragrant
    breath
  The purple violet's head,
And the stargrass in the early spring
  Peeps from the sear leaf's bed.

8

I would no more of strife or tears
  Might on thee ever meet,
But when against the tide of years
  This heart has ceased to beat,
Where the green weeping-willows
    blend
  I fain would go to rest,
Where waters chant, and winds may
    sweep
  Above my peaceful breast.

This spiritually-minded and heavenly-gifted woman took cold one autumn day, out of which tetanus, or lock jaw, developed, that caused her death on Nov. 25th, 1855, at the early age of thirty-one. Like Enoch of old she had walked with God and suddenly was not, for God had taken her.   But though dead she yet speaketh, speaketh through this charming poem and a number of others equally exquisite that make up a volume of poetry entitled "Indian Legends and Other Poems," published the very year she died, and which she dedicated to her father, "as a slight testimonal of a daughter's gratitude and affection."   Let her name be enshrined forever among that galaxy of noble men and women given of God to this church.   The parents of this saint were both members of this church, the mother, Mary C. (L'Hommedieu) Gardiner, uniting March 29th, 1829, and the father, Samuel S. Gardiner, twenty years later, on May 20, 1849.   He had a remarkable conversion at the advanced age of sixty years.   It is said that when he experienced religion he arose and made one of the most marvellous speeches ever made, which is remembered by many to this day.   He was an eminent lawyer and politician.   At the early age of thirty-one he had attained such prominence in the State as to be made secretary of the convention that formed the constitution of the Empire State in 1821.   He was a very stately gentleman, tall, handsome and attractive, always wearing a frilled shirt.   After his conversion he became very useful in the church, which he had already served for a number of years as a trustee, being a teacher in the Sunday school.

We have now reached the summer of 1847 in the tracing down of those who have served the church as pastor or preacher.   Mr. Sheldon's services ceased in June, 1847.   About this time the Rev. Mr. Lord returned to Shelter Island after an absence of thirteen years for rest and recuperation.   During these years he had unceasingly labored as pastor of the Mariners' Church in Boston, and also as agent of the Seamen's Friend Society.   His health had become so broken through these arduous duties that he was forced to leave the city, and in order to regain his accustomed vigor and at the same time provide for his family, he turned to Shelter Island with the purpose of becoming a tiller of the soil.   Settling on Menantic Creek he was soon engaged in farming, with the happy result of restoring to him speedily his wonted powers.   Again he was ready to go forth as a preacher of righteousness, and the Lord of the harvest as speedily pointed out to him what proved to be the last and closing field for his labors. This church being without a preacher needed a supply. It turned to Mr. Lord for the third time in its need. At first it simply asked him to tide over the going and the coming servant of God, whoever he might be, and so one Sabbath in September, 1847, the male members were requested to remain after the close of the meeting for the purpose of consulting "about getting a minister to preach for us (them), and they Voted Unanimous that the Trustees offer Mr. Lord $7.00 per Sabbath to preach for them until they could obtain some one permanently to preach for them." To this invitation Mr. Lord favorably responded, but upon the one condition that when they found a man of their choice to minister to them in the things of Christ he would step aside, and if still residing among them would heartily assist them in his settlement and support. Under these conditions he began his labors. The winter came and went. Each succeeding week strengthened the bond between them, until at last the church became conscious that the man they were seeking and that God had for them was the very man who stood before them. The result was that on Feb. 28th, 1848, the sense of the church was called for, in a meeting held in the school-house, in regard to calling Mr. Lord, not as a supply, according to the custom of the church since the death of Mr. Hall in 1812, but as pastor. The response was unanimous, and the Rev. Daniel M. Lord was thereupon solicited to become the pastor of this church, with a promise of four hundred dollars per annum as salary. After much prayer, counsel and deliberation he assented to their desires, and on the 11th of April, 1848, pursuant to notice given the parish, met in the school-house "for the purpose of making a call for the settling of the Rev. D. M. Lord as our pastor." The meeting was moderated by the Rev. Anson Sheldon, the church's previous supply. He opened it with prayer. But one feeling was expressed, all hearts being united in the desire that the great Head of the Church might appoint the man of their choice to lead them like a shepherd and be a pastor to them. After the prayer this formal action was taken: "Voted unanimously that we make out a call for the settlement of Rev. D. M. Lord as our installed pastor, that we give Rev. Mr. Lord annually the sum of four hundred dollars and the use of the parsonage and three Sabbaths per annum. We, agreeably to the vote, made out a call for the settlement of Rev. D. M. Lord, signed by the moderator and the elders, and will leave it with the Presbytery of

Long Island for them to decide on. Present at the meeting as elders, C. S. Loper and Horace B. Manwaring.

"CALEB S. LOPER, Clerk."

This call was committed to Presbytery. Presbytery then placed it in Mr. Lord's hands. He agreeing to accept, Presbytery constituted this sacred relation between Mr. Lord and this church on the 30th of August, 1848, by duly installing him as pastor of the Shelter Island Presbyterian Church. It was a happy occasion, in which both pastor and people rejoiced. The like of it had never before been seen on this island. It was the first of its kind. Almost two hundred years had now elapsed since the settlement of Shelter Island. And while during that long period this community was never without those who feared God and worked righteousness, while it had been favored with the presence of those who were world-famed evangelists of the glorious news from heaven, while there had lived among them those who were accepted as the ambassadors of the Most High, one of whom was looked upon and acknowledged as pastor of this church, still to the Rev. Daniel M. Lord belongs the honored distinction of being the first duly installed pastor of the church of the living God on Shelter Island. While most of the former preachers of God's infinite grace were as "wayfaring men away from home tarrying as but a night," Mr. Lord's relation, now established, was a permanent and abiding one; indeed, as we shall see in the providence of God, the relation was to last until death should remove him from all earthly toil to the heavenly land of peace and rest. As he has left on record the motive that prompted him and the condition of things spiritually that greeted him as he entered upon this pastoral relation, it seems eminently proper that the same should be repeated here, hence the following: "Permit me to say that in accepting the office of your pastor it was not pecuniary compensation I sought. If it had been my exclusive attention would have been given to the broad acres of Menantic. In this respect my worldly interests have suffered; without this ministry I might have been richer in dollars and cents. I knew this when I acceded to your wishes. Nor do I now regret it. For it was not yours but you I sought. God is my witness how I have longed for your salvation. I entered upon my labors among you in much weakness and through many discouragements. Twelve years had passed since God had blessed this church and congregation with a special dispensation of his

REV. THOMAS H. HARRIES
1864—1884

REV. RANDOLPH CAMPBELL
1834—1837

REV. EZRA YOUNGS
1821—1828

REV. BENJAMIN F. PARLIMAN
1889—1895

REV. DANIEL M. LORD
1827 1832—4 1847—1861

REV. JONATHAN HUNTTING
1828—1832

REV. A. P. BISSELL, D. D. PH. D.
1884—1889

REV. ANSON SHELDON
1842—1847

REV. CHARLES H. HOLLOWAY
1861—1864

spirit. The church had become lukewarm. Some of its members had backslidden, alienation of feeling had taken place between brethren, the cause of Christ was insulted and in some instances trampled upon. The youth were irreverent in the house of God, and in some instances forgetting even the common decencies of the proprieties of life. They were without God and without hope in the world. Their conduct seemed to say, 'Who will show us any good?' But God has been better to me and to you than we had even dared to hope. The fruits of my ministry is fresh in your recollection. Many of you were nine years ago the subjects of renewing grace. In that wonderful refreshing from the presence of the Lord you were made to sing of redeeming grace and dying love. The winter of 1848 and 1849 will be long remembered by this church and congregation as the season of the most powerful and extended work of grace with which this island had been previously blessed. I seem to hear one and then another saying at the slightest recollection of those scenes and those events,

'Amazing grace, how sweet the sound
That saved a wretch like me!' "

You will see from this quotation that a mighty work of grace took place upon this island during the winter of 1848 and 1849.

It was the divine witness of approval to the relation that had but a few months previous been consummated. God set his seal at once upon Mr. Lord's ministry to this people, and that favor attended to it to its very end, for one revival followed another during the fourteen consecutive years that he was privileged to labor here before the Lord said to him, "It is enough, come up higher!" As the result of that divine quickening in 1848-9, thirty-six persons united with the church on May 20th, 1849, now nearly fifty years ago. Of these the name of Archibald R. Havens, of saintly memory, heads the list. Only five of the number continue unto this day, they are Samuel B. Jennings, Mrs. John B. Bowditch, Mrs. Charles T. Chester, Mrs. Daniel Hudson and Mrs. Charles H. Smith, the first three still retaining their membership in this church. Nine years later another revival took place, and on May 4th, 1856, thirty-two united upon their profession of faith in the atoning work of Christ with this church, followed by nine more during that year, making the total forty-one as the precious fruits of that season of refreshing. This was followed by a third revival in the winter of 1857 and 1858, mightier still than any of the many and the mighty that had

preceded it. Behold what God wrought for this people! "It is
the Lord's doings and it is marvellous in our eyes." Fully one-
half of the adult population of this island, as the result of these
mighty outpourings of divine grace, were the open and avowed
professed friends of the Lord Jesus Christ. Many of these still abide
with us. They are Mr. Lord's spiritual children, his joy and crown.
And so he labored with untiring energy and with marvellous success until the Lord strangely took him, translating him most suddenly to the heavenly glories Aug. 26, 1861.

It is no wonder that Mr. Lord has been so enshrined by this
people in their undying affection that the mere mention of his name
makes their pulse to beat more rapidly, their face to grow more
brightly as in memory they behold the beloved face and form of him
who led them so divinely. Few pastors ever wrought themselves
into the very being of their people as did this dear man of God. As I
think of all this, how his radiant form adorns your homes, how his
name is as sweetest smells to your senses, how in labors more abundant the power of Christ was so wondrously displayed, I thank my
God that He hath appointed me as one of his successors in the same
pastoral office, and at the same time invoke His grace to attend
me that I may be faithful in this trust.

His death, already referred to, was both tragic and sudden. It
occurred on Monday, Aug. 26, 1861, while he was making prepara-
tions for the comfort and entertainment of the Presbytery of
Long Island, which was to meet on this island the next day.
Leaving his home in a wagon with three of his children for the
purpose of securing a sheep off his extended farm that was to
be slaughtered and prepared to refresh the members of Presbytery, he was driving along the road when suddenly his horse took
fright at the noise of some boards which a neighbor was removing
from one place to another, and though at first the animal seemed
to be brought under control, it started again, this time throwing
Mr. Lord from the wagon so as to strike on his forehead, inflicting
what speedily proved to be a fatal wound. While lying prostrate
upon the ground a wheel of the wagon likewise passed over his
body, mortally injuring it. Neighbors near by ran to his assistance
and relief. The first words he spoke were words not concerning
himself, but his children, whether "those dear children had been
hurt," and to "take care of them." Then he called for water and
asked that a physician he sent for, at the same time saying that he

must be bled. Loving hands did all they could for him, and then conveyed him to his home.

He realized the fact that death was near, and so he said in a few moments after: "The Lord have mercy, I am going." Though upon reaching his home he showed some signs of consciousness, "neither the voice of his wife nor the kisses of his children could evoke another word of love from those pale lips. God had sealed them with a sacred seal. Twenty minutes more the husband, the father, the brother, the pastor, continued to breathe in the midst of his kindred and friends, and not a groan nor a sigh gave sign of pain. He fell asleep, and no struggle marked his sweet repose."

> "So Jesus slept. God's dying Son
> Passed through the grave and blessed the bed;
> Rest here, blest saint! till from His throne
> The moring break and pierce the shade."

Three days later his funeral took place in this church in the presence of kindred, Presbytery and flock of God, to say nothing of the great circle of friends that mourned over his going, spreading over the New England and the Middle States, all stricken to the dust. And from that day until the present his sacred remains lie sleeping in yonder cemetery awaiting the resurrection of the just, whither tender hands and bleeding hearts bore them that memorable day in August, 1861.

Never having seen Mr. Lord I cannot speak of him but from observation. However, there is one still living who knew him intimately, and who in the providence of God was called upon to perform the kind and solemn office of delivering his funeral sermon, the Rev. Epher Whitaker, D. D., of Southold. It is from a printed copy of that able discourse, abounding with personal and exalted testimony, that the foregoing and the following quotations are given: "It would be impossible in a brief space to set forth even the main points of his character. His peculiar training and wide range of intercourse with other men made him at ease in any presence, but never erased one line from his features, which gave him a charming individuality. He was always and delightfully himself. Having a physical frame of medium size he was able, through all his life, to keep it vigorous, sinewy and symmetrical, and even now, on his lifeless face, we may trace the fair lines of that manly beauty which the friends of his early years so well remember. He usually showed a degree of activity that would have utterly overcome almost any man. Closely allied to this feature of his character was another which made his home the scene of an unbounded and almost unceasing hospitality. His largeness of heart was vast enough to make him desire the welfare of every human being, and the fountain of his cheerfulness was a perpetual spring of delight to all who shared his company. His heart was full of kindness and love for every class, but it knew not the fear of man in any walk of life. He had a special love for the company of Christian ministers.

"And how shall I speak of his virtues in the family—his tender love, his sacred truth, his wise forethought, his delicate sympathy, his unceasing devotion, his supporting hand, his protecting arm, and all those nameless qualities which made him, in so high a degree, the faithful husband, the judicious father, the beloved brother?

"It was Mr. Lord's high and keen sense of moral responsibility, as well as his great love for all his fellow-men, that often called him away from his home. What zeal and power has he not shown in staying the waste and the woe inflicted by the scourge of intemperance? What village of the county has not been thrilled by his startling pictures and carried to unknown heights of enthusiasm by the flood of his manly eloquence? Yes, we have heard from his lips an eloquence which came not from the schools. He was no surface reformer. He laid the foundation of all his work on the solid rock of religion. This was one source of his excellence as a minister of God's word. He had his own style of preaching, and though it was all his own, it was nearer the style of the model Preacher, who uttered the Sermon on the Mount, than any modern invention or resuscitated antiquity used by popular preachers who make their names notorious in the world. He spoke as one having authority. Few men could speak like him in the use of this element of the preacher's power. His unusual success in the ministry is good evidence for us that God approved his work. Few so well deserved to be called Godlike. Few so closely resemble the Son of Man, who came not to be ministered unto but to minister, and to give his life a ransom for many."

Loving tribute fitly spoken. Daniel Minor Lord was born at Lyme, Conn., April 9th, 1800. His father dying while he was yet a boy, he was placed in the care of a relative who was a prominent merchant in the city of New York. There he grew to manhood and experienced religion. Feeling called of God to the ministry, he entered the Academy of Monson, Mass., from whence he went to Amherst College, graduating in 1830. He then entered Princeton Theological Seminary, and there successfully pursued the study of theology, after which he entered upon his labors in this place. Being called to Boston, he left Shelter Island in 1834 to become the pastor of the Mariners' Church in that New England city. There he labored most successfully for thirteen years, until forced to retire in order to recuperate his health. While laboring there he was instrumental in converting, among many others, the Rev. Mr. Jones, who afterwards became the noted chaplain of Sailors' Snug Harbor. This Mr. Jones was a sailor. One day he was sent by his captain over the side of the ship to do some painting. It was an exceedingly stormy day, the sea was so rough that no boat could have been lowered safely into it. As he was painting he all at once looked up and saw to his amazement that two of the strands of the rope that held the scaffold were cut, and that what supported him was the remaining strand. His blood ran cold. Horror came over him, and the thought that arose in his mind prompted the question, "Jones, if that strand had broken where would you have been?" And a voice that seemed to be plainly heard made answer, "Jones, you'd have been in hell!" It rang through his ears and kept ringing. He could not get rid of it until he had made his peace with God. He devoted his life to his Savior's service with the above noted success. And now in the starry diadem of Brother Lord in glory one gem shines with conspicuous brilliancy. It represents the conversion of Rev. Mr. Jones, in which Rev. Mr. Lord was chiefly instrumental. "For that one service alone," said the Rev. Dr. Theodore L. Cuyler to me, "the memory of Mr. Lord will continue blessed." One hundred and thirty-three persons united with this church during his third period of ministry to this church. At the close of the revival of 1856 the church had to be enlarged in order to accommodate the people. This was accomplished in 1858 by the addition of fifteen feet to the length of the building on the north end, which gave room for twenty-eight more pews in the body of the church. At the same time the belfry was added, giving a much more churchly appearance to the building. These improvements were under the care of Martin L. Prince, George G. Penny and Marcellus D. Loper, who were appointed a building committee for the purpose of effecting these improvements at the annual parish meeting held June 15th,

1858. The whole involved an outlay of about one thousand five hundred dollars. Upon its completion the enlarged and improved sanctuary was rededicated by Mr. Lord to the service and glory of God.

Mr. Lord was twice married, his first wife being Miss Brown, whose mother, Mrs. Hannah P. Brown, was the author of that noted hymn, "I love to steal awhile away." Miss Brown lived but a short time after her marriage to Mr. Lord. During his pastorate in Boston Mr. Lord married again a Miss Eliza A. Hardy, of Chatham, Mass., by whom he had seven children. The mother was still living with all her children when we began the preparation of these papers. Two of the sons of Mr. Lord entered the ministry, a third became a prominent business man in Chicago, while two of the daughters are successfully maintaining a new educational enterprise in this State.

CHAPTER VII.

Mr. Lord was succeeded by the Rev. Charles H. Holloway, who was invited to act as stated supply for one year. He accepted and began his labors in September, 1861. He continued in this relation until February, 1863, when he was duly installed by Presbytery as pastor. In this relation he continued until Aug. 2d, 1864, when his pastoral relation was dissolved by his own request. Mr. Holloway possessed great literary ability, and while the equal of his predecessor in this respect did not possess that personal magnetism of Mr. Lord, and so failed to meet the expectations of some of the congregation. By those who knew him his memory is still cherished with affection. He is still living and cherishes most highly the three years of labor he was permitted to engage in here.

It was during his connection with this church that the present parsonage was built, and thus he and his family were the first to occupy it. Previous to this the parsonage was the house now owned and occupied by Mr. Edward P. Baldwin and family, and as such was in turn the home of the Rev. Randolph Campbell, Rev. William Ingmire and the Rev. Anson Sheldon and their families while these clergymen served the Society. The use of it was likewise included in the salary of the Rev. Daniel M. Lord. He, however, did not reside there, having his own home in Menantic, where Mr. Henry Walther now lives, and of which he is the worthy owner. The first parsonage owned by the parish was bought about 1834 with part of the legacy that Mr. Benjamin Conkling bequeathed to the church. It remained in the possession of the church until Mr. Smith Baldwin bought it about 1850. The Rev. Daniel Hall, who organized the church in 1808, and who lived and labored on this island from 1805 to the day of his death in 1812, made his home in the house now owned and occupied by Mr. Charles W. Jennings, while the very first minister to live and labor among the people of this community, the Rev. William Adams, had his home in the mansion of Brinley Sylvester, Esq. These then have been the various homes of God's servants who lived on this island while they labored here. Rev. Ezra Youngs made his home in Greenport, and the Rev. Jonathan Huntting in Southold while they served this Society.

The successor of Rev. Mr. Holloway was the Rev. Thomas H. Harries, who came for the first time to this island on Saturday, Nov.

19th, 1864, in order to supply the pulpit the following day. He did this with such acceptance that five weeks later he again occupied the sacred desk. The day was Christmas. In harmony with the spirit of that glad day this church gave Mr. Harries a call to preach for one year, at a salary of seven hundred dollars. The invitation was accepted and he began his labors with the first Sunday of the new year. Two months had hardly passed by when his services, having proved so acceptable to the people, he was unanimously requested to become their pastor at the increased salary of seven hundred and fifty dollars, together with the use of the parsonage. The call was presented to Presbytery at its spring meeting. Presbytery placed it in the hands of Rev. Mr. Harries, who, having considered it earnestly and prayerfully, accepted the same. Arrangements were made for his installation, and on the evening of the 8th of June, 1865, he was duly inducted into the pastoral office of this church by the following clergy: the Rev. Clark Lockwood, who conducted the opening exercises; the Rev. James T. Hamlin, who preached the sermon and proposed the constitutional questions; the Rev. Edward Stratton, who delivered the charge to the pastor; the Rev. Dr. Epher Whitaker, who charged the people, and the Rev. Mr. Knouse, who offered the concluding prayer, the benediction being pronounced by the newly installed pastor. Rev. Mr. Harries was the third person to be thus placed by Presbytery over this church, and in that pastoral relation he continued to serve the longest of all, a continuous service of nineteen years, and then only brought to a close because of his failing health, which necessitated his retirement in 1884. He proved himself an able and efficient workman in the vineyard of the Lord. He too was used of God to the conversion of many souls. Like Mr. Lord's, his ministry was also attended with revival power and seasons of refreshing. More than two hundred persons were added to the church during his ministry. He greatly endeared himself to this people, and when in the providence of God he was forced to resign, through ill health, it was not without deep regrets that this church parted with him who had so faithfully, so ably and so long served them in the holy office of pastor. What he was, both as a man and brother beloved in Christ, and as a bishop of souls, is best expressed by the following resolutions unanimously adopted by the church at the close of his pastorate:

"Whereas, Our pastor, the Rev. Thomas Harries, on account of ill health, has felt it necessary to tender his resignation as pastor of this church; and

"Whereas, We deplore the circumstances which seem to make it necessary for us to sever the pastoral relation with feelings of heartfelt sadness;

"Resolved, That the twenty years of faithful service rendered by him to this parish have been greatly blessed in upbuilding our church, increasing its membership and creating feelings of Christian fellowship and good will;

"Resolved, That for his ministering to the temporal wants of the poor and the spiritual needs of all, for the tender solicitude and earnest sympathy which always brought him to the bedside of the sick and dying, and for his exertions to ameliorate the condition of suffering humanity at all times and under all circumstances, the members of this parish and the people of this island owe him a debt of gratitude which they can never repay;

"Resolved, That in parting our kindest wishes will ever attend him as one worthy of our full confidence and highest esteem."

Upon leaving Shelter Island Mr. Harries took up his residence in the city of Brooklyn, N. Y., where he passed the remaining days of his earthly life. He fell asleep in Jesus August 4th, 1888, aged seventy-five years. He was born in Wales on the 23d of February, 1813, and came to America when a boy. At first he worked in a large printing house, Henry R. Pitney being his employer. Here he soon, by his zeal, intelligence and attention to business, became his employer's chief man at the early age of twenty-one. It was while thus engaged that he felt called to the gospel ministry and decided to enter the same. Relinquishing his bright business prospects he began his theological studies, at the same time preaching where he had opportunity. And thus he continued until he was twenty-four years of age, when in the month of April, 1837, he was ordained and entered upon the full ministry of the gospel. For the next two or three years he was mainly engaged as an evangelist, after which he became the pastor of Upper Aquebogue Congregational Church, and continued so for a number of years.

Receiving a call from the Mount Sinai Congregational Church he moved to Miller's Place to enter upon the duties of that office. While occupying the pastoral office to the Mount Sinai Church he was largely instrumental in the establishment of Miller's Place Academy, and for over ten years carried it on with advantage to himself and great usefulness to others. From Miller's Place he went to Northville about the beginning of the Civil War to become the minister of the Congregational Church in that community. Here he remained until he was called by this church, on Christmas Day of 1864, to occupy its pulpit. He accepted, as we have seen, was shortly afterward installed as pastor, and served for twenty years. Altogether he was a preacher of righteousness for fifty years. Mr. Harries was married to Miss Joanna Van Zandt Duryea about the year 1839. For forty-three years they lived in blessed union together, her death occurring in 1883 in the present parsonage. They were blessed with four children, named Thomas W., Charles D., Mary W. and Elizabeth.

Mr. Harries was succeeded by the Rev. A. P. Bissell, D. D., who was recommended to this church by the Rev. Dr. Thomas S. Hastings, of Union Seminary, New York City. He preached on three Sundays in November, 1884, and at the close of the morning service of the last Sabbath in that month was unanimously invited to become the Society's stated supply for one year at a salary of one thousand dollars, the use of the parsonage and six Sabbath vacations. Mr. Bissell accepted and began his labors on Sunday, December 15, 1884. He continued in this relation until May 1, 1889. His ministry was attended with the divine blessing, and various additions were made to the membership of the church. A blessed quickening in 1885 resulted in fifteen uniting with the church on Sunday, April 2d of that year.

Mr. Bissell was a very scholarly man, being the only minister of all who have served on this island to receive the degree of Doctor of Divinity, which was conferred upon him by the University of Vermont in 1884. The same year he received the degree of Doctor of Philosophy from the University of Leipsic, Germany, where he was a student from 1882 to 1884.

Dr. Bissell was born in Essex County, N. Y. He graduated from the University of Vermont with high honors. For seven years he was a teacher, after which he studied theology, graduating from Union Theological Seminary in 1868. The next four years he served as pastor, and the following four years as Professor of Hebrew in Blackburn University at Carlinville, Ill. In 1876-7 he was instructor in Hebrew in Lane Seminary. From 1877 to 1882 he served again in the pastorate. The next two years he spent abroad. Upon his return from Europe he began his labors here, and at their close became in 1891 Professor of Hebrew and Greek Exegesis and German in Biddle University, Charlotte, N. C., which high position he still discharges.

Dr. Bissell was followed in the ministerial office here by the Rev. Benjamin F. Parliman, a graduate of Princeton Theological Seminary, who began his services to this people as stated supply in December, 1889, and continued them to September, 1895. He served the church with earnestness and consecration, and his labors were blessed with a remarkable revival of religion in 1891, the fruitage of which was the largest ingathering of souls into this church in its history, forty-five uniting with the church on Sunday, March 15th, 1891. It must have been a memorable occasion. Two of that number have since been called to the assembly of the church of the First Born on high, Miss Leonora Ketcham and Miss Nellie S. Jennings, both young disciples of Christ, who were known and are still lovingly remembered for their holy zeal and good works. "They rest from their labors but their works do follow them."

The former lost her life while bathing. But it was not in vain, for both the manner and suddenness of it made a deep impression upon the community which is felt to this day. The latter's death was likewise speedy and startling, and being but a few months passed, is still fresh in our memory. May every one of their companions, who with them formed that great company on that memorable Sabbath in March, 1891, leave as positive a going "to be with Christ which is far better" when they depart this life, as all acknowledge concerning the two whose names are here given a place in these papers.

Besides this glorious work of grace brother Parliman's ministry is conspicuous for the erection of the present commodious and attractive chapel.

Mr. Parliman was born in Haverstraw, June 19, 1855, graduated from Princeton Seminary in 1887. The same year he was ordained and installed pastor of the church at Salt Point, N. Y., by the Presbytery of North River. He is now the pastor of the First Presbyterian Church in Haverstraw, N. Y., his native place.

After Mr. Parliman came the present incumbent, the author of these papers, who was unanimously called to become the pastor of this church on November 17, 1895. The following January, 1896, he was duly inducted into that sacred office by the Presbytery of Long Island, the following clergymen assisting: Rev. Frederick G. Beebe, moderator of the Presbytery, presided and asked the constitutional questions; Rev. Minot S. Morgan read the Scriptures; prayer was offered by Elder Schuyler B. Horton; the sermon was preached by the Rev. J. J. Dunlop; Rev. Dr. E. C. Lawrence charged the pastor; Rev. Dr. Epher Whitaker, the honored stated clerk of Presbytery for over forty years, charged the people, and the newly installed pastor pronounced the benediction.   Concerning his labors here it will be left for others to speak.   He was born in the city of Brooklyn, N. Y., Sept. 29, 1858, and is the son of Jacob and M. D. C. (Lehnert) Mallmann.   Early in life he felt the need of a Savior and gave his heart to Christ.   Entering into mercantile life he in time became the successor of his father in the baking business.   This he carried on for seven years, when feeling himself called to the gospel ministry he disposed of his business and began to fit himself for the ministry, at first in Springfield, Mass., as one of the original students of the School for Christian Workers, now known as the Bible Normal College, and also under the instruction of a private tutor, after which he entered Princeton Theological Seminary, from which he graduated in 1889.   During the last year in the Seminary, and the first year after graduation, he was minister in charge of Olivet Chapel, under the care of the Lafayette Avenue Presbyterian Church, of which the Rev. Theodore L. Cuyler, D.D., LL.D., at that time was pastor, and of which church before entering the ministry he was a member.   In that chapel he was ordained by the Presbytery of Brooklyn, October 23d, 1889.   In the early part of 1890 he received a unanimous call as pastor from the First Presbyterian Church of Newtown, N. Y., which he accepted, and was installed by the Presbytery of Nassau on the evening of May 8th, 1890.   Here he continued to labor until the fall of 1895.   While serving the Newtown Presbyterian Church he was honored with the great privilege of building one of the finest suburban church buildings in the country, through the munificent bequest of over sixty thousand dollars by John Goldsmith Paynter, Esq., deceased, to that Society.   Immediately upon the close of his labors at Newtown, N. Y., he entered upon his services here, in which he still continues.   On April 11th, 1878, he married Miss Hannah Matilda Robinson, daughter of Charles B. and Catherine (Babcock) Robinson.   Their union has been blessed with three children, two daughters and a son, the latter, named Payson, passing on to the "Father's house" on Aug. 11th, 1885, aged nearly eleven months.   The names of the daughters are Ruth Robinson, now the wife of Dr. F. Everett Benjamin, of Shelter Island, N. Y., and Maria D. Caroline Mallmann. And here the writer wishes to make use of the privilege of rising up and calling the memory of his dear mother "blessed," for he feels that to her parental faithfulness in religious training, untiring efforts for his welfare, and self-denying labors he owes everything under God in that He hath "counted me faithful, putting me into the ministry." Oh, that precious name of "mother!" how sweet it sounds! We shall meet again, dear mother. In the meantime may your "dear boy," by the grace of God, ever prove himself worthy of that care you so unceasingly bestowed upon him.

We turn now to speak of some of the members of this church who have been an honor to it and who have stood in it as "pillars in the temple of our God." We cannot mention every one of them, for space and time will not permit it. If, therefore, any names are omitted that perhaps ought to appear, in charity let it be remembered that some things and some names must of necessity be omitted. Though their names may be wanting here, upon the Lamb's book of life they have been everlastingly entered, and have therefore become inheritors of the eternal glories. Earth's honor roll may be faulty, heaven's never. There even the least are remembered to such a degree that it is said, "Many that are first shall be last, and the last shall be first." At various times in its history this church has been represented by her sons in the gospel ministry. We have already had occasion to speak of several of them. At the present time we have two such honored representatives in the persons of the Rev. Charles E. Havens and the Rev. Nelson B. Chester, who have been appointed of the King to be "watchmen on the walls of Zion."

The first, Rev. Charles E. Havens, is the second son of Stratton M. Havens and Lydia Ann Chester, born on Shelter Island March 13th, 1850. Early in youth he felt the need of the Savior and surrendered his soul into the hands of the Appointed One for safety, being converted to God under the Rev. Mr. Harries at the very beginning of his ministry here. At the age of fifteen he united with the church on July 9th, 1865. Feeling himself called to the ministry, he began his preparation for the same first in the academy at Southold, where he was a student from 1868 to 1870. Here he was fitted for college. In 1870 he entered Hamilton College, from which institution he graduated in 1874. The next four years he devoted to teaching, serving as Principal of Mexico Academy, in Mexico, Oswego county, N. Y. In 1878 he began the study of theology in Union Theological Seminary, New York City, and graduated therefrom in 1881. His first call was from the Presbyterian Church, Green Island, N. Y., where he was ordained and installed September 10th, 1881. Here he remained until September 1st, 1885, when he became the pastor of the Congregational Church of West Lebanon, N. H., which office he continued to discharge until 1893. In that year, having accepted a call to the pastorate of the Congregational Church in Newton Highlands, Mass., he removed thence and began his pastoral duties to that people, in which he still continues. Brother Havens is highly esteemed by his brethren in the ministry, and is greatly beloved by his people, who constitute a strong and flourishing church in that suburb of Massachusett's greatest city. On July 13th, 1881, he was married to Miss Ellen A. Hall, daughter of the Rev. John H. and Julia (Gillespie) Hall, and to them have been born four children, named Ralph Edgar, Elloine L., Leon C. and Maurice H.

Our second living representative in the gospel ministry, the Rev. Nelson Burdick Chester, was born on Shelter Island January 20th, 1864. He is the second son of Charles T. Chester and Eleanor Jennings. His boyhood was passed in the manner usual to country lads, namely, of working on the farm in the summer and of attending the public school in the winter. At the early age of twelve he united with God's people in 1876, being graciously persuaded of the Lord to do so through the instrumentality of the Rev. Mr. Harries, so that that beloved deceased pastor was the honored instrument of turning both of these brethren into heaven's way and toward the holy ministry. In 1881, having decided to enter God's high calling as His appointed ambassador, he entered the Academy at Bridgehampton, L. I., to prepare for college under the guidance of Prof. Lewis Hallock. In the autumn of 1884 he entered Hamilton College and was graduated with honors in 1888. The following summer he studied Hebrew at Chautauqua, and in the autumn of the same year he entered Union Theological Seminary, New York City, and was graduated in May, 1891. Having been licensed by the Presbytery of Long Island in April, 1890, he was ordained by the same Presbytery a year later, and was at once dismissed to the Presbytery of Buffalo to take charge of Bethlehem Presbyterian Chapel in that city. In a few months this chapel was organized into a church, over which brother Chester was installed as pastor, in which relation he continued until the autumn of 1896, when, having received a call to the Presbyterian Church at Youngstown, N. Y., which he accepted, he removed to that place, where he still continues. On July 14,

1891, he was married to Miss Georgia Grant, of Cleveland, O., to whom have been born two children.

After the teaching elder comes the ruling elder in the polity of the Presbyterian Church, and so we come to speak of those who have served this church in that high office ordained of God in His word. We have already spoken at some length of the virtues and excellencies of our first elder, Gen. Sylvester Dering. We therefore begin here with Mr. Jonathan Doughlass, the second elder, who was ordained as such with Gen. Dering and Lodowick Havens on the 27th of March, 1812, the year in which this church was admitted into the Presbytery. Jonathan Doughlass, together with Gen. Dering, were at the same time of their ordination to the eldership appointed deacons, and these two have been the only deacons in the history of this church. In this double capacity of elder and deacon, brother Jonathan Doughlass served the church for the long period of twenty-eight years "with fidelity and greatly to the edification" of the Society. "He ruled well," and the church was not regardless of the divine injunction. "Let the elders that rule well be counted worthy of double honor," said the Rev. Mr. Harries. "He shared largely of the respect, confidence and love of the church and congregation." He and his wife were original members of this Society. Mr. Doughlass was a member of the building committee that had charge of erecting this our sanctuary. He was most faithful in his office, as the sessional records will show, constantly appointed by the brethren to plead with the erring and to the discharge of special duties. He was born in Waterford, Conn., and removed to this island about the year 1800. His worth was immediately recognized by the community, being chosen to double office in 1800. He served in public office for many years, chiefly as school commissioner. Upon the death of his honored colleague in the eldership, Gen. Sylvester Dering, he was chosen as his successor in the Board of Trustees and continued to serve until 1837, a term of seventeen years. His last years were spent in feebleness. Unable to recline upon his bed he passed away serenely and sweetly while sitting in his chair on the 24th of September, 1840, in the seventy-third year of his age. He was the father of six children, one of whom, named Charles G. Doughlass, is still living, at the advanced age of eighty-eight years, a highly respected citizen of Sag Harbor, N. Y.

The third elder was Lodowick Havens, chosen by the church at the same time elders Dering and Doughlass were chosen. These three were ordained together. Rev. Mr. Harries has left an extended biographical sketch of Mr. Havens and of a number of his successors, from which I shall quote freely. Speaking of our present subject he says: "Mr. Lodowick Havens was born on Shelter Island on the 17th of January, 1774, two months after the passage of the Boston Port Bill by the British Parliament, and two years and a half before the Declaration of Independence. Like Timothy, he had been favored with the instruction and example of a godly mother and a remarkably pious grandmother, Mrs. Mary (Budd) Parker. The sacred truths they instilled into his tender mind, gently and habitually as the descent of nightly dew, leavened his entire spiritual being and exerted a plastic influence upon his whole life of eighty years. At thirteen years of age he prayed regularly in secret, and at eighteen obtained, as he then thought, a saving interest in the oblation of Calvary. But after a season adverse influences abated the fervor of his love and obscured the lustre of his hallowed light. In the closing year of the last century, when about twenty-five years of age, he was wedded to Miss Mary Annable. Soon after that event their attention was called to the subject of personal salvation by a peculiarly solemn and impressive providence. As his impenitent father lay in the agony of remorse upon the margin of the tomb, he summoned his children around his dying couch and warned them of the fearful consequences of deferring a preparation for death until a dying hour. He besought them with tear-bedimmed eyes and all the tender yearnings of a fond parent not to follow his example, but to seek an interest, without delay, in the Friend of Sinners. His spirit then took its flight to its eternal destiny, but his warning failed not of its gracious purpose. A younger son began at once to secure a preparation for a life of union and felicity with God. In fourteen days after his father's death that son followed his steps through the portals which admit us to an eternal state. The fearful manner in which the father died, together with the sudden and unexpected death of the younger brother, were blessed by the Holy Spirit to the quickening and saving of the elder. His conviction of the evil of sin and of his own ill deserts was so deep and overwhelming as to compel him to deprecate unceasingly his self-righteousness and to abandon forever his former hope, and at times to discontinue his secular pursuits. While digging clams in West Neck Creek he was so tortured with remorse, with a sense of approaching judgment and of his own eternal ruin, that he abandoned his work. Prostrate in his boat he cried with trembling and tears for mercy. God heard his pleas and filled his soul with the raptures of pardon as he drank of the cup of salvation. He thus describes his delightful experience in that glorious hour:

'Oh what immortal joys I felt, and raptures all divine,
When Jesus told me I was his and my beloved mine.'

"This change produced the ripened fruits of genuine piety for more than half of a century. During the first eight years after his conversion his religious privileges were exceedingly limited, for the ministrations of the sacred word occurred only occasionally on the island. His golden opportunities were like angels' visits to our earth, few and far between; still he held on to the even tenor of his Christian course. The organization of this church in 1808 deeply interested him. From that period he was favored with the means of grace, aided in their maintenance, enjoyed their luxuriant spiritual benefits and developed their golden fruits in a life of unblemished piety and Christian activity. For many years he was as metal in the crucible, and subjected to the fiercest fire of affliction. Thirty years before his death he was crippled by the incision of an axe into his right ankle. During the last sixteen years of his pilgrimage his sufferings were intense, so that he was confined like a caged bird to his domicile. Still he aspired with almost impatient longings to visit the Lord's house. His heart would devoutly exclaim, 'Oh, God, my soul thirsteth for Thee, to see Thy power and Thy glory in Thy earthly habitation so as I have seen Thee in Thy sanctuary in days of old.' But this priceless immunity was denied him until his remains—weighed down with the infirmities of fourscore years—were brought here to be committed to 'the house appointed for all living.' He was eminently a man of Christian devotion. It seemed as if he made but one prayer in his life, which began at the time of his espousal to Jesus and ended as his spirit winged its way to nestle in His bosom. Christ was his only hope. His presence was his delight. It made his humble abode appear as the vestibule to his celestial mansion. His death was as peaceful as his life was happy. He fell asleep in Jesus on the eleventh of November, 1854. He was a Town officer for many years, serving in various capacities, mostly as Town Clerk, which position he discharged from 1828 to 1849, a period of twenty-one years.

The fourth person to be elevated to the office of elder was Mr. Abraham Sherril. He came to this place from Easthampton and was received by letter from the Presbyterian Church in that locality on the 27th day of March, 1814, just two years after the election of our first elders. The same day he was received he was chosen and ordained an elder over this church, something rather unusual, and implying high esteem and great appreciation on the part of the church for the new comer. Doubtless his fidelity and usefulness had preceded him. His former pastor, the Rev. Ebenezer Philips, had the great pleasure of ordaining his departed member as elder in this house of God. Mr. Sherril was a man of sterling qualities, for which he was usually styled by the people "a good old man." He continued as elder in this church for seven years, to the edification of the church and the glory of his God, after which he returned to Easthampton, where he resided until called to serve in the upper and more glorious sanctuary where they worship unceasingly Him that sitteth on the Throne and the Lamb once slain.

Our fifth elder was Richard F. Nicoll, he being elected on June 30, 1816, and ordained at the same time. It was that memorable Sabbath when so many united with the church who were the fruits of that first and mighty revival of which we have had occasion to speak at length:

"When heaven came down their souls to greet
And glory crowned the mercy-seat."

Rev. Dr. Woolworth and the Rev. Stephen Tracey were in the pulpit, and the sacrament of the Lord was the joyous feast. Shortly after his ordination, as has already been stated, Mr. Nicoll began the study of theology, and in time was ordained to the gospel ministry. As a minister he served various churches. At one time he carried on a private school in the tenant house on the Horsford estate close by the creek. At the close of his public ministry he returned to this island, his native place, and there he continued to live until his death, in 1857. His earthly remains were deposited in the silent grave in the family plot a little north of this building. In 1809 he was married to Margaret S. Dering, daughter of Gen. Sylvester Dering. Their union was blessed with ten children.

The sixth elder was John C. Chester. He united with this church the same Sabbath that Mr. Nicoll was ordained to the eldership. As a church member he walked in the fear of the Lord to the great commendation of the church, who, beholding his good works, chose him to rule over them for four years after his union with them, namely, on the 6th of November, 1820, being ordained at the same time by the Rev. John D. Gardiner, of Sag Harbor. He greatly magnified his office. Though never abounding in wealth, it is said he was proverbial for his hospitality towards God's servants, his house being called the "clergyman's tavern." One of the first missionaries to the Sandwich Islands, a Mr. Bingham, preached in this church on the Lord's day previous to the sailing of the ship which was to carry him to his far-off field of labor, and while here was entertained at Elder Loper's house. He sailed from Sag Harbor, according to our information, in the ship "Thomas," and reached the Sandwich Islands in a most providential time, when the natives, through the failure of their gods to respond to their cries for help and deliverance in a season of great drought and physical suffering, threw their idols into the sea, and having no gods, were eager to hear the glorious gospel of the only living and true God. Marvellous was the power of God upon them through the preached Word. Between the years 1845 and 1848 the son of Elder Chester, our brother in Christ, Charles T. Chester, visited those islands several times, remaining several weeks each visit. He attended their religious services and was impressed with the solemnity and reverence of the worshippers, no trifling being engaged in by any of the large congregations gathered to hear the precious inestimable news of Jesus and His dying love for sinners. And now those very islands are a part of our own national domain and those idolaters, transformed and in their right minds, our fellow citizens. One's thoughts, in view of such things, find fitting expression in the words of Cowper:

"God moves in a mysterious way his wonders to perform;
He plants his footsteps on the sea, and rides upon the storm.
Deep in unfathomable mines of never-failing skill,
He treasures up his bright designs and works his sovereign will."

Elder Chester was a man rich in faith and full of good works. In him there was no guile. Always open in action, honest in speech, frank in dealing and true at heart, his life was an epistle clear and eligible, so as to be read by all men. And in return he was esteemed and loved by all who knew him, who manifested their faith in him by actions of trust and confidence. The love of Christ constrained him to all faithfulness. Though in old age and weary with daily toil, his place in the sanctuary was seldom vacant. Distance did not hinder him in his weekly attendance at the service of prayer and praise. God's house was his delight, and when the church was strained financially, he would step forward to do the humblest work. Literally, he would rather be a doorkeeper in the house of our God than dwell in the tents of wickedness. As "Jacob served seven years for Rachel, and they seemed unto him but a few days, for the love he had to her," so Mr. John C. Chester served the church forty-seven years in the eldership, and it seemed to him but a brief period for the love he had to Zion. When fifteen years of age he turned unto the Lord, and for sixty-three years he was a worthy member of this church. He died July 10th, 1863, at the age of seventy-eight years. He was a native of Rhode Island, from whence he removed to this place in his boyhood. He married Miss Nancy Cartwright, and to them were born a number of children, several of whom still continue with us. A son and a grandson, since his departure, have been called to serve as elders in this church, so that since 1820 there has been, without interruption, a Chester in the eldership of this church.

The next brother chosen to be ruling elder was Jeremiah Case. He was born in the "city," on Shelter Island. While visiting the South on business in 1816, he obtained a hope in Christ. In a short time he returned home and united with this church. Some fifteen years after, on the 13th of November, 1831, he was appointed a ruling elder and ordained by the Rev. Jonathan Huntting. His contemporaries esteemed him as a devoted Christian, whose godly life everywhere exemplified the excellency of the gospel and commended it to the world "as a faithful saying and worthy of all acceptation." Though invested with the authority of a ruler in the church, he did not "lord it over God's heritage," but magnified his office by the exhibition of a meek and quiet spirit, which is in the sight of God of "great price." He was "clothed with humility." Modesty was his daily habitude and meekness beautified, like a polished gem in a coronet, his whole life. But though free from a self-asserting, vaunting, demonstrative nature, he was not a weak, negative character, nor easily turned from the line of Christian duty. Though conciliating, he was neither vacillating nor pusillanimous in the maintenance of his own opinions. Though ready to yield to the better reason, he was firmly wedded to his own convictions, when justified by such reason. While gentle as a lamb and amiable as the exile of Patmos, he was still an earnest, laborious, self-sacrificing Christian, and a prudent, efficient officer in the church of God. When well stricken in years and weighed down with infirmities, he moved to Greenport to reside with his daughter. There he remained until released from the ills of mortal life. The Master called him. Happy death! He went home to the banquet of love and the rest prepared for the people of God. He lived long, for he lived well, and his deathbed was a field of conquest, for on such a battleground death itself dies.

On the 3d of December, 1843, the church made choice of its eighth and ninth elders in the persons of Caleb S. Loper and Horace B. Manwaring. They were "at the same time solemnly ordained, according to the Directory by the Rev. Jonathan Huntting." These two brethren were true yoke-fellows in the work of the Lord's house, continuing in this happy relation until death called the former, in 1860, to his heavenly home. Elder Loper was a native of Noyac, in the Town of Southampton, where he was born December 2d, 1802. At the age of eleven years his parents moved to this island. He experienced the joys of sins forgiven in the great revival under the Rev. Jonathan Huntting in 1831. Two years after he removed to Greenport to engage in business, and when the Presbyterian Church was organized in that place, Feb. 7th, 1833, transferred his membership to it, being one of its original members. Here he remained but two years, when his business being destroyed by fire, he again moved to this island, at the same time transferring his membership to this his mother church. And here he continued to live until his death, on the 3d of October, 1860, in the fifty-eighth year of his age. Altogether he was a member of this church for twenty-seven years, and an elder for seventeen years. He possessed a strong, active mind, great decision of purpose, a large capacity for business, and an almost intuitive perception of character. He had only to look at another to reach a just conclusion respecting his moral worth. When he took a position in regard to any subject, however unpopular it might be, he was ready to avow and vindicate it. When the temperance enterprise was in its infancy, despised and sneered at, and not a few were predicting that it would die in its cradle, and that its swaddling clothes would be its winding-sheet, he rallied under its banner, and was the first on the island, hiring farm labor, who pledged not to furnish spirituous liquors to his workmen. This was a hazardous step, as but few persons would work on such terms, yet he adhered to the right regardless of consequences. He was too ingenuous and transparent to be ever guilty of duplicity, low cunning or double dealing. He filled the office of Justice of the Peace with wisdom, impartiality and equity, and was as just to an enemy as to a friend. Society very generally respected him for his ability, integrity, piety and usefulness. He was emphatically "a devout man, and one who feared God." This church ought ever to hold his name in grateful remembrance, for he toiled, watched, wept, prayed and sacrificed no little to promote its welfare. He "ruled well" in God's house, and is therefore "worthy of double honor." His death was an unmeasured loss to this Society, but to him it was like the freeing of a bird from its cage. His spirit, released from its prison house, hasted away to revel in the bliss of endless life, where "the smile of the Lord is the feast of the soul." He passed from mortal sight

"As sets the sun at eve, to rise in splendor where
His kindred luminaries shine, their heaven of bliss to share;
Beyond the battlefield, he reigns and triumphs now,
Sweeping a harp of wondrous song with glory on his brow."

Caleb S. Loper was a Town officer almost continuously from 1824 to the day of his death, in 1860, serving in various positions, from the lowest to the highest, being chosen five times as Supervisor. He was also for a number of years a Trustee of this church. In 1826 he was married to Hepsibah P. Douglass, daughter of Elder Jonathan Douglass, by whom he had four children, one of whom was chosen as an Elder and in time became as distinguished for piety and usefulness as his father, in this church and community.

The ninth elder, Horace B. Manwaring, was born in East Lyme, Conn., March 6th, 1805. When nineteen years old he made a public profession of faith in Christ and united with the Baptist Church in his native place. Nine years later, namely, about 1834, he removed to this island. Here he stayed until about 1838, when he moved to Gull Island, there to become the lighthouse keeper. This position he discharged for four years, at the expiration of which he once more took up his residence on this island, and continued here until his death. In 1842 he united with this church upon profession of faith in Christ. His views concerning baptism hindered him not in fellowshiping with those who differed with him regarding that ordinance. He loved the fellowship of those who honored God and enjoyed the communion of the Lord's Table with them. In less than a year after his uniting with this church he was chosen elder, and in this office served the church with zeal and wisdom for twenty-three years, or until his death, on the 19th of February, 1866, in the sixtieth year of his age. He was noted for his good sense and extraordinary prudence.

As a neighbor he was peaceful and accommodating. His friendship was warm and abiding, his integrity universally recognized,
and his sincere piety undoubted. He was not subject to changes in
his devout habits, but was "always engaged in religion." Judgment
and prudence distinguished his administration, while his power in
prayer and remarkable gift in exhortation made him unusually rich
and edifying in his devotional exercises. His life was a testimony
and his death a demonstration of the excellency of our holy religion.
He approached life's closing hour calmly,

"Like one who wraps the drapery of his couch about him
And lies down to pleasant dreams."

So serenely he closed his eyes on this fading, fleeting world to
feast his clarified vision on the ever-enduring glories of heaven.

Mr. Manwaring was the son of Adam Manwaring and Temperance Dennison. He was twice married, his second wife being
Nancy A. Havens, daughter of Elder Lodowick Havens. He possessed a wonderful gift of language, which he exercised to the great
delight and profit of those who heard him testify of the goodness
of God and supplicate the throne of grace. For many years he served
the Town as one of its officers in various capacities, among them as
Town Clerk from 1854 to 1857. Upon his death, in 1866, the whole
community was overshadowed by sorrow in losing such a noble soul
in the very midst of his powers, he being but sixty years old.

The tenth person chosen as elder was Charles T. Chester, elected
the 25th of January, 1856, and ordained by the Rev. Daniel M. Lord.
Mr. Chester was the son of Elder John C. Chester, and was born on
Shelter Island. He united with the church July 1, 1849. In 1892 he
was, at his own request, dismissed to the brethren. Being still a
resident of this island we forbear speaking of his services and usefulness to the church at this time. He is the honored father of one of
our present efficient elders and of the Rev. Nelson B. Chester already referred to.

The eleventh elder was Marcellus D. Loper, chosen and ordained
at the same time with Elder Charles T. Chester. Mr. Loper was
the son of Caleb S. Loper and grandson of Jonathan Douglass, both
of whom had served so conspicuously in the eldership before him.
He was born May 1, 1827, and united with the church January 16th,
1848. He continued his membership until his death, December
11th, 1895. As elder he served for nearly forty years. During all
these years he was noted for his great love and zeal for Zion. He
constantly had upon his heart the welfare of the church, and was a

most devout Christian. There was not a position of trust and honor in the gift of this church to which he was not called. Of him it can be said that he fulfilled the exhortation of Christ to "Let your light so shine before men that they may see your good works and glorify your Father which is in heaven." Being of such a pronounced Christian character the community gladly chose him, like the church, to almost every position of trust within its power, from the lowest to the highest. At the time of his death he was the Clerk of the Town, and in the church an Elder, Clerk of the Session, Trustee and Librarian of the Sabbath School. One can readily see from these how useful a citizen and member of the church he was. Well does the author of these papers remember the two visits he made upon Mr. Loper while supplying the pulpit of this church in the month of November, 1895. Mr. Loper was at the time seriously ill with the illness that resulted in his death. In these brief visits he impressed me as sweetly resigned to God's will; firm in his faith, having the triumph over death that comes by faith in the Son of God. The second visit was on the Monday after the Sunday on which the church extended the call to the author to become their pastor. Not being present at that meeting, he assured me personally of his hearty acquiescence in it, at the same time expressing the hope of its acceptance. The day after my arrival at home I received a letter from him, written after my leaving him, in which he again urged upon me the acceptance of the call, and explaining that the reason why he wrote was that he felt he had not been urgent enough at the time of my visit. These things are stated here simply to show the good, earnest character of the man who, though dangerously ill and near his death, lest he should not have been urgent enough pens his message to make sure of it. That letter is sweetly treasured, for the hand that penned it was soon struck with death, and the first service devolving upon the pastor elect the day after his arrival to take up his residence and work upon this island was the funeral service of this faithful soul. And in his going another soul was fixed in its eternal state among the multitude that have gone up to glory and the Father's house from this community and church. How large a company has already gathered on that Shining Shore. As a testimonial to his worth the following is a part of what was entered upon the sessional records:

"Whereas, Our Heavenly Father has taken from among us in the person of Marcellus D. Loper one whom we had learned to love and respect, whose counsel we sought and whose commendation we

PUBLIC SCHOOL BUILDING

OLD DUTCH GRIST MILL

PUBLIC LIBRARY

prized, the session feels called upon at this time to recognize the faithfulness with which he served the church and to pay a tribute to his memory.   Therefore be it

"Resolved, That in the removal of our Senior Elder, M. D. Loper, from the scenes of his earthly activity our church has lost a most faithful servant, the cause of Christ a valiant champion and the community at large a valuable citizen.

"For forty years he has stood in the front ranks of our church workers, his whole life bound up in the welfare of the church militant, a firm defender of 'the faith once delivered to the saints.' Through this devotion to the cause of Christ we feel it can be said of him as of one of old, 'He being dead yet speaketh.' "

In 1858 Elder Loper was married to Mary S. Horton, who survives him.   They were blessed with three sons, all of whom grew to manhood and are still living.

Archibald R. Havens was the twelfth person selected as Elder, being chosen April 23, 1865, and ordained by the Rev. Mr. Harries on the following 11th of June.   Mr. Havens was born on this island Oct. 9th, 1816, to Obadiah and Nancy (Robinson) Havens.   On May 20th, 1849, he united with the church, and continued as a member until his death, Nov. 20th, 1894, a period of forty-five years.   Concerning him it is the universal testimony of those who knew him that you cannot say too much about his noble Christian character.   He was a model among men, always looked up to and highly esteemed, implicitly trusted, a saint on earth.   One who ever had a word for Jesus.   Carrying on a country store, he would follow his customers to the door to drop a word concerning the Savior and His dying love for men.   He was indeed a remarkable man.   Faithful in attendance upon the state means of grace of the sanctuary and ever ready to testify for Jesus.   He cherished the words and oft repeated them that "They that feared the Lord spake often one to another; and the Lord hearkened and heard it, and a book of remembrance was written before Him for them that feared the Lord and that thought on His name.   And they shall be mine, saith the Lord of Hosts, in that day when I make up my jewels, and I will spare them as a man spareth his own son that serveth him."   He was constantly encouraging others into the Kingdom, and was instrumental in cheering at least one soul on to the Savior who is now an honored Elder of this church.   How many such jewels are set in his immortal crown we cannot at present tell, but shall know some day,

"When the mists have rolled in splendor from the beauty of the hills,
And the sunlight falls in gladness on the river and the rills,
And we come with joy and gladness up to the great white throne,
Face to face with those that love us, then we'll know as we are known."

Though full of cares at times yet never a word of discouragement did he utter. He dwelt upon the innumerable promises of the Most High. They were to him as a sweet morsel rolled under the tongue. Like one of old, he esteemed the Word of God more than his necessary food. And as he lay upon his bed in his last illness in a state of coma those that sat beside him heard him repeating those everlasting and abiding promises upon which his soul was fixed. They were his comfort in the death valley. His parting words, repeated a number of times, were "I'm going home, I'm going home," and his spirit left its earthly tabernacle to occupy the "building of God, an house not made with hands, eternal in the heavens."

Mr. Havens was postmaster of Shelter Island for nearly fifty years, one of the longest terms of office on record in the Postal Department of these United States. In 1839 he married Miss Caroline A. Hughes, by whom he had six children.

Our thirteenth elder, chosen and ordained with Elder Havens in 1865, was Horace G. Manwaring, the son of Elder Horace B. and Nancy (Havens) Manwaring, born on Nov. 21, 1838, and died Sept. 18, 1883. He continued as an elder of this church about three years, when he moved to Westfield, Mass. During his short term as Elder of this church he served with great credit, being a young man of good parts and ability. It was therefore with sorrow and reluctance that the church parted with this young servant when Providence removed him to another place. He died at the early age of forty-five years.

On Dec. 7, 1872, the church elected its fourteenth, fifteenth and sixteenth elders in the persons of Benjamin C. Cartwright, Timothy P. Congdon and Smith Baldwin. These three were ordained on Jan. 12, 1873, by the Rev. Mr. Harries, who devoted the entire service that Sabbath morning to the consideration of the office of elder and its duties. The first of the three above mentioned brethren was the last to leave this earth, the order of their departure being just the reverse of their selection. Benjamin C. Cartwright, our fourteenth elder, was a native of Shelter Island, born May 13th, 1815, of George and Lucretia (Conkling) Cartwright. He passed triumphantly away on Dec. 11th, 1896, in his eighty-second year. For more than fifty years he was a conspicuous member of this church. All who knew him honored him. In early life he followed the sea, making a number of voyages in a whaler. In this profession he early attained a position of responsibility, becoming commander of the ship. Here his life was conspicuous for at least one thing, namely, he never resorted to the use of oaths or profane language of any kind, so general a custom among seamen. His mouth was clean; no corrupt communication proceeded from between his lips. After retiring from the pursuit of the whale he established himself in business of various kinds in turn on this island. Soon his services were called upon in town affairs and he was chosen to public office.

And nearly to the time of his death did he continue in office, serving the town in almost every capacity, among them as Supervisor, for thirteen years. He was a man who stood firm for his principles, never compromising with evil but always true to his God. He could no more be turned by bribery or intimidation from what he esteemed to be right than you could turn the sun from out its course. He illustrated in all its truth the saying, now a maxim, "An honest man is the noblest work of God." Would that all the men of our community were of his noble, faithful spirit! Never did his pastor want for an attentive, inspiring listener so long as he remained with the church militant. One had but to turn his eye in his direction when it would be cheered by his encouraging countenance. And the warm grasp of the hand at the close of the service was a silent "God bless you, my pastor," that cannot easily be forgotten. That hand was constantly extended in doing good. He was the poor man's friend. His generous soul led him to sacrifice himself for the welfare of others. "He went about doing good," and when he came to leave this earth God took care that this devoted servant should have one of the sweetest departures ever granted to mortal man. It was the nearest approach to Enoch's translation that has ever come under our notice. "He walked with God, and was not for God took him." Conscious almost to the very last moment, speaking with the loved ones around his dying bed, telling his children of the happy meeting with mother who had gone on some eight years before, and in all confidence of his being brought into the desired haven, his final words were "Safe into port." Then he closed his eyes in that sleep which knows no waking here but which is the sweetest of all sleeps, a repose upon the breast of Jesus, and devout men carried him to his burial as they carried Stephen, and made great lamentations over him because "a prince and a great man had fallen in Israel."

As a tribute to his memory the following resolutions were spread upon the sessional minutes:

"Whereas, It has pleased our Heavenly Father to take from among us, in the person of Elder Benjamin C. Cartwright, a brother in the Lord, whose fidelity through an unusually long term of service entitled him to be considered by his fellow men as holding a first place among those who love our Lord and strove to do His will. Therefore be it

"Resolved, That by the removal of Elder Cartwright from the scenes of his earthly labors the Presbyterian Church of Shelter Island loses an honorable member, a faithful servant and an efficient officer, one deeply interested in all that concerned the church, both in spiritual and temporal lines, well fitted for service in the former by his simple faith, his hopeful courage and his charitable judgment of others; and for the latter by his natural ability, the experience gained in a long business career and the open-handed liberality with which he responded to all appeals made for the needs of the church.

"Resolved, That we extend our sympathy to the bereaved family of our departed brother with the assurance that we share their sorrow in the loss of a beloved father and a faithful and wise counsellor, consoled, however, by the knowledge that while we miss his familiar form from among us his life remains among us and that we can apply to him that most glorious testimony received from heaven, 'Blessed are the dead that die in the Lord from henceforth. Yea, saith the Spirit, that they may rest from their labors and their works do follow them.'"

Brother Cartwright was married in 1838 to Hannah Maria Tuthill, and unto them were born ten children. Two of his sons were in time chosen by the church as elders. He was most happy in his domestic relations, surrounded as he was by a large family of children, grandchildren and great grandchildren, all devotedly attached to this dear old servant of God, this grand old man.

"Servant of God, well done!   Soldier of Christ, well done!
  Rest from thy loved employ;   Praise be thy new employ;
The battle fought, the victory won,   And while eternal ages run,
  Enter thy Master's joy!   Rest in thy Saviour's joy!"

Mr. Timothy P. Congdon was the fifteenth elder chosen by this church. Early in life he surrendered himself into the hands of the Savior with the purpose to be his as long as life should last, and this vow he kept religiously until his death Jan. 6th, 1888. At the age of seventeen he united with this church. He was a member of the church for nearly fifty-five years and an elder for fifteen years. At one time in life he had the ministry in view, and to that end entered Amherst College. He was, however, providentially turned from this purpose, and passed his life on this island cultivating the farm inherited from his father. He was a man who possessed natural gifts of unusual power, among them a fine voice, which he knew how to use with great effect in oratory. Being of an emotional temperament, there were times when his soul would mount, as it were, into the third heaven, and the strain would become so great that he would have to desist from attending services in seasons of revival, so strongly did they appeal to him. Having a large home, he freely opened and offered it for prayer meetings and other religious services. He was constant in his attendance upon the sanctuary, and ready with his services when called upon. His testimonies and his prayers were listened to and united in with delight and profit. He taught the Word of God to the young and served as superintendent of the Sabbath school. He was a man well versed in scripture and could use it with great effectiveness.

Mr. Congdon was born at South Kingston, R. I., on May 20, 1815, of Joseph and Elizabeth (Peckham) Congdon. At the age of eleven years he removed with his parents to this island. Here he married Miss Amanda A. Bennet, daughter of Lewis L. and Asenath (Wright) Bennet, a very earnest Christian woman, on the 29th of October, 1843. To them were born seven children, several of whom are our most worthy members at the present time.

The sixteenth elder was Mr. Smith Baldwin. He united with the church in July, 1856, and died on June 23, 1884, at the age of sixty-eight years. In early life he sailed the seas, and in time became a sea captain in the whaling industry. In one of his voyages, while touching at the island of St. Helena, his wife gave birth to their first child, a daughter, who was named Ella Carroll Baldwin, after the daughter of the Governor of the island. Retiring from a seaman's life, he carried on for a number of years the milling business in the old Dutch mill. Upon his conversion in the great revival of 1856 he became a most devout follower of Christ. In speaking of him recently with one who knew him well it was said, "You can say everything that is good of this man and yet not say too much." He was a most conscientious man, and rather than come short in any duty would perform that duty twice. Kind, noble-hearted and generous to a fault. Often would he be found in his mill on his knees praying to God for himself, his loved ones, his neighbors; yea, everybody, mentioning one after another in prayer before the throne of grace. He was a man of humble and devout spirit, untiring in his services for the glory of his Risen Master. So deeply conscious of the awfulness of sin and the absolute need of a Savior, of man's lost condition outside of the Lord Jesus Christ, that at times he would wonder whether he had a standing in Christ. His was more the negative than the positive disposition. While his saintly wife was just the opposite, so that the two together formed a most perfect couple. One day a stranger was being conveyed across this island, and as he was riding along he said to his conveyor: "Does Smith Baldwin still live on this island?" Being told that he did, he said: "I wish you would take me to where he lives if it isn't too much out of your way, and I will pay you extra for it, as I want to see that man because I have learned to respect and greatly esteem him. Early in life I sailed the seas with him, and it was while in the midst of an awful storm that I learned to regard him so highly. Things looked black aboard ship at that time. All hands felt fearful, but Smith Baldwin stood calm, self-possessed and confident, and I could not help but admire him as he gave his orders to the men, all of which were readily obeyed, and if ever I learned to respect a man it was Smith Baldwin." It is needless to say that he was carried to his friend's house, and the exchange of greetings was so warm and hearty that the time seemed very short ere the evening was upon them. May the stranger and his honored captain renew their friendly greetings in the better land.

The following minute was entered upon the records the day of Brother Baldwin's death: "Our esteemed brother, Smith Baldwin, having been removed by death on the morning of this day, we enter the following minute, namely:

"With humble submission to the dispensation of God's holy providence, the session records the death of one of its members, Smith Baldwin, who departed this life on Monday, the 23d day of June, 1884, in the sixty-ninth year of his age."

Mr. Baldwin was born in 1816 at Babylon, Long Island. His parents were John and Phebe Smith Baldwin. On June 7, 1847, he married Miss Maria Cartwright, daughter of Anderson and Cynthia (Payne) Cartwright, a most devoted servant of Christ. To them were born several children, only one of whom, a son, Edgar P., lived to grow to manhood.

What a remarkable body of men has God given unto this church as elders. How nobly have they served and what glory have they brought to this high office in the church of God. Besides these sixteen brethren the church has chosen the following also as elders, namely: Winfield S. Cartwright, Byron Griffing, J. Edward Chester, Arthur S. Cartwright, E. Havens Payne and Scudder Smith, making twenty-two in all. These are all still living and rendering most efficient service. Of these the first, Winfield S. Cartwright, having removed from the island, has ceased to exercise his office in this church. He is, however, still an active elder, serving as such in the Presbyterian Church of Islip, where he now resides. He was elected on June 5, 1881, and ordained by the Rev. Mr. Harries the following Sunday, June 12, 1881.

The three following Mr. Cartwright, namely, Mr. Byron Griffing, Mr. John Edward Chester and Mr. Arthur S. Cartwright, were elected elders on Nov. 8, 1891. At the same time the church adopted the rotary system of eldership in the place of the life eldership, which had prevailed up to this time, but now having adopted the rotary, or term system, these brethren were elected for three years, two years and one year respectively. Two weeks later they were solemnly ordained to their office by the Rev. B. F. Parliman, and they have continued in active service until the present time, being reelected whenever their term has expired. On Nov. 2, 1896, the remaining two brethren, E. Havens Payne and Scudder Smith, were chosen as the successors of Archibald R. Havens and Marcellus D. Loper, deceased. One month later they were ordained by the present pastor. Propriety seems to forbid any extended remarks concerning these brethren at this time. But the writer wishes at least to state that as a body of advisers and helpers they have been most faithful, considerate and brotherly. In all his relations with them he has received nothing but kindness and encouragement. The spirit of unity and of love has been the spirit of them all, making the relations of the pastor with them nothing but of the pleasantest kind. They have my highest regards. I esteem them for their work's sake and am ready to declare that thus far they have been loyal and earnest co-laborers with me in the solemn responsibility of the oversight of this flock of God, forming a body of elders of which the church may be justly proud. May God spare them for many years unto this church, and may they by His grace more and more magnify their office, as we feel this to be their heart's desire. And when their course is run may the portals of heaven swing open wide for the incoming, and may the King greet them with the words of highest praise, "Well done, thou good and faithful servant, enter into the joys of thy Lord."

"How beautiful it is for man to die upon the walls of Zion! to be called, Like a watch-worn and weary sentinel, to put his armor off and rest —in heaven."

And here a tribute is due to the men who have had the care of the material things of this church; in other words, to the Board of Trustees, organized in 1785, and in continuous existence until the present time, a period of more than a hundred and thirteen years. The various members of this body who have served in all these years are tabulated elsewhere.   The existence of this board antedates the organization of the church by twenty-three years.   The congregation for which they acted at first, however, properly dates its existence from the building of the first meeting house in 1743, a hundred and fifty-five years ago.   We have spoken of a number of these men to their deserved praise.   And in that praise the present members of the board can justly be included for their wise, judicious and faithful service in looking after the material things of this religious corporation.   The present excellent condition of the church's property, the freedom from debt and the safe investment of funds now in their hands proclaim their efficiency most effectively.

There are still others who have been of great service to this Society whose names have not yet been mentioned.   As we have already said, some names must be omitted.   We cannot enumerate all those who have been conspicuous in this church for holy living, extended usefulness and Godlike character.

One of them, however, must be here enshrined, because he has left behind him a name that is like precious ointment poured forth. I refer to Martin L. Prince, one of nature's noblemen, a whole-souled follower of the Lord Jesus Christ.   A man whose consecration was a living sacrifice acceptable unto God.   Who literally gave himself for the good of this community, neither sparing effort or money to bring about the largest results in matters and movements that elevated and refined.   He was the most useful man in the whole community.   A leading spirit in temperance reform and in the cultivation of music, raising them both to such a high stage of effectiveness and efficiency as to make Shelter Island famous abroad in both of these departments of laudable and praiseworthy effort.   How sweetly is his name cherished by the older portion of this community. In his day a notable trio lived on this island in the persons of the Rev. Daniel M. Lord, Archibald R. Havens and himself, Martin L. Prince. These were so conspicuous, each in his department, that it led one eminent man to remark that the Shelter Island community ought to be a very happy people with a "Lord" for a pastor, a "Prince" living among them and a "Haven" on dry land.

All hail to the name of Martin L. Prince! And as regards the women of this church, as much could be said to their praise as has been recited of the other sex in these papers. Some have already been alluded to. Along with those already mentioned we enroll the names of Mrs. Thomas Dering, Mrs. Mary Parker, Mrs. Esther Case, three spiritually minded women who used to unite their prayers under the shadow of a haystack before ever a church was organized on this island. Other women since then have carried the light of God aloft, as Mrs. Lucretia Cartwright, a remarkably devoted woman; Mrs. Smith Baldwin, as remarkable an example of filial affection and untiring service to both high and low, rich and poor, knowing no creed or caste in her self-denying labors. Among the younger women there shines out the name of Mrs. Esther (Tuthill) Loper with those already mentioned.

But we must forbear, though many appeals come to us from Sunday-school and Young People's societies, from temperance organizations and missionary bodies, pleading for a place and a rehearsal. Concerning each one of which a noble record could be given. Perhaps another hand will pen their immortal deeds. As the conclusion to this historical review, I am more than pleased to be able to give the following poem written by Elder Byron Griffing for the rededicatory services in 1897, and entitled "Hallowed Echoes," since it so beautifully refers to these varied persons and departments of work connected in the past with this honored church of God.

1.

As stronger hands have from the past
  The curtain drawn aside,
And on their efforts borne us back
  O'er time's unchanging tide,
'Twould seem that angel fingers swept
  Harps long in silence lain,
And woke from out the vanished years
  Their sleeping chords again.

2.

For as o'er altar, aisle and pew
  This sunset glory lays,
Streaming across the wrecks of time
  From light of "former days,"
We catch these harmonies long hushed
  That once this temple filled,
And throbbing hearts again respond
  To hearts forever stilled.

3.

How vast yet varied are the tones
  These hallowed echoes bring,
What gracious messages they bear,
  What countless changes ring!
They plead from o'er the sacred desk,
  From off this altar call,
And from yon lonely gallery
  In tuneful cadence fall.

4.

They rise from 'midst those lonely woods
  And stacks of new-mown hay,
Where saintly women years ago
  Gathered to praise and pray.
They peal from out the tempest blast
  That forest monarchs felled,
Whose hearts of oak for fourscore years
  This temple hath upheld.

5.

They break from hillsides rough and steep
  Where sturdy pilgrims trod,
Who came with grateful heart and voice
  To give this house to God.
Not "that which cost them naught" was
    then
  Upon God's altar laid,
But that for which they long had sought
  And labored for and prayed.

6.

They steal from hidden, thorny paths
  That weary feet have pressed,
Where patient souls with steadfast faith
  Waited the promised rest.
They bear the sweet, submissive song
  Of spirits sorely tried,
Who 'mid life's darkest hours could sing
  There's " light at eventide."

7.

They tell of burdens bravely borne,
  Of tears in secret wept,
Of pleadings none but God and heaven
  Hath in remembrance kept.
They tell of hallowed moments spent
  Around some mercy seat,
Where with the Master kindred souls
  Have held communion sweet.

8.

They sound from yonder library's walls,
  Ring with past Christmas cheer,
And o'er Mount Auburn fondly breathe
  A sweet memorial here.
They drop from those mosaic panes
  Whispering the name they bear,
And fall on grateful hearts to stamp
  Its deeper impress there.

9.

They tell of one whose life and work
  Were love and tenderness,
Whose tireless feet were swift to seek,
  Whose hands as swift to bless.
Who knew no station, age nor sex,
  No color, race nor creed;
Her ministries, like those divine,
  Encircled all in need.

10.

They tell us how with faltering steps
  An aged saint had come,
Content that at God's holy feast
  His soul should find a crumb.
Nor thought that from his morsel shared
  With those in greater need
A fragment, though long years should
    fall,
  Our hungry souls to feed.

11.

For what were all these conflicts waged,
  These holy triumphs won,
These trials patiently endured,
  These deeds of kindness done ?
Methinks an hallowed echo doth
  Yon chapel's silence break,
And in a pastor's thrilling tones
  Answers, "For Jesus' sake."

12.

O! temple of the living God,
  In thy new beauty dressed,
May he who hath enriched thy past
  Be still thy constant guest;
And when the present's sunset glow
  Is o'er the future cast,
Still may as hallowed echoes fall
  As ring from out thy past!

A LIST OF THE TOWN OFFICERS

From the Founding of the Town, in 1730, down to the year 1815.

1730.—William Nicoll, Supervisor; John Havens and Samuel Hudson, Assessors; Edward Havens, Collector; Edward Gilman, Constable.

1731.—William Nicoll, Supervisor; Joel Bowditch and William Nicoll, Assessors; Abraham Parker, Collector and Constable.

1732.—Brinley Sylvester, Supervisor; Brinley Sylvester and Jonathan Havens, Assessors; Sylvester L'Hommedieu, Collector and Constable.

1733.—Brinley Sylvester, Supervisor and Clerk; Jonathan Havens and Henry Havens, Assessors; Samuel Hopkins, Collector and Constable.

1734.—Brinley Sylvester, Clerk; William Nicoll, Supervisor; John Havens and Samuel Hudson, Assessors; Henry Havens, Collector and Constable.

1735.—William Nicoll, Supervisor; Joel Bowditch and George Havens, Assessors; Samuel Vail, Constable and Collector; Brinley Sylvester and John Havens, Overseers of the Poor.

1736.—William Nicoll, Supervisor; Jonathan Havens, Jr., and Abraham Parker, Assessors; Joel Bowditch, Jr., Constable and Collector; Joel Bowditch and Samuel Hudson, Overseers of the Poor, Brinley Sylvester, Clerk.

1737.—William Nicoll, Supervisor; Joel Bowditch and Jonathan Havens, Jr., Assessors; Brinley Sylvester, Clerk; Joseph Havens, Constable and Collector; Samuel Hudson and John Havens, Overseers of the Poor.

1738.—Brinley Sylvester, Clerk; William Nicoll, Supervisor. Brinley Sylvester and Jonathan Havens, Assessors; Abraham Parker and George Havens, Overseers of the Poor: John Bowditch, Constable and Collector.

1739.—Brinley Sylvester, Clerk; William Nicoll, Supervisor; John Havens and Thomas Conkling, Assessors; Joel Bowditch and Noah Tuthill, Overseers of the Poor; Charles Gilham, Constable and Collector.

1740.—Brinley Sylvester, Clerk; William Nicoll, Supervisor; Joel Bowditch and Jonathan Havens, Jr., Assessors; Elisha Pain, Constable and Collector; Brinley Sylvester and Jonathan Havens, Overseers of the Poor

1741.—Brinley Sylvester, Clerk; William Nicoll, Supervisor; Jonathan Havens and Joel Bowditch, Jr., Assessors; Thomas Conkling, Constable and Collector; Henry Havens and Samuel Vail, Overseers of the Poor.

1742.—Brinley Sylvester, Clerk; Jonathan Havens, Supervisor; Joel Bowditch and William Nicoll, Assessors; Samuel Case, Constable and Collector; Abraham Parker and William Havens, Overseers of the Poor.

1743.—Brinley Sylvester, Clerk; Jonathan Havens, Jr., Supervisor; Noah Tuthill and Henry Havens, Assessors; William Havens, Jr., Constable and Collector; John Havens and Brinley Sylvester, Overseers of the Poor.

1744.—Brinley Sylvester, Clerk; Brinley Sylvester, Supervisor; William Nicoll and John Havens, Assessors; Abraham Parker, Jr, Constable and Collector; Joel Bowditch and Noah Tuthill, Overseers of the Poor.

1745.—Brinley Sylvester, Clerk; Brinley Sylvester, Supervisor; Daniel Brown and Jonathan Havens, Jr., Assessors; William Bowditch, Constable and Collector; Abraham Parker and William Havens, Overseers of the Poor.

1746.—Brinley Sylvester, Clerk; Brinley Sylvester, Supervisor; William Havens and Noah Tuthill, Assessors; Thomas Conkling and Henry Havens, Overseers of the Poor; George Duvall, Constable and Collector.

1747.—Daniel Brown, Supervisor; Samuel Landon and Jonathan Havens, Jr., Assessors; Brinley Sylvester and Henry Havens, Overseers of the Poor; Thomas Conkling, Constable and Collector; Brinley Sylvester, Clerk.

1748.—Daniel Brown, Supervisor; Renselear Nicoll and Henry Havens, Assessors; Brinley Sylvester and Henry Havens, Overseers of the Poor; Elisha Pain, Constable and Collector; Brinley Sylvester, Clerk.

1749.—Brinley Sylvester, Supervisor; William Nicoll and Jonathan Havens, Assessors; Noah Tuthill and William Havens, Overseers of the Poor; George Havens, Constable and Collector; Brinley Sylvester, Clerk

1750.—Daniel Brown, Supervisor; Noah Tuthill and Brinley Sylvester, Assessors; Jonathan Havens and Henry Havens, Overseers of the Poor; Samuel Case, Constable and Collector; Brinley Sylvester, Clerk.

1751.—Daniel Brown, Supervisor; Henry Havens and William Havens, Assessors; Samuel Case and Abraham Parker, Jr., Overseers of the Poor; John Daval, Constable and Collector; Brinley Sylvester, Clerk.

1752.—Daniel Brown, Supervisor; William Nicoll and Jonathan Havens, Assessors; Brinley Sylvester and Henry Havens, Overseers of the Poor; Abraham Parker, Jr., Constable and Collector; Brinley Sylvester, Clerk.

1753.—Daniel Brown, Supervisor; George Daval and Abraham Parker, Jr., Assessors; William Havens and Elisha Pain, Overseers of the Poor; Joseph L'Hommedieu, Constable and Collector; William Nicoll, Clerk.

1754.—Daniel Brown, Supervisor; Jonathan Havens and Thomas Fanning, Assessors; Thomas Conkling and George Havens, Overseers of the Poor; George Daval, Constable and Collector; William Nicoll, Clerk.

1755.—Daniel Brown, Supervisor; Daniel Brown and Henry Havens, Assessors; Thomas Conkling and George Havens, Overseers of the Poor; John Daval, Constable and Collector; William Nicoll, Clerk.

1756.—Daniel Brown, Supervisor; Nicoll Havens and William Nicoll, Assessors; Henry Havens and Abraham Parker, Jr., Overseers of the Poor; John Daval, Constable and Collector; William Nicoll, Clerk.

1757.—Daniel Brown, Supervisor; Jonathan Havens and Daniel Brown, Assessors; Thomas Conkling and Thomas Fanning, Overseers of the Poor; Benjamin Sawyer, Constable and Collector; William Nicoll, Clerk.

1758.—Daniel Brown, Supervisor; William Havens and Nicoll Havens, Assessors; William Havens (John's son) and Samuel Case, Overseers of the Poor; Benjamin Sawyer, Constable and Collector; William Nicoll, Clerk.

1759.—Daniel Brown, Supervisor; Thomas Conkling and George Havens, Assessors; William Havens, (John's son) and Samuel Case, Overseers of the Poor; Joseph L'Hommedieu, Collector and Constable; Nicoll Havens, Clerk.

1760.—Daniel Brown, Supervisor; William Havens and William Nicoll, Overseers of the Poor; Joseph L'Hommedieu, Collector and Constable; Nicoll Havens, Clerk.

1761.—Daniel Brown, Supervisor; William Havens, Jr., and Daniel Brown, Assessors; Thomas Conkling and William Havens, Overseers of the Poor; Joseph L'Hommedieu, Collector and Constable; Nicoll Havens, Clerk.

1762.—Daniel Brown, Supervisor; Nicoll Havens and William Havens, Assessors; William Havens, Jr. and Samuel Case, Overseers of the Poor; Joseph L'Hommedieu, Collector and Constable; Nicoll Havens, Clerk.

1763.—Daniel Brown, Supervisor; William Nicoll and Samuel Case, Assessors; Joel Bowditch and William Havens, Overseers of the Poor; George Havens, Collector and Constable; Nicoll Havens, Clerk.

1764.—Daniel Brown, Supervisor; Nicoll Havens and Daniel Brown, Assessors; Abraham Parker, Jr., and William Havens, Overseers of the Poor; Shadrach Conkling, Collector and Constable; Nicoll Havens, Clerk.

1765.—Daniel Brown, Supervisor; James Havens and Jonathan Havens, Assessors; George Havens and Samuel Case, Overseers of the Poor; Benjamin Sawyer, Collector and Constable; Nicoll Havens, Clerk.

1766.—Nicoll Havens, Clerk; Thomas Dering, Supervisor; Jonathan Havens and James Havens, Assessors; William Havens and Abraham Parker, Jr., Overseers of the Poor; Benjamin Conkling, Collector and Constable; Joel Bowditch and George Havens, Fence Viewers.

1767.—Nicoll Havens, Clerk; Thomas Dering, Supervisor; Jonathan Havens and James Havens, Assessors; Samuel Case and George Daval, Overseers of the Poor; Joseph L'Hommedieu, Collector and Constable; George Daval and Nicoll Havens, Fence Viewers; Nicoll Havens and Joseph Havens, to make out and levy the quit rents.

1768.—Nicoll Havens, Clerk; Thomas Dering, Supervisor; William Nicoll and Joseph L'Hommedieu, Assessors; Joseph L. Hommedieu and Thomas Dering, Overseers of the Poor; Moses Horton, Collector and Constable; William Havens and Joel Bowditch, Fence Viewers.

1769.—Nicoll Havens, Clerk; Thomas Dering, Supervisor; Joseph Havens and Daniel Brown, Assessors, both for Town and County Rates; Nicoll Havens and Samuel Case, Overseers of the Poor; Shadrach Conkling, Collector and Constable; Joel Bowditch and William Havens, Fence Viewers.

1770.—Nicoll Havens, Clerk; Nicoll Havens, Supervisor; James Havens and Thomas Dering, Assessors; Joel Bowditch and Benjamin Sawyer, Overseers of the Poor; Jonathan Havens, Jr., Collector and Constable; Joel Bowditch and William Havens, Fence Viewers.

1771.—Nicoll Havens, Clerk; Nicoll Havens, Supervisor; George Daval and Shadrach Conkling, Assessors; Benjamin Sawyer and James Havens,

Overseers of the Poor; Obadiah Havens, Collector and Constable; Benjamin Sawyer and James Havens, Fence Viewers.

1772.—Nicoll Havens, Clerk; Nicoll Havens, Supervisor; Nicoll Havens and John Daval, Assessors; Nicoll Havens and James Havens, Overseers of the Poor; George Daval, Collector and Constable; William Havens and Joel Bowditch, Fence Viewers.

1773.—Nicoll Havens, Clerk; Nicoll Havens, Supervisor; Jonathan Havens and James Havens, Assessors; Nicoll Havens and James Havens, Overseers of the Poor; George Daval. Collector and Constable; William Havens and Joel Bowditch, Fence Viewers.

1774.—Nicoll Havens, Clerk; Nicoll Havens, Supervisor; Jonathan Havens and James Havens, Assessors, for Town and County Rates; George Daval, Collector and Constable; Nicoll Havens and William Havens, Overseers of the Poor; Shadrach Conkling and Obadiah Havens, Fence Viewers.

1775.—Daniel Brown, Moderator; Nicoll Havens, Clerk; Nicoll Havens, Supervisor; Daniel Brown and Obadiah Havens, Assessors; Nicoll Havens and Daniel Brown, Overseers of the Poor; Nathan Hand, Collector and Constable; Joel Bowditch and Shadrach Conkling, Fence Viewers.

1776.—Thomas Dering, Moderator; Nicoll Havens, Clerk; Nicoll Havens, Supervisor; Nicoll Havens and Thomas Dering, Assessors; William Havens and Obadiah Havens, Overseers of the Poor; Samuel Havens, Collector and Constable; Joel Bowditch and Benjamin Sawyer, Fence Viewers.

1777.—Joel Bowditch, Moderator; Daniel Brown, Clerk; Samuel Case, Jr., Supervisor; Daniel Brown and John Bowditch, Assessors; Samuel Case and Benjamin Sawyer, Overseers of the Poor; Walter Havens, Collector and Constable; Joel Bowditch and John Duvall, Fence Viewers.

1778.—John Duvall, Moderator; Daniel Brown, Clerk; Samuel Case, Jr., Supervisor; James Havens and William Brown, Assessors; Noah Terry and Obadiah Havens, Overseers of the Poor; John Bowditch, Constable and Collector; Benjamin Sawyer and William Havens, Fence Viewers.

1779.—John Duvall, Moderator; Daniel Brown, Clerk; Samuel Case, Jr., Supervisor; James Havens and William Brown, Assessors; Noah Terry and Obadiah Havens, Overseers of the Poor; John Bowditch, Constable and Collector; William Havens and Benjamin Sawyer, Fence Viewers.

1780.—John Duvall, Moderator; Samuel Case. Jr., Supervisor; James Havens and William Brown, Assessors; Noah Terry and Ebenezer Havens, Overseers of the Poor; John Bowditch, Collector and Constable; Benjamin Sawyer and Shadrach Conkling. Fence Viewers; Nicoll Havens, Clerk.

1781.—Samuel Case, Jr., Moderator; Noah Terry, Supervisor; William Bowditch and Noah Terry, Assessors; Obadiah Havens and Ebenezer Havens, Overseers of the Poor; John Bowditch, Constable and Collector; Walter Havens and John Bowditch, Fence Viewers.

1782.—Daniel Brown, Moderator; Noah Terry, Supervisor; Samuel Case, Jr., and Nicoll Havens, Assessors; Nicoll Havens and Joshua Youngs, Overseers of the Poor; John Bowditch, Constable and Collector; Obadiah Havens and Walter Havens, Fence Viewers; Nicoll Havens, Clerk.

1783. — Daniel Brown, Moderator : Nicoll Havens, Supervisor; Nicoll Havens and James Havens, Assessors; Shadrach Conkling and Rufus Paine, Overseers of the Poor: John Bowditch, Constable and Collector; John Bowditch and Walter Havens, Fence Viewers; Nicoll Havens, Clerk.

November 4, 1783, Special Meeting. --Daniel Brown, Assessor; James Havens, Supervisor; Jonathan N. Havens, Clerk.

December 22, 1783, Special Meeting.—Daniel Brown, Moderator; James Havens, Supervisor; Daniel Brown and James Havens, Assessors; Rufus Paine and Shadrach Conkling, Overseers of the Poor; John Bowditch, Constable and Collector; John Bowditch and Walter Havens, Fence Viewers; Jonathan Nicoll Havens, Clerk.

1784. — Daniel Brown, Supervisor ; James Havens and Daniel Brown, Assessors; Obadiah Havens and Sylvester Dering, Overseers of the Poor ; Rufus Paine, Constable and Collector ; William Bowditch and Samuel Havens, Fence Viewers; Jonathan N. Havens, Clerk.

1785.—Daniel Brown, Moderator ; Jonathan N. Havens, Supervisor; James Havens, William Bowditch and Sylvester Dering, Assessors; James Havens and William Bowditch, Overseers of the Poor ; Ezekiel Havens and Obadiah Havens, Fence Viewers; Ezekiel Havens, Constable and Collector; Jonathan N. Havens, Clerk.

1786.—Daniel Brown, Moderator; Jonathan N. Havens, Supervisor; William Bowditch, James Havens and Sylvester Dering, Assessors; James Havens and William Bowditch, Overseers of the Poor; Samuel Havens, Constable and Collector; Walter Havens and Ezekiel Havens, Fence Viewers; Jonathan N. Havens, Clerk.

1787.—Sylvester Dering, Clerk; Jonathan N. Havens, Supervisor; William Bowditch, Sylvester Dering and James Havens, Assessors; Benjamin Nicoll and Ezekiel Havens, Overseers of the Poor; Samuel Havens, Constable and Collector; Ezekiel Havens and Francis Havens, Fence Viewers, Noah Terry, Trustee.

1788.—William Bowditch, Moderator; Sylvester Dering, Clerk; Jonathan N. Havens, Supervisor ; Benjamin Nicoll, James Havens and Jonathan N. Havens, Assessors; James Havens and Noah Terry, Overseers of the Poor; Sylvester Dering and Ezekiel Havens, Fence Viewers; Samuel Havens, Constable and Collector; Sylvester Dering, Trustee.

1789.—Jonathan N. Havens, Supervisor; Sylvester Dering, Town Clerk; Sylvester Dering, William Bowditch and Ezekiel Havens, Assessors; Ezekiel Havens, Collector and Constable; William Bowditch and Jonathan N. Nicoll, Overseers of the Poor; Noah Terry and Samuel Havens, Fence Viewers; William Bowditch, Trustee.

1790.—Jonathan N. Havens, Supervisor; Sylvester Dering, Town Clerk; Sylvester Dering and William Bowditch and Shadrach Conkling, Assessors; Gillum Case, Collector and Constable; Sylvester Dering and William Bowditch, Overseers of the Poor; Shadrach Conkling and William Bowditch, Fence Viewers; Jonathan N. Havens, Trustee.

1791.—Jonathan N. Havens, Supervisor; Sylvester Dering, Town Clerk; Benjamin Nicoll, Shadrach Conkling and Sylvester Dering, Assessors; Ezekiel Havens, Constable and Collector; William Bowditch and Sylvester Dering, Overseers of the Poor; Shadrach Conkling and Samuel Havens, Fence Viewers; Samuel Havens, Pound Master; Sylvester Dering, Trustee; Benjamin Nicoll and James Havens, Commissioners to Build a Pound.

1792.—Jonathan N. Havens, Supervisor; Sylvester Dering, Town Clerk; Sylvester Dering, William Bowditch and James Havens, Assessors; Ezekiel Havens, Constable and Collector; Sylvester Dering and William Bowditch, Overseers of the Poor; Shadrach Conkling and Samuel Havens, Fence Viewers; Moses Griffing, Pound Master; William Bowditch, Trustee.

1793.—Sylvester Dering, Supervisor; Sylvester Dering, Town Clerk; Sylvester Dering, William Bowditch and James Havens, Assessors; Ezekiel Havens, Constable; Ezekiel Havens and Sylvester Dering, Overseers of the Poor; James Havens and William Bowditch, Commissioners of Highways, also Sylvester Dering; Gordon Havens and Ezekiel Havens, Fence Viewers; Moses Griffing, Pound Master.

1794.—William Bowditch, Supervisor; Sylvester Dering, Town Clerk; Sylvester Dering, William Bowditch and James Havens, Assessors; Ezekiel Havens, Constable and Collector; William Bowditch and Samuel Reeve, Overseers of the Poor; Francis Havens and Ezekiel Havens, Overseers of the Roads; Walter Havens and Shadrach Conkling, Fence Viewers; Henry Haines, Pound Master.

1795.—William Bowditch, Supervisor; Sylvester Dering, Town Clerk; James Havens, Sylvester Dering and William Bowditch, Assessors; Ezekiel Havens, Constable and Collector; William Bowditch and Ezekiel Havens, Overseers of the Poor; Walter Havens and Shadrach Conkling, Fence Viewers; James Havens, Pound Master.

1795.—William Bowditch and Ezekiel Havens, Overseers of the Poor for the town of Shelter Island; Jonathan N. Havens and John Hurlbut, Justices of the Peace of the County of Suffolk.

1796.—Sylvester Dering, Supervisor; Sylvester Dering, Town Clerk; Ezekiel Havens, Shadrach Conkling and William Bowditch, Assessors; Gordon Havens, Constable and Collector; Sylvester Dering and Ezekiel Havens, Overseers of the Poor; Shadrach Conkling and Walter Havens, Fence Viewers; James Havens, Pound Master: Sylvester Dering, William Bowditch and Benjamin Nicoll, Commissioners of Schools.

1797.—Benjamin Nicoll, Supervisor; Sylvester Dering, Town Clerk; Shadrach Conkling, Benjamin Nicoll and William Bowditch, Assessors; Jonathan Reeve, Constable and Collector; William Bowditch and Ezekiel Havens, Overseers of the Poor; Ephraim King and Shadrach Conkling, Fence Viewers; Samuel Havens, Pound Master; Sylvester Dering, Benjamin Nicoll and William Bowditch, Commissioners of Schools.

1798.—Shadrach Conkling, Supervisor; Sylvester Dering, Town Clerk; William Bowditch, Shadrach Conkling and Francis Havens, Assessors; Jonathan Reeve, Constable and Collector; Wm. Bowditch and Sylvester Dering, Overseers of the Poor; Walter Havens and Shadrach Conkling, Fence Viewers; Francis Havens, Pound Master; Sylvester Dering, Benjamin Nicoll and William Bowditch, Commissioners of Schools.

1799.—William Bowditch, Supervisor; Sylvester Dering, Town Clerk; William Bowditch, Sylvester Dering and Francis Havens, Assessors; Henry Havens, Constable and Collector; William Bowditch and Sylvester Dering, Overseers of the Poor; Shadrach Conkling and William Bowditch, Fence Viewers; Francis Havens, Pound Master; Sylvester Dering, Wm. Bowditch and Benjamin Nicoll, Commissioners of the Schools.

1800.—Sylvester Dering, Clerk; Obadiah Havens, Supervisor; James Havens and Henry Haines and Ezekiel Havens, Assessors; Henry Haines, Constable and Collector; William Bowditch, Sylvester Dering, Overseers of the Poor; Gordon Havens and Shadrach Conkling, Fence Viewers; James Havens, Pound Master; Sylvester Dering, William Bowditch and Benjamin Nicoll, Commissioners of Schools.

1801.—William Bowditch, Supervisor; Sylvester Dering, Town Clerk; Shadrach Conkling, William Bowditch and Sylvester Dering. Assessors; Jonathan Reeve, Constable and Collector; William Bowditch and Ezekiel Havens, Overseers of the Poor; Shadrach Conkling and Jonathan Douglass, Fence Viewers; Samuel Havens, Pound Master; Jonathan Douglass, Sylvester Dering and Benjamin Nicoll, Commissioners of Schools.

1802.—William Bowditch, Supervisor; Sylvester Dering, Town Clerk; Sylvester Dering, William Bowditch and Obadiah Havens, Assessors; Jonathan Reeve, Constable and Collector; William Bowditch and Shadrach Conkling, Overseers of the Poor; Jonathan Reeve and Gordon Havens, Fence Viewers; Samuel Havens, Pound Master; Sylvester Dering, Benjamin Nicoll and Jonathan Douglass, Commisioners of Schools.

1803.—William Bowditch, Supervisor; Sylvester Dering, Town Clerk; Sylvester Dering, Benjamin Nicoll and William Bowditch, Assessors; Ezekiel Havens, Constable and Collector; Joseph Congdon and Benjamin Nicoll, Overseers of the Poor; Joseph Congdon and Ezekiel Havens, Fence Viewers; William Bowditch, Pound Master.

1804.—Sylvester Dering, Clerk; William Bowditch, Supervisor; John Bowditch, William Bowditch and Ezekiel Havens, Constable and Collector; Jonathan Douglass and Phineas King, Overseers of the Poor; Shadrach Conkling and Joseph Congdon, Fence Viewers; William Bowditch, Pound Master.

1805.—Sylvester Dering, Town Clerk; Wm. Bowditch, Supervisor; Benjamin Nicoll, John Bowditch and Wm. Bowditch, Assessors; Jonathan Reeve, Constable and Collector; Ezekiel Havens and Phineas King, Overseers of the Poor; Jonathan Douglass and John Bowditch, Fence Viewers; Wm. Bowditch, Pound Master.

1806.—William Bowditch, Supervisor; Sylvester Dering, Town Clerk; William Bowditch, Benjamin Nicoll and Jonathan Douglass, Assessors; Jonathan Reeve, Constable and Collector; William Bowditch, and Obadiah Havens, Overseers of the Poor; Shadrach Conkling and Joseph Congdon, Fence Viewers; William Bowditch, Pound Master.

1807.—William Bowditch, Supervisor; Sylvester Dering, Town Clerk; William Bowditch, Jonathan Douglass and John Bowditch, Assessors; William Bowditch and Jonathan Douglass, Overseers of the Poor; Jonathan Reeve, Constable and Collector; Joseph Congdon and Shadrach Conkling, Fence Viewers; William Bowditch, Pound Master.

1808.—William Bowditch, Supervisor; Sylvester Dering, Town Clerk; John Bowditch, William Bowditch and Jonathan Douglass, Assessors; Jonathan Reeve, Constable; Henry Hains, Collector; Phineas King and Jonathan Douglass, Overseers of the Poor; Joseph Congdon and Shadrach Conkling, Fence Viewers; William Bowditch, Pound Master.

1809.—William Bowditch, Supervisor; Sylvester Dering, Town Clerk; John Bowditch, Benjamin Nicoll and Jonathan Douglass, Assessors; Jonathan Reeve, Constable; Henry Haines, Collector; Benjamin Nicoll and Sylvester Dering, Overseers of the Poor; Phineas King and Joseph Congdon Fence Viewers; William Bowditch, Pound Master.

1810.—William Bowditch, Supervisor; Sylvester Dering, Town Clerk; Jonathan Douglass, John Bowditch and William Bowditch, Assessors; Jonathan Reeve, Constable; Henry Haines, Collector; Joseph Congdon and Benjamin Nicoll, Overseers of the Poor; Joseph Congdon and Jonathan Douglass, Fence Viewers; William Bowditch, Pound Master.

1811.—William Bowditch, Supervisor; Sylvester Dering, Town Clerk; John Bowditch, William Bowditch and Jonathan Douglass, Assessors; Jonathan Reeve, Constable; Phineas King, Collector; Phineas King and Daniel W. Pierson, Overseers of the Poor; Joseph Congdon and William Bowditch, Fence Viewers; William Bowditch, Pound Master.

1812.—William Bowditch, Supervisor; Sylvester Dering, Town Clerk; William Bowditch, John Bowditch and Francis Havens, Assessors; Jonathan Reeve, Constable; Francis Havens, Collector; Sylvester Dering and Francis Havens, Overseers of the Poor; Benjamin Nicoll and William Bowditch, Fence Viewers; William Bowditch, Pound Master.

1813.—William Bowditch, Supervisor; Sylvester Dering, Town Clerk; William Bowditch, Jonathan Douglass and John Bowditch, Assessors; Jonathan Reeve, Constable and Collector; Jonathan Douglass and Lodowick Havens, Overseers of the Poor; Phineas King and William Bowditch, Fence Viewers; William Bowditch, Pound Master; Sylvester Dering, Benjamin Nicoll and Jonathan Douglass, Commissioners; William Bowditch, Benjamin Glover and Frederick Chase, Inspectors.

September 27, 1813.—Sylvester Dering, Moderator; Benjamin Glover, Remington Havens and Frederick Chase, Trustees; Sylvester Dering, District Clerk; Remington Havens, District Collector.

1814.—William Bowditch, Supervisor; Sylvester Dering, Town Clerk; Benjamin Nicoll, Obadiah Havens and John Bowditch, Assessors; Frederick Chase, Collector and Constable; Henry Conklin and Frederick Chase, Overseers of the Poor; Lodowick Havens and Obadiah Havens, Fence Viewers; William Bowditch, Pound Master; Benjamin Nicoll, Jonathan Douglass and Sylvester Dering, Commissioners of Schools; John Bowditch, Henry Conklin and William Bowditch, Inspectors of Schools.

1814.—Benjamin Glover, Remington Havens and Obadiah Havens, Trustees; Sylvester Dering, Clerk; Frederick Chase, Collector.

1815.—William Bowditch, Supervisor; Sylvester Dering, Clerk; John Bowditch, Benjamin Nicoll and Henry Conklin, Assessors; Frederick Chase, Constable and Collector; Henry Conklin and Frederick Chase, Overseers of the Poor; Obadiah Havens and Lodowick Havens, Fence Viewers; William Bowditch, Pound Master; Benjamin Nicoll, Jonathan Douglass and Sylvester Dering, Commissioners of Schools; John Bowditch, Henry Conklin and Obadiah Havens, Inspectors of Schools; Benjamin Glover, George W. Congdon and Sineus Conklin, Trustees; Frederick Chase, Collector.

VARIOUS MEMBERS OF THE BOARD OF TRUSTEES OF THE PRESBYTERIAN CHURCH, SHELTER ISLAND, N. Y., FROM ITS ORGANIZATION, APRIL 26th, 1785.

1785..Jon. N. Havens, Syl. Dering, Wm. Bowditch.		
1786.. " " "		
1787..Noah Terry, " "		
1788.. " " "		
1789.. " " "		
1790..Jon. N. Havens, " "		
1791.. " " "		
1792.. " " "		
1793.. " " "		
1794.. " " "		
1795.. " " "		
1796.. " " "		
1797.. " " "		
1798.. " " "		
1799.. " " "		
1800..Obadiah Havens, " "		
1801.. " " "		
1802.. " " "		
1803.. " " "		
1804.. " " "		
1805.. " " Benj. Nicoll.		
1806.. " " "		
1807.. " " "		
1808.. " " Wm. Bowditch.		
1809..Benj. Nicoll, " "		
1810.. " " "		
1811.. " " "		
1812.. " " "		
1813.. " " "		
1814.. " " "		
1815.. " " "		
1816.. " " "		
1817.. " " "		
1818.. " " "		
1819.. " " "		
1820.. " " "		
1821..Phin. P. King, Jon. Douglass, Samuel Lord.		
1822.. " " Jos. C. Havens.		
1823.. " " "		
1824..John C. Chester, " "		
1825.. " " Josiah Mayo.		
1826.. " " "		
1827..Caleb S. Loper, " "		
1828.. " " "		
1829.. " " "		
1830.. " " Sam'l S. Gardiner.		
1831.. " " "		
1832..Jeremiah Case, " "		
1833..Henry Conklin, " "		
1834.. " " "		
1835.. " " "		
1836..Caleb S. Loper, " "		
1837.. " " "		
1838.. " Jas. D. Tuthill, John C. Chester.		
1839.. " " "		
1840.. " " "		
1841.. " " "		

1842..Sam'l B. Nicoll, J. D. Tuthill, J. C. Chester.		
1843.. " " "		
1844.. " Caleb S. Loper, "		
1845. Benj. Cartwright, " "		
1846.. " " Sam'l B. Nicoll.		
1847.. " " Arch. Havens.		
1848.. " " "		
1849.. " " "		
1850.. " Sam'l B. Nicoll, "		
1851.. " " "		
1852.. " " "		
1853.. " " "		
1854.. " " "		
1855.. " " "		
1856.. " " "		
1857.. " " "		
1858.. " C. D. Manwaring, "		
1859.. " " "		
1860.. " " "		
1861.. " " "		
1862..M. D. Loper, " "		
1863.. " Benj. Cartwright, "		
1864.. " " "		
1865.. " " "		
1866.. " " "		
1867.. " " Chas. T. Chester.		
1868.. " " "		
1869.. " " "		
1870.. " " "		
1871.. " " "		
1872.. " " "		
1873.. " " "		
1874.. " " "		
1875.. " " "		
1876.. " " "		
1877..Byron Griffing, " "		
1878.. " " "		
1879.. " " "		
1880..G. R. Havens, " "		
1881.. " " "		
1882.. " " E. H. Payne		
1883.. " " "		
1884.. " " "		
1885.. " " "		
1886.. " " "		
1887.. " " "		
1888.. " " "		
1889.. " " "		
1890.. " " "		
1891.. " " "		
1892.. " " "		
1893.. " Scudder Smith, "		
1894.. " " "		
1895.. " " "		
1896.. " " "		
1897.. " " "		
1898.. " " "		
1899.. " Irving Clark, "		

PART SECOND.

GENEALOGICAL TABLES

OF THE DESCENDANTS OF

JOHN HAVENS,
  HENRY HAVENS, } p. 163.
    BRINLEY SYLVESTER, p. 177.
      SAMUEL HOPKINS, p. 182.
        JOEL BOWDITCH,
          JOHN BOWDITCH, } p. 198.
            SAMUEL HUDSON, p. 203.
              JONATHAN HAVENS,
                GEORGE HAVENS, } p. 239.
                JOSEPH HAVENS,
                  NOAH TUTHILL, p. 292.
Who helped to   THOMAS CONKLING, p. 300.
found the Town of Shelter Island,   ABRAHAM PARKER, p. 305.
in 1730.   DANIEL BROWN, p. 307.
                    SYLVESTER L'HOMMEDIEU, p. 310.

AND

Rev. DANIEL HALL,
  LUCRETIA HALL, } p. 311.
    SYLVESTER DERING,
      E. SARAH DERING, } p. 117, sec. 177.
        JONATHAN DOUGLASS,
          ABIGAIL DOUGLASS, } p. 312.
            EPHRAIM KING,
              MEHITABLE KING, } p. 315.
                MARY MAYO, p. 316.
                  EUNICE CASE,
Founders of the   ESTHER CASE, } p. 320.
Church,   ANNA BOISSEAU,
September 28, 1808.   LODOWICK HAVENS, p. 247, sec. 49.
                    ELIZABETH HAVENS, p. 242, sec. 17.
                      ABIGAIL SAWYER, p. 325.

NOTE.—The Compiler of these tables will esteem it a great kindness on the part of those who, discovering an error, or able to supply what may be lacking in them, will kindly inform him of it or send the same to his address. He would also suggest writing upon the margin the additions and corrections which have come to hand, opposite the sections to which they belong.

KEY TO THE FOLLOWING TABLES,

Taking as an Example the Record on the Opposite Page.

THE TABLES ARE DIVIDED INTO SECTIONS, EACH SECTION REPRESENTING A FAMILY AND FOLLOWING EACH OTHER IN NUMERICAL ORDER.

The numeral "1" in all cases is assigned to the family of the person whose name heads the table. Thus the numeral "1" on the opposite page will be seen to stand at the top of the family record of John Havens. The letters of the alphabet act in the same capacity, only that they are assigned to the families through whom the person's ancestry is to be traced, which is given in each table so far as the compiler has been able to trace it in this country. Thus Mr. John Havens' ancestors are here given under the letters "A" and "B" back to the first Havens who came to America, and who in this case was his grandfather, namely, William Havens. The line through which Mr. John Havens descended from William Havens is indicated by the letter "B" which will be seen to stand before the son George of the first William Havens. This letter, like the numerals that appear in the subsequent family records, intimate that the person before whose name the letter or number stands, not only married, but had a family, and that the record of that family can be found under that letter or number in the table of which it is a part. Thus under the letter "B" is to be found the family record of George Havens, who in this case was the father of Mr. John Havens. In the record of George Havens it will be seen that the numeral "1" precedes the name of John, which refers the reader for the record of his family to the record that appears under that number, and so on through the table. By this arrangement the ancestors and descendants of any person whose name appears in any of the following tables, save of the parents of those who have married into the family, can be easily traced. In some of the sections, as for instance in section No. 16, page 185, it will be noticed that the names of both of the parents are set in small capitals. This is to indicate that the marriage between those persons was a consanguineous one, that is, between blood relations, they having descended from the same ancestor.

ABBREVIATIONS.—b., born; bap., baptised; m., married; da., daughter; ch. or child, child or children; wid., widow; s., son; d., died; d. s. p., died without issue; d. unm., died unmarried; ae., aged.

162

ANCESTORS.

A.

*WILLIAM HAVENS, s.
    b. in England.   m.   d.   1683.
Dionis   da.
    b.   d. after 1692.

11 ch. *John*, b.   *Sarah*, b.   m.   Tyler.   *Thomas*, b.   *Robert*, b.
    B. *George*, b.   m.   Eleanor Thurston.
    Mary, b.   m. { 1st,   Thomas Cook.
                2d,   Jeremiah Brown.
    Ruth, b.   m. Card. *Dinah*, b.   *Rebecca*, b.   *William*, b.   *Margaret*, b.
(*) In 1638 he was admitted an inhabitant of the Island of Aquidneck, having submitted himself to the government that is, or shall be established.
On April 30, 1639, he and twenty-eight others, signed the following compact: " We whose names are underwritten, do acknowledge ourselves the legal subjects of His Majesty, King Charles, and in his name do hereby bind ourselves into a civil body politicke unto his laws according to matters of justice." In 1644, he had a grant of four acres. On May 23, 1650, he and five others were appointed to make and mend all arms presented by inhabitants of any of the Towns. 1680, March 30, date of Will. Proved Sep. 25, 1683. In it all the above names are mentioned, and wife Dionis is appointed Executrix.

B.

*GEORGE HAVENS, s. William and Dionis (   ) Havens.
   b.   1653.   m.   1674.   d. Feb. 21, 1706-7.
Eleanor Thurston, da. °Edward and Elizabeth (Mott) Thurston.
   b. Mar.   1655.   d. Nov. 7, 1747.
8 ch. ∥*George*, b.   m.   Mary
    Jonathan, b. Feb. 22, 1681; m. Jan. 1. 1706-7. Hannah Brown.
    William, b.   d. unm.   1746.   *Abigail*, b.
  1. *John*, b.   m.   Sarah
    Content, b.   m.   Cornelius Payne.
    Patience, b.   m.   Soper.
    Desire, b.   m.   Gardiner.
(*) 1680, Freeman. 1687, Taxed in Kingston, R. I. 1695, July 15, Jamestown, Constable.
(°) b. in 1617, d. Mar. 1st, 1707. Married June, 1647, Elizabeth Mott, da. of Adam Mott, b. in 1629 and d. Sep. 2, 1694. Edward Thurston was the first person of that name in the Colony of Rhode Island. He was the third on the record of the "Society of Friends" at Newport and therefore a Quaker. In 1655, Freeman; 1663, Commissioner; 1667-71-74; 80-86, Deputy; 1675, 86, 90-91, Assistant.
On Aug. 26, 1686, he signed an address with the other Quakers to the King in regard to the Writ of Quo Warranto. They desired to be excused from bearing arms, being a peaceable people and willing to pay all just rates and duties for carrying on the Commonwealth affairs.
On Jan. 30, 1690, he, with five other Assistants and Deputy Governor Greene, wrote a letter to William and Mary congratulating them on their accession to the crown, and informing them that since the deposition of Sir Edmund Andros, the former Government under the Charter had been resumed, mentioning also the seizure of Andros in Rhode Island on his flight from confinement in Massachusetts, and his return to Massachusetts on demand of that Colony.
Date of Will, Jan. 11, 1704. Proved, Mar. 12, 1707.
(∥) This George Havens, the first son of George and Eleanor (Thurston) Havens, is said to have been born on Shelter Island. In a deed, dated Shelter Island, Nov. 19, 1701, given by George Havens of Kingstown, he calls himself George, son of George of Shelter Island. He married a lady whose given name was Mary and had the following children: Joseph, Edward who m. Desire Terry in 1724, George, William, Ebenezer, Thurston who m. Jerusha Polly in 1752, John, Eleanor who m. a Mr. Davilt, Abigail who m. a Mr. Fish, Hannah, Mary and Ruth. These are all mentioned in his Will, dated Fisher's Island, Oct. 31, 1726, and proved Apr. 13,1738.

1.

JOHN HAVENS, s. George and Eleanor (Thurston) Havens.
    b.   m.   d. 1750.
Sarah   da.
   b.   d.
9 ch. *Henry*, b.   m.   °Abigail Tuthill.
  2. *William*, b.   m.   Ruth
  3. *Jonathan*, b.   m. Oct. 29, 1733, Patience Tuthill.
  4. *Benjamin*, b.   m.   Abigail Strong.
  5. *Phebe*, b.   m.   Nathaniel Jessup.
    Eleanor, b.   *Sarah*, b.   *Desire*, b.
    ∥*Mary*, b.   m. Dec. 21, 1735, Daniel Brown.
(*) One of the founders of the town.   (°) da. of Daniel and Mehitable (Horton) Tuthill, b. Apr. 7, 1710.   (∥) See Brown genealogy No. 1.

2.

WILLIAM HAVENS, s. John and Sarah (   ) Havens.
    b.   m.   d.
* (?) Ruth   da.
   b.   1720.   d. Feb. 18, 1759.

8 ch.   *Ebenezer*, b.   d. unm. 1787.   *Eunice*, b.   d.   °*Joseph*, b.   m.
   6. *William*, b.   m.   Bethiah Bowditch.
   †*Daniel*, b.   m.   *Lydia*, b.   *John*, b.
   ‖*Hannah*, b. Dec. 10, 1751; m.   Phineas Parker.

(*) In memory of Ruth, ye wife of William Havens, d. Feb. 18, 1759 in ye 39th yr. of her age.—Headstone in North Church Yard.   (o) Had a s. Augustus mentioned in his Uncle Ebenezer's will. also 2 more s.; see Sag Harbor census of 1776.   (†) Had 2 s. in 1776; see Sag Harbor census of 1776.   (‖) See Parker genealogy No. 3.

3.

JONATHAN HAVENS, s. John and Sarah (   ) Havens.
   b. in 1711.   m. Oct. 29, 1733.   d. Nov. 5. 1797.

Patience Tuthill, da. Daniel and Mehitable (Horton) Tuthill.
   b. Mar. 11, 1716.   d.
8 ch.   **7.** *Mehitable*, b.   m. Nov. 30, 1758, John Moore.
   Nathaniel, b.   m. Sep.   1778, Parmelia   ; probably no issue.
   8. *John*, b. July 14, 1748; m. 1st,   Abigail Bostwick.
   9. *Bethiah*, b. in 1750; m.   Daniel Rackett.   *Charlotte*, b.
   10. *Jeremiah*, b.   m. { 1st, Dec. 19, 1780, Mehitable Brown.
    { 2d,   Conklin.
   *Benjamin, b.   m.   °Lucretia Payne.
   Jerusha, b.   m. Jan. 8, 1788, Elcanah Smith.
(*) Had 1 ch. Nancy.   °da. of John and Phebe Payne, d. June 22. 1792, ae. 32.

4.

BENJAMIN HAVENS, s. John and Sarah (   ) Havens.
   b.   m.   d.

Abigail Strong, da. Selah and Abigail (Terry) Strong.
   b. May 8, 1706.   d. Feb. 2, 1761.
3 ch.   vens, b. Apr. 20, 1755 ; d. Jan. 29. 1785.
   *Selah, b.   m.   Sarah Strong ; no issue.   °*Susannah*, b.   m.   Daniel Voorhees.
(*) d. in 1786.   (°) Had 2 ch., Benjamin, and Phebe who m. a Mr. Webster.

5.

PHEBE HAVENS, da. John and Sarah (   ) Havens.
   b.   m.   d.

Nathaniel Jessup, s.
   b.   d.
1 ch.   **11.** *Phebe*, b. Mar. 3, 1736.   m. Nov. 11, 1756, Daniel Fordham.

6.

WILLIAM HAVENS, s. William and (?) Ruth (   ) Havens.
   b.   m.   d. Mar. 26, 1780.

*Bethiah Bowditch, da. Joel and Bethiah (Case) Bowditch.
   b. Sep. 9, 1755.   d. Dec. 14, 1830.
3 ch.   A son.
   12. *Desire L.*, b. June 22, 1775; m. July 29, 1802, Oliver Fowler.
   13. *Henry Bowditch*, b. Oct. 13, 1780; m. Jan. 9, 1806, Hannah Sayre.
(*) She m. a 2d time, a Mr. Phineas Parker; see Parker genealogy No. 3.

7.

MAHETABLE HAVENS, da. Jonathan and Patience (Tuthill) Havens.
   b.   m. Nov. 30, 1758.   d.

John Moore, s. John and Rachel (Conklyn) Moore.
   b.   d. Feb. 6, 1811.
9 ch.   *Mahetable, b.   m. Dec. 24, 1795, James Griffing.
   14. *Elizabeth*, b.   m. Luther Tuthill.
   Rachel, b.   d. Oct. 11, 1780.   *John*, b.   d. unm.   *Patience*, b.   d. unm.
   15. *Daniel*, b. Mar. 8, 1764; m.   Ruth Vail.
   16. *Shadrach*, b. Oct. 28. 1767; m.   Mahitable Rackett.
   17. *Joseph*, b.   1771; m. July 2. 1806, Anna Cleveland.
   18. *Mary*, b.   m. Nov. 30, 1786, John Wiggins.
(*) Had 8 ch., Daniel, David, Joseph, Benjamin, Daniel, Benjamin. William H., Deziah.

8.

*JOHN HAVENS, s. Jonathan and Patience (Tuthill) Havens.
   b. July 14, 1748; m.   d. June 18, 1810.

Abigail Bostwick, da. Merriby and Mary (Strong) Bostwick.
   b. July 4, 1746.   d. Nov. 9, 1801.
9 ch.   *Mary*, b. May 6, 1770, d. unm. Dec. 1, 1812.   *Nathan*, b. Mar. 6, 1772, d. unm. Feb. 27, 1797
   19. *Jeremiah*, b. July 6, 1774; m. Mar. 6, 1795, Bethiah Youngs.
   °*Charity*, b. Jan. 8, 1777; m.   William Hawkins or Havens.
   Sarah, b. June 13, 1779, d. June 6, 1782.   *Abigail*, b. Apr. 13, 1782. d. May 3. 1782.
   ‖*Charles H.*, b. Dec. 4, 1784; m.   †Betsy Sherrill.
   20. *John*, b. Nov. 14, 1787; m. Sep. 17, 1823, Eliza Ketcham.
   21. *Sarah*, b. May 6, 1791; m. June,   1814, Dr. Nathaniel Miller.
(*) John Havens married a second time, a widow, by whom he had no issue.   (°) Had 2 ch., John, and Abigail who m. Charles Hawkins.   (‖) Had 3 ch., Robert Emmet who married Maria Eldridge, Juliet who died unm. and Mary who m. Charles Little.   (†) da. of Jacob Sherrill.

9.

*BETHÍAH HAVENS, da. Jonathan and Patience (Tuthill) Havens.
    b. in 1750.   d. Oct. 15, 1816, ae. 66.

Daniel Rackett, s. Jonathan and Hannah (King) Rackett.
    b. about 1744.   d. May 18. 1800.

1 ch. **22.** *Daniel H.*, b.   m.   1795, Deziah Vail.

10.

JEREMIAH HAVENS, s. Jonathan and Patience (Tuthill) Havens.
    b.   m. 1st, Dec. 19, 1780.   2d,   d. Aug. 21, 1829.
1st, Mehitable Brown, da.
    b. Mar. 31, 1760.   d. Sep. 10. 1807.

2d,   Conklin, da.
    b.   d.

7 ch.   *Patience*, b. *Joseph Conkling*, b. 1781, d. June 3, 1807. *Mehetable*, b. d. Sep. 2, 1793.
    23. *Daniel Tuthill*, b. June 9, 1789; m. Feb. 1815, Betsey Raynor.
    *Jerusha, b. about 1791; m.   °Coe S. Downing; no issue.
    24. *John Symus*, b. 1796; m.   Nancy F. Smith.
    25. *Maria S.*, b. Jan. 9, 1810; m. May 10, 1836, Nathaniel N. Munsell.
(*) d. s. p. Apr. 17, 1876.   (°) d. Sep. 2, 1847, ae. 46 yrs.

11.

PHEBE JESSUP, da. Nathaniel and Phebe (Havens) Jessup.
    b. Mar. 3, 1736.   m. Nov. 11, 1756.   d. Nov. 4, 1806.

Daniel Fordham, s. Nathan and Abigail (Bowditch) Fordham.
    b. Dec. 6, 1730.   d. June 12, 1816.

10 ch.   *Nathan*, b. Aug. 7, 1757, d. Jan. 7, 1838.   A child, b. Aug. 18, 1759, d. Aug. 29, 1759.
    Frances, b. Dec. 4, 1761; m.   Wentworth.
    Charlotte, b. Mar. 7, 1763; m.   Kirtland.
    Frederick, b. Mar. 27, 1765, d. June 27, 1782. *Jares*, b. Aug. 2, 1767, d. July 24, 1831
    26. *Thaddeus*, b. July 29, 1769; m. Jan. 26, 1796. Clarissa Havens.
    Samuel, b. Nov. 14, 1771, d. Feb. 27, 1803. *Joel*, b. Apr. 4, 1774, d.
    Daniel, b. June 2, 1779, lost at sea in 1806.

12.

DESIRE LYDIA HAVENS, da. William and Bethiah (Bowditch) Havens.
    b. June 22, 1775.   m. July 29, 1802.   d. Dec. 16, 1828.

Oliver Fowler, s. Richard and Mary (   ) Fowler.
    b. July 1, 1778.   d. Feb. 16, 1866.

5 ch. **27.** *Charles H.*, b. Apr. 22, 1805; m. Apr. 4, 1838. Iantha Titus.
    *Nancy H., b. Apr. 14, 1807; m. Nov. 8. 1825, Samuel Kip.
    Elizabeth, b. Jan. 6, 1809, d. Nov. 1, 1810. *Frances E.*, b. Apr. 10, 1812, d. Oct. 22, 1813.
    28. *Charlotte M.*, b. Mar. 27, 1814; m. Nov. 19, 1834, Richard Berry.
(*) See Jonathan Havens genealogy No. 90.

13.

HENRY BOWDITCH HAVENS. s. William and Bethiah (Bowditch) Havens.
    b Oct. 13, 1780.   m. Jan. 9, 1806.   d. Oct. 2, 1877.

Hannah S. Sayre, da. David and   (Wickham) Sayre.
    b. Jan. 13, 1783.   d. Apr. 20, 1850.

8 ch. **29.** *Wickham Sayre*, b. Oct. 23, 1806; m.   Sarah W. Darling.
    30. *Harriet Elmira*, b. Aug. 23, 1809; m. Aug. 19, 1827, William Rysam Mulford.
    Henry Thomas, b. Sep. 14, 1811, d. Jan. 4, 1812.
    Silas Sayre, b. Mar. 20, 1814, d. May 8, 1815.
    *Mary Parker, b. Aug. 16, 1816; m. Sep. 6, 1837, †Rev. Albert Williams.
    ‖*Henry Thomas*, b. Apr. 5, 1819; m.   Kate Isaacs.
    °*Caroline*, b. Aug. 2, 1821; m.   ‡Anson Brown.
    Elizabeth Wickham, b. Apr. 1. 1825, d. June 7, 1827.
(*) d. July 2, 1888; had 3 ch., Henry W., Albert, and Harriet M. who m. Dr. John C. Barron
(†) b. Apr. 29, 1809, d. June 4, 1893. (‖) Had 3 ch., Charles, Catherine and Edward. (°) Had several
ch., Alice, Gertrude, Silas H. who d. Apr. 19, 1897, and others. (‡) b. Oct. 9, 1814, d. July 16, 1892.

14.

ELIZABETH MOORE, da. John and Mehetable (Havens) Moore.
    b. about 1775.   m.   d. Oct. 10, 1861.

Luther Tuthill, s. Jeremiah and Lois (King) Tuthill.
    b. about 1788.   d. in 1854.

2 ch.   *Elizabeth A.*, b. May 21, 1810; m. Aug. 2, 1832, Orrin Reeves; no issue.
    31. *Patience Ann*, b. Mar. 22, 1814; m. Nov. 19, 1835, Harvey Brown.

15.

DANIEL MOORE, s. John and Mehetable (Havens) Moore.
    b. Mar. 8, 1764.   m.   d. July 30, 1835.

Ruth Vail, da. Stephen and Ruth (Terry) Vail.
    b. July 27, 1764.   d. Oct. 4, 1817.

10 ch. *Lucretia*, b.   m.   James Brown.   *Benjamin*, b.   *Nathaniel*, b.   d.
        Bethiah, b. Nov. 20. 1787; m. Jan. 3, 1828, Jeremiah Rackett ; no issue.
        Elizabeth, b.   m.   Smith.   *Roxanna*, b.   d. unm.   *Sophronia*, b.   m.
   32. *Mary E.*, b.   m.   Robert Mack.   *Selah*, b.   d.   *Clinton*, b.   d.

16.

SHADRACH MOORE, s. John and Mehetable (Havens) Moore.
        b. Oct. 28, 1767.   m.   d. July 30, 1833.

Mehitable Rackett, da.
        b. Apr. 2, 1769.   d. Nov. 31, 1848.

8 ch. 33. *Erastus*, b. Aug. 2, 1794 ; m. { 1st, Jan. 2, 1819, Elizabeth Walton.
                                          { 2d, Oct. 27, 1822, Jennette Rackett.
       34. *Sarepta*, b. Feb. 14, 1796 ; m. Oct. 3, 1835, James Wiggins.
       35. *Rachel*, b. Sep. 19, 1797 ; m. Aug. 28, 1818, Charles Tea Overton.
          **Mehetable*, b. Mar. 27, 1799 ; m. Sept. 10, 1826, °Moses Griffing.
           Sarah Ann, b. Jan. 31, 1801 ; m. Apr. 23, 1825, Elias M. Richmond.
       36. *Lydia*, b. Feb. 4, 1807 ; m. Apr. 29, 1830, Terry V. Racket.
           David, b. Nov. 25, 1810, d. unm. June 16, 1847.
           Hannah Maria, b. Apr. 25, 1813, d. in 1815.
(*) Died Apr. 30, 1881. Had 2 ch., Daniel H., b. Dec., 1826, d. Feb. 2, 1854. ; Hannah D., b. Dec. 4, 1829, d. Jan. 26, 1858.   (°) Son of Milton Griffing, b. Dec., 1796, d. Mar. 22, 1856.

17.

JOSEPH MOORE, s. John and Mehetable (Havens) Moore.
        b.   1768.   m. July 2, 1806.   d. Dec. 7, 1842.

Anna Cleveland, da.   of Southold, L. I.
        b.   1770-1.   d. Mar. 6, 1838.

1 ch.   *Joseph Cleveland*, b. 1809, drowned Oct. 29, 1835.

18.

MARY MOORE, da. John and Mehetable (Havens) Moore.
        b.   m. Nov. 30, 1786.   d.

John Wiggins, s.
        b.   d.

5 ch.   *Mary*, b.   m.   Harvey Beebe.   *Patience*, b.   m. Jan. 8, 1809, Daniel Vail.
       37. *John Shepherd*, b. Aug. 14, 1792; m. Jan. 26. 1819, Rhoda Youngs.
       38. *Sarah*, b. Jan. 9, 1796; m. Jan. 27, 1818, Benjamin F. Youngs.   *Harvey*, b.

19.

JEREMIAH HAVENS, s. John and Abigail (Bostwick) Havens.
        b. July 6, 1774.   m. Mar. 6, 1795.   d. Feb. 11, 1862.

Bethiah Youngs, da.
        b. July 10, 1776.   d. Mar. 5, 1849.

11 ch. 39. *Jane*, b. Sep. 23, 1796; m. Jan. 21, 1818, Joseph Burnett.
       40. *Nathan*, b. Sep. 23, 1798; m.   Mahala Wilson.
       41. *Abigail*, b. Jan. 16, 1801; m.   Samuel Lewis.
       42. *Betsey*, b. Mar. 6, 1803; m.   Henry Reed.
       43. *David Y.*, b. Dec. 22, 1805; m. { 1st, June 12, 1827, Mary Rose.
                                            { 2d, Sep. 23, 1841, Mary L. Carrington.
           Mary Ann, b. Mar. 15, 1808, d. July 19, 1810.
          **Augustus*, b. Mar. 20, 1811; m.   Mary Ann Stewart.
       44. *Charles W.*, b. Apr. 20, 1813; m. Oct. 5, 1838, Mary P. Baldwin.
           John S., b. Mar. 11, 1816, d. in the army.
           Bethia A., b. Mar. 19, 1818; m.   Willard Stewart.
           Cornelia L., b. July 7, 1820; m.   Henry Terpening.
(*) d. Feb. 2, 1869; had 7 ch., Harriet who m. Mr. Dreiman,   David Y. who m. Maria S. Tice, Willard S., Sarah C., Augustus J., Maria and Charles.

20.

JOHN HAVENS, s. John and Abigail (Bostwick) Havens.
        b. Nov. 14, 1787.   m. Sep. 17, 1823.   d. Apr. 24, 1850.

Eliza Ketcham, da. Scudder and Eliza (Rose) Ketcham.
        b. Jan. 3, 1796.   d. May 1, 1863.

5 ch. 45. *Jerusha*, b. Oct. 9, 1824 ; m. Apr. 10, 1850, Willet Green.
       46. *John S.*, b. Oct. 20, 1826 ; m. June 14, 1865, Mary A. Pelletran.
       47. *Sarah*, b. June 30, 1828 ; m. July 1, 1857, William Wickham.
           Juliet, b. Aug. 4, 1832, d. unm. May 1, 1878.
       48. *Charles S.*, b. Aug. 26, 1834 ; m. Dec. 14, 1858, Nancy M. Williamson.

21.

SARAH HAVENS, da. John and Abigail (Bostwick) Havens.
        b. May 6, 1791.   m. June, 1814.   d. Oct. 11, 1863.

Dr. Nathaniel Miller, s. Elisha and Abigail (   ) Miller.
        b. Apr. 17, 1783.   d. May 7, 1863.

9 ch. **49.** *Nathaniel*, b. Sep. 15, 1815 ; m. Oct. 5, 1823, Ellen Carmen.
     **Mary A.*, b. Aug. 25, 1817 ; m. Feb. 16, 1843, °William D. Andrews.
  50. *Caroline E.*, b. May 10, 1819 ; m. Oct. 26, 1853, Caleb Green.
  51. *Jerusha K.*, b. Nov. 4, 1822 ; m. Jan. 5, 1848, Caleb Parshall.
     Dewitt Clinton, b. June 30, 1825, d. Nov. 17, 1826.
     Dewitt Clinton, b. May 19, 1827, d. unm. June 12, 1852.
     Sarah M., b. June 21, 1831 ; m. July 2, 1855, George H. Andrews ; no issue.
  52. *Laura C.*, b. Sept. 3, 1833 ; m. Dec. 19, 1854, George N. Ashby.
     Julia F., b. Sep. 25, 1837, d. unm. Aug. 17, 1888.
(*) d. Oct. 19, 1881 ; had 1 ch., Augusta. (°) s. of Nahum Andrews, b. May, 1818, d. Nov. 26, 1896.

22.

DANIEL H. RACKETT, s. Daniel and Bethiah (Moore) Rackett.
    b.   1773-4.   m.   1795.   d. June 8, 1815.
Deziah Vail, da.
    b. Apr. 20, 1772.   d. Feb. 4, 1856.
6 ch.   *Jeremiah*, b. Dec. 3, 1795; m. Jan. 3, 1828, Bethiah Moore; no issue.
     George, b. Apr. 25, 1797, d. June 20, 1797.   *Neville, b. Feb. 27, 1799; m
     Jennette, b. June 26, 1801. *Daniel*, b. Feb. 20, 1805; m.   *Bethiah*, b. July 15, 1808; m.
(*) d. July 7, 1858; had 4 ch., Julia W. who m. Albert Mapes, Appleton, Catherine J. who m. Henry
  Oakley, and George C.

23.

DANIEL TUTHILL HAVENS, s. Jeremiah and Mehitable (Brown) Havens.
    b. June 9, 1789.   m. Feb.   1815.   d. Feb. 28, 1868.
Betsey Raynor, da. John and Rebecca (Martin) Raynor.
    b. Apr. 13, 1791.   d. Nov. 20, 1861.
     Hettie, b. Jan. 18, 1817; m. Nov. 13, 1836, William Murdock.
10 ch.   *John, b. May 1, 1818; m. { 1st,   Phebe Mosier.
                                 { 2d,   Wid. Netty Petty.
  53. *Rebecca*, b. Nov. 18, 1819; m. May 22, 1839, James P. Baker. *Jeremiah*, b.   d.
  54. *Jeremiah*, b. Aug. 22, 1823; m. July 25, 1850, Mary G. Overton.
     Symms, b. Apr. 19, 1825; m. Phebe Okane. °*Jerusha*, b. Apr. 13, 1827; m. William Kingsland.
     †*Elizabeth*, b. Nov. 5, 1829; m.   Thomas Reeves.
     Matilda, b. Oct. 1831; m.   Elisha Lamb. *Mary J.*, b. June 28, 1833; m.   Charles M. Howell.
(*) Had 3 ch., Isabelle who m. John Howell, and Bessie H. by 1st wife John L. by 2d wife. (°) Had
  ch., Doretta, Lily William, and others. (†) Had 4 ch., Edward, Frank, Nina and Mabel, all m.

24.

JOHN S. HAVENS, s. Jeremiah and Mehitable (Brown) Havens.
    b.   1796.   m.   d. Apr. 6, 1865.
Nancy F. Smith, da. Josiah and Sarah (Brewster) Smith.
    b. Nov. 6, 1796.   d. Oct. 17, 1874.
5 ch.   *Joseph Conkling, b. Oct. 8, 1818; m. Jan. 1, 1848, °Catherine F. Ford.
  55. *Charles S.*, b. Aug. 12, 1820; m. Dec. 12, 1848, Augusta Girard.
  56. *Elizabeth*, b. 1823-4; m.   Henry Getty.
     Julia A., b.   1826, d. July 19, 1827.   *Julia A.*, b. Oct. 12, 1828, d. unm. Sep. 30, 1849.
(*) Had 2 ch., Charles F. who d. and Grace F.   (°) da. Ebenezer and Sarah (Jervis) Ford.

25.

MARIA S. HAVENS, da. Jeremiah and   (Conkling) Havens.
    b. Jan. 9, 1810.   m. May 10, 1836.   d. Mar. 1, 1893.
Nathaniel Nelson Munsell, s. Nathaniel and Dolly (Smith) Munsell.
    b. Oct. 30, 1806.
10 ch.   **Mary L.*, b. Feb. 11, 1837; m. J. Downs. °*Sarah F.*, b. m. Jan. 19, 1881, Charles E. Havens.
  57. *Nathaniel*, b. June 30, 1839; m. June 24, 1866, Eliza Tomlinson.
     Alexander H., b. Oct. 16, 1840, d. Dec. 16, 1861. *Jeremiah*, b. June, 1842, d.
     ‖*Dolly G.*, b. Dec. 7, 1843; m.   Edward D. Baker.
  58. *Isabelle F.*, b. Dec. 16, 1845; m. July 15, 1875, James M. Ashton.
     ¶*Nancy*, b.   m. Robert Raynor. †*Julia*, b. Nov. 12, 1851; m. Nov., 1886, Edward Gordon.
  59. *Jerusha*, b. Oct 14, 1855; m. Mar. 27, 1889, Adam Bubb.
(*) Had 7 ch., Addy E. who m. Frederick Raynor, William who m., Ella who m. William Collins,
  Nettie, d., Alexander, d., Jennie, d., and May. (°) See No. 92. (‖) d Aug., 1875; had 2 ch.,
  Nellie who m. George Fowler, and Eva. (¶) Had 8 ch., Edward, Gracie, d. ae. 14, Ida who m.
  Mr. Hanson, Nelson, Claud A., Robert, Nathaniel and Manly. (†) Has 3 ch., Frank, b. Jan.,
  1888, d. same day, Anna, b. May 9, 1889, Nellie, b. Apr. 19, 1891.

26.

THADDEUS FORDHAM, s. Daniel and Phebe (Jessup) Fordham.
    b. July 29, 1769.   m. Jan. 26, 1796.   d. May 28, 1843.
Clarissa Havens, da. Obadiah and Phebe (Havens) Havens.
    b. July 4, 1773.   d. May 9, 1824.
4 ch.   *Elmira*, b. Sep. 3, 1796, d. May 29, 1797.   *Nancy*, b. May 7, 1798, d. Sep. 20, 1798.
    **George G.*, b. Apr. 18, 1800; m. { 1st, June 11, 1822, °Catherine F. Jones.
                                  { 2d, Aug. 2, 1827, ‖Frances E. Halsey.
     Daniel A., b. Dec. 18, 1810, d. Oct. 19, 1833.
(*) Had 2 ch., Clarissa, b. July 22, 1823, d. Sep. 14, 1824, and Sylvanus who m.
(°) da. of Elias and Jerusha Topping Jones, d. Sep. 4, 1824. (‖) da. of Sylvanus Halsey.

27.

CHARLES H. FOWLER, s. Oliver and Desire L. (Havens) Fowler.
   b. Apr. 22, 1805.   m. Apr. 4, 1838.   d. Sep. 10. 1859.

Iantha Titus, da. Zebulon and Mary (Douglas) Titus.
   b. Nov. 20, 1815.   d. Sep. 5, 1882.
1 ch.   *Mary D.*, b. Jan. 14, 1839; m. Nov. 29. 1888, Stephen W. Gaines; no issue.

28.

CHARLOTTE MARY FOWLER, da. Oliver and Desire L. (Havens) Fowler.
   b. Mar. 27, 1814.   m. Nov. 19, 1834.   d. Sep. 15, 1874.

Richard Berry, s. Abram and Catherine (Terheun) Berry.
   b. Feb. 25, 1804.   d.
7 ch.   *Clinton*, b. Nov. 1835, d. June 16, 1862. **Jacob*, b. m. June 10, 1877. °Isabel Wysham.
     †*Oliver F.*, b. m. Oct. 1870, ‡Mary Andrews. *Annie*, b. d. young.
   60. *Katherine*, b. m. Apr. 27, 1865, John di Zeraga.
     §*Charlotte A.*, b. m. Mar. 15, 1873, ¶David L. Bennet.
   61. *Mary E.*, b. m. Mar. 16, 1876, Francis A. di Zeraga.
(*) Has 3 ch., Richard L., Isabel and Gladys C.   (°) da. of Henry Wysham, of Baltimore.
(†) Has 1 da., Mary Constance.   (‡) da. of Thomas and Mary (Dougherty) Andrews, d. Mar. 1884.
(§) Has 2 ch., Harold L. and Mary B.   (¶) s. of Edward and Mary (La Tourette) Bennet. d. Sep. 1887.

29.

WICKHAM SAYRE HAVENS, s. Henry B. and Hannah S. (Sayre) Havens.
   b. Oct. 23, 1806.   m.   d. Nov. 26, 1880.

Sarah W. Darling, da.
   b. July 4, 1812.   d. Sep. 22, 1890.
10 ch. **62.** *Harriet Mulford*, b. Feb. 10, 1835; m. Sep. 13, 1855, Chauncey Marvin Cady.
     Ripley Filmore, b. Feb. 1, 1838. *Wickham Sayre*, b. Jan. 22, 1840, d. Dec. 17. 1873.
     Charles Carpenter, b. Jan. 8, 1842, d. May 7, 1848.
   63. *Mary Parker*, b. Dec 12, 1845; m. Dec. 25, 1868, Dr. George Sterling.
   64. *Albert William*, b. Mar. 4, 1847; m. Oct. 26, 1876, Marie F. Quinn.
   65. *Frank Colton*, b. Nov. 21, 1848; m. { 1st, Feb. 12, 1874, Sadie P. Bell.
                                   2d, May 7, 1892, Lila Rand.
     Charles Darling, b. July 16, 1850; m. in 1879, Ella Hockkofler.
     **Henry Bowditch*, b. Aug. 21, 1852; m. June 1888, °Alice Crystal.
     William Falconer, b. Apr. 13, 1855, d. Dec. 31, 1888.
(*) d.¹Feb. 1898. Had 5 ch., Eugenia, Pierre who d., Jack, Alice and Cecelia. (°) da. of Peter Crystal.

30.

HARRIET ELMIRA HAVENS, da. Henry B. and Hannah S. (Sayre) Havens.
   b. Aug. 23, 1809.   m. Aug 21, 1827.

William Rysam Mulford, s. Edward and Fanny (Rysam) Mulford.
   b. Oct. 18, 1794.   d. July 24, 1865.
4 ch. **Fanny R.*, b. May 1828; m. { 1st, 1846, †Dr. Cleveland S. Stilwell.
                                  2d, 1885, Rev. John J. Harrison.
    |*Hannah M.*, b. m. Nov. 6, 1865, °Dr. Samuel B. Nicoll; no issue.
    ‡*William*, b., m. Laura Allen. *Edward*, b. d. in infancy.
(*) Has 1 s., Cleveland, b. Feb. 1858. (†) d. Nov. 20, 1879, ae. 60. (|) d. Apr. 25, 1876. (°) s.
of Samuel B. and Sarah (Payne) Nicoll, b. May 31, 1825, d. Jan. 4, 1899. (‡) d. in Civil War;
had 2 ch., Laura, and a s. who also d. in the Civil War.

31.

PATIENCE ANN TUTHILL, da. Luther and Elizabeth (Moore) Tuthill.
   b. Mar. 22, 1814.   m. Nov. 19, 1835.   d.   1898.

Harvey Brown, s. Jeremiah and Phebe (Glover) Brown.
   b. about 1813.   d. Apr. 3, 1843.
2 ch. *Betsey Ann*, b. Sep. 14, 1836, d. unm. May 4, 1860.
     **Adaline Amelia*, b. June 26, 1841; m. °Henry McGinnis.
(*) d. 1869; had 1 ch., Adaline Clark, who m. O. B. Youngs; they have no issue. °Also d.

32.

MARY E. MOORE, da. Daniel and Ruth (Vail) Moore.
   b.   m.   d.

Robert Mack, s.
   b.   d.
2 ch. **Daniel T.*, b. Aug. 9, 1819; m. Bridget McEnroe. *Edwin V.*, b. m. Laura Castle.
(*) d. July 21, 1895; had 3 ch., Mary E. who m. Atwood E. Brown, Carrie, d. Aug. 1893, and Robert.

33.

ERASTUS MOORE, s. Shadrach and Mehetable (Rackett) Moore.
   b. Aug. 2, 1794.   m. 1st, Jan. 2, 1819.   2d, Oct. 27, 1822.   d. Feb. 8, 1871.

1st. Elizabeth Walton, da.
   b. in 1802.   d. Oct 4, 1820.

2d, Jennette Rackett, da. Daniel H. and Desire (   ) Rackett.
   b. June 26, 1787.   d. Apr. 5, 1873.

10 ch.   *Betsey A.*, b. Sep. 16, 1820; m.   Thomas A. Wiggins.
  66. *Caroline A.*, b. July 3, 1823; m. Nov. 16, 1845, Joseph A. Goldsmith.
    °*Daniel G.*, b. Apr. 20, 1825; m. Nov. 2, 1850, Melvina P. Glover.
    Hannah L., b. May 28, 1827, d. Sep. 17, 1855.
    Bethiah A., b. Feb. 17, 1829; m. Feb. 11, 1853, Moses Cleveland; no issue.
  67. *Harriet E.*, b. Oct. 3, 1832; m. Mar. 11, 1853, Henry C. Cleveland.
  68. *Jennette D.*, b. Oct. 8, 1834; m. Aug. 11, 1859, Alexander Horton.
    Mary C., b. Apr. 4, 1837, d. Sep. 25, 1837.
  69. *Benjamin F.*, b. Aug. 25, 1839; m. Oct. 13, 1862, Lydia A. Payne.
  ‖*Mary E.*, b. Feb. 4, 1843; m. May 18, 1863, Theron W. Squires.
(*) She has d.; left 1 s., Thomas Allen.   (°) Had 2 ch., Mervin and Charles.   (‖) Has 5 ch.

34.

SAREPTA MOORE, da. Shadrach and Mehetable (Rackett) Moore.
  b. Feb. 14, 1796.   m. Oct. 3, 1835.   d. Nov. 25, 1888.

James Wiggins, s. David and Mary (Vail) Wiggins.
  b. Feb. 12, 1791.   d. July 4, 1853.

3 ch. **70.** *David A.*, b. Oct. 2, 1836; m. Feb. 25, 1869, Maria Benjamin.
  71. *Frances*, b. Apr. 1, 1840; m Nov. 7, 1857, Aaron Youngs.   *Matilda*, b. Sep. 13, 1841.

35.

RACHEL MOORE, da. Shadrach and Mehetable (Rackett) Moore.
  b. Sep. 19, 1797.   m. Aug. 28, 1818.   d. Dec. 10, 1884.

Charles Tea Overton, s. Eleazer and Mary (Tea) Overton.
  b. Jan. 16, 1797.   d. May 15, 1826.
4 ch.   An infant, b. Dec. 10, 1819, d. Dec. 21, 1819.
  72. *Sarah M.*, b. Aug. 27, 1820; m. May 11, 1843, George M. Fenton.
  73. *Mary T.*, b. Aug. 23, 1822; m. Feb. 11, 1844, Seth T. Wells.
  74. *Charles W.*, b. June 7, 1824; m. Oct. 9, 1847, Mary Howell.

36.

LYDIA MOORE, da. Shadrach and Mehetable (Rackett) Moore.
  b. Feb 4, 1807.   m. Apr. 29, 1830.   d. Aug. 23, 1881.

Terry V. Rackett, s. Abraham and Hannah (Vail) Rackett.
  b. Nov. 4, 1802.   d. Nov. 6, 1836.

3 ch.   *Andras*, b. Dec. 15, 1831; m. Nov. 1857, *Lucinda Clark.
  †*Mary E.*, b. Nov. 14, 1833; m. Oct. 6, 1854, °Francis Clark. *Lydia A.*, b. June 1, 1836.
(*) da. of Francis and Eunice (Rackett) Clark.   (°) s. of Francis and Eunice (Rackett) Clark.
(†) Had a s. named Ambrose, b. July 17, 1855.

37.

JOHN SHEPHERD WIGGINS, s. John and Mary (Moore) Wiggins.
  b. Aug. 14, 1792.   m. Jan. 26, 1819.   d. Mar. 12, 1863.

Rhoda Youngs, da. Thomas and Lydia (Tuthill) Youngs.
  b. Apr. 10, 1788.   d. Aug. 29, 1878.

2 ch. **75.** *John Harvey*, b. Sep. 5, 1823; m. June 3, 1856, Harriet A. Williams.
  76. *Sarah Jane*, b. Oct. 28, 1826; m. Feb. 4, 1863, James J. Jarrett.

38.

SARAH WIGGINS, da. John and Mary (Moore) Wiggins.
  b. Jan. 9, 1796.   m. Jan. 27, 1818.   d. Jan. 19, 1884.

Benjamin Franklin Youngs, s. Thomas and Lydia (Tuthill) Youngs.
  b. Dec. 5, 1790.   d. Dec. 19, 1867.
8 ch.   *Mary W.*, b. Dec. 24, 1818; m. Nov. 10, 1866, *Isaac J. Lake.
  Sarah Ann, b. Dec. 11, 1820, d. Dec. 6, 1851.
  77. *Lydia M.*, b. Aug. 16, 1823; m.   1851, Seymour Shutts.
  Edward, b.   †*Elizabeth*, b. Aug. 2, 1826; m.   Stephen Shutts.
  Julia, b. Sep. 10, 1829, d. Feb. 16, 1862.
  ‡*Seth*, b. May 13, 1823; m. ⎰ 1st, June 1, 1859, Arabella Sprague.
                   ⎱ 2d, Aug.   1890, Mary Bradley.
  William Budd, b. Sep. 1, 1839; m. ⎰ 1st, June 1870, Marietta Loper.
                      ⎱ 2d,   1874, Elizabeth Norman.
(*) d. Oct. 19, 1895.   (†) Has a s. named Alvin.   (‡) Has 1 ch., Edward F., b. July 1, 1860, m. in
1885, Annie Dedrich and has 1 ch., Alton S., b. June, 1886.

39.

JANE HAVENS, da. Jeremiah and Bethiah (Youngs) Havens.
  b. Sep. 23, 1796.   m. Jan. 21, 1818.   d. July 16, 1876.

Joseph Burnett, s. Joseph L. and Huldah (Ogden) Burnett.
  b. Jan. 23, 1793.   d. Aug. 27, 1862.
8 ch.   *Mary Ann*, b. Sep. 24, 1818; m. Oct. 21, 1858, George Champlain; no issue.
  Jane, b. Nov. 8, 1819; m. Sep. 2, 1863, Edmund Brand; no issue.
  Joseph O., b. Mar. 4, 1823, d. Aug. 9, 1870.
  David H., b. Apr. 18, 1827; m.   Angeline Hadcock; no issue.
  78. *George H.*, b. May 12, 1830; m.   Keziah Beverley.
  79. *Huldah E.*, b. Apr. 14, 1832; m. Oct. 24, 1864, William Beare.
  80. *J. Youngs*, b. May 25, 1834; m. summer 1857, Olive A. Smith.
  Charles W., b. July 1, 1837, d. July 27, 1840.
(*) d. Oct. 7, 1890.

40.

NATHAN HAVENS. s. Jeremiah and Bethiah (Youngs) Havens.
  b. Sep. 23, 1798.   m.   d. Aug. 14, 1882.
  Mahala Wilson, da.
    b.
  3 ch.   *Jerusha Cornelia*, b. m. L. G. Hubbard.   *Mary Jane*, b. m. { 1st, Edwin Hubbard.
                                                                            { 2d, Asa Tenant.
          Charles H., b.

41.

ABIGAIL HAVENS, da. Jeremiah and Bethiah (Youngs) Havens.
  b. Jan 16, 1801.   m.   d. Sep. 27. 1884.
  Samuel Lewis, s.
    b.
  5. ch.   *Mary Jane*, b.   m.   Eber C. Merrill.   *Elizabeth*, b.   m.   Layman.
          Rachel, b.   m.   John Lambart.   *J   D.*, b.   m.   Layman.
          Abigail, b.   m.   John Puffer.

42.

BETSEY HAVENS, da. Jeremiah and Bethiah (Youngs) Havens.
  b. Mar. 6, 1803.   m.   d.
  Henry Reed.
    b.   d.
  6 ch.   *Margaret*, b.   m.   Benjamin Tuttle.   *Jane*, b.   m.   J. Monroe Dewey.
          Hester, b.   m.   Stone.   *John F.*, b.   m.   Salina Jump.
          David, b.   m.   Huldah Jump.   *William*, b.   m.   Maria Barger.

43.

DAVID Y. HAVENS, s. Jeremiah and Bethiah (Youngs) Havens.
  b. Dec. 22, 1805.   m. 1st, June 12, 1827.   *2d, Sep. 22, 1841.   d. Apr. 30, 1885.
  1st, Mary Rose, da. Donald and Elizabeth (Grant) Rose.
    b. Apr. 29, 1807.   d. Feb. 25, 1840.
  2d, Mary L. Carrington, da. Miles and Rachel (Hotchkiss) Carrington.
    b.
  5 ch.   *Bethiah E.*, b. Feb 14, 1830; m. Dec. 14, 1852, Charles R. Brewer.
      81. *Katherine R.*, b. Feb. 12, 1832; m. Sep. 28, 1852, Benjamin B. Merchant.
      82. *Jeremiah D.*, b. June 22, 1834; m. Sep. 14, 1862, Frances S. Robinson.
      83. *R. Grant*, b. Feb. 7. 1837; m. Sep. 6. 1864, Lily Ryder Jarvis.
  (*) d. Feb. 25, 1856; had 1 ch., Charles H., b. Mar. 6, 1854; m. Cora Hallenbeck.

44.

DR. CHARLES W. HAVENS, s. Jeremiah and Bethiah (Youngs) Havens.
  b. Apr. 20, 1813.   m. October 5, 1838.   d. Nov. 7, 1891.
  Mary P. Baldwin, da. Daniel and Betsey (Rifenbark) Baldwin.
    b. Feb. 17, 1816.   d. Jan. 2, 1895.
  6 ch.   *Elizabeth A.*, b. Nov. 9, 1839 ; m. { 1st, Feb. 12, 1859, Lester Baum.
                                                { 2d, Feb. 22. 1872, Samuel S. Perry.
          Julia E., b. Sep. 27. 1841 ; m. Sep. 16, 1863, James H. Brown.
          Menzo, b. Dec 23. 1845, d. Dec. 5, 1846.   *Fletcher*, b. May 19, 1848, d. Apr. 27, 1850.
          Charles B., b. Jan. 28, 1852 ; m. Sep. 26, 1878, Anna Reynolds.
          William L., b. Oct. 29, 1858 ; m. Sep. 26, 1878, Emma Dibble.
  (*) Has 2 ch., Ella D., b. Apr. 23, 1863 who m. Clarence Phillips, and Lula, b. Sep. 26, 1874 who m.
      Frederick C. Winters.

45.

JERUSHA HAVENS, da. John and Eliza (Ketcham) Havens.
  b. Oct. 9, 1824.   m. Apr. 10, 1850.   d. Oct. 19, 1889.
  Willet Green, s. Isaac and Charity (Newton) Green.
    b. June 12, 1824.
  3 ch.   *Ella Havens*, b. Jan. 22, 1854, d. unm. May 1, 1881.
      84. *Edgar W.*, b. Feb. 18, 1857; m. Sep. 8, 1887, Annie F. Getty.
          Charles Hoover, b. Feb. 29, 1864; m. Feb. 22, 1887, Mabel Rogers; no issue.

46.

JOHN SCUDDER HAVENS, s. John and Eliza (Ketcham) Havens.
  b. Oct 20, 1826.   m. June 14, 1865.
  Mary A. Pelletrau, da. Jesse and Marion (Michaels) Pelletrau.
    b.   d. Sep. 23, 1898.
  4 ch.   *Eliza*, b. June 13, 1866.   *Archibald S.*, b. Mar. 16, 1868.
          Aimee M., b.   *Sarah M.*, b.

47.

SARAH HAVENS, da. John and Eliza (Ketcham) Havens.
  b. June 30, 1828.   m. July 1, 1857.
  William Wickham, s. William and Anna (Reeve) Wickham.
    b. Oct. 5, 1819.   d. Feb. 27, 1881.
  3 ch.   *James*, b. Oct. 8, 1859.   *William H.*, b. Feb. 3, 1864,   *Julia M.*, b. Dec. 24, 1867.

48.

CHARLES SMITH HAVENS, s. John and Eliza (Ketcham) Havens.
b. Aug. 26, 1834. m. Dec. 14, 1858.

Nancy M. Williamson, da. Samuel and Experience (Penny) Williamson.
b. Apr. 24, 1838.

3 ch. *John L.*, b. Oct. 8, 1859; m. Jan. 3, 1884, Imogene Reeve; no issue.
85. *Lillian*, b. Feb. 19, 1861; m. Oct. 17, 1893. Grosvenor C. Adams.
Hettie L., b. May 11, 1874.

49.

NATHANIEL MILLER, s. Dr. Nathaniel and Sarah (Havens) Miller.
b. Sep. 15, 1815. m. Oct. 5, 1853. d. Dec. 23, 1896.

Ellen Carmen, da. Samuel and Catherine (Homan) Carmen.
b.

6 ch. *Frederick*, b. m. Julia Ashby. *N. Clinton*, b. m. Annie Gerard.
Catherine, b. d. in youth. *Mary* and *Sarah*, twins, both d. *George*, b.

50.

CAROLINE E. MILLER, da. Dr. Nathaniel and Sarah (Havens) Miller.
b. May 10, 1819. m. Oct. 26, 1853. d. June 5, 1883.

Caleb Green, s. Isaac and Charity (Newton) Green.
b. in 1815. d. in 1864 or 5.

1 ch. *Dewitt*, b. Sep. 7, 1854, d. Oct. 2, 1871.

51.

JERUSHA K. MILLER, da. Dr. Nathaniel and Sarah (Havens) Miller.
b. Nov. 4, 1822. m. Jan. 5, 1848.

Caleb Parshall, s. David and Christine (Kidd) Parshall.
b. Nov. 24, 1815. d. Feb. 28, 1886.

3 ch. *Caroline*, b. July 7, 1849. *Sarah*, b. May 4, 1853.
86. *William A.*, b. Dec. 9, 1866; m. June 1, 1893, Christine Senger.

52.

LAURA C. MILLER, da. Dr. Nathaniel and Sarah (Havens) Miller.
b. Sep. 3, 1833. m. Dec. 19, 1854. d. Aug. 17, 1865.

George N. Ashby, s. William and Mary (Carmon) Ashby.
b. about 1832.

3 ch. *George*, b. m. { 1st, Rosa Carmen. *Jennie*, b. *Julia*, b. m. Frederick N. Miller.
{ 2d, Jennie Rogers.

53.

REBECCA HAVENS, da. Daniel T. and Betsey (Raynor) Havens.
b. Nov. 18, 1819. m. May 22, 1839.

James P. Baker, s. William and Chloe (Baker) Baker.
b. Jan. 18, 1817. d. May 2, 1896.

7 ch. **87.** *Elizabeth*, b. July 19, 1840; m. Sep. 30, 1860, Henry F. Brown.
**William W.*, b. Dec. 29, 1842; m. 1861, Hattie Spencer.
°*Charles R.*, b. Apr. 24, 1844; m. Sarah
88. *Jeremiah B.*, b. Sep. 12, 1847; m. { 1st, Henrietta Yarrington.
{ 2d, Maggie Johnson.
89. *J. Symns*, b. Nov. 7, 1852; m. July 5, 1877, Emma Caldwell.
90. *Mary E.*, b. Aug. 2, 1854; m. Apr. 18, 1871, Lewis Hulse Noe.
Daniel M., b. Dec. 12, 1856, d. July 7, 1874.
(*) Has 4 ch. (°) Had 7 ch., Roy L., Bessie H., Charles, Forest, Henry L., Lewis, Adrian.

54.

JEREMIAH HAVENS, s. Daniel T. and Betsey (Raynor) Havens.
b. Aug. 22, 1823. m. July 25, 1850. d. Oct. 28, 1894.

Mary G. Overton, da. Nicoll and Sarah (Glover) Overton.
b. Feb. 5, 1832.

8 ch. **91.** *Nicoll D.*, b. Apr. 21, 1851; m. May 8, 1873, Jennie McAllister.
William A., b. Aug. 20, 1853, d. Oct. 18, 1853. *Elisha R.*, b. Oct. 7, 1855, d. Oct. 12, 1855.
92. *Charles E.*, b. June 19, 1857; m. June 19, 1881, Sarah F. Monsell.
**Joseph C.*, b. Nov. 6, 1860; m. Jan. 22, 1883, Mary J. Anderson.
Elizabeth, b. Sep. 10, 1868, d. Apr. 22, 1869
°*Ella S.*, b. Dec. 3, 1870; m. June 14, 1893, Joseph Corwin. *Almira B.*, b. June 17, 1872.
(*) Has 2 ch. (°) Has 1 ch.

55.

CHARLES S. HAVENS, s. John S. and Nancy F (Smith) Havens.
b. Aug. 12, 1820. m. Dec. 12, 1848. d. Dec. 9, 1880.

Augusta Girard, da. Hiram and Hannah (Newins) Girard.
b. Oct. 9, 1830.

7 ch. **93.** *Julia Anna*, b. Oct. 2, 1849; m. Nov. 18, 1885, John Robert.
Moretta Girard, b. July 30, 1851. *Girard*, b. Oct. 10, 1853.
Charles, b. May 1857, d. Aug. 22, 1859.
94. *Dewitt Miller*, b. Sep. 5, 1858; m. June 20, 1883, Mary Z. Ketcham.
95. *Louise Minturn*, b. Aug. 22, 1860; m. Apr. 18, 1890, Frank Hobby.
Anna Augusta, b. Sep. 27, 1862.

56.

ELIZABETH S. HAVENS, da. John S. and Nancy F. (Smith) Havens.
   b.   1823-4.   m.   d. Jan. 27, 1874.
   Henry Getty, s.   of Ireland.
      b. in 1822.   d.   1876.
   5 ch.   *Mary E.*, b. Mar.   1850, d. July 18, 1851.   *Julia H.* b. Feb.   1852, d. July 18, 1859.
      96. *Sarah Smith*, b. Oct. 8, 1855; m. Sep. 30, 1873, Thomas H. Mickem.
         **Annie F.*, b. Nov. 21, 1862; m. Sep. 8, 1887, Edgar W. Green.
         Harry M., b.   1865, d. Jan. 21, 1887.
(*) See No. 84.

57.

NATHANIEL MUNSELL, s. Nathaniel N. and Maria S. (Havens) Munsell.
      b. June 30, 1839.   m. June 24, 1866.   d. Feb. 1899.
   Eliza A. Tomlinson, da. Charles F. and Eliza (Fawcett) Tomlinson.
      b. Sep. 11, 1849.
   7 ch.   *Marshall A.*, b. Apr. 2, 1867.
      97. *Hattie G.*, b. Jan. 24, 1871; m. Nov. 22, 1893, Dr. Joseph Ogle.
         Laura Estelle, b. Jan. 9, 1875, d. Feb. 28, 1876.   *Willard B.*, b. June 28, 1879.
         An infant, d. in birth, Mar. 1, 1883.   *Frank B.*, b. July 5, 1886.
         Ray Harrison, b. Jan. 9, 1891.

58.

ISABELLE F. MUNSELL, da. Nathaniel N. and Maria S. (Havens) Munsell.
      b. Dec. 16, 1845.   m. July 15, 1875.
   James M. Ashton, s. William and Margaret (Lyle) Ashton.
      b. Jan. 20, 1838.
   4 ch.   *Maria M.*, b. June 18, 1876.   *Alice H.*, b. July 26, 1878.
         Julia I., b. Oct. 6, 1880.   *Frances J.*, b. Oct. 18, 1885.

59.

JERUSHA J. MUNSELL, da. Nathaniel N. and Maria S. (Havens) Munsell.
      b. Oct. 14, 1853.   m. Mar. 27, 1889.
   Adam Bubb, s. Frederick and Johanne (Winter) Bubb.
      b. Oct. 4, 1866.
   3 ch.   *Louis*, b. Jan. 16, 1890.   *Mary E.*, b. Aug. 4, 1894.   *Herman A.*, b. July 18, 1898.

60.

KATHERINE BERRY, da. Richard and Charlotte M. (Fowler) Berry.
      b.   m. Apr. 27, 1865.
   John A. di Zerega, s. John A. and Eliza (Mörch Baroness Von Bretton) di Zerega.
      b.
   2 ch.   *Richard A.*, b. Feb. 16, 1866.
         Charlotte M., b. June 19, 1867; m. Dec. 10, 1890, *Sir Frederick Frankland; no issue.
(*) Tenth Baronet of Sherkleby, d. Mar. 24, 1892.

61.

MARY E. BERRY, da. Richard and Charlotte M. (Fowler) Berry.
      b.   m. Mar. 16, 1876.
   Francis A. di Zerega, s. John A. and Eliza (Mörch Baroness Von Bretton) di Zerega.
      b.
   3 ch.   *Violet*, b.   m. June 23, 1897, *Reginold Arnold.   *Eliza, V'B.*, b.   *Victor P.*, b.
(*) Son of John H. and Josephine A. (Ormsby) Arnold.

62.

HARRIET M. HAVENS, da. Wickham S. and Sarah W. (Darling) Havens.
      b. Feb. 10, 1835.   m. Sep. 13, 1855.
   Chauncey M. Cady, s.
      b. May 16, 1824.   d. June 16, 1889.
   5 ch.   *Harriet*, b. June 29, 1856.   *Charlotte Havens*, b. Oct. 3, 1860.
         Sarah Darling, b. June 15, 1862.   *Henry Landon*, b. Oct. 28, 1869, d. Mar. 20, 1886.
         Chauncey Marvin, b. Mar. 5, 1871, d. Nov. 2, 1880.

63.

MARY PARKER HAVENS, da. Wickham S. and Sarah W. (Darling) Havens.
      b. Dec. 12, 1845.   m. Dec. 25, 1868.
   Dr. George A. Sterling, of Sharon, Conn.
      b.   d. in 1897.
   9 ch.   *Alice Crystal*, b.   d.   *George A.*, b.   m. in 1897, Carrie Rand.
         Wickham H., b.   m.   Lottie Halsey.
         Mary Isabel, b.   m. Aug. 23, 1898, J. Stanford Brown.
         James D., b.   *Flora*, b.   *Madaline*, b.   *Marion*, b.   *Avis Canfield*, b.

64.

ALBERT WILLIAM HAVENS, s. Wickham S. and Sarah W. (Darling) Havens.
      b. Mar. 4, 1847.   m. Oct. 26, 1876.
   Marie Frances Quinn, da. William J. and Frances (Ferris) Quinn.
      b.
   1 ch.   *Marietta B.*, b. Jan. 27, 1878.

65.

FRANK COLTON HAVENS, s. Wickham S. and Sarah W. (Darling) Havens.
b. Nov. 21, 1848.   m. 1st, Feb. 12, 1874.   2d, May 7, 1892.

1st, Sadie P. Bell, da. Rev. Samuel B. and Sophie (Walsworth) Bell.
b. in 1852.   d. Apr. 30, 1886.

2d, Lila Rand, da. David H. and Eliza M. (Abbott) Rand.
b. Feb. 16, 1866.

ch.   *Wickham*, b. Dec. 27, 1874; m. Sep. 22, 1897, Florence J. Walker.
Harold, b. July 26, 1877.   *Said* and *Paul*, b. Apr. 30, 1886.

66.

CAROLINE A. MOORE, da. Erastus and Jennetta (Rackett) Moore.
b. July 3, 1823.   m. Nov. 16, 1845.   d.

Joseph A. Goldsmith, s. Joseph H. and Maria (Case) Goldsmith.
b. July 26, 1824.

5 ch.   **Josepine A.*, b. Feb. 18, 1848; m.   May   1870, Albert L. Conklin.
Addison M., b. Mar. 24, 1850; m.   *Clarence*, b.   m.   DeLacey.
†*Caroline W.*, b. Dec. 19, 1855; m. { 1st, Charles Robinson. { 2d, Thatcher.   *Leroy*, b.   d. ae. 5.
(*) See Conkling genealogy.   (†) 1 ch. by 1st hus., William.

67.

HARRIET E. MOORE, da. Erastus and Jennetta (Rackett) Moore.
b. Oct. 3, 1832.   m. Mar. 11, 1853.   d. July 20, 1869.

Henry C. Cleveland, s. Joseph and Jemima (Abrams) Cleveland.
b. July 23, 1829.

3 ch.   *Florence A.*, b. Mar. 25, 1854.   *Hattie*, b.   *Katie*, b.   All m.

68.

JENNETTE D. MOORE, da. Erastus and Jennette (Rackett) Moore.
b. Oct. 8, 1834.   m. Aug. 11, 1859.

Alexander B. Horton, s. Barnabas and Elizabeth (Case) Horton.
b. Apr. 4, 1835.   d. Apr. 15, 1898.

2 ch.   **Ella Isabelle*, b. June 18, 1860; m. July 3, 1895. Fredericks E. Hutchinson.
William Madison, b. May 7, 1863, d. Oct. 15, 1869.
(*) See King genealogy.

69.

BENJAMIN F. MOORE, s. Erastus and Jennette (Rackett) Moore.
b. Aug. 25, 1839.   m. Oct. 13, 1862.

Lydia A. Payne, da. Alanson and Charity (Hart) Payne.
b. Sep. 9, 1846.

1 ch.   **Franklin C.*, b. Aug. 30, 1865; m.   Elizabeth Smith.
(*) Had 1 s. who d. in infancy.

70.

DAVID A. WIGGINS, s. James and Sarepta (Moore) Wiggins.
b. Oct. 2, 1836.   m. Feb. 25, 1869.   d. Oct. 2, 1872.

Maria Benjamin, da. John and Hattie (Raynor) Benjamin.
b.   d.   1894.

1 ch.   *Adelaide*, b. July 20, 1872.

71.

FRANCES WIGGINS, da. James and Sarepta (Moore) Wiggins.
b. Apr. 1, 1840.   m. Nov. 7, 1857.

Aaron Youngs, s. Jacob and Fanny (Moore) Youngs.
b. July 22, 1836.

2 ch.   **Coralie M.*, b. Nov. 15, 1865; m. Jan. 1, 1887, Willard H. Wiggins.
Herbert A., b. July 22, 1867; m. Nov.   1897, †Jennette R. Wiggins.
(*) See No. 99.   (†) da. of John H. and Harriet A. (Williams) Wiggins, b. Oct. 24. 1868.

72.

SARAH M. OVERTON, da. Charles T. and Rachel (Moore) Overton.
b. Aug. 27, 1820.   m. May 11, 1843.

George Marvin Fenton, s. Marvin and Mary (Hibbard) Fenton.
b. May 19, 1816.   d. May 13, 1887.

1 ch. 98. *Charles Marvin*, b. Sep. 4, 1845; m. { 1st, Jan. 20, 1872, Eva Geen Case. { 2d, Dec. 18, 1892, Ruth Helen Moore.

73.

MARY T. OVERTON, da. Charles T. and Rachel (Moore) Overton.
b. Aug. 23, 1822.   m. Feb. 18, 1844.   d. July 23, 1854.

Seth T. Wells, s. Jonathan and Bethiah (Terry) Wells.
b. June 13, 1821.

3 ch.   *Julia Bethiah*, b. May 22, 1846; m. Jan. 27, 1866, Charles N. Green.
Franklin, b.   *Lida Rachel*, b. May   1849, d. Oct.   1854.

74.

CHARLES W. OVERTON, s. Charles T. and Rachel (Moore) Overton.
  b. June 7, 1824.   m. Oct. 9, 1847

Mary Howell, da. (?) Daniel and Esther (Reeve) Howell.
  b. Feb. 26, 1822.
  2 ch.   *Albro Howell*, b. Oct. 29, 1848, d. July 29, 1849.
      Charles Hanford, b. Feb. 6, 1855; m.   Cora Ackerson.
(*) d. Dec. 9, 1885; had 4 ch., Charles, Albro (both d. in infancy), Ethel and Roberta.

75.

JOHN HARVEY WIGGINS, s. John S. and Rhoda (Youngs) Wiggins.
  b. Sep. 5, 1823.   m. June 3, 1856.

Harriet Amelia Williams, da. John   Williams.
  b. May 4, 1835.
  4 ch.   *Bertha Amelia*, b. Jan. 22, 1861.
    99. *Willard Harvey*, b. June 28, 1863; m. Jan. 1, 1887, Coralie M. Youngs.
       Ernest B., b.   1865, d.   1866.
       Jennette Rhoda, b. Oct. 24, 1868; m. Nov.   1897. *Herbert A. Youngs.
(*) s. of Aaron and Frances (Wiggins) Youngs, b. July 22, 1867; see No. 71.

76.

SARAH JANE WIGGINS, da. John S. and Rhoda (Youngs) Wiggins.
  b. Oct. 28, 1826.   m. Feb. 4, 1863.

James J. Jarrett, s.
  b.
  3 ch.   *Henry Shepherd*, b. Apr. 5, 1864; m. { 1st, Oct. 23, 1887, Elizabeth Thompson.
                                                { 2d,
       Mary Elizabeth, b. Dec. 23, 1865.
       William Parker, b. Jan. 7, 1868; m.   Sarah Bostwick.
(*) Has 2 ch., Henry Wadsworth, b. Sep. 1, 1888, Esther May, b. Aug. 25, 1890.

77.

LYDIA M. YOUNGS, da. Benjamin F. and Sarah (Wiggins) Youngs.
  b. Aug. 16, 1823.   m.   1851.   d. July 4, 1857.

Seymour Shutts, s.
  b.   d. in 1883.
  1 ch.   *John Arthur*, b.   m. { 1st, Apr.   1877, †Adelia Warfield.
                                 { 2d,   Harriet Turner.
(*) Has 3 ch., Neva Lydia, b. Dec. 24, 1882, Isabella, b. Oct. 1892, and Arthur B., b. Mar., 1896.
(†) d. May, 1889.

78.

GEORGE HAVENS BURNETT, s. Joseph and Jane (Havens) Burnett.
  b. May 12, 1830. m.   d. Nov. 5, 1897.

Keziah Beverley, da.
  b.
  6 ch.   *Mary Jane*. b.   m.   John Dayton.   †Pheobe Ann. b.   m.   John Perry.
       °Charles E., b.   m.   Statire Padin.
       Emerson G., b.   Ida H., b.   ‡Carrie, b.   m.   Boukeep.
(*) Has 6 ch., Elsie, Madge, Bertha, Jennie, Mary, Warren.   (†) Has 1 ch., Grace.
(°) Has 6 ch., George, Winfield, Maud, Charles, Edwin, Youngs.   (‡) Has 3 ch.

79.

HULDAH E. BURNETT, da. Joseph and Jane (Havens) Burnett.
  b. Apr. 14, 1832.   m. Oct. 24, 1864.

William Beare, s. Peter and Martha (Smith) Beare.
  b. Jan. 20, 1828.
  1 ch.   *Jennie*, b. Aug. 10, 1865; m. Sep. 12, 1889, Joseph Clegg; no issue.

80.

J. YOUNGS BURNETT, s. Joseph and Jane (Havens) Burnett.
  b. May 25, 1834.   m. 1st,   1857.   2d,   d. Nov. 21, 1893.

1st, Olive A. Smith, da. Brainerd and Rhoda (Conkling) Smith.
  b. Aug. 18, 1835.   d. Oct. 13, 1876.

2d, Ellen E. Kane, da. George and Mary (Brown) Kane.
  b.
  4 ch. 100. *Alice A.*, b. Apr. 22, 1859; m. May 16, 1877, George M. Murphey.
       Hattie J., b. June 7, 1862; m. Aug. 23. 1888, *Lorenzo J. Kendall; no issue.
       Melvin, b. in 1865, d.   1865.   1 ch. by 2d m., *Ida Blanche*, b. Aug. 10. 1880.
(*) s. of Lorenzo and Rosamond (Langmaid) Kendall, b. May 15, 1857.

81.

KATHERINE R. HAVENS, da. David Y. and Mary (Rose) Havens.
  b. Feb. 12, 1832.   m. Sep. 28, 1852.

Benjamin B. Merchant, s. Reuben and Ella (Smith) Merchant.
  b. Oct. 18, 1829.
  2 ch.   *Mary Elise*, b. July 28, 1853; m. May 2, 1888, Frank H. Fisk.
       Frank H., b. May 24, 1856. d. Dec. 26, 1861.
(*) Has 1 s., Anthony Merchant, b. Sep. 16, 1889.

82.

JEREMIAH D. HAVENS, s. David Y. and Mary (Rose) Havens.
  b. June 22, 1834.   m. Sep. 28, 1862.   d. Feb. 12, 1875.
Frances Susan Robinson, da. Phineas and Eliza (Day) Robinson.
  b. Dec. 4, 1833.   d Mar. 31, 1896.
3 ch.   *Thomas Young*, b. Dec. 12, 1863, d. Sep. 20, 1864.   *Robert Grant*, b. July 6, 1865.
  101. *Henry Robinson*, b. Jan. 14. 1869; m. Aug. 15, 1894, Mary A. Atwill.

83.

R. GRANT HAVENS, s. David Y. and Mary (Rose) Havens.
  b. Feb. 7, 1837.   m. Sep. 6, 1864.   d. Dec. 30. 1895.
Lily Ryder Jarvis, da. John J. and Eveline (Ryder) Jarvis.
  b.
8 ch.   *D. Jay*, b. Jan. 25. 1867   *Evelyn J.*, b. June 18. 1868; m. Mar. 28, 1896. E. R. Pearse.
  *Frank B., b. Dec. 12, 1869; m. Mar. 18, 1896. Marie C. Dodge.
  Lydia R., b. July 29, 1876.   *Laura K.*. b. Feb. 9, 1881.   *Robert G.*, b. Dec. 20. 1882.
  Mary Rose, b. Sep. 18. 1886.   *Coreane E.*, b. Aug. 29, 1889.
(*) Has 1 s., William, b. Jan. 20, 1897.

84.

EDGAR W. GREEN, s. Willet and Jerusha (Havens) Green.
  b. Feb. 1857.   m. Sep. 8, 1887.
ANNIE F. GETTY. da. Henry and Elizabeth S. (Havens) Getty.   See No. 60.
  b. Nov. 21, 1862.
1 ch.   *Charles Havens*, b. Aug. 13, 1891.

85.

LILLIAN HAVENS, da. Charles S. and Nancy M. (Williamson) Havens.
  b. Feb. 19, 1861.   m. Oct. 17, 1893.
Grosvenor C. Adams, s. Grosvenor S. and Nancy U. (Cone) Adams.
  b. May 2, 1854.
1 ch.   *Louise Havens*, b. May 7, 1897.

86.

WILLIAM A. PARSHALL, s. Caleb and Jerusha K. (Miller) Parshall.
  b. Dec. 9, 1866.   m. June 1, 1893.
Christine Senger, da. Lewis and Florence (Corwin) Senger.
  b. May 3, 1869.
1 ch.   *Walter Corwin*, b. July 19, 1895.

87.

ELIZABETH BAKER, da. James P. and Rebecca (Havens) Baker.
  b. July 19, 1840.   m. Sep. 30, 1860.
Henry F. Brown, s. David and   (Patterson) Brown.
  b. Sep.   1839.
9 ch.   *Fanny R.*, b. Feb. 23, 1863; m.   William Williams   *Mary*, b. Dec. 24. 1864, d.
  Edna L., b. Apr. 30. 1870, d. unm.   *Lottie*, b.   d.   *Henry M.*, b.   *George D.*, b.
  Clara E., b. June. 1874.   *W. Jay*, b.   1881.   *Flora M.*. b.   d.

88.

JEREMIAH BAKER, s. James P. and Rebecca (Havens) Baker.
  b. Sep. 12, 1847.   m. 1st,   2d,
1st, Henrietta Yarrington, da. George and Sarah (Davis) Yarrington.
  b.   d. Nov.   1886.
2d, Maggie Johnson, da. John Johnson, of Newark, N. J.
  b.
6 ch.   *Sarah E.* b. July 7, 1874.   **Lulu*, b.   1876; m. July   1896, Stephen Drake.
  William, b. July 12, 1881.   *George*, b.   1883.
  Oscar, b. Nov.   1886.   By 2d wife an infant, *Percy H.*   (*) Has 1 ch.

89.

J. SYMMS BAKER, s. James P. and Rebecca (Havens) Baker.
  b. Nov. 7, 1852.   m. July 5, 1867.
Emma Caldwell, da. William and Emma J. (   ) Caldwell.
  b. about 1862.
3 ch.   *Joshua*, b. Jan. 30, 1882.   *Unie*, b. Jan. 31, 1884.   *Minetta*, b. May   1886.

90.

MARY E. BAKER, da. James P. and Rebecca (Havens) Baker.
  b. Aug. 2, 1854.   m. Apr. 18, 1871.
Lewis Hulse Noe, s. Thomas J. and Louisa (Hulse) Noe.
  b. Feb. 8, 1849.
3 ch.   **Grace F.*. b. Nov. 1. 1872; m. July 11, 1893, Allen Herbert Feldmeier.
  Winnie L.. b. Nov. 11, 1879.   *Mamie Lois*. b. May 13, 1898.
(*) 1 ch., Herbert Allen, b. Mar. 12, 1894.

91.

NICOLL D. HAVENS. s. Jeremiah and Mary G. (Overton) Havens.
  b. Apr. 21. 1851.   m. May 8, 1873.
Jennie McAllister, da. Robert and Margaret (McDowell) McAllister.
  b. Aug. 22, 1849.
1 ch.   *Grace M.*, b. May 4, 1874; m. Nov. 17, 1895, Martin W. Hawkins.

92.

CHARLES E. HAVENS, s. Jeremiah and Mary G. (Overton) Havens.
    b. June 19, 1857.   m. Jan. 19, 1881.
  SARAH F. MUNSELL, da. Nathaniel and Maria S. (Havens) Munsell. See No. 25.
          b.
  4 ch.   *Edward,* b.   *Eva Maria,* b.   *William G.,* b.   *Minnie,* b.

93.

JULIA ANNA HAVENS, da. Charles S. and Augusta (Girard) Havens.
    b. Oct. 2, 1849.   m. Nov. 17, 1885.
  John Robert, s. William and Caroline (Smith) Robert.
    b. Aug. 4, 1840.
  1 ch.   *Josiah Smith,* b. June 3, 1887.

94.

DEWITT MILLER HAVENS, s. Charles S. and Augusta (Girard) Havens.
    b. Sep. 5, 1858.   m. June 20, 1883.
  Mary Zoretta Ketcham, da. Townsend V. and Matilda (Rogers) Ketcham.
          b.
  3 ch.   *Zoretta Ketcham,* b. Jan. 11, 1886.   *Charles Smith,* b. May 4, 1887.
          Dewitt Miller, b. Sep. 26, 1896.

95.

LOUISE MINTURN HAVENS, da. Charles S. and Augusta (Girard) Havens.
    b. Aug. 22, 1860.   m. Apr. 18, 1890.   d.
  Frank Hobby, s. Edwin H. and Adelaide A. (Frost) Hobby.
          b.
  1 ch.   *Girard Havens,* b. Nov. 19, 1892.

96.

SARAH SMITH GETTY, da. Henry and Elizabeth S. (Havens) Getty.
    b. Oct. 8, 1855.   m. Sep. 30, 1873.
  Thomas Hamilton Mickem, s. Thomas and Eliza J. (Hamilton) Mickem.
    b. Mar. 5, 1847.
  7 ch.   *Freddie Rotan,* b. Oct. 19, 1875, d. Jan. 20, 1896.
          Welton Elder, b. Oct. 25, 1876, d. Jan. 2, 1878.   *DeWitt Clinton,* b. Feb. 26, 1879.
          Kate Hamilton, b. Sep. 30, 1882, d. Nov. 30, 1882.
          Bessie Floyd, b. Aug. 4, 1887, d. May 16, 1889.
          Arthur Seitz, b. Mar. 11, 1891.   *Walter Hamilton,* b. Mar. 11, 1891.

97.

HATTIE GORDON MUNSELL, da. Nathaniel and Eliza A. (Tomlinson) Munsell.
    b. Jan. 24, 1872.   m. Nov. 22, 1893.
  Dr. Joseph Ogle, s. Joseph and Margerite (Heffernan) Ogle.
    b. Dec. 5, 1859.
  1 ch.   *Hattie Munsell,* b. June 19, 1895.

98.

CHARLES MARVIN FENTON, s. George M. and Sarah M. (Overton) Fenton.
    b. Sep. 4, 1845.   m. 1st, Jan. 20, 1872.   2d, Dec. 18, 1892.
  1st, Eva Geen Case, da. Henry and Mary A. (Ross) Case.
    b. Jan. 12, 1853.
  2d, Ruth Helen Moore, da. Charles B. and Helen F. (Tuthill) Moore.
    b. Oct. 14, 1866.
  1 ch.   *Georgiana Vienna,* b. Sep. 28, 1874, d. Sep. 22, 1877.

99.

WILLARD H. WIGGINS, s. John H. and Harriet A. (Williams) Wiggins.
    b. June 28, 1863.   m. Jan. 1, 1887.
  CORALIE M. YOUNGS, da. Aaron and Frances (Wiggins) Youngs. See No. 71.
    b. Nov. 15, 1865.
  2 ch.   *Ernest,* b. Dec. 20, 1887.   *Lillian B.,* b. May 19, 1890.

100.

ALICE A. BURNETT, da. J. Youngs and Olive A. (Smith) Burnett.
    b. Apr. 22, 1859.   m. May 16, 1877.
  George M. Murphey, s. Jacob and Sarah B. (Gibson) Murphey.
    b. Jan. 29, 1844.
  4 ch.   *Eleanor G.,* b. Aug. 10, 1880.   *Marie B.,* b. in Nov., 1882, d. in Feb., 1883.
          Joseph A., b. Jan. 3, 1884.   *Ralph B.,* b. Feb. 17, 1886.

101.

HENRY ROBINSON HAVENS, s. Jeremiah D. and Frances S. (Robinson) Havens.
    b. Jan. 14, 1869.   m. Aug. 15, 1894.
  Mary A. Atwill, da. George and Eliza J. (Gordon) Atwill.
    b. Aug. 11, 1871.
  2 ch.   *Herbert Grant,* b. Oct. 24, 1895.   *Mildred Frances,* b. Mar. 20 1898.

ANCESTORS.

A.

NATHANIEL SYLVESTER, s. Giles and Mary (Gascoigne) Sylvester.
b. in England.   m. in 1652.   d. in 1680.

Grissel Brinley, da. Thomas and Anne (Wade) Brinley.
b. in England.   d.

11 ch.   *Grissel*, b. Aug. 12, 1654; m.   James Loyd.
   Giles, b. in 1657; m. in 1686, wid. Hannah Gillam, nee Savage.
   B. *Nathaniel*, b. Dec. 31, 1661; m.   Margaret Hobert.
   Peter, b. in 1663; d s. p.
   *Patience, b. in 1664; m. in 1694, Benjamin L'Hommedieu.
   Elizabeth, b. in 1666; m. (after 1695), Jonathan Brown.
   Mary, b.
   Ann, b. in 1669.
   o*Constant*. b. in 1671; m. perhaps a Miss Booth.
   Benjamin, b.   d. s. p. 1689.
   Joshua, b.   d. June 21, 1706.

(*) See L'Hommedieu gen.
(o) d. in 1695.

B.

NATHANIEL SYLVESTER, s. Nathaniel and Grissel (Brinley) Sylvester.
b. Dec. 31, 1661.   m.   d.

Margaret Hobert, da. Isaiah Hobert, of Easthampton, Long Island.
b.   d.

4 ch.   *Nathaniel*, b.   m.
   1. *Brinley*, b. Nov. 23, 1694; m. Dec. 2, 1718, Mary Burroughs.
   Griselda, b.   m.   Cotton.
   *Margaret, b.   m. Oct. 2, 1723, Rev. Ebenezer Prime.

(*) d. Sept. 26, 1726.

1.

BRINLEY SYLVESTER, s. Nathaniel and Margaret (Hobert) Sylvester.
b. Nov. 23, 1694.   m. Dec. 2, 1718.   d. Dec. 24, 1752.

Mary Burroughs, da. Thomas Burroughs, of New York.
b. about 1702.   d. March 1, 1751.

2 ch.   *Margaret. C.*, b.   m. Oct. 8, 1749, David Cheeseborough ; no issue.
   2. *Mary*, b. in 1724; m. March 9, 1756, Thomas Dering.

2.

MARY SYLVESTER, da. Brinley and Mary (Burroughs) Sylvester.
b. in 1724.   m. March 9, 1756.   d. Aug. 19, 1794.

Thomas Dering, s. Henry and Elizabeth (Packer) Dering.
b. May 16, 1770.   d. Sept. 26, 1785.

4 ch.   *Henry Sylvester*, b. Apr. 21, 1757; d. Jan. 28, 1758.
   3. *Sylvester*, b. Nov. 27, 1758; m. Dec. 6, 1787, Esther Sarah Havens.
   4. *Elizabeth*, b. Apr. 21, 1762; m. Jan. 27, 1784, Dr. Nathaniel Gardiner.
   5. *Henry Packer*, b. July 3, 1763; m. Dec. 27, 1793, Anna Fosdick.

3.

SYLVESTER DERING, s. Thomas and Mary (Sylvester) Dering.
b. Nov. 27, 1758.   m. Dec. 6, 1787.   d. Oct. 8, 1820.

Esther Sarah Havens, da. Nicoll and Sarah (Fosdick) Havens.
b. Jan. 31, 1763.   d. July 31, 1839.

7. ch.   **6.** *Margaret S.*, b. Sept. 11, 1789; m. Jan. 5, 1809, Richard F. Nicoll.
   *Charles T., b. Nov. 17, 1790; m. Aug. 14, 1816, o*Eliza Floyd Nicoll*; no issue.
   Sarah Frances, b. Feb 24. 1792; d. unm. Oct. 5, 1833.
   7. *Nicoll H.*, b. Jan. 1, 1794; m. 1st June 6, 1826, Frances Huntington.
                        2nd Oct. 1, 1844, Sarah H Strong.
   8. *Henry S.*, b Sept. 29, 1804; m. Apr. 29, 1839, H. Eliza Hulse.
   Twins who died in infancy.

(*) d. June 7, 1859.   (o) da. of Samuel B. and Anna (Floyd) Nicoll; d. in 1872.

4.

ELIZABETH DERING, da. Thomas and Mary (Sylvester) Dering.
b. Apr. 21, 1762.   m. Jan. 27. 1784.   d. Mar. 18, 1801.'

Dr. Nathaniel Gardiner, s. Abraham and Mary (Smith) Gardiner.
b. Jan. 11, 1759.   d. Mar. 25, 1804.

3 ch.   *Maria Sylvester*, b. in 1784; d. Nov. 9. 1804.
   Robert Smith. b. Sept. 10, 1786; d. unm. Jan. 19, 1824.
   * *Elizabeth Packer*, b. June 4, 1788; m.   Reuben Bromley.

(*) d. s. p. Aug. 7, 1863.

5.

HENRY PACKER DERING, s. Thomas and Mary (Sylvester) Dering.
  b. July 3, 1763.   m. Dec. 22, 1793.   d. Apr. 30, 1822.
Anna Fosdick, da. Dr. Thomas and Anna (Havens) Fosdick.
  b. May 23, 1769.   d. Feb. 21, 1852.

9 ch.   *Frances Mary*, b. Mar. 22, 1795; d. unm. Feb. 18, 1874.
  * *Henry Thomas*, b. Oct. 27, 1796; m. July 20, 1842, o Gloriana Havens; no issue.
    Brinley Sylvester b. Feb. 17. 1799; lost at sea Aug. 19, 1827.
    Lodowick Fosdick, b. Feb. 21, 1801; d. Sept. 6, 1805.
    Gloriana Havens, b. Feb. 28, 1804; d. Oct. 17. 1828.
    Elizabeth Packer, b. Dec. 3, 1805; d. unm. Mar. 31, 1881.
  9. *Lodowick Fosdick*, b. Dec. 27, 1807; m. Apr. 23, 1840, Eliza Gracie Mulford.
 10. *Ann Charlotte*, b. Jan. 2, 1811; m. Jan. 2, 1833, William R. Sleight.
    Nicoll Richard, b. Oct. 29, 1812; d. unm. Mar 16, 1873.
(*) d. Jan. 14, 1854.
(o) da. Rensselaer and Anna (Jenkins) Havens, born Sep. 29, 1800, died Feb. 6, 1879.

6.

MARGARET S. DERING, da. Sylvester and Esther S. (Havens) Dering.
  b. Sept. 11, 1789.   m. Jan. 5, 1809.   d. Aug. 25, 1847.
Rev. Richard F. Nicoll, s. Samuel B. and Anna (Floyd) Nicoll.
  b. Sept. 15, 1785.   d. Feb. 28, 1857.

10 ch.   *Margaret S. D.*, b. Aug. 26, 1810; d. unm. July 4, 1856.
 11. *Richard Floyd*, b. June 25, 1812; m.
    Sarah Ann, b. Nov. 18, 1813; d. unm. Dec. 26, 1846.
    Catherine M, b. Nov. 1, 1816; d. unm.
 12. *Elisabeth G.*, b. June 21, 1818; m. Nov. 1, 1837, Samuel Gardiner.
    Sylvester Dering, b Jan. 28, 1821; d. unm. Sept. 6, 1862.
    Hester Renelche, b. Oct. 26, 1823; d. unm. Dec. 7, 1856.
    Charles Henry, b. Mar. 20, 1826; d unm. Oct. 18, 1858.
 13. *Charity A.*, b. Jan. 20, 1828; m. Nov. 27. 1855, Joseph F. Gavitt.
    Johanna Rachel, b. May 1, 1832; m. * May 25, 1894, Dr. Samuel B. Nicoll.
(*) as his 3d wife; see Haven's genealogy.

7.

NICOLL H. DERING, s. Sylvester and Esther S. (Havens) Dering.
  b. Jan. 1, 1794.   m. 1st June 6, 1826.   m. 2nd Oct. 1, 1844.   d. Dec. 19, 1867.
1st. Frances Huntington, da. Henry and Catherine M. (Havens) Huntington.
  b. Sept. 16, 1799.   d. Feb. 2, 1841.
2nd. Sarah H. Strong, da. Benjamin and Sarah (Weeks) Strong.
  b. Mar. 8, 1796.   d. Feb. 21, 1889.

7 ch. **14.** *Anne Huntington*, b. Aug. 16, 1828; m. July 1, 1856, Charles S. Wilson.
    Sarah Sylvester, b. July 13, 1831; d. unm. May 10, 1893.
    Catherine May, b. Feb. 21, 1833.
    Frances Huntington, b. Nov. 18, 1834.
    Lucy, b. Nov. 23, 1836, d. Jan. 23, 1837.
 15. *Sylvester*, b. Mar. 12, 1838; m. Feb. 24, 1864, Ella Virginia Bristol.
    Henrietta Wright, b. Dec. 25, 1839, d. July 22, 1841.

8.

HENRY S. DERING, s. Sylvester and Esther S. (Havens) Dering.
  b. Sept. 29, 1804.   m. Apr. 29, 1839.   d. Oct. 2, 1871.
Harriet Eliza Hulse, da. Stephen and Eliza (Smith) Hulse.
  b. July 19, 1814.   d. Aug. 19, 1895.

4 ch. **16.** *Sarah F.*, b. Mar. 1, 1840; m. June 10, 1868, Rev. E. P. Sprague.
  * *Charles T.*, b. Jan 21, 1842; m. Oct. 26, 1875, Mary Bailey; no issue.
    Mary S., b. Aug. 28, 1847; m. o Apr. 29, 1896, † Rev. Egbert C. Lawrence.
    Henry, b. Dec. 8, 1850; m. Nov. 19, 1891, ‡ Carrie Sangston.
(*) d. Sept. 23, 1880.   (o) as his 2nd wife.
(†) s. of Silas R. and Lucinda (Hull) Lawrence; b. June 25, 1845.
(‡) da. of Edward and Mary (Morehouse) Sangston.

9.

LODOWICK FOSDICK DERING, s. Henry P. and Anna (Fosdick) Dering.
  b. Dec. 29, 1807.   m. Apr. 23, 1840.   d. June 22, 1860.
Eliza Gracie Mulford, da. Edward and Fanny (   ) Mulford.
  b. in 1813—1814.   d. July 11, 1886.

2 ch. **17.** *Henry Packer*, b. Apr. 3, 1842; m. Apr. 20, 1876, Martha Frederick.
 18. *Edward M.*, b. Aug. 15, 1847; m. Mar. 5, 1880, Helen Field Raynor.

10.

ANN CHARLOTTE DERING, da. Henry P. and Anna (Fosdick) Dering.
     b. Jan. 2, 1811.   o m. as his 2nd wife, Jan. 2, 1833.

William Rysam Sleight, s. Cornelius and Hannah R. (Rysam) Sleight.
     b. June 9, 1802.   d. Jan. 29, 1876.

10 ch.   *Henry Cornelius*, b. Oct. 24, 1833; d. ae. 1 year.
    19. *Brinley Dering*, b. Mar. 11, 1835; m. Oct. 17, 1865, Susan J. Hedges.
       Anna Caroline, b. Jan. 27, 1837; d. July 7, 1843.
       Augustus, b. Feb. 21, 1839; d. Feb. 25, 1839.
    20. *Hannah Rysam*, b. Mar. 30, 1841; m Oct. 29, 1862, David Stewart.
       Charlotte Elizabeth, b. Aug. 10, 1842; d. unm. Sept. 6, 1872.
    21. *William Rysam*, b. Sept. 10, 1844; m. Jan. 12, 1870, Sarah Andrews.
       Cornelius, b. Oct. 27, 1847, d. May 15, 1850.
       Ann Frances, b. April 9, 1851.
      * *Cornelius*, b. Dec. 21, 1853; m. Oct. 6, 1880, Elizabeth Clark; no issue.
(*) d. Aug. 5, 1881.   (o) See Bowditch genealogy.

11.

RICHARD FLOYD NICOLL, s. Rev. Richard F. and Margaret S. (Dering) Nicoll.
     b. June 25, 1812.   m. Oct. 30, 1834.   d. Aug. 20, 1849.

Rebecca Platt, da. Stephen and Rebecca (Velsor) Platt.
     b. Jan. 6, 1815.   d. June 23, 1887.

6 ch.   **22.** *Catherine Parmelia*, b. Aug. 29, 1835; m. Oct. 8, 1853, Thomas Manahan.
    23. *Margaret Dering*, b. May 30, 1837; m. Sep. 28, 1856, James Dickerman.
    24. *Charles Henry*, b. April 29, 1840; m. March 8, 1863, Catherine Crue.
       Rebecca Platt, b. Nov. 9, 1842, d. Sep. 22, 1843.
       Stephen Platt, b. Sep. 1, 1846; m. Oct. 1, 1874, *Fostina Estelle Burton, no issue.
    25. *Pho be Josephine*, b. Nov. 27, 1848; m. William Cotter, b. July 31, 1851.
(*) Daughter of Thomas A. and Elizabeth C. (Hughes) Burton.

12.

ELIZABETH G. NICOLL, da. Rev. Richard F. and Margaret S. (Dering) Nicoll.
     b. June 21, 1818.   m. Nov. 1, 1837.   d. Jan. 31, 1886.

Samuel Gardiner, s. Abraham and Abby (Lee) Gardiner.
     b. Nov. 10, 1812.   d. Mar. 21, 1873.

7 ch.   *Abraham S.*, b. Apr. 14, 1840; d. unm. June 15, 1872.
    26. *Richard F. N.*, b Nov. 6, 1842; m. Feb. 29, 1872, Margaret A. Dyckman.
       Elizabeth N., b. Dec. 25, 1844.   *Mary C.*, b. Apr. 25, 1850.
       Clarence L., b. Oct. 15, 1842.   *Margaret S.*, b. Aug. 21, 1856.
       Murray S., b. June 12, 1860; m. Feb. 19, 1895, *Elizabeth Hall.
(*) da. of John D. and Sarah E. (DeGroff) Hall, b. Feb. 21, 1864.

13.

CHARITY ANTIONETTE NICOLL, da. Rev. Richard F. and Margaret S. (Dering) Nicoll.
     b. Jan. 20, 1828.   m. Nov. 27, 1855.

Joseph Franklin Gavitt, s. Joseph and Thankful (Bliven) Gavitt.
     Lost at sea.

1 ch.   *Cortland N.*, b. Aug. 27, 1856.

14.

ANNE HUNTINGTON DERING, da. Nicoll H. and Frances (Huntington) Dering.
     b. Aug. 16, 1828.   m. July 1, 1856.

Charles S. Wilson, s. David and Mary (Watt) Wilson.
     b. Dec. 20, 1809.

1 ch.   *Frances Huntington*, b. Jan. 9, 1860, d. May 30, 1861.

15.

SYLVESTER DERING, s. Nicoll H. and Frances (Huntington) Dering.
     b. Mar. 12, 1818.   m. Feb. 25, 1864.

Ella Virginia Bristol, da. Willis and Delia S. (Davidson) Bristol.
     b. Nov. 19, 1842.

2 ch.   *Nicoll Havens*, b. May 7, 1865, d. May 23, 1869.   *Brinley Sylvester*, b. May 18, 1874.

16.

SARAH F. DERING, da. Henry S. and Harriet E. (Hulse) Dering.
     b. Mar. 1, 1840.   m. June 10, 1868.

Rev. E. P. Sprague, s. Daniel G. and Caroline (Wood) Sprague.
     b. Oct. 18, 1843.

4 ch.   *Vesta Dering*, b. Nov. 21, 1870.   *Edward*, b. July 24, 1874, d. Sep. 25, 1874.
       Laura W., b. Sept. 29, 1875, d. Sept. 30, 1875.   *Dering J.*, b. Oct. 22, 1877.

17.

HENRY PACKER DERING, s. Lodowick F. and Eliza G. (Mulford) Dering.
  b. Apr. 3, 1842.   m. Apr. 20, 1876.

Martha Frederick, da. Cornelius and Maria (Van Emburg) Frederick.
  b. July 15, 1847.

3 ch.   *Henry P. F.*, b. Apr. 12, 1878.   *Frederick M.*, b. Nov. 3, 1880.
          Lucelle Grace, b. June 27, 1883. d. Aug. 4, 1889.

18.

EDWARD MULFORD DERING, s. Lodowick F. and Eliza G. (Mulford) Dering.
  b. Aug. 15, 1847.   m. Mar. 5, 1880.

Helene Field Raynor, of Poughkeepsie, New York.
  b.

5 ch.   *Marion Raynor*, b. Jan. 18, 1881.   *Helen Field*, b. Aug. 2, 1883.
          Eliza Gracie, b. Sept. 30, 1885.   *Edward Mulford*, b. Aug. 2, 1887.
          Gertrude, b. Jan. 28, 1890.

19.

BRINLEY DERING SLEIGHT, s. William R. and Ann C. (Dering) Sleight.
  b. Mar. 11, 1835.   m. Oct. 17. 1865.

Susan Jane Hedges da. Albert G. and Elmira (Halsey) Hedges.
  b. Nov. 20, 1841.

4 ch.   *Cornelius Rysam*, b. Nov. 19, 1867.
    27. *William J. R.*, b. Oct. 20, 1870: m. Jan.   1894, Fanny McFarland.
          Helen Grant, b. Dec. 13, 1872, d. Sept. 14, 1873.   *Harry Dering*, b. Dec. 20, 1875.

20.

HANNAH RYSAM SLEIGHT, da. William R. and Ann C. (Dering) Sleight.
  b. Mar. 30, 1841.   m. Oct. 29, 1862

David Stewart, s.
  b.

4 ch.   *Anne Charlotte*, b. Aug.   1863; m. Nov,   1889, George H. Gaffga.
          Mary Dalguise, b. Oct. 6, 1866, d. Mar. 6, 1869.
          Frederick Charles, b. Nov. 10, 1870.   *Caroline Sleight*, b. Apr. 24, 1873.

21.

WILLIAM RYSAM SLEIGHT, s. William R. and Ann C. (Dering) Sleight.
  b. Sep. 10, 1844.   m. Jan. 12, 1870.

Sarah Andrews, da. John and Sarah (Gibbs) Andrews.
  b. May 27, 1842.   d. July 20, 1890.

3 ch.   *Mary Rysam*, b. July 11, 1873; m. May 30, 1896, *Edward E. O'Donnell.
          Charles Kingsley, b. Nov. 23. 1875, d. Oct. 25. 1892.
          William Rysam, b. May 10, 1878; m. Nov. 27, 1807, †Annie B. Copp.
(*) Son of John and Mary E. (Kennedy) O'Donnell, b. May 17, 1860.
(†) Daughter of David R. and Laura E. (Butler) Copp, b. Oct. 14, 1878.

22.

CATHERINE PARMELIA NICOLL. da. Richard F. and Rebecca (Platt) Nicoll.
  b. Aug. 29, 1835.   m. Oct. 8, 1853.

Thomas Manahan, s. William and Annie (Walker) Manahan.
  b. July 12. 1832, d. May 29, 1894.

6 ch.   *Mary Alice*, b. Nov. 16, 1854, d. March 19, 1855.   *William Floyd*, b. June 29, 1856.
          Charles Henry, b. April 27, 1860, d. Nov. 12, 1861.   *James Platt*, b. Sep. 28, 1862.
          Estelle, b. June 4, 1872.   *Frank*, b. May 15. 1876.

23.

MARGARET DERING NICOLL, da. Richard F. and Rebecca (Platt) Nicoll.
  b. May 30, 1837.   m. Sep. 28, 1856.

James Dickerman, s. James and Hannah (MacConnel) Dickerman.
  b. April 6, 1828.

4 ch. **28.** *Julia A.*, b. Aug. 29, 1857; m. April 6, 1881, George Turner.
    29. *Agnes*, b. Nov. 22, 1859; m. July 15, 1886, Oliver Mills.
    30. *Susia A..* b. May 18, 1861; m. Oct. 15, 1897, George Powell.
          Ida R., b. June 11, 1864, d. Oct. 12, 1874.

24.

CHARLES HENRY NICOLL, s. Richard F. and Rebecca (Platt) Nicoll.
  b. April 29, 1846.   m. March 8, 1863.

Catherine Crue, da. Mangles and Catherine (Haver) Crue.
  b. May 13. 1843.

11 ch.   *Charles Platt*, b. Jan. 10, 1864, d. Jan. 11, 1885.
  31. *Florence May*, b. Feb. 16, 1866; m. May 29. 1884, Jacob W. Gulick.
  32. *Richard Floyd*, b. March 9, 1868; m. June 11, 1891, Bertha Stiefel.
       George Titchen, b. April 29, 1870.
       William Crue, b. Jan. 25, 1872; m. April 21, 1897, *Grace Gardner Kane.
       Frederick Haver, b. Feb. 6, 1874, d. May 30, 1894.
       Daisy Oliver, b. May 24, 1877.   *Ida Elizabeth*, b. Dec. 26, 1879.
       Elmer Grove, b. Oct. 23, 1882. d. June 5. 1884.
       Elmer Lockwood, b. Sep. 12, 1884.   *Chester Cuthell*, b. July 31, 1887.
(*) Daughter of Lyman E. and Anna (Gardner) Kane, b. Sep. 19, 1872.

25.

PHOEBE JOSEPHINE NICOLL, da. Richard F. and Rebecca (Platt) Nicoll.
    b. Nov. 27, 1848.   m.

William Cotter, s. William and Jane (Cummin) Cotter.
    b.

2. ch.   *William*, b. Sep. 1, 1869.   *Josephine*, b. Dec. 11, 1884.

26.

RICHARD F. N. GARDINER, s. Samuel and Elizabeth G. (Nicoll) Gardiner.
    b. Nov. 6, 1842.   m. Feb. 29, 1872.

Margaret A. Dyckman, da. Peter G. and Sarah (Travis) Dyckman.
    b. Sep. 2, 1841.
4 ch.   *Bertha Floyd*, b. May 18, 1873.   *William Dyckman*, b. Dec. 4, 1875, d. July 21, 1876.
      Gertrude Sherrill, b. Aug. 13, 1878. *Edward Nicoll*, b. Nov. 25, 1881, d. May 16, 1882.

27.

WILLIAM J. R. SLEIGHT, s. Brinley D. and Susan J. (Hedges) Sleight.
    b. Oct. 20, 1870.   m. Jan.   1894.

Fanny McFarland, da.
    b.
2 ch.   *Evangeline Dering*, b. Nov. 6, 1894.   *Brinley Dering*, b. Oct. 13, 1897.

28.

JULIA A. DICKERMAN, da. James and Margaret D. (Nicoll) Dickerman.
    b. Aug. 29, 1857.   m. April 6, 1881.

George Turner, s. George and Ann (Taylor) Turner.
    b. Oct. 24, 1844.
3 ch.   *George*, b. Feb. 25, 1882, d. April 12, 1883.
      Nettie, b. Dec. 16, 1883, d. Dec. 13, 1884.   *Raymond*, b. March 10, 1888.

29.

AGNES DICKERMAN, da. James and Margaret D. (Nicoll) Dickerman.
    b. Nov. 22, 1859.   m. July 15, 1886.

Oliver Mills, s. Isaac C. and Rebecca (Williamson) Mills.
    b. Dec. 26, 1859.
5 ch.   *Ida R.*, b. May 14, 1887, d. July 11, 1887.
      James D., b. July 26, 1888.   *Charles E.*, b. July 10, 1891.
      Mildred, b. Feb. 6, 1894.   *Floyd*, b. July 24, 1895.

30.

SUSIA A. DICKERMAN, da. James and Margaret D. (Nicoll) Dickerman.
    b. May 18, 1861.   m. Oct. 15, 1897.

George Powell, s. Samuel and Harriet (Perry) Powell.
    b. Oct. 10, 1860.
1 ch.   *George Le Roy*, b. March 15, 1898.

31.

FLORENCE MAY NICOLL, da. Charles H. and Catherine (Crue) Nicoll.
    b. Feb. 16, 1866.   m. May 29, 1884.   d. Jan. 21, 1888.

Jacob W. Gulick, s. Andrew and Eliza (Van Derveer) Gulick.
    b. Oct. 12, 1861.
2 ch.   *Charles Platt*, b. May 21, 1885.   *William Henry*, b. Jan. 26, 1887.

32.

RICHARD FLOYD NICOLL, s. Charles H. and Catherine (Crue) Nicoll.
    b. March 9, 1868.   m. June 11, 1891.

Bertha Stiefel, da. Charles and Albertina (Neuman) Stiefel.
    b. April 2, 1875.
1 ch.   *Florence May*, b. Aug. 20, 1896.

ANCESTORS.

A.

* STEPHEN HOPKINS,
     b. in England.   m. 1st   m. 2d March, 1617.   d. in 1644.

2d Elizabeth Fisher.
     b.   d. between 1640-44.

8 ch. by 1st wife—**B.** *Giles*, b. in 1605-6; m. Oct. 9, 1639, Catherine Wheldon.
            Constanta, b. in 1608; m in 1627, Nicholas Snow.
       by 2d wife *Damaris*, b. in 1618; m. in 1646, Jacob Cook.
           ° *Oceanus*, b. in 1620, d. in 1626-7.
           Deborah, b. in 1622; m. in 1646, Andrew Ring.
           Caleb, b.   d. perhaps unm.
           Ruth, b.   *Elizabeth*, b.   d. unm.
(*) Came over to America in the "Mayflower" in 1620.
(°) Born on the "Mayflower" in 1620.

B.

* GILES HOPKINS, s. Stephen Hopkins.
     b. in 1605-6.   m. Oct. 9, 1639.   d. 1690.

Catherine Wheldon, da. Gabriel Wheldon of Yarmouth.
     b.   d.

10 ch.   *Mary*, b in 1640.   *Stephen*, b. in 1642; m. May 22, 1667, Mary Merrick
       John, b. in 1643, d. in infancy.   *Abigail*, b. in 1644.
       Deborah, b. in 1645.   *Caleb*, b. in 1650, d. in 1728.
       Ruth, b. in 1653.   *Joshua*, b. in 1657; m.   Mary Cole.
       C. *William*, b. in 1660; m. Rebecca.   *Elizabeth*, b. in 1664.
(*) Born in England and came over to America with his father in the "Mayflower" in 1620.

C.

WILLIAM HOPKINS, s. Giles and Catherine (Wheldon) Hopkins.
     b. in 1660.   m.   d. June 26, 1718.

Rebecca   , da.
     b.   d. April 23, 1746.

6 ch.   *Sarah*, b.   m. March, 1726, Uriah Glover.
       Ephraim, b.
       Hannah, b.   m. Nov. 21, 1729, Benjamin Emmons.
       John, b. in 1705-6, drowned July 22, 1727.
     1. *Samuel*, b. in 1710; m. Dec. 20, 1733. Dorithy Conklyn.
       Abijah, b.   m. Dec. 26, 1734, Elizabeth King.

1.

SAMUEL HOPKINS, s. William and Rebecca (   ) Hopkins.
     b. in 1710.   m. Dec. 30, 1733.   d. Jan. 12, 1790.

Dorothy Conklyn, da.
     b. in 1703-4.   d. Feb. 15, 1778.
5 ch.   a daughter who d. in Nov. 1740.
       a child who d. in Nov. 1740.
       a child who d. in Nov. 1743.   } from the Salmon Record.
       Jonathan, who d. Nov. 23, 1754. }
     2. *Samuel*, b. Apr. 4, 1744 ; m. 1st in   1773, Elizabeth Robinson.
                         2nd, Nov. 6, 1780, Elizabeth Woodhull,

2.

SAMUEL HOPKINS, s. Samuel and Dorothy (Conklyn) Hopkins.
     b. Apr. 4, 1744.   m. 1st in   1773.   m. 2nd, Nov. 6, 1780.   d. Sept. 8, 1807.

1st. Elizabeth Robinson, da. John and Elizabeth (   ) Robinson.
     b. Apr. 23, 1751.   d. Sept. 28, 1777.

2nd. Elizabeth Woodhull. da. John and Elizabeth (Smith) Woodhull.
     b. Oct. 2, 1759.   d. Nov. 9, 1795.

12 ch.   3. *Elizabeth*, b. Sept. 29, 1774; m. 1st Oct. 23, 1791, Caleb Helme.
                                  2nd Dec. 20, 1804, Nathaniel Davis.
       4. *Martha*, b. Nov. 16, 1776; m. Dec. 23, 1794, Nathaniel Davis.
       5. *Samuel*, b. Nov. 20, 1781; m. Dec. 11, 1816, Maria Woodhull.
       John, b. Nov. 25, 1783; d. Jan. 7, 1800.
       6. *Dorothy*, b Mar. 21, 1785, m. Apr 27, 1805, Daniel Davis.
       7. *Sarah*, b. Oct. 20, 1786; m. June 23, 1809, Dr. Nathaniel Rowell.
       8. *William*, b. July 7, 1788; m. 1st Jan. 26, 1811, Abigail Davis.
                        2nd Aug. 22, 1834, Angeline Davis.
       Sophie, b. July 18, 1790, d. Sept. 11, 1807.
       James, b. July 18, 1790, d. Dec. 7, 1790.
       9. *Gilbert*, b. Aug. 2, 1792; m. Nov. 2, 1819, Deborah Ferris.
     10. *George*, b. Nov. 23, 1793; m. Sept. 24, 1816, Eliza M. Johnson.
       David, b. Oct. 24, 1795, d. Nov. 24, 1795.

3.

ELIZABETH HOPKINS, da. Samuel and Elizabeth (Robinson) Hopkins.
    b. Sept. 29, 1774.   m. 1st Oct. 23, 1791.   m. 2nd Dec. 20, 1804.   d. May 30, 1816.

1st. Caleb Helme, s. Thomas and Hannah (Smith) Helme.
    b. June 27, 1763.   d. Nov. 19, 1798.

2nd. Nathaniel Davis, s. Samuel and Hannah (Roe) Davis.
    b. Sept. 9, 1760.   d. May 16, 1825.

6 ch. **11.** *Eliza*, b. Aug. 8, 1793; m. Sept. 10. 1816, Rev. Ezra King.
  12. *Martha M.*, b. Sept. 19, 1805; m. Jan. 30, 1825, Hiram S. Tuthill.
  13. *Alfred M.*, b. Mar. 9. 1808; m. Oct. 7, 1840, Sophronia Emmons.
  * *Laura S.*, b. Apr 25, 1810; m.   Hiram S. Tuthill.
  14. *Sylvester R.*, b. Mar. 18, 1812; m. Dec. 30, 1834, Elmina Hallock.
  * *Harriet A.*, b. Aug. 15, 1814; m.   Hiram S. Tuthill.

(*) See No. 12.

4.

MARTHA HOPKINS, da. Samuel and Elizabeth (Robinson) Hopkins.
    b. Nov. 16, 1776.   m. Dec. 23, 1794.   d. Apr. 7, 1804.

Nathaniel Davis, s. Samuel and Hannah (Roe) Davis.
    b. Sept. 9, 1760.   d. May 16, 1825.

3 ch. **15.** *Corinna*, b. June 20, 1796; m. Nov. 30, 1820, Charles Miller.
  * *Spafford H.*, b. Nov. 10, 1797; m. Dec. 9, 1824, Maria A. Horton; no issue.
  o *Eliza Catherine*, b. Sept. 17, 1800; m. Dec. 14, 1824, Nathaniel Miller; no issue.

(*) d. about Oct., 1878. (o) d. Jan. 20, 1828.

5.

SAMUEL HOPKINS, s. Samuel and Elizabeth (Woodhull) Hopkins.
    b. Nov. 20, 1781.   m. Dec. 11, 1816.   d. Dec. 9, 1866.

Maria Woodhull, da. Merritt S. and Mary (Davis) Woodhull.
    b. May 11, 1793.   d. Nov. 30, 1880.

10 ch. *Mary Sophia*, b. Oct. 26, 1817, d. Oct. 5, 1819.
  16. *Catherine Ophelia*, b. Jan. 25, 1819; m May 19, 1845, Edwin N. Miller.
  * *Sarah Matilda*, b. Sept. 24, 1820; m. Jan. 24, 1843, Ezra S. King.
  17. *Mary*, b. Mar. 18. 1823; m. Oct. 17, 1849. J. Bryan Marshall.
  Samuel Merritt, b. Sept. 18. 1824, d. Oct. 27, 1825.
  Louisa, b. Aug. 15, 1827, d. Mar. 7, 1893.
  Martha Maria, b. Aug. 10, 1829; m Oct. 29, 1868, Henry A. Brown; no issue.
  Harriet, b. Sept. 2, 1831, d Apr. 1, 1832.
  18. *George Woodhull*, b. Nov. 27, 1833; m. Jan. 2, 1855. Mary M. Tuthill.
  19. *Samuel Judson*, b. Dec. 3, 1836; m. May 16, 1864, Sarah K. Hallock.

(*) See No. 41.

6.

DOROTHY HOPKINS, da. Samuel and Elizabeth (Woodhull) Hopkins.
    b. March 21, 1783.   m. April 27, 1805.   d. Dec. 19, 1849.

Daniel Davis, s. William and Elizabeth (Robins) Davis.
    b. Jan. 13, 1782.   d. July 23, 1829.

8 ch. **20.** *Elizabeth*, b. Feb. 10, 1806; m. Nov. 1828, Lewis R. Overton.
  21. *Lester H.*, b. Sept. 30, 1807; m. Oct. 19, 1836, Clarissa Roe.
  * *Sophia*, b. Feb. 5, 1811: m. Jan. 1839, Hiram S. Tuthill.
  William, b. May 13, 1814, d. May 20. 1814.
  22. *Mary Janet*, b. July 6, 1816; m. Dec. 25, 1837, Thomas J. Ritch.
  23. *Dorothy C.*, b. April 17, 1819; m. Dec. 14. 1835, Van Rensselaer Swesey.
  * *Harriet M.*, b. Nov. 23, 1822; m. 1st, Dec. 21, 1839, Hiram S. Tuthill.
           2d,   1850, Thomas Bayles.
  24. *Daniel Woodhull*, b. Oct. 19, 1824; m. 1st, Jan. 9, 1850, Ann Eliza Davis.
           2d, Dec. 31, 1860, Laura S. Davis.

(*) See No. 12.

7.

SARAH HOPKINS, da. Samuel and Elizabeth (Woodhull) Hopkins.
    b. Oct. 20, 1786.   m. June 23, 1809.   d. March 4, 1830.

Dr. Nathaniel M. Rowell. s. Nathaniel and Juliette (Morse) Rowell.
    b. July 4, 1781.   d. March 17, 1827.

6 ch. **25.** *Hopkins*, b. May 16, 1810; m. Oct. 8, 1849. Mary E. Blood.
  26. *Thompson*, b. Oct. 31. 1812; m. Oct. 23. 1851, Mary R. Talbot.
  27. *Juliette*, b. Jan. 4, 1815; m. April 17. 1833, Henry L. Smith.
  28. *Morse*, b. Aug. 12, 1816; m. 1st, March 3, 1852, Elizabeth M. Van Schoick.
           2d, June 24, 1862, Letitia Crawford.
  29. *Eliza*, b. April 4, 1819; m. Dec. 25, 1845, George Danforth.
  Sarah, b. Oct. 15, 1825, d. Nov. 19, 1825.

8.

WILLIAM HOPKINS, s, Samuel and Elizabeth (Woodhull) Hopkins.
b. July 7, 1788.   m. 1st Jan. 26, 1811.   m. 2d Aug. 22, 1834.   d. July 19, 1869.

1st Abigail Davis, da. Joshua and Abigail (   ) Davis.
b. June 11, 1792.   d. Aug. 5, 1830.

2d Angeline Davis, da. Wells and Bethiah (Hammond) Davis.
b. Dec. 2, 1811.

8 ch.   *Gilbert*, b. March 28, 1812, d. June 22, 1830.
   30. *Charles*, b. Feb. 14, 1814; m. Oct. 17, 1841, Elizabeth Jennings.
   31. *Maria*, b. Nov. 2, 1815; m. 1st, Jan. 13, 1841, George Brown.
                   2d, Nov. 28. 1869. James L. Bradley.
   32. *Elizabeth*, b. Oct. 27, 1818; m. May 28, 1839, Stiles W. Judson.
   33. *Frances Ellen*, b. Oct. 9, 1838; m. Jan. 17, 1858, Washington W. Brown.
   34. *Susan*, b. Oct. 20, 1842; m. 1st. Oct. 25, 1859. Timothy H. Helme.
                   2d, Dec. 3, 1894. Israel C. Terry.
   35. *William Augustus*, b. Dec. 26, 1847; m. Feb. 20, 1878, Emily Sanford.
   Also an infant who died, ae., 3 weeks.

9.

GILBERT HOPKINS, s. Samuel and Elizabeth (Woodhull) Hopkins.
b. Aug. 2, 1792.   m. Nov. 2, 1819.   d. Dec. 4, 1870.

Deborah Ferris, da. Samuel and Phebe (Ferris) Ferris.
b. Dec. 16, 1794.   d. Dec. 25, 1875.

6 ch.   *Elizabeth*, b. Jan. 23, 1821; m. Nov.   1845, George G. Hopkins.
   36. *Samuel Woodhull*, b. Oct. 13, 1822; m. May 26, 1845, Sarah L. Jessup.
   Phebe Ann, b. June 15, 1824, d. March 26, 1841.
   Adeline, b. July 6, 1826, d. Aug. 12, 1827.
   Gilbert W., b. Aug. 28, 1828, killed by Indians. Feb. 17, 1865.
   37. *Judson Hawley*, b. Sep. 29, 1830; m. June 12, 1862, Elizabeth M. Freeman.
(*) see No. 39.

10.

DR. GEORGE HOPKINS, s. Samuel and Elizabeth (Woodhull) Hopkins.
b. Nov. 23, 1793.   m. Sep. 24, 1816.   d. Oct. 28, 1819.

Eliza M. Johnson, da. John and Hannah (   ) Johnson.
b. April 21, 1793.   d. Jan. 13, 1826.

2 ch. **38.** *Samuel Johnson*, b. Jan. 22, 1818; m. May 12. 1845. Mary E. Berrien.
   39. *George Gilbert*, b. Aug. 22, 1819; m. Nov. 1845, Elizabeth Hopkins.

11.

ELIZA HELME, da. Caleb and Elizabeth (Hopkins) Helme.
b. Aug. 8, 1793.   m. as his 2d w. Sep. 10. 1816.   d. Dec. 21, 1733.

Rev. Ezra King, s. Jeremiah and Hannah (Youngs) King.
b. July 24, 1784.   d. Feb. 7, 1867.

6 ch.   **40.** *Caleb H.*, b. Jan. 6, 1818; m. May   1842, Deborah M. Brown.
   41. *Ezra S.*, b. Mar. 25. 1820; m. Jan. 24, 1843. Sarah M. Hopkins.
   42. *Joseph N*, b. June 8. 1823; m. Nov. 17, 1846, Therina Hudson.
   43. *Elisha E.*, b. Dec. 30, 1826; m. May   1850. Catherine S. Davis.
   44. *Hannah Y.*, b. Mar. 22. 1830; m. Dec. 7, 1848, Joseph R. Rowland.
   45. *Maria E.*, b. Jan. 22, 1833; m.   Benjamin B. Bailey.

12.

MARTHA M. DAVIS, da. Nathaniel and Elizabeth (Hopkins) Davis.
b. Sep. 19, 1805.   m. Jan. 30, 1825   d. May 29, 1829.

HARRIET A. DAVIS, da. Nathaniel and Elizabeth (Hopkins) Davis.
b. Aug. 15, 1814.   m.   d. May 21, 1836.

LAURA S. DAVIS, da. Nathaniel and Elizabeth (Hopkins) Davis,
b. Apr. 25, 1810.   m,   d July 9, 1838.

SOPHIA DAVIS, da. Daniel and Dorothy (Hopkins) Davis.
b. Feb. 5, 1811.   m. Jan.   1839.   d. May 20, 1839.

HARRIET M. DAVIS, da. Daniel and Dorothy (Hopkins) Davis.
b. Nov. 23, 1822.   m. 1st Dec. 21, 1839; m. 2d   1850.

*Hiram S. Tuthill, s. Nathaniel and Elizabeth (Skidmore) Tuthill.
b. Apr. 23, 1801.   d. Sept. 16, 1848.

Thomas D. Bayles, s.
b. Sep. 1823.

8 ch. **46.** *Sylvester D.*, b. Dec. 23, 1826; m. Dec. 20, 1849, Ann Eliza Tuttle.
   47. *Nathaniel M.*, b. Dec. 25. 1828; m.   Caroline C. Carll.
   Martha M., b. Nov. 25, 1841, d. Apr. 10 1842.

Joseph W., b. Dec. 12, 1843, d. May 12, 1847.
Hiram S., b.
48. *Harriet W.*, b.   1851; m. June 13, 1878. Seth B. Worth.
49. *Martha M.*, b.   1854; m. Nov. 30, 1876. Herman Aldrich.
    † *Elsie*, b.   1857; m.   1877, ○Charles A. Bayles.
(*)Mr Hiram S. Tuthill had five wives. He married three sisters of one family and two sisters of
another family, all by the name of Davis. His last wife survived him and married as her second
husband Thomas D. Bayles. This is in explanation of the above remarkable record.
(†) Had one child born July 1st, 1898 which died.
(○) Son of Alfred E. and Caroline (Gates) Bayles, born Oct. 25, 1839.

13.

ALFRED M. DAVIS, s. Nathaniel and Elizabeth (Hopkins) Davis.
        b. Mar. 9, 1808.   m. Oct. 7, 1840.   d. July 18, 1877.

Sophronia Emmons, da. Benjamin and Clements (Tuthill) Emmons.
        b. July 10, 1818.   d. July 21, 1886.

8 ch. **50.** *Eliza C.*, b. Oct. 15, 1841; m. Jan. 14, 1867, John S. Randall.
    51. *Nathaniel T.*, b. Sep. 4, 1843; m. 1st, Oct. 10, 1870, Mary M. Beebe.
                            2d, Jan. 19, 1882, M. Salome Rand.
                            3d, Apr. 15, 1891, Mariana J. Davies.
    52. *Elbert M.*, b. Apr. 6, 1845; m. Oct. 11, 1870, Ellen M. Miller.
    53. *Corrina M.*, b. Feb. 11, 1847; m. Oct.   1874, Charles E. Tooker.
        Harriet E., b. Nov. 6, 1849.
    54. *Hewlett H.*, b. Dec. 5, 1853; m. Nov. 21, 1883, Minnie L. Davis.
        Joanna L., b. Aug. 14, 1855, d. unm. Aug. 15, 1882.
    55. *Alfred G.*, b. June 21, 1863, m. Oct. 25, 1884, Elsie Banks.

14.

SYLVESTER R. DAVIS, s. Nathaniel and Elizabeth, (Hopkins) Davis,
        b. Mar. 18, 1812.   m. Dec. 30, 1834.   d. May 25, 1887.

Elmina Hallock, da. Thomas and Mary (Gleason) Hallock.
        b. Apr. 7, 1813.   d. Apr. 30, 1896.

7 ch. **56.** *Joseph W.*, b. Nov. 10, 1835; m. 1st, Oct. 10, 1859, Sarah E. Randall.
                            2d, Dec. 25, 1871, Harriet T. Ritch.
    57. *Merrit W.*, b. Mar. 28, 1837; m. 1st. Oct. 27, 1863, Amelia S. Banks.
                            2d, Mar. 10, 1874, Mary E. Lutz.
        Laura S., b. June 30, 1839; m. Dec. 30, 1860, Daniel W. Davis.
        Roxanna M., b. May 7, 1840; m. Oct. 28, 1867, Benjamin Robertson.
        Spafford P., b. Nov. 30, 1842; m. Aug. 15, 1868, R. Jennie Potter.
        Christena E., b. Mar. 31, 1847; m. Dec. 21, 1868, Edwin J. Banks, no issue.
        ○*Emma J.*, b. Sep. 2, 1850; m. Mar. 11, 1874, Sherman P. Smith.
(*) See No. 24.
(○) Died s. p. Feb. 1, 1897.

15.

CORINNA DAVIS, da. Nathaniel and Martha (Hopkins) Davis.
        b. June 20, 1796.   m. Nov. 30, 1820.   d. Sep. 12, 1872.

Charles Miller, s. Mathaniel and Martha (Miller) Miller.
        b. Jan. 1, 1797.   d. Apr. 23, 1867,
2 ch. * *Edwin N.*, b. Oct. 18, 1821; m. May 19, 1845. Catherine O. Hopkins.
        Spafford D., b. Aug. 23, 1834, d. Apr. 10, 1839.
(*) See next number.

16.

CATHERINE OPHELIA HOPKINS, da. Samuel and Maria (Woodhull) Hopkins.
        b. Jan. 25, 1819.   m. in 1845.   d. Jan. 20, 1888.

EDWIN N. MILLER, s. Charles and Corinna (Davis) Miller.   See previous number.
        b. Oct. 18, 1821.   d. Oct. 23, 1872.

6 ch. * *Ellen Maria*, b. Jan. 16, 1846, m. Oct. 17, 1870, Elbert M. Davis.
    58. *Nathaniel D.*, b. Feb. 7, 1848; m. Dec.   1869, Jane Sophia Snow.
        Charles Ellet, b. Nov. 27, 1849; m.   Elmira Tooker, no issue.
        Catherine Louisa, b. Dec. 1, 1851, d. Oct. 3, 1872.
    59. *Samuel H.*, b. Nov. 7, 1853; m. Sep. 18, 1878, Alilah Y. Tillotson.
        Luetta Judson, b. Aug 23, 1857.
(*) See No. 52.

17.

MARY HOPKINS, da. Samuel and Maria (Woodhull) Hopkins.
        b. Mar. 18, 1823.   m. Oct. 17, 1849.   d. Sep. 22, 1885.

J. Bryan Marshall, s. Joseph and Abigail (Andrew) Marshall.
        b.   d. June 30, 1861.

4 ch. *Maria Woodhull*, b. Aug. 26, 1850.
        Mary Ellen, b. Nov.   1852.
        Lydia Bryan, b. Jan. 15. 1857.
        Francis Matilda, b. Mar. 19, 1859, d. Mar. 11, 1864.

18.

GEORGE WOODHULL HOPKINS, s. Samuel and Maria (Woodhull) Hopkins.
  b. Nov. 27, 1833.   m. Jan. 2, 1855.   d. June 21, 1887.

Mary Miller Tuthill, da. James H. and Charlotte (Miller) Tuthill.
  b. July 18, 1838.
  5 ch. 60. *Fannie Tuthill*, b. July 31, 1858; m. Nov. 19, 1875, Havens J. Davis.
      Lottie Miller, b. July 13, 1862.
      James Hubbard, b. June 16, 1864, m. Sep. 11, 1890, Eliza W. Davis.
      Samuel and *Wilson* both died in infancy.

19.

SAMUEL JUDSON HOPKINS, s. Samuel and Maria (Woodhull) Hopkins.
  b. Dec. 3, 1836.   m. May 16, 1864.

Sarah Katherine Hallock, da. Hendrick H. and Martha R. (Bishop) Hallock.
  b. Nov. 20, 1843.
  4 ch. 61. *Philip Hallock*, b. Jan 29, 1866; m. Oct. 2, 1895, Lulu M. Howland.
      Rupert Henry, b. Nov. 24, 1869.
      Samuel Ernest, b. Jan. 20, 1875.   *Merritt Judson*, b. Nov. 16, 1879.

20.

ELIZABETH DAVIS, da. Daniel and Dorothy (Hopkins) Davis.
  b. Feb. 10, 1806.   m. Nov.   1828.   d. May 4, 1896.
Lewis R. Overton, s. Elisha and Ruth (Roe) Overton.
  b. Dec. 10, 1800.   d. Jan. 4, 1872.
  6 ch. 62. *Lewis Irving*. b. July 8, 1831; m. Aug.   1853, Matilda J. Overton.
      63. *Phebe B.*, b. Jan. 11, 1833; m. June 30, 1853, Edward C. Benedict.
      64. *C. Helen*. b. Mar. 6, 1838; m. Dec. 26, 1860, Charles J. Randall.
      65. *E. Webster*, b. Oct. 8, 1839; m. Mar. 27, 1875, Charlotte L. Overton.
      Sarah O., b. Feb. 9, 1844.
      66. *Hopkins R.*, b. Jan. 14, 1850; m. 1st, in 1875, Christina Johnson.
                      2d, Aug. 30, 1882, Charity A. Thickett.

21.

LESTER H. DAVIS, s. Daniel and Dorothy (Hopkins) Davis.
  b. Sep. 30, 1807.   m. Oct. 19, 1836.   d. Oct. 26, 1886.

Clarissa Roe, da. Azel and Nancy (Jones) Roe.
  b. July 15, 1816.
  12 ch.   *Infant Son*, b. June 5, 1837, d. June 6, 1837.
      Hopkins R., b. May 6, 1838, d. Feb. 10, 1840.
      Mary T.. b. Jan. 26, 1841.
      67. *Harriet S*, b. Nov. 5, 1842; m. Jan. 3, 1866, George P. Schryver.
      Louisa A, b. June 17. 1844.
      68. *Elizabeth J.*, b. Dec. 18, 1846; m. Apr. 8, 1869, James A. Randall.
   * *Amelia A.*, b. July 18, 1848; m. Mar. 16, 1882, John R. Dayton.
      69. *William L.*, b. July 5, 1850; m. 1st, Feb. 20, 1879, Carrie M. Overton.
                      2d, Dec. 5, 1894, Annie M. Smith.
      Ada. b. Mar. 20, 1852; m. Sep. 15, 1898. John R. Dayton.
      70. *Daniel R.*, b. Jan. 5, 1854; m. Dec. 9, 1886, Nellie J. Randall.
      Fannie M., b. Aug. 28, 1855.
      Alice R., b. Mar. 24, 1857; m. Nov. 20, 1895, Joseph H. Randall.
(*) Died Jan. 16, 1884.   **22.**

MARY JANET DAVIS, da. Daniel and Dorothy (Hopkins) Davis.
  b. July 6, 1816.   m. Dec. 25, 1837.

Thomas J. Ritch, s. Lewis and Charity (Hulse) Ritch.
  b. Oct. 20, 1813.
  10 ch.   *Lewis E.*. b. Sep. 16, 1838, d. July 10, 1854.
      71. *Martha J.*. b. Mar. 20. 1840; m. Oct. 29, 1860, Hiram L. Moger.
      Mary J., b. Mar. 29. 1842, d. Oct. 29, 1844.
   * *Harriet T.*, b. Mar. 12, 1844; m. Dec. 25. 1871, Daniel R. Davis.
      72. *Thomas J.*, b. May 19, 1846; m. Oct. 30, 1877, Alice Randall.
      Daniel D., b. July 23. 1848., d. Dec. 19. 1868.
      73. *I. Wilson*, b. Feb. 11. 1851; m. Apr. 1, 1884, Martha A. Freeland.
      74. *Mary J.*, b. Jan. 21. 1853, m. Oct. 28. 1880, Orange T. Fanning.
      75. *Virgil*, b. Aug. 3, 1855; m. Oct. 8, 1885, Ada C. Hawkins.
      Lena E., b. Apr. 7, 1858.
(*) See No. 56.   **23.**

DOROTHY C. DAVIS, da. Daniel and Dorothy (Hopkins) Davis.
  b. Apr. 17, 1819.   m. Dec. 14, 1835.   d. May 21, 1897.

Van Rensselaer Swesey, s. Christopher and Betsey (Downs) Swesey.
  b. Mar. 25, 1810.   d. July 22, 1878.
  2 ch. 76. *Gilbert H.*. b. Apr. 21, 1842; m. Oct. 21, 1873, Susan Emily Miller.
      Van Rensselaer, born and died the same day.

24.

DANIEL WOODHULL DAVIS, s. Daniel and Dorothy (Hopkins) Davis.
    b. Oct. 19, 1824.   m. 1st, Jan. 9, 1850.   m. 2d, Dec. 30, 1860.

1st, Ann Eliza Davis, da. Timothy and Anna (Reeves) Davis.
    b. Oct. 25, 1825.   d. Dec. 4, 1859.

2d, LAURA S. DAVIS, da. Sylvester R. and Elmina (Hallock) Davis. See No. 14.
    b. June 30, 1839.

7 ch.   An infant daughter d. age 4 days.
      Anna R., b. April 13, 1852, d. March 23, 1861.
      Evelyn S., b. Aug. 5, 1854; m. Sep. 22, 1886, *John M. Brown. No issue.
  77. *Timothy J.*, b. Nov. 5, 1856; m. Oct. 15, 1885, Julia B. Hulse.
  78. *William A.*, b. Oct. 15, 1861; m. Feb. 20, 1890, Leonella Davis.
      Lena W., b. June 26, 1863.
  79. *Lester H.*, b. Feb. 26, 1865; m. Feb. 6, 1890, Eloise S. Randall.
(*) Son of Morris and Mary (Bennett) Brown, b. April 9, 1854.

25.

HOPKINS ROWELL, s. Dr. Nathaniel N. and Sarah (Hopkins) Rowell.
    b. May 16, 1810.   m. Oct. 8, 1849.   d. Oct. 1, 1880.

Mary Elizabeth Blood, da. Joel and Laura (Hastings) Blood.
    b. Jan. 21, 1827.

7 ch. **80.** *Jacob Hastings*, b. Sep. 28, 1850; m. Nov. 18, 1885, Mary Maria Palmer.
      Annie Juliet, b. March 1, 1853.
      Joel Nathaniel, b. June, 26, 1855; m. April 21, 1892, *Annie Whitney.
      Laura E. H., b. Dec. 15, 1859.
      Mary Elizabeth, b. June 27, 1864. d. Aug. 28, 1865.
      Hopkins Woodhull, b. June 27, 1864, d. Aug. 19, 1864.
  81. *Sarah Genevieve*, b. Dec. 28, 1865; m. June 15, 1893, Benjamin L. McFadden.
(*) Da. of William A. and Charlotte A. (Buell) Whitney, b. Aug. 23, 1869.

26.

REV. THOMPSON ROWELL, s. Dr. Nathaniel M. and Sarah (Hopkins) Rowell.
    b. Oct. 31, 1812.   m. Oct. 23, 1851.   d. March 6, 1874.

Mary Roxana Talbot, da. Rev. William K. and Mary (Prier) Talbot.
    b. Feb. 6, 1829.

9 ch. **82.** *Mary Antionette*, b. Sep. 17, 1852; m. May 14, 1884, William W. Ross.
      Eliza Juliet, b. Jan. 16 1854, d. April 21, 1854.
  83. *Henry Hastings S.*, b. July 8, 1855; m June 20, 1894, Emily Rudolph.
      Eliza Juliet, b. July 26, 1857, d. Dec. 22, 1880.
      Minnie Loretta, b Oct. 27, 1859, d. Nov. 16, 1868.
      Carrie L. P., b. Feb. 2, 1861, d. Nov. 23, 1872.
      William Talbot, b. Sep. 4, 1865, d. Nov. 19. 1872.
      Nathaniel P., b. Jan. 7, 1869, d. Nov. 17, 1872.
  84. *George Hopkins*, b. Sep. 3, 1870; m. July 20, 1892, Julia Walsh.

27.

JULIETTE ROWELL, da. Dr. Nathaniel M. and Sarah (Hopkins) Rowell.
    b. Jan. 4, 1815.   m. April 17, 1833.   d. Oct. 20, 1875.

Henry L. Smith, s. Levi and   (Ingraham) Smith.
    b. July 31, 1807.   d. Nov. 2, 1869.

4 ch.   *Hopkins Rowell.* b. Nov. 24, 1835; m. Dec. 15, 1858, *Harriet Cooper. No issue.
      Henry Thompson, b. Dec. 18, 1838, d. Feb. 27, 1843.
      George L., b, in 1842. d. unm. Sep. 4, 1866.
      Henry Lewis, b. Jan.   1852, d. Sep. 17, 1852.
(*) Da. John C. and Margaret (Simmons) Cooper, b. Aug. 17, 1838.

28.

REV. MORSE ROWELL, s. Dr. Nathaniel M. and Sarah (Hopkins) Rowell.
    b. Aug. 12, 1816.   m. 1st, March 3, 1852. m. 2d, June 24, 1862.   d. Feb. 2, 1886.

1st Elizabeth M. Van Schoick, of Manasquan, New Jersey.
    b. in 1821-22.   d. July 31, 1860.

2d, Letitia Crawford, da. John and Mary (McLaughlin) Crawford.
    b. Dec. 16, 1842.

7 ch. **85.** *Morse*, b. July 2, 1863; m. Dec. 24, 1888, Belle J. England.
      Sarah, b. July 5, 1865, d. Jan. 19, 1898.
      Mary, b. June 18, 1867, d. Dec. 15, 1891.
      Eliza, b. May 13, 1870; m. May 19, 1896, *James W. Davis.
      John Baird, b. Aug. 25, 1872.
      Margaret Letitia, b. March 2, 1875.
      Grace, b. July 3, 1878, d. Dec. 6, 1894.
(*) Son of James W. and Martha (Hutchingson) Davis, b. Nov. 11, 1863.

29.

ELIZA ROWLAND, da. Dr. Nathaniel M. and Sarah (Hopkins) Rowell.
　　b. Apr. 4, 1819.　　m. Dec. 3, 1844.　　d. Jan. 11, 1878.
George Danforth, s. David J. and Annis (White) Danforth.
　　b. May 24, 1816.　　d. Apr. 1, 1850.
　　1 ch. *Martha Juliet*, b. Jan. 30, 1848.

30.

CHARLES HOPKINS, s. William and Abigail (Davis) Hopkins.
　　b. Feb. 14, 1814.　　m. Oct. 17, 1841.　　d. May 22, 1890.
Elizabeth Jennings, da. Sanford and Eliza (　　　) Jennings.
　　b.
　9 ch.　*Charles Sanford*, b. Oct. 4. 1842, d. Apr. 26, 1862.
　　　　　William Gilbert, b. Nov. 25, 1844. d. Nov. 26, 1861.
　　　　　Abigail Redfield, b. Nov. 6. 1846, d. Mar. 14. 1851.
　　86. *Eliza Willis*, b. Sep 11, 1849; m. Apr. 14, 1868, Francis Hutchinson.
　　　　　Maria Everett, b. Sep. 18, 1852.
　　　　　Frank Wilson, b. Aug 12, 1855. d. Aug. 11, 1875.
　　　　　Fannie Wilson, b. Aug. 12, 1858, d. Sep. 17, 1875.
　　　　　Emma Cornelia, b Aug. 10. 1862, d. Feb. 10, 1864.
　　　　　Sarah Esther, b. July 31, 1865.

31.

MARIA HOPKINS, da. William and Abigail (Davis) Hopkins.
　　b. Nov. 12, 1815.　　m. 1st. Jan. 13. 1841.　　m. 2d, Nov. 28, 1869.　　d. Sep. 8, 1892.
1st, George Brown, s. Samuel and Clarissa (Miller) Brown.
　　b. June 8, 1806.　　d. July 28, 1861.
2d, James L. Bradley, of St. Johns, New Brunswick, N. S.
　　b. June 12, 1813.
　　1 ch. * *Cornelia Abigail*, b. Oct. 28, 1842; m. Dec. 25, 1867, Zophar M. Woodhull.
(*) See Hudson genealogy.

32.

ELIZABETH HOPKINS, da. William and Abigail (Davis) Hopkins.
　　b. Oct 27, 1818.　　m. May 23, 1839.　　d. March 28, 1894.
Stiles Wheeler Judson, of Monroe. Connecticut.
　　b. Sep. 20, 1814.　　d. July 28, 1890.
　2 ch. 87. *Emma Hopkins*, b. Aug. 29, 1841; m. 1st, Oct. 21, 1863, Nathaniel M. Bennett.
　　　　　　　　　　　　　　　　　　　　　　　2d, May 21, 1887. David Thomson.
　　88. *William Henry*, b. Dec. 26, 1652; m. Aug. 2, 1881, Anna L. Andrews.

33.

FRANCES E. HOPKINS, da. William and Angeline (Davis) Hopkins.
　　b. Oct. 9, 1838.　　m. Jan. 15, 1858.
Washington W. Brown, s. Woodhull and Ruth (　　　) Brown.
　　b.　　　1835.
　4 ch.　*Martha W.*, b. July 4, 1859; m. July 9, 1884, Edward Walker, no issue.
　　　　　Annie F., b. May 18, 1863, drowned Feb. 8, 1869.
　　　　　Elvia J., b. Sep. 12, 1871, d, April 4, 1882.
　　　　　Charles G., b. Sep. 18, 1874.

34.

SUSAN HOPKINS, da. William and Angeline (Davis) Hopkins.
　　b. Oct. 20, 1842.　　m. 1st, Oct. 25, 1859.　　m. 2d, Dec. 3, 1894.
1st, Timothy H. Helme, s. Thomas and Julietta (　　　) Helme.
　　b. Sep. 30, 1813.　　d. Apr. 8, 1890.
2d, Israel C. Terry, s. Daniel T. and Eunice (Case) Terry.
　　b. Sep. 14, 1835.
　3 ch.　*Arthur*, b. Nov. 20, 1860.
　　　　　William T., b. April 18, 1863, d. Aug. 21, 1863.
　　89. *Cornelius H.*, b. May 24, 1867; m. March 19. 1892, Marie S. Helme.

35.

WILLIAM AUGUSTUS HOPKINS, s. William and Angeline (Davis) Hopkins.
　　b. Dec. 26, 1847.　　m. Feb. 20, 1878.
Emily Sanford, da.　　　　　　　　　　　Sanford.
　　b.
　1 ch.　*William Floyd*, b. Oct. 25, 1879.

36.

SAMUEL WOODHULL HOPKINS, s. Gilbert and Deborah (Ferris) Hopkins.
 b. Oct. 13, 1822. m. May 26, 1845.

 Sarah Louisa Jessup, da. Jonathan and Sarah (Weed) Jessup.
  b. April 2, 1826.

9 ch. **90.** *Gilbert S.*, b. Dec. 30. 1846; m. July 6, 1874, Ada Augusta Hubbie.
   Clinton F., b. Oct. 8, 1848.
   Judson W., b. July 21, 1850.
   Mary E., b. Aug. 24. 1852; m. Nov. 28, 1876, *S. D. Hall Clark. No issue.
  91. *William*, b. May 31, 1854; Feb. 27, 1877, Elizabeth Clark.
   Louisa, b. Feb. 13, 1856, d. March 10. 1856.
  92. *Adeline*, b. Feb. 6, 1857; m. June 8, 1875, Nelson N. Lockwood.
  93. *Charles*, b. May 24, 1859; m. May 14, 1884, Hattie Blowers.
   Madison, b. June 26, 1862, d. Dec. 1, 1863.
(*) Son of Edward S. and Eliza (Palmer) Clark.

37.

REV. JUDSON H. HOPKINS, s. Gilbert and Deborah (Ferris) Hopkins.
 b. Sep. 29, 1830. m. June 12, 1862. d. July 11, 1897.

 Elizabeth M. Freeman, da. Pliny and Sarah (Mairs) Freeman.
  b. Aug. 14, 1828.

5 ch. *Sarah Freeman*, b. March 20 1864.
  Elizabeth, b. June 2, 1865, d. July 27, 1866.
  George Freeman, b. A g. 16, 1866.
  Judson Gilbert, b. Aug. 11, 1868.
  Henry, b. Oct. 14, 1871.

38.

SAMUEL JOHNSON HOPKINS, s. Dr. George and Elizabeth (Johnson) Hopkins.
 b. Jan. 23, 1818. m. May 12, 1845. d. April 1881.

 Maria Eliza Berrien, da. Daniel Berrien, of New York City.
  b. d. July 29, 1880.

6 ch. **George Gilbert*, b. Aug. 20, 1846; m. an English lady.
  Maria Louisa. b. March 6, 1848, d. Feb. 6. 1849.
  Augusta Berrien, b. Feb. 4. 1855. d. Aug. 25, 1855.
  Gertrude, b. July 20, 1856, d. Aug. 4, 1856.
  Maria Eliza, b. d. May 29, 1880.
  William Berrien, b. Jan. 19. 1862, d. Jan. 7, 1885.
(*) d. in China, Sep. 26, 1887 and left 3 children.

39.

GEORGE G. HOPKINS, s. Dr. George and Elizabeth M. (Johnson) Hopkins.
 b. Aug. 22, 1819. d. Jan. 28, 1898.

 ELIZABETH HOPKINS, da Gilbert and Deborah (Ferris) Hopkins. See No. 9.
  b. Jan. 23, 1821. d. Feb. 3, 1895.

6 ch. *Phebe A.*, b.
  Alonzo, b. m.
  Araminta R., b. d.
  Araminta R., b.
  Grace, b. d.
  Blanche, b. d. ae., 2½ years.

40.

CALEB H. KING, s. Rev. Ezra and Eliza (Helme) King.
 b. Jan. 6, 1818. m. May 1842. d. April 27. 1896.

 Deborah M. Brown, da. John and Phebe (Rogers) Brown.
  b. Dec. 1, 1818. d. Feb. 12, 1871.

3 ch. *John E.*, b. Sept. 1844; m.
  Albert N., b. m.
  94. *G. Howard*, b. Feb. 7, 1855; m. Jan. 14, 1880, Terentia E. Hawkins.

41.

EZRA S. KING, s. Rev. Ezra and Eliza (Helme) King.
 b. March 25, 1820. m. Jan. 24, 1843. d. Aug. 31, 1873.

 SARAH MATILDA HOPKINS, da. Samuel and Maria (Woodhull) Hopkins. See No. 5.
  b. Sept. 24, 1820.

6 ch. *Eliza H.*, b. Jan. 27, 1844, d. March 18, 1844.
  Wilson, b. Feb. 11. 1846, d. Sept. 5. 1849.
  Elmore, b. April 24. 1849, d. July 16, 1849.
  Augustus W., b. April 30. 1851; m. March 22, 1883, * Blanche C. Penfield. No issue.
  Helen A., b. June 21, 1856, d. March 18, 1857.
  Ella Gertrude, b. June 28, 1862.
(*) da. of Edward and Carrie (Ritter) Penfield, b. Jan. 26, 1860.

42.

JOSEPH N. KING, s. Rev. Ezra and Eliza (Helme) King.
b. June 8, 1823.   m. Nov. 17, 1846.

Therina Hudson, da. Horace and Eliza (Davis) Hudson.
b. Feb. 15, 1828.

1 ch.   *Byron Scott*, b. Sept. 3, 1847, d. June 23, 1848.

43.

ELISHA E. KING, s. Rev. Ezra and Eliza (Helme) King.
b. Dec. 30, 1826.   m. May   1850.

Catherine S. Davis, da. Lewis and Hannah (Hawkins) Davis.
d. Feb. 10, 1898.

3 ch.   *Charles E.*, b.   m.   *Ezra*, b.   *Eliza H.*, b.

44.

HANNAH Y. KING, da. Rev. Ezra and Eliza (Helme) King.
b. March 22, 1830.   m. Dec. 7, 1848.

Joseph R. Rowland, s. Jeremiah and Eliza A. (Ridgeway) Rowland.
b.

3 ch.   **95.** *Everett W.*, b. Aug. 8, 1861; m. May 21, 1882, Emily J. Smith.
Lillian J., b. Sep. 13, 1865, d. March 31, 1885.
   96. *Florence V.*, b. Sep. 29, 1870; m. July 13, 1893, Richard M. Bayles.

45.

MARIA E. KING, da. Rev. Ezra and Eliza (Helme) King.
b. Jan. 22, 1833.   m.

Benjamin B. Bailey, s. Samuel and   (Brown) Bailey.
d. Sep. 1, 1874.

2 ch.   *Anna K.*, b.   m.   Hamlyn.   *Burtus B.*, b.   m.

46.

SYLVESTER D. TUTHILL, s. Hiram and Martha M. (Davis) Tuthill.
b. Dec. 23, 1826.   m. Dec. 20, 1849.   d. Feb. 24, 1885.

Ann Eliza Tuttle, da. Nathaniel and Joanna (Mills) Tuttle.
b. Aug. 31, 1828.

3 ch.   **97.** *Frank H.*, b. Aug. 15, 1860; m. Feb. 14, 1883, Ann Eliza Smith.
Nathaniel, b. July 28, 1862, d. March 2, 1863.
Isabel H., b. Aug. 24, 1865.

47.

NATHANIEL M. TUTHILL, s. Hiram and Martha M. (Davis) Tuthill.
b. Dec. 25, 1828.   m.

Caroline C. Carll, da. Gilbert and Fanny (Carll) Carll.
b. June 1, 1831.   d. Nov. 10, 1869.

6 ch.   *Hiram G.*, b. March 25, 1854, d. July 2, 1871.
Florabel, b. March 3, 1857, d. Feb. 9, 1859.
Carrie C., b. Feb. 19, 1860.
   98. *Alfred A.*, b. Dec. 29, 1861; m. April 2, 1891, Emily Rowley.
Egbert P., b. May 11, 1864.
Sylvester, b. Sep. 23, 1867, d. Oct. 4, 1869.

48.

HARRIET W. BAYLES, da. Thomas and Harriet M. (Davis) Bayles.
b.   1851.   m. June 13, 1878.

Seth B. Worth, s. Seth and Katie (Smith) Worth.
b. Dec. 16, 1835.

3 ch.   *Hattie*, b. May 5, 1880.   *Fred. J.*, b. Feb. 25, 1882.   *Estelle*, b. July 18, 1885.

49.

MARTHA M. BAYLES, da. Thomas and Harriet M. (Davis) Bayles,
b.   1854,   m. Nov. 30, 1876.

Herman Aldrich. s. William G. and Mary (Bayles) Aldrich.
b. Nov. 24, 1853.

2 ch.   *Eva B.*, b.   1878; m. May 3, 1897, Rev. H. M. Lowry,
Herman T., b. July 26, 1888.

50.

ELIZA C. DAVIS, da. Alfred M. and Sophronia (Emmons) Davis.
b. Oct. 15, 1841.   m. Jan. 14, 1867.

John S. Randall, s. Sylvester and Frances (Davis) Randall.
b. Oct. 16, 1841.   d. April 29, 1886.

3 ch.   **Eloise S.*, b. Jan. 20, 1868; m. Feb. 6, 1890, Lester H. Davis.
Forrest B., b. Feb. 11, 1870.   *Edna L.*, b. June 24, 1872.

(*) See No. 79.

51.

NATHANIEL T. DAVIS, s. Alfred M. and Sophronia (Emmons) Davis.
b. Sep. 4, 1843.   m. 1st, Oct. 10. 1870.   m. 2d, Jan. 19, 1882.   m. 3d, April 15, 1891.

1st, Mary M. Beebe, da. Theodore and Clarissa (Billard) Beebe.
b. Sep. 6, 1850.   d. July 20, 1877.

2d, M. Salome Rand, da. Stephen and Cornelia (Hathaway) Rand.
b. Nov. 14, 1844.   d. Jan. 14. 1883.

3d, Mariana J. Davies, da. James and Sarah (Andrews) Davies.
b. May 23, 1863.

4 ch.   A son by 2d wife d. in infancy.   *Marion N.*, b. July 3, 1892.
        Walter E., b. Aug. 12, 1894.   *Samuel J.*, b. March 17, 1897.

52.

ELBERT M. DAVIS. s. Alfred M. and Sophronia (Emmons) Davis.
b. April 6, 1845.   m. Oct. 11, 1870.

ELLEN M. MILLER, da. Edwin N. and Catherine O. (Hopkins) Miller.   See No. 16.
b. Jan. 16, 1846.

5 ch.   *Clara Miller*, b. Aug. 27, 1871.   *Catherine Miller*, b. Oct. 8, 1873, d. March 2, 1875.
        Ethel Louise, b. June 10, 1877, d. April 4, 1885.
        Mabel Earle, b. Jan. 1, 1882.   *Harold Elbert*, b. Sep. 9, 1886.

53.

CORRINA M. DAVIS, da. Alfred M. and Sophronia (Emmons) Davis.
b. Feb. 11, 1847.   m. Oct.   1874.

Charles E. Tooker, s. Brewster and Charry (Brewster) Tooker.
b. Sep. 7, 1844.

1 ch.   *George M.*, b. July 14, 1875.

54.

HEWLETT H. DAVIS, s. Alfred M. and Sophronia (Emmons) Davis.
b. Dec. 5, 1853.   m. Nov. 21, 1883.

Minnie L. Davis, da. Lorenzo G. and Ann E. (Hulse) Davis.
b. June 24. 1862.

6 ch.   *Isabel T.*, b. Jan. 4, 1885.   *Kate W.*, b. Nov. 3, 1886.
        Alfred M., b. April 9, 1890.   *Hewlett H.*, b. Oct. 31, 1892.
        James L., b. Jan. 31, 1895.   *Sophronia E.*, b. Oct. 14, 1897.

55.

ALFRED G. DAVIS, s. Alfred M. and Sophronia (Emmons) Davis.
b. June 21, 1863.   m. Oct. 25, 1884.

Elsie Banks, da. William H. and Lucretia (Avery) Banks.
b. June 22, 1860.

3 ch.   *Corrine B.*, b. Dec. 11. 1885.   *Edmund R.*, b. Jan. 12, 1892.
        Elsie Burgess, b. Jan. 3, 1897.

56.

JOSEPH W. DAVIS, s. Sylvester R. and Elmina (Hallock) Davis.
b. Nov. 10, 1835.   m. 1st, Oct. 10, 1859.   2d, Dec. 25, 1871.

1st, Sarah E. Randall, da. Sylvester and S. A. (Morehouse) Randall.
b. June 27, 1842.   drowned Sep. 23, 1865.

2d, HARRIET T. RITCH, da. Thomas J. and Mary J. (Davis) Ritch.   See No. 22.
b. March 12, 1844.

7 ch.   *Hattie B.*, b. Dec. 20, 1863, drowned Sep. 23, 1865.
        Emma W., b. Jan. 8, 1865, drowned Sep. 23, 1865.
        Emma R., b. Dec. 9, 1872. d. Aug. 7, 1885.
        Daniel S., b. June 2, 1874, d. Aug. 31, 1874.
        Clifford W., b. Nov. 3, 1875. d. July 10, 1876.
        Nettie W., b. Nov. 10, 1877.
        Joseph M., b. July 20, 1880, d. Aug. 9, 1885.

57.

MERRIT W. DAVIS, s. Sylvester R. and Elmina (Hallock) Davis.
b. March 28, 1837.   m. 1st, Oct. 27, 1863.   m. 2d, March 10, 1874.

1st, Amelia S. Banks, da. Bradley and Polly P. (Banks) Banks.
b. Jan. 1, 1843.   d. July 4, 1865.

2d, Mary E. Lutz, da. P. Joseph and Eliza A. (Boelyn) Lutz.
b. Nov. 24, 1846.

1 ch.   *William B.*, b. Oct. 9, 1864, d. Sept. 24, 1865.

58.

NATHANIEL D. MILLER, s. Edwin N. and Catherine O. (Hopkins) Miller.
    b. Feb. 7, 1848.   m. Dec.   1869.

Jane Sophia Snow, da. Aaron and Abigail (Hovey) Snow.
    b.

    2 ch. *Aaron Snow, b. Nov.   1870; m. Oct.   1895, Sarah Stannard.
        Florence Ophelia b.   m. June 15, 1898, Alliston B. Gifford.
(*) Have one daughter named Elizabeth.

59.

SAMUEL H. MILLER, s. Edwin N. and Catherine O. (Hopkins) Miller.
    b. Nov. 7, 1853.   m. Sep. 18, 1878.

Alilah Y. Tillotson, da. Richard and Julia A. (Norton) Tillotson.
    b.

    2 ch.   Grace J., b. Sep. 18, 1879.   Alila May, b. May 28, 1881.

60.

FANNY TUTHILL HOPKINS, da. George W. and Mary M. (Tuthill) Hopkins.
    b. July 31, 1858.   m. Nov. 19, 1875.

Havens J. Davis, s. Lorenzo and Ann E. (Hulse) Davis.
    b. Nov. 1, 1858.

    2 ch.   Lorenzo Hopkins, b. Mar. 4, 1876.   William Van Pelt, b. Sep. 21, 1898.

61.

PHILIP HALLOCK HOPKINS, s. Samuel J. and Sarah K. (Hallock) Hopkins.
    b. Jan. 29, 1866.   m. Oct. 2, 1895.

Lulu M. Howland, da. James L. and Mary R. (Spencer) Howland.
    b. June 15, 1875.

    1 ch.   Eleanor Ruth, b. Nov. 24, 1897.

62.

LEWIS IRVING OVERTON, s. Lewis R. and Elizabeth (Davis) Overton.
    b. July 8, 1831.   m. Aug.   1853.

Matilda J. Overton, da. Joshua and Ruth (Hart) Overton.
    b. April 1, 1836.

  15 ch. 99. Woodhull I., b. Aug. 29, 1855; m. { 1st in 187-, Mary Davis.
                                           { 2d, Jan. 8, 1883, Annie W. Overton.
    100. Edgar M., b.   1857; m. Oct. 11, 1878, Mary E. Rose.
    101. William R., b. May 13, 1859; m.   1884, Lottie Clark.
        Ruth E., b. Feb. 3, 1861. d. July 11, 1861.
    102. Elliott J., b. June 7, 1862; m. July 1, 1883, Hattie Davies.
    103. Eliza B., b.   1864; m. Dec. 31, 1885. Scudder T. Smith.
        Daniel J., b. July 30 1866, d. April 16. 1883.
        Carrie, { b. Dec. 3, 1868, { d. Sept. 8, 1869.
        Lelia, {   { d. April 21, 1870.
        Carrie, b. Jan. 28, 1870; d. Jan. 12, 1875.
    104. Frank L., b. June 3, 1871; m. April 30. 1893, Malta Mills.
        Libbie, b. March 28, 1873, d. Jan. 26, 1875.
    105. Jennie S., b. July 13, 1874; m. March 11, 1894, Edward Smith.
        H. Webster, b. Sept. 4, 1876.   John B., b. Aug. 7, 1878.

63.

PHEBE OVERTON, da. Lewis R. and Elizabeth (Davis) Overton.
    b. Jan. 11, 1833.   m. June 30, 1853.   d. June 14, 1895.

Edward C. Benedict, s. Nathaniel and Malinda (Williams) Benedict.
    b. March 19, 1831.

    3 ch. 106. Lewis N., b. June   1856; m. June   1881, Hattie Lockwood.
        Emma M., b. March   1858, d. Feb. 19, 1876.
        Rosetta S., b. Jan.   1865, d. Aug. 1868.

64.

C. HELEN OVERTON, da. Lewis R. and Elizabeth (Davis) Overton.
    b. March 6, 1838.   m. Dec. 26, 1860.

Charles J. Randall, s. Horace and Sabre (Davis) Randall.
    b. Feb. 8, 1837.

    7 ch.   *Nellie J., b. Dec. 18, 1864; m. Dec. 9, 1886, Daniel R. Davis.
        Ada O., b. March 29, 1869.
        Charles H., b. Nov. 16, 1872; d. May 5, 1873.
        Lewis R., { twins, b. Dec. 2, 1873, { d. March 15, 1874.
        Elizabeth D., {   { d. Dec. 4, 1873.
        Cora E., b. Sep. 30, 1875.   Blanche R., b. June 8, 1881.
(*) see No. 70.

65.

E. WEBSTER OVERTON, s. Lewis R. and Elizabeth (Davis) Overton.
b. Oct. 8, 1839.   m. March 27, 1875.

Charlotte L. Overton, da. Sheldon R. and Catherine (Roe) Overton.
b.

4 ch.   *Grace E.*, b. Feb. 8, 1876.   *Christina O.*, b. March 8, 1878.
  Morse R., b. Feb. 18, 1880.   *Lewis S.*, b. Jan. 1, 1883, d. Oct. 24, 1892.

66.

HOPKINS R. OVERTON, s. Lewis R. and Elizabeth (Davis) Overton.
b. Jan. 14, 1850.   m. 1st, 1875.   m. 2d, Nov.   1883.

1st, Christina Johnson, da.
b. June 10, 1847.   d. Aug. 30, 1882.

2d, Charity A. Thickett, da. William and Mary (Terry) Thickett.
b. Sep. 19, 1842.   d. Apr. 14, 1898.

1 ch.   *B. Attosa*, b. March 6, 1890.

67.

HARRIET S. DAVIS, da. Lester H. and Clarissa (Roe) Davis.
b. Nov. 5, 1842.   m. Jan. 3, 1866.

George P. Schryver, s. John E. and Abigail (Bartlett) Schryver.
b. Nov. 19, 1834.

4 ch.   *Ida*, b. March 26, 1868.   *William*, b. Nov. 18, 1872, d. May 1, 1873.
  Infant daughter b. Nov. 27, 1876, d. Feb. 3, 1877.
  Edna, b. Jan. 25, 1878.

68.

ELIZABETH J. DAVIS, da. Lester H. and Clarissa (Roe) Davis.
b. Dec. 18, 1846.   m. April 8, 1869.

James A. Randall, s. Ezra and Mary (Gildersleeve) Randall.
b. Dec. 18, 1845.

5 ch.   *Clifford D.*, b. Mar. 15, 1870, d. Jan. 25, 1892.   *Ernest*, b. Sep. 6, 1872.
  Shirlie, b. Nov. 1, 1874, d. Sep. 1875.   *Fred L.*, b. Aug. 12, 1877.
  Sadie, b. Dec. 25, 1881.

69.

WILLIAM L. DAVIS, s. Lester H. and Clarissa (Roe) Davis.
b. July 5, 1859.   m. 1st, Feb. 20, 1879.   m. 2d, Dec. 5, 1894.

1st, Carrie M. Overton, da. Daniel T. and Charry (Hawkins) Overton.
b. Nov. 19, 1857.   d. March 20, 1893.

2d, Annie M. Smith, da. W. Floyd and Clarissa (Darling) Smith.
b. Nov. 8, 1863.

3 ch.   *J. Percy*, b. Jan. 20, 1880.   *William L.*, b. Jan. 1, 1884.   *Harold F.*, b. Sep. 8. 1885.

70.

DANIEL R. DAVIS, s. Lester H. and Clarissa (Roe) Davis.
b. Jan. 5, 1854.   m. Dec. 9, 1886.

NELLIE J. RANDALL, da. Charles J. and C. Helen (Overton) Randall.   See No. 64.
b. Dec. 18, 1864.

6 ch.   An infant son, b. July 8, 1887, d. July 10, 1887.   *Eleanor T.*, b. Jan. 13, 1889.
  Lester H., b. Feb. 18, 1891.   *Charles R.*, b. Feb. 7, 1893
  Homer W., b. Aug. 30, 1895.   *Vernon R.*, b. Nov. 5, 1897.

71.

MARTHA J. RITCH, da. Thomas J. and Mary J. (Davis) Ritch.
b. March 20, 1840.   m. Oct. 29, 1860.

Hiram L. Moger, s. Henry and Catherine (Tuthill) Moger.
b. Dec. 15, 1832.

5 ch.   *Martha R.*, b. Aug. 17, 1861.   *Lewis E.*, b. Aug. 12, 1863.
  Fannie T., b. Dec. 2, 1866; m. Jan. 16, 1896, *Elmer W. Davis
  Henry T., b. Sep. 11, 1868.   *Irene W.*, b. Aug. 28, 1876.
(*) Son of Joel S. and Clarissa (Norton) Davis, b. March 31, 1861.

72.

THOMAS J. RITCH, s. Thomas J. and Mary J. (Davis) Ritch.
b. May 19, 1846.   m. Oct. 30, 1877.

Alice Randall, da. Buel and Catherine M. (Phillips) Randall.
b. Aug. 5, 1852.

6 ch.   *Mary P.*, b. Sep. 4, 1878.   *Thomas J.*, b. Dec. 12, 1880, d. Aug. 4, 1886.
  Alice C., b. Jan. 21, 1884.   *Daniel D.*, b. Dec. 7, 1885, d. Feb. 21, 1888.
  Helen R., b. April 15, 1888, d. April 20, 1890.
  Rossiter W., b. Dec. 24, 1890.

73.

I. WILSON RITCH, s. Thomas J. and Mary J. (Davis) Ritch.
  b. Feb. 11, 1851.   m. April 1, 1884.

  Martha A. Freeland, da. William H. and Catherine (Ackerman) Freeland.
  b. Sep. 6, 1862.

  4 ch.   *Lena E.*, b. Feb. 17, 1885; d. Jan. 19, 1887.   *I. Wilson*, b. Jan. 6, 1888.
  Alvin B., b. Sep. 30, 1895.   *Marion*, b. March 12, 1898.

74.

MARY J. RITCH, da. Thomas J. and Mary J. (Davis) Ritch.
  b. Jan. 21, 1853.   m. Oct. 28, 1880.

  Orange T. Fanning, s. Jacob and Abigail (Fanning) Fanning.
  b. Oct. 9, 1844.

  2 ch.   *Martin R.*, b. March 18, 1884; d. Dec. 16, 1886.   *Thomas R.*, b. March 17, 1888.

75.

VIRGIL RITCH, s. Thomas J. and Mary J. (Davis) Ritch.
  b. Aug 3, 1855.   m. Oct. 8, 1885.

  Ada C. Hawkins, da. Frederick G. and Almira C. (Hawkins) Hawkins.
  b. June 16, 1863.

  1 ch.   *Myrtle Clair*, b. Nov. 14, 1894.

76.

DR. GILBERT HOPKINS SWESEY, s. Van Rensselaer and Dorothy C. (Davis) Swesey.
  b. April 21, 1842.   m. Oct. 21, 1873.

  Susan Emily Miller, da. Dr. Charles and Sarah (Gifford) Miller.
  b. Feb. 18, 1851.

  8 ch.   *Lillian Corneta*, b. July 10, 1874.   *Dora Catherine*, b. Dec. 22, 1875.
  Van Rensselaer, b. Feb. 11, 1878.   *Sarah Ellis*, b. Aug. 28, 1880.
  Florence, b. Dec. 30, 1881.   *Charlotte, Powell*, b. July 21, 1883.
  Charles Miller, b. Sep. 12, 1888.   *Frank Robinson*, b. Dec. 30, 1897, d. Feb. 14 1898.

77.

TIMOTHY J. DAVIS, s. Daniel W. and Ann Eliza (Davis) Davis.
  b. Nov. 5, 1856.   m. Oct. 15, 1885.

  Julia B. Hulse, da. Barnabas W. and Lucetta P. (Howell) Hulse.
  b. Sep. 15, 1864.

  4 ch.   *Archer Woodhull*, b. May 14, 1888.   *Evvie Brown*, b. Aug. 24, 1891.
  Clara May, b. Oct. 25, 1893.   *Freeman Howell*, b. Nov. 30, 1897.

78.

WILLIAM A. DAVIS, s. Daniel W. and Laura S. (Davis) Davis.
  b. Oct. 15, 1861.   m. Feb. 20, 1890.

  Leonella Davis, da. William A. and Martha (Hutchinson) Davis.
  b. June 22, 1871.

  1 ch.   *Amhurst Woodhull*, b. Oct. 22, 1896.

79.

LESTER H. DAVIS, s. Daniel W. and Laura S. (Davis) Davis.
  b. Feb. 26, 1865.   m. Feb. 6, 1890.

  ELOISE S. RANDALL, da. John and Eliza (Davis) Randall.   See No. 50.
  b. Jan. 20, 1868.

  2 ch.   *Laura W.*, b. June 22, 1892.   *Raymond L.*, b. Dec. 18, 1895.

80.

JACOB HASTINGS ROWELL, s. Hopkins and Mary E. (Blood) Rowell.
  b. Sep. 28, 1850.   m. Nov. 18, 1885.

  Mary Maria Palmer, da. Homer W. and Effie (Palmer) Palmer.
  b. Sep. 8, 1868.

  1 ch.   *Effie Elizabeth*, b. Oct. 7, 1886.

81.

SARAH GENEVIEVE ROWELL, da. Hopkins and Mary E. (Blood) Rowell.
  b. Dec. 28, 1865.   m. June 15, 1893.

  Benjamin L. McFadden, s. Henry W. and Harriet M. (Munson) McFadden.
  b. Nov. 23, 1865.

  1 ch.   *Robert Morse*, b. June 10, 1895.

82.

MARY ANTOINETTE ROWELL, da. Rev. Thompson and Mary R. (Talbot) Rowell.
  b. Sep. 17, 1852.   m. May 14, 1884.

  William Walter Ross, of Detroit, Michigan.
  b. Dec. 22, 1839.

  2 ch.   *Warren Proctor*, b. July 13, 1885.   *Harriet Maria*, b. Sep. 24, 1888.

83.

HENRY H. S. ROWELL, s. Rev. Thompson and Mary R. (Talbot) Rowell.
b. July 8, 1855.   m. June 20, 1894.

Emily Randolph, da. Charles and Fredericka (Borchart) Randolph.
b.

2 ch.   *Ralph Randolph*, b. April 5, 1895.   *Paul Talbot*, b. Feb. 17, 1897.

84.

GEORGE HOPKINS ROWELL, s. Rev. Thompson and Mary R. (Talbot) Rowell.
b. Sep. 3, 1870.   m. July 20, 1892.

Julia Walsh, da. Patrick and Mary (Kahoe) Walsh.
b.

3 ch.   *Henry Sibley*, b. Aug. 13, 1893.   *Ellen Maria*, b. Dec. 4, 1894.
          John Proctor, b. June 6, 1896.

85.

MORSE ROWELL, s. Rev. Morse and Letitia (Crawford) Rowell.
b. July 2, 1863.   m. Dec. 24, 1888.   d. April 5, 1896.

Belle J. England, da. Ira I. and Cynthia M. (Davis) England.
b. Oct. 3, 1857.

4 ch.   *Ira Morse*, b. March 30, 1890.   *Mary Belle*, b. Oct. 24, 1891.
          Marjorie Lillie, b. Nov. 14, 1893.   *Violet England*, b. Aug. 13, 1895.

86.

ELIZA WILLIS HOPKINS, da. Charles and Elizabeth (Jennings) Hopkins.
b. Sep. 11, 1849.   m. April 14, 1868.

Francis Hutchinson, s. Benjamin F. and Minerva (   ) Hutchinson.
b. Jan. 13, 1845.

4 ch.   *Edwin*, b. Oct. 23, 1869, d. Dec. 5, 1870.   *George Herbert*, b. Feb. 8, 1872.
          Willis Everett, b. Jan. 29, 1875.   *Lena Irene*, b. Nov. 3, 1877.

87.

EMMA HOPKINS JUDSON, da. Stiles W. and Elizabeth (Hopkins) Judson.
b. Aug. 29, 1841.   m. 1st, Oct. 21, 1863.   m. 2d, May 21, 1887.

1st, Nathaniel M. Bennet, s. Henry and Mary E. (Martin) Bennet.
b.

2d, David Thomson, s. David and Eliza (Johnson) Thomson.
b. Jan. 13, 1834.

2 ch.   *Elizabeth Judson*, b. March 24, 1865; m. May 28, 1888, *William G. Backhouse.
          Emma Judson, b. March 10, 1869.
(*) Son of Edward T. and Rebecca L. (Cowenhoven) Backhouse, b. June 15, 1862.

88.

WILLIAM HENRY JUDSON, s. Styles W. and Elizabeth (Hopkins) Judson.
b. Dec. 26, 1852.   m. Aug. 2, 1881.   d. Nov. 26, 1894.

Anna L. Andrews, of Cincinnati, Ohio.
b.

1 ch.   *Howard Tilghman*, b. Aug. 14, 1883; d. Jan. 26, 1884.

89.

CORNELIUS H. HELME, s. Timothy H. and Susan (Hopkins) Helme.
b. May 24, 1867.   m. March 19, 1892.

Marie Sweet Helme, adopted da. George P. and Hannah (Burnell) Helme.
b. Dec. 25, 1870.

1 ch.   *George Phillips*, b. March 19, 1893.

90.

GILBERT S. HOPKINS, s. Samuel W. and Sarah L. (Jessup) Hopkins.
b. Dec. 30, 1846.   m. July 6, 1874.

Ada Augusta Hubbie, da. Robert and Angeline (Rosamond) Hubbie.
b. July 5, 1858.

2 ch.   *Frederick Gilbert*, b. May 2, 1875; m.   Elizabeth Thomas.
          Ada Belle, b. Sep. 19, 1877; m.   Paul Otto Hughes.

91.

WILLIAM HOPKINS, s. Samuel W. and Sarah L. (Jessup) Hopkins.
b. May 31, 1854.   m. Feb. 27, 1877.   d. May 24, 1887.

Elizabeth Clark, da. Edward S. and Eliza (Palmer) Clark.
b.

5 ch.   *Samuel Woodhull*, b. Sep. 25, 1877.   *Clinton*, b. June 1882.
          Grover C., b.   *Lillian Agnes*, b.   d. ae., 18 months.
          Cyrus, b.   d. ae., 6 months.

92.

ADALINE HOPKINS, da. Samuel W. and Sarah L. (Jessup) Hopkins.
    b. Feb. 6, 1857.   m. June 8, 1875.

Nelson N. Lockwood, s. Henry S. and Sarah E. (White) Lockwood.
    b. Oct. 14, 1851.
    2 ch. *Grace*, b. May 2, 1876.   *Sarah May*, b. May 29, 1885.

93.

CHARLES HOPKINS, s. Samuel W. and Sarah L. (Jessup) Hopkins.
    b. May 24, 1859.   m. May 14, 1884.

Hattie Blowers, da. Hiram and Rebecca (Herriden) Blowers.
    b. July 22, 1862.
    3 ch. *Clinton Hiram*, b. Oct. 1, 1885.   *Lula Grace*, b. March 20, 1887.
        Hattie May, b. April 15, 1894.

94.

G. HOWARD KING, s. Caleb H. and Deborah M. (Brown) King.
    b. Feb. 7, 1855.   m. June 14, 1880.

Terentia E. Hawkins, da. Nichol S. and Mary C. (Bayles) Hawkins.
    b. March 26, 1854.
    1 ch.   *Orah Mai*, b. May 2, 1886.

95.

EVERETT W. ROWLAND, s. Joseph R. and Hannah Y. (King) Rowland.
    b. Aug. 8, 1861.   m. May 21, 1882.

Emily J. Smith, da. John H. and Caroline K. (Satterly) Smith.
    b. Feb. 22, 1864.
    3 ch.   *Royall*, b. June 27, 1883.   *Wesley*, b. June 13, 1885.
        Lillian, b. June 4, 1889.

96.

FLORENCE V. ROWLAND, da. Joseph R. and Hannah Y. (King) Rowland.
    b. Sep. 29, 1870.   m. July 13, 1893.

Richard M. Bayles, s. Richard M. and Harmony (Swezey) Bayles.
    b. March 23, 1846.
    2 ch.   *Thomas Richard*, b. Feb. 4, 1895.   *Albert Edward*, b. Dec. 23, 1897.

97.

FRANK H. TUTHILL, s. Sylvester D. and Ann E. (Tuttle) Tuthill.
    b. Aug. 15, 1860.   m. Feb. 14, 1883.

Ann Eliza Smith, da. John H. and Roxanna (Satterlee) Smith.
    b. Nov. 7, 1861.
    3 ch.   *Nathaniel*, b. June 10, 1884.   *Henry A. S.*, b. June 8, 1886.
        Anlis Ena, b. April 21, 1890.

98.

ALFRED A. TUTHILL, s. Nathaniel M. and Caroline C. (Carll) Tuthill.
    b. Dec. 29, 1861.   m. April 2, 1891.

Emily Rowley, da. Samuel and Helen (Terry) Rowley.
    b. Sep. 25, 1866.
    1 ch.   *Helen H.*, b. March 21, 1892.

99.

WOODHULL I. OVERTON, s. Lewis I. and Matilda J. (Overton) Overton.
    b. Aug. 29, 1855.   m. 1st, in 187-.   m. 2d. Jan. 8, 1883.
    1st, Mary Davis, da. Stephen and   (   ) Davis.

    2d, Annie W. Overton, da. Gilbert L. and Sarah T. (Overton) Overton.
    b. Sep. 10, 1863.
    3 ch.   *Georgiana E.*, b. June 10. 1885.   *Lillian R. A.*, b. Oct. 30. 1890.
        Alfred Dewey, b. June 19, 1898.

100.

EDGAR M. OVERTON, s. Lewis I. and Matilda J. (Overton) Overton.
    b.   1857.   m. Oct, 11, 1878.

Mary E. Rose, da. George and Melissa (Jones) Rose.
    b.   1863.
    10 ch.   **107.** *Fannie M.*, b. Oct. 7, 1879; m. Jan. 1, 1897, Fred. R. Johnson.
        Fred. L., b. March 6, 1881.   *Elsie C.*, b. Nov. 27, 1892.
        Clara B., b. April 22, 1884.   *Myrtle A.*, b. June 3, 1894.
        Flora A., b. April 10, 1886.   *Edith M.*, b. May 6, 1897.
        Daniel M., b. Feb. 29, 1888.   *Mildred*, b. Aug. 5, 1898.
        Minnie E., b. Jan. 11, 1891.

101.

WILLIAM R. OVERTON, s. Lewis I. and Matilda J. (Overton) Overton.
b. May 13, 1859.   m.   1884.
Lottie Clark. da. James and Elizabeth (Smith) Clark.
b.

6 ch.	*Raymond,* b.	1884.	*Mabel.* b.	1890.
	Fremont. b.	1886.	*Virgil R.,* b.	1892.
	Irene, b.	1888.	*Crawford,* b.	1895.

102.

ELIOTT J. OVERTON, s. Lewis I. and Matilda J. (Overton) Overton.
b. June 7, 1862.   m. July 1, 1883.
Hattie Davies, da. George and Jane (Edwards) Davies.
b. Dec. 27, 1865.

2 ch.	*Ada M.*, b. May 3, 1886.	*G. Arthur.* b. July 12, 1888.

103.

ELIZA B. OVERTON, da. Lewis I. and Matilda J. (Overton) Overton.
b.   1864.   m. Dec. 31, 1885.
Scudder T. Smith, s. Hawkins and Eliza (Terry) Smith.
b. June 11, 1855.

3 ch.	*Bula A.,* b. March 2, 1889.	*Pearl A.,* b. Jan. 5, 1896.
	Elsie B., b. Dec. 10, 1892.	

104.

FRANK L. OVERTON, s. Lewis I. and Matilda J. (Overton) Overton.
b. June 3, 1871.   m. April 30, 1893.
Malta Mills, da. Edward and May (Newton) Mills.
b.

2 ch.	*Howard* b. Nov. 20, 1893.	*Percy* b. Oct. 20, 1897.

105.

JENNIE S. OVERTON, da. Lewis I. and Matilda J. (Overton) Overton.
b. July 13, 1874.   m. March 11, 1894.
Edward Smith, s. J. Carl and Elizabeth (Mackenzie) Smith.
b.

2 ch.	*Stanley,* b. April 20, 1895.	*Marguerite.* b. June 4, 1897.

106.

LEWIS N BENEDICT, s. Edward C. and Phebe (Overton) Benedict.
b. June   1856.   m. June   1881.
Hattie Lockwood, da. George and Lucinda (Fourbush) Lockwood.
b. Aug. 16, 1856.

1 ch.	*Ruth,* b. Aug. 1884.

107.

FANNIE M. OVERTON, da. Edgar M. and Mary E. (Rose) Overton.
b. Oct. 7, 1879.   m. Jan. 1, 1897.
Fred R. Johnson, s. Andrew and Rhoda (Crowell) Johnson.
b. April 19, 1876

3 ch.	*Ruby B.,* b. Aug. 30, 1897; d. Sep. 20, 1898.
	Son and daughter, twins, b. Oct. 23, 1898.

BOWDITCH.

Savage's Genealogical Dictionary says a John Bowditch of Boston, married in 1682, Temperance French, a daughter of John French, the first of Braintree. She died Aug. 12, 1720. A William Bowditch resided in Salem, in 1639. This William is thought to have come from Devonshire, England, as the name Bowditch is frequently found there. In 1643, this William received a grant of land. His wife's given name was Sarah, by whom he had a son, Nathaniel, who was baptized Feb. 12, 1643. Another son, named William, born perhaps in England, was the only son his father-left. This son, William, was a custom officer under the Colonial administration. He died suddenly in 1681, leaving an only son, also named William, born in 1663. This third William became eminent at Salem, for his usefulness. In 1688, he married Mary Gardner, daughter of Thomas Gardner, and died May 28, 1728. He had seven children, one of whom named Ebenezer, born April 26, 1703, married Aug. 15, 1728, Mary Turner, daughter of the Hon. John Turner, and died Feb. 2, 1768. He alone, of the seven children. left male issue ; one of his sons, named Habakkuk, being the father of Nathaniel Bowditch, the very celebrated astronomer and translator of La Place.

1.

JOEL BOWDITCH, s.
   b.   m.   d. Nov. 22. 1746.

Ruth   da.
   b.   d. Sep.   1753.

5 ch.   (*) *Abigail*, b.   m. about 1718, Nathan Fordham.
         Hannah, b.   **John**, b.   °A son, b.   d. July 1, 1714.
   2. *Joel*, b,   m. June 5, 1735, Bethiah Case.

Joel Bowditch, late of Suffolk Co., deceased. Letters granted to his widow, Ruth Bowditch, dated
   Dec. 2, 1747.
Joel Bowditch appears as resident of Easthampton, from 1704-1718. Hedge's Hist., p. 344.
A Joe'm Bowditch appears on the muster roll of a militia company in Easthampton, dated 1715.
* Dec. 23, 1722. The daughter of Joel Bondage, Hannah, baptized upon uniting with the church.
   Easthampton Town Records.
° Taken from the Easthampton Town Records.

2.

JOEL BOWDITCH, s. Joel and Ruth (   ) Bowditch.
   b.   m. June 5, 1735.   d. Nov. 20, 1769.

Bethiah Case, da. Samuel and Zeriah (Horton) Case.
   b.   d. Feb. 10, 1799.

8 ch.   A child, b.   d. Jan. 17, 1739.
         A child, b.   d. April 29, 1739.
         Frances, b.   m. Oct. 4, 1758, John Devall.
         °*Elizabeth*, b.   m. about 1760, James Havens.
   3. *Joel*, b.   m. Sep. 13, 1761, Mary Vail.
   4. *John*, b in 1745-6; m.
   5. *William*, b. in 1751; m. Susannah.
         †*Bethiah*, b. Sep. 9, 1755; m. 1st,   William Havens.
                          2d,   Phineas Parker.

* Probably no issue, none being given on Census lists of 1771 and 1776.
° See Haven's Genealogy.   † See Haven's Genealogy and Parker Genealogy.

3.

JOEL BOWDITCH, s. Joel and Bethiah (Case) Bowditch
   b.   m. Sep. 13, 1761.   d.

Mary Vail, da.
   b.   d.

1 ch.   *Mary*, b.   m.   John Youngs.

4.

JOHN BOWDITCH, s. Joel and Bethiah (Case) Bowditch.
   b. in 1745-46.   m.   d. Jan. 1, 1826.

         b.   d.
5 ch.   *William*, b.   1765-6; m. Oct. 29, 1807, °Hepsibah Harley; no issue.
   6. *John*, b.   m.   Mary Case.
   ‖ *Esther*, b. in 1773; m.   Augustus Havens.
   7. *Samuel C.*, b. Nov. 8, 1780; m. Sep. 13, 1826, Eleanor H. Gardiner.
   8. *Fanny*, b. in 1786; m. Dec. 12, 1809, Sineus Conkling.
*d. Jan. 20, 1828, ae. 62.   °d. Dec. 19, 1808, ae. 33.   ‖ See Haven's Genealogy.
Will of John Bowditch, dated March 31, 1825, names Esther, Fanny and Samuel. Also a grandson,
   John Benedict Bowditch. Wife's name not given. Presumably she had died before her husband,
   Will proved Jan. 9, 1826.

5.

WILLIAM BOWDITCH, s. Joel and Bethiah (Case) Bowditch
   b. in 1751.   m. about 1774.   d. Aug. 8, 1820.

Susannah
   b.   1775.   d. Dec. 11, 1847.

2 ch.   **9.** *Harriet*, b.   1775-76; m. 1st, Sep. 24, 1800, Caleb Smith.
                          2d, June 24, 1810. John Brainerd.
   10. *Julia Ann*, b.   m. April 12, 1807, Nathan Oaks.

6.

JOHN BOWDITCH, s. John and   (   ) Bowditch.
   b.   m.   d. at Farmington, Conn.

Mary Case, da. Samuel and Esther (Budd) Case.
   b.   d. Dec. 8, 1817.

4 ch. **11.** *John Benedict*, b. Aug. 4, 1800; m. 1st, Oct. 25, 1823, Sarah Conklin.
                          2d, Nov. 24, 1825-6, Frances M. Griffing.
   21. *Jonas Blair*. b. Sep. 1, 1803; m. in 1825, Esther Alley.
         Mary Howard, b. Nov. 6, 1806; m. Nov. 19, 1830, ° Isaac S. Wadsworth. No issue.
         Julia Havens, b. Dec. 12, 1808; d. unm., Feb. 16, 1866.
*d. April 21, 1887.   ° s. of Jabez and Anna (Ferguson) Wadsworth, b. March 6, 1805; d. Dec. 8, 1865.

7.

SAMUEL CASE BOWDITCH, s. John and ( ) Bowditch.
    b. Nov. 7, 1780.   m. Sep. 13, 1826.   d. Feb. 7, 1855.

Eleanor Holland Gardiner, da. William and Elizabeth (Brown) Gardiner.
    b. March 2d, 1801.   d. March 25, 1859.
7 ch.   *William S.*, b. Jan. 14, 1828; d. July 22, 1828.
   13. *William Samuel*, b. May 7, 1829; m. 1st, Dec. 31, 1854, Sarah H. Clark.
                              2d, Jan. 11, 1858, Lydia J. Smith.
   14. *Joseph Haddock*, b. June 8, 1830; m. Feb. 2d, 1863, Margaret J. Havens.
   15. *Mary Elizabeth*, b. March 30, 1833; m. Aug. 1853, Stafford Squires.
    Maria Jane, b. April 18, 1835, d. April 13, 1836.
   16. *Nancy Maria*, b. April 11, 1841; m. Nov. 10, 1860, Washington Eddy.
    Theodore Freeling, b. March 13, 1844, d. Oct. 27, 1864.

8.

FANNY BOWDITCH, da. John and ( ) Bowditch.
    b. in 1786.   m. Dec. 12, 1809.   d. Jan. 8, 1840.

Sineus Conkling, s.
    b. Feb. 3, 1786.   d. April 3, 1870.
6 ch.   *Esther*, b.   1810, d. unm., July 28, 1883.
   Frances, b.   1812; m.   John S. Tuthill.
   Nancy, b.   m.   Sanford Hedges. No issue.
   James Lawrence, b. May 1818, d. April 1, 1819.
   Nathaniel, b. Nov. 1822; d. Oct. 7, 1826.
   17. *DeWitt Clinton*, b.   1824; m.   Clarissa Mott.   *Julia*, b.
*See Tuthill Genealogy.

9.

HARRIET BOWDITCH, da. William and Susannah ( ) Bowditch.
    b. in 1775-6.   m. 1st, Sep. 24, 1800.   m. 2d, June 24, 1810.   d. March 15, 1851.

1st, Caleb Smith, s. William and Ruth (Woodhull) Smith.
    b.   1767.   d.   1805.

2d, John Brainerd, s. Phineas and Jerusha (Towner) Brainerd.
    b. Nov. 5, 1757.   d. Nov. 28, 1815.
4 ch.   *Caleb S.*, b. in 1804-5, d. unm., March 6, 1884.
   Elizabeth, b.   m. Sep. 16, 1824, William R. Sleight.
   †*Harriet B.*, b. Jan. 10, 1814; m. 1st, Dec. 25, 1838, °Nathan P. Howell.⎱ No issue.
                     2d, Nov. 21. 1878, ‖Dr. Henry Cook.⎰
   18. *Mary A.*, b. May 10, 1811; m. 1831-32, Edward Mitchell.
*d. s. p. °s. of Silas and Bethiah Howell, b. March 12, 1805, d. Dec. 27, 1869.
†d. Dec. 24, 1891. ‖Of London, Eng., b. Aug. 29. 1814, d. Oct. 9, 1887.

10.

JULIA ANN BOWDITCH, da. William and Susannah ( ) Bowditch.
    b.   m. April 12, 1807.   d.

Nathan Oaks of New Haven, Conn.
    b.   d.
1 ch.   *Julia*, b.   m. Sep.   1835, George Walters, of New Haven, Conn.

11.

JOHN BENEDICT BOWDITCH, s. John and Mary (Case) Bowditch.
    b. Aug. 4, 1800.   m. 1st, Oct. 28, 1823.   m. 2d, May 27, 1825-6.   d. Dec. 13, 1855.

1st, Sarah M. Conklin, da. Henry and Phebe (Conklin) Conklin.
    b. April 12, 1802.   d. Aug. 28, 1824.

2d, Frances M. Griffing, da. Absalom and Sybil (King) Griffing.
    b. Feb. 8, 1803.   d. March 24, 1872.
8 ch. **19.** *Sarah D.*, b. Aug. 20, 1824; m. Nov. 6, 1845, Benjamin Mulford.
   20. *John Boliver*, b. March 2, 1827; m. May 30, 1852, Mary Jane Case.
   Frances Sybil, b. Oct. 15, 1828; m. Jan. 25, 1851, Charles A. Cartwright.
   Moses Griffing, b. Nov. 20, 1830; d. unm., Aug. 28, 1856.
   Jonas Blair, b. Aug. 4, 1836.
   21. *Julia Eugenia*, b. May 4, 1838; m. Oct. 23, 1872, Warren Johnson.
   Edwin Anderson, b. Dec. 12, 1840, d. unm., April 26, 1864.
   Maria Louise, b. April 26, 1843.
*d. s. p., July 4, 1870.

12.

JONAS BLAIR BOWDITCH, s. John and Mary (Case) Bowditch.
    b. Sep. 1, 1803.   m. in 1825.   d. Sep. 27, 1866.

Esther Alley, da. Joseph and Esther (Bradley) Alley,
    b. Nov. 10, 1804.   d. Jan. 15, 1879.
4 ch. **22.** *Edwin B.*, b. Nov. 2, 1826; m. Oct. 2, 1849, Frances S. King.
   Mary E., b. May 8, 1831; m. Nov. 21, 1860, ° Dr. James E. Dwinelle. No issue.
   23. *Esther A.*, b. Feb. 10, 1834; m. Aug. 1854, Edward Ely.
   Emma F., b. June 12, 1841, d. Sep. 8, 1842.
*d. April, 1870. °s. of Justin and Louisa (Whipple) Dwinelle, b. Jan. 30, 1830.

13.

WILLIAM SAMUEL BOWDITCH, s. Samuel C. and Eleanor H. (Gardiner) Bowditch.
b. May 7, 1829.   m. 1st, Dec. 31, 1854.   m. 2d, Jan. 11, 1858.

1st, Sarah Hannah Clark, da. Benjamin and Hannah (Potter) Clark.
b. in 1830.   d. May 28, 1856.

2d, Lydia Jackson Smith, da. Jeremiah and Abigail (Randall) Smith.
b. Oct. 19, 1828.   d. Sep. 7, 1889.

4 ch. **24.** *Howard Clark*, b. April 24, 1856; m. July 15, 1876, Louisa F. King.
   25. *William Joseph*, b. Nov. 11, 1858; m. Nov. 15, 1883, Florrie B. Simmons.
   26. *Nelly Abby*, b. June 18, 1860; m. Oct. 18, 1893, Edward H. Grafton.
   Arthur Smith, b. April 2, 1864, d. Nov. 18, 1865.

14.

JOSEPH HADDOCK BOWDITCH, s. Samuel C. and Eleanor H. (Gardiner) Bowditch.
b. June 8, 1830.   m. Feb. 2, 1863.

Margaret Jane Havens, da. Archibald R. and Caroline A. (Hughes) Havens.
b. March 27, 1841.

3 ch. **27.** *Frederick K.*, b. Nov. 10, 1863; m. April 7, 1887, Laura B. Baldwin.
   Archibald H., b. April 29, 1865.
   28. *Edwin Anderson*, b. Feb. 28, 1869; m.   1890, Christina E. Davidson.

15.

MARY ELIZABETH BOWDITCH, da. Samuel C. and Eleanor H. (Gardiner) Bowditch.
b. March 30, 1833.   m. Aug.   1853.   d. July 8, 1863.

Stafford Squires, s. Richard and Abigail E. (Loper) Squires.
b. May 14, 1830.

5 ch.				
Richard Nelson, b.	1853; m.	*Gilbert Henry*, b.	1855.
William Joseph, b.	1857; m.		
Maria Isabelle, b.	1859; m.	James L. Hull.	
Jesse, b. July , 1863.			

16.

NANCY MARIA BOWDITCH, da. Samuel C. and Eleanor H. (Gardiner) Bowditch.
b. April 11, 1841.   m. Nov. 19, 1860.

Washington Eddy, s. Asa and Betsey (   ) Eddy.
b. in 1837.   d. March 25, 1878.

2 ch. *Eleanor*, b. Aug. 16, 1863, d. Feb. 11, 1885.
   Walter Carlton, b. Sep. 25, 1867; m. April   , 1898, *wid. Celia Hotchkiss.
(*) da. of Leander F. and Ellen S. (Norton) Johnson.

17.

DEWITT CLINTON CONKLING, s. Sineus and Fanny (Bowditch) Conkling.
b.   1824.   m.   d. July 3, 1884.

Clarissa Mott, da. Henry and   (Strong) Mott.
b.   d. Sep. 2, 1897.

2 ch. *Fannie B.*, b. Dec.   1857, d. March 9, 1867.   *Gracie C.*, b. Oct. 15, 1873, d. Aug. 2, 1874.

18.

MARY BRAINERD, da. John and Harriet (Bowditch) Brainerd.
b. May 10, 1811.   m.   1831-32.   d. Jan. 22, 1848.

Edward Mitchell, s. James and Lucy (Cook) Mitchell.
b. Nov. 12, 1799.   d. Aug. 3, 1876.

5 ch. **29.** *Harriet B.*, b. Oct. 11, 1835; m. Feb. 3, 1864, Clark K. Royce.
   30. *James L.*, b. May 17, 1841; m. May 14, 1874, Margaret L. Rendell.
   31. *Lucy*, b. July 12, 1843; m. March   1877, Josiah H. Post.
   32. *John H.*, b. Oct. 5, 1845; m. March 16, 1874, Annie McPherson.
   Mary B., b. Jan. 15, 1848; d. Jan. 27, 1848.

19.

SARAH D. BOWDITCH, da. John B. and Sarah M. (Conklin) Bowditch.
b. Aug. 20, 1824.   m. Nov. 6, 1845.

Benjamin K. Mulford, s. Elisha and Fanny (Terry) Mulford.
b. Aug. 14, 1820.

3 ch. **33.** *Fanny*, b. Aug. 1, 1848; m. Nov. 6, 1872, Dwight Beebe.
   Ernest, b. May 1st, 1850; d. unm., July 5, 1876.
   34. *Adelaide*, b. Nov. 19, 1851; m. Oct. 27, 1874, Edward Latham.

20.

JOHN BOLIVER BOWDITCH, s. John B. and Frances M. (Griffing) Bowditch.
b. March 2, 1827.   m. May 20, 1853.   d. June 17, 1892.

Mary Jane Case, da. Samuel H. and Lydia M. (Cartwright) Case.
b. Oct. 5, 1829.

2 ch. **35.** *John Lay*, b. March 12, 1854; m. 1st, Jan. 30, 1875, Maria L. Payne.
2d, Dec. 25, 1883, Ella L. Smith.
36. *Edith Belle*, b. Feb. 8, 1857; m. Dec. 25, 1876, Sidell E. Fish.

21.

JULIA EUGENIA BOWDITCH, da. John B. and Frances M. (Griffing) Bowditch.
b. May 4, 1838. m. Oct. 23, 1872.

J. Warren Johnson, s. Aholiab and Eliza (Peck) Johnson.
b. Dec. 2, 1828.

2 ch. *Louise Bowditch*, b. May 26, 1874. *Warren Bowditch*, b. March 23, 1876.

22.

EDWIN B. BOWDITCH, s. Jonas B. and Esther (Alley) Bowditch.
b. Nov. 2, 1826. m. Oct. 2, 1849.

Frances S. King, da. Henry F. and Mary E. (Viall) King.
b. April 26, 1825. d. Dec. 17, 1891.

5 ch. *Henry F.*, b. Sep. 23, 1850, d. Feb. 12, 1855.
Edwin E., b. July 12, 1854, d. Jan. 1, 1855.
Henrietta F., b. Jan. 22, 1856; m. July 29, 1880, *Rev. Frederick S. Root. No issue.
37. *Sarah E.*, b. Nov. 25, 1857; m. Nov. 25, 1880, Frank H. Gaylord.
38. *Margaret E.*, b. Sep. 24, 1859; m. Aug. 19, 1885, Arthur B. Woodford.

*s. of La Fayette and Elizabeth (Benham) Root, b. May 7, 1853.

23.

ESTHER ALLEY BOWDITCH, da. Jonas B. and Esther (Alley) Bowditch.
b. Feb. 10, 1834. m. Aug. 1854. d. Oct. 4, 1861.

Edward Ely, s. Elisha and Eloise (Curtiss) Ely.
b. March 2, 1830. d. Dec. 21, 1891.

1 ch. **39.** *Emma Ely*, b. Oct. 1855; m. Sep. 18, 1877, George Quinan.

24.

HOWARD BOWDITCH CLARK, adopted s. Daniel and Sarah ( ) Clark.
b. April 24, 1856. m. July 15, 1876.

Louisa F. King, da. Lewis and Madaline (Karchur) King.
b. in 1859.

7 ch. *Ella Lora*, b. Sep. 7, 1877; m. Winfield C. Rackett.
Mabel Bowditch, b. Oct. 7, 1880, d. April 23, 1894.
William Lewis, b. Dec. 10, 1883. *Maud Alice*, b. March 16, 1886.
Frank, b. Sep. 27, 1889, d. Dec. 1889. *Lila May*, b. July 15, 1891.
Bryant Elwood, b. March 4, 1895.

25.

WILLIAM JOSEPH BOWDITCH, s. William S. and Lydia J. (Smith) Bowditch.
b. Nov. 11, 1858. m. Nov. 15, 1883.

Florie Burnside Simmons, da. George C. and Caroline L. (Burke) Simmons.
b. April 26, 1861.

1 ch. *Mabel Irene*, b. March 1, 1886.

26.

NELLIE ABBY BOWDITCH, da. William S. and Lydia J. (Smith) Bowditch.
b. June 18, 1860. m. Oct. 18, 1893.

Edward H. Grafton, s. Edward H. and Jane E. (Russell) Grafton.
b. June 30, 1860.

2 ch. *Lydia Elizabeth*, b. Jan. 10, 1895. *Marion Bowditch*, b. Jan. 23, 1898.

27.

FREDERICK KLEBER BOWDITCH, s. Joseph H. and Margaret J. (Havens) Bowditch.
b. Nov. 10, 1863. m. April 7, 1887,

Laura Belle Baldwin, da. John and Mary J. (Viercant) Baldwin.
b. Sep. 24, 1866.

3 ch. *Clifford Baldwin*, b. Oct. 14, 1888. *Arthur Willis*, b. Dec. 3, 1892.
John Viercant, b. Oct. 31, 1897.

28.

EDWIN ANSON BOWDITCH, s. Joseph H. and Margaret J. (Havens) Bowditch.
b. Feb. 28, 1869. m. 1890.

Christena Elder Davidson, da. John H. and Christena (Gibson) Davidson.
b. Oct. 12, 1869.

1 ch. *Frank Raymond*, b. Nov. 19, 1890.

29.

HARRIET BRAINERD MITCHELL, da. Edward and Mary (Brainerd) Mitchell.
b. Oct. 11, 1835. m. Feb. 3, 1864.

Clark King Royce, s. Ira and Lucy A. (King) Royce.
b. Jan. 13, 1836. d. Oct. 1897.

3 ch.   *Frank Howell*, b. Dec. 24, 1864, d. Dec. 18, 1893.   *Robert Mitchell*, b. Aug. 22, 1871.
         Mary Brainerd, b. Feb. 6, 1874, d. April 13, 1897.

30.

JAMES L. MITCHELL, s. Edward and Mary (Brainerd) Mitchell.
    b. May 17, 1841.   m. May 14, 1874.
    Margaret L. Rendell, da. John and Caroline M. (Smith) Rendell.
        b. Sep. 17, 1844.
2 ch.   *Harry Brainerd*, b. June 14, 1878.   *Marguerite*, b. March 7, 1882.

31.

LUCY MITCHELL, da. Edward and Mary (Brainerd) Mitchell.
    b. July 12, 1843.   m. March, 1877.
    Josiah H. Post, s. George O. and Julia (Howell) Post.
        b. Dec. 10, 1844.
1 ch.   *Lucy Mitchell*, b. Jan. 31, 1883.

32.

JOHN HOWELL MITCHELL, s. Edward and Mary (Brainerd) Mitchell.
    b. Oct. 5, 1845.   m. March 16, 1874.   d. June 24, 1898.
    Annie McPherson, da. Alexander and Catherine W. (Devoe) McPherson.
        b. March 4, 184-.
1 ch.   *Edward McPherson*, b. March 30, 1876, d. Aug. 5, 1876.

33.

FANNY MULFORD, da. Benjamin K. and Sarah D. (Bowditch) Mulford.
    b. Aug. 1, 1848.   m. Nov. 6, 1872.
    Dwight Beebe, s. Joseph and Nancy (Hughes) Beebe.
        b. Feb. 10, 1845.
2 ch.   *Edwin Mulford*, b. Feb. 22, 1878.   *Joseph Claire*, b. Feb. 22, 1883.

34.

ADELAIDE MULFORD, da. Benjamin K. and Sarah D. (Bowditch) Mulford.
    b. Nov. 19, 1851.   m. Oct. 27, 1874.
    Edward Latham, s. Daniel T. and Lydia (Webb) Latham.
        b. May 23, 1847.
3 ch.   *Maud Mulford*, b. Feb. 6, 1876.   *Fanny Lucilla*, b. April 29, 1878.
         Daniel Terry, b. Oct. 16, 1885.

35.

JOHN LAY BOWDITCH. s. John B. and Mary J. (Case) Bowditch.
    b. March 12, 1854.   m. 1st, Jan. 30, 1875.   m. 2d, Dec. 25, 1883.
    1st, Maria Louisa Payne, da. Elias W. and Louise (Havens) Payne.
        b. Sep. 3, 1853.   d. Aug. 7, 1875.
    2d, Ella L. Smith, da. Oliver and Adelaide V. (Stevenson) Smith.
        b. Jan. 13, 1861.
6 ch.   *Sybil H.*, b. Oct. 28, 1884.   *Catherine C.*, b. Jan. 21, 1887.
         John B., b. Oct. 10, 1889.   *Henry*, b. March 12, 1891, d. March 14, 1891.
         Edith Byron, b. Aug. 9, 1895.   *Belle B.*, b. Nov. 18, 1896.

36.

EDITH BELLE BOWDITCH, da. John B. and Mary J. (Case) Bowditch.
    d. Feb. 8, 1857.   m. Dec. 25, 1876.
    Siddell E. Fish, s. George H. and Ann (Russell) Fish.
        b. April 3, 1846.
4 ch.   *Edith B.*, b. Sep. 17, 1880, d. Nov. 8, 1890.   *Mary H.*, b. Sep. 10, 1882.
         Russell S., b. July 3, 1885.   *George H.*, b. Nov. 22, 1886, d. Nov. 7, 1893.

37.

SARAH E. BOWDITCH, da. Edwin B. and Frances S. (King) Bowditch.
    b. Nov. 25, 1857.   m. Nov. 25, 1880.
    Frank H. Gaylord, s. Ebenezer H. and Harriet J. (Phelps) Gaylord.
        b. Nov. 13, 1854.
2 ch.   *Edwin Blair Bowditch*, b. Oct. 29, 1883.

38.

MARGARET E. BOWDITCH, da. Edwin B. and Frances S. (King) Bowditch.
    b. Sep. 24, 1859.   m. Aug. 19, 1885.
    Arthur B. Woodford, s. John and Laura (Burnham) Woodford.
        b. Oct. 7, 1861.
2 ch.   *Frances Bowditch*, b. March 21, 1897.   *Burnham Bowditch*, b. March 19, 1898.

39.

EMMA ELY, da. Edward and Esther A. (Bowditch) Ely.
> b. Oct.   1855.   m. Sep. 18, 1877.

George Quinan, s. Henry E. and Mary (Stephenson) Quinan.
> b. March 12, 1846.

2 ch.   *George Ely*, b. Oct. 26, 1878.   *Arthur Stanley*, b. Aug. 29, 1881, d. Sep. 28, 1890.

SAMUEL HUDSON.

ANCESTORS.

JONATHAN HUDSON,
> b. in England, May 8, 1658.   m. June 17, 1686.   d. Apr. 5, 1729.

Sarah
> b.   d.

9 ch.   *Sarah*, b. Mar. 27, 1687 ; m.   Abraham Parker.
Deborah, b. Oct. 27, 1688; m.   Parker.
*Jonathan, b. Jan. 6, 1690; m. May 30, 1728, Mary Jennings.
Hannah, b. Apr. 6, 1693.
Richard, b.   { m. 1st, June 8, 1723, °Hannah Booth.
                       { m. 2d, Mar. 1746, Caturah Goldsmith.
Asenath, b.   m.   Spencer.
‖ *Mary*, b.   m. Feb. 22, 1727, John L'Hommedieu.
1. *Samuel*, b.   m   Grissel L'Hommedieu.
Joseph, b.   d. 1720-21.

(*) d. in Albany, 1745.   (°) d. Nov. 18, 1734.   (‖) Aug. 11, 1727.

1.

SAMUEL HUDSON, s. Jonathan and Sarah (   ) Hudson.
> b.   m.   d. Oct. 12, 1781.

Grissel L'Hommedieu, da. Benjamin and Patience (Sylvester) L'Hommedieu.
> b. Apr. 20, 1701.   d. Oct. 16, 1776.

9 ch.   *Samuel*, b. June, 1727, d. Oct. 7, 1738.
Nathaniel, b.   1729, d. May 26, 1735.
Sarah, b.   d. unm. Feb. 10, 1789.
Elizabeth, b. Dec. 10, 1733, d. Sep. 21, 1738.
2. *Henry*, b.   1735; { m. 1st. Apr. 10, 1766, Jemina Havens.
                               { m. 2d, Oct. 11, 1787, wid. Esther Brown.
3. *Nathaniel*, b. ·   m. Jan. 31, 1760, Margaret Swesey.
4. *Samuel*, b.   m. July 30, 1761, Elizabeth Terry.
5. *Elizabeth*, b. July 31, 1741; m.   Nathan Tuthill.
John, b.   d. Oct. 4, 1755.

2.

HENRY HUDSON, s. Samuel and Grissel (L'Hommedieu) Hudson.
> b. in 1735.   m. 1st, Apr. 10, 1766.   m. 2d, Oct. 11, 1787.   d. Mar. 3, 1815.

1st, Jemima Havens, da. (?) George and Patience (Booth) Havens.
> b.   d. Feb. 3, 1786.

2d, wid. Esther Brown (*nee* Fanning), da. Phineas and Mehitable (Wells) Fanning.
> b.   d. Aug., 1817.

7 ch.   6. *Henry*, b. July 21, 1767; m.   Mary Petty.
Benjamin, b.   d. July 22, 1776.
7. *Jemima*, b.   m. June 11, 1793, Zebulon Woodhull.
8. *Joseph*, b. Oct. 18, 1778; m. Sep. 20, 1801, Mehitable Fanning.
George, b.   d. July 2, 1785.
9. *Mehitable*, b. in 1792; m.   Azariah G. Phelps.
Esther, b.   d. unm.

3.

NATHANIEL HUDSON, s. Samuel and Grissel (L'Hommedieu) Hudson,
> b.   m. Jan. 31, 1760.   d. in 1800.

Margaret Swesey, da.
> b.   d.

5 ch.   10. *Nathaniel*, b. Nov. 17, 1760; m.   Hannah Wells.
*John, b.   m. Mar. 18, 1790, Patience Hallock.
Richard, b.   m.
Sarah, b.   m.   Homan.
°*Linah*, b.   m. after 1800,   Squires.

(*) Had three daughters, Margarite, Miriam and Orpha, who are supposed to have d. unm.
(°) Supposed to have d. s. p.

4.

SAMUEL HUDSON, s. Samuel and Grissel (L'Hommedieu) Hudson.
   b. in 1738-9.   m. July 30, 1761.   d. Mar. 7, 1812.

Elizabeth Terry, da. Daniel and Elizabeth (Tuthill) Terry.
   b. in 1742.   d. Nov. 3, 1820.

8 ch.	*Samuel*, b.	d. Oct. 24, 1776.	*Deborah*, b.	d. Oct. 29, 1776.

   Thomas, b.   d. Nov. 30, 1776.   *Oliver*, b.   d. Mar. 11, 1795.
   11. *Deziah*, b.   1767-8; m.   Richard Brown.
   12. *Samuel*, b. Feb. 10, 1778; m.   Mary Reeve.
   13. *Daniel*, b. Apr. 3, 1779; m. Oct. 4, 1813, Rachel Skillman.
   14. *Charity*, b.   { m. 1st,   Oliver Hudson.
                          { m. 2d,   Silas Reeve.

5.

ELIZABETH HUDSON, da. Samuel and Grissel (L'Hommedieu) Hudson.
   b. July 31, 1741.   m.   d. Apr. 20, 1831.

Nathan Tuthill, s. Nathan and Mary (Tuthill) Tuthill.
   b. Mar. 9, 1742.   d. Jan. 18. 1803.

10 ch.   *John*, b. July 6, 1763.
         Elizabeth, b. Dec. 28, 1764; m.   Youngs, of Cayuga Co.
   15. *Hannah*, b. Feb. 13, 1766; m.   Frederick Hallock.
   16. *Jemima*, b. Apr. 14, 1768; m.   Abraham Luse.
   17. *Nathan*, b. Mar. 2, 1770; m.   Esther Parshall.
   18. *Samuel*, b. Feb. 7, 1772; m.   Karon Howell.
   19. *Sarah*, b. Nov. 9, 1774; m.   Peter Fournier.
   20. *Daniel*, b. Sep. 14, 1776; m.   Keturah Terry.
   21. *Mehitable*, b. Feb. 19, 1778; m. Jan. 24, 1798, John Terry.
   22. *Mary*, b. Dec. 10, 1779; m.   Richard Hallock.

6.

HENRY HUDSON, s. Henry and Jemima (Havens) Hudson.
   b. July 21, 1767.   m.   d. Sep. 17, 1851.

Mary Petty, da.
   b. in 1770.   d. Feb. 24, 1832.

9 ch. **23.** *Henry*, b. May 1, 1791; m. Julianer S. Brewster.
   24. *George*, b. Feb. 3. 1793; m.   Patience Wells.
   25. *Albertus*, b.   1796; m.   Clarissa Woodhull.
         Susan, b. Jan.   1798, d. Feb. 4, 1798.
         Jemima, b.   1800; m.   Caleb Raynor, no issue.
   26. *Charles*, b. Oct. 20, 1802; m.   Hannah Woodhull.
   27. *Eliza*, b. Apr. 6, 1804;   { m. 1st,   Randall.
                                       { m. 2d,   John Tyler.
   28. *Benjamin F.*, b. May 28, 1806; m. Jan. 24, 18—, Elizabeth Wells.
   29. *Mary*, b. Jan. 12, 1810; m. Nov. 10, 1829, Ezra Beach.

7.

JEMIMA HUDSON, da. Henry and Jemima (Havens) Hudson.
   b.   m. June 11, 1793.   d.

Zebulon Woodhull, s. Zebulon and   (   ) Woodhull.
   b.   d.

5 ch. **30.** *Hudson*, b. July 6, 1794; m. July 31, 1823, Ann Miller.
   Joseph, b.   d. unm.   *Fannie*, b.   d. unm.
   31. *Claudius*, b. July 16, 1800; m. Feb. 22, 1827, Sophia Miller.
   Roxanna, b.   m.   Whimster.

8.

JOSEPH HUDSON, s. Henry and Jemima (Havens) Hudson.
   b. Oct. 18, 1778.   m. Sep. 20, 1800.   d. Mar. 5, 1854.

Mehitable Fanning, da. Nathaniel and Anna (Wells) Fanning.
   b. June 3, 1782.   d. Feb. 6, 1868.

11 ch. **32.** *Nerva Newton*, b. Sep. 25, 1801; m.   Mary Gulliver.
   33. *Phineas*, b. Aug. 20, 1803; m. Mar. 30, 1826, Hannah R. Brown.
   34. *Caroline*, b. Apr. 23, 1805; m. Jan. 26, 1832, Thomas P. Young.
   ***Jemima H.*, b. Oct. 4, 1807; m. Oct. 4, 1855, °Thomas J. Nevins; no issue.
   35. *Joseph B.*, b. Apr. 22, 1810;   { m. 1st, Oct. 19, 1836, Maria L. Griffing.
                                           { m. 2d.   1846, Mary A. Havens.
   36. *Daniel*, b. June 3, 1812; m. Mar. 13, 1855, Mary C. Griffing.
   37. *Anna Wells*, b. Mar. 15, 1815;   { m. 1st, Nov. 27, 1838, William H. Cook.
                                             { 2d,   Thomas P. Young.
   38. *Matthew H.*, b. Sep. 22, 1818; m. Apr. 30, 1846, Esther P. Hallock.
   39. *Nathaniel*, b. May 11, 1821;   { m. 1st, July 27, 1847, Cordelia Sammis.
                                           { m. 2d, Oct. 1862, Lydia A. Jones.
   Mehitable, b. Oct. 15, 1822.
   †*George*, b. Mar. 13, 1824; m. Dec. 22, 1853, !wid. Ada M. Elliott; no issue.

(*) d. Jan. 11, 1891.   (°) b. June 5, 1795, d. Jan. 14, 1862.   (†) d. Apr. 12, 1898.   (!) d. May 17, 1897.

9.

MEHITABLE HUDSON, da. Henry and Jemima (Havens) Hudson.
 b. in 1792. m.   d. Oct. 13, 1847.
Azariah Gaylor Phelps, s. Azariah and Azuba (Warner) Phelps.
 b. Nov. 25. 1786. d. Jan. 12, 1843.
7 ch. **40.** *Catherine M.*, b. Mar. 7, 1816; m. Nov. 30. 1843, James M. Griswold.
  Alfred, b. June 19, 1818, d. unm. Dec. 19, 1869.
  Henry H., b. Mar. 21, 1820, d. in infancy.
  41. *Esther F.*, b. Nov. 22, 1822; m. Nov. 30, 1843. Virgil H. Griswold.
  42. *Henry H.*. b. June 22. 1824; m. Ellen J.
  43. *Azariah G.*, b. June 22, 1826; m. Nov. 25, 1868, Charlotte E. Warriner.
  Samuel O., b. Nov. 14, 1827, d. unm. May 6. 1871.

10.

NATHANIEL HUDSON, s. Nathaniel and Margaret (Swesey) Hudson.
 b. Nov. 17, 1760. m.   d.
Hannah Wells, da. John and Mary (Wells) Wells.
 b. Nov. 11, 1764.   d.
10 ch. **44.** *Hannah*, b. Apr. 25, 1787; { m. 1st, Lewis Parshall.
           { m. 2d,   Still.
  Polly, b. Dec. 2. 1788; m. Carlon. *Sally*, b. Dec. 14, 1790, d. unm. July 28, 1875.
  Nathaniel, b. Mar. 19, 1793, d. unm. Feb. 21, 1874.
  Cleo, b. Oct. 17, 1795, m. Andrew Still.
  *Daniel, b. Dec. 24, 1797; m. Fanny Mills.
  45. *Horace*, b. Apr. 6, 1800; m. Oct. 22, 1823, Eliza Davis.
  Temperance, b. Oct. 24, 1802, d. unm. Apr. 19, 1885.
  46. *Eliza*, b. Dec. 30, 1805; m. Nov. 1843, Henry Carter.
  47. *Isaac*, b. Apr. 6, 1808; m. Sep. 1828, Sally Roe.
(*) had four das., Margarite, Anna, Emma and Prudence, who m. a Mr. Arthur.

11.

DEZIAH HUDSON, da. Samuel and Elizabeth (Terry) Hudson.
 b. in 1767-8. m.   d. Feb. 21, 1854.
Richard Brown, s.
 b.   d.
5 ch. **48.** *Richard*, b. Feb. 1786; m. Elizabeth Howell.
  49. *John*, b.   1788; m. Eunice Reeve.
  Elizabeth, b. d. unm. *Charity*, b. 1804; d. unm. Feb. 22, 1869.
  Van Rensselaer, b. 1807, d. unm. March 4, 1871.

12.

SAMUEL HUDSON, s. Samuel and Elizabeth (Terry) Hudson.
 b. Feb. 10, 1778. m. d. Aug. 5, 1833.
Mary Reeve. da.
 b. June 1779.   d.
6 ch. *Samuel*, b. Feb. 28, 1805.
  50. *Joel*, b. Apr. 8, 1808; m. Martha S. Glover.
  51. *David*, b. Mar. 4, 1811; { m. 1st Charry Davis.
           { m. 2d Mary C. Hawkins.
  Charity, b. Nov. 18, 1815; m. Fowler.
  Daniel, b. June 21, 1817; m. Jane Tyler.
  Sylvanus, b. Nov. 23, 1819; m. Mary Edwards.

13.

DANIEL HUDSON, s. Samuel and Elizabeth (Terry) Hudson.
 b. Apr. 3, 1779. m. Oct. 4, 1813. d. Aug. 12, 1875.
Rachel Skillman, da. Thomas and Jerusha (Rogers) Skillman.
 b. Jan. 3, 1792.   d. May 21, 1876.
13 ch. **52.** *Charity W.*, b. July 1, 1814; m. July 29, 1838, Joseph La Rose.
  Elizabeth, b. Jan. 30, 1816, d. May 20, 1816.
  53. *Samuel*, b. July 1, 1817; m. Oct. 13, 1837, Angeline Downs.
  Elizabeth, b. Jan. 20, 1819; m. Jan. 24, 1837, Bethuel E. Hallock.
  Thomas S., b. Nov. 11, 1820, d. Oct. 1, 1837.
  54. *Daniel*, b. July 20, 1822; m. Dec. 16, 1845, Ann M. Wells.
  55. *Jerusha R.*, b. Feb. 24, 1824; m. June 14, 1838, Wilkinson W. W. Wells
  Sarah S., b. Oct. 30, 1825, d. April 5, 1828.
  Else Ann, b. July 25, 1827, d. April 23, 1828.
  56. *Desire Ann*, b. Jan. 20, 1829; m. Nov. 4, 1850, Benjamin T. Griffin.
  57. *Maria S.*, b. Aug. 23, 1830; m. Dec. 5, 1849, Elisha Wells.
  Oliver F., b. Apr. 12, 1832, d. Oct. 25, 1849.
  58. *Rachel J.*, b. Apr. 7, 1835; m. Nov. 7, 1855, Albert B. Terry.

14.

CHARITY HUDSON, da. Samuel and Elizabeth (Terry) Hudson.
 b. m. 1st m. 2nd d.
1st, Oliver Hudson, of Wading River, Long Island.
 b.   d.
2nd, Silas Reeve, of Moriches, Long Island.
 b.   d.

7 ch. **59.** *Fanny*, b.   m.   Simons.
      Tersey, b.   d. unm.
      Catherine, b.   m.   William Van Dyke; no issue.
   60. *Sarah*, b.   m.   Collins Holcom.
   61. *Frederick*, b.   m. Aug. 19, 1826, Mehitable Penny.
      Terry, b.   d. young.
      *Susan, b.   m.   Nicholas Downs.
(*) had one ch., Benjamin; d. in youth.

15.

HANNAH TUTHILL, da. Nathan and Elizabeth (Hudson) Tuthill.
    b. Feb. 13, 1766. m.   d.

Frederick Hallock, s.
    b.   d.

10 ch. **62.** *Hannah*, b.   m.   Lewis Mills.
   63. *James*, b. Jan. 15, 1788; m.   Rhoda Hallock.
   64. *Frederick*, b. Dec. 20, 1790; m.   Nancy Bishop.
   65. *Amelia*, b. Dec. 20, 1796; m. Aug. 12, 1814, Rev. William Benjamin.
   66. *Anna*, b.   m.   Oliver or Zophar Cooper.
   67. *Benjamin*, b.   m. { 1st, Sarah Hobby. 2d, Betsey ——. 3d, wid. Betsey Frankfort.
      Harvey, b.   d. unm.
   68. *Peter*, b.   m.   Catherine Roe.
   69. *Eliza*, b.   m.   Halsey Stevens.
   70. *Sarah*, b.   m. { 1st, Joseph Wood. 2d, Daniel Haff.

16.

JEMIMA TUTHILL, da. Nathan and Elizabeth (Hudson) Tuthill.
    b. April 14, 1768; m.   d. Jan. 20, 1850.

Abraham Luce, s. Eleazer and Prudence (Youngs) Luce.
    b. Oct. 176-, d. March 15, 1848.

3 ch. **71.** *John T.*, b. Nov. 7, 1785; m. { 1st, Rachel Terry. 2d, Mary Wells.
   72. *Eleanor*, b. Nov. 25, 1786; m.   Merritt Howell.
   73. *Abraham*, b.   1790; m. { 1st, Nov. 19, 1812, Abigail Howell. 2d, wid. Elizabeth R. Noyce.

17.

NATHAN TUTHILL, s. Nathan and Elizabeth (Hudson) Tuthill.
    b. Mar. 2, 1770; m.   d.

*Esther Parshall, da. David and Elizabeth (Sweezy) Parshall.
    b.   d.

7 ch.   *Nathan*, b.
   74. *Elizabeth*, b. Oct. 1792; m.   David Benjamin.
      Caleb Halsey, b.
      Roxanna, b.   m.   Youngs.
      Hannah, b.   m.   Clark.
      Harriet, b.
      Laura O., b.
(*) m. a 2d time, Daniel Terry and had children.

18.

SAMUEL TUTHILL, s. Nathan and Elizabeth (Hudson) Tuthill.
    b. Feb. 7, 1772. m.   d.

Karen Howell, da.
    b.   d.

5 ch. *John.*   *Hudson.*   *Electa.*   *Caroline.*   *Ann.*

19.

SARAH TUTHILL, da. Nathan and Elizabeth (Hudson) Tuthill.
    b. Nov. 9, 1774. m. Sep. 17, 1794. d.

Peter Fournier, s. Francis and Esther (Clark) Fournier.
    b.   d.

7 ch. *Sophia*, b.   m.   Lewis Scott. *Hiram*, b.   1800, d. unm.
  75. *Peter*, b. Dec. 8, 1803; m. May 10, 1828, Maria Bishop.
    John, b.   d. unm.   *Franklin*, b.
    Eliza, b.   d. unm.   *Maxie*, b.   m.   William H. Harris.

20.

DANIEL TUTHILL, s. Nathan and Elizabeth (Hudson) Tuthill.
    b. Sep. 14, 1776. m.   d. June 28, 1827.

Keturah Terry, da. Daniel and Mary (   ) Terry.
    b.   1778.   d. Sep. 14, 1861.

6 ch. **76.** *Daniel M.*, b. Dec. 29, 1798; m   Maria Downs.
77. *Jehiel*, b. June 5, 1802; m. Oct. 14. 1826, Johannah Hallock.
78. *Mary.* b. Apr. 5, 1807; m.   Moses Reeve.
79. *Mehitable*, b. June 11, 1809; m. Sep. 21, 1826, Nathan Corwin.
80. *Elizabeth*, b. Dec. 31, 1811; m. May 2, 1833, Christopher N. Downs.
81. *Amanda*, b. Apr. 3, 1818; m.   1837. Joseph F. Hallock.

21.

MEHITABLE TUTHILL, da. Nathan and Elizabeth (Hudson) Tuthill.
     b. Feb. 19, 1778.   m. Jan. 24, 1798, as his 2d wife.   d. Mar. 3, 1872.

John Terry, s. John C. and Abigail M. (King) Terry.
     b. Mar. 29. 1771.   d. Apr. 28, 1856.
6 ch. **82.** *John*, b. in 1798; m. June 15, 1820, Maria T. Tice.
83. *Van Rennsslaer*, b. Mar. 5, 1801; m. Sep. 29, 1824, Elizabeth W. Moffat.
84. *Puah*, b. June 21, 1807; m.   1825, Jedidiah Conklin.
85. *Lewis H.*,   } b. Jan. 2, 1810;   m. Jan. 14. 1835, Harriet Fanning.
   *Benjamin C.   }   m.   Adaline Smith.
   °*William F.*, b. Sep. 15, 1812; m.   Maria Sweezey.

(*) Had 5 ch., James, Samuel, Catherine, Lucy, ———.   (°) Had 3 ch., Sarah and 2 who d. young.

22.

MARY TUTHILL, da. Nathan and Elizabeth (Hudson) Tuthill.
     b. Dec. 10, 1779.   m.   d.

Richard Hallock, s.
     b.   d.
3 ch. **86.** *Nathan T.*, b.   m. Jan. 4, 1825, Mary Dunster.
87. *Elizabeth A.*, b. July 17, 1806; m. Feb. 12, 1828, Benjamin G. Hallock.
Fanny, b.   d. young.

23.

HENRY HUDSON, s. Henry and Mary (Petty) Hudson.
     b. May 1, 1791.   m.   d. May 7, 1877.

Julianer S. Brewster, da.
     b. Aug. 12, 1803.   d. July 10, 1875.
7 ch.   *Hester Ann*, b. Dec. 13, 1824. d. unm. Aug. 12, 1856.
    Julia Augusta, b. Oct. 14, 1830, d. Mar. 28, 1832.
    Malissa B., b. Mar. 20, 1832, d. unm. June 16. 1854.
    Mary M., b. Oct. 22, 1835, d. unm. July 30. 1862.
88. *John Henry*, b. Jan. 11, 1838; m. Jan. 22, 1873, Emeline H. Raynor.
    Brewster H., b. Jan. 11, 1840, d. unm. Oct. 18, 1862.
    Sarah S., b. Nov. 14, 1844, d. unm. Jan. 23, 1873.

24.

GEORGE HUDSON, s. Henry and Mary (Petty) Hudson.
     b. Feb. 3, 1793.   m.   d. Mar. 3, 1870.

Patience Wells, da. Rev. David and Huldah (Tuthill) Wells.
     b. Apr. 13, 1798.   d. Jan. 12, 1846.
1 ch.   **Georgiana*, b. Aug. 1, 1822; m.   Elias H. Luce.
(*) See No. 167.

25.

ALBERTUS HUDSON, s. Henry and Mary (Petty) Hudson.
     b. 1796.   m.   d. Oct. 22, 1826.

Clarissa Woodhull, da. Benjamin and Ruth (   ) Woodhull.
     b. May   1797.   d. Nov. 30, 1862.
1 ch.   *Lorenzo W.*, b. Nov. 24, 1823; m.   Mary Hutchingson; no issue.

26.

CHARLES HUDSON, s. Henry and Mary (Petty) Hudson.
     b, Oct. 20, 1802.   m.   d. May 22, 1857.

Hannah Woodhull, da. Terry and Nancy (Emmons) Woodhull.
     b. Sep.   1818.   d. Aug. 2, 1878,
8 ch.   *Woodhull*, b.   d. unm.
    Charles W., b. July 23, 1837, d. unm. Oct. 27, 1858.
    Mary Ellen, b. Aug. 26, 1839, d. unm. Nov. 1, 1858.
    Hannah E., b. Sep. 20, 1842, d. Dec. 11, 1859.
    Benjamin F., b.   *Charles V.*, b.
89. *Ellsworth*, b. Apr. 15, 1850; m. Dec. 6, 1877, Emma R. Gallagher.
    Orphelia, b. Mar. 29, 1853, d. Nov. 15, 1868.

27.

ELIZA HUDSON, da. Henry and Mary (Petty) Hudson.
     b. Apr. 6, 1804.   m. 1st,   m. 2d, Jan. 1, 1827.   d. Aug. 5, 1877.

1st,   Randall, s. John and   (Worth) Randall.
     b.   d.

2d, John Tyler, s. Nathaniel and Nancy (Stockwell) Tyler.
     b. Oct. 1, 1806.   d. June 4, 1870.

6 ch. **90.** *Mary H.*, b. June 30, 1829; { m. 1st, Jan. 20, 1847, Moses H. Ackerly.
{ m. 2d, Jan. 27, 1869, Richard T. Osborn.
91. *Charles H.*, b. Oct. 21. 1831; m. July 4, 1880. Jerusha Hancock.
92. *Elizabeth S.*, b. Oct. 6, 1833; m. Dec. 1, 1849. Lester Mills.
93. *Joseph B.*, {
Josephine, { b. Sep. 14. 1837; { m. Oct. 21, 1868, Louise A. Thorne.
{ d. Jan. 9, 1839.
Edwin, b.

28.

BENJAMIN FRANKLIN HUDSON, s. Henry and Mary (Petty) Hudson.
b. May 28, 1806.   m. Jan. 24, 18—.   d. Mar. 3. 1864.

Elizabeth Wells, da. Rev. David and Huldah (Tuthill) Wells.
b. Apr. 13, 1812.   d. July 1, 1891.

5 ch. **94.** *Helen*, b. Dec. 17. 1833; m. Sep. 15, 1852, Ellsworth Tuthill.
George, b. July 16, 1836; m. Nov. 27. 1857. °Elizabeth Miller; no issue.
95. *Georgiana*, b. May 8, 1839; m. Nov. 26, 1857, William H. Skidmore.
An infant da..   d. ae., 3 months.
Arabella, b. Mar. 5, 1849; m. Oct. 20. 18—, David T. Young.

(*) d. Feb. 1896.   (°) da. Sylvester and Emily (Tuthill) Miller, b. Dec. 31. 1832.

29.

MARX HUDSON, da. Henry and Mary (Petty) Hudson.
b. Jan. 12, 1810.   m. Nov. 10, 1829.   d. Oct. 3, 1889.

Ezra Beach, of Northford, Conn.
b. Apr. 16, 1806.   d. Nov. 29, 1865.

5 ch. **96.** *Albertus*, b.   1830; m. Sep. 6, 1853, Margaret E. Whitney.
Alvira, b. Apr. 1, 1833. d. unm., Sep. 29. 1863.
97. *Mary*, b. Apr. 19, 1835; m.   Samuel Budd.
Ezra, b. Nov. 9, 1837, d. unm., Oct. 2, 1860.
98. *Ophelia R.*, b. Aug. 2, 1842; m. Aug. 12, 1869, Dr. Zebulon S. Webb.

30.

HUDSON WOODHULL, s. Zebulon and Jemima (Hudson) Woodhull.
b. July 6, 1794.   m. July 31, 1823.   d. Sep. 28, 1824.

Ann Miller, da. Zophar and Betsey (Davis) Miller.
b. May 15, 1803.   d. June 1, 1892.

1 ch. **99.** *Annie H.*, b. Aug. 31, 1824; m. Jan. 7, 1850, Rev. Andrew F. Dickson.

31.

CLAUDIUS WOODHULL, s. Zebulon and Jemima (Hudson) Woodhull.
b. July 16, 1800.   m. Feb. 22, 1827.   d. May 26, 1881.

Sophia Miller, da. Zophar and Betsey (Davis) Miller.
b. Mar. 23, 1808.   d. May 23, 1870.

7 ch. **100.** *Maria M.*, b. Mar. 3, 1831; m. Aug. 31, 1852, William C. J. Hall.
101. *Joseph H.*, b. Oct. 2, 1834; m. Jan. 19, 1859, Hannah Aldrich.
102. *Zophar M.*, b. Sep. 1, 1837; m Dec. 25, 1867, Cornelia A. Brown.
103. *Sylvester H.*, b. Jan. 6, 1841; m. { 1st, Nov. 19, 1870, Mary C. Darling.
{ 2d, June 19, 1873, Emma Marshall.
104. *Emily T.*, b. June 4, 1843; m. Jan. 10, 1866, Leonard R. Aldrich.
105. *Alfred K.*, b. Mar. 20, 1847; m. { 1st, April 27, 1870, Martha Darling.
{ 2d, Jan. 1, 1887, Catherine Durin.
106. *Mitchell H.*, b. Mar. 17, 1849; m.   1876, Fanny Reeve.

32.

NERVA NEWTON HUDSON, s. Joseph and Mehitable (Fanning) Hudson
b. Sep. 25, 1801.   m.   d. Oct. 28, 1865.

Mary Gulliver, da.
b. Feb. 11, 1807.   d. Mar.   1883.

9 ch.   *Anne*, b. June 1, 1828; m.   Thomas Walker.
Joseph, b. Oct. 11, 1829; m.   Gertrude
107. *William*, b. Mar. 19, 1831; m. Nov. 8, 1853, Catherine M. Tuttle.
108. *Jeanette W.*, b. Nov. 4. 1833; m. Dec. 6, 1855, William C. Bunce.
Robert, b. Sep 26, 1834; m.
Henrietta, b.   m.   Jordan.
Mehitable, b.   d. unm.   *Mary*, b.   d. unm.
Sarah, b.   d. unm.

(*) Had one child.

33.

PHINEAS HUDSON, s. Joseph and Mehitable (Fanning) Hudson.
b. Aug. 20, 1803.   m. Mar. 30, 1826.   d. Sep. 11, 1872.

Hannah Rackett Brown, da. Beriah and Hannah (Hallock) Brown
b. Dec. 5, 1804.   d. Feb. 23, 1891.

7 ch.   *Catherine A.*, b. Sep. 5, 1827, d. unm. Apr. 29, 1866.
      ***George B.**, b. Jan. 21, 1830; m. June 1, 1863, Elmira Whitney.
109. **Henry D.**, b. May 21, 1832; m. May 21, 1867, Mary C. Mulford.
      Lewis H., b. Jan. 22, 1835, d. Oct. 17, 1835.
      Phineas, b. Oct. 29, 1836; m. Oct. 12. 1877, Louisa A. Carr; no issue.
      Matthew H., b. Nov. 19, 1839; m. Dec. 22, 1886. Helen Augusta White; no issue.
110. **Hannah A.**, b. Sep. 23, 1842; m. Aug. 1, 1866, Thomas W. Mulford.
(*) d. Nov. 4, 1883. Had 2 ch., Mary B. and George B., both of whom died in infancy.

34.

CAROLINE HUDSON, da. Joseph and Mehitable (Fanning) Hudson.
    b. Apr. 23, 1805.   m. Jan. 26, 1832.   d. Nov. 30, 1865.

*Thomas Perkins Young, s. Thomas and Esther (Perkins) Young.
    b. Sep. 28, 1808.   d. Aug. 8, 1880.

7 ch.   **111.** *Laetitia*, b. Apr. 23, 1833; m. Oct. 31. 1855, George B. Reeve.
    112. *Daniel H.*, b. June 30, 1835; m. { 1st, Mar. 1, 1864, Mary Harries.
                                         { 2d, Mar. 9, 1874, Sophia Benjamin.
       John Perkins, b. Apr. 1, 1837, d. unm. Oct. 8, 1856.
    113. *Thomas*, b. Jan. 10, 1840; m. Dec. 7. 1870, Martha L. Williams.
       Lucius Comstock, b. Nov. 19. 1841.   *Joseph Fanning*, b.   *George*, b.   d.
(*) m. a second time. See No. 37.

35.

JOSEPH BELLAMY HUDSON, s. Joseph and Mehitable (Fanning) Hudson.
    b. Apr. 22, 1810.   m. 1st, Oct. 19, 1836.   2d,   1846.   d. Mar. 22, 1859.

1st, Maria Louisa Griffing, da. Moses and Asenath (Conkling) Griffing.
    b. Apr. 7, 1819.   d. Aug. 20, 1841.

2d, Mary Ann Havens, da. Obadiah and Nancy (Robinson) Havens.
    b. Dec. 10, 1811.   d. Feb.   1881.

8 ch. **114.** *Maria Jane*, b. Mar. 30, 1838; m. Oct. 26, 1861, Dr. William Stimson.
      Joseph H., b. Jan. 9, 1840, d. unm. May 7, 1862.
    115. *Benjamin C.*, b. Aug. 10, 1841; m. May 29, 1867, Sarah A. Cartwright.
    116. *Adriana L.*, b. Nov. 25, 1847; m. June 21, 1871, Nathaniel L. Pope.
      Adelaide A., b. Aug. 7, 1850.
    117. *Florence D.*, b. Feb. 20, 1852; m. Oct. 24, 1877, George Miller.
      Clarence H., b. Nov. 12, 1856, d. unm. Feb. 19, 1898.   *George C.*, b. Aug. 8, 1858.

36.

DANIEL HUDSON, s. Joseph and Mehitable (Fanning) Hudson.
    b. June 3, 1812.   m. Mar. 13, 1855.

Mary Clarissa Griffing, da. Charles and Maria (Havens) Griffing.
    b. Apr. 4, 1833.

2 ch. **118.** *Charles G.*, b. June 13, 1856; m.   1884, Pauline A. Schaible.
      Caroline Fanning, b. Dec. 17, 1860, d. Oct. 6, 1861.

37.

ANNA WELLS HUDSON, da. Joseph and Mehitable (Fanning) Hudson.
    b. Mar. 15, 1815.   m. 1st, Nov. 27, 1838.   2d,   d. June 21, 1882.

William H. Cook, s.
    b. in 1796.   d. Dec. 7, 1863.

Thomas P. Young, s. Thomas and Esther (Perkins) Young.
    b. Sep. 28, 1808.   d. Aug. 8, 1880.

5 ch.   *Anna Maria*, b. Apr. 26, 1840, d. unm. March   1886.
    119. *William H.*, b. March 29, 1842; m. June 20, 1870, Emily A. Wells.
      George Hudson, b. Aug. 19, 1844, d. Nov. 19, 1844.
    120. *Lafayette H.*, b. Mar. 25, 1849; m. Jan. 25, 1875, Mary E. Corwin.
    121. *Joseph R.*, b. Dec. 15, 1852; m.   Ida Leek.

38.

DR. MATTHEW HENRY HUDSON, s. Joseph and Mehitable (Fanning) Hudson.
    b. Sep. 22, 1818.   m. Apr. 30, 1846.

Esther Perkins Hallock, da. Ezra and Lydia E. (Young) Hallock.
    b. Dec. 25, 1826.

5 ch. **122.** *John Q. A.*, b. Feb. 9, 1849; m. Dec. 25, 1873, Sarah M. Newville.
    123. *Estella E.*, b. Mar. 26, 1852; m. Sep. 22, 1875, Benjamin F. Reed.
    124. *Henry H.*, b. Mar. 18, 1857; m. Apr. 28, 1886, Cora E. Morford.
    125. *George C.*, b. May 10, 1860; m. Dec. 31, 1892, Abbia M. Burgan.
      Joseph E., b. Mar. 9, 1868.

39.

DR. NATHANIEL HUDSON, s. Joseph and Mehitable (Fanning) Hudson.
    b. May 11, 1820.   m. 1st, July 27, 1847.   2d, Oct.   1862.

1st, Cordelia Sammis, da. Daniel and   (Ketchum) Sammis.
    b. July 14, 1822.   d. May   1857.

2d, Lydia Ann Jones, da.   (Black) Jones.
    b. in 1847.   d. in 1882.

3 ch. **126.** *Joseph N.*, b. Aug. 20, 1852; m. { 1st, Jan. 14, 1874, Susia A. Frakes.
{ 2d, Nov. 8, 1887, Martha A. Reel.
   127. *Ione May*, b. Oct. 21, 1863; m. Sep. 3, 1888, Arthur Philbrick.
    George O. O. H., b. Dec. 23, 1865.

40.

CATHERINE M. PHELPS, da. Azariah G. and Mehitable (Hudson) Phelps.
    b. Mar. 7, 1816.   m. Nov. 30, 1843.   d. Mar. 16, 1875.
James Monroe Griswold, s.
    b. Aug. 17, 1818.   d. May 28, 1852.
3 ch. **128.** *Mary C.*, b. May 18, 1845; m. Mar. 22, 1863, George C. Whiton.
    129. *Sarah M.*, b. Aug. 29, 1846; m. Oct. 14, 1874, Dr. Erastus E. Case.
    130. *James A.*, b. Feb. 18, 1848; m. Jan. 13, 1875, Sarah E. Warner.

41.

ESTHER F. PHELPS, da. Azariah G. and Mehitable (Hudson) Phelps.
    b. Nov. 22, 1822.   m. Nov. 30, 1843.   d. Dec.   1871.
*Virgil Hilton Griswold, s.
    b.   d.
3 ch.   *William B.*, b. Oct. 2, 1846.   *Lucy Griswold*, b. May 2, 1848, d. May 23, 1848.
    °*Ella Gillette*, b. June 8, 1862, d. May 14, 1882.
(*) m. a 2d time, Wid. Fannie A. Murphy of Urbana, Ohio, and had 1 ch., Hilton A., b. Jan.   1888.
(°) She was m. the Dec. previous to her death.

42.

HENRY H. PHELPS, s. Azariah G. and Mehitable (Hudson) Phelps.
    b. June 22, 1824.   m.   d. July 19, 1864.
Ellen J.   da.
    b.   1832.   d. Oct. 23, 1862.
2 ch.   *Gilbert H.*, b. Oct. 31, 1854, d.   1881.   *Alfred C.*, b. May 11, 1860.

43.

AZARIAH G. PHELPS, s. Azariah G. and Mehitable (Hudson) Phelps.
    b. June 22, 1826.   m. Nov. 25, 1868.   d. June 26, 1897.
Charlotte E. Warriner, da. Zebina and Esther (Potter) Warriner.
    b. Nov. 26, 1835.   d. July 16, 1893.
2 ch. **131.** *Mary C.*, b. Dec. 8, 1870; m. Dec. 20, 1892, Dr. George Deacon.
    Lewis Azariah, b. Aug. 11, 1875, d. Oct. 13, 1877.

44.

HANNAH HUDSON, da. Nathaniel and Hannah (Wells) Hudson.
    b. Apr. 25, 1787.   m. 1st,   2d,   d. Jan. 12, 1847.
1st, Lewis Parshall.
    b.   d.
2d, Jonah Still, s.
    b.   d.
6 ch.   *Sydney*, b.   *Adolphus*, b.   *Hudson*, b.   *Polly*, b.   *Charles*, b.   *Josiah*, b.

45.

HORACE HUDSON, s. Nathaniel and Hannah (Wells) Hudson.
    b. Apr. 6, 1800.   m. Oct. 22, 1823.   d. July 20, 1881.
Eliza Davis, da. Samuel and Elizabeth (Robbins) Davis.
    b. July 24, 1806.
3 ch.   *Charles F.*, b. May 31, 1824, d. Aug. 19, 1824.
    *Therina, b. Feb. 15, 1828; m. Nov. 17, 1846, Joseph N. King.
    132. *Elizabeth R.*, b. Aug. 8, 1836; m. June 23, 1857, William H. Tyler.
(*) See Hopkins genealogy, No. 42.

46.

ELIZA HUDSON, da. Nathaniel and Hannah (Wells) Hudson.
    b. Dec. 30, 1805.   m. Nov.   1843.   d. Sep. 18, 1890.
Henry Carter, s. Noah D. and Ruth (Turner) Carter.
    b. Mar. 4, 1803.   d. Dec. 19, 1897.
1 ch. **133.** *Frances T.*, b. Mar. 29, 1846; m. May 25, 1865, Gilbert Peterson.

47.

ISAAC HUDSON, s. Nathaniel and Hannah (Wells) Hudson.
    b. Apr. 6, 1808.   m. Sep.   1828.   d. Dec. 17, 1860.
Sally Roe. da. Stephen and Sally (Smith) Roe.
    b. Apr.   1809.   d. in 1841.
2 ch. **134.** *Charles S.*, b. Oct. 15, 1829; m. Oct. 3, 1855, Martha Terry.
    Frances, b. Dec.   1834; m. in 1879, Joseph Lockitt; no issue.

48.

JOHN BROWN, s. Richard and Deziah (Hudson) Brown.
b. 1788-9.　m.　d. Feb. 18, 1864.

Eunice Reeve, da. Isaac and Sarah (Cheeseborough) Reeve.
b. Nov. 10, 1788.　d. Dec. 23, 1862.

2 ch.　*Laurins*, b. 1814, d. unm. Oct. 24, 1844.　*Deborah*, b. 1817. d. unm. Aug. 17, 1839.

49.

RICHARD BROWN, s. Richard and Deziah (Hudson) Brown.
b. Feb. 1786.　m.　d. Apr. 17, 1855.

Elizabeth Howell, da. Richard and　　　　(　　　) Howell.
b. Jan. 1787.　d. Aug. 8, 1853.

5 ch.　*Oliver*, b. May 10, 1813, d. Jan. 21, 1889.
　　　Amanda, b.　　m. { 1st, Nov. 8, 1840, William Dicks.
　　　　　　　　　　　　{ 2d, James Crouter.
　　　Charles, b. May　　1819, d. Feb. 25, 1835.
　　　Daniel, b. Feb. 1822, d. Sep. 12, 1840.　*Elizabeth*, b. Oct. 1828. d. Dec. 9, 1835.
(*) Had 2 ch., Charles L., b. Mar. 19, 1842, d. Nov. 1, 1842.　William H., b. Aug. 13, 1843, d. Mar. 26, 1847.

50.

JOEL HUDSON, s. Samuel and Mary (Reeve) Hudson.
b. Apr. 8, 1808.　m.　d. Sep. 17, 1885.

Martha S. Glover, da. Benjamin and Mary (Hulse) Glover.
b. Sep.　1824.　d. Mar. 24, 1890.

2 ch. 135. *Eugene M.*, b. Mar. 19, 1854; m. Jan. 6, 1886, Lelia L. Hulse.
　　　Charles Benjamin, b. Sep. 17, 1863; m.

51.

DAVID HUDSON, s. Samuel and Mary (Reeve) Hudson.
b. Mar. 4, 1811.　m. 1st,　　2d,　　d. June 2, 1854.

1st, Charry Davis, da. Elisha and Julianor (　　　) Davis.
b. Dec. 8, 1808.　d. Aug. 25, 1841.

2d, Mary Catherine Hawkins, da. Joseph and Lucy (　　　) Hawkins.
b. Dec. 1. 1824.　d. Jan. 29, 1896.

3 ch.　*Caleb Mapes*, b. Oct. 7, 1835, d. Mar. 2, 1857.
　．　*Albert Nelson*, b. Aug. 23, 1839.　*Joseph Allen*, b. June 4. 1851.

52.

CHARITY W. HUDSON, da. Daniel and Rachel (Skillman) Hudson.
b. July 1, 1814.　m. July 29, 1838.　d. Jan. 19, 1863.

Joseph La Rose, of Venice, Italy.
b.　　d.

1 ch.　*Sarah*, b.　　m. July 29, 1858, James Wheeler.

53.

SAMUEL HUDSON, s. Daniel and Rachel (Skillman) Hudson.
b. July 1, 1817.　m. Oct. 13, 1837.　d. Dec. 17, 1882.

Angeline Downs, da. Joshua and Matsey (Terry) Downs.
b. Sep. 22, 1816.　d. Nov. 2, 1876.

1 ch. 136. *S. Terry*, b. Nov. 24, 1843; m. Oct. 13. 1864, Mary E. Wells.

54.

DANIEL HUDSON, s. Daniel and Rachel (Skillman) Hudson.
b. July 20, 1822.　m. Dec. 15, 1845.　d. Jan. 23, 1894.

Ann M. Wells, da. Joshua and Deborah (Youngs) Wells.
b. May 10, 1827.　d. Sep. 25, 1860.

5 ch.　*Mary A.*, b. Mar. 28, 1847; m.　　　　　1866, °George W. Aldrich; no issue.
　　　Julia F., b. May 30, 1850.
　　137. *Charles H.*, b. Apr. 3, 1854; m. Nov. 24, 1874, Sarepta E. Sayre.
　　　Daniel W., b. Aug. 9, 1856, d. Oct. 31, 1860.　*John W.*, b. July 31, 1858, d. Mar. 28, 1861.
(*) d. in 1879.　(o) s. of Elisha and Mary (Wells) Aldrich, b. Mar. 10, 1840.

55.

JERUSHA ROGERS HUDSON, da. Daniel and Rachel (Skillman) Hudson.
b. Feb. 24, 1824.　m. June 14. 1838.　d. June 17, 1870.

Wilkinson W. W. Wells, da. Rev. Eurystheus H. and Mary (Corwin) Wells.
b. Dec. 24, 1818.

4 ch.　An infant, b. Jan. 13, 1842, d. Jan. 20, 1842.
　　　Jane Rosaline, b. Aug. 20, 1843; m. Jan. 11, 1865, James E. Bayles.
　　　Bethia Howell, b. Jan. 12, 1848, m. Feb.　　1877, George A. Jennings.
　　　Milnor H., b. June 6, 1856.

56.

DESIRE ANN HUDSON, da. Daniel and Rachel (Skillman) Hudson.
　　b. Jan. 20, 1829.　m. Nov. 4, 1850.　d. Jan. 30, 1879.
　Benjamin T. Griffin, s. James and Elizabeth (Tuthill) Griffin.
　　b. Oct. 16, 1823.
　4 ch.　*Elizabeth*, b. Jan 31, 1852.　*James E.*, b. Apr. 29, 1855; m.　Jagella Terry.
　　　　　Edward. b. 1859, d. 1860.　*Daniel H.*, b. Feb. 1, 1865; m. June 27, 1895, Eleda Ryan.
　(*) Has 3 ch., Eva, Benjamin, Leroy.

57.

MARIA SKILLMAN HUDSON, da. Daniel and Rachel (Skillman) Hudson.
　　b. Aug. 23, 1830.　m. Dec. 5, 1849.
　Elisha Wells, s. Salem and Elsie M. (Terry) Wells.
　　b. June 17, 1830.　d. May 6, 1895.
　11 ch. 138. *Miander*, b. Jan. 9, 1851; m. June 20, 1867, Albert T. Downs.
　　　　139. *Elsie Maria*, b. Nov. 6, 1852; m. Nov. 6, 1869, Addison J. Wells.
　　　　140. *Oliver F.*, b. Oct. 4, 1854; m. Nov. 23, 1875, Henrietta J. Fanning.
　　　　141. *Rachel H.*, b. June 5, 1856; m. Sep. 3, 1872, John T. Downs.
　　　　142. *Lucy K.*, b. Aug. 3, 1858; m. Dec. 6, 1882, Franklin B. Reeve.
　　　　143. *Elisha W.*, b. Aug. 13, 1860; m. Dec. 8, 1881, Emma E. Genther.
　　　　144. *Louisa E.*, b. Sep. 26, 1862; m. Dec. 24, 1881, Louis F. Jennings.
　　　　145. *Etta E.*, b. May 17, 1866; m. May 17, 1887, Frederick B. Conklin.
　　　　146. *De Forrest*, b. Mar. 18, 1868; m. Sep. 11, 1890, Nancy L. Robinson.
　　　　　　　Ida Schenck, b. Apr. 22, 1870.
　　　　147. *Charles S.*, b. Jan. 30, 1872; m. Dec. 10, 1891, Eula C. Hallock.

58.

RACHEL JANE HUDSON, da. Daniel and Rachel (Skillman) Hudson.
　　b. Apr. 7, 1835.　m. Nov. 7, 1855.　d. Apr. 28, 1892.
　Albert B. Terry, s. Walter and　　　(　　　) Terry.
　　b. Mar. 22, 1829.　d. Nov.　1897.
　8 ch.　*Fanny E.*, b. m. Jacob White.　*Almeda V.*, b. m. Nov. 29, 1874. John H. Smith.
　　　　　Rachel S., b. m.　Frederick Turner.　*Edward A.*, b.　*Ira W.*, b.
　　　　　Ida W., b. m. Porter.　*Laura*, b.　*Pervilla J.*, b.　d.

59.

FANNY HUDSON, da. Oliver and Charity (Hudson) Hudson.
　　b.　　　m.
　　　Simons, s.
　　b.
　2 ch.　*Sarah Catherine*, b.　　m.　　Hudson Hewitt.　*William*, b.

60.

SARAH HUDSON, da. Oliver and Charity (Hudson) Hudson.
　　b.　　　m.
　　Collins Holcom, s.
　　b.
　3 ch.　*Sarah*, b.　　*Collins*, b.　　A third.

61.

FREDERICK HUDSON, s. Oliver and Charity (Hudson) Hudson.
　　b.　　m. Aug. 19, 1826.　d.
　Mehitable Penny, of Cutchogue, Long Island.
　　b.　　d.
　5 ch.　*Jerusha*, b.　　1828, d. Mar. 18, 1834.　*Lucy Jane* b. 1829-30, d. Jan. 18, 1832.
　　　　　George, b.　m. Ann　no issue.
　　　　　William, b　d. unm.　**Charity*, b.　m.　Charles Field.
　(*) Had 1 son who d. unm.

62.

HANNAH HALLOCK, da. Frederick and Hannah (Tuthill) Hallock.
　　b.　　　m.
　Lewis Mills, s.
　　b.
　4 ch.　*Algernon*, b.　　m. { 1st,　Anna Hallock.
　　　　　　　　　　　　　　　{ 2d,　Rebecca Brewster.
　　　　　Alfred, b.　m.　Jones.　*Frederick*, b.　d. unm.　*Elizabeth*, b.　d. unm.

63.

JAMES HALLOCK, s. Frederick and Hannah (Tuthill) Hallock.
　　b. Jan. 15, 1788.　m.　　d. Aug. 24, 1868.
　Rhoda Hallock, da. William and Rhoda (Corwin) Hallock.
　　b. Apr. 22, 1797.　d. May 8, 1874.
　5 ch.　*James S. Y.*, b. Mar. 24, 1819.
　　　　　William O., b. Oct. 1, 1820; m.　Jerusha Herrick.
　　　　148. *Selencia F.*, b. Dec. 5, 1823; m. Nov. 29, 1848, William C. Wells.
　　　　　Harvey F., b. Nov. 8, 1826, d. unm. Feb. 6, 1851.
　　　　149. *Avis Rhoda*, b. Dec. 21, 1828; m. Dec. 2, 1853, Eurystheus H. Wells.

64.

FREDERICK HALLOCK, s. Frederick and Hannah (Tuthill) Hallock.
  b. Dec. 20, 1790.   m.   d. Aug.   186-.
Nancy Bishop, da. Nathan and Hulda (Culver) Bishop.
  b.   1794.   d. Aug.   1856.

8 ch. **150.** *Frederick*, b. Feb. 20, 1817; m. Nov. 23, 1859, Elizabeth M. Hallock.
  151. *Nathan B.*, b. Dec. 6, 1818; m.   Hannah A. Goodale.
  152. *Hannah*, b. Feb. 20, 1821; m.   Harvey Rose.
        Harvey, b. Feb. 15, 1823; m. } 1st,   1850, Elizabeth M. Hawkins.
                                        } 2d, Jan. 23, 1884, Wid. Hulda M. Overton.
  153. *Hulda F.*, b. Mar.   1825; m.   Asher Benedict.
        *Fanny, b. May   1827; m,   Sylvanus Squires.
        †John D., b. Jan. 28, 1829; m. Feb. 17. 1857, Sarah E. Aldrich.
        Franklin B., b.   1831; d. unm. April 17, 1863.
(*) has one ch. Sylvanus, who m.   (†) had one ch. William, who d. in infancy.

65.

AMELIA HALLOCK, da. Frederick and Hannah (Tuthill) Hallock.
  b. Dec. 20, 1796.   m Aug. 12, 1814.   d. Mar. 3, 1884.
Rev. William Benjamin, s. Richard and Nancy (Fanning) Benjamin.
  b. July 13, 1790.   d. Oct. 13, 1860.

5 ch. **154.** *William F.*, b. Feb. 24, 1816; m. Oct. 6, 1838, Elizabeth L. Terry.
  155. *Richard H.*, b. Oct. 2, 1820; m. Dec. 4, 1847, Hannah S. Smith.
  156. *James H.*, b. April 4, 1823; m. Dec. 15, 1852, Harriet H. Raynor.
        Frederick H., b. May 16, 1829, d. Aug. 16, 1832.
        Frederick H., b. Nov. 10, 1834, d. unm. Oct. 10, 1857.

66.

ANNA HALLOCK, da. Frederick and Hannah (Tuthill) Hallock.
  b.   m.
Oliver or Zophar Cooper, s. Obadiah and   (   ) Cooper.
  b.

3 ch. **157.** *Eliza Ann*, b.   m. Jan. 24, 1842, Matthew P. Wells.
        Amelia, b.   m.   Moses Sweezey.
        Franklin, b.   m. } 1st,   Huldah Rogers.
                                } 2d,

67.

BENJAMIN F. HALLOCK, s. Frederick and Hannah (Tuthill) Hallock.
  b.   m. 1st.   m. 2d.   m. 3d.   d.
  1st, Sarah A. Hobby, da.
    b.
  2d, Betsey
    b.
  3d, Wid. Betsey Frankfort, (*nee* Bishop)
    b.
2 ch. **158.** *Anna*, b.   m.   David W. Benjamin.
  159. *Theresa*, b. June 13, 1837; m. Dec. 29, 1853, George Syrene Wells.

68.

PETER HALLOCK, s. Frederick and Hannah (Tuthill) Hallock.
  b.   m.
Catherine Roe, da.
  b.

5 ch.   **Mary*, b.   m. Alexander Rogers.   *Maria*, b.   m. Abbott.
        Ann, b. m. Algernon Mills.   *Amelia F.*,   m. Lockitt.
        Catherine, b.   *†Peter R.*, b.   m.
(*) had one daughter.   (†) had one son named Frederick, who died unm.

69.

ELIZA HALLOCK, da. Frederick and Hannah (Tuthill) Hallock.
  b.   m.
Halsey Stevens, s.
  b.

8 ch.   *Frederick H.*, b.   d. unm.   *Caroline*, b.   d. unm.
        William, b.   m.   *Thomas*, b.   m.
        Forest, b.   m. Griffin.   *Hiram*, b.
        Elizabeth, b.   m. Clark.   *Zacheus F.*, b.   m.

70.

SARAH HALLOCK, da. Frederick and Hannah (Tuthill) Hallock.
  b.   m. 1st,   m. 2d,
  1st, Joseph Wood, s.
    b.
  2d, Daniel Haff, s.
    b.

6 ch.   *John*, b.   m. Vail.   *Hannah*, b.   m. Smith.   *Amelia*, b.
        Mary, b.   m. Soper.   *Elizabeth*, b.   m. Wells.   *Daniel*, b.

71.

JOHN T. LUCE, s. Abraham and Jemima (Tuthill) Luce.
       b. Nov. 7, 1785.   m. 1st   m. 2nd   d. Nov. 22, 1852.
   1st, Rachel Terry, da. Daniel and Phebe (Howell) Terry.
       b. July 31, 1788.   d. June 1, 1842.
   2nd, Mary Wells, da. James and Lydia (Terry) Wells.
       b.   1803-4.   d. Apr. 18, 1856.
                                    ⎧ 1st,   Charity W. Hallock.
   7 ch. 160. *George O.*, b. Oct. 18, 1806; m. ⎨ 2nd,   Betsy G. Reeve.
                                    ⎩ 3rd,   Deborah A. Wells.
       161. *John T.*, b. May 28, 1808; m.   Mary B. Tuthill.
       162. *Phebe T.*, b. Jan. 11, 1812; m.   Benjamin Warner.
       163. *Jemima*, b. Mar. 1, 1820; m. June 1837, George H. Tuthill.
            Daniel T., b. Sep. 25, 1823, d. Mar. 15, 1839.
            Charles, b. Aug. 23, 1828, d. Sep. 7, 1848.
       164. *Daniel T.*, b. June   1846; m. July 1, 1869, Caroline Tuthill.

72.

ELEANOR LUCE, da. Abraham and Jemima (Tuthill) Luce.
       b. Nov. 25, 1786.   m.   d.
   Merritt Howell, s. Merritt and Sarah (Luce) Howell.
       b. Nov. 10, 1783.   d.   18—
   11 ch.   *Bewell*, b. June 8, 1804, d. Dec. 1, 1806.
       165. *Jemima*, b. July 26, 1806; m. Sep. 16, 1823, Daniel Howell.
            Eleanor, b. Aug. 21, 1808, d. Jan. 19, 1823.
            Fanny B., b. Oct. 4, 1810; m.   Rev. Parshall Terry.
       166. *Betsey*, b. May 1, 1814; m.   J. Rock Smith.
            Sally, b. Sep. 26, 1816; m. ⎧ 1st,   Hallock Edwards.
                                        ⎩ 2nd,   David Horton.
            Hampton F., b. Sep. 10, 1812; m.   Maria Raynor; no issue.
            Harriet, b. May 28, 1819; m.   Herman Hallock.
            Frances M., b. Feb. 25, 1826; m.   Sylvester Hallock.
            Merritt B., b. Apr. 21, 1824, d. Dec. 31, 1825.
            Eleanor Lecta, b. Aug. 19, 1829, d. unm.

73.

REV. ABRAHAM LUCE, s. Abraham and Jemima (Tuthill) Luce.
       b.   1790.   m. 1st, Nov. 19, 1812.   m. 2nd   d. Oct. 23, 1865.
   1st, Abigail Howell, da. Elias and Mehitable (Youngs) Howell.
       b. June 5, 1798.   d. Mar. 30, 1849.
   2nd, Wid. Elizabeth R. Noyce, (*nee* Foster) da. Justus and Susan (   ) Foster.
       b. Jan. 7, 1806.   d. Mar. 4, 1860.
   5 ch. 167. *Elias H.*, b.   m.   Georgiana Hudson.
            *Celia J., b.   1820; m.   †Ira Downs.
            Abraham M., b. July 4, 1816, d. Oct. 25, 1818.
            ¶*Abraham B.*, b.   m.   Harriet Benjamin.
       168. *Elmira*, b.   1825; m.   Caleb Hallock.
   (*) d. Apr. 11, 1861; left one son, Daniel. (†) s. of Daniel and Bethiah (Hallock) Downs; d. Jan. 18,
   1895, ae., 80. (¶) had one son, Dr. Jacob Luce.

74.

ELIZABETH TUTHILL, da. Nathan and Esther (Parshall) Tuthill.
       b. Oct.   1792.   m.   d. July 4, 1882.
   David Benjamin, s. Richard and Nancy (Fanning) Benjamin.
       b. Sep. 1787.   d. Oct. 17, 1861.
   9 ch.   **David*, b.   m. ⎧ 1st,   Sophronia Hutchinson.
                                    ⎩ 2d, Mary Hallock.
       169. *Van Rensselaer*, b. Mar. 1, 1813; m. ⎧ 1st,   Mary Wells.
                                              ⎩ 2nd,   Phebe Tuthill.
       170. *Sophronia*, b. Oct. 2, 1815; m. Nov. 28, 1835, Joshua L. Youngs.
            John, b.   m.   Adelia.
       171. *Caleb H.*, b. Mar. 15, 1821; m. ⎧ 1st, Apr. 23, 1843, Hannah M. Youngs.
                                          ⎩ 2nd, Oct. 25, 1870, Gloriana Fanning.
            Albert T., b.   m. ⎧ 1st,   Phebe J. Wells; ⎫ no issue.
                                        ⎩ 2nd,   Carrie Carter; ⎭
            George A., b.   m.   Emily Youngs; no issue.
       172. *Simeon O.*, b. Feb. 24, 1834; m. Oct. 12, 1858, Adelia J. Hallock.
       173. *Mary*, b. May 21, 1838; m. May 29, 1856, James M. Reeve.
   (*) has one ch. who m.

75.

PETER FOURNIER, s. Peter and Sarah (Tuthill) Fournier.
  b. Dec. 8, 1803.   m. May 10, 1828.   d. Apr. 23, 1871.
Maria Bishop, da. John and Jerusha (   ) Bishop.
  b. Apr. 12, 1805.   d. Dec. 22, 1869.
7 ch.   *Frances M.*, b. Jan. 5, 1830, d. Sep. 20, 1842.
     Arabella, b. Nov. 9, 1832; m. *Oct. 2, 1876, Albert Halsey; no issue.
     John F., b. Oct. 13, 1834; m.   Wid. Mary Halsey; no issue.
     °*Justena*, b. Oct. 25, 1840; m. Dec. 10, 1860, James L. Sanford.
  174. *Fanny M.*, b. Jan. 11, 1843; m. June 6, 1867, John E. Aldrich.
  175. *Anne E.*, b. Jan. 27, 1846; m. Feb. 3, 1875, George O. Reeves.
     An infant da., b. Nov. 13, 1846, d. Nov. 13, 1846.
(*) as his 3rd wife; s. of Nathaniel and Amelia Halsey; b. Apr. 17, 1817.   (°) had one ch. now dead.

76.

DANIEL MINOR TUTHILL, s. Daniel and Keturah (Terry) Tuthill.
  b. Dec. 29, 1798.   m.   d. Aug. 31, 1832.
*Maria Downs, da. David and Mehitable (Wells) Downs.
  b.   d.
2 ch.   *Daniel M.*, b.   m.
  176. *Alectha, M.*, b.   m. Feb. 2, 1839, John P. Terry.
(*) m. a 2d time, Rev. Mr. Sewell.

77.

JEHIEL TUTHILL, s. Daniel and Keturah (Terry) Tuthill.
  b. June 5, 1802.   m. Oct. 14, 1826.   d. Aug. 4, 1866.
Johanah Hallock, da. John and Johanah (Wells) Hallock.
  b. Nov. 5, 1808.   d. Nov. 19, 1867.
8 ch. **177.** *Mary Ann*, b. June 28, 1828; m. Oct. 29, 1846, Harvey L. Fanning.
  178. *Daniel M.*, b. Nov. 20, 1830; m. { 1st, Nov. 17, 1852, Mary A. Downs.
                                          { 2d, May 11, 1876, Mary J. Wells.
     Phebe A., b. Aug. 7, 1833; m. Dec. 23, 1851, Walter F. Havens.
     Elizabeth, b. Feb. 2, 1837; m. May 20, 1853, Manasseh Havens.
  179. *Samuel*, b. Aug. 18, 1839; m. Nov. 13, 1866, Eliza T. Wells.
  180. *Johanah W.*, b. June 23, 1843; m. Jan. 31, 1867, Horace B. Horton.
     °*Celia J.*, b. Nov. 15, 1847; m.   Mortimer Smith.
     Hannah M., b. Sep. 25, 1851; m.   J. Wesley Squires; no issue.
(*) See Havens' genealogy.   (°) Had 1 ch., d. in infancy.

78.

MARY TUTHILL, da Daniel and Keturah (Terry) Tuthill.
  b. Apr. 5, 1807.   m.   d. Mar. 5, 1827.
Moses Reeve, s. Paul and Mehitable (   ) Reeve.
  b.
1 ch.   *Mary J.*, b. Feb. 19, 1826; m.   Thomas Mayo. See Mayo Genealogy.

79.

MEHITABLE TUTHILL, da. Daniel and Keturah (Terry) Tuthill.
  b. June 11, 1809.   m. Sep. 21, 1826.   d. Sep. 28, 1887.
Nathan Corwin, s. Matthias and Julia A. (Corwin) Corwin.
  b. Oct. 17, 1801.   d. Apr. 20, 1890.
9 ch. **181.** *Mary E.*, b. Oct. 18, 1827; m. Nov. 5, 1843, Francis Lane.
  182. *Jane*, b. Aug. 12, 1830; m. Nov. 10, 1847, Nathaniel A. Griffin.
     Amanda, b. June 15, 1832, d. unm. Jan. 3, 1894.
     Minor T., b. Sep. 18, 1834, d. Mar. 8, 1839.
  183. *Rosabella*, b. Sep. 1, 1836; m. Oct. 7, 1856, Charles Hallett.
     Maria K., b. Feb. 1, 1840; m. { 1st, June 1, 1870, *Samuel B. Boyer.
                                    { 2d, June 19, 1877, Orville B. Ackerly.
     °*Matthias*, b., June 30, 1842; m.   Caroline Houser.
     Hannibal, Apr. 30, 1845; m. Sep. 10, 1865, ‖Fredericka Houser.
     Wallace, b. Feb. 15, 1848, d. unm. Feb. 28, 1871.
(*) d. Apr. 14, 1875, ae. 36.   (°) Has one da. Annie.   (‖) b. Mar. 9, 1849.

80.

ELIZABETH TUTHILL, da. Daniel and Keturah (Terry) Tuthill.
  b. Dec. 31, 1811.   m. May 2, 1833.   d. May 16, 1849.
Christopher N. Downs, s. Joshua and Matsey (Terry) Downs.
  b. May 2, 1812.   d. Mar. 23, 1896.
5 ch.   *Albert T.*, b. Aug. 31, 1834, d.
     Matsey E., b. Mar. 8, 1837; m. Dec. 18, 1859, Henry Brown.
  184. *Mary J.*, b. Dec. 2, 1839; m. Dec. 16, 1871, John F. Terry.
  185. *John W.*, b. Aug. 21, 1842; m. Jan. 1, 1867, Millicent J. Aldrich.
     Josephine E., b. Apr. 18, 1845; m. Apr. 8, 1872, Thomas J. McClure.

81.

AMANDA TUTHILL, da. Daniel and Keturah (Terry) Tuthill.
  b. Apr. 3, 1818.   m.   1837.

Joseph Edwin Hallock, s. Bethual and Polly (Corwin) Hallock.
  b. Mar. 16, 1816.   d. Sep.   1865.

3 ch. **186.** *Eugene E.*, b. Sep. 16, 1838; m. Nov. 1, 1859, Rosaline Howell.
  Amanda M., b. June 4, 1841, d. unm., Sep. 14, 1884.   *Sarena*. b. Sep. 8, 1851.

82.

JOHN TERRY, s. John and Mehitable (Tuthill) Terry.
  b. Feb. 19, 1798.   m. June 15, 1820.   d. Oct. 17, 1855.

Maria T. Tice, of New York City.
  b. April   1803.   d.

8 ch.   *John N.*, b. June 21, 1821, d. in infancy.
         Chester N., b. June 21, 1823; m. Feb. 7, 1856, Julia M. Bryant.
         John R., b. Nov. 3, 1825, d. unm.   1850.
         †*Eliza M. T.*, b. Dec. 19, 1827; m. Jan.   1844-5, Freeman D. Moore.
         Catherine M., b. Jan. 24, 1830; m.   James D. Tyrer.
         Eugene F., b. Mar. 14, 1832, d. Sep. 10, 1851.
         Maria M., b. Nov. 10, 1836; m. Sep. 3, 1856, Samuel C. Judy.
         Lewis B., b. April 21, 1838, d. Nov. 30, 1862.
(*) one ch. Edward, b. June 6, 1857, d. June 27, 1883.   (†) one ch. John T.

83.

VAN RENSSELAER TERRY, s. John and Mehitable (Tuthill) Terry.
  b. Mar. 5, 1801.   m. Sep. 29, 1824.   d. Jan. 6, 1857.

Elizabeth M. Moffat, da.
  b.   d.

4 ch.   *Catherine M.*, b. June 11, 1825, d. Aug. 15, 1830.
         John R., b. Feb. 4, 1827; m. Mar. 13, 1849, Ellen Gardiner.
         †*Van Rensselaer*, b. Oct. 9, 1828; m. Dec.   1852, Frances Doremus.
         Benjamin F., b. Sep. 16, 1833, d. Jan. 25, 1846.
(*) had 3 ch., John Rufus, Benjamin F., William.   (†) had 3 ch., Ella, Frances, Van Rensselaer.

84.

PUAH TERRY, da. John and Mehitable (Tuthill) Terry.
  b. June 21, 1807.   m.   1825.   d. May 6, 1885.

Jedidiah Conklin, s.
  b.   1798.   d. April 8, 1891.

5 ch.   *John Baker*, b. Dec. 20, 1826, d. unm.
    187. *Dorliska F.*, b. Nov. 10, 1828; m. June 17, 1857, James F. Bassett.
    188. *Catherine M.*, b.   m. Oct.   1859, Dr. John Law.
         Henry T., b.   d. unm.   *Evelyn*, b.

85.

LEWIS HAMPTON TERRY, s. John and Mehitable (Tuthill) Terry.
  b. Jan. 2, 1810.   m. Jan. 14, 1835.   d. Feb. 23, 1886.

Harriet Fanning. da. Peter and Mary (Foster) Fanning.
  b. Mar. 28, 1813.   d. Mar. 8, 1881.

9 ch. **189.** *John L.*, b. Dec. 12, 1835; m. { 1st, Jan. 19, 1859, Sarah E. Buckley.
                                            { 2nd, Dec. 19, 1875, Mary E. Merrill.
                                            { 3rd, June 1, 1893, Wid. Amelia E. Penny.
         Mary M., b. Jan. 29, 1839; m. Oct. 24, 1880, Abram Sully; no issue.
    190. *Dorlisca M.*, b. Jan. 3, 1842; m. Jan.   1869, Horace B. Tuthill.
    191. *Catherine M.*, b. Nov. 20, 1843; m. Dec. 23, 1863, J. Madison Wells.
         Peter F., b. July 3, 1848; m. Jan.   1870, Adella Downs.
         Lillian H., b. Dec. 4, 1851, d. unm. Mar.   1895.
         Franklin H., b. Oct. 4, 1854, d. unm. Aug. 15, 1873.
         Ella S., b. Sep. 4, 1856, d. May 7, 1862.
         °*Ann E.*, b. Aug. 10, 1859; m. { 1st, Feb. 22, 1881, Harry Bubest.
                                       { 2nd,   1895,   Harrington.
(*) had 3 ch. William, Eva, Lena.   (°) had 1 ch. Harriet, b. Dec. 20, 1882.

86.

NATHAN TUTHILL HALLOCK, s. Richard and Mary (Tuthill) Hallock.
  b.   180-.   m. Jan. 4, 1825.   d.   1884.

Mary Dunster, da. Oliver and Mary (Reeve) Dunster.
  b.   1804.

8 ch. **192.** *James Madison*, b. Feb. 14, 1838; m. April 3, 1866, Louise Boutcher.
         James Monroe, b.   m. Jan. 4, 1868, *Mary E. Terry; no issue.
         Horace Henry, b.   d.
    193. *William H. H.*, b.   m. Dec. 7, 1864, Hannah Eldridge.
         Lewis Van Buren, b.   d.
    194. *Martha Adelaide*, b.   m. Dec. 31, 1861, William A. Haynes.
         Ann Judson, b.   d. unm.   1854.
    195. *Frances Mary*, b. Oct. 3, 1832; m. Feb. 5, 1851, Barnabas Wines.
(*) da. of Joshua and Sarah (Davis) Terry.

87.

ELIZABETH A. HALLOCK, da. Richard and Mary (Tuthill) Hallock.
    b. July 17, 1806.   m. Feb. 12, 1828.   d. Apr. 24, 1882.

   Benjamin G. Hallock, s. James and Amelia (Goldsmith) Hallock.
    b. Jan. 6, 1807.   d. Nov. 28, 1890.

4 ch. **196.** *Josephine A.*, b. Oct. 5, 1828; m. May 22, 1849, Dennis K. Halsey.
    197. *James Richard*, b. Apr. 21, 1831; m. { 1st, Oct. 18, 1864, Rosetta Corwin.
                                  { 2d, Dec. 28, 1869, Wid. Mary Jane Reeve.
    198. *Fanny C.*, b. Mar. 16, 1839; m. June 21, 1865, David R. Dayton.
    Mary E., b. June 19, 1841, d. Feb. 18, 1846.

88.

JOHN HENRY HUDSON, s. Henry and Julianer S. (Brewster) Hudson.
    b. Jan. 11, 1838.   m. Jan. 22, 1873.

   Emeline H. Raynor, da.
    b.   1841.

6 ch. *John H.*, b. Sep. 2, 1874.   *George A.*, b. Oct. 31, 1876, d. May 24, 1896.
       Charles F., b. Jan. 24, 1878, d. Apr. 28, 1879. *Carolyn B.*, b. July 9, 1880.
       William T., b. Jan. 14, 1882.   *Edward R.*, b. July 12, 1886.

89.

ELLSWORTH HUDSON, s. Charles and Hannah (Woodhull) Hudson.
    b. Apr. 15, 1850.   m. in 1877.

   Emma R. Gallagher, da. Thomas and Mary S. (Bowler) Gallagher.
    b. Nov. 21, 1852,

9 ch. *Walter E.*, b July 8, 1878.   *George T.*, b. Nov 1, 1879.
       Charles M., b. Oct. 10 1881.   *Maud E.*, b. Aug. 25, 1883.
       Joseph H., b. July 12, 1885.   *Russell B.*, b. Nov. 4, 1888.
       Hannah E., b. July 6, 1890.   *Grace*, b. Aug. 17, 1892.
       Mary B., b. Mar. 24, 1896.

90.

MARY HUDSON TYLER, da. John and Eliza (Hudson) Tyler.
    b. June 30, 1829.   m. 1st, Jan 20, 1847.   m. 2nd, Jan. 27, 1869.

   Moses H. Ackerly, of Patchogue, New York.
    b. Apr. 14, 1821.   d. July 23, 1866.

   Richard Thomas Osborn, s. Jacob and Louisa (Homan) Osborn.
    b. May   1823.

6 ch. **199.** *Edwin F.*, b. Nov. 5, 1847; m. Oct. 10, 1878, Sadie Hawkins.
    200. *John T.*, b. Sep. 15, 1850; m. June 29, 1879, Mary F. Wiggins.
    201. *Evalyn M.*, b. July 9, 1852; m. Oct. 15, 1879, Giles T. Loomis.
    ***Archibald F.**, b. Sep. 24, 1860; m. Aug. 10, 1882, Eugenia Mestri.
    Moses H., b. Oct. 7, 1865; m.   Emma Griffin.
    Louisa A., b. Oct. 30, 1872; m. Dec. 29, 1898, William R. Brown.
(*) had one ch.

91.

CHARLES HUDSON TYLER, s. John and Eliza (Hudson) Tyler.
    b. Oct. 21, 1831.   m. July 4, 1880.

   Jerusha Hancock, da. Joseph and Nancy (Bemis) Hancock.
    b. Aug. 30, 1854.

2 ch. *Mary Hudson*, b. Dec. 29, 1883.   *Charles Joseph*, b. Mar. 22, 1889.

92.

ELIZABETH STOCKWELL TYLER, da. John and Eliza (Hudson) Tyler.
    b. Oct. 6, 1833.   m. Dec. 31, 1849.   d. June 14, 1890.

   Lester Mills, s. Gabriel and Sarah (Tuthill) Mills.
    b. June 17, 1816.

1 ch. ***Charles J.**, b.   m.   Grace Cook.
(*) has one ch. Jerome Tyler, b. Apr. 1895.

93.

JOSEPH BENTON TYLER, s. John and Eliza (Hudson) Tyler.
    b. Sep. 14, 1837.   m. Oct. 21, 1868.

   Louisa A. Thorne, da. Edmund and Amelia (Richmond) Thorne.
    b.

5 ch. *Lizzie J.*, b.   m.   *Lydia E.*, b.   m.
     Amelia B., b.   *Carrie L.*, b.   *Charles B.*, b.

94.

HELEN HUDSON, da. Benjamin F. and Elizabeth (Wells) Hudson.
  b. Dec. 17, 1833. m. Sep. 15, 1852.

Ellsworth Tuthill, s. Nathaniel and Clarissa (Miller) Tuthill.
  b. Apr. 13, 1828.

1 ch. **202.** *Nathaniel S..* b. Aug. 24, 1853; m. Nov. 20, 1877, Susan J. Hawkins.

95.

GEORGIANA HUDSON, da. Benjamin F. and Elizabeth (Wells) Hudson.
  b. May 8, 1839. m. Nov. 26, 1857. d. Oct. 27, 1863.

William Henry Skidmore, s. Walter and Harmony (Warner) Skidmore.
  b. Sep. 24, 1832. d. Dec. 1, 1896.

1 ch. *Lizzie Frank.* b. June 19, 1861.

96.

ALBERTUS HUDSON BEACH, s. Ezra and Mary (Hudson) Beach.
  b. in 1830. m. Sep. 6, 1853. d. Aug. 24, 1887.

Margaret Elizabeth Whitney, da. John and Clarissa (   ) Whitney.
  b. d. Aug. 20, 1854.

1 ch. **203.** *George Hudson,* b. July 23, 1854; m. Dec. 24, 1879, Eliza A. Kidger.

97.

MARY HUDSON BEACH, da. Ezra and Mary (Hudson) Beach.
  b. Apr. 19, 1835. m.

Samuel Budd, s.
  b. 1836.

7 ch. **Alvira Shipman,* b. 1861; m. Caleb G. Evans.
       Gertrude Greenleaf, b. 1864; d. 1866.
 204. *Henry Albert,* b. 1866; m. Julia M. McClave.
       ºMary Hudson, b. 1868; m. Frederick I. Cairns.
       Ophelia Read, b. 1870: m. Howard F. Welsh.
       Elizabeth Scholes, b. 1873; m. John S. Ascough.
       Georgiana Beatrice, b. 1875; m. { 1st, Clarence Cleland.
                                          { 2nd, J. Seargant Cram.

(*) has one ch. Arthur Gaskell. (º) has one ch. Samuel Irwin.

98.

OPHELIA BEACH, da. Ezra and Mary (Hudson) Beach.
  b. Aug. 2, 1842. m. Aug. 12, 1869. d. July 23, 1876.

Dr. Zebulon Swift Webb, s. Charles S. and Catherine (Cheney) Webb.
  b. Sep. 11, 1824.

2 ch. *Catherine Alice,* b. Jan. 15, 1872, d. Jan. 9, 1873.
       Charles Henry, b. July 10, 1876, d. Aug. 26, 1877.

99.

ANNIE HUDSON WOODHULL, da. Hudson and Ann (Miller) Woodhull.
  b. Aug. 31, 1824. m. Jan. 7, 1850. d. Feb. 21, 1867.

Rev. Andrew Flynn Dickson, s.
  b. d. Jan. 8, 1879.

8 ch. *Annie Flynn,* b. July 15, 1851; d. June 20, 1853.
       John Woodhull, b. Jan. 9, 1853; m. May, 2, 1888, Mary Ann Jayne.
       Mary Louise, b. July 3, 1854; m. Robert L. Arrowood.
       Sarah Huldah, b. Dec. 5, 1856, d. May 18, 1861.
       Bartley Fanning, b. Mar. 13, 1859; m. { 1st, July 4, 1881, Kate E. Fignet.
                                               { 2nd, Bessie Andrews.
       Samuel Howard, b. Dec. 5, 1860, d. June 6, 1861.
       *Julia Lee. b. Jan. 11, 1862; m. Braxton B. Hudson.
       Henry Robertson, b. Aug. 12, 1865, d. Oct. 14, 1886.

(*) had three ch. who d. young.

100.

MARIA MILLER WOODHULL, da. Claudius and Zophia (Miller) Woodhull.
  b. Mar. 3, 1831. m. Aug. 31, 1852.

William C. J. Hall, s. William and Julia (Jones) Hall.
  b. Aug. 8, 1828. d. Oct. 30, 1887.

3 ch. *William Woodhull,* b. July 24, 1853; d. Mar. 3, 1864.
 205. *Alfred Eliott,* b. Apr. 25, 1861; m. July 2, 1885, Elizabeth McElroy.
       Sophia Maria, b. Aug. 3, 1873; m. June 9, 1896, Rev. Frank H. Marshall.

101.

JOSEPH HUDSON WOODHULL, s. Claudius and Sophia (Miller) Woodhull.
  b. Oct. 2, 1834. m. Jan. 16, 1859.

Hannah Aldrich, da. Rogers and Hannah (Hallock) Aldrich.
  b. Dec. 28, 1839.

3 ch. **206.** *Carrie Sophia,* b. May 8, 1862; m. Oct. 28, 1885, Charles Fordham.
       Fred Howard, b. Aug. 13, 1872. *Lina Belle,* b. Oct. 8, 1874.

102.

ZOPHAR MILLER WOODHULL, s. Claudius and Sophia (Miller) Woodhull.
b. Sep. 1, 1837.   m. Dec. 25, 1867.

Cornelia Abigail Brown, da. George and Maria (Hopkins) Brown.
b. Oct. 28, 1842.

5 ch. **207.** *George Brown,* b. June 8, 1869; m. Dec. 9, 1896, Georgia K. Lester.
 William Hopkins, b. Jan. 20. 1872. *Angie Maria,* b. Sep. 28. 1874.
 Minnie Cornelia, b. Feb. 28, 1876. *Elizabeth Judson,* b. Nov. 20, 1877.

103.

SYLVESTER HAVENS WOODHULL, s. Claudius and Sophia (Miller) Woodhull.
b. Jan. 6, 1841.   m. 1st, Nov. 19, 1870.   m. 2d, June 19, 1873.

1st, Mary Cornelia Darling, da. Brewster and Margaret (Walker) Darling.
b. Nov. 16, 1848.   d. Apr. 28, 1872.

2d, Emma Marshall, da. Joseph and Elizabeth (Walker) Marshall
b. Sep. 3, 1848.

5 ch. *Mary Cornelia,* b. Apr. 18, 1872.
 Roberta Marshall, b. Apr. 14, 1875; m. Nov. 26, 1896, *Edwin G. Young.
 Louise Walker, b. Sep. 24, 1877.
 Frank Eliott, b. June 6, 1884. *Edith,* b. July 26, 1889.
(*) Son of James and Maria H. (Griffin) Young.

104.

EMILY TUTHILL WOODHULL, da. Claudius and Sophia (Miller) Woodhull.
b. June 4, 1843.   m. Jan. 10, 1866.

Leonard Rogers Aldrich, s. Rogers and Hannah (Hallock) Aldrich.
b. Oct. 27, 1843.

2 ch. *Jennie Hall,* b. Nov. 4, 1866, d. unm. Dec. 9, 1894.
 Annie Woodhull, b. June 19, 1868; m. Oct. 23, 1890, *Harry S. Sayre.
(*) Son of Stephen and Elizabeth (Squires) Sayre, b. Mar. 13, 1865.

105.

ALFRED KETCHAM WOODHULL, s. Claudius and Sophia (Miller) Woodhull.
b. Mar. 20, 1847.   m. 1st, Apr. 27. 1870.   m. 2d, Jan. 1, 1887.   d. Feb. 25, 1887.

1st, Martha Darling, da. Alfred Darling.
b. d. June 16, 1885.

2d, Catherine Durin,
b.

4 ch. *Alfred Ketcham,* b. Apr. 21, 1871. *Lottie Sophia,* b. Aug. 11, 1873.
 Sherman Darling, b. June 13, 1876. *Florence Amelia,* b. Dec. 11, 1880, d. Apr. 10, 1882.

106.

MITCHELL HOWELL WOODHULL, s. Claudius and Zophia (Miller) Woodhull.
b. Mar. 17, 1849.   m.   1876.

Fanny Reeve, da. Edward Y. and Charlotte (Corwin) Reeve.
b. Apr. 5, 1847.

5 ch. *Lillian Maria,* b. Mar. 21, 1877. *Rosa,* b. Oct. 28, 1878, d. June 3, 1885.
 Daisy Cornelia, b. Aug. 6, 1884. *Eva,* b. June 5, 1886.
 Ralph Howell, b. May 25, 1893.

107.

WILLIAM HUDSON, s. Nerva N. and Mary (Gulliver) Hudson.
b. Mar. 19, 1831.   m. Nov. 8. 1853.

Catherine M. Tuttle, da. Daniel and Elizabeth (Merritt) Tuttle.
b. Feb. 26, 1835.

7 ch. *William,* b.   m. Mary W. Gray. *Joseph,* b.   m. Alice Fleet.
 Henrietta, b.   m. Mervin J. Baylis. *Anna,* b.   m. Frank W. Seaman.
 Mary, b.   m. Charles Stevenson. *Charles* and *Frances* d. in youth.
(*) has one ch.   (°) has one ch.

108.

JEANETTE WELLMAN HUDSON, da. Nerva N. and Mary (Gulliver) Hudson.
b. Nov. 4, 1833.   m. Dec. 6, 1855.

William Carrington Bunce, s.
b. May   1818.   d. Dec. 25, 1892.

6 ch. *Joseph Hudson,* b. Dec. 22, 1856. *William Carrington,* b. Apr. 17, 1858, d. Sep. 17, 1872
 208. *Nerva Francis,* b. Sep. 4, 1859; m. July 24, 1882, Virginia E. Fruelson.
 Jennie Nevins, b. Apr. 1, 1864, d. Oct. 6, 1872.
 George R., b. July 31, 1868, d. Dec. 7, 1895. *Henry Nevins,* b. June 12, 1873.

109.

HENRY DAYTON HUDSON, s. Phineas and Hannah R. (Brown) Hudson,
b. Mar. 21, 1832.   m. May 21, 1867.

Mary Clarissa Mulford, da. Edward and Charity (Smith) Mulford.
b.

1 ch. *Henry Mulford,* b. Oct. 10, 1868.

110.

HANNAH ADAMS HUDSON, da. Phineas and Hannah R. (Brown) Hudson.
b. Sep. 22, 1842.   m. Aug. 1, 1866.   d. Nov. 3, 1890.
Thomas Mulford, s. Edward and Charity (Smith) Mulford.
b. Apr. 26, 1829,
2 ch.   *Catherine Adams*, b. Sep. 7, 1868, d. Feb. 23, 1884.
Gertrude Hudson, b. Feb. 16, 1874; m. Apr. 12, 1893, William G. Lowry.

111.

LAETITIA YOUNG, da. Thomas P. and Caroline (Hudson) Young.
b. Apr. 23, 1833.   m. Oct. 31, 1855.
George Benjamin Reeve, s. Edward and Mary A. (Benjamin) Reeve.
b. Oct. 11, 1833.
5 ch. 209. *Ruth Estelle*, b. May 13, 1857; m. Nov. 6, 1878, John F. Booth.
    210. *James Wickham*, b. Apr. 12, 1859; m. Nov. 30, 1887, Kate Booth Wells.
    211. *Lizzie Keyser*, b. Mar. 20, 1861; m. Feb. 2, 1887, William E. Hallock.
    212. *Caroline Hudson*, b. Dec. 22, 1864; m. Oct. 13, 1884, Oliver H. Tuthill.
    Mary Laetitia, b. Nov. 24, 1866.

112.

DANIEL HUDSON YOUNG, s. Thomas P. and Caroline (Hudson) Young.
b. June 30, 1835.   m. 1st, Mar. 1, 1864.   m. 2d, Mar. 9, 1871.   d. June 25, 1872.
1st, Mary Harries, da. Rev. Thomas and Joannah (Duryea) Harries.
b. July 28, 1840.   d. Oct. 16, 1865.
2d, Sophia Benjamin, da. George and Ann (Cook) Benjamin.
b.
2 ch. 213. *David Harries*, b. Apr. 5, 1865; m.   Eva B. Hudson.
    Daniel Anderson, b. Feb. 10, 1871.

113.

THOMAS YOUNG, s. Thomas P. and Caroline (Hudson) Young.
b. Jan. 10, 1840.   m. Dec. 7, 1870.
Martha L. Williams, da. Gilbert and Lucinda (Potter) Williams.
b. Dec. 22, 1844.
3 ch.   *Caroline Williams*, b. Sep. 6, 1871; m. Dec. 1. 1897, Ross W. Downs.
    Ethel Fanning, b. Nov. 4, 1872.   *Bertha Lucinda*, b. Sep. 25, 1875.

114.

MARIA JANE HUDSON, da. Joseph B. and Maria L. (Griffing) Hudson.
b. Mar. 30, 1838.   m. Oct. 26, 1861.
Dr. William Stimson, s. Elam and Susan (Bolles) Stimson.
b.   d. Aug. 27, 1884.
8 ch.   o*William Howard*, b. Nov. 6, 1862; m. Jan. 6, 1894, Mary Remenschneider.
    Benjamin Hudson, b. Aug. 2, 1865.
    214. *Edwin Lawrence*, b. Dec. 15, 1867; m. Oct. 8, 1889, Bertha E. McClure.
    **Joseph Elam*, b. May 18. 1870; m. Jan. 23, 1894, Anna C. Peterson.
    215. *Albert Rutherford*, b. May 9, 1872; m. Dec. 18, 1895, Grace E. Means.
    John Augustus, b. Mar. 17, 1874.   *Florence Carolyn*, b. Jan. 24, 1878.
    Charles Bowles, b. May   1882.
(o) has one ch. Hazel York, b. Jan. 7, 1895.   (*) has one ch. Louise, b. Apr. 28, 1895.

115.

BENJAMIN C. HUDSON, s. Joseph B. and Maria L. (Griffing) Hudson.
b. Aug. 10, 1841.   m. May 29, 1867.   d. Feb. 11, 1868.
Sarah Ann Cartwright, da. Benjamin C. and Hannah M. (Tuthill) Cartwright.
b. Aug. 1, 1847.
1 ch.   **Eva Benjamin*, b. Mar. 22, 1868; m.   David H. Young.
(*) see No 213.

116.

ADRIANA LAWRENCE HUDSON, da. Joseph B. and Maria L. (Griffing) Hudson.
b. Nov. 25, 1847.   m. June 21, 1871.
Nathaniel L. Pope, s. Joshua and Sophia (Barstow) Pope.
b. Aug. 23, 1846.
1 ch.   *Harry Lawrence*, b. July 20, 1876.

117.

FLORENCE DELAPHINE HUDSON, da. Joseph B. and Maria L. (Griffing) Hudson.
b. Feb. 10, 1852.   m. Oct. 24, 1887.
George Miller, s. Joseph and Susan (Blondell) Miller.
b. Oct. 10, 1851.
2 ch.   *Florence Blondell*, b. Feb. 9, 1880.   *Howard Hudson*, b. Feb. 7, 1883, d. June 17, 1887.

118.

CHARLES G. HUDSON, s. Daniel and Mary C. (Griffing) Hudson.
b. June 13, 1856.   m.   1884.

Anna Pauline Schaible, da. Jacob and Catherine (Dietz) Schaible.
b. Dec. 27, 1865.

6 ch.   *George Hudson*, b. June 27, 1885.   *Nathaniel Sylvester*, b. Apr. 2, 1887.
Henry Harrison, b. Feb. 27, 1889.   *Randolph Griffing*, b. Aug. 4, 1891.
Samuel L'Hommedieu, b. July 30, 1894.   *Byron Griffing*, b. Jan. 2, 1897.

119.

WILLIAM HENRY COOK, s. William H. and Anna W. (Hudson) Cook.
b. Mar. 29, 1842.   m. June 19, 1870.

Emily A. Wells, da. Ransford and Julia (Foster) Wells.
b. Jan. 6, 1850.

6 ch.   *Julia Evelyn*, b. Sep. 24, 1873, d. Feb. 11, 1874.   *William Nevins*, b. Apr. 29, 1875.
Estelle Rockwell, b. July 10. 1877, d. Aug. 15, 1878.   *Maud Wells*, b. Sep. 29. 1879.
Daisy Falsom, b. Sep. 22, 1886.   *Rowland*, b. Sep. 17, 1889.

120.

LAFAYETTE HAYWARD COOK, s. William H. and Anna W. (Hudson) Cook.
b. Mar. 25, 1849.   m. Jan. 25, 1875.

Mary Emma Corwin, da. Charles L. and Ann M. (Terry) Corwin.
b. Apr. 3, 1847.

6 ch.   *Lillian Maria*, b. Oct. 3, 1875.   Twin brother, d. Nov. 3, 1875.
Jemima Nevins, b. July 27, 1877.   *Jennie Rockwell*, b. Feb. 22, 1882, d. Aug. 23, 1896.
George Hudson, b. May 30, 1884, d. Feb. 12, 1885. *Lafayette Hayward*, b. Apr. 23, 1889.

121.

JOSEPH ROCKWELL COOK, s. William H. and Anna (Hallock) Cook.
b. Dec. 13, 1852.   m.

Ida Leek, da. Walter Leek of Port Jefferson, N. Y.
b.

1 ch.   *Joseph Rockwell*, d. in infancy.

122.

JOHN Q. A. HUDSON, s. Dr. Matthew H. and Esther P. (Hallock) Hudson.
b. Feb. 9, 1849.   m. Dec. 25, 1873.

Sarah M. Newville.
b. Jan. 18, 1850.

2 ch.   *Minnie Nevins*, b. Aug. 25, 1870.   *Mildred De Etta*, b. Aug. 27, 1884.

123.

ESTELLA E. HUDSON, da. Dr. Matthew H. and Esther P. (Hallock) Hudson.
b. Mar. 26, 1852.   m. Sep. 22, 1875.

Benjamin F. Reed, s. Samuel and Ellen (Bennett) Reed.
b. May 16, 1848.

3 ch.   *Fay F.*, b. May 21, 1877.   *Lee H.*, b. Sep. 22, 1880.   *Ruth E.*, b. Feb. 15, 1886.

124.

HENRY H. HUDSON, s. Dr. Matthew H. and Esther P. (Hallock) Hudson.
b. Mar. 18, 1857.   m. Apr. 28, 1885.

Cora E. Morford, da. William L. and Mary (Hopkins) Morford.
b. Aug. 9, 1862.

3 ch.   *Locke M.*, b. Apr. 11, 1886.   *Henry H.*, b. Mar. 18, 1889.   *Milo G.*, b. Oct. 30, 1893.

125.

GEORGE CHEEVER HUDSON, s. Dr. Matthew H. and Esther P. (Hallock) Hudson.
b. May 10, 1860.   m. Dec. 31, 1892.

Abbie Marie Burgan, da. Daniel M. and Lucy A. (Reeve) Burgan.
b. May 12, 1859.

2 ch.   *George Burgan*, b. Nov. 4, 1894.   *Robert Cheever*, b. Sep. 30, 1896.

126.

JOSEPH NATHANIEL HUDSON, s. Dr. Nathaniel and Cordelia (Sammis) Hudson.
b. Aug. 20, 1852.   m. 1st, Jan. 14, 1874.   2d, Nov. 8, 1887.

1st, Susie A. Frakes, da. Robert and Evaline (Maxwell) Frakes.
b.   d.

2d, Martha A. Reel, da.   (Marrs) Reel.
b. Apr. 5, 1872.

5 ch.   *Leonie Christine.* b. Dec.   1875, d. Sep.   1877.   *Leila May*, b. Jan   1878.
         Frank W., b. June, 1880.   *Joseph E.*, b. Aug. 16, 1888.   *Cordelia E.*, b. Feb. 4, 1896.

127.

IONE MAY HUDSON, da. Dr. Nathaniel and Lydia A. (Jones) Hudson.
    b. Oct. 21, 1863.   m.

Arthur Philbrick, s.
    b.

1 ch.   A daughter, b. June 7, 1890.

128.

MARY CATHERINE GRISWOLD, da. James M. and Catherine M. (Phelps) Griswold.
    b. May 18, 1845.   m. Mar. 22, 1863.

George Calvin Whiton.
    b. Jan. 1, 1840.

2 ch.   *Katie Phelps*, b. Sep. 27, 1864; m. Jan. 12, 1884, Francis P. Leary.
         Jennie Eleanor, b. Apr. 30, 1877.

129.

SARAH MARIA GRISWOLD, da. James M. and Catherine M. (Phelps) Griswold.
    b. Aug. 29, 1846.   m. Oct. 14, 1874.

Dr. Erastus E. Case.
    b. May 28, 1847.

3 ch.   *Herbert Monroe*, b. Sep. 28, 1875.   *Helen Eliza*, b. Nov. 15, 1876.
         Clarence Norton, b. Sep. 29, 1880.

130.

JAMES AZARIAH GRISWOLD, s. James M. and Catherine M. (Phelps) Griswold.
    b. Feb. 18, 1848.   m. Jan. 13, 1875.

Sarah Emma Warner, da.
    b. Dec. 21, 1852.

4 ch.   *Frances Catherine*, b. Apr. 13, 1876.   *Martha Emily*, b. Mar. 28, 1878.
         Emily Warner, b. Feb. 27, 1880.   *Ethel Sarah*, b. Feb. 1, 1889.

131.

MARY CHARLOTTE PHELPS, da. Azariah G. and Charlotte E. (Warriner) Phelps.
    b. Dec. 8, 1870.   m. Dec. 20, 1892.

Dr. George Deacon, s. William and Eliza (Mason) Deacon.
    b. Oct. 25, 1855.

2 ch.   *Charlotte*, b. June 25, 1894.   *Dorothy*, b. Nov. 22, 1896.

132.

ELIZABETH R. HUDSON, da. Horace and Eliza (Davis) Hudson.
    b. Aug. 8, 1826.   m. June 23, 1857.   d. Feb. 1, 1873.

William H. Tyler, s. Benjamin and Eliza (Fowler) Tyler.
    b. Mar. 3, 1834.   d. Apr. 10, 1890.

5 ch.   *Eliza H.*, b. Mar. 11, 1858, d. Aug. 13, 1860.   *William H.*, b. July 1, 1860.
         Horace H., b. Sep. 29, 1862.   *Benjamin F.*, b. Nov. 22, 1864.
         Frederick A. S., b. July 5, 1872, d. Aug. 12, 1872.

133.

FRANCES T. CARTER, da. Henry and Eliza (Hudson) Carter.
    b. Mar. 20, 1846.   m. May 25, 1865.

Gilbert Peterson, s. William and Hannah (Robinson) Peterson.
    b. July 9, 1843.

3 ch.   *Eugene B.*, b. May 6, 1867, d. Oct. 13, 1875.
         Frank D., b. June 22, 1869; m. June 1, 1892, Kitty Conklin.
         Alida B., b. Dec. 5, 1872; m. { 1st, May 3, 1894, Percy L. Smith.
                                        { 2d, Oct. 30, 1898, Robert. J. Potter.

134.

CHARLES S. HUDSON, s. Isaac and Sally (Hudson) Hudson.
    b. Oct. 15, 1829.   m. Oct. 3, 1855.

Martha Terry, da. Brewster and Urania (Davis) Terry.
    b. Nov. 20, 1835.

7 ch.   *Frank T.*, b. Sep. 11, 1856, d. June   1873.
    216. *Charles B.*, b. Nov.   1858; m. Apr.   1878, Elizabeth Tuthill.
    217. *Bryant T.*, b. Oct.   1862; m. June   1888, Martha Roberts.
    218. *Sallie Roe*, b. Oct.   1866; m. Oct. 6, 1885, W. E. Dugen.
    219. *M. Augusta*, b. July   1869; m. Dec.   1893, Edward S. Edwards.
         Lucille G., b. June   1873, d. Oct.   1875.   *Charlotte M.*, b. Oct.   1875; not m.

135.

EUGENE M. HUDSON, s. Joel and Martha (Glover) Hudson.
b. Mar. 19, 1854.   m. Jan. 6, 1886.

Lelia L. Hulse, da. Lewis and Harriet (Jones) Hulse.
b. Jan. 17, 1861.
2 ch.   *Harriet Sophia*, b. Dec. 15, 1886.   *Grace Lelia*, b. Jan. 20, 1893. d. Feb. 3, 1893.

136.

S. TERRY HUDSON, s. Samuel and Angeline (Downs) Hudson.
b. Nov. 24, 1843.   m. Oct. 13, 1864.

Mary Emma Wells, da. J. Edward and Cordelia E. (Youngs) Wells.
b. Apr. 10, 1846.
3 ch. **220.** *Edward G.*, b. Apr. 15, 1866; m.   Sarah E. Reeve.
  221. *Ada Roberts*, b. Apr. 23, 1868; m. Dec. 18, 1890. J. Addison Young.
  Alice Angeline, b. Feb. 2, 1870; m. Dec. 25, 1889, Henry G. Dimond.
(*) See No. 274.

137.

CHARLES H. HUDSON, s. Daniel and Ann M. (Wells) Hudson.
b. Apr. 3, 1854.   m. Nov. 24, 1874.

Sarepta Emma Sayre, da. James and Sarepta E. (King) Sayre.
b. Nov. 6, 1855.
4 ch.   *Daniel Howard*, b. Jan. 23, 1877.   *Carrie Dimon*, b. Sep. 22, 1878, d. Aug. 19, 1885.
  F. Clifford, b. Jan. 15, 1885.   *Raymond D.*, b. July 18, 1888, d. Jan. 2, 1894.

138.

MIANDA WELLS, da. Elisha and Maria S. (Hudson) Wells.
b. Jan. 9, 1851.   m. June 20, 1867.

Albert T. Downs, s. James Y. and Joanna (Tuthill) Downs.
b. Jan. 26, 1842.
6 ch. **222.** *David Lewis*, b. May 11, 1868; m. Nov. 27, 1889, Cora Young.
  223. *Frederick Skillman*, b. June 30, 1870; m. Dec. 4, 1895, Mary A. Howell.
  Charles Albert, b. Dec. 8, 1872   *Oliver Francis*, b. Jan. 30, 1876.
  Lucy Eugenia, b. May 12, 1878.   *Nellie Maria*, b. Jan. 14, 1883.

139.

ELSIE MARIA WELLS, da. Elisha and Maria S. (Hudson) Wells.
b. Nov. 6, 1852.   m. Nov. 6, 1869.

Addison J. Wells, s. Joshua M. and Betsey H. (Youngs) Wells.
b. Feb. 12, 1849.
6 ch. **224.** *Thaddeus Sherman*, b. Aug. 30, 1871; m. Nov. 1, 1893, Isabel H. Otis.
  225. *Eva Almira*, b. Sep. 11, 1872; m. July 12, 1892, Lucien Jarvis Bisbee.
  Horace Joshua, b. Sep. 21, 1875; m. Sep. 17, 1898, *Agnes Brown Binkerd.
  Edith Maria, b. Oct. 2, 1877 ; m. Sep. 11, 1897, °Morrell Smith.
  Howard Addison, b. Dec. 21, 1884.   *Ralph Hudson*, b. Jan. 30, 1887.
(*) da. of Oscar and Emma (Brown) Binkerd, b. Sep. 17, 1875.
(°) s. of Charles H. and Mary A. (Morrell) Smith, b. July 16, 1875.

140.

OLIVER FRANCIS WELLS, s. Elisha and Maria S. (Hudson) Wells.
b. Oct. 4, 1854.   m. Nov. 23, 1875.

Henrietta J. Fanning, da. Franklin T. and Sarah J. (Luce) Fanning.
b. July 10, 1853.
4 ch.   *Leila E.*, b. Dec. 2, 1876; m. Jan. 3, 1893, John Ernest Downs.
  Florence Ettie, b. Dec. 15, 1881.   *Blanche Ethel*, b. Aug. 6, 1884.
  Oliver Francis, b. Jan. 5, 1893.
(*) See No. 257.

141.

RACHEL HUDSON WELLS, da. Elisha and Maria S. (Hudson) Wells.
b. June 5, 1856.   m. Sep. 3, 1872.

John Tuthill Downs, s. James Y. and Joanna (Tuthill) Downs.
b. Sep. 25, 1849.
5 ch.   *Elsie Anna*, b. Aug. 15, 1873.
  226. *Alice Evalyn*, b. Apr. 25, 1875; m. June 1, 1897, Edward P. Wells.
  Rowena Fayett, b. Nov. 5, 1878; m. Oct. 26, 1897, *John T. Luce.
  Inez May, b. Nov. 12, 1880.   *Hattie Griffith*, b. Mar. 12, 1892.
(*) s. of Daniel T. and Caroline (Tuthill) Luce, b. Oct. 24, 1872.

142.

LUCY KARON WELLS, da. Elisha and Maria S. (Hudson) Wells.
b. Aug. 3, 1858.   m. Dec. 6, 1882.

Franklin B. Reeve, s. Francis H. and Phebe A. (Downs) Reeve.
b. June 8, 1858.
2 ch.   *Annie May*, b. Nov. 8, 1884.   *Francis Wells*, b. Mar. 6, 1894.

143.

ELISHA WHEELER WELLS, s. Elisha and Maria S. (Hudson) Wells.
    b. Aug. 13, 1860.   m. Dec. 8, 1881.

Emma Elizabeth Genther, da. George W. and Elizabeth D. (Lang) Genther.
    b. May 12, 1863.   d. Sep. 17, 1895.

3 ch.   *Clifford Rudolph*, b. Sep. 26, 1882.   *Eunice Skillman*, b. Feb. 11, 1886.
        Hudson Genther, b. Oct. 2, 1889.

144.

LOUISA ELIZABETH WELLS, da. Elisha and Maria S. (Hudson) Wells.
    b. Sep. 26, 1862.   m. Dec. 24, 1881.

Louis Frank Jennings, s. Joseph E. and Harriet (Youngs) Jennings.
    b. Apr. 18, 1862.

1 ch.   *Florence Mabel*, b. Sep. 11, 1883.

145.

ETTA EVELYN WELLS, da. Elisha and Maria S. (Hudson) Wells.
    b. May 17, 1866.   m. May 17, 1887.

Frederick B. Conklin, s. Benjamin and Mary A. (Benjamin) Conklin.
    b. Sep. 23, 1865.

3 ch.   *Helen Hudson*, b. Feb. 3, 1890.   *Meta*, b. June 11, 1894.
        Una, b. Feb. 11, 1897, d. Nov. 13, 1898.

146.

DE FORREST WELLS, s. Elisha and Maria S. (Hudson) Wells.
    b. Mar. 18, 1868.   m. Sep. 11, 1890.

Nancy Lucretia Robinson, da. George O. and Nancy L. (Hallock) Robinson.
    b. Feb. 21, 1871.

4 ch.   *Ralph Otis*, b. Aug. 9, 1891.   *Clara Bell*, b. July 30, 1893.
        Mira Mianda, b. Sep. 20, 1894.   *Lulu Anetha*, b. Mar. 5, 1896.

147.

CHARLES SEAMAN WELLS, s. Elisha and Maria S. (Hudson) Wells.
    b. Jan. 30, 1872.   m. Dec. 10, 1891.

Eula Cornelia Hallock, da. David H. and Emilie J. (Wells) Hallock.
    b. Dec. 11, 1871.

2 ch.   *Halsey Minor*, b. Nov. 18, 1894, d. Jan. 29, 1896.   *Emily Maria*, b. Aug. 25. 1897.

148.

SELENCIA FRANKLIN HALLOCK, da James and Rhoda (Hallock) Hallock.
    b. Dec. 5, 1823.   m. Nov. 29, 1848.

William Cravitt Wells, s. John and Lydia (Corwin) Wells.
    b. Mar. 14, 1825.

4 ch. **227.** *William James*, b. Feb. 17, 1850; m. Dec. 13, 1871, Jennie Williams.
        Harvey Hallock, b. July 18, 1853.   *Frederick Howell*, b. Aug. 9, 1858.
        Susan Goldsmith, b. Sep. 24, 1860.

149.

AVIS RHODA HALLOCK, da. James and Rhoda (Hallock) Hallock.
    b. Dec. 21, 1828.   m. Dec. 2, 1853.

Eurystheus H. Wells, s. Rev. Eurystheus and Mary (Corwin) Wells.
    b. June 17, 1829.   d. Mar. 24, 1894.

2 ch.   *A. Rosabelle*, b. Aug. 9, 1856; d. unm. Mar. 3, 1896.
   228. *E. Helen*, b. Jan. 14, 1861; m. June 9, 1884, Rev. David W. Hutchinson.

150.

FREDERICK HALLOCK, s. Frederick and Nancy (Bishop) Hallock
    b. Feb. 20, 1817.   m. Nov. 23, 1859.

Elizabeth M. Hallock, da. Barnabas W. and Urcilla (McLenan) Hallock.
    b. Dec. 10, 1832.

2 ch.   **Frederick W.*, b. Mar. 3, 1861; m. June 5, 1895, °Bessie W. Williamson.
        Frank B., b. Apr. 12, 1864, d. Sep. 5, 1865.
(*) Has 1 ch., Frederick Arthur, b. Apr. 19, 1897.   (°) See Douglass genealogy, No. 9.

151.

NATHAN B. HALLOCK, s. Frederick and Nancy (Bishop) Hallock.
    b. Dec. 6, 1818.   m. Jan. 7, 1845.

Hannah A. Goodale, da. Josiah and Martha (Vail) Goodale.
    b.   d. Mar   1894.

7 ch.   *Susan*, b.   m.   Lozelle Young.
        Nathan B., b.
        Frederick O., b.   m.   Benjamin.
        Asha B., b.   *Richard H.*, b.   *Phebe*, b.   *Fannie*, b.

152.

HANNAH HALLOCK, da. Frederick and Nancy (Bishop) Hallock.
b. Feb. 20, 1821.

Harvey Rose, s.
b.

4 ch.   *Frederick H.*, b.   m.   Sarah E. White.   *Charles*, b.   m.   Anna Strong.
      Sarah, b.   m.   Samuel Arwith.   *Nancy*, b.   m.   Abram Rose

153.

HULDA F. HALLOCK, da. Frederick and Nancy (Bishop) Hallock.
b. Mar.   1825,   m.

Asher Benedict, s.
b.

7 ch.   *Robert M.*, b.   m.   Lamont.
      Walter, b.   m.   *Frederick H.*, b.
      John F., b.   m.   Electa Foster.
      Carrie, b.   d. in youth.   *Fannie*, b.   d. in youth.
      Frank E., b.   m.   Evy Edwards.

154.

WILLIAM FRANK BENJAMIN, s. Rev. William and Amelia (Hallock) Benjamin.
b. Feb. 24, 1816.   m. 1st, Oct. 6, 1838.   m. 2d, Oct. 22, 1852.   d. June 8, 1879.

1st, Elizabeth L. Terry, da. James and Hannah (Cooper) Terry.
b. Aug. 20, 1821.   d. July 20, 1851.

2nd, Clarissa Rathbun, da.
b.

3 ch.   *Simeon*, b. Jan. 20, 1849; m.   Anna
      Elizabeth A., b. Aug. 2, 1841; m. { 1st, Benjamin F. Wells.   *James*, b. July 11, 1846; m.
                                   { 2nd, George Vail.

155.

RICHARD HAMPTON BENJAMIN, s. Rev. William and Amelia (Hallock) Benjamin.
b. Oct. 2, 1820.   m. Dec. 4, 1847.   d. Apr. 26, 1886.

Hannah S. Smith, da. Samuel and Phebe (Goodale) Smith.
b. Oct., 1826.

6 ch.   *H. Amelia*, b. June 3, 1847; m. Mar. 4, 1873, *Dr. Louis Wilson Terry; no issue.
      Phebe S., b.   d.   *Mannasseh Fanning*, b.   d. in youth.
      Elida M., b.   d. in youth.   *M. Louise*, b. July 15, 1857, d. Aug. 27, 1877.
   220. *Maria T.*, b. Oct. 21, 1862; m. Dec. 16, 1886, Louis G. Rathbun.
(*) son of William and Sarah (Green) Terry; b. Dec. 19, 1843, d. May 26, 1894.

156.

JAMES HARVEY BENJAMIN, s. Rev. William and Amelia (Hallock) Benjamin.
b. Apr. 4, 1823.   m. Dec. 15, 1852.   d. May 8, 1896.

Harriet H. Raynor, da. Herrick and Harriet H. (Halsey) Raynor.
b. Dec. 23, 1832.

6 ch.   *Nancy W.*, b. Dec. 28, 1857; m. Apr. 16, 1895, Alfred Rigby.
      Mary A., b. Feb. 15, 1854, d. Apr. 5, 1856. *Harriet H.*, b. Oct. 22, 1856, d. Mar. 22, 1857.
      Amelia H., b. Aug. 25, 1860.   *Henrietta*, b.   d. Aug. 5, 1863.
      William H., b. Dec. 25, 1865; m. Jan. 1, 1891, Florence M. Downs.

157.

ELIZA ANN COOPER, da. Oliver and Anna (Hallock) Cooper.
b.   m. Jan. 24, 1842.

Matthew Phillip Wells, s. Christopher and Susannah (Howell) Wells.
b.

5 ch.   *Susan Howell*, b. Sep. 20, 1842; m.   John Griffin.
      Albert Herbert, b. Feb.   184-, d. June 13, 1847.
      Oliver C., b. Feb. 11, 1848; m.   Ada Wells.
      Mary A., b. June 16, 1850; m.   1868, Simeon Hawkins.
      b. Jan. 6, 1857, d.

158.

ANNA HALLOCK, da. Benjamin F. and Sarah A. (Hobby) Hallock.
b.   m.   d.

David W. Benjamin, s. Wells and Abigail (Hallock) Benjamin.
b. Apr. 14, 1825.

4 ch.   *Isabella*, b.   m.   John Phillips.   *Elizabeth*, b.   d. age 18.
      Emma Jane, b.   m.   John W. Robinson.
      Etta May, b.   m.   Thomas Ellis; no issue.

159.

THERESA HALLOCK, da. Benjamin F. and Sarah A. (Hobby) Hallock.
b. June 13, 1837.   m. Dec. 29, 1853.

George Syrene Wells, s. Thomas and Anne (Wells) Wells.
b. June 7. 1831.

8 ch.   *Benjamin Franklin*, b. Dec. 25, 1854. *Charlotte Althea*, b. Jan. 15, 1856, d. Aug. 5, 1875.
Anne Leonora, b. June 25, 1858.   *Minnie Hallock*, b. Oct. 23, 1862.
Willis Weston, b. Dec. 2, 1864.   *Lillian Florence*, b. Dec. 6, 1866.
Ralph Brunelle, b. Feb. 7, 1874.   *Robert Eugene*, b. Aug. 16, 1876.

160.

GEORGE O. LUCE. s. John T. and Rachel (Terry) Luce.
b. Oct. 17, 1806.   m. 1st, 1836.   m. 2d,   m. 3d,   d. Jan. 17, 1871.

1st, Charity W. Hallock, da. John and Joannah (Wells) Hallock.
b. June 30, 1814.   d. Mar. 3, 1838.

2d, Betsey G. Reeve, da, Jessie   Reeve.
b. 1813.   d. Oct. 12, 1840.

3d, Deborah A. Wells, da. Daniel and Deborah (Terry) Wells.
b. May 1811.   d. Dec. 7, 1871.

8 ch. 230. *Mary T.*, b. Sep. 12, 1837; m. Nov. 5, 1860, Daniel S. Terry.
An infant of Betsey, d. Apr. 12, 1840.   Three infants of Deborah.
Sarah T., b.   m.   Franklin Fanning.
George F., b.   m.   Adelia Griffin.
231. *Charles E.*, b. June 4, 1846; m. Dec. 12, 1867, Lorenia N. Benjamin.

161.

JOHN T. LUCE, s. John T. and Rachel (Terry) Luce.
b. Mar. 28, 1808.   m. 1831.   d. Jan. 7, 1878.

Mary B. Tuthill, da. David and Mary (Howell) Tuthill.
b. Feb. 14, 1812.   d. Oct. 2, 1898.

6 ch.   *Daniel T.*, b. Oct. 27, 1840.   *John T.*, b. Nov. 9, 1831.
232. *Rachel Ann*, b. Sep. 25, 1833; m. Mar. 24, 1851, Rev. Edward K. Fanning.
Henry B., b. Dec. 10, 1835; m.   Ernestine Rogers.
Mary Elma, b. Jan. 4, 1844; m.   Peter Enos; no issue.
Electa Jane, b. May 4, 1847; m.   Henry Wiggins.
(*) Had three ch., Henry, Nathaniel and Nancy F.

162.

PHEBE T. LUCE, da. John T. and Rachel (Terry) Luce.
b. Jan. 11, 1812.   m.   d. Dec. 9, 1874.

Benjamin Warner, s. Benjamin and Anna (Edwards) Warner.
b. Sep. 6, 1802.   d. Mar. 4, 1852.

8 ch.   *Anna A.*, b.   *Ann E.*, b.   m.   William Jones; no issue.
Emma, b.   d. unm. 1892.   *Amelia*, b. May 20, 1833, d. June 3, 1843.
Phebe, b.   m. Guyon.   †*Charles*, b.   m.   Lizzie
George E.. b.   m.   Anna Woodhull; no issue.
Stephen, b.   m.
(*) Has three ch., Walter, b.   Emma, b.   Bessie, b.   (†) Had one ch.

163.

JEMIMA LUCE, da. John T. and Rachel (Terry) Luce.
b. Mar. 1, 1820.   m. June 1837.

George H. Tuthill, s. David and Mary (Howell) Tuthill.
b. Feb. 1817.   d. June 21, 1888.

2 ch. 233. *George H.*. b. Sep. 29, 1838; m. Nov. 21, 1860, Nannie W. Beebe.
234. *Charles S.*, b. Jan. 2, 1844; m. Nov. 1876, Elma H. Petty.

164.

DANIEL T. LUCE, s. John T. and Mary (Wells) Luce.
b. June 1846.   m. July 1, 1869.

Caroline Tuthill, da. John and Lydia (Wells) Tuthill.
b.

1 ch.   *John*, b.   m. Oct. 26, 1897, Rowena F. Downs.

165.

JEMIMA HOWELL, da. Merritt and Eleanor (Luce) Howell.
b. July 26, 1806.   m. Sep. 16, 1823.   d. Oct. 22, 1857.

Daniel Howell, s. Micah and Hannah (Lupton) Howell.
b. Oct. 23, 1797.   d. Mar. 17, 1870.

5 ch. 235. *Eleanor*, b. May 15, 1825; m. Oct. 19, 1841; Daniel Warner.
236. *Hannah Rosetta*, b. Sep. 28,1828; m. Dec. 14, 1849, Jeremiah G. Tuthill.
237. *Henry Harrison*, b. Mar. 31, 1830; m. { 1st, Sep. 8, 1858. Catherine Tuthill.
{ 2d, Dec. 29, 1875, Melinda Young.
238. *Electa H.*, b. Mar. 7, 1834; m. Apr. 15, 1855, Benjamin R. Griffing.
239. *Marinda Ann*, b. Feb. 21, 1841; m. Jan. 4, 1860, H. Beecher Halsey.

166.

BETSEY HOWELL, da. Merritt and Eleanor (Luce) Howell.
      b. May 1, 1814.   m.

J. Rock Smith, s. John and Sarah (Corwin) Smith.
      b. Apr. 9, 1809.   d. Apr. 19, 1881.
6 ch.   *Sarah C., b. 1833; m.   James Fordham.   +Merritt H., b. 1835; m.   Ellen Robbins.
      ‡Amelia A., b. 1838; m.   Albert Norton.   John H., b. 1840, d.   1864.
      Floyd E., b.   1842; m. Sep. 26, 1896, Emily Jason.
      §Gertrude I., b.   184-; m.   Ardin Wicks.
(*) Has six ch.   (†) Has one da., named Jennie R., who m. Hermon H. Wells.
(‡) Has four ch.   (§ Has three ch.

167.

ELIAS H. LUCE, s. Rev. Abraham and Abigail (Howell) Luce.
      b.

GEORGIANA HUDSON, da. George and Patience (Wells) Hudson. See No. 24.
      b. Aug. 1, 1822.   m.   d. Jan. 6, 1895.
1 ch.   Lucelia, b. Aug. 10, 1841; m. June 10, 1873, Francis Woodhull; no issue.

168.

ELMIRA LUCE, da. Rev. Abraham and Abigail (Howell) Luce.
      b.   1825.   m.

Caleb Hallock, s. John and Joanna (Wells) Hallock.
      b.   1824.
3 ch.   *Adaline A., b.   m.   Joseph M. Woodhull.   Twins, who d. in infancy.
(*) Had one ch. Elida, who m. Mr. Van Hovenburgh. They have one ch. named Rudolph.

169.

VAN RENSSELAER BENJAMIN, s. David and Elizabeth (Tuthill) Benjamin.
      b. Mar. 1, 1813.   m. 1st,   m. 2d,   d. July 16, 1879.

1st, Mary Wells, da. Joshua and Deborah (Youngs) Wells.
      b. Sep.   1819.   d. Oct. 27, 1840.

2d, Phebe Tuthill, da. Daniel and Phebe (Wells) Tuthill.
      b.
2 ch. 240. Milford T., b. Aug. 17, 1847; m. Dec. 8, 1880, Deborah J. Hallock.
      George V., b. Mar. 8, 1850, d. Dec. 22, 1862.

170.

SOPHRONIA BENJAMIN, da. David and Elizabeth (Tuthill) Benjamin.
      b. Oct. 2, 1815.   m. Nov. 28, 1835.   d. July 29, 1897.

Joshua Lester Young, s. John and Hannah (Williamson) Young.
      b. Mar. 4, 1813.   d. Mar. 18, 1878.
10 ch. 241. Frances E., b. Jan. 20, 1837; m. Nov. 1, 1854, John Hallock.
      Hannah Janet, b. Mar. 12, 1839; d. May 11, 1859.
      242. John Leonard, b. Apr. 25, 1842; m. Nov. 26, 1862. Harriet E. Robinson.
      243. Adelia Sophronia, b. Apr. 15, 1844; m. Dec. 6, 1864, John Martyn Dimond.
      244. Marietta, b. June 27, 1846; m. Nov. 2, 1868, Chauncey P. Howell.
      245. David Halsey, b. Sep. 12, 1848; m. May 26, 1872, Iona Zytel:a Wells.
      Lillian Evaline, b. Nov. 8, 1850, d. May 13, 1880.
      246. George Lester, b. Mar. 2, 1853; m. Dec. 23, 1875, Mary Ella Hallock.
      Phebe Johnson Hunt, b. Jan. 17, 1856, d. Jan. 25, 1857.
      247. Albert Benjamin, b. Jan. 12, 1858; m. Dec. 10, 1878, Rosaella M. Robinson.

171.

CALEB HALSEY BENJAMIN, s. David and Elizabeth (Tuthill) Benjamin.
      b. Mar. 15, 1821.   m. 1st, Apr. 23, 1843.   m. 2d, Oct. 25, 1870.

1st, Hannah M. Youngs, da. John and Hannah (   ) Youngs.
      b.   d. July 8, 1869.

2d, Glorianna Fanning, d. Dr. Joshua and Elma (Tuthill) Fanning.
      b. Nov. 25, 1825.
3 ch. 248. Maria Elizabeth, b. June 12, 1844; m.   Henry Terry.
      *Lorenia Nancy, b. July 19, 1845; m. Dec. 12, 1867. Charles E. Luce.
      John Halsey, b. July 20, 1855; m. { 1st,   Florie Williams; } no issue.
                                        { 2d, Aug. 1889,   Arminda J. M. Wood; }
(*) see No. 231.

172.

SIMEON O. BENJAMIN, s. David and Elizabeth (Tuthill) Benjamin.
      b. Feb. 24, 1834.   m. Oct. 12, 1858.

Adelia Jane Hallock. da. Herman W. and Arminda (Youngs) Hallock.
      b. Aug. 9. 1841.
4 ch.   *Ella May, b. Aug. 27, 1859; m. Dec. 25, 1882, George Omer Hallock.
      ○Mary Florence, b. Feb. 29, 1868; m.   1887, Joshua T. Fanning.
      Bertha, b. Nov. 2, 1872, d. Mar 20, 1874.   Nina Ethelwyne, b. Mar. 20, 1879.
(*) See Mayo genealogy.   (○) See No. 253.

173.

MARY M. BENJAMIN, da. David and Elizabeth, (Tuthill) Benjamin.
    b. May 21, 1838.   m. May 29, 1856, as his 2d wife.

James M. Reeve. s. Jesse and   (Aldrich) Reeve.
    b. May 2, 1828.

6 ch.   *David O.*, b. Feb. 4, 1857, d. Mar. 2, 1857.   *David B.*, b. Mar. 22 1859, d. May 15, 1859.
        George Harvey, b. Aug. 19, 1861, d. in youth.
        *Henry J., b. Mar. 13, 1863; m. Oct. 12, 1887, Carrie B. Robinson.
        O*Sarah L.*, b.   m.   Edward G. Hudson.
        Herbert M., b. Jan. 31, 1871; m. June 16, 1897, ‖Maud M. Hallock.
(*) Has two ch., Beulah, Irma.   (O) See No. 220.
(‖) Da. of Zachariah and Caroline (Terry) Hallock, b. Feb. 29. 1876.

174.

FANNY M. FOURNIER, da. Peter and Maria (Bishop) Fournier.
    b. Jan. 11, 1843.   m. June 6, 1867.

John E. Aldrich, s. John and Mary (Howell) Aldrich.
    b. Mar. 22, 1842.

4 ch.   *Elliott F.*, b. Jan. 17, 1870.   *Frederick H.*, b. Oct. 9, 1873.
        Mary Louise, b. Oct. 5, 1878.   *Alice Justena*, b. Feb. 22, 1883.

175.

ANN ELIZA FOURNIER, da. Peter and Maria (Bishop) Fournier.
    b. Jan. 27, 1846.   m. Feb. 3, 1875, as his 2d wife.

George O. Reeve, s. Orry and Otsey (Brown) Reeve.
    b. July 1, 1829.   d. Apr. 28, 1890.

3 ch.   *Frank F.*, b. Dec. 18, 1875.   *Ann Maria*, b. June 21, 1878.
        Chauncey Tappen, b. Jan. 30, 1884.

176.

ALECTHA M. TUTHILL, da. Daniel M. and Maria (Downs) Tuthill.
    b.   m. Feb. 2, 1839.   d. June 19, 1871.

*John P. Terry, s. Howell and Hannah (Albertson) Terry.
    b. Sep. 21, 1818.

4 ch.   O*Alonzo P.*, b. June 10, 1842; m. May 2,)863, Annie Amanda Wells.
        Cassius M., b. Feb. 22, 1846; m. Nov. 13, 1871, Mary Molly Bailey.
        Rosabel E., b. Mar. 26, 1858, d Sep. 19, 1859. *Lillie M.*, b. May 26, 1861, d. Oct. 16, 1871.
(*) m. a 2d time.   (O) Had four ch., two of whom d. in youth.

177.

MARY ANN TUTHILL, da. Jehiel and Johanah (Hallock) Tuthill.
    b. June 28, 1828.   m. Oct. 29, 1846.

Harvey L. Fanning, s. Nathaniel and Abigail (Terry) Fanning.
    b. June 13, 1822.   d. Dec. 1, 1889.

7 ch. **249.** *Jane Louise*, b. Mar. 23, 1849; m. Mar. 9, 1869, John Gildersleeve.
    250. *Harvey P.*, b. Apr. 25, 1852; m. Dec. 31, 1877, Zola Goodale.
    251. *Mary Ella*, b. Feb. 20, 1855; m. Mar. 9, 1873, Louis Downs.
        Emily Ann, b. May 9, 1859, d. Aug. 11, 1863.
    252. *Carrie M.*, b. Jan. 3, 1863; m. Feb. 11, 1890, John Henry Carlton.
        Addie Woodhull, b. Feb. 26, 1866, d. Jan. 19, 1877.
    253. *Joshua T.*, b. Feb. 2, 1869; m.   Mary F. Benjamin.

178.

DANIEL MADISON TUTHILL, s. Jehiel and Johanah (Hallock) Tuthill,
    b. Nov. 30, 1830.   m. 1st, Nov. 17, 1852.   m. 2d, May 11, 1876.

1st, Mary A. Downs, da. Nicoll and Hannah (Wells) Downs.
    b. Dec. 9, 1830.   d. Oct. 14, 1875.

2d, Mary J. Wells, da. Joseph and Jane (Benjamin) Wells.
    b.

3 ch.   **Elsworth*, b.   m.   Hattie E. Weeks.
        Rosamond, b. June 14, 1855, d. Apr. 6, 1856.
        Rosamond I., b. Sep. 23, 1859, d. Nov. 23, 1860.
(*) Had a da. who d. Apr. 20, 1895, ae., 1 yr. 6 mo. and 8 days.

179.

SAMUEL TUTHILL, s. Jehiel and Johanah (Hallock) Tuthill.
    b. Aug. 18, 1839.   m. Nov. 13, 1866.

Eliza T. Wells, da. Salem and Elsie M. (Terry) Wells.
    b. Aug. 18. 1849.

3 ch.   *Samuel Terry*, b. Nov. 27, 1869, d. Sep. 14, 1870.
    254. *Emerson Sherwood*, b. Nov. 8, 1871; m. Nov. 10, 1891, Nellie L. Brown.
        Elsie May, b. May 22, 1875, d. Aug. 19. 1875.

180.

JOHANAH WELLS TUTHILL, da. Jehiel and Johanah (Hallock) Tuthill.
    b. June 23, 1843.   m. Jan. 31, 1867.

Horace B. Horton, s. Alvah and   (   ) Horton.
    b.

1 ch.   **Elizabeth*, b.   m.   Robert Gosman.
*) Has three ch.

181.

MARY E. CORWIN, da. Nathan and Mehitable (Tuthill) Corwin.
  b. Oct. 18, 1827.   m. Nov. 5, 1843.

  Francis Lane, s. Joseph and   (   ) Lane.
    b. Feb. 7, 1815.   d. Jan. 2, 1872.
  4 ch.   *Alice, b.   m.   James Vail; no issue.
    255. *Herbert W.*, b. Jan. 7, 1849; m. Dec. 20, 1870, Jennie R. Wells.
      Fannie, b. Sep. 8, 1851, d. unm.
    256. *Frank C.*, b. Oct. 15, 1867; m.   Rosabell Reeve.
  (*) d. Mar. 11, 1897.

182.

JANE CORWIN, da. Nathan and Mehitable (Tuthill) Corwin.
  b. Aug. 12, 1830.   m. Nov. 10, 1847.   d. Dec. 25, 1870.

  Nathaniel A. Griffin, s. Wells and Hannah (Wiggin) Griffin.
    b. Oct.   1823.
  3 ch.   *Ellen Jane*, b. May 27, 1849.   *Minnie Amanda*, b. May 12, 1851, d. Dec. 22, 1859.
    Nathan Corwin, b. May 7, 1863, d. Aug. 11, 1865.

183.

ROSABELLA CORWIN, da. Nathan and Mehitable (Tuthill) Corwin.
  b. Sep. 1, 1836.   m. Oct. 7, 1856.

  Charles Hallett, s. John and   (   ) Hallett.
    b. Oct. 3, 1833.
  4 ch.   *John Fred.*, b. Aug. 4, 1858; m. { 1st,   Nina Terry.
                                            { 2d,   Effie Lawrence.
    Frank Carl, b. Apr. 18, 1860; m.   Ella Bunce.
    Archibald Corwin, b. July 12, 1865.   *Jennie Avah*, b. Aug. 20, 1877.
  (*) Had one ch. by 1st wife, named Carll A., b. Mar. 21, 1883, and one ch. by 2d wife, named Valdemar, b. Feb. 25, 1898.

184.

MARY JANET DOWNS, d. Christopher N. and Elizabeth (Tuthill) Downs.
  b. Dec. 2, 1839.   m. Dec. 16, 1871.

  John Francis Terry, s. James and Emeline (Petty) Terry.
    b. Aug. 25, 1839.
  2 ch.   *John Newton*, b. Feb. 10, 1875; m. Aug. 6, 1897, Josephine Wallen.
    James Ellwood, b. Mar. 5, 1878, d. Jan. 24, 1881.
  (*) Had one ch. who d. in infancy.

185.

JOHN WASHINGTON DOWNS, s. Christopher N. and Elizabeth (Tuthill) Downs.
  b. Aug. 21, 1842.   m. Jan. 1, 1867.

  Millicent Jane Aldrich, d. Gershom and Mary L. (King) Aldrich.
    b. Mar. 22, 1850.
  2 ch. **257.** *John Earnest*, b. Aug. 10, 1870; m. Jan. 3, 1894, Leila E. Wells.
    Lulu Mary, b. Feb. 26, 1884.

186.

EUGENE E. HALLOCK, s. Joseph E. and Amanda (Tuthill) Hallock.
  b. Sep. 16, 1838.   m. Nov. 1, 1859.

  Rosalene Howell, da. George and Mary (Wells) Howell.
    b. Mar. 1838.
  4 ch.   *Keturah*, b. Aug. 28, 1863.   *Joseph Edwin*, b. Jan. 15, 1867.
    Frederick W., b. Mar. 2, 1871.   *Archibald*, b. Mar. 21, 1873, d. May 17, 1874.

187.

DORLISKA F. CONKLIN, da. Jedediah and Puah (Terry) Conklin.
  b. Nov. 10, 1828.   m. June 17, 1857.

  James Fordham Bassett, s. John and Frances (Fordham) Bassett.
    b. Nov. 5, 1824.
  4 ch.   *Frank Congdon*, b. June 10, 1858, d. Feb. 14, 1872.
    258. *Katherine Evelyn*, b. Nov. 14, 1860; m. Sep. 19, 1889, Walter Kimball
    Bertha Brown, b. Jan. 27, 1867; m. Sep. 19, 1897, Dr. John M. Lewis.
    George Hawley, b. Dec. 23, 1875.

188.

CATHERINE M. CONLIN, s. Jedediah and Puah (Terry) Conklin.
  b.   m. Oct.   1859.

  Dr. John Low, s.
    b.
  3 ch.   *Elizabeth B.*, b. Nov. 28, 1860.   *Edward H.*, b.   d.
    Frances B., b. Dec. 26, 1867, d. 1872.

189.

JOHN LEWIS TERRY, s. Lewis H. and Harriet (Fanning) Terry.
b. Dec. 12, 1835. m. 1st, Jan. 19, 1859. m. 2d, Dec. 19, 1875. m. 3rd, June 1, 1883. d. June 10, 1897.

1st, Sarah E. Buckley, da. Oliver K. and   (Penny) Buckley.
b. Oct. 1, 1841.   d. Mar. 17, 1873.

2d, Mary Emily Merrills, da. Henry and   (Beebe) Merrills.
b. Mar 27, 1849.   d. Apr. 17, 1884.

3d, Wid. Amelia E. Penny, *nee* Waterhouse, da. William and Cynthia E. (Booth) Waterhouse.
b. Oct. 4, 1838.

6 ch.   *Oliver H.*, b. Feb. 13, 1862; m. Oct. 30, 1889, Anna Corwin.
       Loreta B., b. Oct. 18, 1865; m. July 10, 1889, Daniel Dimon.
       Harriet M., b. Dec. 20, 1868; m. June 10, 1894, George Horton.
       Henrietta M., b. Aug. 17, 1876; m. Mar. 4, 1897, Charles S. Sage.
       John L., b. Dec. 14, 1877; d. July 29, 1878.   *Sarah E.*, b. Feb. 23, 1879.

190.

DORLISCA M. TERRY, da. Lewis H. and Harriet (Fanning) Terry.
b. Jan. 3, 1842.   m. Feb. 14, 1861.

Horace B. Tuthill, s. Isaac and Hannah (Benjamin) Tuthill.
b. Apr. 8, 1834.

4 ch.   *Ella Sophia*, b. Sep. 4, 1862; m. Feb. 16, 1885, George B. Horton.
       Annie S., b. Apr. 4, 1866; m. July 1890, George H. Prince.
       Lulu M., b. Feb. 14, 1874.   *Harold W.*, b. Oct. 8, 1893, d. May 18, 1894.

191.

CATHERINE M. TERRY, d. Lewis H. and Harriet (Fanning) Terry.
b. Nov. 20, 1843.   m. Dec. 23, 1863.

J. MADISON WELLS, s. Alden and Jane (Wells) Wells.
b. Apr. 28, 1842.

6 ch. **259.** *James Clarence*, b. Oct. 3, 1864; m. Sep. 1, 1888, Elida Trimnal.
       Joshua Sheridan, b. Jan. 14, 1867.   *Henry Alden*, b. Oct. 19, 1868.
   260. *Adriana*, b. Feb. 23, 1870; m. Sep. 21, 1894, Leonard G. Venn.
       °*Frank Terry*, b. May 14, 1874; m. Dec. 16, 1896, Fanny Jetter.
       Kate, b. Dec. 20, 1885.
(°) Has one ch., Florence.

192.

JAMES MADISON HALLOCK, s. Nathan T. and Mary (Dunster) Hallock.
b. Feb. 14, 1838.   m. Apr. 3, 1866.

Louise Boutcher, da. John and Rosanna (Brice) Boutcher.
b.

10 ch.   *Charles*, b.   m.   Jeanette Morris.
       William, b.   d.   *Howard*, b.   *Clarence*, b.
       Roy, b.   *Clifford*, b.   *John*, b.
       Annie, b.,   m.   Elma Bond.   *Bertha*, b   *Rosa*, b.

193.

WILLIAM H. H. HALLOCK, s. Nathan T. and Mary (Dunster) Hallock.
b.   m.   Dec. 7, 1864.

Hannah Eldridge, da. Samuel and Mary (King) Eldridge.
b.   1840.   d. Jan. 19, 1876.

5 ch.   *Mary*, b. Nov. 9, 1866.
       ✦William Seymour, b. Feb. 29, 1868; m. Dec. 18, 1889, Jennie E. Raynor.
       °*Graham Greenwood*, b. June 9, 1870; m. June 10, 1892. Libby G. Payne.
       Everett Harrison, b. Nov. 25, 1873.   *Herbert*, b. Jan. 16, 1876. d. Aug. 18, 1886.
(✦) Has one ch., Henry Franklin, b. Jan. 18, 1896.   (°) Has one ch., Freemont.

194.

MARTHA ADELAIDE HALLOCK, da. Nathan T. and Mary (Dunster) Hallock.
b.   m. Dec. 31, 1861.

William A. Haynes, s. Halsey and Mary (Horton) Haynes.
b.

4 ch.   *Annie*, b.   d.   *William*, b.   d.   *Monroe Halsey*, b.   d.
       Adda, b.   m.   Charles Hubbard.

195.

FRANCES MARY HALLOCK, da. Nathan T. and Mary (Dunster) Hallock.
b. Oct. 3, 1832.   m. Feb. 5, 1851.

Barnabas Wines, s. Barnabas and Temperance (Woodhull) Wines.
b. Apr. 14, 1823.

2 ch.   *Mary Frances*, b. Oct. 19, 1852.   *Horace Brewster*, b. Oct. 14, 1855.

196.

JOSEPHINE A. HALLOCK, da. Benjamin G. and Elizabeth A. (Hallock) Hallock.
  b. Oct. 5, 1828.   m. May 22, 1849.

Dennis K. Halsey, s. Harvey and Sarah L. (Kimberly) Halsey.
  b. Sep. 24, 1825.

3 ch. **261.** *Mary Sophia*, b.   m. Dec. 22, 1864, Josiah P. Howell.
       Fanny G., b.   m.   Ahasuerus Franckin; no issue.
    262. *Louise Kimberly*, b.   m. Oct. 31, 1878, Henry Gardiner.

197.

JAMES RICHARD HALLOCK, s. Benjamin C. and Elizabeth A. (Hallock) Hallock.
  b. Apr. 21, 1831.   m. 1st, Oct. 18, 1864.   m. 2d, Dec. 28. 1869.   d. June 1, 1898.

1st, Rosetta H. Corwin, da. Daniel and Huldey (Goodale) Corwin.
  b. May 29, 1842.   d. Aug. 24, 1865.

2d, Wid. Mary J. Reeve, *nee* Aldrich, da. Hiram and Miriam (Brown) Reeve.
  b. Oct. 1, 1828.

1 ch.   *Annie Tessora*, b. Nov. 27, 1870. d. Jan. 8, 1871.

198.

FANNY C. HALLOCK da. Benjamin G. and Elizabeth A. (Hallock) Hallock.
  b. Mar. 16, 1839.   m. June 21, 1865.

David R. Dayton, s. Eleasor and Elizabeth (Robinson) Dayton.
  b. Sep.   1841.

5 ch.   *Elizabeth*, b. Jan. 3. 1866, d unm. Apr. 3, 1890.
       Rossa H., b. Oct. 21, 1867; m. Oct. 30, 1894, George A. Reeve.
       Eleasor J. B., b July 27, 1869.   *La Rosseau C.*, b. Oct. 6, 1873.
       Helen C., b. May 8, 1876; m. Feb. 12, 1895, Robert A. Culver.

199.

EDWIN FORREST ACKERLY, s. Moses H. and Mary H. (Tyler) Ackerly.
  b. Nov. 5, 1847.   m. Oct. 10, 1878.

Sadie Hawkins, da. Brewster and   (   ) Hawkins.
  b.

3 ch.   *Julia M.*, b. Dec. 30, 1879.   *Edna*.   Another child.

200.

JOHN TYLER ACKERLY, s. Moses H. and Mary H. (Tyler) Ackerly.
  b. Sep. 15, 1850.   m. June 29, 1879.

Mary Floyd Wiggins, da. Floyd and Emily (King) Wiggins.
  b.

2 ch.   *Maud E.*, b. Apr.   1883.   *Floyd*, b.

201.

EVELYN MARIA ACKERLY, da. Moses H. and Mary H. (Tyler) Ackerly.
  b. July 9, 1852.   m. Oct. 15, 1879.   d. June 10, 1887.

Giles Turner Loomis, s. C. C. and   (Turner) Loomis.
  b.

2 ch.   *Agnes*, b.   d. Apr. 30, 1897.   *Guy*, b.

202.

NATHANIEL STRONG TUTHILL, s. Ellsworth and Helen (Hudson)Tuthill.
  b. Aug. 24, 1853.   m. Nov. 20, 1877.

Susan Jane Hawkins, da. Ebenezer and Mary L. (Albertson) Hawkins.
  b. Jan. 10, 1856.

1 ch.   *Clara Strong*, b. Oct. 13, 1878.

203.

GEORGE HUDSON BEACH, s. Albertus H. and Margaret E. (Whitney) Beach.
  b. July 23, 1854.   m. Dec. 24, 1879.

Eliza Agnes Kidger, da. Thomas and Mary (Wilson) Kidger.
  b. Dec. 1, 1858.

1 ch.   *George Albertus*, b.   d.

204.

HENRY ALBERT BUDD, s. Samuel and Mary H. (Beach) Budd.
  b.   1866.   m.

Julia Martha McClave, da. John and Charlotte L. (Wood) McClave.
  b. Apr. 16, 1873.

1 ch.   *Hudson*, b. Aug. 19, 1896.

205.

ALFRED ELIOTT HALL, s. William C. J. and Maria M. (Woodhull) Hall.
  b. Apr. 25, 1861.   m. July 2, 1885.

Elizabeth McElroy, da.
  b.

4 ch.   *William McElroy*, b. July 25, 1886, d. Mar. 10, 1893.   *Alfred Irwin*, b. Dec. 1, 1888.
       Carol Miller, b. May 22, 1892.   *Shirley McElroy*, b. July 10, 1895.

206.

CARRIE SOPHIA WOODHULL, da. Joseph H. and Hannah (Aldrich) Woodhull.
b. May 8, 1862.   m. Oct 28, 1885.

Charles Fordham, s. James and Amanda (   ) Fordham.
b. Mar. 15, 1848.

1 ch.   *Leroy W.*, b. Nov. 8, 1894.

207.

GEORGE BROWN WOODHULL, s. Zophar and Cornelia A. (Brown) Woodhull.
b. June 8, 1869.   m. Dec. 9. 1896.

Georgia Keeney Lester, da. Cornelius and Mary S. (Cartwright) Lester.
b. June 14, 1871.

1 ch.   *Sterling Brown*, b. Jan. 31, 1899.

208.

NERVA FRANCIS BUNCE, s. William C. and Jeanette W. (Hudson) Bunce.
b. Sep. 4, 1859.   m.   1882.

Virginia E. Fruelson, da.
b.

5 ch.   *Mabel T.*, b. Jan. 7, 1883.   *William F.*, b. Aug. 29, 1884.   *Jeanette H.*, b. Aug. 16, 1888.
         Clara S., b. Oct. 5, 1891.   *Lillian V.*, b. June 20, 1894.

209.

RUTH ESTELLE REEVE, da. George B. and Laetitia (Young) Reeve.
b. May 13, 1857.   m. Nov. 6, 1878.

John Francis Booth, s. John F. and Mary (Wells) Booth.
b.

1 ch.   *John Carlton*, b. Aug. 20, 1891.

210.

JAMES WICKHAM REEVE, s. George B. and Laetitia (Young) Reeve.
b. Apr. 12, 1859.   m. Nov. 20, 1887.

Kate Booth Wells, da. John and Minerva (Hooper) Wells.
b.

1 ch.   *Esther Leslie*, b. Nov. 5, 1888.

211.

LIZZIE KEYSER REEVE, da. George B. and Laetitia (Young) Reeve.
b. Mar. 20, 1861.   m. Feb. 2, 1887.

William Edward Hallock, s. Charles and Rachel (Adamson) Hallock.
b.

2 ch.   *Marjorie*, b. Feb. 15, 1888.   *George Reeve*, b. Dec. 1891,

212.

CAROLINE HUDSON REEVE, da. George B. and Laetitia (Young) Reeve.
b. Apr. 12, 1859.   m. Oct. 13, 1884.

Oliver Howard Tuthill, s. Warren L. and Sarah (Wells) Tuthill.
b. Sep. 23, 1864.

2 ch.   *Madeline*, b. May 3, 1885.   *Grace Reeve*, b. Nov. 24, 1887.

213.

DAVID HARRIES YOUNG, s. Daniel H. and Mary (Harries) Young.
b. Apr. 5, 1865.   m.

*EVA BENJAMIN HUDSON, da. Benjamin C. and Sarah A. (Cartwright) Hudson.
b. Mar. 22, 1868.

2 ch.   *Helen Hudson*, b. Apr. 25, 1887.   *Thomas Tuthill*, b. July 30, 1892.
(*)See No. 115.

214.

EDWARD LAWRENCE STIMSON, s. Dr. William and Maria J. (Hudson) Stimson.
b. Dec. 15, 1867.   m. Oct. 8, 1889.

Bertha Estelle McClure, da. Jacob and Annie (Hill) McClure.
b. Dec. 25, 1868.

2 ch.   *Bessie M.*, b. Oct. 5, 1890.   *Edwin Rex*, b. Nov. 3, 1896.

215.

ALBERT RUTHERFORD STIMSON, s. Dr. William and Maria J. (Hudson) Stimson.
b.

Grace Ellen Means, da. William and Lydia T. (Catlett) Means.
b. May 28, 1868.

1 ch.   *Alberta Grace*, b. Nov. 25, 1896.

216.

CHARLES B. HUDSON, s. Charles S. and Martha (Terry) Hudson.
  b. Nov.   1858.   m. Apr. 16, 1879.
*ELIZABETH H. TUTHILL, da. Jeremiah G. and Hannah R. (Howell) Tuthill.
  b. Mar. 13, 1855.
2 ch.   *Brewster Terry*, b. Jan 12, 1880.   *Howard*, b. Apr. 18, 1882.
(*) See No. 236.

217.

BRYANT T. HUDSON. s. Charles S. and Martha (Terry) Hudson.
  b. Oct.   1862.   m. June   1888.
Martha Roberts. da. Joseph and Susan (Rowe) Roberts.
  b. June 1864.
3 ch.   *Bryant C.*, b. Sep.   1889.   *Sallie Roe*, b.   1891.   *Joseph Roberts*, b.   1893.

218.

SALLIE ROE HUDSON. da. Charles S and Martha (Terry) Hudson.
  b. Oct.   1866.   m. Oct. 6, 1885.
William E. Dugan, s. John Dugan, of Rochester, N. Y.
  b.   1859.
2 ch.   *Charles Hudson*, b. July   1886.   *William Ed.*, b. Dec.   1889

219.

M. AUGUSTA HUDSON, da. Charles S. and Martha (Terry) Hudson.
  b. July   1869.   m. Dec.   1893.
Edward S. Edwards, s. Edward Edwards, of Patchogue, N. Y.
  b.   1868.
1 ch.   *Urania Hudson*, b. Dec. 14, 1894.

220.

EDWARD G. HUDSON, s. S. Terry and Mary E. (Wells) Hudson.
  b. Apr. 15, 1866.   m.
*SARAH ELIZABETH REEVE, da. James M. and Mary M. (Benjamin) Reeve.
  b.
3 ch.   *Bertha Arabella*, b. Aug. 31, 1890.   *James Russell*, b. Jan. 23, 1893.
         Myron Terry, b. Feb. 7, 1896.   (*) See No. 173.

221.

ADA ROBERTS HUDSON, da. S. Terry and Mary E. (Wells) Hudson.
  b. Apr. 23, 1868.   m. Dec. 18, 1890.
J. Addison Young. s. J. Halsey and Lucy (Young) Young.
  b. Sev. 14. 1866.
2 ch.   *Walter Halsey*, b. Mar. 29, 1892.   *Helen Alice*, b. Apr. 8, 1895, d. Aug. 1, 1896.

222.

DAVID LEWIS DOWNS, s. Albert T. and Mianda (Wells) Downs.
  b. May 11, 1868.   m. Nov. 27, 1889.
Cora Ethelyn Young, da. John L. and Harriet E. (Robinson) Young.
  b. May 3, 1873.
3 ch.   *Ethelyn E.*, b. Jan. 3, 1891.   *Viola Althea*, b. Sep. 15, 1894.
         Iva Adelle, b. Mar. 8, 1897; d. Dec. 16, 1898.

223.

FREDERICK SKILLMAN DOWNS, s. Albert T. and Mianda (Wells) Downs.
  b. June 30, 1870.   m. Dec. 4, 1895.
Mary Augusta Howell, da. Chauncey P. and Marrietta (Young) Howell.
  b. Jan. 6, 1875.
2 ch.   *Eloise Brown*, b. Oct. 25, 1896.   *Marrietta*, b. June 3, 1898.

224.

THADDEUS SHERMAN WELLS, s. Addison J. and Elsie M. (Wells) Wells.
  b. Aug. 31, 1870.   m. Nov. 1, 1893.
Isabel H. Otis, da. Edward T. and Margaret (Vredenburg) Otis.
  b. Dec. 10, 1870.
2 ch.   *Margaret*, b. Aug. 18, 1896.   *Dorothy*, b. Feb. 9, 1898.

225.

EVA ALMIRA WELLS, da. Addison J. and Elsie M. (Wells) Wells.
  b. Sep. 11, 1872.   m. July 12, 1892.   d. Jan. 10, 1899.
Lucian Jarvis Bisbie, s. John F. and Eliza (O'Brien) Bisbie.
  b.   21, 1867.
1 ch.   *Elsie Eliza*, b. June 29, 1893.

226.

ALICE EVELYN DOWNS, da. John T. and Rachel H. (Wells) Downs.
  b. Apr. 25, 1875.   m. June 1, 1897.
Edward P. Wells, s. Joshua M. and Betsey H. (Young) Wells.
  b. Jan. 9, 1868.
1 ch.   *Russell Lenwood*, b. Mar. 23, 1898.

227.

WILLIAM JAMES WELLS, s. William C. and Seleucia F. (Hallock) Wells.
  b. Feb. 17, 1850.   m. Dec. 13, 1871.
Jennie Williams, da. Samuel and Janet (Nevins) Williams.
  b. Dec. 24, 1852.
2 ch.   *Maud*, b. Nov. 4, 1872.   *Jessie*, b. June 7, 1874.

228.

E. HELEN WELLS. da. Eurystheus and Avis R. (Hallock) Wells.
  b. Jan. 14, 1861.   m. June 9, 1884.
  Rev. David W. Hutchinson, s. James and Sarah (McMaster) Hutchinson.
    b. Dec. 8, 1863
3 ch.   *David*, b. May 17, 1885.   *Harold* and *Russell*, (twins), b. July 7, 1895.

229.

MARIA TUTHILL BENJAMIN, da. Richard H. and Hannah (Smith) Benjamin.
  b. Oct. 21, 1862.   m. Dec. 16, 1886.   d. Apr. 4, 1898.
  Louis Goldsmith Rathbun, s. John T. and Sarah (Benjamin) Rathbun.
    b. Oct. 28, 1858.
4 ch.   *Louis Goldsmith*, b. June 2, 1882, d. Mar. 10, 1898.   *John Hampton*, b. Jan. 3, 1889
         Mina Recar, b. July 9, 1890.   *Sarah Louise*, b. Nov. 16, 1892.

230.

MARY T. LUCE, da. George O. and Charity W. (Hallock) Luce.
  b. Sep. 12, 1837.   m. Nov. 5, 1860.
  Daniel S. Terry, s. Daniel C. and Lorinda (Benjamin) Terry.
    b. Jan. 26, 1839.
6 ch.   *Henrietta*, b.   m.   Herbert W. Wells.
         Leslie L., b.   Four children died in infancy.

231.

CHARLES E. LUCE, s. George O. and Deborah (Wells) Luce.
  b. June 4, 1846.   m. Dec. 12, 1867.
  *LORENIA N. BENJAMIN, da. Caleb H. and Hannah M. (Youngs) Benjamin.
    b. July 19, 1845.
3 ch.   †*Orvis H.*, b. Oct. 31, 1868; m. Oct. 17, 1893, Winona L. Hallock.
         George E., b. Apr. 13, 1872.   *Eva V.*, b. Sep. 29, 1881.
(*) See No. 171.   (†) Has 1 ch. Annie L., b. June 1897.

232.

RACHEL ANN LUCE, da. John T. and Mary B. (Tuthill) Luce.
  b. Sep. 25, 1833.   m. Mar. 24, 1851.
  Rev. Edward K. Fanning, s. Nathaniel and   Fanning.
    b. June 30, 1820.
3 ch.   *Edward Olin*, b. Sep. 15, 1852.
         Rachel Emma, b. Mar. 15, 1857; m.   William S. S. Powell.
         **Annie Marietta*, b. Oct. 17, 1863; m.   Rev. Samuel Gurney.
(*) d. June 13, 1894.

233.

GEORGE H. TUTHILL, s. George H. and Jemima (Luce) Tuthill.
  b. Sep. 29, 1838.   m. Nov. 21, 1860.
  Nannie M. Beebe, da. Daniel and Nancy (Terry) Beebe.
    b. Sep. 7, 1840.
4 ch. **263.** *Epher Whitaker*, b. June 16, 1863; m. { 1st, Nov. 23, 1887. Eva M. Jackson.
                                                     { 2nd, May 29, 1890. Ardella Luce.
      264. *Frederick H*, b. July 31, 1865; m. Nov. 23, 1886, Ruth Albertson.
      265. *Rose Elma*, b. Aug. 4, 1872; m. Nov. 5, 1890. Louis E. Downs.
         Cuyler B., b. July 20, 1874; m. Feb. 22, 1898, Cynthia May.

234.

CHARLES S. TUTHILL, s. George H. and Jemima (Luce) Tuthill.
  b. Jan. 2, 1844.   m. Oct. 28, 1876.
  Elma H. Petty, da. Sylvester and Joannah (Reeve) Petty.
    b. Oct. 6, 1853.
1 ch.   *Laura H.*, b. Aug. 29, 1885.

235.

ELEANOR HOWELL, da. Daniel and Jemima (Howell) Howell.
  b. May 15, 1825.   m. Oct. 19, 1841.
  Daniel Warner, s.
    b. June 9, 1818.

13 ch. *Allen M.*, b. Oct. 6, 1842; m. { 1st, Achsa Howell.
2nd, Isabel Howell.
3rd, Kate Fordham.

266. *Frances M.*, b. July 11, 1844; m. A. H. Corwin.
Josephine A, b. May 27, 1846. d. Oct. 17, 1848.
Martha R., b. Mar. 3, 1848; m. Daniel Goldsmith.
Eunice E., b. Feb. 19, 1850; m. Hiram F. Howell.
Agnes M., b. Dec. 16, 1851; m. C. A. Edwards.
Julia H., b. Dec. 14, 1853; d. May 10, 1871.
Waldo D., b. Feb. 11, 1856; m. Mary Howell.
Charles H., b. May 11, 1858; m. Ella Terry.
Eleanor B., b. July 20, 1860; m. John
John B., b. Aug. 12, 1862; m. Carrie Terry.
Eugene G., b. Nov. 27, 1864; m. { 1st, Leta Hallock.
2nd, Alice Hammond.
Frnk E., b. Jan. 5, 1868; m. Grace McNey.

236.

HANNAH ROSETTA HOWELL, da. Daniel and Jemima (Howell) Howell.
b. Sep. 28, 1828. m. Dec. 14, 1849.

Jeremiah Goldsmith Tuthill, s. Ira B. and Elizabeth (Goldsmith) Tuthill.
b. Dec. 24, 1826. d. July 1, 1898.

8 ch. *Ella C.*, b. July 11, 1851, d. Dec. 17, 1860.
*Harrison H., b. April 11, 1853; m. June 14, 1877, Rhoda Gildersleeve.
OElizabeth H., b. Mar. 13, 1855; m. Apr. 16, 1879, Charles Hudson.
Ira B., b. Mar. 13, 1855, d. Aug. 3, 1855.
‖H. Rosetta, b. Nov. 18, 1857; m. May 31, 1883, Dr. Arthur Terry.
†Jeremiah G., b. July 19, 1861; m. Dec. 10, 1884, Hattie Hildreth.
§Howard G., b. Nov. 14, 1863; m. { 1st, June 13, 1887, Adaline Ahillict.
2nd, June 12, 1895. Irene Conkling.
¶John T., b. Sep. 19, 1867; m. Dec. 12, 1892, Harriet B. Knight.

(*) has 2 ch. Goldsmith B., b. Aug. 22, 1878 and Harrington H., b. May 19, 1885. (O) See No. 216.
(‖) has 3 ch. Arthur H., b. May 18, 1884; Rosetta and Robert, twins, b. Feb. 27, 1889; Robert, d.
Nov. 14, 1897. (†) has 3 ch. Harry H., b. June 16, 1887; Marian G., b. Apr. 10, 1891; Bruce C.,
b. Mar. 28· 1895. (§) has 1 ch. Ruth C., b. Oct. 4, 1896. (¶) has 2 ch., John T. and Elizabeth.

237.

H. HARRISON HOWELL, s. Daniel and Jemima (Howell) Howell.
b. Mar. 31, 1830. m. 1st, Sep. 8, 1858. m. 2nd, Dec. 29, 1875.

1st, Catherine Tuthill, da. Charles and Phebe (Raynor) Tuthill.
b. Oct. 15, 1836. d. Aug. 7, 1874.

2nd, Melinda Young, da. Samuel and Jane (Cook) Young.
b. Sep. 18, 1841.

1 ch. **267.** *Harry Micah*, b. Nov. 24, 1859; m. Feb. 22, 1889, Hannah C. Vail.

238.

ELECTA HOWELL, da Daniel and and Jemima (Howell) Howell.
b. Mar. 7, 1834. m. Apr. 15, 1855.

Benjamin R. Griffing, s. Moses and Hettie A. (Moore) Griffing.
b. Nov. 25, 1831.

3 ch. **268.** *Hettie D.*, b. July 24, 1858; m. Dr. H. P. Terry.
*Daniel H., b. Sep. 17, 1860; m. Emma Richards.
Maria T., b. Oct. 26, 1872.
(*) has one ch. Paul R., b. Mar. 25, 1886.

239.

MARINDA ANN HOWELL, da. Daniel and Jemima (Howell) Howell.
b. Feb. 7, 1840. m. Jan. 4, 1860.

H. Beecher Halsey, s. Hiram and Melissa (Tuthill) Halsey.
b. Mar. 9, 1833.

3 ch. **269.** *Lizzie Beecher*, b. Jan. 15, 1865; m. W. C. Rogers.
270. *Benjamin Griffing*, b. Apr. 10, 1867; m. Feb. 7. 1889, Josephine M. Jagger.
Ruth Amelia, b. Sep. 19, 1876, d. Jan. 22, 1877.

240.

MILFORD T. BENJAMIN, s. Van Rensselaer and Phebe (Tuthill) Benjamin.
b. Aug. 17, 1847. m. Dec. 8, 1880.

*Deborah J. Hallock, da. Benjamin L. and Mary J. (Mayo) Hallock.
b. June 26, 1853.

2 ch. *Mary Ethel*, b. Jan. 19, 1884. *Albert Halsey*, b. June 19, 1896.
(*) See Mayo genealogy.

241.

FRANCES E. YOUNG, da. Joshua L. and Sophronia (Benjamin) Young.
b. Jan. 20, 1837. m. Nov. 1, 1854.

John Hallock, s. John F. and Sophronia (Wells) Hallock.
b. Dec. 4, 1832.

4 ch.   *Alice Evelyn*, b. Mar. 1, 1856, d. Jan. 25, 1865.
       Hannah Janet, b. Mar. 8, 1860, d. Feb. 24, 1865.
       John Alden, b. Dec. 11. 1864, d. Mar. 4. 1865.
  271. *John Morse*, b. Jan. 8, 1868; m. Dec. 15, 1886, Ellenmietta Hallock Woodhull.

242.

JOHN LEONARD YOUNG, s. Joshua L. and Sophronia (Benjamin) Young.
    b. Apr. 25, 1842.   m. Nov. 26, 1862.

Harriet E. Robinson, da. Joshua and Mary (Benjamin) Robinson.
    b. July 15, 1843.

6 ch. **272.** *Ida May*, b. Jan. 15, 1864; m.   William H. Corwin.
    273. *Clarence Joshua*, b. Mar. 10, 1866; m.   Ida D. H. Dayton.
      Cora Ethaline, b. May 3, 1873; m.   David Lewis Downs.
      Chauncey Hallock, b. Mar. 12, 1877.   *Anetha Genevieve*, b. Apr. 17, 1880.
      John Ross, b. July 4, 1884, d. Apr. 5, 1885.

243.

ADELIA SOPHRONIA YOUNG, da. Joshua L. and Sophronia (Benjamin) Young.
    b. Apr. 15, 1844.   m. Dec. 6, 1864.

John Martyn Dimond, s. Daniel and Harriet E. (Davis) Dimond.
    b. May 18, 1843.

3 ch. **274.** *Henry Goldsmith*, b. Sep. 5, 1866; m. { 1st, Dec. 25, 1889, Alice A. Hudson.
                                  { 2nd, Oct. 27, 1897, Lottie M. Gooding.
      John Frank, b. Sep. 2, 1872; m. Dec. 24, 1895, Hattie M. Jennings.
      Daniel Young, b. Mar. 22, 1874; m. Aug. 24, 1897, Huldah A. Taft.

244.

MARIETTA YOUNG, da. Joshua L. and Sophronia (Benjamin) Young.
    b. June 27, 1846.   m. Nov. 2, 1868.

Chauncey P. Howell, s. Sylvester and Nancy (Young) Howell.
    b. Oct. 5, 1845.

4 ch.   *Addie Evelyn*, b. Nov. 19. 1870, d. Aug. 20, 1873.
      Alice Janet, b. Aug. 12, 1872, d. Aug. 15, 1873.
      May Augusta, b. Jan. 6, 1875; m. Dec. 4, 1895, Frederick S. Downs.
      Elizabeth Frances, b. Sep. 13, 1881.

245.

DAVID HALSEY YOUNG, s. Joshua L. and Sophronia (Benjamin) Young.
    b. Sep. 12, 1848.   m. May 26, 1872.

Iona Zytella Wells, da. George F. and Mary P. (Young) Wells.
    b. Sep. 21, 1855.

6 ch.   *David Addison*, b. Apr. 23, 1873; m. Dec. 18, 1895. Eva May Taft.
      Harriet Elizabeth, b. Feb. 3. 1875; m. Jan. 15, 1896, Arthur W. Wells.
      Charles Ernest, b. Oct. 21, 1878.   *William Halsey*, b. Mar. 18, 1883
      Lucy May, b. Dec. 8, 1890, d. Oct. 17,1891.   *Nellie Iona*, b. Aug. 28, 1893.

246.

GEORGE LESTER YOUNG, s. Joshua L. and Sophronia (Benjamin) Young,
    b. Mar. 2, 1853.   m. Dec. 23, 1875.

Mary Ella Hallock. da. Terry and Elizabeth (Youngs) Hallock.
    b. Dec. 17, 1855.

2 ch.   *Emily Veola*, b. July 20, 1878 .   *Addison Lester*, b. July 29, 1882.

247.

ALBERT BENJAMIN YOUNG, s. Joshua L. and Sophronia (Benjamin) Young.
    b. Jan. 8, 1858.   m. Dec. 10, 1878.

Rosaella M. Robinson, da Christopher and Mary (Benjamin) Robinson.
    b. Oct. 17, 1857.

2 ch.   *Ethel May*, b. May 11, 1880, and *Archie Ray*, b. July 4, 1891, d. Oct. 4, 1891.

248.

MARIA ELIZABETH BENJAMIN, da. Caleb H. and Hannah M. (Youngs) Benjamin.
    b. June 12, 1844.   m.

Henry Terry, s. Conklin and Laura (Benjamin) Terry.
    b.

3 ch.   *Hannah*, b. Aug. 27, 1872; m.   1897,   Salmon.
      Irving L., b. Apr.   1877.   *Mabel*, b.

249.

JANE LOUISE FANNING, da. Harvey L. and Mary A. (Tuthill) Fanning.
    b. Mar. 23, 1849.   m. Mar. 9, 1869.

John Gildersleeve, s. Andrew and Annie (Reeve) Gildersleeve.
    b.

4 ch.   *Fannie Louise*, b. Oct.   1874.   *Jennie May*, b.   d.
      John Andrew, b. Feb. 2, 1884.   *Merriam Kirkup*, b. Sep.   1887.

250.

HARVEY P. FANNING, s. Harvey L. and Mary A. (Tuthill) Fanning.
  b. Apr. 25, 1852. m. Dec. 31, 1877.
Zola Goodale, da. Oscar and Betsey (Davis) Goodale.
  b.
4 ch. *Addie*, b. *Oscar Ford*, b. May 1879. *Cora*, *May*, b. Feb. 1886.

251.

MARY ELLA FANNING, da. Harvey L and Mary A. (Tuthill) Fanning.
  b. Feb. 20, 1855. m. Mar. 9, 1873. d. Dec. 14, 1886
Louis Downs, s. Sylvester and Angeline (Corwin) Downs.
  b.
2 ch. *Louis*, b. Nov. 1874. *James Harvey*, b. Sep. 1876.

252.

CARRIE M. FANNING, da. Harvey L. and Mary A. (Tuthill) Fanning.
  b. Jan. 3, 1863. m. Feb. 11, 1890.
John H. Carlton, s. John Carlton.
  b.
3 ch. *William M.*, b. Jan. 10, 1891. *George H.*, b. Aug 28, 1893. *Margaretta*, b. July 8, 1897.

253.

JOSHUA T. FANNING, s. Harvey L. and Mary A. (Tuthill) Fanning.
  b. Feb. 2, 1869. m.
MARY F. BENJAMIN, da. Simeon O. and Delia J. (Hallock) Benjamin. See No. 172.
  b. Feb. 29, 1868.
2 ch. *Marjorie May*, b. July 30, 1887. *Florence Adelia*, b. Feb. 14, 1894.

254.

EMERSON S. TUTHILL, s. Samuel and Eliza T. (Wells) Tuthill.
  b. Nov. 8, 1871. m. Nov. 10, 1891.
Nellie L. Brown, da. Philetus and Millicent (Warner) Brown.
  b. May 29, 1875.
1 ch. *Rollo Samuel*, b. June 27, 1895.

255.

HERBERT W. LANE, s. Francis and Mary E. (Corwin) Lane.
  b. Jan. 7, 1849. m. Dec. 20, 1870.
Jennie R. Wells, da. John R. and Maria T. (Hegeman) Wells.
  b.
1 ch. *Harold M.*, b. May 22, 1873; m. Dec. 6, 1893, Ella G. Linds.

256.

FRANK C. LANE, s. Francis and Mary E. (Corwin) Lane.
  b. Oct. 15, 1867. m.
Rosabell Reeve, da. Oliver and Juliaetta (   ) Reeve.
  b.
2 ch. *Mary Alice*, b. Dec. 7, 1889. *Vivian F.*, b. Mar. 30, 1893.

257.

JOHN EARNEST DOWNS, s. John W. and Millicent J. (Aldrich) Downs.
  b. Aug. 10, 1870. m. Jan. 3, 1894.
LEILA E. WELLS, da. Oliver F. and Henrietta J. (Fanning) Wells. See No.
  b. Dec. 2, 1876.
1 ch. *Hazel Marie*, b. June 22, 1897.

258.

KATHERINE EVELYN BASSETT, da. James F. and Dorliska F. (Conklin) Bassett.
  b. Nov. 14, 1860. m. Sep. 19, 1889.
Walter Kimball, s. Charles W. and Mary E. (Town) Kimball.
  b. May 4, 1861.
2 ch. *Fordham Bassett*, b. Nov. 10, 1890. *Stuart English*, b. Nov. 24, 1893.

259.

JAMES CLARENCE WELLS, s. J. Madison and Catherine M. (Terry) Wells.
  b. Oct. 3, 1864. m. Sep. 1, 1888.
Elida Trimnal, da.
  b.
4 ch. *J. Madison*, b. Aug., 1890. *Marjorie*, b. Nov. 1893, d. Aug. 1894.
       Adriana P., b. Feb., 1895. *Frank*, b. Aug. 2, 1897.

260.

ADRIANA WELLS, da. J. Madison and Catherine M. (Terry) Wells.
  b.
Leonard G. Venn, of Westfield, N. J.
  b.
2 ch. *Howard*, b. June 19, 1895, d. Sep. 21, 1895. *Beatrice*, b. Mar. 19, 1897.

261.

MARY SOPHIA HALSEY, da. Dennis K. and Josephine A. (Hallock) Halsey.
b.   m. Dec. 22, 1864.
  Josiah P. Howell, s. John H. and Nancy (Oakley) Howell.
  b. July 27, 1843.
  2 ch.   *Helen McE.* b.   *Josiah P.* b.

262.

LOUISE KIMBERLY HALSEY, da. Dennis K. and Josephine A. (Hallock) Halsey.
b.   m. Oct. 31, 1878.
  Henry Gardiner, s. Henry and Mary J. (Jessup) Gardiner.
  b. Feb. 20, 1855.
  3 ch.   *Henry H.*, b. Oct. 14, 1881.   *Josephine L.*, b. Sep. 29, 1883.   *Lion*, b. Sep. 20, 1891.

263.

EPHER WHITAKER TUTHILL, s. George H. and Nannie M. (Beebe) Tuthill.
  b. June 16, 1863.   m. 1st, Nov. 22, 1887.   m. 2d, May 29, 1890.
  1st, Eva M. Jackson, da. Marshall and Mary Ann (Foster) Jackson.
  b.   d. Dec. 28, 1888.
  2d, Ardella Y. Luce, da. Hallock and Betsey J. (Young) Luce.
  b. May 29, 1863.
  3 ch.   *Vernon M.*, b. Dec. 24, 1888.   *George L.*, b. Apr. 14, 1891.   *Milly E.*. b. Feb. 4, 1897.

264.

FREDERICK H. TUTHILL, s. George H. and Nannie M. (Beebe) Tuthill.
  b. July 31, 1865.   m. Nov. 23, 1886.
  Ruth Albertson, da. Richard and Sarepta (Aldrich) Albertson.
  b.
  3 ch.   *Wayne*, b. Nov. 25, 1888.   *Irene*, b. Oct., 1891.   *Kenneth*, b. June 16, 1897.

265.

ROSE ELMA TUTHILL, da. George H. and Nannie M. (Beebe) Tuthill.
  b Aug. 4, 1872.   m. Nov. 5, 1890.
  Louis E. Downs, s. Sheldon and Matilda (Hallock) Downs.
  b.
  2 ch.   *Florence*. b. Nov., 1891.   *Louis L.*, b. Nov., 1893.

266.

FRANCES M. WARNER, da. Daniel and Eleanor (Howell) Warner.
  b. July 11, 1844.   m.
  A   H. Corwin, s.
  b.
  2 ch.   **William H.*, b. Mar. 20, 1865; m.   Mary B. Fanning.
          °Clifford E., b. Dec. 15, 1866; m.   Elizabeth Stimson.
  (*) Has one son, Henry F., b. Nov. 16, 1891.   (°) Has one da., Julia S., b. June 7, 1896.

267.

HARRY MICAH HOWELL, s H. Harrison and Catherine (Tuthill) Howell.
  b. Nov. 25, 1859.   m. Feb. 22, 1889.
  Hannah C. Vail, da. Daniel and Ada (Smith) Vail.
  b.
  1 ch.   *Eric V.*, b. Aug. 29, 1891.

268.

HETTIE D. GRIFFING, da. Benjamin R. and Electa (Howell) Griffing.
  b. July 24, 1858.   m.
  Dr. H. P. Terry, s.
  b.
  4 ch.   *Eva*, b. Jan. 24, 1880.   *Rose Parsons*, b. Jan. 19, 1882.
          Hettie G., b. Feb. 10, 1886.   *Henry P.*, b. June 6, 1888, d. Mar., 1894.

269.

LIZZIE BEECHER HALSEY, da. H. Beecher and Marinda A. (Howell) Halsey.
  b. Jan. 15, 1865.   m.
  W   C. Rogers, s. Hermon and Phebe A. (Young) Rogers.
  b.
  3 ch.   *Howard H.*, b. Nov. 5, 1886.   *Frank B.*, b. Apr. 4, 1888.   *George C.*, b. Sep. 16, 1890.

270.

BENJAMIN GRIFFING HALSEY, s. H. Beecher and Marinda A. (Howell) Halsey.
  b. Apr. 10, 1867.   m. Feb. 7, 1889.
  Josephine M. Jagger, da. Andrew J. and Rachel (Bishop) Jagger.
  b. May 22, 1863.
  4 ch.   *Genevieve Adell*, b. Apr. 12, 1890.   *Harold Beecher*, b. Sep. 20, 1891.
          Andrew Jagger, b. Mar. 13, 1894.   *Wilmot Benjamin*, b. July 13, 1895.

271.

JOHN MORSE HALLOCK, s. John and Frances E. (Young) Hallock.
 b. Jan. 8, 1868. m. Dec. 15, 1886.

 *Ellennietta H. Woodhull, da. John W. and Rosalene E. (Hallock) Woodhull.
  b. Aug. 28, 1866.

 1 ch. *Alice Evelyn*, b. Dec. 6, 1889.

(*) See Mayo genealogy, No. 28.

272.

IDA MAY YOUNG, da. John L. and Harriet E. (Robinson) Young.
 b. Jan. 15, 1864. m. Dec. 21, 1882.

 William H. Corwin, s. John H. and Phebe A. (Corwin) Corwin.
  b. Aug. 20, 1858.

 2 ch. *Charles E.*, b. Nov. 26, 1885, d. Jan. 12, 1887. *Raymond C.*, b. Aug. 12, 1888.

273.

CLARENCE JOSHUA YOUNG, s. John L. and Harriet E. (Robinson) Young.
 b. Mar. 10, 1866. m. June 4, 1893.

 Ida D. H. Dayton, da. Webb and Mary E. (Corwin) Dayton.
  b. Nov. 9, 1872.

 2 ch. *John Lawrence*, b. June 23, 1894. *Harry Lynias*, b. Mar. 14, 1896.

274.

HENRY GOLDSMITH DIMOND, s. John M. and Adelia S. (Youngs) Dimond.
 b. Sep. 5, 1866. m. 1st, Dec. 25, 1889. m. 2d, Oct. 27, 1897.

 1st, ALICE ANGELINE HUDSON, da. S. Terry and Mary E. (Wells) Hudson; see No.
  b. Feb. 2, 1870. d. Jan. 21, 1895.

 2d, Lottie M. Gooding, da. Seth and Mary ( ) Gooding.
  b. July 23, 1870.

 4 ch. *Agatha*, b. July 19, 1891. *Henry Hudson*, b. May 8, 1893.
   Alice, b. Jan. 11, 1895. *Mary Adelia*, b. 1898.

JONATHAN, GEORGE AND JOSEPH HAVENS.

1.

JONATHAN HAVENS, s. George and Eleanor (Thurston) Havens.
 b. Feb. 2, 1681. m. Jan. 1, 1706-7. d. Aug. 5, 1748.

 Hannah Brown, da.
  b. 1788-9. d. Aug. 4, 1754.

 10 ch. **2.** *George,* b. m. Mary.
   3. *Jonathan,* b. Jan. 29, 1709; m. Jan. 27, 1728, Catherine M. Nicoll.
   4. *Constant,* b. in 1713; m. { 1st, Abigail.
             { 2d, Feb. 18, 1752, Wid. Elizabeth Crook.
   5. *Joseph,* b. in 1714; m. { 1st, Widow Mary Watts.
             { 2d, Nov. 22, 1769, Jemima Glover.
   6. *William,* b. 1719; m. Sarah Case.
   Sarah, b. m. Dec. 15, 1737, *Alexander King. *Hannah*, b.
   Jemima, b. in 1726; m. George Duvall.
   Keziah, b. m. Jan. 25, 1756, Joshua Hempstead. *Walter*, b. d. Jan. 19, 1740.

(*) Son of John and Katherine (Osborne) King.

2.

GEORGE HAVENS, s. Jonathan and Hannah (Brown) Havens.
 b. m. d. in 1733-4.

 Mary
  b.

 1 ch. **7.** *George,* b. m. { 1st, Patience Booth.
           { 2d, Amy Johnson.

3.

JONATHAN HAVENS, s. Jonathan and Hannah (Brown) Havens.
 b. Jan. 29, 1709. m. Jan. 27, 1728. d. Nov. 1, 1774.

 Catherine Nicoll, da. William and Anna (Van Rensselaer) Nicoll.
  b. Oct. 12, 1700. d. May 1779.

7 ch. **8.** *Anna*, b. Apr. 25, 1729; m. Nov. 28, 1748, Thomas Fosdick.
9. *Elizabeth*, b. Jan. 1, 1731; m. Jan. 20, 1751, David Howell.
10. *Nicoll*, b. Feb. 10, 1733; m. { 1st, Nov. 24, 1755, Sarah Fosdick.
{ 2d, Mar. 29. 1770, Desire Brown.
11. *Catherine*, b. May 25, 1735; m. Dec. 7, 1752, Thomas Mumford.
Frances, b. Feb. 18, 1737; m.   Ephraim Baker.
Hannah, b. May 19, 1739; m.   William Chadwick.
Margaret, b. Dec. 6, 1741, d. unm. Sep. 23, 1762.
†*Gloriana*, b. Oct. 22, 1745; m. (as his 2d wife,) Charles Eldridge.

(*) d. Apr. 24, 1758. Had one da. who m. a Coit.   (†) d. s. p.

4.

CONSTANT HAVENS, s Jonathan and Hannah (Brown) Havens.
b.   1713.   m. 1st.   m. 2d, Feb. 18, 1752.   d. Jan. 3, 1761.

1st, Abigail
b.   1706.   d. Sep. 19, 1751.

*2d, Wid. Elizabeth Crook, *nee* Hopkins, da. William and Rebecca (   ) Hopkins.
b.   d. Nov.   1784.

7 ch. **12.** *Constant*, b.   m. { 1st, Oct. 15,1756, Bethiah Brown.
{ 2d,   Martha.
{ 3d,   Temperance.
13. *Mary*, b. Aug. 1735, m. Nov. 22, 1759, Nathaniel Tuthill.
14. *Abigail*, b.   m. 1752, Thomas Terry.
15. *Jonathan*, b. 1738; m.   Abigail Tiley.
16. *Lucretia*, b. 1741; m. James Howell.
Elizabeth, b. 1743, d. unm. Dec. 9, 1823.   *Walter*, b. Oct. 1757, d. Mar. 10, 1759.

(*) Wid. of Samuel Crook.   Samuel Crook m. Elizabeth Hopkins, Nov. 24, 1742.   S. R.

5.

JOSEPH HAVENS, s. Jonathan and Hannah (Brown) Havens.
b.   1714.   m. 1st   m. 2nd, Nov. 22, 1769.   d. May 31, 1775.

1st, Madam Mary Watts, wid. of John Watts.
b.   1690.   d. Aug.   1768.

2nd, Jemima Glover,   of Southampton.
b.   d. May 18, 1772.
1 ch.   *Joseph*, b. May 18, 1772, d. Oct. 13, 1775.

6.

WILLIAM HAVENS, s. Jonathan and Hannah (Brown) Havens.
b.   1719.   m.   d. May 4, 1763.

Sarah Case, da.
b.   1719.   d. Oct. 8, 1769.

9 ch. **17.** *James*, b. Feb. 12, 1742; m.   Elizabeth Bowditch.
18. *Walter*, b.   m.   Lois.
19. *Samuel*, b.   m.   Mary Parker.
Peter, b.   d. Sept. 3, 1775.
20. *Ezekiel*, b.   1759; m. { 1st,   Mary Stratton.
{ 2nd, Mar.   1793, Jemima Case.
21. *William*, b.   m.
Phebe, b.   1749; d. Oct. 28, 1752.
Desire, b.   1750; m.   William Havens.
22. *Phebe*, b. Apr. 22, 1753; m.   Joseph Havens.

(*) d. Nov. 5, 1771.

7.

GEORGE HAVENS, s. George and Mary (   ) Havens.
b.   m. 1st, Feb. 9, 1747.   2d, Sep. 2, 1762.   d. Aug. 1770.

1st, Patience Booth, d.
b. in 1823-4.   d. May 30, 1762.

2d, Amy Johnson, d.
b.

23. *Obadiah*, b.   1747, m. about 1769-70, Phebe ?Havens
Jemima, b. 1749, m. Apr. 10, 1766, Henry Hudson.
George, b.   m. Nov. 22, 1781, Lucretia Denison.
John, b. 1755, d. d. Oct. 6, 1709.
24. *Jonathan*, b.   m.   Susannah Horton.   *Keziah*,

(*) See Hudson Genealogy.

Will of George Havens dated Shelter Island, July 4, 1770, speaks of wife Anna; sons Obadiah, John
and George; daughter Keziah, another son Jonathan, another daughter Jemima who appears to
be married. Appoints his trusty friend Capt. David Brown, cousin Nicoll Havens, Executors.
Witnesses, William Havens, yeoman; George Duvall, tanner and Robert Hemsteed. Prov. Aug.
27, 1770.

A George Havens was bap. Dec. 1754.   Southold ch. R.   Obadiah was bap. Jan. 21, 1755.   Headstone in ch. yard.   John Havens drowned Oct. 6, 1789, in the 34th year of his age.

8.

ANNA HAVENS, da. Jonathan and Catherine (Nicoll) Havens.
b. Apr. 25, 1729.   m. Nov. 28, 1748.   d. Sep. 24, 1782.

Thomas Fosdick. s. Thomas and Esther (Updike) Fosdick.
b. Apr. 30. 1725.   d. Apr.   1776.

10 ch. **25.** *Nicoll,* b. Apr. 18, 1750; m. Jan. 19, 1784, Abigail Eldredge.
Mary, b. Feb. 19, 1752, d. Jan. 11, 1753.
26. *Thomas Updike,* b. Mar. 6, 1754; m. June 17, 1783, Sarah Howe.
Lodowick, b. July 9, 1756, d. Sep. 18, 1773.   *Jonathan,* b. May 5, 1758, d. in childhood.
Frances, b. Mar. 28, 1760, d. in childhood.   *Giles,* b. May 13, 1762, d. in childhood.
Frances. b. Apr. 10, 1764, d. Nov. 13, 1790.
27. *Richard,* b. Nov. 28, 1765; m. Sep. 20, 1796, Phebe L'Hommedieu.
*Anna, b May 23, 1769; m. Dec. 22, 1793, Henry Packard Dering.
(*) See Sylvester genealogy, No. 5.

9.

ELIZABETH HAVENS. da. Jonathan and Catherine (Nicoll) Havens.
b. Jan. 1, 1731.   m. Jan. 20, 1751.   d.

David Howell, s. Israel and Abigail (   ) Howell, of Moriches, N. Y.
b. June   1724.   d. Feb. 13, 1803.

6 ch.   **Frances.* b.   m. Jan. 13, 1773, Rev. Joshua Hartt.   *Elizabeth,* b.   1756, d.   1780.
Abigail. b.   m.   Dr.   Howard.   *Nicoll,* b.   1760, d.   1764.
†Margaret, b.   1763; m.   Ebenezer Hartt.   *Charles,* b.   1766, d.   1788.
(*) Had one ch. named Frances, who m. Col. Hunt, of Sag Harbor, N. Y.
(†) Had one ch. named Elizabeth Rose, who m. Horace Jerome, and had one son named Horace.

10.

NICOLL HAVENS, s. Jonathan and Catherine (Nicoll) Havens.
b. Feb. 10, 1733.   m. 1st, Nov. 14, 1755.   m. 2d, Mar. 29, 1770.   d. Sep. 7, 1783.

1st, Sarah Fosdick. da. Thomas and Esther (Updike) Fosdick.
b. Apr. 9, 1730.   d. Aug. 4, 1767.

2d, Desire Brown, da. Daniel and Mary (Havens) Brown.
b. Sep. 17, 1744.   d. Mar. 31, 1828.

10 ch.   *Jonathan Nicoll,* b. Jan. 18, 1757, d. unm. Oct. 25, 1799.
Esther, b. Sep. 4, 1759, d. Aug. 4, 1762.
*Esther Sarah, b. Jan. 31, 1763; m. Nov. 27, 1787, Sylvester Dering.
28. *Mary Catherine.* b. Sep. 25, 1765; m. June 15, 1803, Ezra L'Hommedieu.
29. *Catherine Mary,* b. Apr. 20, 1771; m. Feb. 26, 1797, Henry Huntington.
30. *Rensselaer,* b. Mar. 13, 1773 ; m. { 1st, May 9, 1799, Anna Jenkins.
{ 2d, July 20, 1818, Catherine Cebra Webb.
31. *Gloriana,* b. Dec. 11, 1774; m. Sep. 15, 1794, Rev. Whitfield Cowles.
Frances, b. Sep. 7, 1776, d. unm. Apr. 9, 1811. *Watson,* b. Nov. 21. 1779, d. Mar. 11, 1785.
Henrietta, b. Nov. 6, 1781, d. Apr. 16, 1784.
(*) See Sylvester genealogy, No. 3.

11.

CATHERINE HAVENS, da. Jonathan and Catherine (Nicoll) Havens.
b. May 25, 1735.   m. Dec. 7, 1752.   d. Dec. 2, 1778.

*Thomas Mumford, s. Thomas and Abigail (Cheeseborough) Mumford.
b. Sep. 10, 1728.   d. Aug. 30, 1799.

8 ch. **32.** *Catherine,* b. Sep. 16, 1754; m.   Peter Richards.
Thomas Cheeseborough, b. Mar. 22, 1756, d. Oct. 18, 1764.
Silas, b. Apr. 17, 1759; m.   A son, b. Aug. 15, 1760, d. Aug. 16, 1760.
33. *Hannah,* b. May 12, 1767; m. Mar. 23 1786, Zacariah Huntington.
A daughter, b. Sep. 11, 1769, d. Sep. 11, 1769.   *Frances,* b. June 23, 1771, d. Sep. 30, 1771.
34. *Benjamin Maverick,* b. July 28, 1772; m. June 19, 1802, Harriet Bowers.
(*) Thomas Mumford was thrice married.

12.

CONSTANT HAVENS, s. Constant and Abigail (   ) Havens.
b.   1734.   m 1st, Oct. 15, 1756.   m. 2d,   m. 3d,   d. Sep.   1797.

1st, Bethiah Brown, da.
b.   d.

2d, Martha
b.   1744-5.   d. Feb. 25, 1774.

3d, Temperance
b.

13 ch. **35.** *Walter,* b   m. { 1st, Oct. 17, 1784, Hannah Downs.
{ 2d,   Disie Goodale.
Constant,   *Abigail,*   *Lucretia,*   *Peggy,*   *Jerusha,*   *Hannah,*
Polly,   *Nancy,*   *Jeremiah,*   *Biram,*   *David,*   *Gordon,*

13.

MARY HAVENS, da Constant and Abigail (   ) Havens.
b. July 20, 1735.   m. as his 2d wife, Nov. 22, 1759.   d. Nov.   1822.

Nathaniel Tuthill, s. Nathaniel and Hannah (King) Tuthill.
b. July 3, 1731.   d. Apr. 8, 1768.

5 ch.   *Mary*, b. Jan.   1761, d. in her 85th year.
        Hannah, b. May   1762, d. Jan. 8, 1855.
        *Elizabeth, Aug.   1764; m.   °Joseph King.   *Abigail*, b. Oct.   1766.
        Lucretia, b. July 14, 1768, d. May 18, 1849.
(*) Had a son named Tuthill, b. 1804, who m. wid. Susannah Hubbard.   (°) Had 4 wives.

14.

ABIGAIL HAVENS, da. Constant and Abigail (   ) Havens.
    b.   m.   1752, as his 2d wife.   d.

Thomas Terry, s. Thomas and Mehitable (Tuthill) Terry.
    b. about 1726.   d. about 1777.
4 ch.   **Ruth*, b. Dec. 2, 1752; m. Feb. 1, 1770, Daniel Tuthill.
  36. *Abigail*, b. about 1753; m. { 1st,   1777, Benjamin King.
                    { 2d, Nov. 18, 1784, John Cleaves Terry.
  37. *Elizabeth*, b.   1761; m.   Christopher Tuthill.
    °*Mehitable*, b. Sep. 21, 1764; m.   1780, Richard Chadwick.
(*) See Tuthill genealogy, No. 3.
(°) Had four ch., Nancy, b. 1781; Mary, b. 1783; Betsey, b. 1791; George W., b. 1793.

15.

JONATHAN HAVENS, s. Constant and Abigail (   ) Havens.
    b.   1738.   m.   d. Apr. 26, 1801.

Abigail Tiley or Tyler.
    b.   1735.   d. Sep. 5, 1820, ae., 85.
9 ch.   *Barret*, b.   m.
  38. *John Tiley*, b.   1765; m. June 14, 1806, Phebe Havens.
    *Gabriel, b.   m.   Cynthia Stanton.   *Philetus*, b.   d. unm.
    Jenet, b.   1769, d. unm. June 12, 1852, ae., 83.   *Harriet*, b.   d. unm.
  39. *Abigail T.*, b.   1777; m.   Rev. Jabez Munsell.   *Henrietta*, b.   m.   Crary.
    Ptolemy, b.   1779, d. Nov. 3, 1798.
(*) Had one ch. named Harriet, who d. in infancy.

16.

LUCRETIA HAVENS, da. of Constant and Abigail (   ) Havens.
    b.   1741.   m.   d. Nov. 14, 1791.

James Howell, s. Nathan or Ezekiel Howell of Sag Harbor.
    b. Oct. 15, 1734.   d. Dec. 12, 1808.
6 ch.   *Lucretia*, b. 1760, d. 1767.   *Mary*, b.   1762; m. July 29, 1783, Nathan Fordham.
  40. *Matthew*, b. Jan. 24, 1764; m.   Hannah Latham.
    Jerusha, b. Sep. 6, 1768; m. Oct. 11, 1800, Stephen Holt.
  41. *Elizabeth*, b. Dec. 23, 1770; m. Nov. 8, 1794, Samuel Kip.
    Abigail, b. May 9, 1776; m. Oct. 2, 1798, John Price.

17.

JAMES HAVENS, s. William and Sarah (Case) Havens.
    b. Feb. 12, 1742.   m.   d. Mar. 15, 1810.

Elizabeth Bowditch, da. Joel and Bethial (Case) Bowditch.
    b. Nov. 12, 1742.   d. Mar. 15, 1828.
11 ch.   *Frances*, b. Oct. 22, 1761, d. Aug. 10, 1763.
                     { 1st, Apr. 16, 1797, Martha J. Lay.
  42. *Francis*, b. Nov. 16, 1763; m. { 2d, Jan. 26, 1803, Phebe Payne.
                     { 3d, Feb. 10, 1810, Mary Eldridge.
  43. *Frances*, b. Dec. 21, 1766; m.   Matthias Davis.
  44. *Gordon*, b. Nov. 29, 1768; m.   Esther Clark.
  45. *Julia*, b. May 30, 1771; m. July, 1796, David Gardiner.
  46. *Elizabeth*, b. May 19, 1773; m. July 4, 1796, Jonathan Thompson.
    Sidney, b. May 20, 1775, d. by drowning, Oct. 6, 1789.
    Lucretia, b. June 1, 1777, d. unm. July 14, 1849, ae., 72.
    *David, b. June 3, 1780; m. Aug. 2, 1801, Mary Mayo.
  47. *Henry P.*, b. Dec. 13, 1782; m. Mar. 12, 1811, Hannah Corlies.
    Sarah, b. Feb. 23, 1786, d. Aug. 23, 1790.
(*) Had one son, Sidney, who d. in 1831.

18.

WALTER HAVENS, s. William and Sarah (Case) Havens.
    b.   m.   d. May 1st, 1806.

Lois,
    b.   d. Sep. 1813.
3 ch.   **William*, b.   m. Dec. 1814, Sarah Frances Havens.
    Hannah, b.   d. prob. unm. Nov. 1815.
  48. *Remington*, b.   m. Jan. 13, 1803, Jemima Tuthill.
(*) See No. 98.

19.

SAMUEL HAVENS, s. William and Sarah (Case) Havens.
    b.   m.   d.

Mary Parker, da. Abraham and Mary (Budd) Parker.
    b.   d.

3 ch.   *Sarah*, bap. July 6, 1772.
    49. *Lodowick*, b. Jan. 17, 1774; m. Oct. 30, 1799, Mary Annabal.
    50. *Lucinda*, bap. Jul. 19, 1782; m. June 11, 1808, William C. Congdon.

20.

EZEKIEL HAVENS, s. William and Sarah (Case) Havens.
    b. 1759.   m. 1st,   m. 2d, March, 1793.   d. Nov. 29, 1821.

1st, Mary Stratton, da.
    b.   1763.   d. June 30, 1792.

2d, Jemima Case, da.
    b.   d.

4 ch.   *Jemima*. b.   m.
    51. *Stratton*, b.   m. Feb. 26, 1808, Abigail F. Hamilton.
    52. *Sarah Phina*, b. Mar. 1, 1789; m. Oct. 29, 1807, Robert Harlow.
    53. *Philena*, b. Mar. 1, 1789; m. Aug. 27, 1806, Abraham Mulford.

21.

WILLIAM HAVENS, s. William and Sarah (Case) Havens.
    b.   m.   d. about 1802.

5 ch.   *William*, b.   d. by drowning.
    54. *Catherine M.*, b.   1787; m. { 1st,   John M. Isaacs.
                                  { 2d, July 28, 1842, William Davenport.
    55. *Ezekiel*, b. about 1789; m. May 10, 1810, Roxanna Case.
    56. *Sarah*, b.   m. Jan. 17, 1811, Sayre House.
    57. *Eunice Maria*, b. Dec. 25, 1791; m. Dec. 23, 1810, Samuel Stratton Dayton.

22.

PHEBE HAVENS, da. William and Sarah (Case) Havens.
    b. Apr. 22, 1753.   m.   d. Mar. 12, 1806.

Joseph Havens, s,
    b.   1745.   d. Oct. 18, 1827.

8 ch. **58.** *Augustus*, b. Nov. 19, 1768; m.   Esther Bowditch.
    Caleb, b. Feb. 9, 1773, d. at sea, unm., Sep. 6, 1795.
    William, b. June 16, 1776, d. Apr. 25, 1791.
    *Nathaniel S., b. Sep. 18, 1778; m.   Abigail Stewart.
    59. *Jacob*, b. Mar. 25, 1783; m.   Elizabeth Bennet.
    Joseph Caleb, b. Oct. 3, 1786, d. unm. June 17, 1842.
    Cynthia, b. Jan. 25, 1789, d. unm., June 11, 1883.
    Charles Alfred, b. June 21, 1795, d. July 2, 1808.
(*) d. Mar. 24, 1829, left one s., Austin L., b. in 1813, who m. and had ch., several of whom d. young.

23.

OBADIAH HAVENS, s. George and Patience (Booth) Havens.
    b. in   1747.   m. about   1769-70.   d. Aug. 22, 1786.

Phebe (?) Havens,
    b. in   1750-1.   d. June 15, 1831.

6 ch.   **Phebe*, b. May 27, 1771; m. June 14, 1806, John Tiley Havens.
    †*Clarissa*, b. July 4, 1773; m. Jan. 26, 1796, Thadeus Fordham.
    Elmira, b. Mar. 17, 1775; d. unm. Feb. 27, 1799.
    60. *Obadiah*, b. Feb. 26, 1777; m. July 1, 1799, Nancy Robertson.
    °*Patience*, b. Mar. 7, 1784; m. Aug. 25, 1823, ‖Lewis Howell; no issue.
    61. *George H.*, b. Nov. 5, 1786; m. Jan. 17, 1808, Sarah Haynes.
(*) See No. 38. (†) See John and Henry Havens' genealogy, No. 38. (°) d. Mar. 13, 1837. (‖) Son
of Stephen and Eunice Howell, b. Mar. 10, 1776; d. Jan. 24, 1851.

24.

JONATHAN HAVENS, s. George and Patience (Booth) Havens.
    b.   m.   d. May 2, 1771.

Susannah Horton, da.
    b.

2 ch.   **Silas*, b.   m.   Proculah, b.   *Patience*, b.
(*) Had at least 3 ch., Cordelia, b. Oct. 1, 1791, d. Sep. 1, 1792; Proculah, b. Feb. 1, 1796, d. Feb. 6,
1796; John N., b. May 14, 1797, d. Oct. 6, 1798.
Will of Jonathan Havens, Jr., dated Shelter Island, Mar. 30, 1781, speaks of wife Susannah, son Silas
and daughter Patience, both under age. Appoints trusty friend Nicoll Havens and wife Executors. Witness: George Daval, shoemaker; John Daval, joiner; and Obadiah Havens.
Prov. May 25, 1771.

25.

NICOLL FOSDICK, s. Thomas and Anna (Havens) Fosdick.
    b. Apr. 18, 1750.   m. Jan. 19, 1784.   d. Jan. 21, 1821.

Abigail Eldredge, da. Charles and Mary (Starr) Eldredge.
    b. May 11, 1761.   d. Oct. 23, 1809.

9 ch.   *Nicoll*, b. Nov. 9, 1785; d. unm.   1868.
    Lodowick, b. Feb. 27, 1788; m. May 12, 1811 ⁰Elizabeth Smith; no issue.
  62. *Abby*, b. Mar. 8, 1790; m. July 24, 1811, John Billings.
    Charles, b. July 19, 1793; m.   Maria Duvcare.
    Thomas, b. Jan. 19, 1795; d. Sep. 26, 1795.
  63. *Mary Ann*, b. Aug. 19, 1796; m. May 14, 1817, Thomas Mussey.
    Gloriana, b. Oct. 17, 1798; d. Oct. 27, 1800.
  64. *Frances Eliza*, b. Jan. 28, 1801; m. Oct. 2, 1834, George Jones.
    Gloriana, b. Jan. 22, 1803; m.   Warren Green; no issue.
(*) d. July 14, 1826.   (⁰) da. of Joseph Smith; d. Feb. 9, 1853.

26.

THOMAS UPDIKE FOSDICK, s. Thomas and Anna (Havens) Fosdick.
    b. Mar. 6, 1754.   m. June 17, 1780.   d. Aug. 11, 1811.

Sarah Howe, da.
    b.   d.
1 ch. 65. *Thomas Updike*, b. Apr. 19, 1784; m. Oct. 9, 1804, Rachel Armstrong.

27.

RICHARD FOSDICK, s. Thomas and Anna (Havens) Fosdick.
    b. Nov. 28, 1765.   m. Sep. 20, 1796.   d. Aug. 20, 1837.

Phebe L'Hommedieu, da. Samuel and Sarah (White) L'Hommedieu.
    b. July 3, 1776.   d. Nov. 3, 1826.
7 ch.   *Thomas Richard*, b. June 22, 1797; m.   Wid. Drake.
  66. *Sylvester L'H.*, b. May 6, 1799; m. Apr. 30, 1821, Harriet R. Raymond.
  67. *Samuel*, b. Mar. 21, 1801; m. Jan. 12, 1836, Sarah Ann Wood.
    Anna Sybil, b. Feb. 23, 1803; d. Mar. 22, 1824.
  68. *Betsy Eliza*, b. Feb. 9, 1805; m. June 21, 1841, Rev. Benjamin P. Aydelott.
  69. *Henry Nicoll*, b. Sep. 21, 1808; m. June 28, 1836, Harriet Harkness.
    Charles Updike, b. May 15, 1815; d. Jan. 6, 1835.
(*) d. Aug. 1, 1829; had 1 ch. named William, who d. unm. 1869, ae. 41.

28.

MARY CATHERINE HAVENS, da. Nicoll and Sarah (Fosdick) Havens.
    b. Sep. 25, 1765.   m. June 15, 1803.   d. July 25, 1843.

Ezra L'Hommedieu, s. Benjamin and Martha (Browne) L'Hommedieu.
    b. Aug. 30, 1734.   d. Sep. 11, 1811.
1 ch. 70. *Mary Catherine*, b. July 8, 1806; m. Aug. 7, 1823, Samuel S. Gardiner.

29.

CATHERINE MARY HAVENS da. Nicoll and Sarah (Fosdick) Havens.
    b. Apr. 20, 1771.   m. Feb. 26, 1797.   d. Mar. 11, 1839.

Henry Huntington, s. Benjamin and Anne (Huntington) Huntington.
    b. May 28, 1766.   d. Oct. 15, 1846.
10 ch. 71. *Catherine H.*, b. Dec. 3, 1797; m. Mar. 26, 1833, William Williams.
    Frances, b. Sep. 16, 1799; m. June 6, 1826, Nicoll H. Dering.
    Anne, b. Feb. 23, 1801, d. Oct. 3, 1823.
  72. *Henrietta Desire*, b. June 15, 1803; m. Dec. 9, 1828, Benjamin H. Wright.
    Gloriana, b. Feb. 1, 1806, d. Dec. 3, 1808.
    Lucy, b. Feb. 2, 1818, d. Feb. 28, 1837.
    Gloriana, b. June 7, 1808, d. June 3, 1837.
    ⁰*Elizabeth*, b. Aug. 6. 1811, m. Aug. 4, 1836, ‖Charles C. Young; no issue.
    Henry, b. July 11, 1813, d. Mar. 21, 1854.
    †*Benj. Nicoll*, b. May 5, 1816; m. Jan. 24, 1855, ‡Mable Limbrick Utley.
(*) See Sylvester genealogy, No. 7.   (⁰) d. Jan. 19, 1838.   (‖) s. of John and Mary S. (White) Young;
  b. July 13, 1804; d. Jan. 8, 1893.   (†) d. Nov. 10, 1882; had 2 ch. Benjamin N., b. Nov. 16, 1855;
  d. June 12, 1860, and Henry b. June 13, 1864.   (‡) da. of Rufus Utley.

30.

RENSSELAER HAVENS, s. Nicoll and Desire (Brown) Havens.
    b. Mar. 13, 1773.   m. 1st, May 9, 1799.   m. 2nd, July 20, 1818.   d. Feb. 8, 1854.

1st, Anna Jenkins, da. Thomas and Mary (Barnard) Jenkins.
    b. Dec. 9, 1780.   d. Aug. 24, 1816.

2nd, Catherine Cebra Webb, da. Orange and Elizabeth (Cebra) Webb.
    b. Jan. 25, 1801.   d. Apr. 24, 1897.
14 ch.   *Gloriana*, b. Sep. 29, 1800; m. July 20, 1842, Henry Thomas Dering; no issue.
    Charlotte Mary, b. Sept. 5, 1802, d. unm. Jan. 25, 1889.
    ⁰*Rensselaer Nicoll*, b. Aug. 24, 1804; m. Aug. 29, 1833, ¶Elizabeth S. Dwight; no issue.
    ‖*Henry Watson*, b. Feb. 10, 1807; m.   †Susan Clark; no issue.
    Thomas Jenkins, b. July 23, 1809, d. Feb. 20, 1810.
  73. *Sarah Jenkins*, b. Mar. 4, 1812; m. Dec. 24, 1844, Edward Bement.
  74. *Howard Havens*, b. Apr. 26, 1820; m. June 14, 1856, Asenath C. Randall.
  75. *Frances Maria*, b. July 15, 1821; m. Dec. 4, 1839, Rev. Samuel B. S. Bissell.
    Anna Jenkins, b. June 25, 1823, d. May 29, 1830.
    Catherine, b. July 24, 1827, d. Jan. 16, 1828.
  76. *Sylvester Dering*, b. Mar. 3, 1829; m. Feb. 25, 1851, Rachel Kay Phillip.
    Anna Jenkins, b. June 22, 1830, d. Apr. 1, 1832.
  77. *Charles Edward*, b. May 6, 1832; m. Sep. 4, 1855, Mary J. Tracy.
    Katherine Elizabeth, b. Aug. 6, 1839.
(*) See Sylvester genealogy, No. 5.   (⁰) d. July 11, 1876.   (¶) da. James and Aurelia (Darling)
  Dwight, b. July 20, 1812; d. May 30, 1848.   (‖) d. June 22, 1873.   (†) d. in 1870.

31.

GLORIANA HAVENS, da. Nicoll and Desire (Brown) Havens.
 b. Dec. 11, 1774. m. Sep. 15, 1794. d. Apr. 12, 1802.

*Rev. Whitfield Cowles, s. Josiah Cowles, of Southington, Conn.
 b. June 3, 1764. d. Nov. 19, 1840.
2 ch. **78.** *Rensselaer Watson*, b. Feb. 18, 1796; m. Sep. 20, 1818, Laura Kilbourne.
 °*Mary Henrietta*, b. Jan. 21, 1801; m. Byron Kilbourne.
(*) d. June 24, 1837, had two ch., Gloriana and Lucy Fitch, who d. in childhood.
(°) See Brown genealogy.

32.

CATHERINE MUMFORD, da. Thomas and Catherine (Havens) Mumford.
 b. Sep. 16, 1754. m. d. Sep. 7, 1805.

Peter Richards, s. Guy and Elizabeth (Harris) Richards.
 b. 1754. d. Sep. 6, 1781.
2 ch. *Thomas Mumford*, b. d. ae. 9 months.
 79. *Catherine Havens*, b. m. Oct 23, 1802, Levi Huntington.

33.

HANNAH MUMFORD, da. Thomas and Catherine (Havens) Mumford.
 b. May 12, 1767. m. Mar. 23, 1786. d. Mar. 13, 1823.

Zachariah Huntington, s. Jabez and Hannah (Williams) Huntington.
 b. Nov. 2, 1764. d. June 23, 1850.
3 ch. **80.** *Thomas Mumford*, b. Dec. 28, 1786; m. in 1819, Mary B. Campbell.
 Jabez Williams, b. Nov. 8, 1788; m. May 22, 1833, Sally Ann Huntington: no issue.
 **Elizabeth, M.*, b. Oct. 5, 1793; m. May 16, John Griswold.
(*) Is supposed to have died soon after her marriage, and to have had no issue.

34.

BENJAMIN MAVERICK MUMFORD, s. Thomas and Catherine (Havens) Mumford.
 b. July 28, 1772. m. June 19, 1802. d.

Harriet Bowers, da. Henry and Mary (Myer) Bowers.
 b. Apr. 23, 1782. d.
10 ch. **81.** *Samuel Jones*, b. May 23, 1803; m. { 1st, June 2, 1830, Caroline Givens Astor.
    { 2d, Sep. 27, 1836, Hariette Viser Innes.
 Mary Bowers, b. Aug. 22, 1804, d. Aug. 15, 1805.
 Catherine, b. Jan. 23, 1806, d. Oct. 30, 1806.
 82. *Harriet B.*, b. Sep. 7, 1807; m. July 11, 1832, Alonzo C. Paige.
 Henry Bowers, b. Aug. 27, 1810, d. Aug. 10, 1811.
 Mary Bowers, b. Feb. 8, 1812, d. Aug. 22, 1813. *Mary*, b. July 2, 1813, d. Aug. 31, 1814.
 Benjamin, b. Aug. 4, 1815, d. Feb. 25, 1816. *Thomas*, b. Aug. 18, 1817.
 Hannah, b. Mar. 11, 1819.

35.

WALTER HAVENS, s. Constant and
 b. m. 1st, Oct. 17, 1784, 2d, d.

1st, Hannah Downs, da.
 b. d. Aug. 19, 1785.

2d, Disie Goodale, da. Joseph Goodale.
 b. d.
5 ch. **83.** *Ezra*, b. 1786; m. { 1st, Elizabeth Jagger.
      { 2d, Rosetta Sinclair.
 Bethiah, b. m. Nathan King; no issue.
       { 1st, Nov. 28, 1820, Anna Benjamin.
 84. *Walter*, b. Sep. 23, 1799; m. { 2d, Dec. 12, 1844, Sarah Homan.
       { 3d, June 24, 1851, Clarissa Benjamin.
       { 4th, Wid. Susan Benjamin, (*nee* Downs.)
 85. *Mehetable*, b. m. Joel Sweesey.
 Juliet, b. m. Sweesey.

36.

ABIGAIL TERRY, da. Thomas and Abigail (Havens) Terry.
 b. about 1753. m. 1st, 1777. m. 2d, Nov. 18, 1784. d. Mar. 5, 1823.

1st, Benjamin King, s. Benjamin and Betsy ( ) King.
 b. Sep. 23, 1750. d. April 19, 1780.

2d, John Cleaves Terry, s. William and Elizabeth (Cleaves) Terry.
 b. Feb. 8, 1744. d. Sep. 6, 1823.
2 ch. **86.** *Edward Conkling*, b. Aug. 2, 1778; m. Sarah Tignor.
 **Benjamin*, b. June 13, 1780; m. about 1805, Payne; no issue.
(*) d. April 12, 1850.

37.

ELIZABETH TERRY, d. Thomas and Abigail (Havens) Terry.
 b. 1761. m. d. April 23, 1825, ae. 64.

Christopher Tuthill, s. Christopher and Phebe (Youngs) Tuthill.
 b. 1760. d. Nov. 26, 1823, ae. 63.
3 ch. **87.** *William H.*, b. Aug. 5, 1793; m. Jan. 28, 1823, Sophia Petty.
 Joshua, b. m. Polly Downs. *Henry*, b.

38.

JOHN TILEY HAVENS, s. Jonathan and Abigail (Tiley) Havens.
    b.   1765.   m. June 14, 1806.   d. June 25, 1839.
Phebe Havens, da. Obadiah and Phebe ([?] Havens) Havens.
    b. May 27, 1771.   d. Feb. 3, 1850.
3 ch.   *Jonathan, b.   m.   †Wid. Cynthia Stanton Gleason, nee Vandevoort; no issue.
        Frances M., b.   1811, d. unm. Mar. 4, 1858.
        Julia, b.   m.   Elisha Belcher Sackett; no issue.
(*) Died Jan. 24, 1880.   (†) d. July 9, 1883.

39.

ABIGAIL T. HAVENS, da. Jonathan and Abigail (Tiley) Havens.
    b.   1777.   m.   d. July 3, 1858.
Rev. Jabez Munsell, s.
    b.   1772.   d. Aug. 1, 1832.
5 ch.   Abigail, b.   m.   Sweetzer.   Elizabeth, b.   m.   Cornelius Sleight.
        Henry, b.   m.   Jabez, b.   Jonathan H., b,   1807.   d. Jan. 20, 1842

40.

MATTHEW HOWELL, s. James and Lucretia (Havens) Howell.
    b. Jan. 24, 1764.   m.   d. about 1827.
Hannah Latham, da.
    b. Aug. 17, 1767.   d. June 19, 1834.
1 ch. 88. Charles J., b. June 19, 1797; m.   1827, Lydia Hinchman Spear.

41.

ELIZABETH HOWELL, da. James and Lucretia (Havens) Howell.
    b. Dec. 23, 1770.   m. Nov. 8, 1794.   d. Feb. 4, 1846.
Samuel Kip, s. Samuel and Ann (Harring) Kip.
    b. Oct. 20, 1771.   d. Jan. 25, 1833.
6 ch.   Mary, b. Sep. 14, 1795, d. unm. June 21, 1835.
        James, b. Mar. 9, 1797, d. unm. Sep. 11, 1860.
    89. Elbert S., b. Oct. 8, 1799; m. Oct. 17, 1843, Elizabeth Goelet.
    90. Samuel, b. Sep. 8, 1801; m. Nov. 8, 1825, Nancy H. Fowler.
                                                (1st,   1845, Elizabeth Abbott.
    91. Henry, b. July 25, 1807; m. { 2d,   1852, Catherine Gates.
                                                (3d,   1885, Geraldine Gardiner.
        George W., b. Mar. 13, 1813, d. unm. Feb. 7, 1851.

42.

FRANCIS HAVENS, s. James and Elizabeth (Bowditch) Havens.
    b. Nov. 16, 1763.   m. 1st, Apr. 16, 1797. 2d, June 26, 1804. 3d, Feb. 10, 1810. d. Nov. 8, 1829.
1st, Martha J. Lay, da.
    b.   1778.   d. Feb.10, 1802.
2d, Phebe Payne, da. John and Phebe (   ) Payne.
    b.   1774.   d. Oct. 20, 1805, ae., 29.
3d, Mary Eldredge, da.
    b.   1782.   d. Mar. 28, 1848.
9 ch.   Phebe Lay, b.   d. unm.   Martha J., b.
        Nancy, b.   (of the 2d wife.)
    92. Frances Hand, b. Feb. 18, 1811; m. July 9, 1831, Zachariah Rogers.
        Henrietta T., b. Oct. 23, 1812.   James Monroe, b. Aug. 10, 1814, d. Sep. 20, 1815.
                                                        (1st,   °Mary B. Cory.
        *James Monroe, b. July 17, 1816; m. { 2d,   ‖Cordelia Latham.
        Mary Jane, b. Jan. 20, 1819   Elizabeth Bowditch, b. May 26, 1822.
(*) d. Jan. 23, 1892, had two ch., J. Monoe, who d. 1852, ae., 4 months, and Henry H., who d. 1879,
    ae., 38.   (°) d. Apr. 21, 1852, ae., 31.   (‖) d. Jan. 24, 1892, ae., 82.

43.

FRANCES HAVENS, da. James and Elizabeth (Bowditch) Havens.
    b. Dec. 21, 1766.   m.   d. Apr. 20, 1831.
Matthias Davis, s.
    b. Oct. 14, 1761.   d. Dec. 12, 1849.
6 ch.   Frances Havens, b. Aug. 20, 1793, d. unm. May 29, 1828.
    93. Nancy B., b. Nov. 6, 1795; m. Uriah Valentine.
    94. Charles Havens, b. Mar. 13, 1798; m. { 1st,   Crossman.
                                                        { 2d, July 20, 1831, Hulda Ann Richardson.
    95. Elvira, b. Sep. 10, 1800; m. { 1st,   James Davis.
                                                { 2d,   Smith Conklin.
    96. Julia Gardiner, b. June 29, 1804; m.   1833, Charles S. Loper.
    97. Mary C., b. Nov. 7, 1807; m. Jan. 2, 1833, Strong Conklin.

44.

GORDON HAVENS, s. James and Elizabeth (Bowditch) Havens.
  b. Nov. 29, 1768. m. d. Mar. 16, 1825.
Esther Clark, da.
  b. in 1772. d. Nov. 14, 1828.
7 ch. **98.** *Sarah Frances*, b. Feb. 18, 1796; m. { 1st, Dec. 28, 1814, William Havens.
                                                 { 2d, Apr. 18, 1818, Richard Lester.
  99. *Nancy*, b. Dec. 18, 1797; m. June 4, 1822, Henry M. Chatfield.
  100. *Esther E.*, b. Feb. 21, 1800; m. Nov. 22, 1828, Nathaniel B. Tyndal.
  101. *Abigail D.*, b. Mar. 10, 1803; m. about 1834-5, Frances Burdick.
  102. *Albert Gallatin*, b. June 4, 1806; m. { 1st, Sep. 7, 1833, Elizabeth Valentine.
                                               { 2d,   wid. Mehetable H. Parker.
  103. *James Henry*, b. Dec. 15, 1809; m. { 1st,   Mary Jane Phelps.
                                             { 2d, Oct. 6, 1845, Margaret Vanderberg.
  Charles Rensselaer, b. Dec. 20, 1813; m. Priscilla Stills.
(*) Had 13 ch.: Charles G., now d. left two ch.; Laura, now d. left one ch.; Albert, killed by R.R. left 3 ch.; Rennselaer, d. unm.; Gertrude. now d. had one ch. which d.; Elmira, now d. left one ch. which d.; Josephine; Vinton has four ch.; Ada; the other four d. in infancy.

45.

JULIA HAVENS, da. James and Elizabeth (Bowditch) Havens.
  b. May 30, 1771. m. July 1796. d. July 3, 1806.
David Gardiner, s. David and Jerusha (Buell) Gardiner.
  b. Feb. 29, 1772. d. Apr. 6, 1815.
3 ch. *Charles*, b. May 7, 1797; m. { 1st, Aug. 29, 1821, °Lucy Stedman.
                                    { 2d, June 25. 1825, Nancy Gibbs Elliott.
  104. *David*, b. Jan. 1, 1799; m. Feb. 20, 1820, Marietta Huntington.
  John Lyon, b. June 27, 1801, d. unm. Sep. 3, 1824.
.(*) d. Mar. 12, 1827. (°) d. Jan. 10, 1824.

46.

ELIZABETH HAVENS, da. James and Elizabeth (Bowditch) Havens.
  b. May 19, 1773. m. July 4, 1796. d. May 31, 1868.
Jonathan Thompson, s. Isaac and Mary (Gardiner) Thompson.
  b. Dec. 7, 1773. d. Dec. 30, 1846.
6 ch. **105.** *David*, b. May 3, 1798; m. Sarah Didodati Gardiner.
  106. *Mary G.*, b. Mar. 23, 1807; m. Samuel B. Gardiner.
  Elizabeth, b. Jan. 12, 1811; m. Alonzo Brown; no issue.
  107. *Jonathan*, b. Feb. 1, 1814; m. Katherine Todhunter.
  108. *Abraham G.*, b. Aug. 10. 1816; m. Apr. 17, 1851, Sarah E. Strong.
  109. *George W.*, b. Feb. 25, 1817; m Eliza Prall
(*) d. Dec. 12, 1889.

47.

HENRY P. HAVENS, s. James and Elizabeth (Bowditch) Havens.
  b. Dec. 13, 1782. m. Mar. 12, 1811. d. Sep. 17, 1856.
Hannah Corlies, da. Asher and Rachel (Hance) Corlies.
  b. Nov. 14, 1790. d. Oct. 4. 1872.
5 ch. **110.** *Elizabeth C.*, b. Mar. 26, 1812: m. Mar. 30, 1830. David B. Keeler.
  111. *Margaret B.*, b. Apr. 23, 1814; m. Sep. 1, 1831. Theodore Crane.
  112. *Rachel C.*, b. July 14, 1816; m. Jan. 25, 1838, William C. Russell.
  113. *Asher Corlies*, b. Aug. 24, 1819; m. { 1st, Feb. 20, 1845, Rachel S. Chardavoyne.
                                             { 2d. Nov. 26, 1862, Jane A. Crane
  Henry P., b. Aug 20, 1821, d. Dec. 2, 1841.

48.

REMINGTON HAVENS, s. Walter and Louise ( ) Havens.
  b. m. Jan. 13, 1803. d. Sep. 16, 1815.
Jemima Tuthill, da. Jeremiah Tuthill.
  b. 1781, d. Sep. 12, 1866.
6 ch. *Charlotte Maria*, b. Sep. 14, 1803; m. July 5, 1873, Nathaniel Havens.
  114. *Jeremiah Tuthill*, b. Apr. 26, 1805: m. { 1 st, Apr. 5, 1828, Phebe Foster.
                                                   { 2d, Oct. 30, 1832, Eliza Sayre.
  115. *Walter*, b. Apr. 25, 1807; m. Mar. 1830, Beulah M. Case,
  116. *Jemima*, b. Mar. 13, 1810; m. May 14, 1831, Edward Conkling.
  117. *Remington*, b. Sep. 4, 1812; m. May 1, 1836, Anna P. Cartwright.
  118. *Louise*, b. Sep. 28, 1814; m. Feb. 7, 1839, Elias Woodruff Payne.
(*) See No. 132.

49.

LODOWICK HAVENS, s. Samuel and Mary (Parker) Havens.
  b. Jan. 17, 1774. m. Oct. 30, 1799. d. Nov. 11, 1854.
Mary Annabal, da.
  b. Oct. 15, 1782. d. Mar. 4, 1859.
6 ch. *Giles S.*, b. Aug. 18, 1800; m. Dec. 23, 1824, °Esther Sherril; no issue.
  ‖*Mary P.*, b. Feb. 3, 1803; m. June 19, 1824, †Charles Griffing; no issue.
  119. *Nancy A.*, b. Jan 15, 1805; m. Sep. 25, 1836, Horace Manwaring.
  Lucinda, b. Mar. 3, 1807, d. unm. May 16, 1885.
  Sarahfina, b. Mar. 10, 1810, d. unm., Mar. 6, 1897.
  120. *Esther S.*, b. Oct. 9, 1817; m June 23, 1840, George Penny.
(*) d. Dec. 3, 1843. (°) da. Abraham and Mehetable (Terry) Sherril, b. Jan. 4, 1806, d. Feb. 25, 1886.
(‖) d. May 5, 1926. (†) See No.

50.

LUCINDA HAVENS, da. Samuel and Mary (Parker) Havens.
    b.   1782.   m. June 11, 1808.   d. Sep. 12, 1840.

William D. Congdon, s. Joseph and Abigail (Dockray) Congdon.
    b.   1785.   d. Aug. 27, 1862.

6 ch. **121.** *Samuel H.*, b. June 22, 1810; m. Oct. 7, 1841, Cornelia Philena Van Gandron.
    **Abigail D.*, b. June 17, 1812; m. June 4, 1859, ⁰Joseph Hildreth; no issue.
    ‖*Mary P.*, b. Sep. 6, 1816; m. Sep. 23, 1860, †Jeremiah Mulford; no issue.
    Nancy M., b. Aug. 27, 1819, d. May 25, 1834.
    Sarah M., b. Oct. 1823, d. Oct. 28, 1857.
    ‡*Elizabeth*, b. Oct. 1823; m. Oct. 9, 1869, ¶William Verity; no issue.
(*) d. Dec. 6, 1875. (⁰) b. Apr. 7, 1807, d.   1875. (‖) d. Apr. 18, 1878. (†) b. 1796, d. Mar., 1880.
(‡) d. May 3, 1893. (¶) b. in 1818, d. May 14, 1875.

51.

STRATTON HAVENS, s. Ezekiel and Mary (Stratton) Havens.
    b.   m. Feb. 26, 1809.   d.   1812.

Abigail F. Hamilton, da.
    b.   d.
1 ch. **122.** *Stratton M.*, b. Mar. 19, 1810; m. { 1st, Feb. 11, 1840, Lydia Ann Chester.
                                        { 2d, Feb. 22, 1870, wid. Elizabeth Flowers.

52.

SARAH PHINA HAVENS, da. Ezekiel and Mary (Stratton) Havens.
    b. Mar. 1, 1789.   m. Oct. 29, 1807.   d. July, 1850.

Robert Harlow, s. Robert and Phebe (Brown) Harlow.
    b. Oct. 26, 1772.   d. Nov. 20, 1834.

13 ch. **123.** *James Madison*, b. Oct. 6, 1808; m. Aug. 15, 1839, Abby M. Osborn.
    Robert Thomas, b. Feb. 10, 1810; m.
    Stratton H., b. Nov. 19, 1811; m.   Russell.   *Edgar*, b. Nov. 22, 1813, d. July,   1815.
    Mary Philena, b. Jan. 7, 1815; m.   Henry Cone.
    Daniel Brown, b. Mar. 16, 1817; m. { 1st, Mary Baird.
                                   { 2d, Catherine Abbott.
    Andrew J., b. Mar. 21, 1818, d. May 31, 1823.
    Sarah P., b. Oct. 30, 1821; m.   Lewis Jagger.
    Ezekiel, b. Apr. 12, 1823.   *Andrew J.*, b Jan. 14, 1824
    Alexander, b. Jan. 22, 1825; m. { 1st, Sophiah R. Woodruff.
                          { 2d, Frances Reeve.
    Henry Addison, b. Nov. 8, 1830; m. Nov. 18, 1857, Rebeccah R. Olden.
124. *Charles*, b. Jan. 6, 1834; m. Oct. 19, 1859, Ency J. Reeve.

53.

PHILENA HAVENS, da. Ezekiel and Mary (Stratton) Havens.
    b. Mar. 1, 1789.   m. Aug. 27, 1806.   d. Sep. 18, 1810.

Abraham Mulford, s. Abraham and Joanna (Miller) Mulford.
    b.   1781.   d. Dec. 29, 1864.

1 ch. **125.** *Alva Stratton*, b. Feb.   1808; m. Sep. 10, 1829, Bethiah Horton

54.

CATHERINE M. HAVENS, da. William and   Havens.
    b.   1788.   m. 1st,   2d, July 28, 1842.   d. July 21, 1862.

1st, John M. Isaacs, s.
    b.   d.

2d, William Davenport, s. John and Prudence (Bell) Davenport.
    b.   Mar. 25, 1781.   d. Jan. 16, 1860.
3 ch.   An infant, d. Sep. 6, 1824, ae. 10 months.
126. *Frances Maria*, b.   m. May 2, 1842, Amzi Benedict Davenport.
    Clarissa, bap. May 27, 1820; m.   Rosencrans.
No issue by 2d husband.

55.

EZEKIEL HAVENS, s. of William and   Havens.
    b.   1789.   m. May 10, 1810.   d.   1812.

Roxanna Case, da. Gillum and Esther (Hand) Case.
    b. Aug. 28, 1793.   d. Feb. 17, 1863.

1 ch. **127.** *Anna Maria*, b Mar. 3. 1812; m. June 16, 1824, Charles C. Griffing.

56.

SARAH HAVENS, da. William and   Havens
    b.   m. Jan. 17, 1811.   d.

Sayre House, s.
    b.   d.

4 ch. **128.** *Ezekiel*, b. July 28, 1812; m. Dec. 17, 1846, Hannah Osborne
    *William Havens, b.   m. { 1st, Harriet Thorpe.
                               { 2d, Almira Mills.
129. *Eliza*, b.   m.   David Williams. ⁰*Egbert*, b.   m.
(*) Had eight ch.   (⁰) Has d. leaving a widow, two sons and one da. named Eliza.

57.

EUNICE MARIA HAVENS, da. William and   Havens.
  b. Dec. 25, 1791.   m. Dec. 23, 1810.   d. Jan. 7, 1872.

Samuel Stratton Dayton, s. John and   Dayton.
  b. Nov. 24, 1788.   d. Mar. 16, 1843.

3 ch. **130.** *John Havens*, b. Sep. 8, 1811; m. 1835, Frances Jane Nichols.
       131. *Betsey Smith*. b. Mar. 11, 1816; m.   1837. Richard Parsons Smith.
              David Stratton, b. Jan. 7, 1821, d. unm. July 14, 1848.

58.

AUGUSTUS HAVENS, s. Joseph and Phebe (Havens) Havens.
  b. Nov. 19, 1768.   m.   d. June 4, 1830.

Esther Bowditch, da. John and   Bowditch.
  b.   1773.   d. Nov. 14, 1828.

9 ch.   *Caleb*, b. Feb. 28, 1798, d. May 28, 1798.   *Sally B.*, b. June 4, 1800, d. Nov. 14, 1801.
     132. *Nathaniel*, b. Feb. 24, 1802; m. July 5, 1823, Charlotte M. Havens.
     133. *Joseph Caleb*, b. Mar. 16, 1804; m. { 1st,   Hannah Brown.
                                                    { 2d, May 21, 1845. Hannah M. Brown.
     134. *Benedict*, b.   1806; m { 1st,   Phebe
                                              { 2d,
     135. *Sarah Ann*, b.   m. Sep. 17, 1826, David Cartwright.
     136. *Augustus*. b.   m. Sep. 14. 1839, Phebe Jennings.
     137. *Bethiah M.*, b.   1811; m. Feb. 8, 1831, Sylvanus B. Havens.
          Cynthia Esther, b.   1817; m. Apr. 3, 1873; °Orange Petty; no issue.
(*) d. June 2, 1897.   (°) d. June 3, 1881.

59.

JACOB HAVENS, s. Joseph and Phebe (Havens) Havens.
  b. Mar. 25, 1783.   m.   d. Dec. 23, 1819.

Elizabeth Bennet, da. Jeremiah and Elizabeth (Van Scoy) Bennet.
  b.   d. July 12, 1848.

4 ch.   *Phebe Elizabeth*, b. Nov. 16, 1809; m. Jan.   1837, Ezra A. Tuthill.
         Nancy Maria, b.   d. unm., ae. 19.
     138. *Charles Alfred*, b. Jan. 31, 1813; m. Jan. 18, 1841, Phebe Tuthill.
     139. *Jacob*, b. May 10, 1815; m. July 27, 1840, Ann Eliza Hamilton.
(*) See Tuthill genealogy No. 20.

60.

OBADIAH HAVENS, s. Obadiah and Phebe ([?] Havens) Havens.
  b. Feb. 26, 1777.   m. July 1, 1799.   d. May 19 or 26, 1817.

Nancy Robertson, da. Archibald and Sylthia (Allen) Robertson.
  b. Mar. 29, 1780.   d. Sep. 1, 1865.

8 ch. **140.** *John Steward*, b. Aug. 8, 1800; m. June 1, 1828, Nancy Torrey.
       Sidney, b. Jan. 1. 1802, d. unm. Dec. 13, 1830.
       Elmira, b. Oct. 1, 1803; m. Jan. 21, 1823, °Calvin M. Griffing.
       ‖*Obadiah*, b. June 26, 1805; m. about 1830-31, wid. Prudence Goff; no issue.
       Archibald R., b. Aug. 7, 1807, d. Apr. 11, 1809.
       †*Mary Ann*. b. Dec. 10, 1811; m.   1846, Joseph B. Hudson.
       ‡*Margaret C.*, b. Apr. 25, 1814; m. Mar. 6, 1834, James D. Tuthill.
     141. *Archibald R.*, b. Oct. 9, 1816; m. May 23, 1830, Caroline A. Hughes.
(*) d. Aug. 8, 1827, had 2 ch. Sylvester and Charles, both d. unm.   (°) s. of Absalom and Sybil (King)
Griffing, d. Dec. 24, 1871, ae. 73.
(‖) d. Aug. 9, 1832,   (†) See Hudson Genealogy, No. 35.   (‡) See Tuthill Genealogy, No. 17.

61.

GEORGE H. HAVENS, s. Obadiah and Phebe ([?] Havens) Havens.
  b. Nov. 5, 1786.   m. Jan. 17, 1808.   d. May 29, 1858.

Sarah Haynes, da. Henry and   (Rugg) Haynes.
  b. Apr. 6, 1787.   d. Sep. 15, 1856.

11 ch.   *George Howell*, b. Feb. 23, 1807, d Oct. 5, 1827.
         Henry H., b. July 1, 1810, d. Oct. 5, 1827.
     142. *Nicoll J.*, b. July 1, 1811; m.   Adeline Jennings.
     143. *Phebe H.*, b. Feb. 10, 1813; m.   John C. Wells.
          Sarah A.. b. Mar. 27, 1815; m.   Jerry Aldridge; no issue.
          °*Silas R.*, b. Mar. 13, 1817; m. { 1st,   Elizabeth Wood.
                                            { 2d,   Abby Lyons.
          ‖*Philetus*, b. Aug. 30, 1819; m. Sep. 15. 1847. Mary Elmira Myer: no issue.
     144. *Obadiah*, b. Mar. 6, 1822; m. { 1st, Jan. 4, 1844, Mary Ann Cowles.
                                             { 2d, July 5, 1887, Johannah P. White.
     145. *Clarissa F.*, b. May 7, 1824; m. Sep. 10, 1843. Don Alonzo Miller.
          †*Dewitt*, b. Apr. 12, 1826; m.   ‡Albina King; no issue.
     146. *Henry M.*, b. July 11, 1829; m.   1848, Frances Delia Ross.
(*) d. July 17, 1849.   (°) had 2 ch. by 1st wife. Mary Elizabeth and Nellie, both of whom are dead.
(‖) d. April 5, 1864.   (†) d. Nov. 16, 1854.   (‡) da. of Henry King of New Suffolk.

62.

ABBY FOSDICK, da. Nicoll and Abigail (Eldredge) Fosdick.
   b. Mar. 8, 1790.   m.   d. July 31, 1813.

John Billings, s. Daniel and Katherine (   ) Billings.
   b.   d.

2 ch.   *Abby Fosdick, b. Dec. 29, 1812; m.   OFranklin Stanton.   John, b.   d. young.

(*) Had 1 ch. John Billings, b. June 27, 1851, d. Aug. 1, 1891.   (O) b. May 27, 1814, d. Oct. 19, 1873.

63.

MARY ANN FOSDICK, da. Nicoll and Abigail (Eldredge) Fosdick.
   b. Aug. 19, 1796.   m. May 14, 1817.   d. Dec. 31, 1882.

Thomas Mussey, s. John and Martha (Pierson) Mussey.
   b. July 1, 1773.   d. Jan. 21, 1853.

10 ch. 147. Abby Eldredge, b. May 4, 1818; m. May 7, 1838, George W. Browne.
   148. Elizabeth Fosdick, b. Dec. 8, 1819; m. Apr. 22, 1844, Charles Ramsdell.
   149. Mary Ann, b. May 9, 1822; m. Sep. 27, 1848, Henry Ramsdell.
   150. Martha Pierson, b. Nov. 22, 1824; m. Sep. 4, 1850, Horace F. Ash.
   151. Frances Eliza, b. Mar. 16, 1826; m. Jan. 4, 1853, Rev. James W. Dennis.
      Thomas Nicoll, b. Jan. 8, 1828, d. Nov. 14, 1831.
      Lodowick Fosdick, b. July 10, 1830, d. unm. 1870.   Gloriana Fosdick, b. Nov. 28, 1832.
   152. Jane Hobert, b. Apr. 19, 1835; m. Sep. 2, 1861, Rodney R. Crowley.
      *Letitia Howard, b. May 15, 1835; m. Jan, 7, 1866, ORev. Elmer H. Capen.

(*) d. Sep. 5, 1872, had 1 ch. Paul B., b. Oct. 9, 1871, d. May 18, 1873.   (O) s. of Samuel and Almira (Paul) Capen, b. Apr. 5, 1838.

64.

FRANCIS ELIZA FOSDICK, da. Nicoll and Abigail (Eldredge) Fosdick.
   b. Jan. 28, 1801.   m. Oct. 2, 1834.   d. Dec. 2, 1859.

George Jones, s. John and Mary Ann (Elcock) Jones.
   b. Feb. 14, 1789.   d. Mar. 16, 1861.

4 ch. 153. John Elcock, b. June 11, 1835; m. June 20, 1859, Olivia Jarvis.
   154. Nicoll Fosdick, b. July 31, 1836; m. Apr. 4, 1866, Deborah Merwin.
   155. Abby Maria, b. Aug. 6, 1838; m. Jan. 31, 1865, William H. Ganung.
   156. William, b. Aug. 26, 1840; m. June 16, 1875, Asenath C. Holmes.

65.

THOMAS UPDIKE FOSDICK, s. Thomas U. and Sarah (Howe) Fosdick.
   b. Apr. 19, 1784.   m. Oct. 9, 1804.   d. Oct. 6, 1854.

Rachel Armstrong, da. Solomon Armstrong, of Norwich, Conn.
   b. Jan. 5, 1785.   d. Feb. 5, 1856.

9 ch. 157. Orville, b, Nov. 19, 1805; m. { 1st,   1828, Elizabeth Johnson.
                                          { 2nd, June 11, 1845, Hannah McCollock.
   158. Julia A., b. Feb. 28, 1808; m. Feb. 22, 1831, Richard Mann.
      Samuel, b. 1811, d. young.   Polly, b. 1813, d. young.   Sarah, b. 1815, d. young.
   159. Olive A., b. Jan. 21, 1818; m.   Alonzo Finney.
   160. Louisa A., b. Feb. 19, 1819; m.   1847, Samuel Hackley.
      Mary A., b. Aug. 31, 1821; m.   Gideon Yarlat.
   161. Edward W., b. July 12, 1822; m. { 1st, July 24, 1850, Helen G. Totten.
                                         { 2nd, Mar. 27, 1859, Ruan M. Brandon.
                                         { 3rd, Sep. 17, 1878, Elizabeth H. Fetterhoff.

66.

SYLVESTER L. H. FOSDICK, s. Richard and Phebe (L'Hommedieu) Fosdick.
   b. May 6, 1799.   m. Apr. 30, 1821.   d. Mar. 14, 1833.

Harriet A. Raymond, da. Silas and Mary (   ) Raymond, of Sag Harbor, N. Y.
   b.   1796.   d. June 30, 1844.

5 ch.   Richard Thomas, b. Mar. 15, 1822, d. Sep. 29, 1822.
      Samuel Nicoll, b. Mar. 12, 1824, d. Apr. 26, 1826.
      *Charles Raymond, b. June 4, 1826; m. Oct. 4, 1853, Frances Begham.
      Sylvester L. H., b. Nov. 20, 1827, d. Apr. 12, 1832.
      Anna Mason, b. Nov. 30, 1830, d. Apr. 28, 1885.

(*) d. Dec. 8, 1896, had one son named Dering who d. Aug. 7, 1894.

67.

SAMUEL FOSDICK, s. Richard and Phebe (L'Hommedieu) Fosdick.
   b. Mar. 21, 1801.   m. Jan. 12, 1836.   d. Aug. 5, 1881.

Sarah Ann Wood, da. John and Sarah (   ) Wood.
   b.   d.

8 ch.   Richard L'H., b. Oct. 1, 1836, d. Oct. 4, 1842.   Wood, b. Dec. 24, 1838.
   162. Frances Dering, b. June 30, 1841; m. May 30, 1866, Fred J. Jones.
      Anna Maria, b. July 22, 1843, d. Nov. 23, 1876.
      Samuel, b. Oct. 21, 1845, d. Nov. 14, 1847.   Sarah L'H., b. May 9, 1848, d. Aug. 12, 1874.
      Ella, b. Sep. 11, 1850, d. Dec. 20, 1851.   Charles Updike, b. Nov. 10, 1852, d. Sep. 2, 1876.

68.

BETSEY ELIZA FOSDICK, da. Richard and Phebe (L'Hommedieu) Fosdick.
  b. Feb. 9, 1805.   m. June 21, 1841.   d. Mar. 6, 1890.

Rev. Benjamin Parkam Aydelott, s. Benjamin and Margaret (Parkam) Aydelott.
  b. Jan. 7, 1795.   d. Sep. 10, 1880.
3 ch.   *Louisa E.*, b. Aug. 11, 1843.   *David B.*, b. Sep. 26, 1848, d. July 24, 1864.
  Charles U., b. Nov. 18, 1848.

69.

HENRY NICOLL FOSDICK, s. Richard and Phebe (L'Hommedieu) Fosdick.
  b. Sep. 21, 1808.   m. June 28, 1836.   d. Sep. 6, 1841.

Harriet Harkness, da. Anthony and Mary (   ) Harkness.
  b.

3 ch. **163.** *Sylvester Updike*, b. Jan. 16, 1837; m. Jan. 20, 1859, Anna M. Gasgoigne.
  164. *Mary Ann*, b. Oct. 31, 1838; m. Nov. 4, 1858. Francis M. Doughlas.
  Elizabeth Nicoll, b. Oct. 16, 1840, d. Jan. 5, 1864.

70.

MARY CATHERINE L'HOMMEDIEU, da. Ezra and Mary C. (Havens) L'Hommedieu.
  b. July 6, 1806.   m. Aug. 7, 1823.   d. Jan. 28, 1838.

Samuel Smith Gardiner, s. Abraham and Phebe (Dayton) Gardiner.
  b. May 5, 1789.   d. Mar. 21, 1859.
3 ch. **165.** *Mary L'Hommedieu*, b. Sep. 27, 1824; m. Aug. 4, 1848, Eben Norton Horsford.
  *Phebe D., b. Aug. 15, 1826; m. July 22, 1860, Eben Norton Horsford.
  166. *Frances Eliza*, b. Aug. 31, 1832; m. July 22, 1857, George Martin Lane.
(*) See No. 165.

71.

CATHERINE H. HUNTINGTON, da. Henry and Catherine M. (Havens) Huntington.
  b. Dec. 3, 1797.   m. Mar. 26, 1833, as his 2d wife.   d. Sep. 10, 1856.

William Williams, s. Thomas and Susannah (David) Williams.
  b. Oct. 12, 1787.   d. June 10, 1850.
2 ch.   *Henry H.*, b. May 28, 1834, d. Aug. 15, 1835.   *George H.*, b. July 26, 1837, d. Oct. 22, 1855.

72.

HENRIETTA DESIRE HUNTINGTON, da. Henry and Catherine M. (Havens) Huntington.
  b. June 15, 1803.   m. Dec. 9, 1828.   d. Sep. 23, 1865.

Benjamin H. Wright, s. Benjamin and Philomela (Waterman) Wright.
  b. Oct. 19, 1801.   d. May 13, 1881.
5 ch.   A daughter d. in infancy.   *Henry H.*, b. Aug. 24, 1832, d. July 17, 1833.
  167. *Benjamin Huntington*, b. Jan. 6, 1835; m. Jan. 28, 1868, Florence Melvine Cossitt.
  Henrietta Huntington, b. Sep. 2, 1840.   *Albert W.*, b. Aug. 8, 1845, d. Jan. 7, 1852.

73.

SARAH JENKINS HAVENS, da. Rensselaer and Anna (Jenkins) Havens.
  b. Mar. 4, 1812.   m. Dec. 24, 1844.   d. Dec. 30, 1882.

Edward Bement, s. William and Deborah (Nichols) Bement.
  b. Apr. 15, 1795.   d. Apr. 27, 1866.
1 ch.   *Edward*, b. May 30, 1848.

74.

HOWARD HAVENS, s. Rensselaer and Catherine C. (Webb) Havens.
  b. Apr. 26, 1820.   m. June 14, 1856.

Asenath Cummings Randall, da. Isaac and Elizabeth (Cummings) Randall.
  b. Apr. 3, 1829.   d. Apr. 19, 1890.
3 ch. **168.** *Charles Rensselaer*, b. June 24, 1858; m. July 15, 1890, Mary Lizzie Whipple.
  169. *Howard Cummings*, b. Dec. 1, 1861; m. Sep. 7, 1887, Mary Florence Cutter.
  Ella Mary, b. Dec. 1, 1861.

75.

FRANCES MARIA HAVENS, da. Rensselaer and Catherine C. (Webb) Havens.
  b. July 15, 1821.   m. Dec. 4, 1839.   d. May 1, 1864.

Rev. Samuel Burr Sherwood Bissell, s. Clark and Sally (Sherwood) Bissell.
  b. Feb. 16, 1812.   d. Aug. 23, 1894.
10 ch. **170.** *Eleanor Anderson*, b. Sep. 26, 1840; m. Feb. 6, 1867, Brayton Ives.
  Samuel Sherwood, b. Sep. 17, 1842.
  171. *Katherine Havens*, b. Oct. 5, 1844; m. May 10, 1865, LeGrand Lockwood.
  172. *Rensselaer Havens*, b. Apr. 27, 1848; m. Nov. 10, 1869, Fredericka Belden.
  173. *Frances Maria*, b. June 9, 1854; m. May 9, 1878, Theodore Cuyler Patterson.
  Clark, b. Dec. 13, 1855, d. June 29, 1881.
  174. *Morris Jesup*, b. July 28, 1857; m. Oct. 29, 1889, Leila Ida Lormor.
  Frederick Packard, b. July 30, 1859, d. June 25, 1886.
  Howard Havens, b. Apr. 16, 1864, d. July 29, 1886.
  James Miller, b. Feb. 20, 1868, d. Nov. 27, 1875.

76.

SYLVESTER DERING HAVENS, s. Rensselaer and Catherine C. (Webb) Havens.
    b. Mar. 3, 1829.   m. Feb. 25, 1851.

Rachel Kay Phillip, da. John and Jacobina (Wilson) Phillip.
    b. Apr. 14, 1831.   d. Mar. 14, 1885.

7 ch.   *Catherine Frances. b. Dec. 8, 1851; m. Nov. 6, 1877, Peter O. Peterson.
    °Anna Jenkins. b. July 9, 1854; m. July 25, 1892, George F. Bowman.
    Sarah Bement, b. May 9, 1857; m. Sep. 16, 1890, †Frederick A. Senechal; no issue.
    Charlotte Mary, b. Apr. 9, 1859, d. Aug. 30, 1860.   Rensselaer, b. June 4, 1861.
    |John Phillip, b. May 10. 1867; m. Aug. 23, 1891, Margaret Roche.
    Charlotte Gloriana, b. July 11, 1869; m. Oct. 10, 1892, Clifford T. Whiting; no issue.
(*) Had one ch. named Oliver Haven, b. Jan. 14, 1884.   (°) Has two ch. named George F., b. July
25, 1893, and Charles N., b. Feb. 16, 1895,   (|) Has two ch., Margie Catherine, b Oct. 18, 1892,
and John P., b. Mar. 21, 1896.   (†) da. of Oliver and Josephine (Allaire) Senechal.

77.

CHARLES EDWARD HAVENS, s. Rensselaer and Catherine C. (Webb) Havens.
    b. May 6, 1832.   m. Sep. 4, 1855.   d. Mar. 7, 1865.

Mary J. Tracy, of Horicon, Wisconsin.
    b.   d. Apr. 17, 1859.
1 ch.   *Alice Mary, b. Apr. 4, 1856; m. $\begin{cases} \text{1st,} \\ \text{2d,} \end{cases}$ John B. Church.
                                    Wilfred Peters Price.
(*) Has one ch. by first husband, named Valeria E.

78.

RENSSELAER WATSON COWLES, s. Rev. Whitfield and Gloriana (Havens) Cowles.
    b. Feb. 18. 1796.   m. Sep. 20, 1818.   d. May 3, 1842.

Laura Kilbourne, da. James and Lucy (Fitch) Kilbourne.
    b. May 26, 1797.   d. Jan. 11, 1867.
12 ch.   Havens, b. Oct. 3, 1819; m. Oct. 24, 1866, *Charlotte Sedgwick; no issue.
175.   Cynthia, b. Mar. 8, 1821; m. May 1, 1842, Henry Livingston Richards.
    °Hector Kilbourne, b. Mar. 1, 1823; m. Jan. 17, 1872, †Sarah Porter; no issue.
    Mary Antoinette, b. Dec. 7, 1824, d. Jan. 19, 1852.
    James Whitfield, b. Jan. 11, 1827, d. Aug. 12, 1828.
176.   Geraldine Dering, b. Feb. 17, 1829; m. Apr. 7, 1853. John Adder McDowell.
    Rensselaer Whitfield, b. Nov. 18, 1830, d. Mar. 20, 1834
    Laura Kilbourne, b. July 28, 1832, d. Aug. 21. 1832.
    Granville, b. Aug. 18, 1833, d. Sep. 21, 1835.   Gertrude. b. Sep 7, 1835, d. Nov. 12, 1846.
177.   Byron Kilbourne, b. Oct. 21, 1837; m. Dec. 12, 1867, Lucy G. Buckingham.
    Whiting Day, b. Jan. 26, 1842, d. Sep. 7, 1875.
(*) da. Theodore and Hannah C. (Frink) Sedgwick.   (°) d. Sep. 14, 1878.   (†) d. Feb. 17 1881.

79.

CATHERINE HAVENS RICHARDS, da. Peter and Catherine (Mumford) Richards.
    b.   m. Oct. 23, 1802.   d.

Levi Huntington, s. Levi and Anna (Perkins) Huntington.
    b. Dec. 29, 1777.   b. July 1, 1838.
5 ch.   Joseph Otis, b. Aug. 14, 1803; m. Nov. 4, 1843, Elizabeth C. Otis.
    Catherine Anna, b. Sep. 27, 1806; m. Dec. 9, 1834, William Root.
    Peter Richards, b. Aug. 20, 1809; m. Feb. 21, 1834, Jane Simmons.
178.   John Griswold, b. Feb. 24, 1814; m. Sep. 1, 1836, Mary Isham.
    *Hannah Mumford, b. Sep. 14, 1816; m.   William C. Barns.
(*) Had 5 ch., Margaret P., Catherine R., Josephine O., Emma E., William C.

80.

THOMAS MUMFORD HUNTINGTON, s. Zachariah and Hannah (Mumford) Huntington
    b. Dec. 28, 1786.   m. in 1819.   d. Sep. 11, 1851.

Mary Bowers Campbell, da.
    b. June 27, 1802.   d. in New York City.
5 ch.   Thomas L. Bowers, b. Nov. 6, 1819, d. July 4, 1827.
179.   John Myers, b. Apr. 3, 1821; m. Sep. 2, 1856, Mary A. Parks.
    Henry Bowers, b. Feb. 16, 1823; m. Oct. 18, 1853, Lucinda Willis.
180.   George Wolcott, b. Apr. 6, 1825; m. $\begin{cases} \text{1st, June 23, 1848, Catherine L. Childs.} \\ \text{2d, June 15, 1854, Alice Henderson.} \end{cases}$
    *Mary Elizabeth, b. Sep. 16, 1829; m.   Dr. Timothy Childs.
(*) Has one s. named Huntington.

81.

SAMUEL JONES MUMFORD. s. Benjamin M. and Harriet (Bowers) Mumford.
    b. May 23, 1803.   m. 1st, June 2, 1830.   2d, Sep. 27, 1836.   3d, Oct. 6, 1842.   d. Sep. 9, 1850.

1st, Caroline Givens Astor, adopted da. Henry and Dorothy (   ) Astor.
    b. Apr. 8, 1806.   d. Feb. 4, 1834.

2d, Harriet Viser Innes, da. John and Elizabeth   Innes.
    b. Jan. 25. 1814.   d. Mar. 9, 1838.

3d, Eliza Hooker Strong, da. Elisha B. and Dolly (Goodwin) Strong.
    b. Dec. 10, 1822.   d. June 5, 1844.

4 ch. **181.** *Dora Astor*, b. May 17, 1831; m. Apr. 28, 1850, Alonzo C. Jackson.
 Caroline Harriet. b. Dec. 19, 1833, d. July 30, 1834
 Harriet Viser, b. Sep. 12, 1837, d. Feb. 7, 1884.
 182. *Margaret Hyslop*, b. Aug. 23, 1843; m. Oct. 15, 1867, Charles B. Northrop.

82.

HARRIET MUMFORD, da. Benjamin M. and Harriet (Bowers) Mumford
  b. Sep. 7, 1807.   m. July 11, 1832.   d. Mar. 31, 1867.
 Alonzo Christopher Paige, s. Rev. Winslow and Clarissa (Keyes) Paige.
  b. July 31, 1796.   d. Mar. 31, 1868.
5 ch. *Benjamin Mumford*, b. Jan. 20, 1834, d. June 6, 1838.
  Clara Keyes, b. Aug. 4, 1836; m.   Rev. William Payne.
  Harriet B. M., b. May 17, 1838; m.   Douglas Campbell.
  Caroline Mumford, b. Apr. 14, 1840; m.   Henry Lansing.
  Edward Winslow, b. July 11, 1844.

83.

EZRA HAVENS, s. Walter and Disie (Goodale) Havens.
  b.   1786.   m. 1st,   m. 2d,   d. Nov. 20, 1869.
 1st. Betsey Jagger, da. Stephen and Miriam (Wicks) Jagger.
  b.   1788.   d. Jan. 19, 1845.
 2d, Rosetta Sinclair, da.
  b.
12 ch. **183.** *Jeremiah Jagger*, b. Apr.   1809; m.   Mary B. Rowland.
 184. *William*. b.   m.   Betsey A. Jackson.
 185. *Fanny*. b. Feb. 9, 1812; m. Oct. 16, 1830, Samuel White.
  Charry, b.   m.   William Ruland. **Sarah*. b.   m.   Marshall Loomis.
                                 { 1st,   William Ruland.
 186. *Mary*, b. Apr. 11, 1822; m. { 2d, Apr. 10, 1845, Jasper Vail.
                                 { 3d,   B. Louis Terrill.
  °Bethiah, b.   m.   Walter Sweesy.
 187. *Nancy*, b. June 8, 1824; m.   Harry Warner.
 188. *Hannah*, b. Oct. 15, 1826; m. Dec. 21, 1843, David Petty.
  Lorenzo, b.   m. *Melissa*, b.   m. *Ellen M.*, b.   m.   Edward Aumack.
(*) Had 7 ch., Daniel, Nancy, Eugene, Ezra, Marshall, Henry, William.   (°) See No. 193.

84.

WALTER HAVENS, s. Walter and Disie (Goodale) Havens.
  b. Sep. 23, 1799.   m. 1st, Nov. 28, 1820.   m. 2d, Dec. 12, 1844.   m. 3d, June 24, 1851.
  m. 4th,   d. Apr. 8, 1875.
 1st, Anna Benjamin, da. of James
  b.   d. Feb. 19, 1844.
 2d, Sarah Homan,
  b.   d. Sep. 12, 1850.
 3d, Clarissa C. Benjamin, da. Zachariah and Polly (Wicks) Benjamin.
  b.   d.
 4th, Susan Benjamin, wid. (*nee* Downs), d. of Benjamin and   Downs
  b.
7 ch. *Ann Eliza*, b. Sep. 13, 1822, d. ae. 18.   A ch., d. in infancy.
                                 { 1st, Oct. 10, 1843, Harriet L. Fanning.
 189. *Daniel S.*, b. July 6, 1824; m. { 2d, Sep. 1, 1869, Nancy R. Fanning.
                                 { 3d, Jan. 17, 1883, Jennie E. Fanning.
 190. *Walter F.*, b. June 5, 1828; m. Dec. 23, 1851, Phebe A. Tuthill.
 191. *Manasseh*. b. Dec. 11, 1830; m. May 20, 1853, Elizabeth Tuthill.
 192. *Frances Rosella*, b. Jan. 6, 1834; m. Dec. 24, 1851, Prosper King Benjamin.
  George Washington, b. Aug. 8, 1842. d. Oct. 12, 1843.

85.

MEHETABLE HAVENS, da. Walter and Disie (Goodale) Havens.
  b.   m.   d.
 Joel Sweesy, s.
  b.
1 ch. **193.** *Walter*, b.   m.   Bethiah Havens.

86.

EDWARD CONKLING KING, s. Benjamin and Abigail (Terry) King,
  b. Aug. 2, 1778.   m.   d. Oct. 12, 1827.
 Sarah Tignor,
  b.   1786.   d. Oct. 2, 1855.
3 ch. **Sarah Ann*, b.   m.   1830, William G. Bryan.
  °Elizabeth, b.   m.   1832, Charles Slover. *Harriet*,   b.   d. unm, 1866.
(*) Had 11 ch. (°) Had 7 ch.

87.

WILLIAM H. TUTHILL, s. Christopher and Elizabeth (Terry) Tuthill.
  b. Aug. 5, 1793.   m. Jan. 28, 1823.   d. Dec. 5, 1860.
 Sophia Petty, da. David and Prudence (Terry) Petty.
  b. Oct. 4, 1798.   d. Mar. 30, 1876.

2 ch. **194.** *Betsey M.*, b. Oct. 20, 1823, m. Mar. 22, 1848, John B. Brown.
     William H., b. July 5, 1827, d. June 13, 1828.

88.

CHARLES JAMES HOWELL, s. Matthew and Hannah (Latham) Howell.
    b. June 17, 1797.   m. about 1827.   d. Apr. 20, 1881.

Lydia Hinchman Spear, of Boston, Mass.
    b. Dec. 1, 1803.   d. Sep. 30, 1878.

10 ch.   *Charles J., b. Apr. 7, 1828; m.   Mary Moore Dubois.
       oMatthew, b. May 12, 1829; m.   Julia Gilmore.
       Samuel Spear, b. Mar. 7, 1831, d. Dec. 5, 1858.
       William Henry, b. Oct. 26, 1832, d. July 26, 1833.
      ‖Maria Adelaide, b. Dec. 23, 1834; m.   Horace B. Fisher.
   195. William Perkins, b. May 24, 1837; m. { 1st, Nov. 15, 1866, Cecelia Ray Hunting.
                                       { 2nd, Apr. 14, 1870, Lydia George Cockroft.
       Mary Perkins, b. May 6, 1840.
       Henry Terbell, b. Feb. 22, 1842; m. Maria Relyea; no issue.
       Lydia H., b. Apr. 16, 1846, d. Sep. 26, 1846.
      †John Hancock, b. Dec. 13, 1847; m   Agnes Liston.

(*) d. Sep. 1, 1887, had 3 ch. all of whom m. (o) Had 3 ch. Matthew, William and Harriet. (‖) Has 2 ch. Marion and Howell. (†) Has 2 ch. John H. and Samuel S.

89.

ELBERT S. KIP, s. Samuel and Elizabeth (Howell) Kip.
    b. Oct. 8, 1799.   m. Oct. 17, 1843.   d. July 26, 1876.

Elizabeth Goelet, da. Robert R. and Margaret (Buchanan) Goelet.
    b. Mar. 19, 1808.   d. Feb. 15, 1882.

2 ch. **196.** *George Goelet*, b. Jan. 15, 1845; m. May 23, 1867, Anna M. Geissenheimer.
     Margaret Goelet, b. Mar. 27, 1847, d. June 27, 1854.

90.

SAMUEL KIP, s. Samuel and Elizabeth (Howell) Kip.
    b. Sep. 8, 1801.   m. Nov. 8, 1825.   d.

Nancy H. Fowler, da. Oliver and Desire L. (Havens) Fowler.
    b. Apr. 14, 1807.

7 ch.   An infant, d. Mar. 28, 1830.
   197. Lydia F., b. Nov. 16, 1838; m.   1858, Edward B. Underhill.
   198. Thomas C., b. Nov. 18, 1840; m. July 10, 1866, Mary A. Hodgson.
      *Caswell, b.   m.
   199. Elizabeth, b.   m.   George Harrison.
      oSamuel, b.   m.   Mary, b.

(*) Has d. leaving one ch. (*) Has d.; left 3 ch. Parunel, who d., Charlotte M., and Ethel, who m. Oct. 14, 1898, Charles L. Carberry.

91.

HENRY KIP, s. Samuel and Elizabeth (Howell) Kip.
    b. July 25, 1807. m. 1st, 1845. m. 2nd, 1852. m. 3rd, 1885. d. 1893.

1st, Elizabeth Abbott, da. Robert and Deborah (Minturn) Abbott.
    b.   d.   1857.

2nd, Catherine Gates, da.
    b.   d.

3rd, *Geraldine Gardiner, da. Samuel L'H. and Annie (Shaler) Gardiner.
    b.

2 ch. **200.** *Cornelia*, b. Oct. 28, 1848; m. June 10, 1874, William H. Burr.
    201. *Elizabeth Abbott*, b. Aug. 17, 1851; m. Jan. 19, 1875, Samuel Chase Coale.
(*) See L'Hommedieu genealogy.

92.

FRANCES HAND HAVENS, da. Francis and Phebe (Eldredge) Havens.
    b. Feb. 18, 1811.   m. July 9, 1831.   d. Nov.   1879.

Zachariah Rogers.
    b.

4 ch. **202.** *Frances Elizabeth*, b. Dec. 16, 1834; m. June 29, 1864, Rev. Gordon Huntington.
     Amelia J., b. June 19, 1837, d. Sep. 8, 1838. *Morgan Z.*, b. Jan. 14, 1840, d. Sep. 5, 1858.
     *Robert Francis, b. Sep. 8, 1842; m. Jan. 1866, Emma De Sames.
(*) Has one ch. Eugenia, b. Jan. 1867.

93.

NANCY B. DAVIS, da. Matthias and Frances (Havens) Davis.
    b. Nov. 6, 1795. m.   d.

Uriah Valentine, s.
    b.   d.

3 ch.   Elizabeth Havens, b.   m.   Lewis Flowers.
   203. Frances Davis, b.   m.   Silas Cocks Searing.
      A son, b.   d. in youth.

94.

CHARLES HAVENS DAVIS, s. Matthias and Frances (Havens) Davis.
  b. Mar. 13, 1798. m. 1st m. 2nd, July 20, 1831. d. Sep. 27. 1870.

1st,   Crossman, da. Gilbert and   (   ) Crossman.
  b.   d.

2nd, Hulda Ann Richardson, da. Lemuel and Ann S. (Hoffman) Richardson.
  b.   d. Mar. 11, 1877.

9 ch. *Henry Clinton*, b.   d. Jan. 26, 1837. *Charles Homer*, b.   m.
  Lemuel Richardson, b. May 1, 1833, d. Dec. 16, 1836.
  Gilbert Crossman, b. Jan. 2, 1835, d. Jan. 16, 1837.
  Lemuel Richardson, b. Nov. 7, 1837, d. Mar. 18, 1840.
 204. *Maria Rapyhea*, b. Feb. 21, 1840; m. Apr. 25. 1861, Egbert Quimby.
 205. *Josephine*, b. July 27, 1842; m. June 12, 1867, Joshua Thurston Haws.
  John Luther, b. Apr. 12, 1847; m. Oct. 29, 1873, Emma L. Smith.
 206. *Mary Frances*, b. Apr. 2, 1849; m. Dec. 16, 1867, Richard Byrne.

95.

ELVIRA DAVIS, da. Matthias and Frances (Havens) Davis.
  b. Sep. 10, 1800. m. 1st, in 1816. 2d,   d. about 1878.

1st, James Davis, s.
  b.   d. in 1820.

2d, Smith Conklin, s.
  b.   d.

2 ch. **Thomas H.*, b. Apr. 5, 1820; m.   Elizabeth Powell.
 207. *Catherine A.*, b. Nov. 28, 1817; m. June 18, 1840, Alfred F. Chatman.
(*) Had 7 ch. John H., Thomas N., who d., Katie E., Julia L., Sarah, James W., and George P.

96.

JULIA GARDINER DAVIS, da. Matthias and Frances (Havens) Davis.
  b. June 20, 1810. m.   d. Jan. 19, 1874.

Charles S. Loper, s. Cabet and Mary (Squires) Loper.
  b.   d. Dec. 1, 1884.

3 ch. *Mary Frances*, b. Nov. 1835, d. Jan. 25, 1840.
 208. *Mary Frances*, b. July 13, 1841; m. Apr. 13, 1859, Thomas S. Marlor.
 209. *Julia M.*, b. May 16, 1845; m. Jan. 30, 1868, Robert J. Clyde.

97.

MARY C. DAVIS, da. Matthias and Frances (Havens) Davis.
  b. Nov. 7, 1807. m. Jan. 2, 1833. d. July 5, 1884.

Strong Conklin, s. Samuel and Martha (Smith) Conklin.
  b. Nov. 3c, 1807. d. Nov. 1, 1887.

4 ch. *Orry*, b. May 23, 1834, d. Feb. 25, 1835.
  Dewitt C., b. Mar. 15, 1841; m. June 13, 1869, Mary F. Hart.
  **Isabella S.*, b. Sep. 20, 1844; m. May 8, 1863, °George H. DeLong.
  Martha F., b. Apr. 17, 1846, d. Oct. 12, 1848.
(*) d. Dec. 22, 1866, had twins who d. in birth. (°) s. of Jacob and Mary DeLong.

98.

SARAH FRANCES HAVENS, da. Gordon and Esther (Clark) Havens.
  b. Feb. 18, 1794. m. 1st, Dec. 28, 1814. m. 2nd, Apr. 18, 1818. d. Sep. 11, 1843.

1st, William Havens, s. Walter and Louise   Havens.
  b.   d. Aug. 19, 1815.

2nd, Richard Lester, s. David and Louise (Talmadge) Lester.
  b. Apr. 13, 1797.   d. Mar. 27, 1879.

5 ch. *Richard Henry*, b. Dec. 4, 1819, d. unm. Sep. 23, 1850.
 210. *Nancy Havens*, b. Oct. 18, 1820; m. Dec. 1, 1835, John Worth.
 211. *William Havens*, b. Dec. 4, 1825; m. Aug. 31, 1854, Elizabeth Hand.
  Esther Elizabeth, b. Jan. 1827, d. Jan. 1827.
 212. *George Lewis*, b. July 8, 1831; m. Apr. 13, 1853, Hatty Osborn.

99.

NANCY HAVENS, da. Gordon and Esther (Clark) Havens.
  b. Dec. 18, 1797. m. June 4, 1822. d.

Henry M. Chatfield, s. Henry and Rebecca (Mulford) Chatfield.
  b.   1801.   d. Mar. 29, 1867.

3 ch. **213.** *Julia A.*, b.   1824; m.   Samuel Haines Howell.
 214. *John H.*, b. Jan. 20, 1826; m. Oct. 1857, Esther Edwards.
  Charles, b.   d. in infancy.

100.

ESTHER E. HAVENS, da. Gordon and Esther (Clark) Havens.
  b. Feb. 22, 1800. m. Nov. 22, 1828. d. July 20, 1881.

Nathaniel Tyndall, s. Amah and Anna ( ) Tyndall.
  b. Aug. 18, 1804.   d. June 21, 1877.

2 ch. **215.** *George*, b. Sep. 1, 1832; m. May 6, 1857, Nancy Maria Havens.
  William, b. Sep. 14, 1835.

101.

ABIGAIL DAVIS HAVENS, da. Gordon and Esther (Clark) Havens.
>b. Mar. 10, 1803.   m. 1834 or 5.   d. Jan. 29, 1871.

Francis Burdick, s. Jonathan and Elizabeth (Vansteiman) Burdick.
>b. Mar. 13, 1804.   d. Mar. 14, 1886.

3 ch.   *Jonathan Havens, b.   1836; m.   186-. °Frances Anna Loomis.
>Francis Lodowick. b.   1846, d. Aug. 25, 1864.
>Esther Elizabeth. b.

(*) d. Dec. 24, 1870, left 2 ch. Francis L. and Elizabeth L.   (°) da. George and Hannah (Burdick)
Loomis.

102.

ALBERT GALLATIN HAVENS, s. Gordon and Esther (Clark) Havens.
>b. June 4, 1806.   m. 1st, Sep. 7, 1833; 2d, Apr. 6, 1849.   d. May 16, 1873.

1st, Elizabeth Valentine, da. Philip Valentine and   Huntington.
>b. Jan. 29, 1815.   d. July 22, 1848.

2d, Wid. Mehetable H. Parker, da.
>b.   d.

6 ch. 216. Valentine, b. Aug. 24, 1834; m. Nov. 15, 1854, Sarah Gertrude Britton.
>*Jonathan Nicoll, b. Aug. 25, 1836; m. { 1st,   Augustus Chamberlain.
>   { 2d,   Alpherseyn Kidd.
>Esther Ann. b. Jan. 16, 1839.
>217. Mary Elizabeth, b. Mar. 9, 1842; m. Nov. 28, 1866, William Geery.
>James Henry, b. Dec. 1, 1843, d. July 18, 1848.
>Sarah Frances, b. Aug. 10, 1846, d. Sep. 17, 1847.

(*) Has two sons, Walter E., b. (of 1st w.) Jan. 13, 1867, and William Westerfield.

103.

JAMES HENRY HAVENS, s. Gordon and Esther (Clark) Havens.
>b. Dec. 15, 1809.   m. 1st,   2d, Oct. 6, 1845.   d. June 17, 1884.

1st, Mary Jane Phelps, da.
>b.   d. s. p. Nov.   1844.

2d, Margaret Vandenburg, da. John A. and Christiana M. (Glenn) Vandenburg.
>b. Aug 6, 1824.

8 ch. 218. James Henry, b. Feb. 15, 1847; m. Dec. 11, 1872, Mary C. Oliver.
>Christiana, b. May 18, 1849, d. July 18, 1851.
>‖Margaret. b. Dec. 23, 1851; m.   John Edward Sharp.
>*Sarah Esther, b. Nov. 27, 1854; m.   Nathan Merrit.
>John W., b. Mar. 12, 1857, d. Mar. 12, 1857.
>†William. b. Sep. 8, 1858; m.   Florence Parker.
>°Ella, b. Apr. 19, 1861; m.   Marcus Groll.
>Frances M., b. June 11, 1865, d. July 25, 1865.

(*) 3 ch., William Etta, Maggie.   (†) 1 ch., William.   (‖)1 ch. Margaret G., d. 1898, ae. 23.
(°) 2 ch., Harry, Edward.

104.

DAVID GARDINER, s. David and Julia (Havens) Gardiner.
>b. Jan. 1, 1799.   m. Feb. 20, 1820.   d. Feb. 25, 1880.

Marietta Huntington, da. Abel and Frances (Lee) Huntington.
>b.   1800.   d. Feb. 1, 1882.

3 ch.   *Frances Lee, b. May 30, 1821; m. Oct. 15, 1856, °Rev. Carlton P. Maples.
>John Lyon, b. May 6, 1823; m. { 1st, July 14, 1848, ‖Mary E. Osborne; } no issue.
>   { 2d, Nov. 12, 1867, †Mary E. Jackson; }
>219. Charles Huntington, b. June 10, 1826; m. Sep. 26, 1865, Anna E. Lennon.

(*) d. Mar. 21, 1890, (°) b. May 19, 1840, d. Jan. 19, 1879. (‖) da. Samuel and Mary (Smith) Osborne,
b. Oct. 8, 1825, d. May 11, 1865.   (†) da. Septer W. and Mehetable (Bellows) Jackson, b.
Mar. 19, 2847.

105.

DAVID THOMPSON, s. Jonathan and Elizabeth (Havens) Thompson.
>b. May 3, 1798.   m.   d. Feb. 22, 1871.

Sarah Diodati Gardiner, da. John L. and Sarah (Griswold) Gardiner.
>b. Nov. 1, 1807.   d. Mar. 8, 1891.

7 ch.   *Sarah Gardiner, b. May 23, 1816; m. David Lion Gardiner.
>Elizabeth, b.   Gardiner, b. July 23, 1835.
>Charles Griswold, b.   Mary Gardiner, b.
>Frederick Diodati, b.   John Lyon Gardiner, b.   d.

(*) Has 3 ch., Sarah Diodati, David and Robert Alexander.

106.

MARY GARDINER THOMPSON, da. Jonathan and Elizabeth (Havens) Thompson.
>b. Mar. 23, 1807.   m.   d. Aug. 5, 1887.

Samuel B. Gardiner, s. John Lyon and Sarah (Griswold) Gardiner.
>b. Apr. 6, 1815.   d. Jan. 5, 1882.

5 ch.   *Mary Thompson*, b.   m. Dec. 25, 1866, Wm. R. Sands; no issue.
        David Johnson, b.
220. *John Lyon*. b.   m. Elizabeth C. L. Jones.
      Jonathan Thompson, b.
      Sarah Griswold, b.   m.   John Alexander Tyler.
(*) Had 2 ch., Gardiner who d. young and Lillian Horsford, d. Sep. 1, 1883.

107.

JONATHAN THOMPSON, s. Jonathan and Elizabeth (Havens) Thompson.
    b. Feb. 1, 1814.   m.   d. Nov. 14, 1872.
   Katherine Todhunter, da.
      b.   d. May 9, 1878.
4 ch.   *Elizabeth T.*, b. Dec.   1845; m. June 9, 1884; Elijah Pendleton Smith.
      Harry, b.   d. Mar. 22, 1860.   *Mary*, b.   m.   oWilliam Brewster Westcote.
     221. *Joseph T.*, b. Jan. 10, 1860; m. Apr. 29, 1884, Jane Remsen.
(*) Has 3 ch., Kitty T., Robert D., and William T.   (o) s. of William J. Westcote.

108.

ABRAHAM G. THOMPSON, s. Jonathan and Elizabeth (Havens) Thompson.
    b. Aug. 10, 1816.   m. Apr. 17, 1851.   d. Sep. 26, 1887.
   Sarah Elizabeth Strong, da. Ellis and Mary (Jackson) Strong.
      b.   d.
6 ch.   *Robert Maurice*, b. Aug. 12, 1853. d. Sep. 23, 1873.
     222. *Milton Strong*, b. Feb. 8, 1855; m. Dec. 24, 1889, Abigail A. Johnson,
      Samuel Ludlow, b. Jan. 20, 1860.   *Elizabeth Havens*, b. Apr. 19, 1862, d. July 17, 1864.
      Helen, b. Jan. 10, 1864, d. July 17, 1864.   *Gracie*, b. Jan. 8, 1867, d. Jan. 23, 1867.

109.

GEORGE W. THOMPSON, s. Jonathan and Elizabeth (Havens) Thompson.
    b. Feb. 25, 1817.   m.   d. Jan. 8, 1884.
   Eliza Prall, da.
      b. Dec 16, 1817.   d. May 7, 1886.
4 ch.   *Anna*, b. Dec. 17, 1846; m.   oWilliam Thorne.
     ‖*William Prall*, b. May 4, 1850; m. Dec. 1, 1875, †Grace Hollister.
     Thomas DeWitt, b. Feb. 27, 1853, d. unm.   *George W.*, b.   d. in youth.
(*) Has 1 ch. Lydia A.   (o) Son of Jonathan Thorne.   (‖) Has 2 ch. Edith C., b. Mar. 4, 1877, and
   George W., b. Apr. 7, 1878.   (†) da. of John Jay Hollister.

110.

ELIZABETH C. HAVENS, da. Henry P. and Hannah (Corlies) Havens.
    b. Mar. 26, 1812.   m. Mar. 30, 1830.   d. Oct.   1863.
   David B. Keeler, s. David and Esther (Bradley) Keeler.
      b. Nov. 23, 1803.   d. May 26, 1884.
3 ch. **223.** *Henry P. H.*, b. July 4, 1832; m. Nov. 11, 1856, Rachel C. Crane.
     224. *David B.*, b. Feb. 17, 1835; m. Apr. 8, 1858, Jennie L. Fleet.
     225. *Rachel C.*, b. June   1837; m. June   1858, William D. Baker

111.

MARGARET B. HAVENS, da. Henry P. and Hannah (Corlies) Havens.
    b. Apr. 23, 1814.   m. Sep. 1, 1831.   d. Nov. 25, 1891.
   Theodore Crane, s. Benjamin T. and Jane (Low) Crane.
      b. Oct. 8, 1809.   d. Mar. 12, 1871.
6 ch. **226.** *Hannah L.*, b.   1832; m. Apr. 27, 1853, William H. Decker.
     Jane E., b. in 1835, d. in 1838.
     227. *Jane E.*, b. in 1839; m. Oct. 17, 1860, William L. Andrews.
     Margaret H., b.   1842; m. Dec. 2, 1863, William H. Hurlburt.
     ‖*Mary Elsey*, b.   1844; m. Apr.   1875, George N. Gardiner.
     o*Ella*, b.   1852; m. Sep. 17, 1879, William McClure.
(*) Has 2 ch. Bertha L., who m. L. Stuart Wing and Margaret Crane.
(‖) Has 5 ch. George H., Elsey C., Edith, Bently, and Hilda.
(o) Had 1 ch. Margaret Crane, d. Nov. 7, 1891, ae. 6 months.

112.

RACHEL CORLIES HAVENS, da. Henry P. and Hannah (Corlies) Havens.
    b. July 14, 1816.   m. Jan. 25, 1838.   d. Apr. 13, 1864.
   William C. Russell, s. Emanuel and Betsey (Williams) Russell.
      b. Mar. 29, 1813.   d. Nov. 15, 1843.
3 ch. **228.** *Henry Emanuel*, b. Nov. 23, 1838; m. January 7, 1864, Mary A. Hance.
     229. *Harriet Corlies*, b. Dec. 24, 1840; m. June 15, 1865, James P. Allen.
     230. *William Cowley*, b. Dec. 14, 1842; m. { 1st, Jan. 4, 1866, Caroline E. LaFetra.
                                       { 2d, Apr. 27, 1893, Cordelia W. Guion.

113.

ASHER CORLIES HAVENS, s. Henry P. and Hannah (Corlies) Havens.
    b. Aug. 24, 1819.   m. 1st, Feb. 20, 1845.   2d, Nov. 26, 1862.   d. Mar. 14, 1884.
   1st, Rachel Chardavoyne, da. William and Rachel (Brower) Chardavoyne.
      b.   d. Apr. 23, 1861.
   2d, Jane A. Crane, da. Benjamin and Amanda (Chardavoyne) Crane.
      b. Nov. 29, 1838.

11 ch. **231.** *Henry P.*, b. Dec. 4, 1845; m. Oct. 25, 1883, Marion Herrick.
232. *Rachel C.*, b. July 10, 1847; m. { 1st, Nov. 21, 1867, Alfred Abeel.
{ 2d, Oct. 31, 1882, John H. Johnson.
Adeline A., b. July 4, 1849, d. Dec. 10, 1851. *William C.*, b. Apr. 8, 1852, d. Apr. 8, 1853.
Asher C, b. Mar. 1, 1854, d. in infancy. *Abraham*, b., Mar. 1, 1854, d. in infancy.
233. *Gertrude*, b. July 29, 1855; m. Nov. 21, 1883, Henry N. Tift.
Eliza Matilda, b. Nov. 2, 1857; m. Dec. 14, 1881, *Charles E. Thorne; no issue.
Susan Mary, b. Dec. 1, 1868. *Asher C.*, b. Aug. 19, 1871, d. in infancy.
Thomas Chardavoyne, b. Apr. 24, 1874.
(*) s. of Elwood and Sarah E. (Bennett) Thorne, b. Mar. 27, 1859.

114.

JEREMIAH TUTHILL HAVENS, s. Remington and Jemima (Tuthill) Havens.
  b. Apr. 26, 1805.   m. 1st, Apr. 5, 1828.   2d, Oct. 30, 1832.   d. Jan. 8, 1862.

  1st, Phebe Foster, da. Obadiah and Phebe (   ) Foster.
    b. Jan. 11, 1803.   d. Nov. 12, 1829.

  2d, Eliza Gardiner Sayre, da. Paul and Mary (   ) Sayre.
    b. Oct. 18, 1808.   d. Sep. 23, 1889.

2 ch.   *Phebe Foster*. b. Aug. 8, 1829.
  234. *James S.*, b. May 11, 1834; m. Mar. 15, 1865, Mary Mulford Hand.

115.

WALTER HAVENS, s. Remington and Jemima (Tuthill) Havens.
    b. Apr. 25, 1807.   m. Mar. 4, 1830.   d. Mar. 20, 1869.

  Beulah M. Case, da. Gilbert and Betsey (Vail) Case.
    b. Feb. 23, 1810.   d. July 25, 1897.
7 ch. **235.** *Walter Remington*, b. Oct. 19, 1835; m. May 25, 1857, Margaret E. Wells.
  236. *Malissa B.*, b. Jan. 20, 1838; m. Oct. 31, 1859, Theodore P. Clark.
  Silas G., b. May 18, 1832.   *Elizabeth S.*, b. May 8, 1841.
  Edwin G., b. July 5, 1843, d. Jan. 12, 1844.   *Edward S.*, b.   m.   ºEmily Latham.
  Addele L., b. Jan. 5, 1847, d. July 31, 1848.
(*) Has 2 ch., Walter and Virginia.   (º) da.   and Jemima (Terry) Latham, d. in 1898.

116.

JEMIMA HAVENS, da. Remington and Jemima (Tuthill) Havens.
    b. Mar. 13, 1810.   m. Mar. 14, 1831.

  Edward Conklin. s. Henry and Phebe (Conklin) Conklin.
    b. Jan. 23, 1804.   d. Aug. 7, 1860.
8 ch. **237.** *Edward Henry*, b. May 24, 1833; m.   Maggie Osborn.
  Havens C., b. Aug. 13, 1834, d. July 12, 1843.
  238. *Charlotte Ann*, b. Sep. 23, 1836; m. Apr. 28, 1857, William King Cort.
  239. *Phebe J.*, b. July 20, 1839; m. { 1st, Sep. 5, 1863, Benjamin G. Eldredge.
{ 2d, Jan. 7, 1877, Richard Jeffrey Nicholl.
  James Monroe, b. Aug. 29, 1842, d. Feb. 5, 1871.
  240. *Benjamin Pettit*, b. Nov. 19, 1844; m. Jan. 23, 1872, Mary C. Payne.
  Mary Louisa, b. Apr. 22, 1847, d. Aug. 23, 1863.
  241. *Franklin Pierce*, b. July 9, 1852; m. { 1st, Feb. 20, 1877, Belle B. Sherman.
{ 2d,   1882, Phebe O. Rutan.

117.

REMINGTON HAVENS, s. Remington and Jemima (Tuthill) Havens.
    b. Sep. 4, 1812.   m. May 1st, 1836.   d. Sep. 9, 1865.

  Anna P. Cartwright, da. George and Lucretia (Conkling) Cartwright.
    b. Oct. 20, 1817.   d. Feb. 7, 1870.
7 ch.   *Eugenia Cartwright*, b. Sep. 30, 1839; m. Oct.   1874, ºCharles Griffing; no issue.
  242. *Harriet Winslow*, b. Sep. 6, 1843; m. Dec. 24, 1863, John C. Beebe.
  243. *George Remington*, b. Jan. 30, 1847; m. Dec. 22, 1874, Elizabeth M. Jennings.
  Anna Parker, b. Feb. 9, 1851.   *Emily Judson*, b. June 29, 1853.
  244. *Sophia Woodruff*, b. June 10, 1856; m. Oct. 3, 1878, Willett Green Smith.
  ‖*Marietta*, b. Aug. 4, 1858; m. Sep. 23, 1881, †John Milton Griffing; no issue.
(*) d. June 4, 1875.   (º) s. Calvin and Abigail (Congdon) Griffing.   (‖) d. Dec. 22, 1881.
(†) s. Joseph Griffing, of East Marion, L. I.

118.

LOUISA HAVENS, da. Remington and Jemima (Tuthill) Havens.
    b. Sep. 18, 1814.   m. Feb. 7, 1839.   d. Oc. 14, 1896.

  Elias Woodruff Payne, s. Phineas and Hannah (Woodruff) Payne.
    b. Jan. 30, 1816.   d. Sep. 24, 1881.
5 ch.   *Walter*, b. June 25, 1840, d. July 28, 1840.
  245. *Elias Havens*, b. Nov. 5, 1843; m. Oct. 30, 1877, Mary R. W. Cartwright.
  246. *William Otis*, b. Jan. 30, 1850; m. Feb. 13, 1878, Catherine Dillon Burns.
  Maria Louisa, b. Sep. 3, 1853; m. Jan. 30, 1875, John Lay Bowditch.
  Annie Elizabeth, b. Aug. 27, 1855.
(*) See Bowditch genealogy No. 35.

119.

NANCY A. HAVENS, da. Lodowick and Mary (Annabal) Havens.
b. Jan. 15, 1805.   m. Sep. 25, 1836, as his 2d wife.   d. Feb. 19, 1868.

Horace Manwaring, s. Adam and Temperance (Dennison) Manwaring.
b. Mar. 6, 1805.   d. Feb. 21, 1866.

3 ch. **247.** *Horace G.,* b. Nov. 21, 1838; m. June 16, 1862, Ruth H. Brown.
248. *Lodowick H.,* b. Oct. 21, 1840; m. Oct. 19, 1872, Mary E. Raynor.
249. *Giles A.,* b. Dec. 30, 1844; m. Feb. 11, 1867, Florence E. Carr.

120.

ESTHER S. HAVENS, da. Lodowick and Mary (Annabal) Havens.
b. Oct. 9, 1817.   m. June 23, 1840.   d. July 22, 1859.

George G. Penny, s. Joseph and Harmony (Squires) Penny.
b.   1816.   d. Dec. 28, 1888.

7 ch. **250.** *Mary L.,* b. May 2, 1841; m. Apr. 30, 1868, Daniel R. Cox.
*Harmony M., b. June 17, 1844; m. Dec. 23, 1863, John S. Tuthill.
Hiram G., b. Sep. 19, 1846, d. Sep. 3, 1848.
Caroline I., b. Sep. 30, 1848; m.   †Silas Clark; no issue.
251. *Lilian F.,* b. Apr. 18, 1852; m. Dec. 16, 1872, Luther B. Cox.
252. *George L.,* b. Apr. 15, 1855; m. } 1st, Nov.   1877, Mary Ella Squires.
} 2d, Dec. 16, 1880, Emma Squires.
253. *Alexander C.,* b. July 16, 1859; m. Apr. 4, 1883, Julia Frances Reeve.
(*) See Tuthill genealogy No. 43.   (†) Son Silas and Esther Clark.

121.

SAMUEL HAVENS CONGDON, s. William C. and Lucinda (Havens) Congdon.
b. June 22, 1810.   m. Oct. 7, 1841.   d. Feb. 9, 1891.

Cornelia Philena Van Gandron, da. Cornelius and Abigail (Hamilton) Van Gandron.
b. June 10, 1820.   d. Aug. 21, 1869.

8 ch.   *Isabel G.,* b. July 22, 1843.   *Stratton Havens,* b. Jan. 21, 1846.
254. *Mary Lucinda,* b. July 14, 1847; m. June 4, 1879, Richard M. Johnston.
*William Woodruff, b. Feb. 17, 1850; m. Apr. 5, 1874, †Maria Jane Dickerson.
255. *John Cornelius,* b. Mar. 28, 1852; m. Oct. 18, 1875, Harriet B. Ryder.
Sarah Isadora, b. Dec. 25, 1854.
256. *Charles Anderson,* b. July 4, 1856; m. Apr. 21, 1887, Clara A. Harlow.
George Tabor, b. Jan. 10, 1860, d. Mar. 28, 1863.
(*) d. June 4, 1877; left one ch. Wilhelmina, b. July 4, 1877. (†) da. Nathan P. and Susan Dickerson.

122.

STRATTON M. HAVENS, s. Stratton and Abigail F. (Hamilton) Havens.
b. Mar. 19, 1810.   m. 1st, Feb. 11, 1840.   m. 2d, Feb. 22, 1870.   d. Feb. 11, 1886.

1st, Lydia Ann Chester, da. John T. and Nancy (Cartwright) Chester.
b. Feb. 14, 1812.   d. June 21, 1866.

2d, Wid. Elizabeth Flowers, da.
b.   d.

6 ch. **257.** *Elizabeth S.,* b. Mar. 17, 1842; m. May 29, 1865, Samuel G. Clark.
258. *Adelaide M.,* b. Jan. 1, 1844; m. Sep. 29, 1868, David Y. Clark.
259. *Chester S.,* b. Nov. 7, 1846; m. Dec. 24, 1868, Ann Maria Louise White.
Fanny C., b. Feb. 14, 1848; m. Oct.   1869, *Edward Wilcox; no issue.
260. *Charles E.,* b. Mar. 13, 1850; m. July 13, 1881, Ellen A. Hall.
Martha A., b. Mar. 25, 1852.
(*) Son Joseph and Betsey (Crumb) Wilcox, b. Oct. 12, 1840.

123.

JAMES MADISON HARLOW, s. Robert and Sarah P. (Havens) Harlow.
b. Oct. 6, 1808.   m. Aug. 15, 1839.   d. Dec. 12, 1894.

Abby M. Osborn, da. Daniel and Esther (Mulford) Osborn.
b. July 21, 1818.   d. Sep. 21, 1894.

6 ch. **261.** *James S.,* b. Dec. 24, 1840; m. Dec. 12, 1866, Sarah E. Dudley.
262. *Julia,* b. Aug. 8, 1843; m.   1867, F. Stuart Gray.
263. *Benjamin F.,* b. May 12, 1854; m. Nov. 4, 1880, Anna C. Brown.
Cortlandt V., b. Apr. 11, 1858; m. Aug. 14, 1894, Catherine Rheams.
264. *Daniel O.,* b. Aug. 8, 1847; m. Mar. 23, 1875, Eugenia Sheldon.
Mary T., b. Dec. 18, 1850; m. Oct. 14, 1874, Charles D. Ayers.

124.

CHARLES HARLOW, s. Robert and Sarah P. (Havens) Harlow.
b. Jan. 6, 1834.   m. Oct. 19, 1859.

Ency J. Reeve, da. Hewlett and Maria (Reeve) Reeve.
b. Jan. 6, 1840.

1 ch. **265.** *Carrie E.,* b. Aug. 29, 1860; m. Apr. 7, 1891, William S. Hubbard.

125.

ALVA STRATTON MULFORD, s. Abraham and Philena (Havens) Mulford.
b. Feb. 1808.   m. Sep. 10, 1829.   d. Mar. 20, 1858.

Bethiah Horton, da. David and Mary (Case) Horton.
b. Aug. 5, 1810.   d. June 7, 1887.

4 ch. **260.** *David Horton*, b. Oct. 7, 1830; m. Apr. 5, 1855, Emma Holden Guilder.
    *Benjamin Prince, b. Apr. 30, 1838; m. } 1st,   Fanny Dean.
                              } 2d, June 1869, Mary Williams.
  267. *Mary Catherine*, b. Apr. 24, 1841; m. June 9, 1862, Daniel Edward Davis.
  268. *Isabelle Lucretia*, b. Dec. 1, 1849; m. June 14, 1870, Samuel Irving Mitchell.

(*) Had 4 ch. By 1st w. Alva and Charles, both d. By 2d w. Benjamin P. and Grace W.

126.

FRANCES MARIA ISAACS, da. John and Catherine (Havens) Isaacs.
    b.   m. May 2, 1842.   d. June 9, 1848.

  Amezi Benedict Davenport, s. William and Abigail (Benedict) Davenport.
    b. Oct. 30, 1817.   d. Aug. 13, 1894.

3 ch. **269.** *John Isaacs*, b. May 16, 1843; m. Nov. 14, 1866, Louise E. Post.
  270. *Albert Barnes*, b. Apr. 3, 1845; m. Nov. 24, 1868. Delia M. Crofut.
    Frances Maria, b. Feb. 27, 1848, d. Aug. 13, 1848.

127.

ANNA MARIA HAVENS, da. Ezekiel and Roxanna (Case) Havens.
    b. Mar. 3, 1812.   m. June 11, 1829, as his 2d w.*   d. Mar. 24, 1868.

  Charles C. Griffing, s. Absalom and Sybil (King) Griffing.
    b. Feb. 2, 1802.   d. Oct. 7, 1847.

5 ch. °*Mary C.*, b. Apr. 4, 1833; m. Mar. 13, 1855, Daniel Hudson.
  271. *Charles Markus*, b. Mar. 20, 1838; m. Nov. 14, 1864, Abigail T. Cartwright.
    Byron, b. Aug. 4, 1840.   *Randolph C.*, b. Apr. 3, 1843, d. Dec. 10, 1861.
    Oliver, b. June 18, 1846.

(*) See No. 49.   (°) See Hudson genealogy No. 36.

128.

EZEKIEL HOUSE, s. Sayre and Sarah (Havens) House.
    b. July 28, 1812.   m. Dec. 17, 1846.   d. July 16, 1884.

  Hannah Osborne, da. Henry and Elnora (Baker) Osborne.
    b. Apr. 12, 1823.

1 ch. **272.** *Ellen*, b. Mar. 14, 1855; m.   Henry Hedges.

129.

ELIZA HOUSE, da. Sayre and Sarah (Havens) House.
    b.   m.   d.

  David Williams, s.
    b   d.

4 ch. *Sarah, b.   m.   Herbert Leek.
    Hannah, b.   1853; m.   1890, Eugene Cook.
    Harriet, b.   d. unm.   °
    Egbert, b. Sep. 6, 1855; m. July 6, 1890, °Alice Homan.

(*) d. left 1 ch. Mabel.   (°) da. of Henry H. and Mary E. Homan, b. June 26, 1874.

130.

Dr. JOHN HAVENS DAYTON, s. Samuel S. and Eunice M. (Havens) Dayton.
    b. Sep. 8, 1811.   m.   1835.   d. July 27, 1850.

  Frances Jane Nichols, da.
    b. Sep. 9, 1815.

3 ch. **273.** *Sarah*, b. Apr. 2, 1838; m. Dec. 23, 1874, Richard Lay Hull.
  274. *Frederick L.*, b. Apr. 13, 1840; m.   1865, Almira Olds Reeder.
    b.

131.

BETSY SMITH DAYTON, da. Samuel S. and Eunice M. (Havens) Dayton.
    b. Mar. 11, 1816.   m.   1837.   d. Jan. 16, 1854.

  Richard Parsons Smith, of Sag Harbor, New York.
    b.

2 ch. An infant b.   1838, d. 1838.
  275. *Maria Josephine*, b. May 15, 1845; m. Aug. 14, 1867, Morgan Pierson.

132.

NATHANIEL T. HAVENS, s. Augustus and Esther (Bowditch) Havens.
    b. Feb. 24, 1802.   m. July 5, 1823.   d. Jan. 4, 1802.

  CHARLOTTE M. HAVENS, da. Remington and Jemima (Tuthill) Havens. **See No. 48.**
    b. Sep. 14, 1803.   d. Feb. 25, 1871.

5 ch. *Hannah Maria*, b. Nov. 2, 1824, d. Oct. 12, 1827.
    William Hull, b. Dec. 12, 1826, d. Oct. 29, 1827.   *William Wallace*, b. Aug. 25, 1828.
    *Nancy Maria, b. Oct. 22, 1831; m. May 6, 1857, George Tindall.
    Esther Sarah, b. Dec. 19, 1838.

(*) See No. 215.

133.

JOSEPH CALEB HAVENS, s. Augustus and Esther (Bowditch) Havens.
    b. Mar. 16, 1804.   m. 1st,   2d, May 21, 1845.   d. Aug. 28, 1892.

  1st, Hannah Brown, da. Peter and Phebe (   ) Brown.
    b. Mar. 16, 1804.   d. Sep. 3, 1844.

  2d, Hannah M. Brown, da. Peter and Phebe (   ) Brown.
    b. Sep. 22, 1807.   d. Jan. 31, 1888.

1 ch. **276.** *Edwin Brown*, b. Jan. 19, 1847; m. Oct. 5, 1870, Maria Elizabeth Scholes.

134.

BENEDICT HAVENS, s. Augustus and Esther (Bowditch) Havens.
    b.   1806.   m. 1st.   2d,   d. Sep. 9, 1849.

  1st, Phebe
    b.   d. 1830.
  2d,
    b.

4 ch. **277.** *Joseph A.*, b.   m.   Kate Bennett.   **Charles O.*, b.   m.   Rebecca Kingsland.
    And 2 others.

(*) Had 2 ch., Charles K. and Floyd.

135.

SARAH ANN HAVENS, da. Augustus and Esther (Bowditch) Havens.
    b.   m. Sep. 17, 1826.   d.

  Capt. David Cartwright, s.
    b.   1804.   d. Apr. 8, 1856.

2 ch. **278.** *Julia Adeline*, b. July 31, 1831; m.   Daniel A. Eldridge.
    Sarah, b.

136.

AUGUSTUS HAVENS, s. Augustus and Esther (Bowditch) Havens.
    b.   m. Sep. 14, 1839.   d.

  Phebe Jennings, da. James and Phebe (Sanford) Jennings.
    b. Sep. 4, 1819.   d. Jan. 29, 1865.

4 ch.   *Charles H.*, b. 1840, d. Nov. 15, 1862. *Helen M.*, b. Mar. 22, 1843, d. unm. Mar. 27, 1856.
    Mary B., b.   d. unm. Sep. 10, 1896.   *Augustus*, b.   d. in infancy.

137.

BETHIAH M. HAVENS, da. Augustus and Esther (Bowditch) Havens.
    b.   1811.   m. Feb. 8, 1831.   d. June 26, 1847.

  SYLVANUS B. HAVENS, s. Sylvanus and Rosannah (Bennet) Havens.
    b.   1807.   d. Nov. 16, 1847.

2 ch. **279.** *Frances M.*, b. Sep. 1, 1843; m. Apr. 15, 1875, Eugene Havens Mulligan.
    280. *Sylvanus M.*, b. May 17, 1846; m.   1872, Kate Condon.

138.

CHARLES ALFRED HAVENS, s. Jacob and Elizabeth (Bennet) Havens.
    b. Jan. 31, 1813.   m. Jan. 18, 1841.   d. June 22, 1864.

  Phebe Tuthill, da. Thomas and Abigail (Terry) Tuthill.
    b. Nov. 14, 1823.   d. Feb. 3, 1894.

3 ch. **281.** *Maria*, b. Mar. 21, 1843; m. Aug. 24, 1864, Jesse R. Edwards.
    282. *Mary*, b. Nov. 1, 1849; m. Nov. 22, 1877, William Blinn.
    Alice, b. Jan. 8, 1854; m. June 1893. *Kirby Beers.
(*) s. of Luke H. and Susan S. (Gough) Beers, b. Aug. 31, 1862.

139.

JACOB HAVENS, s. Jacob and Elizabeth (Bennet) Havens.
    b. May 20, 1815.   m. July 27, 1840.

  Ann Eliza Hamilton, da. Benjamin and Nancy (Gardiner) Hamilton.
    b. Sep. 12, 1818.

3 ch. **283.** *Helen J.*, b. Mar. 11, 1843; m. { 1st, Mar.   1860, George A. Oaks.
        { 2d, May 1, 1881, William H. Brown.
    **Charles M.*, b. May 14, 1846; m.   °Isabella Doxey.
    |*Arthur*, b. Feb. 15, 1851; m.   †Emma Corwin.
(*) Has 5 ch., Ella, George, Frank, Oscar and Norman C.   (°) da. of Charles Doxey.
(|) Has 4 ch., Grace, Goldie, Arthur and Everett.   (†) da. of Harvey Corwin.

140.

JOHN STEWARD HAVENS, s. Obadiah and Nancy (Robinson) Havens.
    b. Aug. 8, 1800.   m. June 1, 1828.   d. Apr. 6, 1838.

  Nancy Torrey, da. Abner and Susannah (Hobert) Torrey.
    b. May 25, 1800.   d. Sep. 10, 1843.

4 ch. **284.** *Ann Maria*, b. Apr. 6, 1829; m. June 1, 1853, Thomas P. Bundy.
    Isabella Dawson, b. Apr. 13, 1831, d. Oct. 11, 1832.
    Isabella Dawson, b. Apr. 19, 1833, d. Mar. 19. 1836.
    285. *Elmira Amanda*, b. Feb. 19, 1835; m. Oct. 6, 1858, George W. Stickney.

141.

ARCHIBALD R. HAVENS, s. Obadiah and Nancy (Robinson) Havens.
    b. Oct. 9, 1816.   m. May 23, 1839.   d. Nov. 20, 1894.

Caroline A. Hughes, da. Joseph B. and Betsey E. (Miner) Hughes.
    b. Oct. 24, 1816.   d. Aug. 16, 1890

6 ch.   *Margaret J., b. Mar. 27, 1841; m. Feb. 2, 1863, Joseph H. Bowditch.
    286. Elizabeth M., b. Mar. 29, 1843; m. Nov. 30, 1878, Caleb Dawson.
        Harriet L., b. Apr. 9, 1845.   Nancy M., b. Jan. 9, 1847, d. Feb. 15, 1848.
        Archibald, b. Feb. 9, 1851, d. Oct. 8, 1859.
    287. William G., b. Oct. 24, 1853, m. June 3, 1891, Isabelle C. Reynolds.
(*) See Bowditch genealogy, No. 14.

142.

NICOLL J. HAVENS, s. George H. and Sarah (Haynes) Havens.
    b. July 1, 1811.   m.   d. Oct. 6, 1884.

Adeline Jennings, da. Elias and Dorothy (Purple) Jennings.
    b. Apr. 17, 1813.   d. Nov. 15, 1896.

2 ch.   *Egbert H., b. July 5, 1834; m. Nov. 5, 1856, Kate D. Exley.
        °Sidney, b. Apr. 15, 1842; m.

(*) Has 4 ch., Arthur E., Maud A., Ada S. and Caroline B.
(°) Has 4 ch., Addie P., Annie S., Florence and Eva.

143.

PHEBE HAVENS, da. George H. and Sarah (Haynes) Havens.
    b. Feb. 10, 1813.   m.   d. July   1875.

John C. Wells, s. John C. and Amy (Homan) Wells.
    b.   1782.   d. Nov.   1850.

1 ch. 288. John C., b. May 25, 1838; m.   Margaret Callahan.

144.

OBADIAH HAVENS, s. George H. and Sarah (Haynes) Havens.
    b. Mar. 6, 1822.   m. 1st, Jan. 4. 1844.   2d, July 5, 1887.

1st. Mary Ann Cowles, da. Thaddeus and Phebe (Haynes) Cowles.
    b. Oct.   1824.   d. Apr. 26. 1886.

2d, Johannah P. White, da. Ebenezer and Johannah (Pierson) White.
    b. Nov. 6, 1823.

6 ch. 289. Sidney P., b. Oct. 24, 1844; m. Aug. 11, 1868, Alice G. Vail.
        Asher C., b. Jan. 26, 1846. d. Feb. 18, 1856.
        Charles B., b. May 18, 1850; m. Feb. 20, 1878. *Mamie E. Rackett; no issue.
        Oscar H., b. Dec. 6, 1853; m. Dec. 6, 1877, °Helen M. Snooks; no issue.
        Alice Isabelle, b. Feb. 3, 1856.
    290. Asher W., b. Mar. 24, 1862; m. in 1893, Harriet B. Lester.
(*) da. of Henry C. and Dorinda (Petty) Rackett. b. May 8, 1850.
(°) da. of George Snooks, of England, b. Oct. 18, 1845, d. Aug. 18, 1885.

145.

CLARISSA FRANCES HAVENS, da. George H. and Sarah (Haynes) Havens.
    b. May 7, 1824.   m. Sep. 14, 1843.

Don Alonzo Miller, s. Thomas and Phebe (Canfield) Miller.
    b.

4 ch. 291. Arrabella M., b. Dec. 5. 1844; m. in 1863, Loren C. Terry.
    292. Sarah C., b. June 20, 1847; m.   1865, *Henry G. Hewlett.
        Alonzo, b. Aug. 4, 1850, d. Apr. 10, 1852.
        Dora Phoebe, b. June 4, 1854; m.   1874, *John A. Williams.
(*) d. July 20, 1885. ae., 31, leaving one ch. who d. Nov. 21, 1891, ae. 16.

146.

HENRY M. HAVENS, s. George H. and Sarah (Haynes) Havens.
    b. July 11, 1829.   m. in 1848.   d. Dec. 8, 1878.

Frances Delia Ross, da. Henry and Nancy (Lane) Ross.
    b. Sep. 8, 1829.

9 ch. 293. Ida W., b. Apr. 8, 1849; m. Aug. 26, 1866, George Dutcher.
        *Garrie P., b. July. 15, 1853; m.   Henry Payne; no issue.
        George H., b. Jan. 3, 1855, d. Mar. 15, 1856.
        Henrietta G., b. Nov. 19, 1856; m. Louis R. Edwards.
        Minnie E., b. July 9, 1860, d. unm. June 5, 1893.
        George H., b. July 13, 1862; m. Mar. 20 1888, Mary Potter.
    294. Sarah A., b. Feb. 16, 1866; m. Feb. 16, 1886, William Litell.
    295. Asher C., b. Jan. 21, 1868; m. Feb. 7, 1894, Mamie F. Collard.
        William H., b. Apr. 8, 1871.
(*) d. Aug. 20, 1882.

147.

ABBY ELDREDGE MUSSEY, da. Thomas and Mary Ann (Fosdick) Mussey.
    b. May 4, 1818.   m. May 7, 1838.   d. Mar. 14, 1875.

George W. Browne, s. Benjamin and Hannah (Rogers) Browne.
    b. Mar. 3, 1816.   d. Aug. 11, 1891.

4 ch.　　*Benjamin*, b. Mar. 27, 1839, d. Feb. 8, 1873.
　　　　　　Thomas Nicoll, b. Aug. 10, 1840; m. { 1st,　　Jane Baldy.
　　　　　　　　　　　　　　　　　　　　　　　{ 2d,　　Frances Briggs Dennis.
　　　　　　George W., b. May 28, 1842, d. Mar. 27, 1843.　　*Elizabeth Mussey*, b. Feb. 27, 1844.

148.

ELIZABETH FOSDICK MUSSEY, da. Thomas and Mary Ann (Fosdick) Mussey.
　　b. Dec. 8, 1819.　　m. Apr. 22, 1844.　　d. Oct. 4, 1893.

Charles Ramsdell, s. Isaiah and Clarissa (Collins) Ramsdall.
　　b. Mar. 8, 1809.　　d. Nov. 12, 1881.

6 ch.　　*Charles*, b. June 22, 1845, d. Mar. 11, 1849.
296. *Elizabeth Mussey*, b. Mar. 15, 1847; m. Nov 17, 1871, Edward Miller Ketcham.
　　　　　Sarah Hollister, b. May 13, 1850, d. Feb. 9, 1853.
　　　　　Thomas Mussey, b. Sep. 28, 1851, d July 30, 1853.
　　　　　Frederick Miner, b. Sep. 22, 1855, d. June 12, 1890.
　　　　　Gertrude, b. Apr. 4, 1857; m. Jan. 2, 1890, *John Dennison Bentley; no issue.
(*) Son of Henry F. and Mary H. (Wheeler) Bentley, b. Nov. 4, 1846.

149.

MARY ANN MUSSEY, da. Thomas and Mary A. (Fosdick) Mussey.
　　b. May 9, 1822.　　m. Sep. 27, 1848.　　d.

Henry Ramsdell, s.
　　b.

8 ch.　　*Mary Fosdick*, b. May 19, 1850, d. Mar. 17, 1868.
　　　　　Anna Mussey, b. Aug. 29, 1853, d. May 17, 1893.
297. *Henry Thomas*, b. Mar. 26, 1855; m. June 11, 1884, Kate H. Miller.
　　　　　**Jane Letitia*, b.　　　　m.　　　　Oscar L. Harris.
298. *Lorin P. Waldo*, b. Nov. 4, 1859; m. Feb. 19, 1889, Lucy Story.
　　　　　George Mussey, b. July 6, 1862; m. Apr. 10, 1890, °Elizabeth May Williams.
　　　　　Elizabeth, b.
299. *William M.*, b. July 13, 1864; m. Mar. 15, 1894, Margaret S. Adams.
(°) Has 1 son William Edward.　　(°) da. James C. and Harriet M. (Johnstone) Williams.

150.

MARTHA PEARSON MUSSEY, da. Thomas and Mary A. (Fosdick) Mussey.
　　b. Nov. 22, 1824.　　m. Sep. 4, 1850.

Horace T. Ash, s. Ebenezer and Hannah (Floyd) Ash.
　　b. June 2, 1814.　　d. June 20, 1852.

3 ch.　　*Elizabeth Fosdick*, b. May 9, 1851, d. May 19, 1851.
300. *Jane Letitia*, b. June 2, 1852; m. Sep. 13, 1871, Robert Massie.
　　　　　Abby Eldridge, b. Sep. 6, 1853, d. Jan. 15, 1854.

151.

FRANCES ELIZA MUSSEY, da. Thomas and Mary A. (Fosdick) Mussey.
　　b. Mar. 16, 1826.　　m. Jan. 4, 1853.

Rev. James W. Dennis, s. John and Rachel (　　　　) Dennis.
　　b. Aug. 25, 1825.　　d. Dec.　　1863.

2 ch.　　*Letitia Manning*, b. May 31, 1854, d. Feb. 8, 1884.
　　　　　Gertrude Fosdick, b. Aug. 20, 1858, d. Aug. 10, 1859.

152.

JANE HOBERT MUSSEY, da. Thomas and Mary A. (Fosdick) Mussey.
　　b. Apr. 19, 1835.　　m. Sep. 2, 1861.

Rodney R. Crowley, s. Rufus and Permilia (Crowley) Crowley.
　　b. Nov. 12, 1836.

2 ch. **301.** *Frederick Bowen*, b. Aug. 19, 1865; m. June 29, 1891, Clara Lillie Hall.
　　　　　Mary Gloriana, b. Mar. 6, 1872.

153.

JOHN ELCOCK JONES, s. George and Frances E. (Fosdick) Jones.
　　b. June 11, 1835.　　m. June 20, 1859.

Olivia Jarvis, da.
　　b. May 27, 1841.

1 ch.　　*Eva*, b. Apr. 17, 1868; m. May 17, 1892, Albert T. Lehanan, b. Mar. 6, 1859.

154.

NICOLL FOSDICK JONES s. George and Frances E. (Fosdick) Jones.
　　b. *July 31, 1836.　　m. Apr. 4, 1866.

Deborah Merwin, da. Eber and Julia (Todd) Merwin.
　　b. Aug. 23, 1842.

5 ch. **302.** *Samuel Fosdick*, b. Feb. 18, 1867; m. Feb. 22, 1888, Hattie M. Couch.
　　　　　Lucy Olive, b. Dec. 28, 1868.　　　　　*Frances Eliza*, b. Feb. 24, 1872.
　　　　　Mary Rebecca, b. June 7, 1874; m. Dec. 29, 1897, *Kirk Fowler.
　　　　　William Lodowick, b. Jan. 15, 1879.
(*) s. of George and Julia (Rumsey) Fowler, b. Oct 22, 1870.

155.

ABBY MARIA JONES, da. George and Frances E. (Fosdick) Jones.
  b. Aug. 6, 1838.   m. Jan. 31, 1865.

William H. Ganung, s. Nelson and Malissa (Norton) Ganung.
  b. Apr. 7, 1840.

2 ch.   *Wilhelmina*, b. Aug. 20, 1866.
  303. *Cora M.*, b. Mar. 16, 1868; m. June 14, 1894. Oliver H. Galbraith.

156.

WILLIAM JONES, s. George and Frances E. (Fosdick) Jones.
  b. Aug. 26, 1840.

Asenath Chandler Holmes, da. Stephen and Mahala (Bartlett) Holmes.
  b. Mar. 20, 1851.

3 ch.   *Lodowick Holmes*, b. July 7, 1876.   *Carlton William*, b. Apr. 29, 1878, d. Apr. 27, 1883.
  Chandler William, b. May 21, 1882, d. May 26, 1883.

157.

ORVILLE FOSDICK, s. Thomas U. and Rachel (Armstrong) Fosdick.
  b. Nov. 19, 1805.   m. 1st,   1828.   2d, June 11, 1845.   d. Nov. 6, 1869.

1st, Elizabeth Johnson, da.
  b.   d. s. p.   1842.

2d, Hannah McCollock, da. John and Susana (Lowry) McCollock.
  b.

9 ch.   An adopted son named Thomas M., ——1836–37.
  Edward Wheeler, b. Mar. 4. 1847, d. Mar. 3, 1868.
  Oscar Murray, b. Nov. 26, 1848, d. Aug. 20, 1875.
  304. *Richard Calvin*, b. May 20, 1850; m. Oct. 3, 1883, Mary F. Mullen.
  *Julia Adaline, b. Dec. 30, 1851; m. June 19, 1873, John Alter.
  Francis Marion, b. July 14, 1853.   *Lucinda*, b. Aug.   1855, d. 1857.
  °Rachel Jane, b. May 19, 1858; m. June 15, 1873, John Woolsey.
  George W., b. Apr. 26. 1862, d. Aug. 20, 1885.
(*) Has 2 ch., May, b. Apr. 13, 1874, and Ethelena, b. Sep. 29, 1879, d. Nov. 11. 1881.
(○) Has 2 ch., Margaret, b. May 18, 1874, who m. Louis Fulton, and Fannie, b. July 17, 1878.

158.

JULIA A. FOSDICK, da. Thomas U. and Rachel (Armstrong) Fosdick.
  b. Feb. 28, 1808.   m. Feb. 22, 1831.   d. Dec. 23, 1884.

Richard Mann, s. Nathan   Mann.
  b.   d. Jan. 6, 1847.

7 ch.   *Sarah*, b. Apr. 12, 1832; m.   William A. Cain.
  William C., b. Dec. 31, 1833; m.   *Maria A.*, b. Aug. 1, 1836, d. June 24, 1859.
  Olive H., b. Oct. 24, 1838, d. Jan. 7, 1847.
  Thomas O., b. May 1, 1841; m.   Minerva J. Conner.
  *Rachel L., b. Sep. 28, 1843; m. Jan. 1, 1872, ○Willliam H. McAnultey.
  Laura L., b. Feb. 2, 1846, d. Jan. 27. 1849.
(*) Has ch., her oldest s. d. Mar. 23, 1897.   (○) s. of Robert McAnultey.

159.

OLIVE A. FOSDICK, da. Thomas U. and Rachel (Armstrong) Fosdick.
  b. Jan. 21, 1818.   m.   d.   1877.

Alonzo Finney, s.
  b.

3 ch.   *Erastus*, b.   m.   1865, Sophia Evy.
  305. *Sarah*, b. Dec. 27, 1845; m. Jan. 1, 1865, John Imhoff.   *George W.*, b.   m.

160.

LOUISA A. FOSDICK, da. Thomas U. and Rachel (Armstrong) Fosdick.
  b. Feb. 19, 1819.   m.   1847.

Samuel Hackley, s.
  b.   d. Sep. 3, 1865.

1 ch. 306. *Alice*, b. Oct. 12, 1848; m. 1865, Thomas Hendryx.

161.

EDWARD WHEELER FOSDICK, s. Thomas U. and Rachel (Armstrong) Fosdick.
  b. July 12, 1822.   m. 1st, July 24, 1850.   2d, Mar. 27, 1859.   3d, Sep. 17, 1878.   d.

1st, Helen G. Tatten, da.
  b.   d. May 23, 1856.

2d, Ruan M. Brandon, da.
  b.   d. Apr. 4, 1860.

3d, Elizabeth Harriet Fetterhoff, da.
  b.

2 ch.   *Emma Angeline*, b. Aug. 11, 1852, d. Aug. 15, 1856.
  Edward Lawton, b. May 1, 1856; m.   Josie McCarter.

162.

FRANCES DERING FOSDICK, da. Samuel and Sarah A. (Wood) Fosdick.
    b. June 30, 1841.   m. May 30, 1866.

Frank Johnston Jones, s. John D. and Elizabeth (Johnston) Jones.
    b.

5 ch.   *Anna Fosdick*, b. July 8, 1868; m. Mar. 31, 1891, Edward H. Ernst.
    Charles Davis, b. Apr. 3, 1871.   *Samuel Fosdick*, b. Aug. 4, 1874.
    Frances L'Hommedieu, b. Mar. 20. 1877.   *Edmund Lawrence*, b Oct. 9, 1879.

163.

SYLVESTER UPDIKE FOSDICK, s. Henry N. and Harriet (Harkness) Fosdick.
    b. Jan. 16, 1837.   m. Jan. 21, 1859.   d. Apr. 5, 1873.

Anna Mortimer Gascoigne, da. Charles and Deborah (Post) Gascoigne.
    b.

3 ch.   *Robert Cunningham*. b. Oct. 23, 1859.   *Henry H.*, b. Sep. 20, 1864, d. Nov. 10, 1894.
    Sylvester Doughlas, b. Sep. 27, 1871.

164.

MARY ANN FOSDICK, da. Henry N. and Harriet (Harkness) Fosdick.
    b. Oct. 31, 1838.   m. Nov. 4, 1858.   d. June 13, 1867.

Francis Marion Doughlas, s.
    b.

3 ch.   **Anna Mortimer*, b. Aug. 26, 1859; m. Henry McClure. *Mary Doughlas*, b. Aug. 5, 1861.
    Elizabeth Doughlas, b. June 6, 1865; m. Thomas Pulling.

(*) Has one s. living.

165.

MARY L'HOMMEDIEU GARDINER, da. Samuel S. and Mary C. (L'Hommedieu) Gardiner.
    b. Sep. 27, 1824.   m. Aug. 4, 1847.   d. Nov. 25, 1855.

PHEBE D. GARDINER, da. Samuel S. and Mary C. (L'Hommedieu) Gardiner.
    b. Aug. 13, 1826.   m. July 22, 1860.

Eben Norton Horsford, s. Jerediah and Charry M. (Norton) Horsford.
    b. July 27, 1818.   d. Jan. 1, 1893.

5 ch.   *Lillian*, b. Sep. 18. 1848.   *Mary Catherine*, b. Oct. 24, 1850.
307. *Gertrude Hubbard*, b. July 9, 1852; m. June 20, 1878, Andrew Fiske.
308. *Mary Gardiner*, b. Aug. 27, 1855; m. Oct. 24, 1877, Benjamin Robbins Curtis.
    Cornelia Conway Fenton, b. Sep. 25, 1861.

166.

FRANCES ELIZA GARDINER, da. Samuel S. and Mary C. (L'Hommedieu) Gardiner.
    b. Aug. 31, 1832.   m. July 22, 1857.   d. Aug. 5, 1876.

George Martin Lane, s. Martin and Lucretia (Swan) Lane.
    b. Dec. 24, 1824.   d. June 30, 1897.

3 ch.   *Gardiner M.*, b. Apr. 30, 1858; m. June 8, 1898, Emma L. Gildersleeve.
    Louise G., b. Nov. 25, 1860; m. Nov. 2, 1880, William Bayard Van Rensselaer; no issue.
    Katherine W., b. Mar. 6, 1862, d. Oct. 28, 1893.

167.

BENJAMIN HUNTINGTON WRIGHT, s. Benj. H. and Henrietta D. (Huntington) Wright.
    b. Jan. 6, 1835.   m. Jan. 28, 1868.   d. July 27, 1889.

Florence Melvina Cossitt, da. George G. and Lucy (Mann) Cossitt.
    b. May 13, 1848.

1 ch.   *Florence Henrietta*, b. Apr. 20. 1870.

168.

CHARLES RENSSELAER HAVENS, s. Howard and Asenath C. (Randall) Havens.
    b. June 24, 1858.   m. July 15, 1890.

Mary Lizzie Whipple, da. Hugh L. and Helen B. (Gardiner) Whipple.
    b. May 27, 1867.

1 ch.   *Helen Randall*, b. Sep. 13, 1891.

169.

HOWARD CUMMINGS HAVENS, s. Howard and Asenath C. (Randall) Havens.
    b. Dec. 1, 1861.   m. Sep. 7, 1887.

Mary Florence Cutter, da. James H. and Jane A. (Beach) Cutter.
    b. Mar. 7, 1863.

3 ch.   *Helen*, b. June 24, 1888.   *Florence*, b. Dec. 7, 1891.   *Arthur W.*, b. May 31, 1893.

170.

ELEANOR ANDERSON BISSELL, da. Rev. Samuel B. S. and Frances M. (Havens) Bissell.
    b. Sep. 26, 1840.   m. Feb. 6, 1867.

Brayton Ives, s. William A. and Julia (Root) Ives.
    b. Aug. 23, 1840

4 ch.   *Winifred*, b. Sep. 4, 1869.   *Sherwood Bissell*, b. Dec. 30, 1870.
    Eunice, b. Nov. 24, 1872.   *Francis Havens*, b. July 16, 1875.

171.

KATHERINE HAVENS BISSELL, da. Rev. Samuel B. S. and Frances M. (Havens) Bissell.
  b. Oct. 5, 1844.   m. May 10, 1865.

Le Grand Lockwood, s. Le Grand and Anna L. (Benedict) Lockwood.
  b. June 5, 1841.   d. Apr. 1, 1887.

4 ch.   *Fanny Havens*, b. Dec. 31, 1867, d. Feb. 20, 1875.   *Katherine Bissell*, b. July 5, 1872.
         Louise Benedict, b. Oct. 31, 1873.   *Hilda Le Grand*, b. Oct. 29, 1881.

172.

RENSSELAER HAVENS BISSELL, s. Rev. Samuel B. S. and Frances M. (Havens) Bissell.
  b. Apr. 27, 1848.   m. Nov. 10, 1869.

Frederika Belden, da. Frederick and Catherine E. (Grumans) Belden.
  b. Sep. 28, 1849.

3 ch.   *Samuel B. S.*, b. May 13, 1872.   *Frederick B.*, b. Oct. 1, 1874, d. Aug. 28, 1875.
         Catherine Van Rensselaer, b. June 9, 1876.

173.

FRANCES MARIA BISSELL, da. Rev. Samuel B. S. and Frances M. (Havens) Bissell.
  b. Jan. 9, 1854.   m. May 9, 1878.

Theodore Cuyler Patterson, s. Joseph and Jane (Cuyler) Patterson.
  b. Dec. 22, 1848.

2 ch.   *Elizabeth Stuart*, b. Nov. 25, 1882, d. Dec. 24, 1890.   *Maria Jessup*, b. Oct. 4, 1884.

174.

MORRIS JESSUP BISSELL, s. Rev. Samuel B. S. and Frances M. (Havens) Bissell.
  b. July 28, 1857.   m. Oct. 29, 1889.

Leila Ida Lormor, da. George W. and Adelaide (West) Lormor.
  b. Dec. 25, 1866.

2 ch.   *Morris Lormor*, b. Nov. 13, 1893, d. Aug. 21, 1895.   *Eleanor Anderson*, b. Aug. 23, 1896.

175.

CYNTHIA COWLES, da Rensselaer W. and Laura (Kilbourne) Cowles.
  b. Mar. 8, 1821.   m. May 1, 1842.

Henry Livingston Richards, s. William S. and Isabelle (Mower) Richards.
  b.

5 ch.   *Laura Isabelle*, b. Mar. 10, 1843.   *Henry L.*, b. Oct. 28, 1846.
         William Doughlas, b. Aug. 18, 1848.   *Havens Cowles*, b. Nov. 8, 1851.
         Mary, b. Dec. 20, 1856.

176.

GERALDINE DERING COWLES, da. Rensselaer W. and Laura (Kilbourne) Cowles.
  b. Feb. 17, 1829.   m. Apr. 7, 1853.

John Adair McDowell, s. Abram I. and Eliza S. (Lord) McDowell.
  b.   d July 4, 1887.

6 ch. 309. *Gerald Rensselaer*, b. Feb. 6, 1854; m. June 26, 1894, Helen S. Bain.
         Lucy Fitch, b. Oct. 18, 1855; m. Aug. 10, 1892, *Rev. Joseph A. Milburn.
      310. *Malcolm Hector*, b. Nov. 15, 1857; m. June 6, 1889, Maud Stowe.
         Louis Havens, b. July 22, 1859, d. Sep. 1860.
         °*Selden Lord*, b. Aug. 3, 1864; m. Apr. 6, 1892, Lucy M. Nowland.
         Jennie, b. June 30, 1867, d. Aug. 13 1867.
(*) s. of John G. and Charlotte (Dodds) Milburn.   (°) Has 1 ch. Eloise McDowell, b. Feb. 1894.

177.

BYRON KILBOURNE COWLES, s. Rensselaer W. and Laura (Kilbourne) Cowles.
  d. Oct. 21, 1837.   m. Dec. 12, 1867.

Lucy G. Buckingham, da. Harvey R. and Lucy (Curtis) Buckingham.
  b.

3 ch.   *Harvey Lafayette*, b. Sep. 26, 1868; m. June 1, 1892, Caroline Jensen.
         Laura Kilbourne, b. May 5, 1870.   *Byron Kilbourne*, b. Feb. 11, 1874.

178.

JOHN GRISWOLD HUNTINGTON, s. Levi and Catherine H. (Richards) Huntington.
  b. Feb. 24, 1814.   m. Sep. 1, 1836.   d.

Mary Isham, da.
  b.

2 ch. 311. *Jedidiah*, b. Aug. 7, 1837; m.   Annie E. Hazard.
         John R., b. Sep. 1848; m.
(*) d. in 1884, left 4 ch., Effie, Mary, George and James.

179.

JOHN MYERS HUNTINGTON, s. Thomas M. and Mary B. (Campbell) Huntington.
  b. Apr. 3, 1821.   m. Sep. 2, 1856.

Mary A. Parks, da. Elisha Parks, of Boston, Mass.
  b. Mar. 11, 1825.

1 ch. *Austin Parks, b. Dec. 7, 1857; m.   Mary Freeman.
(*) Had 3 ch. Mildred S., b. Nov. 25, 1889. The first two d. in infancy.

180.

GEORGE WOLCOTT HUNTINGTON, s. Thomas M. and Mary B. (Campbell) Huntington.
    b. Apr. 6. 1825.   m. 1st, June 23, 1848, m. 2d, June 15, 1854.   d.   1859.

1st, Catherine L. Childs, da. Henry M. Childs, of Pittsfield.
    b.   d. June 20, 1852.

2d, Alice Henderson, da. Henry and Delia (Alden) Hendrickson.
5 ch.   *Annie Childs*, b. May 25, 1849, d. Feb. 18, 1852.   *Thomas Myers*, b. May 6, 1852.
         Kate Mary, b. May 6, 1852, d. Aug 12, 1853.   *Timothy Campbell*, b. May 6, 1855.
         Alice Henderson, b. Sep. 17, 1856.

181.

DORA ASTOR MUMFORD, da. Samuel J. and Caroline G. (Astor) Mumford.
    b. May 17, 1831.   m. Apr. 28, 1850.

Alonzo Clinton Jackson, s. Allan H. and Diana C. (Paige) Jackson.
    b. Dec. 17, 1823.   d. Mar. 31, 1853.

2 ch. **312.** *Helen*, b. May 30, 1851; m. Oct. 21, 1875, John T. M. Rowland.
         Jones Mumford, b. Aug. 5, 1852.

182.

MARGARET HYSLOP MUMFORD, da. Samuel J. and Eliza H. (Strong) Mumford.
    b. Aug. 23, 1843.   m. Oct. 15, 1867.

Charles Barzillai Northrop, s. Sylvester and Mahala (   ) Northrop.
    b. May 11, 1836.

3 ch.   *Cornilia Winiler*, b. Jan. 26, 1869.
    313. *Bertha Strong*, b. Mar. 28, 1870; m. May 16, 1891, Edward Orr.
         Arthur Kimball, b. Feb. 2, 1873.

183.

JEREMIAH JAGGER HAVENS, s. Ezra and Betsey (Jagger) Havens.
    b.   1808.   m.   1829.   d. Jan. 1, 1893.

Mary Bethiah Rowland, da. Daniel and Betsey (Hubbard) Rowland.
    b.   d. Sep.   1872.

6 ch.   *Fanny Maria*, b.   m.   Benjamin Fisher.
         °*Henry Harrison*, b.   m.   Mary Frances Corwin.
         Daniel Rowland, b.   m.   Oliver Ames; no issue.
    314. *Hannah Rosina*, b.   m.   George L. Benjamin.
         |*Ann Eliza*, b.   m. { 1st,   Henry C. Hammond.
                                      { 2d,   George Beebe.
    315. *William Hampton*, b. Aug. 19, 1842; m. Sep. 11, 1864, Louisa Park.
(*) Had 5 ch. John F., Mary, both d. in infancy; Fanny, who m. Wm. Crowley; Amanda and Dehlia.
(°) Has one son, John Franklin, who is m.   (|) Had one ch. Olive Ann, who d. unm.

184.

WILLIAM HAVENS, s. Ezra and Betsey (Jagger) Havens.
    b. Oct. 27, 1817.   m.   d. Aug. 3, 1874.

Betsey A. Jackson, da. Nathaniel and Betsey (Davis) Jackson.
    b. Aug. 9, 1817,   d. Aug. 30, 1892.

12 ch.   *Mehetable B.*, b.   Moses W. Downs.
    316. *David Andrew*, b. June 14, 1841; m. Aug. 10, 1861, Marietta L'Hommedieu.

    317. *Sarah Emma*, b.   m. { 1st,   James J. Verity.
                                          { 2d,   John Loving.

         Thomas J., b.   m. { 1st,   Betsey McGuire.
                                     { 2d,   Ella Crosby.
         John Wesley, b.   m.   Mary Ripley.
         Reeves Howell, b. Feb. 9, 1845, d. Jan. 23, 1865.   *Nathan B.*, b.   m. Sarah J. Hulse.
         William Alonzo, b.   *Mary Jane*, b.   m. Amos Davis.
         Ann Amelia, b. Sep. 20, 1843; m. { 1st,   Isaac Fields.
                                             { 2d, July 28, 1870, William Henry Smith; no issue.
                                          { 1st,   Andrew Dayton.
         Betsey Virginia, b.   m. { 2d,   John McDonald.
                                          { 3d,   William H. Jacobs.
                                          { 1st,   Sophie Van Nort.
         Jeremiah J., b.   m. { 2d,   Phebe Loomis.
                                       { 3d,   Anna J. Marrion.
(*) Had 15 ch.

185.

FANNY HAVENS, da. Ezra and Betsey (Jagger) Havens.
    b. Feb. 9, 1812.   m. Oct. 26, 1830.   d. Feb. 13, 1854.

Samuel White, s. Elias and Keziah (Penny) White.
    b. Oct. 9, 1806.   d. May 23, 1883.

10 ch.   *Sophronia, b. Oct. 25, 1831; m.   William Elton.
   318. Juliet, b. Nov. 8, 1833; m.   James Reeves.
   319. Mary E., b. May 28, 1835; m.   John T. Skidmore.
          °William F., b. Oct. 12, 1838; m.   Mary J. Simmons.
   320. Henry H., b. Sep. 1, 1841; m. Jan. 11, 1867, Abigail Hubbard.
          John Harvey, b. May 17, 1843; m.   Louisa Skidmore; no issue.
          Ann Maria, b. Nov. 1, 1845; m.   Josiah Fordham.
          Joseph M., b. May 11, 1848, d. unm. Feb. 3, 1874.
          |Charry, b. Aug. 9, 1850; m.   Edward Buddington.
          Isaac P., b. Aug. 20, 1853, d. unm. Dec. 15, 1872.

(*) Had 6 ch.   (°) Was drowned Oct. 6, 1876, had 4 ch., all of whom d. young.
(|) Had 1 ch., Edith Buddington, who d. in infancy.

186.

MARY HAVENS, da. Ezra and Betsey (Jagger) Havens.
       b. Apr. 11, 1822.   m. 1st,   m. 2d, Apr. 10, 1845, m. 3d,

   1st, William Ruland, s. William Ruland, of Red Creek, N. Y.
       b.   d.   ae. 51.

   2d, Jasper Vail, s. Peter   Vail, of Riverhead.
       b. May 8, 1786.   d.

   3d. B. Louis Terril, s. Lewis Terril, of Port Jefferson.
       b.   d. Mar. 18, 1897.

7 ch.   *John, b. Nov. 3, 1842; m. } 1st,   Bennet.
                                    } 2d,   Hannah Jane Hulse.
          Fannie, b. Jan. 19, 1846, d. unm.
          °Henry H., b. June 30, 1848; m.   Nancy Downs.
          |James A., b. Dec. 7, 1849; m.   Isabella Jennings.
          Hannah G., b. June 7, 1851, d. unm.   Joseph W., b. Dec. 10, 1854, d. unm.
          Mary Louise, b. Apr. 5, 1858; m.   John Q. Adams.

(*) Has 5 ch.   By 1st wife, Annie, Fannie and Grace; by 2d wife, Lottie and Susie.
(°) Has 2 ch., one of whom is m.   (|) Has 13 ch.

187.

NANCY HAVENS, da. Ezra and Betsey (Jagger) Havens.
       b. June 8, 1824.   m.

   Harry Warner, s.
       b.

7 ch.   James, b.   d. unm.   Ann Maria, b.   m. Joshua Warner.
          Hannah J., b.   m. William Brooker.
          Daniel, b.   Louisa, b.   m. Alfonzo Hand.
          Betsey J., b.   m. William Jackson.   Charles, b.

188.

HANNAH HAVENS, da. Ezra and Betsey (Jagger) Havens.
       b. Oct. 15, 1826.   m. Dec. 21, 1843.   d. Nov. 7, 1882.

   David Petty, s. David and Hannah (Norton) Petty.
       b. Mar. 20, 1824.

8 ch.   *Henry W., b. June 8, 1846; m. Dec. 31, 1871, Maria G. Bennet; no issue.
   321. David O., b. Dec 25, 1848; m. Feb. 6, 1870, Sarah J. Newey.
          Edward B., b. Aug. 14, 1852, d. June 29, 1856.
          Ella Gertrude, b. Mar. 5, 1858, d. June 28, 1858.
          Sarah Elizabeth, b. Apr. 19, 1859; m. Jan. 25, 1875, °George F. Holly; no issue.
          Hannah Maria, b. Oct. 19, 1861, d. Dec. 25, 1870.
   322. Minnie Etta, b. Oct. 23, 1863; m. Oct. 10, 1880, Charles L. Newey.
          Adda L., b. Oct. 14, 1867, d. Dec. 13. 1870.

(*) d. June 24, 1872.   (°) s. of George and Catherine (Russell) Holly.

189.

DANIEL SHEPARD HAVENS, s. Walter and Anna (Benjamin) Havens.
       b. July 6, 1824.   m. 1st, Oct. 10, 1843; m. 2d, Sep. 1, 1869; m. 3d, Jan. 17, 1883.

   1st, Harriet L. Fanning, da. Nathaniel and Abigail (Goodale) Fanning.
       b. Mar. 24, 1830.   d. Oct. 12, 1868.

   2d, Nancy R. Fanning, da. Nathaniel and Abigail (Goodale) Fanning.
       b. Jan. 3, 1851.   d. July 10, 1880.

   3d, Jennie E. Fanning, da. Nathaniel and Abigail (Goodale) Fanning.
       b. June 17, 1849.

8 ch.   Daniel Wesley, b. Dec. 11, 1844, d. Dec. 8, 1864.
          Walter Willis, b. Mar. 9, 1847, d. Oct. 7, 1865.
          Anna L., b. Mar. 10, 1849, d. Feb. 17, 1851.
   323. Edward Shepard, b. June 15, 1852; m. Jan. 27, 1871, Alice K. Stubbs.
   324. Ulman Rose, b. June 28, 1854; m. Jan. 9, 1874, Ida W. Albertson.
          Annie, b. Jan. 15, 1857, d. Apr. 24, 1864.   An infant by 2d wife d. in infancy.
          Lillian B., b. Dec. 26, 1874; m. Jan. 23, 1895, *Leander H. Pohly.

(*) s. of Andrew and Semoriah (Eldrich) Pohly, b. Dec. 24, 1869.

190.

WALTER FRANKLIN HAVENS, s. Walter and Anna (Benjamin) Havens.
    b. June 5, 1828.   m. Dec. 23, 1851.

Phebe Annette Tuthill, da. Jehiel and Johannah (Hallock) Tuthill,
    b. Aug. 7, 1823.

5 ch.   *Leslie Franklin*, b. Aug. 27, 1855, d. Apr. 27, 1858.
    325. *George Leslie*, b. Jan. 19, 1859; m. May 30, 1895, Mary B. Drake.
        An infant, b. Feb. 23. 1862, d. Feb. 24, 1862.   *Ada Annette*, b. Apr. 2, 1864.
    326. *Annie May*, b. Sep. 21, 1868; m. June 18, 1895, Israel D. Luce.

191.

MANASSEH HAVENS, s. Walter and Anna (Benjamin) Havens.
    b. Dec. 11, 1830.   m.   1853.   d. Jan. 18, 1893.

Elizabeth Tuthill, da. Jehiel and Johanna (Hallock) Tuthill.
    b. Feb. 3, 1837.

4 ch. **327.** *Chauncey M.*, b. Dec. 9, 1854; m. { 1st, Jan. 8, 1876, Louise Carter.
                                                { 2d, Feb. 20, 1886, Mary Squires.
    328. *Daniel Madison*, b. May 19, 1858; m. Dec. 19, 1880, Georgiana Edwards.
        Edward, b. Oct. 13, 1861, d. Aug. 29, 1879.
        Arthur M., b. Apr. 27, 1867.

192.

FRANCES ROSELLA HAVENS, da. Walter and Anna (Benjamin) Havens.
    b. Jan 6, 1834.   m. Dec. 24, 1851.   d. Feb. 17, 1875.

Prosper King Benjamin, s. W. Phillips and Hannah (Fanning) Benjamin.
    b. Sep. 24, 1830.

7 ch.   *Anna Rosella*, b Dec. 2, 1852; m.   Gilbert Newton.
    Mary Ellen, b. Dec. 5, 1855. d. unm. Nov. 23, 1875.
    Walter P., b. Aug. 31, 1857, d. Oct. 18, 1858.   *Havens K,.* b. Oct 23. 1859, d. Oct. 8. 1860.
    Gilbert L., b. Oct. 27, 1862; m. May 24, 1884, Ella Raynor.
    Charles H., b. Nov. 6, 1865.   *Herbert J.*, b. Oct. 13, 1867, d. Apr. 25. 1874.

193.

WALTER SWESEY, s. Joel and Mehetable (Havens) Swesey.
    b.   m.

BETHIAH HAVENS, da. Ezra and Betsey (Jagger) Havens.
    b.   d.

6 ch.   *Sarah E.*, b.   *Henry Harrison*, b.   *Mehetable*, b.   *Nathan*, b.   Two more.

194.

BETSEY M. TUTHILL, da. William H. and Sophia (Petty) Tuthill.
    b. Oct. 20, 1823   m. Mar. 22, 1848.   d. Sep. 7. 1893.

John B. Brown, s. John and Phebe K. (Taber) Brown.
    b. Aug. 1813.   d. June 28, 1867.

3 ch. **329.** *John Henry*, b. Apr. 22, 1852; m. Dec. 8, 1875, Lydia Terry.
    Lorin Waldo, b. July 24, 1854; m. Dec. 31. 1891, *Lucy Corwin Goldsmith; no issue.
    William Tuthill, b. July 3, 1857; m. Dec. 21, 1882, °Theresa Booth; no issue.
(*) da. of Ezra L. and Lucy L. (Corwin) Goldsmith, b. Apr. 13, 1862.   (°) da. of William and
    Wilamena (Dunkle) Booth.

195.

WILLIAM PERKINS HOWELL, s. Charles J. and Lydia H. (Spear) Howell.
    b. May 24, 1837.   m. 1st, Nov' 15, 1866.   2d, Apr. 14, 1870.

1st, Cecelia Ray Huntting, da. James M.   Huntting.
    b. Sep. 28, 1842.   d. Jan. 10, 1867.

2d, Lydia George Cockcroft, da. Dr. William   Cockcroft.
    b. Oct. 4, 1844.   d. May 2, 1897.

9 ch.   *Lillian Cecelia*, b. Oct. 9, 1871.   *Louise*, b. Nov. 27, 1872.
    Eleanor, b. Aug. 21, 1874.   *William P.*, b. Mar. 13, 1876.   *Eva*, b. Dec. 14, 1877.
    Frances, b. June 20, 1879.   *Lucretia*, b. July 27, 1881.
    Charlotte, b. Feb. 15, 1884.   *Lydia*, b. June 21, 1888.

196.

GEORGE GOELET KIP, s. Elbert S. and Elizabeth (Goelet) Kip.
    b. Jan. 15, 1845.   m. May 23, 1867.   [haimer.

Anna M. Geissenhaimer, da. Rev. Augustus T. and Amelia S. (Havemeyer) Geissen-
    b. Oct. 6, 1847.   d. Apr. 5, 1893.

3 ch.   *Charles Augustus*, b. Aug. 14, 1870.   *Elbert S.*, b. Apr. 10, 1874.
    Ann Elizabeth. b. Dec. 22, 1880.

197.

LYDIA FOWLER KIP, da. Samuel and Nancy (Fowler) Kip.
    b. Nov. 16, 1838.   m.   1858.

Edward B. Underhill, s. Charles and Elvira A. (Beekman) Underhill.
    b. Dec. 9, 1835.

4 ch. **330.** *Edward B.*, b. June 8, 1859; m. Mar. 13, 1896. Kate Isaacson.
    331. *Rawson*, b. Sep. 27, 1861; m. June 11, 1880, Jessie Crowley.
    332. *Jacob B.*, b. May 27, 1867; m. Nov. 2, 1892, Elizabeth Aldrich.
    Gerard B., b. June 13, 1876.

198.

THOMAS COCHRAN KIP, s. Samuel and Nancy (Fowler) Kip.
    b. Nov. 18, 1840.   m. July 10, 1866.   d. Dec. 29, 1890.

Mary A. Hodgson, da. Edward W. and Anna (Keeshan) Hodgson.
    b. July 22, 1845.

7 ch.   *Maud Irene*, b. Oct. 7, 1868.   *John Prentice*, b. Aug. 16, 1870.
    Anna Maud, b. Sep. 21, 1872.   *Walter Stanton*, b. Jan. 14, 1875.
    Charles H., b. Aug. 20, 1879, d. Apr. 2. 1880.
    Charles H.. b. Sep. 25, 1880.   *George Curtis*, b. July 21. 1884.

199.

ELIZABETH KIP, da. Samuel and Nancy (Fowler) Kip.
    b.   m.

George Harrison, of England.
    b.   d.

3 ch.   *George*, b.   d.   **Nancy*, b.   m.   Charles A. Poe.
    Mary, b.   m.   Pettit.

(*) She and her husband are dead; they left two ch., Samuel and Clinton; the last is dead.

200.

CORNELIA KIP, da. Henry and Elizabeth (Abbott) Kip.
    b. Oct. 28, 1848.   m. June 10, 1874.

William H. Burr, s. Melancthon and Euphenia J. (Cooper) Burr.
    b. July 4, 1844.

6 ch.   *May Mentum*, b. Apr. 12, 1875.   *Nellie Kip*, b. Sep. 7, 1876.
    William Henry, b. Sep. 17, 1877, d. May 30, 1878.
    Nina Cooper, b. May 15, 1880, d. Sep. 7, 1883.   *Harold Cooper*, b. June 11. 1884.
    Sherley Hinsdale, b. Nov. 9, 1892, d. Aug. 3, 1893.

201.

ELIZABETH ABBOTT KIP, da. Henry and Elizabeth (Abbott) Kip.
    b. Aug. 17, 1851.   m. Jan. 19, 1875.

Samuel Chase Coale, s. Samuel C. and Sarah (English) Coale.
    b.   1846.

3 ch.   *Elizabeth Kip*, b. July 23, 1876; m. Nov. 15, 1894, *James L. Hammer.
    Sarah Chase, b. Mar. 9, 1878.   *Sarah English*, b. Aug. 4. 1883.

(*) s. of Frederick and Margaret (Thompson) Hammer.

202.

FRANCES ELIZABETH ROGERS, da. Zachariah and Frances H. (Havens) Rogers.
    b. Dec. 16, 1834.   m. June 29, 1864.

Rev. Gordon Huntington, s.
    b.

3 ch.   *Wolcott E.*, b. Apr. 18, 1866, d. May 7. 1884.   *C. Genevieve*, b. Dec. 6, 1868.
    Frances E., b. May 10, 1871; m. Apr. 27, 1898, Charles Lewis Corwin.

203.

FRANCES DAVIS VALENTINE, da. Uriah and Nancy (Davis) Valentine.
    b.   m.

Silas Cocks Searing, s.
    b.

8 ch. **333.** *Phebe B.*, b.   m. Daniel Van Velsor.   **Whitson M.*, b.   m. Eliza Golding.
    334. *Harriet A.*, b.   m. William E. Townsend.   °*Laura A.*, b.   m. Samuel Rudyard.
    ‡*Charles V.*, b.   m Wilhelmina Harris.   ‡*Frances*, b.   m. William Moore.
    †*Orlanda Coe*, b.   m. Ella Baker.   ¶*Mary E.*, b.   m. Carman A. Vernon.

(*) Has 7 ch., Eleanor, Maria, Susan. Grace, Willet, Corydon and Edwin.
(°) Has 1 ch., Clarence A.   (¶) Has 2 ch., Edith and Elsie.
(‡) Has 4 ch., Olive, Lois, Carrie and Cecilia.   (†) Has 2 ch., Ruth and Emily.
(¶) Has 3 ch., Agnes, Charles and Lois.

204.

MARIA RAPYLEA DAVIS, da. Charles H. and Hulda A. (Richardson) Davis.
    b. Feb. 21, 1840   m. Apr. 25, 1861.

Egbert Quimby, s. Daniel and Rachel (Pirgo) Quimby.
    b.

1 ch.   *Henry Richardson*, b. Apr. 18, 1862; m. *Carrie May Hodgson.

(*) da. of Valentine M. and Eliza J. (Requa) Hodgson.

205.

JOSEPHINE DAVIS, da. Charles H. and Hulda A. (Richardson) Davis.
b. July 27, 1842.   m. June 12, 1867.

Joshua Thurston Haws, s. Henry H. and Louisa (Thomson) Haws.
b.

2 ch.   *Charles Davis*, b. Dec. 3, 1870.
Laura Josephine, b. Sep. 5, 1868; m. Oct. 15, 1890, *Andrew Kneeland Dunn.

(*) s. of Andrew and Catherine (Germain) Dunn.

206.

MARY FRANCES DAVIS, da. Charles H. and Hulda A. (Richardson) Davis.
b. Apr. 2, 1849.   m. Dec. 16, 1867.

Richard Byme, s. Richard Byme, of White Plains, N. Y.
b.   d. June 17, 1896.

2 ch.   The 1st d. young.
Lilian, b. June 16, 1870; m. July 5, 1895, Frederick Calhoun.

207.

CATHERINE A. DAVIS, da. James and Elvira (Davis) Davis.
b. Nov. 28, 1817.   m. June 18, 1840.   d. June 30, 1891.

Alfred F. Chatman, s. James and Susan (Emmons) Chatman.
b. Feb. 25, 1814.   d. July 29, 1860.

4 ch. 335. *James W.*, b. Mar. 7, 1841; m. Dec. 25, 1861. Sarah L. Annin.
Alfred F., b. Dec. 27, 1843, d. in Civil War, Sep. 7, 1863.
**Robert D.*, b. Jan. 1, 1845; m. June 1870, °Almira Taylor.
Kate E., b. Mar. 6, 1848; m. Apr. 19, 1882, Richard E. Mott.

(*) d. Aug. 13, 1885, had 1 ch., Byron T., b. 1874. d. Jan. 6, 1881.   (°) d. Nov. 25. 1884.

208.

MARY FRANCES LOPER, da. Charles S. and Julia G. (Davis) Loper.
b. July 13, 1841.   m. Apr. 13, 1859.

Thomas S. Marlor, s. Henry S. and Jane (Dare) Marlor.
b. Dec. 10, 1839.   d. Dec. 23. 1898.

3 ch.   *Charles S.*, b. July 12, 1860.   *Lillian Frances*, b. Aug. 11, 1863. d. Aug. 21, 1865.
Edwin M., b. Jan. 6, 1867.

209.

JULIA M. LOPER, da. Charles S. and JULIA G. (Davis) Loper.
b. May 16, 1845.   m. Jan. 30, 1868.

Robert J. Clyde, s. George and Isabella (Black) Clyde.
b. Feb. 12, 1838.

2 ch.   *Julia L.*, b. Aug. 12, 1872.   *Robert Nicoll*, b. Apr. 19, 1878.

210.

NANCY HAVENS LESTER, da. Richard and Sarah F. (Havens) Lester.
b. Oct. 18, 1820.   m. Dec. 1, 1858.

John Worth, s. James and Nancy (Tooker) Worth.
b. Aug. 4, 1813.   d. May 7, 1894.

1 ch. 336. *Alice Havens*, b. Oct. 21, 1859; m. Aug. 22, 1888, Manuel Boutcher.

211.

Rev. WILLIAM HAVENS LESTER, s. Richard and Sarah F. (Havens) Lester.
b. Dec. 4, 1825.   m. Aug. 31, 1854.

Julia Elizabeth Hand, da. Thomas B. and Harriet (Hedges) Hand.
b. Nov. 21, 1828.   d. Jan. 30, 1898.

3 ch. 337. *William Hand*, b. Apr. 5, 1856; m. { 1st, June 15, 1882, Sarah Margaret Anderson.
{ 2d, Nov. 21, 1887, Carrie Macfarland Field.
Nathaniel Tallmage, b. Apr. 5, 1858.   *Hadassah Elizabeth*, b. Apr. 29, 1866.

212.

GEORGE LEWIS LESTER, s. Richard and Sarah F. (Havens) Lester.
b. July 8, 1831.   m. Apr. 13, 1853.   d. July 12, 1865.

Hatty Osborn, da. Isaac and Catherine (Glover) Osborn.
b. about 1837.

3 ch.   *Sarah Frances*, b. Feb. 18, 1854; m   Frank Edwards; no issue.
George Osborn, b. Dec. 8, 1857, d. in infancy.
Catherine Glover, b. Jan. 15, 1860; m. { 1st, Aug. 7, 1883, *Phineas Terry; } no issue.
{ 2d, Sep. 7, 1892, °James Robinson; }

(*) s. of Phineas Terry, of Bridgehampton, N. Y., d. Oct. 14, 1890, ae. 34.
(°) s. of James and Lucinda (Lamphier) Robinson.

213.

JULIA A. CHATFIELD, da. Henry M. and Nancy (Havens) Chatfield.
b. 1824.   m.

Samuel H. Howell, s. William and Frances (Haines) Howell.
b.

2 ch.   *William H., b. Aug.   1849; m. { 1st,   +Mary Edwards.
                                          { 2d,   Matilda Latham.
    338. Elmer Ellsworth, b. Jan. 11, 1864; m.   Minnie Smith.
(*) Had 1 s. who d. in infancy.   (†) da. Henry and Sarah (Webb) Edwards.

214.

JOHN CHATFIELD, s. Henry M. and Nancy (Havens) Chatfield.
    b. Jan. 20, 1826.   m. Oct. 1857.   d. Dec. 26, 1865.
    Esther Edwards, da. Henry and Eliza (Edwards) Edwards.
    b. Nov. 27, 1829.

4 ch. 339. Anna C., b. Jan. 11. 1859; m.   Stephen E. Rose.
        John G., b. Oct. 2, 1861.
        Lydia H., b. July 18, 1863; m. June 1888, *J. Everett Hand.
    340. Henry H., b. Mar. 17, 1866; m. May 23, 1893, Charlotte M. Peterson.
(*) s. of Albert and Charity (Hedges) Hand, b. June 28, 1861.

215.

GEORGE TINDALL, s. Nathaniel and Esther E. (Havens) Tindall.
    b. Sep. 1, 1832.   m. May 6, 1857.
    NANCY M. HAVENS, da. Nathaniel T. and Charlotte M. (Havens) Havens.   See No.
    b. Oct. 22, 1831.   d. Feb. 27, 1898.   [132.

3 ch.   George Herbert, b. July 14, 1861.   Minnie Elloise, b. Sep. 15, 1866.
        Everett Lex, b. Feb. 3, 1873.

216.

VALENTINE HAVENS, s. Albert G. and Elizabeth (Valentine) Havens.
    b. Aug. 24, 1834.   m. Nov. 15, 1854.   d. Apr. 23, 1870.
    Sarah Gertrude Britton, da. Abraham and Gertrude (Van Cleef) Britton.
    b. Feb. 21, 1830.   d. Oct. 1, 1868.

5 ch.   *Elizabeth, b. Aug. 24, 1856; m.   °William H. Atwood.
        Albert Gallatin, b. Apr. 3, 1858.
    341. Abraham Britton, b. May 27, 1860; m. Jan. 27, 1887, Lila Hoyt Beckwith.
    342. Edwin Taylor, b. Sep. 30, 1862; m. Apr. 21, 1886, Lillie E. Murphy.
        Valentine, b. Nov. 2, 1866.
(*) Has 3 ch., Albert W., Edwin H. and Heman.   (°) s. of John A. and Abigail Atwood.

217.

MARY ELIZABETH HAVENS, da. Albert G. and Elizabeth (Valentine) Havens.
    b. Mar. 9, 1842.   m. Nov. 28, 1866.
    William Geery, s. William and Mary (Blair) Geery.
    b. Apr. 2, 1842.

4 ch. 343. William, b. Oct. 29, 1867; m. May 30, 1889, Isabel M. Christie.
    344. Mary, b. Jan. 11, 1869; m. Dec. 27, 1888, George T. Brown.
        Esther, b. Nov. 29, 1871, d. Sep. 25, 1874.
    345. Elizabeth, b. June 28, 1873; m. Oct. 9, 1895, James H. Isbills.

218.

JAMES HENRY HAVENS, s. James H. and Morgan (Vandenburg) Havens.
    b. Feb. 15, 1847.   m. Dec. 11, 1872.
    Mary C. Oliver, da. Benjamin F. and Mary A. (James) Oliver.
    b. May 12, 1849.

6 ch.   Harry Franklin, b. Mar. 27, 1874.   Emily Augusta, b. Aug. 18, 1876.
        William Edward, b. Dec. 21, 1877; m. Nov. 10, 1898, Mary La Grasse.
        Ella Esther, b. Sep. 24, 1879.   Ida May, b. July 5, 1881, d. Jan. 21, 1882.
        Lauretta, b. July 9, 1883.

219.

REV. CHARLES HUNTINGTON GARDINER, s. David and Marietta (Huntington) Gardiner.
    b. June 10, 1826.   m. Sep. 26, 1865.
    Anna E. Lennon, da. John and Ann (Crooker) Lennon.
    b. Oct. 31, 1834.

1 ch.   David, b. Mar. 11, 1869, d. Oct. 10, 1860.

220.

JOHN LYON GARDINER, s. Samuel B. and Mary G. (Thompson) Gardiner.
    b.   m.
    Elizabeth C. Livingstone Jones, da. Oliver H. and Louisa (Livingstone) Jones.
    b.

5 ch.   Coralie L.,   Adele G.,   Lyon,   John,   Winthrop.

221.

JOSEPH TODHUNTER THOMPSON, s. Jonathan and Katherine (Todhunter) Thompson.
    b. Jan. 10, 1860.   m. Apr. 29, 1884.
    Jane Remsen, da. William and Jane (Suydam) Remsen.
    b.

3 ch.   Jonathan, b. Jan. 31, 1885.   Jane Remsen, b. Nov. 11, 1887.
        Elizabeth Remsen, b. Feb. 16, 1894.

222.

MILTON STRONG THOMPSON, s. Abraham G. and Mary J. (Strong) Thompson.
b. Feb. 8, 1855.   m. Dec. 24, 1889.

Abigail Adams Johnson, da. William C. and Mary C. (Nicholson) Johnson.
b.

2 ch.   *Sarah Elizabeth*, b. Oct. 11, 1890.   *Gardiner*, b. Oc·. 29, 1892.

223.

HENRY P. H. KEELER, s. David B. and Elizabeth C. (Havens) Keeler.
b. July 4, 1832.   m. Nov. 11, 1856.   d. Apr. 14, 1873.

Rachel C. Crane, da. Benjamin T. and Amanda H. (Chardavoyne) Crane.
b. July 31, 1835.

1 ch. 346. *David B.*, b. May 22, 1858; m. Oct. 11, 1888, Caroline S. Stayner.

224.

DAVID B. KEELER, s. David B. and Elizabeth C. (Havens) Keeler.
b. Feb. 11, 1835.   m. Apr. 8, 1858.

Jennie L. Fleet da. Jonathan G. and Eliza (Gardiner) Fleet.
b. June 27, 1838.

3 ch. 347. *Annie H.*, b. Aug. 29, 1861; m. Oct. 1, 1885, William Babcock
       Edward B., b. Feb. 7, 1866; m. Nov. 1, 1888, Emma M. Hebert; no issue.
   348. *Elizabeth C.*, b. Oct. 10, 1871; m. Sep. 14, 1892, Torquato Tasso Fischer.

225.

RACHEL C. KEELER, da. David B. and Elizabeth C. (Havens) Keeler.
b. June 1837.   m. June 3, 1858.

William D. Baker s. Dobbell and Mary (Corlies) Baker.
b. Sep. 18, 1829.   d. July 6, 1868.

3 ch. 349. *Elizabeth K.*, b. June 4, 1859; m. June 4, 1883, John Porter.
   350. *Mary S.*, b. Dec. 19, 1860; m. Oct. 29, 1879, William Williams.
   351. *Margaret C.*, b. May. 12, 1862; m. Nov. 25, 1879, John H. Bonnell.

226.

HANNAH L. CRANE, da. Theodore and Margaret B. (Havens) Crane.
b.   1832.   m. Apr. 27, 1853.

William H. Decker, s.
b.

8 ch.   *Margaret L.*, b.   *Clara*, b.   *Theodore C.*, b.   d.   *Jane E.*, b.
       Alfred, b.   *William H.*, b   m.   Nellic Keller.
       Charles C., b.   d.   *Austin A.*, b.

227.

JANE ELIZABETH CRANE, da. Theodore and Margaret B. (Havens) Crane.
b.   1839.   m. Oct. 17, 1860.

William Loring Andrews, s. Loring and Catherine (Delamater) Andrews.
b. Sept. 9, 1837.

2 ch.   *Loring William*, b. Aug. 26, 1861, d. Oct. 21, 1882.
       Theodore Crane, b. July 2, 1863, d. Oct. 20, 1878.

228.

HENRY EMANUEL RUSSELL, s. William C. and Rachel C. (Havens) Russell.
b. Nov 23, 1838.   m. Jan. 7, 1864.

Mary Augusta Hance, da. William and Margaret (Hance) Hance.
b. Jan. 30. 1840.

5 ch. 352. *Isaac D.*, b. Dec. 4, 1866; m. Apr. 19, 1892, Elizabeth Rockwell.
   353. *Margaret E.*, b. Mar. 28, 1871; m. June 5, 1895. Dwight P. Chamberlain.
       Harriet Corlies, b. Sep. 28, 1873; m. Dec. 11, 1895, *Alex. W. Stanley.
       Echet Crowley, b. Feb. 23, 1875.   *Beatrice*, b. Jan. 9, 1882.
(*) s. of Frederick N. and Mary (Welch) Stanley, b. Feb. 2, 1872.

229.

HARRIET CORLIES RUSSELL, da. William C. and Rachel C. (Havens) Russell.
b. Dec. 24, 1840.   m. June 15, 1865.

James P. Allen.
b.

10 ch.   *Rachel Russell*, b. Apr. 9, 1866.   *Catherine Trafford*, b. Dec. 5, 1867, d. Dec. 15, 1868.
       Charles Gordon, b July 14, 1869, d. Apr. 16, 1873.
       Jennie Andrews, b. Nov. 28, 1871, d. Feb. 27, 1872.
       William Russell, b. Jan 25, 1873, d. July 24, 1873.   *Mary Augusta*, b. Apr. 23, 1874.
       Elsie Edith, b. Nov. 25, 1876.   *Charles Gordon*, b. July 19, 1878, d. Aug. 14, 1878.
       Theodore Henry, b. Oct. 5, 1881.   *Jane Crowell B.*, b. May 26, 1884.

230.

WILLIAM COWLEY RUSSELL, s. William C. and Rachel C. (Havens) Russell.
b. Dec. 14, 1842.   m. 1st, June 4, 1866.   2d, Apr. 27, 1893.

1st, Caroline E. La Fetra, da. Edward and Mary B. (Brindley) La Fetra.
b   d. July 3, 1886.

2d, Cordelia W. Guion, da. Franklin G. and Caroline L. (Warner) Guion.
b.

3 ch.   *Rachel Corlies*, b. Oct. 18, 1866.   *Mary La Fetra*, b. July 23, 1871.
William Cowley, b. Aug. 12, 1882.

231.

HENRY P. HAVENS, s. Asher C. and Rachel (Chardavoyne) Havens,
b. Dec. 4, 1845.   m. Oct. 25, 1883.

Marion Herrick, da. Richard and Georgiana (Nash) Herrick.
b. Apr. 10, 1861.

4 ch.   *Georgiana Herrick*, b. Feb. 27, 1885.   *Marion Chardavoyne*, b. Nov. 3, 1886.
Alice, b. Sep. 13, 1888.   *Mildred*, b. Aug. 3, 1893.

232.

RACHEL C. HAVENS, da. Asher C. and Rachel (Chardavoyne) Havens.
b. July 10, 1847.   m. 1st, Nov. 21, 1867.   2d, Oct. 31, 1882.

1st, Alfred Abeel, s. John H. and Catherine E. (Strobel) Abeel.
b. Oct. 3, 1844   d. May 8, 1871.

2d, John H. Johnson, s. John and Emily (   ) Johnson.
b.   d. Dec. 6, 1887.

3 ch.   *Alfred H.*, b. Oct. 20, 1869.   *Rachel H.*, b. Nov. 16, 1884.
Frederick C., b. Jan. 6, 1886.

233.

GERTRUDE HAVENS, da. Asher C. and Rachel (Chardavoyne) Havens.
b. July 29, 1855.   m. Nov. 21, 1883.

Henry A. Tifft, s.
b.

2 ch.   *Gertrude*, b. Sep. 24, 1884.   *Henry Neville*, b. July 30, 1889.

234.

JAMES SAYRE HAVENS, s. J. Tuthill and Eliza G. (Sayre) Havens.
b. May 11, 1834.   m. Mar. 15, 1865.

Mary Mulford Hand, da. William C. and Ann N. (Blair) Hand.
b. Nov. 9, 1833.

2 ch.   *Anna Blair*, b. Sep. 15, 1870.   m. Nov. 11, 1896, *John Tuthill Young.
Mary Elizabeth, b. July 6, 1872.

(*) s. of Moses T. and Lucy J. (Tuthill) Young, b. Jan. 28, 1867.

235.

WALTER REMINGTON HAVENS, s. Walter and Beulah M. (Case) Havens.
b. Oct. 19, 1835.   m. May 25, 1857.

Margaret E. Wells, da. Calvin and Caroline (Horton) Wells.
b. Apr. 15, 1838.

6 ch. 354. *Herbert Remington*, b. Apr. 19, 1858; m. Sep. 13, 1883, Louise Heimerdinger.
Caroline Moore, b. May 8, 1862.   *Louise Wells*, b. Oct. 19, 1867.
Walter, b. July 16, 1870.   *Theodore Clark*, b. May 2, 1872.   *Ralph R.*, b. Oct. 27, 1874.

236.

MALISSA B. HAVENS, da. Walter and Beulah M. (Case) Havens.
b. Jan. 20, 1838.   m. Oct. 31, 1859.

Theodore Parshall Clark, s. John and Maria J. (Davis) Clark.
b. July 9, 1831.   d. Apr. 16, 1898.

1 ch.   *Virginia Havens*, b. Dec. 18, 1878.

237.

EDWARD HENRY CONKLIN, s. Edward and Jemima (Havens) Conklin.
b. May 24, 1833.   m.   d. Sep. 22, 1884.

Maggie Osborne, da.
b.   d. Oct. 13, 1884.

4 ch. 355. *James Monroe*, b. May 21, 1867; m. Jan. 20, 1895, Margaret McGuire.
Edward H., b. May 31, 1869; m. Nov. 25, 1897, *Henrietta Thompson.
Nellie, b. Sep. 7, 1872 or 4.   *Walter*, b. Aug. 29, 1876.   d. Feb. 9, 1889.

(*) da. of John and Fanny (Johnson) Thompson, b. Aug. 7, 1875.

238.

CHARLOTTE ANN CONKLIN. da. Edward and Jemima (Havens) Conklin.
b, Sep. 23, 1836.   m. Apr. 28, 1857.
William King Cort, s. Nicholas and Elizabeth (King) Cort.
b. Mar. 3, 1829.

5 ch.   *Ida Elizabeth, b. May 10, 1858; m. Nov. 14, 1883, George Leeds Davenport.
    Lottie A., b. Jan. 25, 1860.   Mary Etta, b. Dec. 23, 1866.   d. Jan 4, 1868.
356. May Isabel, b. Sep. 19, 1868; m. Dec. 18, 1889, William Clayton Black.
    Marion Willa, b. July 6, 1876.
(*) Had 1 ch., William Cort, b. Nov. 15, 1884, d. Jan 27, 1891.

239.

PHEBE J. CONKLIN, da. Edward and Jemima (Havens) Conklin.
b. July 20, 1839.   m. 1st, Sep. 5, 1863.   2d, Jan. 7, 1877.
1st, Benjamin G. Eldredge, s. Enoch and Evelina G. (Crowell) Eldredge.
b. Aug. 6, 1838.

2d, Richard Jeffrey Nichols, s. Henry and Prudence (Brainerd) Nichols.
b. Feb. 5, 1813,   d. Aug. 7, 1885.

2 ch. 357. Lottie L., b. Feb. 22, 1866; m. Dec. 24, 1891, Frank W. Whitby.   Richard, b. Nov. 24, 1877.

240.

BENJAMIN PETTIT CONKLIN, s. Edward and Jemima (Havens) Conklin.
b. Nov. 19, 1844.   m. Jan. 23, 1872.
Mary C Payne, da. Richard and Mary A. (Carney) Payne.
b. Jan. 3, 1844.

1 ch. 358. Russell Havens, b. Dec. 23, 1873; m. June 1, 1897. Minnie S. Hoyt.

241.

FRANKLIN PIERCE CONKLIN, s. Edward and Jemima (Havens) Conklin.
b. July 9, 1852.   m. 1st, Feb. 20, 1877.   2d,   1882.
1st, Belle B. Sherman, da. Samuel and Arabella (Case) Sherman.
b. Sep. 19, 1858.   d. Oct. 22, 1878.

2d, Phebe O. Rutan, da. Robert J. and Adelia (Lauterman) Rutan.
b. Dec. 26, 1860.

2 ch.   James Monroe, b. Apr. 23, 1883.   Lawrence Ambler, b. May 23, 1886.

242.

HARRIET WINSLOW HAVENS, da. Remington and Anna P. (Cartwright) Havens.
b. Sep. 6, 1843.   m. Dec. 24, 1863.
John C. Beebe, s. Thomas and Maria N. (Chester) Beebe.
b. Apr. 16, 1842.

7 ch. 359. Adelaide H., b. Sep. 29, 1864; m. June 26, 1886, Charles H. Smith.
360. Harriet Winslow, b. Sep. 26, 1867; m.   1886, Willis W. Worthington.
    George C., b. June 25, 1871, d. July 8, 1891.   Merriam E., b. Jan. 26, 1876.
    Warren L., b. Sep. 6, 1878.   Marietta, b. Aug. 27, 1883.   Arthur L., b. Jan. 3, 1885.

243.

GEORGE REMINGTON HAVENS, s. Remington and Anna P. (Cartwright) Havens.
b. Jan. 30, 1847.   m. Dec. 22, 1874.
Elizabeth M. Jennings, da. Morancy P. and Frances H. (Chester) Jennings.
b. Mar 7, 1854.

2 ch.   Walter Remington, b. Jan. 14, 1876.   George R. b. Aug. 25, 1890.

244.

SOPHIA WOODRUFF HAVENS, da. Remington and Anna P. (Cartwright) Havens.
b. June 10, 1856.   m. Oct. 3, 1878.
Willett Green Smith, s. Nehemiah and Elizabeth (Green) Smith.
b. Nov.   1850.   d. Feb. 11, 1896.

3 ch.   Rachel Elizabeth, b. Sep. 4, 1879.   Willett Green, b. July 29, 1881.
    Clarence Havens, b. July 5, 1886.

245.

ELIAS HAVENS PAYNE, s. Elias W. and Louise (Havens) Payne.
b. Nov. 5, 1843.   m. Oct. 30, 1877.
Mary R. W. Cartwright, da. Benjamin C. and Hannah M. (Tuthill) Cartwright.
b. Dec. 31, 1852.

3 ch.   Matt Taylor, b. Dec. 11, 1879, d. Nov. 25, 1888.   Kenneth Havens, b. July 29, 1881.
    Esther Sanford, b. Feb. 25, 1887.

246.

WILLIAM OTIS PAYNE, s. Elias W. and Louise (Havens) Payne.
b. Jan. 30, 1850.   m. Feb. 13, 1878.
Catherine Dillon Burns, da. John and Catherine D. (Aitken) Burns.
b. Aug. 27, 1855.

6 ch.   *Edward Otis*, b. May 5, 1879.   *Maria Louise*, b. Feb. 5, 1881.
        Katherine Aitken, b. Apr. 20, 1884.   *Fannie Margaret*, b. Sep. 8, 1887.
        Helen Sutton, b. Dec. 19, 1891.   *Dorothy Baldwin*, b. Apr. 6, 1896.

247.

HORACE G. MANWARING, s. Horace B. and Nancy A. (Havens) Manwaring.
    b. Nov. 21, 1838.   m. June 16, 1862.   d. Sep. 18, 1883.

Ruth H. Brown, da. James and Hannah (   ) Brown.
    b.

5 ch.   **Ella A.*, b. Mar. 12, 1863; m.   George Bartlett.
        Grace, b. May 17, 1867, d. Oct. 15, 1870.   *Florence*, b. Feb. 18, 1870.
        Edith, b. May 14, 1874.   *Myra*, b. Sep. 28, 1876, d. Feb. 1, 1877.
(*) Has had two ch., Alfred, b. Mar. 19, 1896; the other (first born) has died.

248.

LODOWICK H. MANWARING, s. Horace B. and Nancy A. (Havens) Manwaring.
    b. Oct, 21, 1840.   m. Oct. 19, 1872.   d. Dec. 21, 1893.

Mary E. Raynor, da. David and Hannah (Ross) Raynor.
    b. Oct. 13, 1856.

6 ch.   *Horace B.*, b. Jan. 1, 1875. *Arthur H.*, b. Sep. 16, 1876. *William H.*, b. Aug. 17, 1879.
        George, b. Jan. 23, 1884. *Nelson*, b. Aug. 14, 1886. *Elsie*, b. Dec. 19, 1889.

249.

GILES A. MANWARING, s. Horace B. and Nancy A. (Havens) Manwaring.
    b. Dec. 30, 1844.   m. Feb. 11, 1867.   d. Jan. 6, 1892.

Florence E. Carr, da. John and Lydia (   ) Carr.
    b.

4 ch.   **Giles E.*, b. Apr. 16, 1868, m. Oct. 9, 1892, †Ida Cornell.
        Leslie, b. Apr. 30, 1870, d. Sep. 5, 1872. *Halsey*, b. Oct. 14, 1875.
        William, b. June 11, 1877, d. Sep. 30, 1880.
(*) Has one ch., Giles M., b. Dec. 3, 1897.   (†) Daughter of Henry and Carrie Cornell.

250.

MARY L PENNY, da. George G. and Esther S. (Havens) Penny.
    b. May 2, 1841.   m. Apr. 30, 1868.

Daniel R. Cox, s. John and Fanny (Reeve) Cox.
    b. Sep. 6, 1844.

4 ch.   *Everett Cortland*, b. Oct. 6, 1869.
    361. *Quincy Ward*, b. May 29, 1872; m. Apr.   1896, Mary Louisa Scott.
        Fanny Esther, b. Nov. 6, 1874.   *Mabel Benjamin*, b. Mar. 26, 1882.

251.

LILLIAN FOSTENIA PENNY, da. George G. and Esther S. (Havens) Penny.
    b. Apr. 18, 1852.   m. Dec. 16, 1872.

Luther Benjamin Cox, s. Samuel and Bethiah (Reeve) Cox.
    b. Oct. 24, 1842.

2 ch.   *Harry Goldsmith*, b. Feb. 27, 1877.   *Shirley Gordon*, b. Apr. 15, 1883.

252.

GEORGE LODOWICK PENNY, s. George G. and Esther S. (Havens) Penny.
    b. Apr. 15, 1855.   m. 1st,   1877.   2d, Dec. 16, 1880.

1st, Mary Ella Squires, da. Alvin and Mary (Jennings) Squires.
    b. June 1854.   d. Aug. 1, 1879.

2d. Emma Jennings Squires, da. Alvin and Mary (Jennings) Squires.
    b. June 1852.

6 ch.   *Ella Squires*, b. July 31, 1879, d. Aug. 3, 1880.   *Mary Squires*, b. Oct. 16, 1881.
        Arthur Havens, b. Apr. 19, 1884.   *Edith*, b. Mar. 13, 1887.
        George Lodowick, b. July 9, 1889.   *Marjorie*, b. June 1, 1891.

253.

ALEXANDER CARTWRIGHT PENNY, s. George G. and Esther S. (Havens) Penny.
    b. July 16, 1859.   m. Apr. 4, 1883.

Julia Frances Reeve, da. James F. and May E. (Wines) Reeve.
    b. June 24, 1858.

4 ch.   *Clifford Adee*, b. Dec. 3, 1885.   *Alexis Clark*, b. Dec. 14, 1887.
        Harold Reeve, b. Aug. 12, 1890.   *Alice Thornton*, b. Apr. 21. 1893.

254.

MARY LUCINDA CONGDON, da. Samuel H. and C. Philena (Van Gandron) Congdon.
    b. July 14, 1847   m. June 4, 1879.

Richard Montgomery Johnston, s. George and Catherine (Austin) Johnston.
    b. Feb. 28, 1854.

2 ch.   *George Clarence*, b. Apr. 15, 1880.   *William Bathgate*, b. Dec. 18, 1887.

255.

JOHN CORNELIUS CONGDON, s. Samuel H. and C. Philena (Van Gandron) Congdon.
  b. Mar. 29, 1852.　　m. Oct. 18, 1875.
  Harriet Branard Ryder, da. James and Eliza (Sherman) Ryder.
  b. Jan. 24, 1852.
3 ch.　*George Wesley*, b. Oct. 23, 1879.　*Rachel R.*, b. Aug. 10, 1882, d. May 20, 1889.
  Ralph Havens, b. Sep. 6, 1890, d. Apr. 7, 1891.

256.

CHARLES ANDERSON CONGDON, s. Samuel H. and C. Philena (Van Gandron) Congdon.
  b. July 4, 1856.　　m. Apr. 21, 1887.
  Clara A. Harlow, da. Daniel and Elizabeth (Ryder) Harlow.
  b. Apr. 22, 1867.
2 ch.　*Maud E.*, b. Mar. 1, 1889.　*Lawrence Havens*, b. July 7, 1891.

257.

ELIZABETH S. HAVENS, da. Stratton M. and Lydia A. (Chester) Havens.
  b. Mar. 17, 1842.　　m. May 29, 1865.
  Samuel G. Clark, s. Samuel G. and Hannah (Young) Clark.
  b. Feb. 17, 1839.
1 ch. **362.** *Irving I.*, b. Mar. 2, 1869; m. Oct. 4, 1892, Alice Parliman.

258.

ADELAIDE M. HAVENS, da. Stratton M. and Lydia A. (Chester) Havens.
  b. Jan. 1, 1844.　　m. Sep. 29, 1868.
  David Y. Clark, s. Samuel G. and Hannah (Young) Clark.
  b. Sep. 6, 1845.
1 ch. **363.** *Clifford Young*, b. Sep. 21, 1872; m. Nov. 11, 1896, Phebe Elizabeth Halsey.

259.

CHESTER S. HAVENS, s. Stratton M. and Lydia A. (Chester) Havens.
  b. Nov. 7, 1846.　　m. Dec. 24, 1868.
  Ann Maria L. White, da. Matthew and Louise (Tryon) White.
  b. Dec. 11, 1848.
3 ch.　*Lillian*, b. Apr. 4, 1873, d. Mar.　1877.
  Tracy C., b. Jan. 9, 1876; m. Jan. 16, 1898, *Lillian Belle Homan.
  Matthew, b. Nov. 11, 1878.
(*) da. George F. and Jennie E. (Raynor) Homan, b. Aug. 13, 1874.

260.

REV. CHARLES E. HAVENS, s. Stratton M. and Lydia A. (Chester) Havens.
  b. Mar. 13, 1850.　　m. July 13, 1881.
  Ellen A. Hall, da. Rev. John H. and Julia (Gillespie) Hall.
  b. Aug. 20, 1852.
4 ch.　*Ralph Edgar*, b. Feb. 11, 1883.　*Elloine L.*, b. July 13, 1885.
  Leon C., b. Aug. 6, 1891.　　*Maurice*, b. Jan. 26, 1894.

261.

JAMES S. HARLOW, s. James M. and Abby M. (Osborn) Harlow.
  b. Dec. 24, 1840.　　m. Dec. 12, 1866.　d. Dec. 27, 1875.
  Sarah E. Dudley, da. James Dudley, of Bath, N. Y.
  b.
3 ch.　*{Clara O.*, b. Jan. 7, 1868, d. Mar. 19, 1868. $\left.\begin{array}{l}\textit{Augustus De Puyster,}\\ \text{A brother, d. unm.}\end{array}\right\}$ twins, b. Dec. 30, 1871.

262.

JULIA HARLOW, da. James M. and Abby M. (Osborn) Harlow.
  b. Aug. 8, 1843.　　m. in 1867.　d. Mar. 27, 1878.
  F. Stuart Gray, of York, New York.
  b.
5 ch.　*Marion*, b. Jan. 8, 1868.　　*Ruth*, b. Aug. 12, 1869.
  Ralph S., b. May 14, 1873, d. Feb. 14, 1874.　*Abby*, b. Nov. 9, 1874; d. Nov. 15, 1875.
  Benjamin S., b. Feb. 8, 1878, d. Apr. 21, 1878.

263.

BENJAMIN F. HARLOW, s. James M. and Abby M. (Osborn) Harlow.
  b. May 12, 1854.　　m. Nov. 4, 1880.
  Anna C. Brown, of Shortsville, N. Y.
  b. Jan. 28, 1858.　d. June 2, 1885.
2 ch.　*H. Loyd*, b. June 5, 1882, d. Apr. 9, 1884.　*Hazel V.*, b.　　d. June 2, 1885.

264.

DANIEL O. Harlow, s. James M. and Abby M. (Osborn) Harlow.
   b. Aug. 8, 1847.   m. Mar. 23, 1875.   d. Apr. 2, 1893.

   Eugenia Sheldon, da. Chauncey Sheldon, of Shortsville, N. Y.
   b.

3 ch.   *James C.*, b. Jan. 11, 1876.   *Ruth*, b. Apr. 9, 1877.   *Cortland V.*, b. Dec. 12, 1882.

265.

CARRIE E. HARLOW, da. Charles and Ency J. (Reeve) Harlow.
   b. Aug. 29, 1860.   m. Apr. 7, 1891.

   William S. Hubbard, s. Nathaniel E. and Elizabeth (Raynor) Hubbard.
   b. Apr. 7, 1858.

1 ch.   *Charles S.*, b. Aug. 21, 1895.

266.

DAVID HORTON MULFORD, s. Alva S. and Bethiah (Horton) Mulford.
   b. Oct. 7, 1830.   m. Apr. 5, 1855.   d. Oct. 5, 1892.

   Emma Holden Gilder, da. Rev. John L. and Emma (Holden) Gilder.
   b. July 1836.

5 ch.   *Nellie Corse*, b. June 1856, d. June 1858.   *Florence*, b. Aug. 29, 1858.
         Mabel, b.   1860, d. in infancy.
         Leonard Stratton, b. July 19, 1862; m. Apr. 5, 1887, Alice Holbrook.
         Kate, b.   1870, d. in infancy.
(*) Has three ch., Marjorie, b. Apr. 25, 1888; Beatrice, b. Nov. 8, 1889, and Holbrook, b. Sep. 2, 1892.

267.

MARY CATHERINE MULFORD, da. Alva S. and Bethiah (Horton) Mulford.
   b. Apr. 24, 1841.   m. June 9, 1862.

   Daniel Edward Davis, s. Samuel and Lucy (Edwards) Davis.
   b.

5 ch.   *Arthur Mulford*, b. Apr. 1, 1863, d. May 1882.   *Robert Winthrop*, b. Oct. 24, 1871.
         Lillian, b. Feb. 1865, d. Dec. 1867. *Alva B.*, b. Feb. 24, 1877.   *Lucy P.*, b. Dec. 23, 1878.

268.

ISABELLA LUCRETIA MULFORD, da. Alva S. and Bethiah (Horton) Mulford.
   b. Dec. 1, 1849.   m. June 14, 1870.

   Samuel Irving Mitchell, s. Jesse and Mary V. (Coulter) Mitchell.
   b. Oct. 5, 1837.

4 ch.   *May*, b. May 2, 1871, d. May 2, 1871.   *Daisy Isabelle*, b. Mar. 17, 1874.
         Catherine Mulford, b. July 24, 1876.   *Jesse Myron*, b. July 19, 1894.

269.

JOHN ISAACS DAVENPORT, s. Amzi B. and Frances M. (Isaacs) Davenport.
   b. May 16, 1843.   m. Nov. 14, 1866.

   Louise E. Post, da. Dr. Louis Post, of St. Louis.
   b.

4 ch.   *Louis Post*, b. Sep. 4, 1867.   *Benjamin Butler*, b. May 16, 1871.
         John Havens, b. Jan. 21, 1873, d.   *May*, b. Aug. 3, 1874; m.

270.

ALBERT BARNES DAVENPORT, s. Amzi B. and Frances M. (Isaacs) Davenport.
   b. Apr, 3, 1845.   m. Nov. 24, 1868.

   Delia M. Crofut, da. Henry Crofut, of Danbury, Conn.
   b. Nov. 18, 1848.

2 ch.   *Albert Shelton*, b. Mar. 26, 1872.   *Laura Nichols*, b. Apr. 3, 1875.

271.

CHARLES MARKUS GRIFFING, s. Charles C. and Anna M. (Havens) Griffing.
   b. Mar. 20, 1838.   m. Nov. 14, 1864.

   Abigail T. Cartwright, da. Benjamin C. and Hannah M. (Tuthill) Cartwright.
   b. Dec. 24, 1841.

4 ch. **364.** *Lulu Terry*, b. Apr. 1, 1866; m. Dec. 28, 1886, George A. Griffin.
      365. *Royal Markus*, b. Dec. 1, 1874; m. Jan. 19, 1895, Clara Juvette Edwards.
         Floyd Cartwright, b. Oct. 4, 1880.   *Benjamin Lawrence*, b. July 16, 1885.

272.

ELLEN HOUSE, da. Ezekiel and Hannah (Osborn) House.
   b. Nov. 14, 1855.   m.

   Henry D. Hedges, s. Stephen L. and Minerva (Cartwright) Hedges.
   b. Nov. 14, 1854.

3 ch.   *Fanny P.*, b. Sep. 14, 1877.   *Henry H.*, b. July 28, 1885.
         Phillip L., b. June 20, 1888, d. Sep., 1888.

273.

SARAH DAYTON, da. Dr. John H. and Frances J. (Nichols) Dayton.
    b. Apr. 2, 1838.   m. Dec. 23, 1874.

Richard Lay Hull, s. Alfred.   Hull.
    b.

2 ch.   *Alfred*, b. May 7, 1868, d. an infant.
        **Une*, b. Nov. 9, 1876; m. Oct. 12, 1897, Francis Edward Greene.
(*) Has one ch., John Dayton, b. July 8, 1898.

274.

FREDERICK LORD DAYTON, s. Dr. John H. and Frances J. (Nichols) Dayton.
    b. Apr. 13, 1840.   m. Aug. 26, 1865.

Almira Olds Reeder, of Muscatina, Iowa.
    b.

1 ch.   *John Havens*, b. Feb. 2, 1869; m. Apr. 14, 1896, Nancy Maupin Reed.

275.

MARIA JOSEPHINE SMITH, da. Richard P. and Betsy S. (Dayton) Smith.
    b. May 15, 1845.   m. Aug. 14, 1867.

Morgan Pierson, of Clinton, Conn.
    b.

3 ch.   *John Dayton*, b. July 17, 1876, d. Jan 12, 1877.   *Mary Morgan*, b. Aug. 16, 1878.
        George Havens, b. Feb. 27, 1883.

276.

EDWIN BROWN HAVENS, s. Joseph C. and Hannah M. (Brown) Havens.
    b. Jan. 19, 1847.   m. Oct. 5, 1870.

Maria Elizabeth Scholes, da. Frederick and Ann M. (Boyce) Scholes.
    b. Sep. 9, 1848.

3 ch.   *Frederick Joseph*, b. Nov. 27, 1871; m. Feb. 25, 1896, *Gertrude May Smith.
        Clayton Scholes, b. Dec, 10, 1876, d. July 25, 1877.   *Charles Scholes*, b. Mar. 28, 1880.
(*) da. of John and May A. (Sherman) Smith, b. July 2, 1875.

277.

JOSEPH A. HAVENS, s. Benedict and   Havens.
    b.   m.

Kate Bennet, da.
    b.

2 ch. 366. *Mary J.*, b. Oct. 25, 1869. m. July 16, 1889, Tunis R. Barns.
        **Charles A.*, b. Sep. 28, 1871; m. Aug.   1896, Mary Sampson.
(*) Has 1 ch., Catherine H.

278.

JULIA ADELINE CARTWRIGHT, da. David and Sarah A. (Havens) Cartwright.
    b.   m.   d.

Daniel Atwood Eldridge, s.
    b.

8 ch.   *Ella Wentworth*, b.   m.   Lawrence Bogart.
        **Henry Cartwright*, b.   m.   Mary Hull.
        Daniel Atwood, b.   d.
        †*Addie Lucretia*, b.   m.   Winfield Walkley.
        ‡*Pheobe Josephine*, b.   m.   Palmer Townsend.
        §*Frank Stutzer*, b.   m.   Emma Snyder.
        ‖*Charles Randolph*, b.   m.   Mary Forman.   *Hanford Wentworth*, b.
(*) Has 6 ch., Daniel (Maud, Henry, Mary are d.), Julia A. and Frank.   (†) Has 1 ch., Clarence.
(‡) Has 1 ch., Atwood Halsey.   (§) Has 1 ch., Dorothy.   (‖) Has 1 ch., Harold.

279.

FRANCES M. HAVENS, da. Sylvanus B. and Bethiah M. (Havens) Havens.
    b. Sep. 1, 1843.   m. Apr. 15, 1875.

Eugene Havens Mulligan, s. Patrick and Margaret (Gallhager) Mulligan.
    b. June 9, 1850.

1 ch.   *Genie H.*, b. Feb. 28, 1876, d. Sep. 21, 1880.

280.

SYLVANUS M. HAVENS, s. Sylvanus B. and Bethiah M. (Havens) Havens.
    b. May 17, 1846.   m.   1872.   d. July   1883.

Kate Condon, of New London, Conn.
    b.

5 ch.   *Johanna*, b. d. July 19, 1893, ae. 36.   *John J.*, b. 1874.   *Edward*, b. 1877, d. 1895.
        Frances R., b. Aug. 18, 1879.   *Joseph S.*, b. June 8, 1881.

281.

MARIA HAVENS, da. Charles A. and Phebe (Tuthill) Havens.
    b. Mar. 21, 1843.   m. Aug. 24, 1864.

Jesse B. Edwards, s. Nathaniel and Irene (Bennet) Edwards.
    b. Oct. 14, 1835.

4 ch.   *Ella T.*, b. July 22, 1865.
    367. *Clinton H.*, b. Nov. 22, 1866; m. June 5, 1895, Mamie E. Ward.
        Carrie B., b. June 21, 1874.   *Lena M.*, b. July 18, 1878.

282.

MARY HAVENS, da. Charles A. and Phebe (Tuthill) Havens.
  b. Nov. 1, 1849.   m. Nov. 22, 1877.
  William Blinn, s. Wardsworth and Jane E. (Tryon) Blinn.
  b.
  1 ch.   *Jennie Maria*, b. Oct. 20, 1878.

283.

HELEN HAVENS, da. Jacob and Ann E. (Hamilton) Havens.
  b. Mar. 11, 1843.   m. 1st,   1860.   2d, May 1, 1881.
  1st, George A. Oaks, s. Cornelius and Hannah (Tuthill) Oaks.
  b.   1842.   d. Mar.   1880.
  2d, William H. Brown, s.
  b.
  3 ch. **368.** *Anna A.*, b. Aug. 3, 1865; m. Mar. 24, 1889, David H. Hamilton.
        Celia Emma, b. Oct. 13, 1883.   *Grace May*, b. June 25, 1885.

284.

ANN MARIA HAVENS, da. John S. and Nancy (Torrey) Havens.
  b. Apr. 6, 1829.   m. June 1, 1853.   d. Sep. 13, 1888.
  Thomas P. Bundy, s. Ezra S. and Helen M. (Patrick) Bundy.
  b. May 20, 1831.
  2 ch. **369.** *Susan Adelaide*, b. Apr. 10. 1854; m. Oct. 7, 1891, Horace N. Plummer.
        Helen Elmira, b. Apr. 4, 1856.

285.

ELMIRA AMANDA HAVENS, da. John S. and Nancy (Torrey) Havens.
  b. Feb. 19, 1835.   m. Oct. 6, 1858.
  George W. Stickney, s. Charles and Sarah M. (Fairchild) Stickney.
  b. Aug. 22, 1833.
  8 ch.   *George Parkhurst*, b. May 28, 1859. d. July 27, 1859.
        Charles Henry, b. May 28, 1859, d. Aug. 10, 1859.
        Ella Luida, b. July 5, 1860, d. Oct. 3, 1861.
        Henrietta Havens, b. Aug. 25, 1862, d. Aug. 28, 1865.
  370. *Minnie Foster*, b. July 14. 1864; m. Oct. 17, 1888, James S. Marshall.
        George Washington, b. July 19, 1866, d. Oct. 15. 1866.
        Anna Grace. b. Nov. 17, 1867; m. June 1, 1887, *John S. McNeal; no issue.
        Herbert Walter, b. July 9, 1870; m. Jan. 26, 1898, °Clara J. Potter.
  (*) s. Charles F. and Margaret (Sott) McNeal, b. Jan. 20, 1864.
  (°) da. Thomas and Isabella (Chisholm) Potter, b. Oct. 5, 1869.

286.

ELIZABETH M. HAVENS, da. Archibald R. and Caroline A. (Hughes) Havens.
  b. Mar. 29, 1843.   m. Nov. 30, 1879. (as his 2d wife.)
  Caleb Dawson, s. Caleb and Charlotte (Maplestone) Dawson.
  b. Apr. 23, 1837.
  3 ch.   *Carrie H.*, b. Oct. 21 1876, d. in infancy.   *Carrie Havens*, b. Aug. 5, 1879.
        Fanny Griffing, b. July 21, 1881.

287.

WILLIAM G. HAVENS. s. Archibald R. and Caroline A. (Hughes) Havens.
  b. Oct. 24, 1853.   m. June 3, 1891.
  Isabelle C. Reynolds, da. Austin L. and Mary E. (Cornell) Reynolds.
  b. Feb. 8, 1858.
  2. ch.   *Archibald Reynolds*, b. June 17, 1892, d. July 29, 1892.
        William Gleason, b. Apr. 22, 1894, d. Apr. 22, 1894.

288.

JOHN C. WELLS. s. John C. and Phebe (Havens) Wells.
  b. May 25, 1838.   m.
  Margaret Callahan, da. Bryan and Julia (   ) Callahan.
  b. May 26, 1841.
  2 ch.   *John C.*, b. July 10, 1868.   *George B.*, b. Feb. 6, 1870.

289.

SIDNEY P. HAVENS, s. Obadiah and Mary A. (Cowles) Havens.
  b. Oct. 26, 1844.   m. Aug. 11, 1868.
  Alice G. Vail, da. Halsey   Vail.
  b.
  1 ch.   *Roy Vail*, b. March 8, 1874, d. May 9, 1874.

290.

ASHER WICKHAM HAVEN, s Obadiah and Mary A. (Cowles) Havens.
b. Mar. 24, 1862. m. in 1893.

Harriet B. Lester, da. James W. and Sarah F. (Loper) Lester.
b. July 4, 1875.

2 ch. *William H.*, b. Jan. 1, 1894. *Mary Isabella*, b. Sep. 2, 1896.

291.

ARABELLA MELLISSA MILLER, da. Don Alonzo and Clarissa F. (Havens) Miller.
b. Dec. 5. 1844. m. 1863.

Loren C. Terry, s.
b.

3 ch. **Clara Bell*, b. m. Clinton Ripley. °*Yula*, b. m. Isaac White.
  Arrebell, b. m. Frank Forbes.
(*) Has 3 ch., Sherman, Bradford and Kenneth.
(°) d. in 1894, ae. 22, had 1 ch., Raymond Terry.

292.

SARAH CANFIELD MILLER, da. Don Alonzo and Clarissa F. (Havens) Miller.
b. June 20, 1847. m. 1865.

Henry G. Hewlett. s.
b.

3 ch. **Alice Bell*, b. m. Clayton Woodward. *Roy*, b. *Alonzo*, b.
(*) Has 2 ch., Marion and Robert.

293.

IDA W. HAVENS, da. Henry M. and Frances D. (Ross) Havens.
b. Apr. 8. 1849. m. Aug. 26, 1866.

George Dutcher, s. Samuel and Esther M. (Fields) Dutcher.
b. Nov. 22, 1847.

4 ch. °*Samuel S.*, b. Mar. 8, 1868; m. June 22, 1892, Sarah Wilson.
  *Henry H., b. Sep. 23, 1871; m. Oct. 28, 1891, Lola Green
  Frank F., b. July 13. 1875; m. Nov. 1897, May Palmer.
  Walter H., b. May 26, 1877.
(*) Has one son, Wesley. (°) Has a son named Clifford, b. Apr. 8, 1893.

294.

SARAH A. HAVENS, da. Henry M. and Frances D. (Ross) Havens.
b. Feb. 16. 1866. m. Feb. 16, 1886.

William Litell, s. John and Amanda (Tompkins) Litell.
b.

3 ch. *Alice A.*, b. Jan. 8, 1888, d. Nov. 13, 1894. *Minnie H.*, b. May 9, 1894.
  Stafford A., b. Jan. 6, 1896.

295.

ASHER C. HAVENS, s. Henry M. and Frances D. (Ross) Havens.
b. Jan. 21, 1868. m. Feb. 7, 1894.

Mamie F. Collard, da. Steven Collard.
b.

3 ch. *Beatrice D.*, b. Aug. 16, 1895. *Ruth A.*, b. Mar. 14, 1897. *Titus R.*, b. July 30, 1898.

296.

ELIZABETH MUSSEY RAMSDELL, da. Charles and Elizabeth (Fosdick) Ramsdell.
b. Mar. 15, 1847. m. Nov. 17, 1871.

Edward Miller Ketcham, s. Alonzo R. and Sarah (Hinsdale) Ketcham.
b. Feb. 5, 1844.

3 ch. *Edith Ramsdell*, b. Aug. 6, 1872. *Howard Platt*, b. Dec. 4, 1878.
  Charles Ramsdell, b. Dec. 8, 1882.

297.

HENRY THOMAS RAMSDELL, s. Henry and Mary A. (Mussey) Ramsdell.
b. Mar 26, 1855. m. June 11, 1884.

Kate Hoyt Miller, da. Charles and Louise L. (Noxon) Miller.

4 ch. *Mary Louise*, b. Jan. 27, 1887. *Charles Miller*, b Mar. 23, 1985.
  Henry Thomas, b. Oct. 17, 1891. *Frederick Gillette*, b. Sept. 3. 1896.

298.

LORIN PINCKNEY WALDO RAMSDELL, s. Henry and Mary A. (Mussey) Ramdsell.
b. Nov. 4, 1859. m. Feb. 19, 1889.

Lucy Story, da. Samuel and Mary C. (Dayton) Story.

3 ch. *Eleanor Story*, b. May 7, 1891. *Dorothy A.*, b. Aug 11, 1893.
  Samuel Story, b. July 6, 1896.

299.

WILLIAM M. RAMSDELL, s. Henry and Mary A. (Mussey) Ramsdell.
  b. July 13, 1864.   m. Mar 15, 1894.

*Margaret Scott Adam, da. John and Jean F. (Adam) Scott.
  b.

3 ch.   *Margaret Adam*, b. Feb 5, 1895.   *Grace Harriet*, b. May 8, 1896.
    Robert Adam, b. June 12, 1898.

(*) Was adopted by her uncle, R. B. Adam, upon which she changed her name from Scott to Adam.

300.

JANE LETITIA ASH, da. Horace T. and Martha P. (Mussey) Ash.
  b. June 2, 1852.   m. Sep. 13 1871.

Robert Dyas Massie, s. William J. B. and Elizabeth G. (Ashton) Massie.
  b. May 8, 1849.

4 ch.   *Horace Floyd*, b. Jan. 10, 1874.
    371. *Emily Benton*, b. July 30, 1877; m. July 30, 1896, James J. Farrell.
    Robert Dyas, b. Jan. 22, 1884.   *Charles Henry*, b. Feb. 21, 1886.

301.

FREDERICK BOWEN CROWLEY, s. Rodney R. and Jane H. (Mussey) Crowley.
  b. Aug. 19, 1865.   m. June 29, 1891.

Clara Lillie Hall, da. John and Mary A. (Merredyth) Hall. ·
  b. Feb. 14, 1870.

1 ch.   *Rodney Edward*, b. Sep. 14, 1892.

302.

SAMUEL FOSDICK JONES, s. Nicoll F. and Deborah (Merwin) Jones.
  b. Feb. 18, 1867.   m. Feb. 22, 1888.

Hattie M. Couch, da. Samuel and Viaren (Woodward) Couch.
  b. June 15, 1869.

2 ch.   *Mary Evalyn*, b. June 5, 1892.   *Avonia L.*, b. Aug. 11, 1894.

303.

CORA M. GANUNG, da. William H. and Abby M. (Jones) Ganung.
  b. Mar. 16, 1868.   m.   1894.

Oliver Howard Galbraith, s. Isaiah J. and Sarah J. (Smith) Galbraith.
  b. June 19, 1871.

3 ch.   *John Eldredge*, b. Feb. 17, 1895.   *Nicoll Fosdick*, b. May 19, 1896.
    William Jones, b. July 21, 1897.

304.

RICHARD CALVIN FOSDICK, s. Orville and Hannah (McCollock) Fosdick.
  b. May 20, 1850.   m. Oct. 3, 1883.

Mary Ellen Mullen, da. James and Ann (Pegnam) Mullen.
  b.

5 ch.   *Rachel Ann*, b. Feb. 5, 1885.   A da., b. Mar 13, 1886, d. at birth.
    Mary Elizabeth, b. Aug. 26, 1888, d. July 6, 1889.
    Ralph Abraham, b. July 1, 1894, d. July 3, 1894.   *Esther Mullen*, b. July 13, 1895.

305.

SARAH FINNEY, da. Alonzo and Olive A. (Fosdick) Finney.
  b. Dec. 27, 1845.   m. Jan. 1, 1865.

John Imhoff, s.
  b.

10 ch.   *Frank*, b. Mar. 21, 1866; m.   *Clark*, b. Oct. 6, 1867.
    Ida, b. Jan. 12, 1869, d. Sep. 18, 1869.   *George*, b. Feb. 10, 1870, d. Sep. 23, 1870.
    John, b. May 31, 1872.   *William*, b. Mar. 7, 1874.   *Millie M.*, b. Dec. 1, 1875.
    Earnest, b. Sep. 13, 1877, d. Oct. 12, 1877.
    Marley, b. Feb, 16, 1879, d. July 26, 1879.   *Jacob*, b. Sep. 1, 1881.

306.

ALICE HACKLEY, da. Samuel and Laura A. (Fosdick) Hackley.
  b. Oct. 13, 1848.   m.   1865.

Thomas Hendryx, s.
  b.

7 ch.   *Emma*, b.   1866; m.   M. Fields.   *Samuel*, b.   1867.   *Dana*, b.   1869.
    John, b.   1871.   *Clyde*, b.   1874.   *William*, b.   1879.   *Hester*, b.   1882.

307.

GERTRUDE HUBBARD HORSFORD, da. Eben N. and Mary L'H. (Gardiner) Horsford.
  b. July 9, 1852.   m. June 20, 1878.

Andrew Fiske, s. Augustus H. and Hannah (Bradford) Fiske.
  b. June 4, 1854.

6 ch.   *Gertrude Horsford*, b. Apr. 16, 1879.   *Augustus Henry*, b. May 28, 1880.
        Eben Norton Horsford, b. May 6, 1883.   *Gardiner Horsford*, b. Sept. 14, 1892.
        Cornelia Horsford, b. Aug. 20, 1895.   *Hannah Bradford*, b. Sep. 22, 1897.

308.

MARY GARDINER HORSFORD, da. Eben N. and Mary L'H. (Gardiner) Horsford.
    b. Aug. 27, 1855.   m. Oct. 24, 1877.   d.   1893.

Benjamin Robbins Curtis, s. Benjamin R. and Anna (Curtis) Curtis.
    b. June 8, 1855.   d. Jan. 21, 1891.

3 ch.   *Benjamin Robbins*, b. Aug. 13, 1878.   *Mary Gardiner*, b. July 5, 1879.
      Helena Pelham, b. Oct. 3, 1880.

309.

GERALD RENSSELAER MCDOWELL, da. John A. and Geraldine (Cowles) McDowell.
    b. Feb. 6, 1854.   m. June 26, 1894.

Helen S. Bain, da. Lewis and Sarah (Frary) Bain.
    b.

1 ch.   *Lewis B. A* , b. Sep. 15, 1895.

310.

MALCOLM HECTOR MCDOWELL, s. John A. and Geraldine (Cowles) McDowell.
    b. Nov. 15, 1857.   m. June 6, 1889.

Maud Stowe, of Brattleboro, Vermont.
    b.

2 ch.   *Adair*, b. May 30, 1890.   *Geraldine Gerry*, b. Sep. 29, 1891.

311.

JEDIDIAH HUNTINGTON, s. John G. and Mary (Isham) Huntington.
    b. Aug. 7. 1837.   m   d. Oct. 9. 1885.

Annie E. Hazard, da. Carder and Eliza (Watson) Hazard.
    b.

2 ch.   **Annie*, b.   m.   William F. Davis.
      °Lillian, b.   m.   Henry M. Hills.
(*) Has one ch., Marion H., b. July 3, 1889.   (°) Has one ch., Huntington, b. July 23, 1892.

312.

HELEN JACKSON, da. Alonzo C. and Dora A. (Mumford) Jackson.
    b. May 30, 1851.   m. Oct. 21, 1875.

John T. M. Rowland, s. Isaac and Catherine A. (Mason) Rowland.
    b. Mar 9, 1844.

5 ch.   *Dora Mumford*, b. July 2, 1876.   *Stevens Thomson*, b. July 3, 1880.
      Gertrude Franchot, b. July 6, 1882.
      Armistead Thomson, b. Apr. 23, 188–, d. Oct. 16, 1887.   *Alonzo C. J.*, b. July 19, 1894.

313.

BERTHA STRONG NORTHROP, da. Charles B. and Margaret H. (Mumford) Northrop.
    b. Mar. 28, 1870.   m. May 16, 1891.   d. Feb. 3, 1895.

Edward Orr, s.
    b.

3 ch.   *Margaret Mary*, b. Mar. 19, 1892.   *Edward*, b. Nov. 27, 1893.
      Bertha Gertrude, b. Feb. 2, 1895.

314.

HANNAH ROSINA HAVENS, da. Jeremiah J. and Mary B. (Rowland) Havens.
    b.   m.

George Lawson Benjamin, s. Nathan and Mary A. (Howell) Benjamin.
    b.

1 ch. 372. *Hampton H.*, b. Jan. 13, 1871; m. July 4, 1891, Edna S. Woodhull.

315.

WILLIAM HAMPTON HAVENS, s. Jeremiah J. and Mary B. (Rowland) Havens.
    b. Aug. 19, 1842.   m. Sep. 11, 1864.

Louisa Park, of Greenport, New York.
    b.

2 ch.   *William Henry*, b. Aug. 18, 1872; m.   Lena Blanche Tieter.
      Edward Coit, b. Dec. 17, 1875.

316.

DAVID ANDREW HAVENS, s. William and Betsey (Jackson) Havens.
    b. June 14, 1841.   m. Aug. 10, 1861.   d. Nov. 17, 1874.

Marietta L'Hommedieu, da. Joseph B. and Susan P. (Higby) L'Hommedieu.
    b. July 23, 1840.   d. Jan. 20, 1882.

3 ch. 373. *Meriam E.*, b. Apr. 4, 1865; m. July 8, 1885, Charles A. Day.
    374. *Gracie May*, b. Apr. 3, 1867; m. Nov. 29, 1885, William B. Newton.
      Joseph Ellsworth, b. Feb. 6, 1868, d. Feb. 17, 1868.

317.

SARAH EMMA HAVENS, da. William and Betsey (Jackson) Havens.
  b.   m. 1st.   2d.

  1st, James J. Verity, s. Obadiah and Sarah (   ) Verity.
  b.
  2d, John Loving.
  b.
  4 ch. by 1st hus. *Lena M., b. Nov.   1871; m.   William Walker.
              Nathan Verity, b. Jan. 4, 1874; m. July 3, 1897, Martha E. Nesbitt.
              Walter, b.   d.   Ernest, b.   d.
(*) Has 1 ch., William.

318.

JULIET WHITE, da. Samuel and Fanny (Havens) White.
  b. Nov. 8, 1833.   m.   d. June 9, 1884.

James H. Reeves.
  b.
  11 ch.   William S., b.   James H., b.   David, b.   Edward, b.
            George E., b. June 1, 1856; m. Dec. 27, 1885, Ida M. Peckham.
            *Fanny M., b.   m.   William Clark; no issue.
            Adelaide M., b.   m.   William Phillips.
            Jennie b..   Two others, who d.
(*) d.

319.

Mary E. White, da. Samuel and Fanny (Havens) White.
  b. May 28, 1835.   m.   d. Jan. 27, 1874.

John T. Skidmore, s. John A. and   Skidmore.
  b.
  7 ch.   James H., b.   d. young.   Edgar, b.   d. young.   Charles A., b.   1857, d.
            Ida Bell, b.   m.   Fred   English.
            Hattie, b.   m.   Samuel McKeaver, Glen Cove.
            Annie M., b.   d. unm.   George E., b.

320.

HENRY H. WHITE, s. Samuel and Fanny (Havens) White.
  b. Sep. 1, 1841.   m. Jan. 11, 1867.

Abigail Hubbard, da. Henry and Nancy (Marshall) Hubbard.
  b. June 30, 1845.
  9 ch.   *Fannie H., b. Feb. 15, 1869; m.   Franklin Robinson.
            James H., b. Sep. 29, 1872, d.
            Alice M., b. Sep. 29, 1872; m. Mar.   1898, Edward Rowley.
            John H., b. May 16, 1874.   Samuel E., b. Aug. 21. 1876.
            Arthur T., b. Aug. 20, 1878.   Washington, b. Apr. 22, 1880.
            Frederick S., b. Dec. 20, 1882.   Etta S., b. Oct. 19, 1888.
(*) Has had 4 ch., Percy, Harold who died, Mabel, and Ralph Henry.

321.

DAVID OLIVER PETTY, s. David and Hannah (Havens) Petty.
  b. Dec. 25, 1848.   m. Feb. 6, 1870.

Sarah Jane Newey, da. Charles and May (Darling) Newey.
  b. June 1, 1848.
  6 ch. 375. Oliver Walestine, b. Dec. 24, 1870; m. Mar. 31, 1895, Grace H. Smiley.
            Millie Briggs, b. Nov. 3, 1872.   Ada Reast, b. Oct. 6, 1874.
            Frederick M., b. Dec. 7, 1876, d. Mar. 17, 1886
            Lillie Janet, b. Dec. 6, 1878; m. Apr. 10, 1898, *Elliott R. L'Hommedieu.
            Arthur Eldredge, b. Nov. 27. 1887.
(*) Son of Daniel and   (Bunce) L'Hommedieu, b. Sep.,   1877.

322.

MINNIE ETTA PETTY, da. David and Hannah (Havens) Petty.
  b. Oct. 23, 1863.   m. Oct. 10, 1880.

Charles L. Newey, s. Charles and Mary (Darling) Newey.
  b. June 27, 1856.
  1 ch.   Ethel R., b. May 26, 1884.

323.

EDWARD SHEPARD HAVENS, s. Daniel S. and Harriet L. (Fanning) Havens.
  b. June 15, 1852.   m. Jan. 27, 1871.

Alice K. Stubbs, da. Charles and Angeline (Seaman) Stubbs.
  b. Oct. 13, 1854.
  7 ch.   *De Forrest E., b. Nov. 20, 1871; m. June 15, 1893, Mabel Highmam.
            Charles E., b. Feb. 3, 1873.   Percey Shepard, b. July 1, 1878, d. Nov. 27, 1883.
            Edgar Glen, b. Oct. 4, 1880.   Hattie M., b. Mar. 4, 1883.
            Amos Barton and Carl Duncan, twins, b. June 15, 1886.
(*) Has 2 ch., Mabel, b. June 1894, and Olive Kenyon.

324.

ULMAN ROSE HAVENS, s. Daniel S. and Harriet L. (Fanning) Havens.
b. June 28, 1854.   m. Jan. 9, 1874.

Ida. W Albertson, da. William and Martha (Terry) Albertson.
b. Mar. 19, 1853.

4 ch. *Gracie A.*, b. Apr. 1880, d. May 9, 1895. *Daniel*, b. Mar. 1882, d. Aug. 27, 1887.
Martha A., b. Mar. 21, 1885. *Le Roy*, b. June 6, 1889.

325.

GEORGE LESLIE HAVENS, s. Walter F. and Phebe A. (Tuthill) Havens.
b. Jan. 19, 1859.   m. May 30, 1895.

Mary Belle Drake, da. Almon L. and Ann A. (Squires) Drake.
b. Sep. 20, 1867.

1 ch. *Walter Kenneth*, b. June 13, 1896.

326.

ANNIE MAY HAVENS, da. Walter F. and Phebe A. (Tuthill) Havens.
b. Sep. 21, 1868.   m. June 18, 1895.

Israel Denton Luce, s. N. Alfred and Theressa A. (Conklin) Luce.
b. Nov. 4, 1863.

1 ch. *Genevieve A.*, b. Oct. 7, 1897.

327.

CHAUNCEY M. HAVENS, s. Manasseh and Elizabeth (Tuthill) Havens.
b. Dec. 9, 1853.   m. 1st, Jan. 8, 1876.   2d, Feb. 20, 1886.

1st, Louise Carter, da. Tuthill and Charity (Squires) Carter.
b. Jan. 24, 1859.   d. July 8, 1885.

2d, Mary A. Squires, da. Harvey and Jemima (Fanning) Squires.
b. Feb. 2, 1857.

9 ch. *Frederick C.*, b. Nov. 14, 1876. *Elizabeth*, b. Sep. 10, 1882. *Louisa*, b. June 27, 1885.
Edward M., b. Nov. 26, 1886. *Mary A.*, b. June 5, 1888, d. Aug. 8. 1888
Rebecca A., b. June 3, 1889, d. Nov. 15, 1889. *Irving T.*, b. Apr. 28. 1890.
Frank G., b. Oct. 17, 1891, d. Aug. 10. 1892. *Natalie M.*, b. May 7, 1894.

328.

DANIEL MADISON HAVENS, s. Manasseh and Elizabeth (Tuthill) Havens.
b. May 19, 1858.   m. Dec. 19, 1880.

Georgiana Edwards, da. Spafford and Mary S. (Raynor) Edwards.
b. Oct. 17, 1863.

5 ch. *Leslie W.*, b. July 19, 1882. *Mary Sophia*, b. July 18, 1884.
Everett E., b. Mar. 31, 1887. *Florence M.*, b. Apr. 23, 1889. *Cora*, b. May 25, 1895.

329.

JOHN HENRY BROWN, s. John B. and Betsey M. (Tuthill) Brown.
b. Apr. 22, 1852.   m. Dec. 8, 1875.

Lydia Terry, da. William T. and Julia (Case) Terry.
b.

2 ch. *Julia Edna*, b. Mar. 18, 1879. *Eva Angeline*, b. July 18. 1882.

330.

EDWARD BEEKMAN UNDERHILL, s. Edward B. and Lydia F. (Kip) Underhill.
b. June 8, 1859.   m. Mar. 13. 1896.

Kate Isaacson, da.   and Virginia (Caldwell) Isaacson.
b.   1878.

1 ch. *Lydia Virginia*, b. Dec. 5. 1897.

331.

RAWSON UNDERHILL, s. Edward B. and Lydia F. (Kip) Underhill.
b. Sep. 27, 1861.   m. June 11, 1880.

Jessie Crowley, da. James and Mary (Mills) Crowley.
b.   1863.

2 ch. *Rawson Kip*, b. Mar. 13, 1881. *Dorothy Edna*, b. Oct. 7. 1885.

332.

JACOB BERRY UNDERHILL, s. Edward B. and Lydia F. (Kip) Underhill.
b. May 27. 1867.   m. Nov. 2, 1892.

Elizabeth Aldrich, da. William Aldrich, of New York City.
b.   1871.

2 ch. *Jacob Berry*, b. Aug. 19. 1893. *William Beekman*, b. Sep. 9. 1896.

333.

PHOEBE B. SEARING, da. Silas C. and Frances D. (Valentine) Searing.
b.   m.

Daniel Van Velsor, s.
b.

2 ch.   *Annie Augusta, b.   m.   Sidney B. Walters.
         °Florence N., b.   m.   Sylvanus S. Hayden.
(*) Has 4 ch., Belmont S., Howard, Florence N. and Arthur V.
(°) Has 2 ch., Sylvia A. and Raymond L.

334.

HARRIET A. SEARING, da. Silas C. and Frances D. (Valentine) Searing.
         b.   m.

William E. Townsend, s.
         b.

1 ch.   *Rosa Belle, b.   m.   Dr. C. H. G. Steinsieck.
(*) Has 2 ch., William T. and Egbert C.

335.

JAMES W. CHATMAN, s. Alfred F. and Catherine A. (Davis) Chatman.
         b. Mar. 7, 1841.   m. Dec. 25, 1861.

Sarah L. Annin, da. William and Catherine (Goetchins) Annin.
         b.
6 ch.   *Kate L., b. Oct. 1, 1862.   m. Dec. 25, 1885, W. Scott Boyenton.
         Alene F., b. May 18, 1865.   William A., b. May 30, 1867.
         °Florence, b. Nov.   1872.   m. Nov.   1895, Harold Kelley.
         Grace B., b. Aug.   1881.   Amy, b. Sep.   1885.
(*) Has 2 ch., Alene F. and Catherine L.   (°) Has 1 ch., Harold, b. Oct.   1896.

336.

ALICE HAVENS WORTH, da. John and Nancy H. (Lester) Worth.
         b. Oct. 21, 1859.   m. Aug. 22, 1888.

Manuel Boutcher, s. John and Elizabeth (Brice) Boutcher.
         b. Apr. 18, 1858.
2 ch.   Nancy Worth, b. June 13, 1889.   John Worth, b. Sep. 30, 1891.

337.

Rev. WILLIAM HAND LESTER, s. Rev. William H. and Julia E. (Hand) Lester.
         b. Apr. 5, 1856.   m. 1st, June 15, 1882.   2d, Nov. 21, 1887.

1st, Sarah Margaret Anderson, da.
         b. Oct. 17, 1857.   d. July 30, 1884.
2d, Carrie Macfarland Field, da,
         b. Feb. 22, 1863.
4 ch.   William Harold, b. July 23, 1884.   Sarah Margaret, b. Sep. 21, 1888.
         Robert MacElroy, b. Feb. 7, 1890.   Elizabeth Jeanette, b. Dec. 26, 1895.

338.

ELMER ELLSWORTH HOWELL, s. Samuel H. and Julia A. (Chatfield) Howell.
         b. Jan. 11, 1864.

Minnie Smith, da. Edward and Phebe (Rogers) Smith.
         b.
1 ch.   A da., b. Feb.   1899.

339.

ANNA C. CHATFIELD, da. John and Esther (Edwards) Chatfield.
         b. Jan. 11, 1859.   m.

Stephen E. Rose, s. Henry M. and Betsey (Cook) Rose.
         b. Sep. 9, 1858.
1 ch.   Ernestine, b. Mar. 19, 1880.

340.

HENRY HAVENS CHATFIELD, s. John and Esther (Edwards) Chatfield.
         b. Mar. 17, 1866.   m. May 23, 1893.

Charlotte M. Peterson, da. Gilbert and Carrie (Hallock) Peterson.
         b. June 18, 1869.
2 ch.   Harry E., b. Aug. 24, 1894, d. Nov. 31, 1895.   Burton H., b. Aug. 6, 1897.

341.

ABRAHAM BRITTON HAVENS, s. Valentine and Sarah G. (Britton) Havens.
         b. May 27, 1860.   m. Jan. 27, 1887.

Lila Hoyt Beckwith, da. William S. and Anne M. (Collyer) Beckwith.
         b. Jan. 17, 1860.
4 ch.   Gertrude, b. Dec. 17, 1887.   Beckwith, b. May 29, 1890.
         Henrietta Bartlett, b. July 15, 1892.   Herbert, b. May 18, 1894.

342.

EDWIN TAYLOR HAVENS, s. Valentine and Sarah G. (Britton) Havens.
         b. Sep. 30, 1862.   m. Apr. 21, 1886.

Lillie E. Murphy, da. William and Anna (Leston) Murphy.
         b. Oct. 18, 1863.
3 ch.   Anna Leston, b. Feb. 26, 1888, d. Aug. 2, 1888.   Valentine Britton, b. July 11, 1869.
         Donald, b. Sep. 15, 1892.

343.

WILLIAM GEERY, s. William and Mary E. (Havens) Geery.
  b. Oct. 29, 1867.   m. May 30, 1889.

Isabel M. Christie, da. Alexander and Isabel (Lindsey) Christie.
  b. June 10, 1869.
3 ch.   *William Monroe*, b. Mar. 5, 1890.   *Albert Havens*, b. Dec. 20, 1892.
          Isabel Christie, b. Mar. 7, 1896, d. Aug. 14, 1898.

344.

MARY GEERY, da. William and Mary E. (Havens) Geery.
  b. Jan. 11, 1869.   m. Dec. 27, 1888.

George T. Brown, s. Thomas C. and Annie (Thomas) Brown.
  b. Jan. 19, 1867.
2 ch.   *George T.*, b. Aug. 16, 1893.   *Gordon Havens*, b. Jan. 31, 1896.

345.

ELIZABETH GEERY, da. William and Mary E. (Havens) Geery.
  b. June 28, 1873.   m. Oct. 9, 1895.

James H. Isbills, s. Edmund and Frances E. (Mallet) Isbills.
  b. Nov. 12, 1869.
1 ch.   *Edmund Geery*, b. Dec. 21, 1897.

346.

DAVID B. KEELER, s. Henry P. H. and Rachel C. (Crane) Keeler.
  b. May 22, 1858.   m. Oct. 11, 1888.

Caroline S. Stayner, of Paterson, New Jersey.
  b. Dec. 11, 1866.
2 ch.   *Violet*, b. Jan. 20, 1891.   *Fanny*, b. July 23, 1894.

347.

ANNIE H. KEELER, da. David B. and Jennie L. (Fleet) Keeler.
  b. Aug. 29, 1861.   m. Oct. 1, 1885.

William Babcock, s. John and Alice C. (Bell) Babcock.
  b.
1 ch.   *Christine Bell*, b. Oct. 29, 1891.

348.

ELIZABETH C. KEELER, da. David B. and Jennie L. (Fleet) Keeler.
  b. Oct. 10, 1871.   m. Sep. 14, 1892.

Torquato Tasso Fischer, s. Charles S. and Helena W. (Beilby) Fischer.
  b.
2 ch.   *Edith Linden*, b. July 10, 1893.   *Bradley Marshall*, b. Aug. 19, 1897.

349.

ELIZABETH KEELER BAKER, da. William D. and Rachel C. (Keeler) Baker.
  b. June 4, 1859.   June 4, 1883.

John Porter, s. Charles T. and Harriette S. (Morgan) Porter.
  b. Aug. 11, 1854.
4 ch.   *Esther Baker*, b. Mar. 28, 1884.   *John*, b. Sep. 18, 1887.
          Charles Talbot, b. Nov. 13, 1885.   *David Burr*, b. Apr. 25, 1892.

350.

MARY SARAH BAKER, da. William D. and Rachel C. (Keeler) Baker.
  b. Dec. 19, 1860.   m. Oct. 29, 1879.

William M. Williams, s. Philip H. and Rachel J. (Flanagan) Williams.
  b.
4 ch.   *Alice Mary*, b. Sep. 27, 1880.   *Eleanor*, b. Sep. 29, 1883.
          Madeline Baker, b. Oct. 25, 1881, d. July 10, 1882.   *Hilda Ray*, b. Nov. 17. 1889.

351.

MARGARET CRANE BAKER. da. William D. and Rachel C. (Keeler) Baker.
  b. May 12, 1862.   m. Nov. 25, 1879.

John Harper Bonnell, s. Alexander and Tamasin (Harper) Bonnell.
  b.
6 ch.   *Elsie Harper*, b. Sep. 13, 1880.   *John Harper*, b. Apr. 13, 1887.
          Margaret Elizabeth, b. Jan. 8, 1882.   *Winifred Harper*, b. May 19, 1889.
          Beatrice Harper, b. Dec. 5, 1885.   *Geoffrey Harper*, b. Nov. 15, 1890.

352.

ISAAC D. RUSSELL, s. Henry E. and Mary A. (Hance) Russell.
  b. Dec. 4, 1866.   m. Apr. 19, 1892.

Elizabe.h Rockwell, da. George P. and Eliza S. (Ames) Rockwell.
  b. Feb. 27, 1869.
3 ch.   *Elsie Rockwell*, b. May 26, 1893.   *Constance Mary*, b. June 22, 1894.
          Julia, b. Feb. 16, 1896.

353.

MARGARET E. RUSSELL, da. Henry and Mary A. (Hance) Russell.
    b. Mar. 28, 1871.   m. June 5, 1895.

    Dwight P. Chamberlain, s. Dwight S. and Katherine (Parshall) Chamberlain.
        b. Mar. 1, 1869.

1 ch.   *Dwight Russell*, b. Oct. 10, 1896.

354.

HERBERT REMINGTON HAVENS, s. Walter R. and Margaret E. (Wells) Havens.
    b. April 19, 1858.   m. Sep. 13, 1883.

    Louise Heimerdinger, da. John and Katherine (   ) Heimerdinger.
        b.

3 ch.   *Walter Wells*, b. Aug. 17, 1884, d. Nov. 27, 1886.   *Margaret R.*, b.   1887.
        Katherine L., b.   1892.

355.

JAMES MONROE CONKLIN, s. Edward H. and Maggie (Osborn) Conklin.
    b. May 21, 1867.   m. Jan. 20, 1895.

    Margaret McGuire, da. Albert and Margaret (Richardson) McGuire.
        b. Nov. 27, 1874.

2 ch.   *Edward Henry*, b. Jan. 5, 1896.   *Margaret*, b. Apr. 9, 1897.

356.

MAY ISABEL CORT, da. William K. and Charlotte A. (Conklin) Cort.
    b. Sep. 19, 1868.   m. Dec. 18, 1889.

    William Clayton Black, s. Thomas A. and Annie E. (Foulk) Black.
        b. Jan. 16, 1866.

3ch.   *Lottie Cort*, b. Apr. 16, 1891.   *William Clayton*, b. July 31, 1892.
        Jean Van Holland, b. June 23, 1895.

357.

LOTTIE LILLIAN ELDREDGE, da. Benjamin G. and Phebe (J. Conklin) Eldredge.
    b Feb. 22, 1866.   m. Dec. 24, 1891.

    Frank Warren Whitby, s. Thomas G. and Martha J. (Thompson) Whitby.
        b. Feb. 11. 1857.

2 ch.   *Frank Gilmer*, b. May 12, 1893.   *Linton Conklin*, b. July 5. 1894

358.

RUSSELL HAVENS CONKLIN, s. Benjamin P. and Mary C. (Payne) Conklin.
    b. Dec. 23, 1873.   m. June 1, 1897.
    Minnie S. Hoyt, da. Samuel and Helen (Walrath) Hoyt.
        b. Apr. 12, 1873.

1 ch.   *Benjamin Hoyt*, b. Apr. 15, 1898.

359.

ADELAIDE H. BEEBE, da. John C. and Harriet W. (Havens) Beebe.
    b. Sep. 29. 1864.   m. June 26, 1886.

    Charles H. Smith, s. Charles H. and Sarah E. (Manwaring) Smith.
        b. June 22, 1860.

2 ch.   *Albert R.*, b. Oct. 19, 1887.   *Sarah E.*, b. Oct. 24, 1889.

360.

HARRIET WINSLOW BEEBE, da. John C. and Harriet W. (Havens) Beebe.
    b. Sep. 26. 1867.   m.   1886.

    Willis W. Worthington, s. George and Mary C. (Raynor) Worthington.
        b. Nov. 14, 1860.

4 ch.   *Mary C.*, b. Mar. 14, 1887.   *Anna M.*, b. Aug. 22, 1890.
        George K., b. June 22, 1896.   *John Edward*, b. Jan. 31, 1899.

361.

QUINCY WARD COX, s. Daniel R. and Mary L. (Penny) Cox.
    b. May 29, 1872.   m. Apr. 25, 1896.

    Mary Louisa Scott, da. Walter and Louisa (Jennings) Scott.
        b. Dec. 29, 1870.

1 ch.   *Russell Scott*, b. June 17, 1897.

362.

IRVING I. CLARK, s. Samuel G. and Elizabeth (Havens) Clark.
    b. Mar. 2, 1869.   m. Oct. 4, 1892.

    Alice Parliman, da. Isaac W. and Marietta (Coe) Parliman.
        b. June 8. 1867.

1 ch.   *Franklin Irving*, b. Mar. 23, 1894.

363.

CLIFFORD YOUNG CLARK, s. David Y. and Adelaide M. (Havens) Clark.
b. Sep. 21, 1872.   m. Nov. 10, 1896.

Phebe Elizabeth Halsey, da. William M. and Martha T. (Ludlow) Halsey.
b. Oct. 8, 1873.

1 ch.   *Donald Havens*, b. Mar. 5, 1898.

364.

LULU TERRY GRIFFING, da. Charles M. and Abigail T. (Cartwright) Griffing.
b. Apr. 1, 1866.   m. Dec. 30, 1886.

George A. Griffin, s. Samuel and Caroline (Halsey) Griffin.
b.   1864.

2 ch.   *Grace*, b. Apr. 25. 1889.   *Reba*, b. Nov.   1892.

365.

ROYAL MARKUS GRIFFING, s. Charles M. and Abigail T. (Cartwright) Griffing.
b. Dec. 1, 1874.   m.

Clara Juvette Edwards, da. Elmer W. and Clara J. (Dennis) Edwards.
b.   1874-5.

2 ch.   *Ethel Juvette*, b. Sep. 30, 1895.   *Edith*, b. Sep. 30, 1897.

366.

MARY J. HAVENS, da. Joseph A. and Kate (Bennet) Havens.
b. Oct. 25, 1869.   m. July 16, 1889.

Tunis R. Barns, s. Thomas B. and Adelaide T. (Huntting) Barns.
b. Jan. 9, 1867.

2 ch.   *Ray H.*, b. May 8, 1890.   *Thomas M.*, b. Dec. 6, 1891.

367.

CLINTON H. EDWARDS, s. Jesse B. and Maria (Havens) Edwards.
b. Nov. 22, 1866.   .n. June 5, 1895.

Mamie E. Ward, da. James H. and Josephine M. (Manwaring) Ward.
b. Dec., 1867.

2 ch.   *Marion T.*, b. Sept., 1898, and a twin boy (still-born).

368.

ANNA A. OAKS, da. George and Helen (Havens) Oaks.
b. Aug. 3 1865.   m. Mar. 24, 1889.

David H. Hamilton, s. Henry and Catherine (Lester) Hamilton.
b. July 29, 1865.

4 ch.   *David Raymond*, b. Feb. 6, 1890.   *George Henry*, b. Feb. 4, 1893.
          Floyd Havens, b. Jan. 10, 1895.   *Edward Webb*, b. Mar. 26, 1898.

369.

SUSAN ADELAIDE BUNDY, da. Thomas P. and Ann M. (Havens) Bundy.
b. Apr. 10, 1854.   m. Oct 7, 1891.

Horace N. Plummer, s. Alva and Priscilla (Littlefield) Plummer.
b. Dec. 15, 1848.

1 ch.   *Raymond Phinney*, b. Jan. 15, 1893.

370.

MINNIE FOSTER STICKNEY, da. George W. and Elmira A. (Havens) Stickney.
b. July 14, 1864.   m. Oct. 17, 1888.

James S. Marshall, s. Alexander and Fanny (Lewis) Marshall.
b. Dec. 2, 1861.

3 ch.   *Elmira*, b. Oct. 11, 1889.   *Fannie*, b. Apr. 4, 1893.   *Grace*, b. Sep. 30, 1897.

371.

EMILY BURTON MASSIE, da. Robert D. and Jeanie L. (Ash) Massie.
b. July 30, 1877.   m. July 30, 1896.

James Joseph Farrell, s. Martin and Ellen (Carnody) Farrell.
b. Sep. 7, 1881.

1 ch.   *Martin*, b. May 7, 1898.

372.

HAMPTON H. BENJAMIN, s. George L. and Hannah R. (Havens) Benjamin.
b. Jan. 13, 1871.   m. July 4, 1891.

Edna S. Woodhull, da. Brewster   Woodhull.
b. Sep. 15, 1872.

1 ch.   *George Lawson*, b. Dec. 12, 1892.

373.

MERIAM ELIZABETH HAVENS, da. David A. and Marietta (L'Hommedieu) Havens.
    b. Apr. 4, 1856.   m. July 8, 1885.

Charles Albert Day, s. Charles M. and Mary C. (Banta) Day.
    b. Jan. 6, 1863.

6 ch.   *Charles Lincoln*, b. Dec. 18, 1886.   *Albert Mortimer*, b. July 9, 1888.
        David Andrew, b. Feb. 7, 1890, d. Apr. 5, 1892.   *Samuel Foster*, b. Feb. 1, 1893.
        Meriam Elizabeth, b. July 13, 1894.   *Mary Catherine*, b. June 14, 1896.

374.

GRACIE MAY HAVENS, da. David A. and Marietta (L'Hommedieu) Havens.
    b. Apr. 3 1867.   m. Nov. 29, 1885.

William Benjamin Newton, s. William E. and Catherine R. (Rhodes) Newton.
    b. Apr. 29, 1859.

7 ch.   *Samuel Edgar*, b. Aug. 22, 1886.   *Irene Rozilla*, b. Jan. 11, 1889.
        Willie, b. June 20, 1891, d. Aug. 8, 1891.   *Walter Lewis*, b. June 9, 1892.
        Chester Loving, b. Feb. 11, 1894.   *Florence Cornelia*, b. Sep. 2, 1895.
        Francis Albert, b. Oct. 18, 1897.

375.

OLIVER WALESTEINE PETTY s. David O. and Sarah J. (Newey) Petty.
    b. Dec. 24, 1870.   m. Mar. 31, 1895.

Grace H. Smiley, da. Charles and Jennie (Yale) Smiley.
    b. May 18. 1873.

1 ch.   *Millicent Devine*, b. June 8, 1896.

SUPPLEMENT.

A.

DEWITT C. CONKLIN, s. Strong and Mary C. (Davis) Conklin.   See No. 97.
    b. Mar. 15, 1841.   m. June 13, 1869.

Mary F. Hartt, da. Charles and Harriet E. (Knapp) Hartt.
    b. Mar. 14, 1852.   d. Dec. 1, 1891.

1 ch.   **B.** *Harriet I.*, b. Jan. 24, 1876; m. July 15, 1896, Walter V. Tuttle.

B.

HARRIET ISABELLE CONKLIN, da. Strong and Mary (Davis) Conklin.
    b. Jan. 24, 1896.   m. July 15, 1876.

Walter V. Tuttle, s. George W. and Mary A. (Miller) Tuttle.
    b. Oct. 26, 1863.

1 ch.   *Harold Leroy*, b. Apr. 27, 1897.

1.

*WILLIAM HAVENS, s.
    b.   m.   d.   1797.

    b.   d.

7 ch.   **2.** *Hamutal*, b. about 1777-8; m. Nov. 28, 1799, John Conklin.
        °*Lucretia*, b. about 1789; m. Sep. 4, 1812, Henry Pierson.
        ‖*Nancy*, b.   m.   Phineas F. Corey.   †*Mary*, b.   m.   William White.
        3. *Elizabeth*, b. about 1786; m. Oct. 23, 1805, Elias Mathias Cooper.
        ¶*Sabrina*, b.   m.   Joseph Gawley.   *Henry*, b.   supposed to have been lost at sea.

(*) This William Havens was a noted captain of various privateers during the Revolution. Whose son
    he was or whom he married we have been unable to discover. Should the reader know whose son
    he was, the compiler of these records will be greatly obliged for the information.
(°) d. June 11, 1830. Had 1 ch., Jerusha H., b. June 13, 1813, d. at 17.
(‖) Had 2 ch., Eliza Ann and Nancy Maria.   (†) Had 2 ch.
(¶) Had 4 ch., Samuel, Joseph, Mary, and Elizabeth, all of whom m.

2.

HAMUTAL HAVENS, da. William   Havens.
    b. about 1777-8.   m. Nov. 28, 1799.   d. Apr. 4, 1847.

John Conklin, s.
    b. about 1776   d. Dec. 15, 1814.

4 ch.   *Nancy*, b.   m. May 8, 1833, George Halsey.
        4. *Charles J.*, b. about 1811; m.   Fanny P. Hand.
        Henry C., b.   1801. d. unm. May 9, 1874.
        5. *John H.*, b. about   1809; m.   Sarah M. Sheffield.
(*) d. in 1895, had 1 ch., Mary Van Scoy, who m. William J. Thorn, they have 1 ch. named **Dunbar.**

3.

ELIZABETH HAVENS, da. William   Havens.
    b. about 1786.   m. Oct. 23, 1805.   d. July 29, 1843.

   Elias Mathias Cooper, s. Elias and Ruth (Rogers) Cooper.
     b. May 21, 1769.   d. Dec. 11, 1842.

4 ch.   *William Havens, b.   1807; m. June 19, 1831, °Roxanna Stuart.
      6. Edward Mortimer, b.   m.   Mary Havens.
      7. Elizabeth Havens, b. Apr. 24, 1814; m. June 4, 1833, Joseph Stanton.
      †Jane, b.   m.   John Harrison.
(*) d. May 28, 1877. Had 3 ch.; 2 d. in infancy, Henry S. d. unm. Sep. 7, 1860, at 25.
(°) da. of Nathan and Roxanna (Fordham) Stuart, b.   1807, d. May 20, 1877.
(†) Had 2 ch., Edward and Frances, both of whom m.

4.

CHARLES J. CONKLIN, s. John and Hamutal (Havens) Conklin.
    b. about 1811.   m.   d. July 17, 1882.

   Fanny P. Hand, da. Ahira and Betsey (   ) Hand.
     b. about 1814.   d. Apr. 17, 1872.

3 ch.   Fanny, b. June 3, 1839; m. Feb.   *James E. Dickerson; no issue.
      Anna, b. Aug.   1845; m.   Joseph Bennet.
      Charles, b. Dec. 1846.
(*) s. of James and Jane Dickerson.

5.

JOHN HOWARD CONKLIN, s. John and Hamutal (Havens) Conklin.
    b. about 1809.   m.   d. about 1862.

   Sarah M. Sheffield, da.
     b   d. Feb. 18, 1870.

8 ch.   William H., b.   d. unm.   John H., b. d. unm.   David S., b.   d. unm.
      *Mary Emma, b.   m. { 1st, May 5, 1861, Charles Wiggins.
                                { 2d,   Orlando Gould.
      Sarah Hamutal, b.   m. Apr. 22, 1868, °Joel F. Raynor.
      ‖George Albert, b. Mar. 24, 1852; m.   1874, Selina J. Baker.
      †Carrie Isabel, b.   m.   Theodore Lyons.
      8. Fred Stanley, b. Sep. 12, 1859; m. July 20, 1885, Hannah M. Hendrickson.
(*) Had 1 ch by 1st hus., May. By 2d. hus. 5 ch., Walter, Fred, Charles, Minnie, and one who d.
(°) d. leaving 2 ch., Isaac Merwin and Mary E. F., both of whom are m.
(‖) Has 2 ch., George L., b. Apr. 14, 1875, and Sadie May, b. Nov.   1876, and m. to Wm. Brown;
    have 1 ch.   (†) Had 6 ch.: Georgiana, who is m., Louis, Fred, Sadie, Carrie and Edith.

6.

EDWARD MORTIMER COOPER, s. Elias and Elizabeth (Havens) Cooper.
    b.   m.   d.

   Mary Havens, da.
     b. Apr. 27, 1809.   d. May 5, 1880.

8 ch.   James H., b.   m.   Lilla Lafave.   Mary E. b.
      Hannah, b, Nov. 10, 1836, d. Jan. 29, 1842.   Robert H., b. Apr. 20, 1837, d. Apr. 10, 1838.
      Edward M., b.   m.   Sophia
      *Anna G., b. about 1845; m. 1st,   Silvera.   2d, C. H. Atkins.
      °Robert E., b.   m.   Inas Atkins.   ‖Jane P., b   m.   Edwin Gawley.
(*) d. s. p. Jan. 7, 1895.   (°) Has 1 ch. Edward Mortimer, b. 1897.   (‖) Has 2 ch., May and Edna.

7.

ELIZABETH HAVENS COOPER, da. Elias and Elizabeth (Havens) Cooper.
    b. Apr. 24, 1814.   m. June 4, 1833.   d. Feb. 26, 1892.

   Joseph Stanton, s. Joseph and Fanny (Minor) Stanton.
     b.   1804.   d. Oct 22, 1866.

8 ch.   Oscar F., b. July 18, 1834; m. July 6, 1859, Caroline E. Gardiner.
      William C., b. Apr. 14, 1836, d. unm. Sep. 2, 1863.
      Charles W., b. Mar. 29, 1839, d. Oct. 1, 1839.   Harriet F., b. June 29, 1840, d. June 27, 1843.
      10. Joseph B., b. Oct. 20, 1843; m. June 18, 1874, Jane Eden.
      Mary E., b. Jan. 10, 1846.   Emma, b. Mar. 22, 1848, d. Sep. 29, 1849.
      11. Helen A., b. Mar. 10, 1850; m. Apr. 26, 1876, Harold A. Booth.

8.

FRED STANLEY CONKLIN, s. John H. and Sarah M. (Sheffield) Conklin.
    b. Sep. 12, 1859.   m. July 20, 1885.

   Hannah M. Hendrickson, da. James and Caroline (Dorland) Hendrickson.
     b. Aug. 30, 1859.

2 ch.   Fred Stanley, b. July 26, 1886.   Frank Elton, b. Sep. 19, 1888.

9.

OSCAR F STANTON, s. Joseph and Elizabeth (Havens) Stanton.
    b. July 18, 1834.   m. July 6, 1859.

   Caroline E. Gardiner, da. Charles F. and Eliza A. (Corey) Gardiner.
     b. Nov.

2 ch. **12.** Fannie Gardiner, b. Oct. 18, 1867; m. Mar. 28, 1888, Daniel Latham.
      Elizabeth, b. Sep. 3, 1875.

10.

JOSEPH B. STANTON, s. Joseph and Elizabeth (Havens) Stanton.
     b. Oct. 20, 1843.   m. June 18, 1874.

    Jane Eden, da. Mark and Rachel (   ) Eden.
       b. June

    1 ch.   *William Havens, b. Jan 4, 1875; m. Nov. 1, 1896, Mary Bell.
    (*) Has 1 ch., Mary E., b. Sep. 1, 1897.

11.

HELEN A. STANTON, da. Joseph and Elizabeth (Havens) Stanton.
     b. Mar. 10, 1850.   m. Apr. 26, 1876.

    Harold A. Booth, s. John H. and Sarah (Price) Booth.
       b. June,   1854.   d. Jan. 14, 1892.

    2 ch.   Florence May, b. Jan. 22, 1877.   Ethel Stanton, b. Feb. 6, 1879.

12.

FANNY GARDINER STANTON, da. Oscar F. and Caroline E. (Gardiner) Stanton.
     b. Oct. 18, 1867.   m. Mar. 28, 1888.

    Daniel Latham, s. Donald and Ann (Strickland) Latham.
       b.

    1 ch.   Stanton, b. May. 12, 1890.

ELISHA PAYNE.
ANCESTORS.
A.

CONTENT HAVENS, da. George and Eleanor (Thurston) Havens.
     b.   m.   d.

    Cornelius Payne, s. (?) Thomas Payne.
       b.   d. Feb. or Mar., 1715-16.

    2 ch.   Thomas, b.   d. Jan. 14, 1725.
       1. Elisha, b.   m. Oct. 31, 1748, Deliverance Tuthill.

1.

*ELISHA PAYNE, s. Cornelius and Content (Havens) Payne.
     b.   m. Oct 31, 1748.   d. Feb. or Mar., 1761.

    Deliverance Tuthill, da. [?] Nathaniel and Mary (Petty) Tuthill.
       b.

    4 ch.   °Mary, bap. Nov. 5, 1752; m. Nov. 24, 1771, Thomas Harley.
       |Elisha, b.   m. or d. before the census of 1776.
       A son named, perhaps, Rufus.   A daughter.
    (*) Will of Elisha Payne dated at Southold, Feb. 17, 1761. Speaks of wife Deliverance, sons and
       daughters, but mentions no names. Appoints wife Deliverance Ex. Proved Mar. 20, 1761. See
       also census list of 1771.   (°) Had at least 1 ch. named Elisha who was bap. Oct. 18, 1786, at
       Southold.   (|) Appears on Association paper of 1775.

NOAH TUTHILL.
ANCESTORS.
A.

JOHN TUTHILL, s. Henry and Bridget (   ) Tuthill.
     b. in England, July 16, 1635.   m. 1st, Feb. 17, 1657.   2d, May 28, 1690.   d. Oct. 12, 1717.

    1st, Deliverance King, da. William and Dorothy ([?] Hayne) King.
       b. in 1640.   d. Jan. 25, 1689.

    2d, Sarah Youngs [?] (nee Frost) da. John Frost.
       b.   d. Nov. 8, 1727.

    10 ch.   John, b. Feb. 14, 1658; m. about 1685, Mehitable Wells.
       Elizabeth, b. Apr. 19, 1661; m. June 1, 1681, William Wells.
       Henry, b. May 1, 1665; m. before 1690, Bethiah Horton.
       Hannah, b. Nov. 7, 1667; m. Jan. 19, 1686, Joshua Wells.
       Abigail, b. Oct. 17, 1670; m. { 1st, Nov.   1690, Joseph Conklin.
                                       { 2d,   John Parker.
       Dorthy, b. Oct. 16, 1674, d. Feb. 24, 1684.   Deliverance, b. Aug. 2, 1677, d. Sep. 17, 1683.
    B. Daniel, b. Jan. 23, 1679; m. in 1705, Mehitable Horton.
       Nathaniel, b. Nov. 10, 1683, d. Dec. 18, 1705.   Mary, b.   1691, d. Jan. 11, 1699.

B.

DANIEL TUTHILL, s. John and Deliverance (King) Tuthill.
  b. Jan. 23, 1679.   m. in 1705.   d. Dec. 7, 1762.

Mehitable Horton, da. Jonathan and Bethiah (Wells) Horton.
  b. Feb. 17, 1679.   d. Sep. 7, 1757.

8 ch. *Mehitable*, b. Sep. 9, 1706; m.   1723-4, Thomas Terry.
  Nathaniel, b. July 1, 1708; m. about 1730, Hannah King.
  Abigail, b. Apr. 9, 1710; m.   Henry Havens.
  Daniel, b. Jan. 15, 1712; m. { 1st, Mar. 17, 1728, Sarah Comstock.
   { 2d, Oct. 29, 1733, Mehitable Budd.
  1. *Noah*, b. Mar. 13, 1714; m. Nov. 2, 1738, Hannah Tuthill.
  Patience, b. Mar. 11, 1716; m. Oct. 24, 1733, John Havens.
  Lydia, b. May 6, 1718; m. Sep. 19, 1737, Jonathan Terry.
  Mary, b. June 30, 1721; m   Nathan Tuthill.

1.

NOAH TUTHILL, s. Daniel and Mehitable (Horton) Tuthill.
  b. Mar. 13, 1714.   m. Nov. 2, 1738.   d. May 18, 1766.

Hannah Tuthill, da. [?] John and Elizabeth ([?] Brown) Tuthill.
  b. in   1719.   d. Sep. 4, 1770.

7 ch. *Elizabeth*, b. Feb. 12, 1740, d. July 14, 1754. *Jemima*, b. Aug. 30, 1742, d. Aug. 11, 1754.
  2. *Mehitable*, b. Jan 1, 1745; m. Oct 13, 1763, Abraham King.
  3. *Daniel*, b. Mar. 13, 1747; m. Feb. 1, 1770, Ruth Terry.
  Hannah, b. Oct. 20, 1750, d. July 9, 1770. *Noah*, b. Sep. 8, 1754, d. July 29, 1756.
  Elizabeth, b. Dec 23, 1757, d. Apr. 21. 1784.

2.

MEHITABLE TUTHILL, da. Noah and Hannah (Tuthill) Tuthill.
  b. Jan 1, 1745.   m. Oct. 13, 1763.   d.   1827.

Abraham King, s. John and Mary (Corey) King.
  b. Dec. 13, 1741.   d. Aug. 31, 1782.

6 ch. **4.** *Abraham*, b. Nov. 4, 1765; m.   Parshall.
  *Luther, b.   1769; m.   °Hannah Tuthill; no issue.
  Gamaliel, b. Nov. 22, 1773, d. unm. Dec. 14 1795.
  Nathaniel, b.   1776, d. unm. Jan. 19, 1858.
  5. *Tuthill*, b. 1782; m.   Lydia Tuthill. *Mehitable*, b.   1779, d. unm. Dec. 30, 1850.
  (*) d. Sep. 11, 1849.   (°) da. of James and Temperance (Moore) Tuthill, b. Sep. 1, 1777, d. July 26. 1851.

3.

DANIEL TUTHILL, s. Noah and Hannah (Tuthill) Tuthill.
  b. Mar. 13, 1747.   m. Feb. 1, 1770.   d. July 17, 1830.

Ruth Terry, da. Thomas and Abigail (Havens) Terry.
  b. Dec. 2, 1752.   d. Nov. 12, 1802.

6 ch. **6.** *Noah*, b. in 1770; m. { 1st, Mar. 27, 1794, Polly Tuthill.
   { 2d,   Abigail Terry.
  Hannah, b. Oct. 15, 1771, d. Apr. 6, 1775. *Mehitable*, b. Mar. 11, 1773, d. Mar. 11, 1775.
  7. *Thomas*, b. Feb. 23, 1777; m. { 1st, Oct. 14, 1798, Abigail Terry.
   { 2d, Sep. 10, 1838, Esther Taber.
  Hannah, b. Mar. 15, 1779, d. Mar. 9, 1816.
  8. *Seth*, b. Aug. 16, 1784; m. { 1st, Nov. 16, 1809, Mary Lewis.
   { 2d,   Wid. Hetty Cleaves.

4.

ABRAHAM KING, s. Joseph and Mehitable (Tuthill) King.
  b. Nov. 4, 1765.   m.   d. July 26, 1801.

Parshall, da.
  b.   d.

1 ch. **9.** *Gamaliel*, b. Dec. 1, 1795; m. June 16, 1819, Catherine Oliver Snow.

5.

TUTHILL KING, s. Joseph and Mehitable (Tuthill) King.
  b.   1782.   m.   d. May 2, 1833.

Lydia Tuthill, da. James and Temperance (Moore) Tuthill.
  b.   1769.   d.

2 ch. **10.** *Lester*, b. Oct. 22, 1810; m.   Mary Corwin.
  Hannah, b. Oct. 25, 1820. d. Oct. 12, 1821.

6.

NOAH TUTHILL, s. Daniel and Ruth (Terry) Tuthill.
  b. Apr. 20, 1770.   m. 1st, Mar. 27, 1794.   2d,   d. Nov. 8, 1826.

1st, Polly Tuthill, da. Rufus and Mary (Dimon) Tuthill.
  b.   d.

2d, Abigail Terry, da. Constantine and Sybil (Case) Terry.
  b.   1788.   d. Aug. 25, 1826.

6 ch.   *Oren*, b.   d. ae. 30 or 35.   *Seth*, b.   d. ae. 2.

11. *Moses*, b. Oct. 26, 1808; m. { 1st, Nov. 1, 1832, Jane Neely.
                                    { 2d, Mar. 4, 1841, Lydia Collins.

12. *Eli*, b. June 13, 1811; m. { 1st, Oct. 23, 1842, Nancy Tabor.
                                { 2d, July 25, 1853, Nancy Tuthill.

13. *Hiram*, b. Jan. 26, 1815; m. { 1st, Jan. 1, 1839, Maria Delamater.
                                  { 2d, Feb. 16, 1851, Freelove Camburn.
                                  { 3d, Apr. 12, 1857, Sarah E. Rogers.

14. *Enoch*, b. Feb. 23, 1823; m.   Ann Thompkins.

7.

THOMAS TUTHILL, s. Daniel and Ruth (Terry) Tuthill.
    b. Feb. 23, 1777.   m. 1st, Oct. 14, 1798.   2d, Sep. 10, 1838.   d. July 17, 1850.

1st, Abigail Terry, da. Thomas and Esther (Tuthill) Terry.
    b. Sep. 13, 1780.   d. Nov. 5, 1835.

2d, Esther Taber, da. Frederick and Esther (Vail) Taber.
    b.   d.

11 ch. 15. *Thomas Gallin*, b. Dec. 20, 1799; m. { 1st, in 1823, Elsie Ann Nealy.
                                                  { 2d, Apr. 17, 1834, Elsie Ann Davis.

16. *Aaron Burr*, b. Jan. 4, 1801; m. { 1st,   Clarette Brooks.
                                       { 2d,   Wid. Katherine Wells.

17. *James Downs*, b. Feb. 10, 1803; m. Mar. 6, 1834, Margaret C. Havens.
    Seth Higgins, b. Apr. 5, 1805; m   Ellen Mc   ; no issue.
18. *David Terry*, b. May 26, 1807; m.   Agnes V. Powell.
19. *John Stuart*, b. Sep. 30, 1809; m.   Frances Conklin.
20. *Ezra Allen*, b. Mar. 4, 1812; m.   1840, Phebe E. Havens.
    Hannah Maria, b. Apr. 10, 1814; m. May 5, 1838, Benjamin C. Cartwright.
21. *Daniel Theodore*, b. July 17, 1817; m. Apr. 10, 1841, Rosina D. Cartwright.
    Joseph Conkling, b. Mar. 17, 1819, d. unm. Feb. 21, 1843.
    °*Phebe Terry*, b. Nov. 14, 1823; m. Jan. 18, 1841, Charles Alfred Havens.

(*) See Conkling genealogy, No. 14.   (°) See Jonathan Havens genealogy, No. 138.

8.

DR. SETH TUTHILL, s. Daniel and Ruth (Terry) Tuthill.
    b. Aug. 16, 1784.   m. 1st, Nov. 16, 1809.   2d,   d.

1st, Mary Lewis, da.
    b. Oct 13, 1789.   d. Jan. 3, 1840.

2d, Wid. Hetty Cleaves. da.
    b.   d.

7 ch.   *Ruth*, b. Sept. 8, 1810.
22. *Joseph L.*, b. July 18, 1812; m. Mar. 20, 1835, Elizabeth Brown Dyer.
    Mary, b. Mar. 5, 1814, d. unm. Jan. 3, 1840.   *Henrietta*, b. Jan. 13, 1816, d. Dec. 5, 1870.
    Jane Amelia, b. July 16, 1820, d. unm. June 22, 1843.   *Thomas Storrs*, b. July 15, 1825.
    Walter Scott, b. Sept. 12, 1833, d. July 9, 1834.

9.

GAMALIEL KING, s. Abraham and   (Parshall) King.
    b. Dec. 1, 1795.   m. June 19, 1819.   d. Dec. 6, 1875.

Catherine Snow, adopted da. John Snow, of Brooklyn, N. Y.
    b. Nov. 25, 1799.   d. Nov. 25, 1874.

6 ch. 25. *George L.*, b. Mar. 15, 1828; m. Mar. 6, 1854, Martha R. Aldrich.
    23. *Mary E.*, b. Sep. 23, 1822; m. Nov. 23, 1842, James H. Cornwall.
    26. *Sarah S.*, b. Sep. 8, 1831; m. July 9, 1856, George B. Jellison.
    Robert S., b. May 1, 1824. d. Sep. 17, 1825.   *Orpha V.*, b. Apr. 20, 1834.
    24. *Martha M.*, b. Jan. 12, 1826; m. Feb. 28, 1846, Alfred Bridgeman.

10.

LESTER KING, s. Tuthill and Lydia (Tuthill) King.
    b. Oct. 22, 1810.   m.   d. July 9, 1882.

Mary Corwin, da. Jed   Corwin.
    b. Apr. 9, 1812.   d. Aug. 14, 1879.

3 ch. 27. *Sarah M.*, b. Apr. 22, 1841; m. Dec. 28, 1864, Charles Conkling.
    Wesley T., b. Dec. 25, 1844, d. Dec. 3, 1852.
    Willis L., b. Aug. 27, 1850, d. unm. Sep. 29, 1884.

11.

MOSES TUTHILL, s. Noah and Abigail (Terry) Tuthill.
    b. Oct. 26, 1808.   m. 1st, Nov. 1, 1832.   2d, Mar. 4, 1841.   d. Feb.   1881.

1st, Jane Neely, da.
    b.   d.

2d, Lydia Collin, da.
    b.   d.

2 ch.   *Hiram*, b. Nov.   1838; m.   °Florence Sparks.
    28. *Noah*, b Dec. 20, 1843; m. Feb. 17, 1869, Margaret H. Tuthill.
(*) d. Dec.   1885; had 1 ch., Paul, who m. Cora Gates and has 3 ch.   (°) d. about 1880.

12.

ELI TUTHILL, s. Noah and Abigail (Terry) Tuthill.
  b. June 13, 1811.   m. 1st, Oct. 23, 1842.   2d, July 25, 1853.   d. July 2, 1855.

1st, Nancy Tabor, da. Frederick and Polly (   ) Tabor.
  b.   1818.   d. Nov. 9, 1843.

2d, Nancy A. Tuthill, da. Lewis and Polly (   ) Tuthill.
  b.

2 ch.   An infant, b.   d. Jan. 24, 1844.   *Eli, b. Sep. 6, 1855; m.   °Augusta Finger.
(*) had 5 ch., Lewis, Floyd, Gertrude, Carl, Earl.   (°) d. July 25, 1892.

13.

HIRAM TUTHILL, s. Noah and Abigail (Terry) Tuthill.
  b. Jan. 26, 1815.   m. 1st, Jan. 1, 1839.   2d, Feb. 16, 1851.   3d, Apr. 12, 1857.

1st. Maria Delamater, da. Isaac and Diadana (Barnes) Tuthill.
  b. Mar. 29, 1820.   d. Apr. 27, 1849.

2d, Freelove Camburn, da. Joseph and Roxana (Shattuck) Camburn.
  b. Sep. 10, 1826.   d. May 27, 1854.

3d. Sarah E. Rogers, da. James L. and Charrilla (Curtis) Rogers.
  b. Nov. 6, 1819.

3 ch. **29.** *Burr*, b. Sep. 13, 1840; m. { 1st, Oct. 21, 1862, Nealy Farnsworth.
                                            { 2d, Mar.   1882, Marion A. Rogers.
  30. *Frances*, b. Jan. 7, 1843; m. Jan. 20, 1864, Fred C. Rogers.
  31. *Mary*, b. Nov. 27, 1847; m. Feb. 6, 1876, A. S. Hilton.

14.

ENOCH TUTHILL, s. Noah and Abigail (Terry) Tuthill.
  b. Feb. 23, 1823.   m.   d. Jan. 4, 1895.

Ann Thompkins, da.
  b.
1 ch.   *Maria*, b.   m.   Frank Joslin.
(*) d. Aug. 17, 1879; had 2 ch., Seth, who m. Ina Crispell, and John, who m. Beneta Crispell.

15.

THOMAS GALLIN TUTHILL, s. Thomas and Abigail (Gerry) Tuthill.
  b. Dec. 20, 1799.   m. 1st,   1823.   2d, Apr. 17, 1834.   d. Jan. 18, 1858.

1st, Elsie Ann Neely, da. John   (   ) Neely.
  b. Apr. 25, 1801.   d. May 16, 1838.

2d, Elsie Ann Davis, da. of Matthew Davis, of Orange County, N. Y.
  b. Mar. 20, 1813.   d. Apr. 13, 1879.

8 ch.   *John N.*, b. Sep. 18, 1825; d. unm.
  32. *Seth H.*, b. Feb. 28, 1829; m.   Content Alemy Chase.
  33. *Adelia*, b. Jan. 28, 1835; m. Dec. 24, 1854, Melvin B. Nichols.
  34. *George W.*, b. Sep. 30, 1836; m. June 20, 1858, Elizabeth Howe.
  Mary E., b. Jan. 24, 1839.   *Charles D.*, b. Oct. 31, 1842.
  *Margaret H., b. Aug. 27, 1846; m. Feb. 17, 1869, Noah Tuthill.
  Thomas G., b. Feb. 22, 1850.
(*) See No. 28.

16.

AARON BURR TUTHILL, s. Thomas and Abigail (Terry) Tuthill.
  b. Jan. 4, 1801; m. 1st,   2d,   d.

1st, Claretta Brooks, of New London, Conn.
  b.   d.

2d, Wid. Katherine Wells, da.
  b.   d.

1 ch. **35.** *Charles Henry*, b. July 22, 1832; m. Sep. 24, 1854, Sarah E. Wells.

17.

JAMES DOWNS TUTHILL, s. Thomas and Abigail (Terry) Tuthill.
  b. Feb. 10, 1803.   m. Mar. 6, 1834.   d. Feb. 4, 1884.

Margaret C. Havens, da. Obadiah and Nancy (Robinson) Havens.
  b. Apr. 25, 1814, d. Sep. 13, 1843.

3 ch.   *Jane E.*, b. Dec. 23, 1834, d. June 14, 1838.   *Margaret C.*, b. Sep. 2, 1836, d. July 2, 1838.
  Margaret Jane, b. Sep. 5, 1840, d. Jan. 8, 1841.

18.

DAVID TERRY TUTHILL, s. Thomas and Abigail (Terry) Tuthill.
  b. May 26, 1807.   m. in 1834.   d. Nov. 12, 1877.

Agnes V. Powell, da. William and Harriet (Valentine) Powell.
  b. Aug. 31, 1811.   d. Sep. 29, 1848.

5 ch.   *Harriet A.*, b. Jan. 7, 1835.   *Thomas P.*, b. Dec. 14, 1838., d. unm. Apr. 16, 1868.
  William H. H., b. Mar. 14, 1841.   *Agnes, A.*, b. June 9, 1846, d. Nov. 3, 1898.
  Leamel Edwin, b. Aug. 24, 1851.

19.

JOHN STUART TUTHILL, s. Thomas and Abigail (Terry) Tuthill.
  b. Sep. 30, 1809. m. d. July 28. 1839.

*Frances Conklin, da. Sinens and Fanny (Bowditch) Conklin.
  b. 1812. d. Aug. 8, 1836.
  1 ch. oFanny Abigail, b. m. Dr. Thompson, of Iowa.
(*) See Bowditch genealogy, No. 8. (o) Had children.

20.

EZRA ALLEN TUTHILL, s. Thomas and Abigail (Terry) Tuthill.
  b. Mar. 4, 1812. m. Jan. 1837. d. May 10, 1889.

Phebe Elizabeth Havens, da. Jacob and Elizabeth (Bennet) Havens.
  b. Nov. 16, 1809. d. Aug. 7, 1895.

3 ch. 36. Maria F., b. May 10, 1840; m. Nov. 6, 1862, Thomas R. Wade.
  37. Ella T., b. Dec. 19, 1842; m. Nov. 14, 1865, Charles J. Barnes.
  38. J. Wickham, b. Apr. 26, 1844; m. June 16, 1873, Emma Harriet Parker.

21.

DANIEL THEODORE TUTHILL, s. Thomas and Abigail (Terry) Tuthill.
  b. July 17, 1817. m. Apr. 10, 1841. d. Sep. 27, 1889.

Rosina D. Cartwright, d. William R. and Nancy (Howe) Cartwright.
  b.

3 ch. 39. John Stewart, b. Mar. 13, 1842; m. Dec. 23, 1863, Harmony M. Penny.
  40. Alfred Theodore, b. Nov. 5, 1847; m. June 27, 1883, Emma L. Dickerson.
  41. Nancy Howe, b. Feb. 27, 1852, m. June 11, 1890, Theodore C. Hance.

22.

JOSEPH L. TUTHILL, s. Dr. Seth and Mary (Lewis) Tuthill.
  b. July 16, 1812. m. Mar. 20, 1835. d. Oct. 14, 1886.

Elizabeth B. Dyer, da. Caleb and Mehitable (Brown) Dyer.
  b. Sep. 3, 1815. d. Sep. 23, 1876.

3 ch. 42. Oscar Fitzerland, b. May 10, 1836; m. Oct. 24, 1861, Frances A. Conklin.
  43. Stratton Huntting, b. Aug. 31, 1840; m. Dec. 28, 1864, Harriet M. Young.
  44. Roswell Howe, b. Oct. 3, 1848; m. Jan. 10, 1869, Fannie L. Fournier.

23.

MARY ELIZABETH KING, da. Gamaliel and Catherine O (Snow) King.
  b. Sep. 23, 1822. m. Nov. 23, 1842. d. May 4, 1887.

James H. Cornwall, s. Richard and Mary (Herbert) Cornwall.
  b. Dec. 29, 1820. d. Feb. 26, 1883.

6 ch. Mary M., b. June 1844, d. Jan. 24, 1846.
  *James H., b. July 8, 1847; m. Nov. 13, 1872, Frederica B. Kline; no issue.
  45. George L., b. Dec. 29, 1849; m. Apr. 9, 1873, M. Fanny Jacobs.
  Catherine K., b. Oct. 2, 1851, d. Dec. 15, 1852.
  46. Robert G., b. Jan. 20, 1854; m. Oct. 17, 1881, Florence H. Conklin.
  Edward W., b. July 26, 1857, d. Mar. 27, 1861.
(*) d. Dec. 21, 1877.

24.

MARTHA M. KING, da. Gamaliel and Catherine O. (Snow) King.
  b. Jan. 12, 1826. m. Feb. 28, 1846. d. May 27, 1898.

Alfred Bridgeman, s. Thomas and Catherine (Eastmond) Bridgeman.
  b. 1818.

5 ch. Julia K., b. 1846, d unm. 1866.
  47. Alfred, b. 1849; m. 1887, Jennie Adams.
  48. Katherine H., b. 1852; m. 1872, Charles St. John Vail.
  Walter, G., b. 1855, d. unm. 1883.
  49. Ella M., b. 1860; m. 1881, Augustus W. Bell.

25.

GEORGE LUTHER KING, s. Gamaliel and Catherine O. (Snow) King.
  b. Mar. 15, 1828. m. Mar. 6, 1854. d. June 30, 1869.

Martha Rosetta Aldrich, da. Daniel (?) Aldrich.
  b.

3 ch. Elbert Gamaliel, b. m. Orpha Virginia, b. George Lester, b.

26.

SARAH S. KING, da. Gamaliel and Catherine O. (Snow) King.
  b. Sep. 8, 1831. m. July 9, 1856.

George B. Jellison, s. William and Julia A. (Tisdale) Jellison.
  b. June 14, 1831. d. Apr. 12, 1891.

1 ch. William G., b. May 27, 1858, d. unm. Mar. 5, 1893.

27.

SARAH M. KING, da. Lester and Mary (Corwin) King.
 b. Apr. 22, 1841. m. Dec. 28, 1864.

*Charles Conkling, s. Thomas P. and Harriet (Woodhull) Conkling.
 b. May 23, 1834.
1 ch. *Archie K.*, b. July 21, 1866, d. ae. 21.
(*) m. a 2d time, a Miss Elizabeth Hallock, da. William Hallock.

28.

NOAH TUTHILL, s. Moses and Lydia (Collins) Tuthill.
 b. Dec. 20, 1843. m. Feb. 17, 1869.

Margaret H. Tuthill, da. Thomas G. and Elsie A. (Davis) Tuthill.
 b. Aug. 27, 1846.
2 ch. *Zada*, b. m. Jefferson Smith.
  Edna, b.
(*) Has 2 ch., Clarence and Fred.

29.

BURR TUTHILL, s. Hiram and Maria (Delamater) Tuthill.
 b. Sep. 13, 1840. m. 1st, Oct. 21, 1862. 2d, Mar. 1882.

1st, Nealy Farnsworth, da. Charles and Anna (Bush) Farnsworth.
 b. July 3, 1843. d. Oct. 3, 1880.

2d, Marion A. Rogers, da. James L. and Charrilla (Curtis) Rogers.
 b. Oct. 18, 1836.
3 ch. *Maria K.*, b. Sep. 26, 1863; m. Charles Van Schoick.
  °*Frank S.*, b. Aug. 28, 1866; m. Lena Wetmore. *Guy Burr*, b Nov. 27, 1876.
(*) Has 4 ch., Cary, Burr, John and Margarite. (°) Has 1 ch , Chauncey Wetmore.

30.

FRANCES TUTHILL, da. Hiram and Maria (Delamater) Tuthill.
 b. June 7, 1843. m. June 20, 1864.

Fred. C. Rogers, s. James L. and Charrilla (Curtis) Rogers.
 b. Mar. 15, 1841.
9 ch. *F. Willis*, b. Aug. 12, 1867; m. Mary Harold.
  Ira C., b. May 22, 1870. *George B.*, b. June 16, 1872.
  I. Walter, b. Jan. 30, 1875. *Elizabeth H.*, b. Mar. 19, 1878.
  Hiram T., b. Dec. 21, 1879, d. Feb. 7, 1885. *Linton J.*, b. June 4, 1882, d. Feb. 27, 1885.
  Bernice, b. June 24, 1885. *Mary*, b. Mar. 22, 1888.
(*) Has 1 ch., Fred. H.

31.

MARY TUTHILL, da. Hiram and Maria (Delamater) Tuthill.
 b. Nov. 27, 1847. m. Feb. 6, 1876. d. Jan. 4, 1895.

A. S. Hilton, s. Robert and Betsy (Young) Hilton.
 b. Sep. 1, 1852.
5 ch. *Ralph*, } twins, b. Nov. 24, 1876. *Edwin B.*, b. Jan. 8, 1880.
  Hiram, }
  Sarah, b. Jan. 31, 1884. *Sardh*, b. Jan. 31, 1887, d. Sep. 4, 1889.

32.

SETH H. TUTHILL, s. Thomas G. and Elsie A. (Nealy) Tuthill.
 b. Feb. 28, 1839. m.

Content Almy Chase, da. William and Ruth (Gifford) Chase.
 b
2 ch. 50. *Isabella Josephine*, b. Oct. 28. 1858; m. May 2, 1882, Rev. Thomas E. Bartlett.
  William Henry, b. May 31, 1860.

33.

ADELIA TUTHILL, da. Thomas G. and Elsie A. (Nealy) Tuthill.
 b. Jan. 28, 1835. m. Dec. 24, 1854.

Melvin B. Nichols, s. Elam and Sophia (Davis) Nichols.
 b. Oct. 12, 1828.
3 ch. 51. *Ada*, b. Apr. 25, 1864; m. Apr. 23, 1885, Louis E. Draper.
  May, b. July 4, 1867. *George T.*, b. Apr. 2, 1875.

34.

REV. GEORGE W. TUTHILL, s. Thomas G. and Elsie A. (Nealy) Tuthill.
 b. Sep. 30, 1836. m. June 20, 1858.

Elizabeth Howe, da. Luther and Mary (Eager) Howe.
 b. Nov. 7, 1837.
9 ch. 52. *Ella*, b. July 22, 1859; m. Sep. 29, 1880, Thomas Dorsey. *Erta*, b. Dec. 6, 1862.
  Jay R., b. Oct. 31, 1864; m. Nov. 20, 1890, °Mable Monroe. *George T.*, b. Dec. 31, 1866.
 53. *Margaret C.*, b. Sep. 18, 1868; m. Feb. 23, 1887, Dr. Ralph P. Beebe.
  Elisabeth, b. Oct. 19, 1871. *B. Cartwright*, b. July 5, 1873.
  Mary Ellen, b. June 2, 1875. *Fanny Mayor*, b. July 6, 1877.
(*) Has 1 ch., Monroe R. (°) da. of Dr. and Aggis (Aber) Monroe.

35.

CHARLES HENRY TUTHILL, s. Aaron B. and Clarette (Brooks) Tuthill.
b. July 22, 1832.   m. Sep. 24, 1854.   d.   1897.

Sarah E. Wells, da. Daniel D. and Evalina (Booth) Wells.
b. Dec. 27, 1834.

1 ch.   *J. Clarence*, b. Oct. 13, 1859; m. Dec. 4, 1884, Rosa B. Terry.

36.

MARIA F. TUTHILL, da. Ezra A. and Phebe E. (Havens) Tuthill.
b. May 10, 1840.   m. Nov. 6, 1862.

Thomas R. Wade, of Brooklyn, New York.
b. Mar. 26, 1836.

2 ch. **54.** *W. Cortland*, b. Sep. 4, 1864; m. in   1890, Mary K. Osborn.
Florence A., b. Dec. 27, 1869.

37.

ELLA T. TUTHILL, da. Ezra A. and Phebe E. (Havens) Tuthill.
b. Dec. 19, 1842.   m. Nov. 14, 1865.

Charles J. Barnes, s. David and Fanny (Baker) Barnes.
b. Aug. 6, 1834.

2 ch.   **David W.*, b. Apr. 7, 1867; m.   Minnie Cately.   *Harry H.*, b. Aug. 16, 1886.
(*) Has 2 ch., Robert C., b. Oct.   1894, and Marjorie T., b. Oct.   1895.

38.

J. WICKHAM TUTHILL, s. Ezra A. and Phebe E. (Havens) Tuthill.
b. Apr. 26, 1844.   m. June 16, 1873.

Emma Harriet Parker, da. Jonas and Mehitable B. (Silver) Parker.
b. Oct. 7, 1848.

1 ch.   *Amie A.*, b. Mar. 8, 1879.

39.

JOHN STEWART TUTHILL, s. Daniel T. and Rosina D. (Cartwright) Tuthill.
b. Mar. 13, 1842.   m. Dec. 22, 1863.

Harmony M. Penny, da. George G. and Esther S. (Havens) Penny.
b. June 17, 1844.

1 ch.   **Esther A.*, b. May 20, 1866; m. Dec. 23, 1890, William D. Loper.
(*) See Douglass genealogy, No. 20.

40.

ALFRED THEODORE TUTHILL, s. Daniel T. and Rosina D. (Cartwright) Tuthill.
b. Nov. 5, 1847.   m. June 27, 1883.

Emma Louisa Dickerson, da. Nathan P. and Louisa B. (Simpson) Dickerson.
b. July 28, 1860.

3 ch.   *Alfred Theodore*, b. Mar. 28, 1885, d. Mar. 4, 1893.
Gertrude Louise, b. June 13, 1888.   *Thomas E. C.*, b. July 9, 1894.

41.

NANCY HOWE TUTHILL, da. Daniel T. and Rosina D. (Cartwright) Tuthill.
b. Feb. 27, 1852.   m. June 11, 1890.

Theodore Crane Hance, s. Joseph L. and Caroline (Borden) Hance.
b. Mar. 20, 1842.

1 ch.   *Theodore Crane*, b. Nov. 21, 1891.

42.

OSCAR F. TUTHILL, s. Joseph L. and Elizabeth B. (Dyer) Tuthill.
b. May 10, 1836.   m. Oct. 24, 1861.   d. Aug. 22, 1897.

Frances A. Conklin, da. William and Phebe (Beebe) Conklin.
b. Sep. 16, 1837.

2 ch.   *William Conklin*, b. Oct. 23, 1866; m. Sep. 20, 1892, *Mary J. Young.
°*Irving Mansfield*, b. Oct. 1, 1871; m. June 27, 1896, Mary Goudey.
(*) da. of George W. and Maria (King) Young, b. May 30, 1866.
(°) Had 1 ch., Irving Mansfield, b. Feb. 12, 1898, d. Feb. 26, 1898.

43.

STRATTON H. TUTHILL, s. Joseph L. and Elizabeth B. (Dyer) Tuthill.
b. Aug. 31, 1840.   m. Dec. 28, 1864.

Harriet M. Young, da. Barzilia and Abigail (Latham) Young.
b. Oct. 25, 1836.

2 ch. **55.** *Alexander Huntting*, b. Aug. 28, 1866; m.   Estelle M. Potter.
56. *Roscoe Stevenson*, b. July 5, 1868; m. Dec. 11, 1888, Frances Isabel Rackett.

44.

ROSWELL H. TUTHILL, s. Joseph L. and Elizabeth B. (Dyer) Tuthill.
   b. Oct. 3, 1848.   m. Jan. 10, 1869.

Fannie L. Fournier, da. John and Maria (Fithian) Fournier.
   b. Jan. 8, 1848.

3 ch.   *Charles Lewis*, b. Jan. 20, 1871; m. Nov.   1897, Grace Lyon Grant.
   Lyle Fournier, b. Dec. 23, 1875.   *Roy Eldredge*, b. Nov. 22, 1879.

45.

GEORGE L. CORNWALL, s. James and Mary (King) Cornwall.
   b. Dec. 29, 1849.   m. Apr. 9, 1873.   d.

M. Fanny Jacobs, da. John and Rebecca (Carrier) Jacobs.
   b.

2. ch.   *John Edward*, b. Apr. 29, 1874.   *George Francis*, b. Sep. 22, 1875.

46.

DR. ROBERT CORNWALL, s. James and Mary (King) Cornwall.
   b. Jan. 20, 1854.   m. Oct. 17, 1881.

Florence H. Conklin, da. Benjamin F. and Arminda H. (Aldridge) Conklin.
   b. Sep. 11, 1857.

4 ch.   *May*, b. Jan. 12, 1883.   *Benjamin C.*, b. Mar. 5, 1885.
   Robert L., b. Mar. 20, 1887, d. May 14, 1888.   *Raymond*, b. May 25, 1890.

47.

ALFRED BRIDGEMAN, s. Alfred and Martha M. (King) Bridgeman.
   b.   1849.   m.   1887.

Jennie Adams, da. George and Sarah E. (Van Velsor) Adams.
   b.   1855.

1 ch.   *Walter A.*, b.   1889.

48.

KATHERINE H. BRIDGEMAN, da. Alfred and Martha M. (King) Bridgeman.
   b.   1852.   m.   1872.

Charles St. John Vail, s. Walter S. and Emma (Nash) Vail.
   b.   1846.

2 ch.   **Walter S.*, b.   1873; m.   1896, Ella H. Sleicher.
   Martha B., b.   1875, m.   1897, Charles E. Leicht.

(*) Has 1 ch., Charles St. John, b.   1897.

49.

ELLA M. BRIDGEMAN, da. Alfred and Martha M. (King) Bridgeman.
   b.   1860.   m.   1881.

Augustus W. Bell, s. Augustus W. and Caroline (Johnes) Bell.
   b.   1855.

2 ch.   *Alfred Augustus*, b.   1884.   *Caroline A.*, b.   1886.

50.

ISABELLA JOSEPHINE TUTHILL, da. Seth H. and Content A. (Chase) Tuthill.
   b. Oct. 28, 1858.   m. May 2, 1882.

Rev. Thomas E. Bartlett, s. Jonathan and Sarah (Shute) Bartlett.
   b. Sep. 20, 1853.

3 ch.   *Ruth E.*, b. Apr. 2, 1885, d. July 13, 1888.   *Florence E.*, b. Apr. 20, 1888.
   Faith, b. Jan. 30, 1891.

51.

ADA NICHOLS, da. Melvin B. and Adelia (Tuthill) Nichols.
   b. Apr. 25, 1864.   m. Apr. 23, 1885.

Louis E. Draper, s.
   b. Anr. 25, 1864.

4 ch.   *Carrie May*, b. July 6, 1886.   *Rena E.*, b. Dec. 30, 1887.
   L   E., b. Mar. 28, 1889.   *Agnes T.*, b. Aug. 8, 1890.

52.

ELLA TUTHILL, da. Rev. George W. and Elizabeth (Howe) Tuthill.
   b. July 22, 1859.   m. Sep. 29, 1880.

Thomas Dorsey, s. William A. and Margarette (Kinney) Dorsey.
   b.

2 ch.   *Elsie Theo*, b. Oct. 12, 1884.   *Carl Lester*, b. Sep. 21, 1888.

53.

MARGARET C. TUTHILL, da. Rev. George W. and Elizabeth (Howe) Tuthill.
   b. Sep. 18, 1868.   m. Feb. 23, 1887.

Dr. Ralph Palmer Beebe, s. Albert and Mary J. (Murray) Beebe.
   b.

1 ch.   *Ralph J.*, b. Oct. 18, 1888.

54.

W. CORTLAND WADE, s. Thomas R. and Maria F. (Tuthill) Wade.
  b. Sep. 4, 1864.   m.   1890.

  *Mary K. Osborn, da. David C. and Josephine (Case) Osborn.
  b. May 10, 1873.

3 ch.   *Julia C.*, b. Apr. 23, 1891.   *Zelina O.*, b. Aug. 28, 1894.   *Ezra T.*, b. Mar. 19, 1896.
(*) See Case genealogy, No. 12.

55.

ALEXANDER H. TUTHILL, s. Stratton H. and Hattie M. (Young) Tuthill.
  b. Aug. 28, 1866.   m.

  Estelle M. Potter, da. William T. and Lucinda G. (Latham) Potter.
  b. Feb. 1, 1870.

1 ch.   *Reginald Huntting*, b.

56.

ROSCOE S. TUTHILL, s. Stratton H. and Hattie M. (Young) Tuthill.
  b. July 5, 1868.   m. Dec. 11, 1888.

  Frances I. Rackett, da. George K. and Phebe (Edwards) Rackett.
  b. Aug. 26, 1868.

6 ch.   *Marion Isabel*, b. Nov. 18, 1889.   *Abby Elizabeth*, b. Feb. 17, 1891.
        Edgar Stratton, b. July 24, 1892.   *William Chatfield*, b. Oct. 7, 1893.
        George Lewis, b. Oct. 9, 1894.   *Cora Amelia*, b. Mar. 21, 1896.

THOMAS CONKLING.
ANCESTORS.

A.

JOHN CONKLING, s. John and Mary (   ) Conkling.
  b.   m. about 1680.   d. Mar. 4, 1705–6.

  Sarah Horton, da. Barnabas and Mary (   ) Horton.
  b.   1663.   d. Aug. 18, 1753.

7 ch. 1. *Thomas*, b.   1695; m. June 29, 1732, Rachel Moore.
       John, b.   1687; m.   1728, Abigail Rider.
       Henry, b   1690; m. { 1st, Jan. 1, 1716–7, Temperance Bayley.
                                     { 2d,   1742, Wid. Mary Budd.
       Joseph, b.   *Sarah*, b.   d. (?) unm.
       **Rachel*, b.   m. Jan. 13, 1731–2, John Moore.
       Mary, b.   m.   1716–7, Benjamin L'Hommedieu.
(*) Rachel may have had two husbands, the first being Ebenezer Loper, m. Jan 13, 1726–7.

1.

THOMAS CONKLING, s. John and Sarah (Horton) Conkling.
  b.   1695.   m. June 29, 1732.

  Rachel Moore, da. Benjamin and Abigail (   ) Moore.
  b. 1703–4.   d. Mar. 4, 1782.

5 ch. 2. *Thomas*, b.   1733; m. July 30, 1760, Phebe Glover.
       Mary, b.   1734–5, d. unm. Jan. 19, 1809.   *Shadrach*, b.   1739–40, d. unm. Jan. 23, 1827.
       James, b. May 10, 1742, d. Oct. 23, 1754.
       Benjamin, b. Apr. 8, 1744, d. unm. Feb. 21. 1826.

2.

THOMAS CONKLING, s. Thomas and Rachel (Moore) Conkling.
  b.   1733.   m. July 30, 1760.   d. Feb. 4, 1783.

  Phebe Glover, da.
  b.   d.

6 ch.   *Thomas*, b.
       3. *Benjamin*, b.   1761; m.   Anna Parker.
       4. *Lewis*, b. Sep. 18, 1768; m.   Lydia Tuthill.   *Rachel*, b.
       Phebe, b.   *James*, b. Nov.   1770.

3.

BENJAMIN CONKLING, s. Thomas and Phebe (Glover) Conkling.
  b.   1761.   m.   d. Aug. 26, 1803.

  Anna Parker, da. Abraham and Mary (Budd) Parker.
  b. July 24, 1759.   d. Feb. 24, 1802.

4 ch. 5. *Asenath*, b. July 15. 1780; m. Aug. 6, 1817, Moses Griffing.
       Mary Ann, b.   1791–2, d. unm. Mar. 16, 1832.   *Harvey*, b.   d. unm.
       Lucretia, b. Sep. 10, 1794; m. Mar. 10, 1814, George Cartwright.

4.

LEWIS CONKLING, s. Thomas and Phebe (Glover) Conkling
    b. Sep. 18, 1768.   m.   d. Jan. 27, 1832.

  Lydia Tuthill, da. James and Elizabeth (Mack) Tuthill.
    b. Jan. 2, 1770.   d. July 25, 1833.

7 ch. *Thomas,* b. Feb. 17, 1790, d. unm. June 27, 1840.
     **Nancy,* b. Jan. 29, 1792; m.   Ezekiel Raynor.
     7. *Phebe,* b. Sep. 10, 1795; m. { 1st,   Devoe.
                           { 2d,   Thomas Brewer.
     8. *Lewis,* b. Jan. 6, 1798; m. May 26, 1827, Polly M. Tuthill.
     9. *Lydia,* b. Oct. 8, 1800; m.   Gershom Howell.
     °*Joel,* b. June 15, 1803; m.   Mary A. King.
     10. *Polly M.,* b. Feb. 28, 1808; m.   Vincent J. Clark.
(*) d. Feb. 5, 1854. had 3 ch., Tuthill, Phebe C. and Elijah. (°) d. Feb. 24, 1865, had 2 ch., William Lewis who d. in infancy, and Fannie, who m. and has 2 ch.
NOTE.—This family wrote their name without the " g."

5.

ASENATH CONKLING, da. Benjamin and Anna (Parker) Conkling.
    b. July 15, 1789.   m. Aug. 6, 1817.   d. Aug. 13. 1865.

  Moses D. Griffing, s. Moses and Sybil (King) Griffing.
    b. Aug. 2, 1790.

7 ch. **Maria Louise,* b. Apr. 7, 1819; m. Oct. 19, 1836, Joseph B. Hudson.
     Mary Ann, b. May 8, 1821; m. Oct. 13, 1841, ‡Samuel W. Sherman.
     11. *Asenath,* b. Oct. 29, 1823; m. June 5, 1855, Thomas M. Duvall.
     Napoleon B., b. Oct. 1, 1825.
     12. *Glorian,* b. Apr. 15, 1827; m. Apr. 26, 1863, Thomas Johnston.
     Isabella, b. Sep. 20, 1828.
     13. *Nicholas C.,* b. Oct. 9, 1830; m. Nov. 24, 1853, Harriet Kinne.
(*) See Hudson genealogy, No. 35.   (°) d., had twins who d.   (‡) See Case genealogy, No. 10.

6.

LUCRETIA CONKLING, da. Benjamin and Anna (Parker) Conkling.
    b. Sep. 10, 1794.   m. Mar. 10, 1814.   d. Sep. 16, 1879.

  George Cartwright, s. Edward and Lydia (Kenyon) Cartwright.
    b. Jan. 27, 1794.   d. Feb. 16, 1837.

6 ch. **14.** *Benjamin C.,* b. May 23, 1815; m. May 5, 1838, Hanna M. Tuthill.
     **Anna P.,* b. Oct. 20, 1817; m. May 1, 1836, Remington Havens.
     °*Lucretia C.,* b. Nov. 1, 1820; m. May 10, 1839, ‖Martin L. Prince; no issue.
     †*George,* b. Feb. 23, 1823; m.   ‡Louisa N. Tuthill.
     Sarah Ann, b. Sep. 7, 1827, d.   *Mary Eugenia,* b. Dec. 21, 1831, d.
(*) See Jonathan Havens genealogy, No. 117.   (°) d. Apr. 14, 1877   (‖) s. of Ezra and Phebe (Horton) Prince, b. Nov. 17, 1812, d. Oct. 13, 1883.   (†) d. July 26, 1895, had 1 ch., George, who d. in infancy.   (‡) da. of James G. and Cleora (Rackett) Tuthill.

7.

PHEBE CONKLIN, da. Lewis and Lydia (Tuthill) Conklin.
    b. Sep 10, 1795.   m. 1st,   2d,   d. July 1, 1877.

  1st,   Devoe, s.
    b.   d.

  2d, Thomas Brewer, s.
    b.   d.

2 ch. **Lydia A.,* b.   m. Nov. 9, 1857, Albert L. Conklin.
     15. *Alva G.,* b. June 7, 1838; m. Nov. 13, 1861, Harriet A. Palmer.
(*) See No. 16.

8.

LEWIS CONKLIN, s. Lewis and Lydia (Tuthill) Conklin.
    b. Jan. 6, 1798.   m. May 26, 1827.   d. July 24, 1877.

  Polly M. Tuthill, da. David and Mary (Terry) Tuthill.
    b. July 13, 1801.   d. July 3, 1878.

8 ch. *Lydia A.,* b. Sep. 28, 1828, d. Oct. 14, 1828.
     16. *Albert L.,* b. June 27, 1830; m. { 1st, Nov. 9, 1857, Lydia A. Brewer.
                           { 2d, May 2, 1870. Josephine A. Goldsmith.
     Thomas H., b. July 26, 1823, d. Oct. 24, 1853. *Eugene,* b. Oct. 25, 1835, d. Sep. 14, 1862.
     17. *David T.,* b. Oct. 8, 1839; m. Aug. 21, 1862, Julia L. Wells.
     **Joel S.,* b. Oct. 8, 1839; m. Oct. 22, 1867, Sarah E. Moulton; no issue.
     18. *Mary M.,* b. Feb. 13, 1842; m. Aug. 23, 1862, Ansel D. Griffing.
     Charles T., b. Mar. 14, 1845, d. Dec. 24, 1867.
(*) d. Sep. 26, 1871.

9.

LYDIA CONKLIN, da. Lewis and Lydia (Tuthill) Conklin.
    b. Oct. 8, 1800.   m.   d. Dec. 16, 1880.

  Gershom H. Howell, s. Isaac and Mary (Hawkins) Howell.
    b. May 28, 1804.   d.

7 ch. *William L.*, b. Feb. 27, 1825, d. Mar. 26, 1825.
  Lydia C., b. May 16, 1826, d June 3, 1826. *William L.*, b. Apr. 15, 1829, d. May 15, 1829.
 19. *Joel C.*, b. July 12, 1832; m. Sep. 24, 1854, Phebe H. Carter.
  Sarah M., b. July 18, 1835. **Lucy A.*, b. Dec. 16, 1837. †*Alfred B.*, b. Apr. 10, 1842.
(*) is m. and has 3 ch. (†) is m. and has 3 ch.

10.

POLLY M. CONKLIN, da. Lewis and Lydia (Tuthill) Conklin.
  b. Feb. 28, 1808. m. d. Aug. 8, 1886.
Vincent J. Clark, s. John and Elizabeth (Corwin) Clark.
  b. Oct. 29, 1807. d. Dec. 25, 1877.
2 ch. *Annie E.*, b. Aug. 2, 1843.   *George W.*, b. July 16, 1855.

11.

ASENATH GRIFFING, da. Moses and Asenath (Conkling) Griffing.
  b. Oct. 29. 1823. m. June 5, 1855. d. Sep. 27, 1898.
Thomas Markus Duvall, of North Haven, Long Island.
  b. Mar. 26, 1826. d. Mar. 31, 1870.
2 ch. *Isabel G.*, b. Aug. 9, 1858.   *Ralph G.*, b. Sep. 7, 1861.

12.

GLORIAN GRIFFING, da. Moses and Asenath (Conkling) Griffing.
  b. Apr. 15, 1827. m. Apr. 26, 1863. d. Dec. 2, 1880.
Thomas Johnston, s. William and Alice (Cairns) Johnston.
  b. Dec. 12, 1816.
2 ch. *Thomas H.*, b. Mar. 20, 1866.
 20. *Jesse Louise*, b. Apr. 14, 1868, m. Mar. 18, 1890, Fred B. Filmore.

13.

NICHOLAS C. GRIFFING, s. Moses and Asenath (Conkling) Griffing.
  b. Oct. 9, 1830. m. Nov. 24, 1853.
Harriet Kinne, da. William and Eliza (Evans) Kinne.
  b. Aug. 21, 1832.
2 ch. **Eliza Ann*, b. Aug. 23, 1854; m. Feb. 10, 1879, Winfield Cartwright.
  Moses Bowditch, b. Aug. 18, 1860; m. May 18, 1897, °Phebe E. Smith.
(*) See No. 22. (°)da. of Scudder and Mary J. (Kent) Smith, b. June 3, 1885.

14.

BENJAMIN C. CARTWRIGHT, s. George and Lucretia (Conkling) Cartwright.
  b. May 13, 1815. m. May 5, 1838. d. Dec. 11, 1896.
Hannah M. Tuthill, da. Thos. and Abigail (Terry) Tuthill. See Tuthill genealogy, No. 7.
  b. Apr. 10, 1814. d. Feb. 21, 1888.
10 ch. *Oscar D. B.*, b. June 1, 1840.
  *Abigail Terry, b. Dec. 24, 1841; m. Nov. 14, 1864, Charles Markus Griffing.
  Martin L. P., b. Mar. 17, 1843, d. Oct. 17, 1863.
  Benjamin C., b. Nov. 9, 1845; m. { 1st, May 28, 1867, °Mary Woodruff. } no isssue.
              { 2d, Dec. 25, 1889, ‖Minnie Chichester. }
  †*Sarah Ann*, b. Aug. 1, 1847; m. May 29, 1867, Benjamin C. Hudson.
  Arthur Stewart, b. Sep. 19, 1849; m. Dec. 6, 1871, ¶Ella E. Sanford; no issue.
 21. *Hannah T.*, b. June 19, 1851; m. Dec. 6, 1875, Gilbert W. Rogers.
  ‡*Mary R. W.*, b. Dec. 31, 1852; m. Oct. 30, 1877, Elias Havens Payne.
 22. *Winfield Scott*, b Feb. 24, 1855; m. Feb. 10, 1879, Eliza Evans Griffing.
 23. *Clarence C.*, b. Mar. 24, 1857; m. Jan. 19, 1887, Frances C. Cullum.
(*) See Jonathan Havens genealogy, No. 271. (°) da. of Laurence V'B. and Mary (Sayre) Woodruff,
b. Feb. 14, 1842, d. Oct. 14, 1888. (‖) da. of Mahlon and Harriet (Walker) Chichester, b. Jan.
8, 1858. (†) See Hudson genealogy, No. 115. (¶) da. of Alfred H. and Esther A. (Case)
Sanford, b. Apr. 19, 1852. (‡) See Jonathan Havens genealogy, No. 245.

15.

ALVA G. BREWER, s. Thomas and Phebe (Conklin) Brewer.
  b. June 7, 1838. m. Nov. 13, 1861. d. May 13, 1887.
Harriet Alice Palmer, da. Wilman and Susan (Bradley) Palmer.
  b.
8 ch. **24.** *Nellie Rose*, b. Sep. 24, 1862; m. Apr. 18, 1888, Richard H. Woodruff.
  Albert Conklin, b. June 24, 1864; m. Jan. 6, 1896, FannieL. Fowler.
 25. *Fannie Conklin*, b. Jan. 23, 1867; m. Dec. 6, 1892, Lovell R. Stone.
 26. *Elizabeth Hill*, b. Jan. 2, 1870; m. William H. Blatchley.
  Angeline Brewer, b. Feb. 11, 1872. *Harry Rogers*, b. July 8, 1878.
  Mary Brewer, b. Jan. 30, 1883. *Harriet Alice*, b. Mar. 29, 1884.

16.

ALBERT L. CONKLIN, s. Lewis and Polly M. (Tuthill) Conklin.
b. June 27, 1830.   m. 1st, Nov. 9, 1857.   2d, May   1870.

1st, Lydia A. Brewer, da. Thomas and Phebe (Conklin) Brewer.
b.   d. Feb. 17, 1868.

2d, Josephine A. Goldsmith, da. Joseph A. and Caroline (Moore) Goldsmith.
b.

2 ch.   *Albert L.*, b. Nov. 1, 1871; m. Feb. 16, 1898, Jessica Ives.
Chandler G., b. Dec. 4, 1875.

17.

DAVID T. CONKLIN, s. Lewis and Polly M. (Tuthill) Conklin.
b. Oct. 8, 1839.   m. Aug. 21, 1862.

Julia L. Wells, da. Henry and Hannah (Landon) Wells.
b. Aug. 24, 1844.

2 ch. **27.** *Eugene L.*, b. May 28, 1866; m. Sep. 12, 1894, Agnes C. Richardson.
M. Louise, b. Dec. 13, 1873.

18.

MARY M. CONKLIN, da. Lewis and Polly M. (Tuthill) Conklin.
b. Feb. 13, 1842.   m. Aug. 23, 1862.

Ansel D. Griffing, of Westhampton, Long Island.
b.   d. Aug. 4, 1871.

3 ch.   *Lewis E.*, b. Nov. 4, 1863.   *Albert C.*, b. Oct. 3, 1868, d. Apr. 28, 1869.
Hannah M., b. July 6, 1870.

19.

JOEL C. HOWELL, s. Gershom H. and Lydia (Conklin) Howell.
b. July 12, 1832.   m. Sep. 24, 1854.

Phebe H. Carter, da. Silas and Selina (Raynor) Carter.
b. Sep. 21, 1834.

7 ch. **28.** *Rinelche H.*, b. Jan. 3, 1856; m. Nov. 8, 1876, Willard F. Hallock.
29. *Thomas H.*, b. Dec. 10, 1857; m. Dec. 21, 1882, Grace A. Tripp.
30. *Silas H.*, b. July 13, 1859; m. Sep. 1, 1886, Lizzie C. Denham.
31. *Lydia C.*, b. Apr. 15, 1861; m. Mar. 17, 1880, F. Porter Howell.
32. *J. Ernest*, b. July 17, 1866; m. Nov. 29, 1887, Sydney R. Burgess.
33. *Caroline A.*, b. Aug. 14, 1868; m. Sep. 8, 1886, Arthur H. Tuthill.
Alfred V. B., b. Feb. 13, 1871.

20.

JESSIE LOUISE JOHNSTON, da. Thomas and Glorian (Griffing) Johnston.
b. Apr. 14, 1868.   m. Mar. 18, 1890.

Fred B. Filmore, s. James S. and Mary E. (Fawcett) Filmore.
b. Oct. 17, 1867.

3 ch.   *Fred Donald*, b. June 13, 1891.   *Ralph Johnston*, b. Dec. 5, 1893.
Glorian, b. Dec. 15, 1895.

21.

HANNAH T. CARTWRIGHT, da. Benjamin C. and Hannah M. (Tuthill) Cartwright.
b. June 19, 1851.   m. Dec. 6, 1875.

Gilbert W. Rogers, s. Anson and Lucretia (Beebe) Rogers.
b. Sep. 27, 1846.

1 ch.   *Edna*, b. June 12, 1881.

22.

WINFIELD SCOTT CARTWRIGHT, s. Benj. C. and Hannah M. (Tuthill) Cartwright.
b. Feb. 24, 1855.   m. Feb. 10, 1879.

ELIZA ANN GRIFFING, da. Nicholas C. and Harriet (Kinne) Griffing. See No. 13.
b. Aug. 23, 1854.

2 ch.   *Benjamin Conkling*, b. Jan. 11, 1880.   *Winfield Scott*, b. May 16, 1881.

23.

CLARENCE C. CARTWRIGHT, s. Benjamin C. and Hannah M. (Tuthill) Cartwright.
b. Mar. 24, 1857.   m. Jan. 19, 1887.

Frances C. Cullum, da. Richard and Frances M. (Cartwright) Cullum.
b.

4 ch.   *George Paul*, b. Feb. 16, 1890.   *Ralph Cullum*, b. Apr. 2, 1892.
Clifford Tuthill, b. Nov. 22, 1895.   *Clarence Clermont*, b. May 22, 1898.

24.

NELLIE ROSE BREWER, da. Alva G. and Harriet A. (Palmer) Brewer.
b. Sep. 26, 1862.   m. Apr. 18, 1888.

Richard H. Woodruff, s. Eleazure and Harriet (Davis) Woodruff.
b.

3 ch.   *Harriet A.*, b. May 29, 1889.   *Alva B.*, b. Mar. 29, 1891.   *Raymon E.*, b. Dec. 17, 1892.

25.

FANNIE CONKLIN BREWER, da. Alva G. and Harriet A. (Palmer) Brewer.
b. Jan. 23, 1867. m. Dec. 6, 1892.
Lovell R. Stone, s. Alvord A. and Lydia (Eaverats) Stone.
b.
1 ch. *Forest Brewer*, b. Mar. 6, 1896.

26.

ELIZABETH HILL BREWER, da. Alva G. and Harriet A. (Palmer) Brewer.
b. Jan. 2, 1870. m.
William H. Blatchley, s. Joel H. and Mary (Davis) Blatchley.
b.
2 ch. *Angeline B.*, b. Sep. 7, 1892. *Joel A.*, b. Mar. 8, 1898.

27.

REV. EUGENE L. CONKLIN, s. David T. and Julia L. (Wells) Conklin.
b. May 28. 1866. m. Sep. 12, 1894.
Agnes C. Richardson, of Webster, New York.
b.
1 ch. *Florence Jeannette*, b. July 1, 1896.

28.

RINELCHE HALLOCK HOWELL, da. Joel C. and Phebe H. (Carter) Howell.
b. Jan. 3, 1856. m. Nov. 8, 1876.
Willard F. Hallock, s. Joel Hallock.
b. July 1855. d. Nov. 12, 1897.
3 ch. *Willard Howell*, b. Nov. 1878. *Robert Fletcher*, b. May 1880. *Victor*, b. June 1892.

29.

THOMAS HENRY HOWELL, s. Joel C. and Phebe H. (Carter) Howell.
b. Dec. 10, 1857. m. Dec. 21, 1882.
Grace A. Tripp, da. Gideon and Betsey (Brewster) Tripp.
b. Sep. 21, 1863.
2 ch. *Ernest Tripp*, b. June 5, 1887. *Henry Merton*, b. July 20, 1892.

30.

SILAS HAWKINS HOWELL, s. Joel C. and Phebe H. (Carter) Howell.
b. July 13, 1859. m. Sep. 1, 1886.
Lizzie C. Dunham, da. William H. and Caroline (Griffin) Dunham.
b. Oct. 1, 1861.
2 ch. *Raynor Dunham*, b. Mar. 29, 1890. *Caroline Carter*, b. Oct. 30, 1894.

31.

LYDIA C. HOWELL, da. Joel C. and Phebe H. (Carter) Howell.
b. Apr. 15, 1861. m. Mar. 17, 1880.
F. Porter Howell, s. Hiram and Belinda (Raynor) Howell.
b. 1859.
5 ch. *Edward Fanning*, b. Dec. 1880. *Ellen Belinda*, b. July 1888.
Lila Lillian, b. Aug. 1, 1890. *Freddie Raynor*, b. Oct. 1892. *Bessie*, b. Sep. 1896.

32.

J. ERNEST HOWELL, s. Joel C. and Phebe H. (Carter) Howell.
b. July 17, 1866. m. Nov. 29, 1887.
Sydney R. Burgess, da. Robert and Sarah (Donnelley) Burgess.
b. Feb. 22, 1868.
3 ch. *Willard Henry*, b. Aug. 20, 1888. *Phoebe Ernestine*, b. Aug. 4, 1890.
Marguerite, b. Aug. 4, 1896.

33.

CAROLINE A. HOWELL, da. Joel C. and Phebe H. (Carter) Howell.
b. Aug. 14, 1868. m. Sep. 8, 1886.
Arthur H. Tuthill, s. Daniel and Caroline (Wells) Tuthill.
b. 1858.
2ch. *Lillie*, b Dec. 24, 1888. *Tracy Emerson*, b. June 1891.

1.

ABRAHAM PARKER,
    b. in England.   m 1st,   m. 2d, Nov. 9, 1742.   d. Mar.   1768.
  1st, Sarah Hudson. da. Jonathan and Sarah (   ) Hudson.
    b. Mar. 27, 1687.
  2d, Wid. Mary Hudson, (*nee* Jennings).
    b.
2 ch.   *Sarah*, b.   m. { 1st, Nov. 3, 1737, John Baldwin, of Hempstead.
                         { 2d,
  2. *Abraham*. b.   m.   Mary Budd.

2.

ABRAHAM PARKER, s. Abraham and Sarah (Hudson) Parker.
    b.   1720.   m.   d. Jan. 12, 1796.
  Mary Budd, da.
    b.
10 ch. **3.** *Phineas*, b. May 20, 1749; m. } 1st.   Hannah Havens.
                             } 2d.   Wid. Bethiah Havens (*nee* Bowditch.)
    Benjamin, bap. June 16. 1751, d. perhaps in 1756.
  4. *William*, bap. July 11, 1752; m. { 1st, Asenath
                               { 2d, Phebe
    James, bap. Apr. 27, 1755, d. Aug. 22, 1773.   *Mary, b.   m.   Samuel Havens.
    °*Anna*, b.   m.   Benjamin Conkling.   *Patience*. b.   d.
  5. *Joseph*, b. 1762; m. Oct. 21, 1787, Experience Cleaves.   *Deborah*, b. 1759, d. Oct. 16. 1761.
    ¦*Sarah*, b.   m. Oct. 1, 1773, †Noah Terry.
(*) See Jonathan Havens genealogy, No. 19. (°) See Conkling genealogy, No. 3.
(¦) Had 5 ch., Phineas, Sarah, Lydia, Lucretia and Jaspar who m. Tinah Barthoff.
(†) Son of Jonathan and Lydia (Tuthill) Terry, b. Sep.   1747, d. Oct.   1815; had a second wife.

3.

PHINEAS PARKER, s. Abraham and Mary (Budd) Parker.
    b. May 20, 1749.   m. 1st,   2d.   d.
  1st, Hannah Havens, da. William and Ruth (   ) Havens.
    b. Dec. 10, 1751.   d. Apr. 7, 1783.
  2d, Wid. Bethiah Havens (*nee* Bowditch), da. Joel and Bethiah (Case) Bowditch.
    b. Sept. 9, 1755.   d.
8 ch.   *Deborah*, b. Nov. 5, 1769.   *Eunice*, b. Oct. 12, 1771, d. Jan. 17, 1772.
    Benjamin, b. Apr. 25, 1774.
  6. *James*, b. Dec. 19, 1776; m. { 1st, Jan. 28, 1802. Hannah Hildreth.
                                    { 2d, Aug. 22, 1826, Rebecca Foster.
    Giles, b. April 24, 1779.   *Phineas*, bap. Jan. 30, 1784.
  7. *Mary*, b. Jan. 19, 1789; m. May,   1817, Arnold Van Scoy.
  8. *Milton*, b. Aug. 29, 1795; m. Feb. 8, 1826, Fanny J. Frothingham.
(*) See John and Henry Havens genealogy, No. 6.

4.

WILLIAM PARKER, s. Abraham and Mary (Budd) Parker.
    b.   1754.   m. 1st, about 1775.   2d.   d. Oct. 2, 1832.
  1st, Asenath   da.
    b.   d. 1786.
  2d, Phebe   da.
    b.   d.
8 ch.   *Henry S.*, b.   1777, d, Oct. 21, 1840.
    *William, bap. July 19. 1782; m. Aug. 26, 1800, °Mary Abigail Fordham.
    Elizabeth, bap. July 19, 1782; m. Dec. 30, 1805, David Gelston, Jr.
    Gilbert, bap. July 19, 1782, d. Nov. 11, 1804.
    A son, b.   1792, drowned July 20, 1796.   *Abraham*. b.   m.   †Nancy
    George. b.   1802, d. Nov. 28, 1822.   *Nancy Maria*. b.   1806, d. Oct. 12, 1828.
(*) Had 1 ch., an infant da. who d. Mar. 5, 1807. (°) d. July 11, 1807. ae. 26. (†) d. Jan. 8, 1813, ae. 26.

5.

JOSEPH PARKER, s Abraham and Mary (Budd) Parker.
    b.   1762.   m. Oct. 21, 1787.   d. Apr. 7, 1835.
  Experience Cleaves, da.
    b.   1763.   d. June 18, 1823.
4 ch.   *Simeon*, b.   d. Apr. 10. 1797.   *Phebe C.*, b.   1790, d. July 31, 1856.
    John, b.   1795, d. Dec. 6, 1832.   *Eliza*, b.   m. May 25, 1824, Michael Burke.

6.

JAMES PARKER, s. Phineas and Hannah (Havens) Parker.
    b. Dec. 19, 1776.   m. 1st, Jan. 28, 1802.   2d, Aug. 22, 1826.   d. June 28, 1848.
  1st, Hannah Hildreth, da.
    b.   1783.   d. Aug. 16, 1825.
  2d, Rebecca Foster, da.   and Sally (   ) Foster.
    b.   1801.   d. Sep. 26, 1848.

5 ch.   *Hetty W.*, b. Nov. 1803, d. Apr. 26, 1870.   *James H.*, b. July 1813. **d. Mar. 25, 1849.**
        Charles, b.   °*Maria*, b. 1811; m. Nov. Highby.   *Carolina, b. m. Lansing Lambert.
(*) Both dead and supposed to have had no issue   (°) d. Apr. 27, 1832, ae. 21.   A James Parker of Sag Harbor m. June 12, 1828. Phebe Whitle of Southampton, according to Sag Harbor Pres. Ch. records.

7.

MARY PARKER, da Phineas and Bethiah (Bowditch) Parker.
     b. Jan. 19, 1789.   m May 8, 1817.   d.

Arnold Van Scoy, s. Isaac and Temperance (Payne) Van Scoy.
     b. Sep. 19, 1793.   d. Aug. 18, 1857.

4 ch.   9. *Marietta*, b. May 26, 1818; m. Oct. 11, 1836, Dr. P. Parker King.
        Charles H., b. Nov. 27, 1820, d. Aug. 4, 1822.
        Charles H., d. Dec. 30, 1823; m. June 19, 1849, Mary G. Johnson; no issue.
     10. *Isaac*, b. Aug. 30, 1827; m. Sep. 5, 1853, Elizabeth T. Harkness.

8.

MILTON PARKER, s. Phineas and Bethiah (Bowditch) Parker.
     b. Aug. 29, 1795.   Feb. 8, 1826.   d. Dec. 10, 1870.

Fanny J. Frothingham, da David and Nancy (Pell) Frothingham.
     b.   1808.   d. July 22, 1874.

5 ch.   *David F.*, b. Dec. 23, 1827, d. June 4, 1858.   *Giles M.*, b. Oct. 23, 1830, d. Apr. 1, 1893.
     Henry H., b. Aug. 11, 1833; supposed to have been lost at sea.
     Edmund A., b. Dec. 23, 1836, d. Jan. 6, 1837.
     11. *Anna Bethiah*, b. Apr. 23, 1839; m. Oct. 21, 1861, Edward Burke.

9.

MARIETTA VAN SCOY, da. Arnold and Mary (Parker) Van Scoy.
     b. May 29, 1818.   m. Oct. 11, 1836.   d. Aug. 16, 1860.

Dr. P. Parker King, s Phineas and Eleanor (Parker) King.
     b.   1800.   d. Aug. 11, 1856.

6 ch.   *Mary*, b. 1838, d. June 19, 1857.
     12. *Eleanor*. b. May 18, 1840;   m. { 1st, Dec.   Charles H. Fordham.
                                         { 2d, Oct. 2, 1887, Arthur Ludlow.
        Charles, b.   1840, d. Sep. 10. 1874.   *Clarence*, b. May   1842, d. unm. Dec. 12. 1874.
        *Harriet. b.   m.   George Stephens.   °*Charlotte*, b.   m.   George Palmer.
(*) Had 2 ch.. Grace who m. Mr. Rogers and has d. had 1 ch., and Mabel.
(°) Has 3 ch.. Maud, George H., both dead, and Marietta who m. William Bole.

10.

ISAAC VAN SCOY, s. Arnold and Mary (Parker) Van Scoy.
     b. Aug. 30, 1827.   m. Sep. 5, 1853.

Elizabeth T. Harkness, da. Aaron and Phebe (Bennet) Harkness.
     b. Mar. 31, 1834.

4 ch.   *Frederick C.*, b. Aug. 28, 1854, d. Sep. 1856.
     *Florence, b. Sep. 11, 1857; m. Oct. 24, 1878, °Stephen Crowell.
     Lillian, b. Sep. 22, 1872.   *Mary K.*, b. Sep. 3, 1875, d. Oct. 1876.
(*) d. Nov. 13, 1801; 2 ch., Laura. d. in infancy and Edward, b. Apr. 27, 1882, d. Sep. 5, 1891. (°) d. 1897.

11.

ANNA BETHIAH PARKER, da. Milton and Fanny S. (Frothingham) Parker.
     b. Apr. 23, 1839.   m. Oct. 21, 1861.

Edward Burke, s. William and Elizabeth (   ) Burke.
     b. Feb. 15, 1824.

1 ch. 13. *Fanny Pell*, b. Oct. 25, 1862; m.   1881, Harry Bisgood.

12.

ELEANOR KING, da. Dr. P. Parker and Marietta (Van Scoy) King.
     b. May 18, 1840.   m. 1st,   2d, Oct. 2, 1887.

1st, Charles Henry Fordham, s. John and Emma (Raynor) Fordham.
     b. June 22, 1835.   d. May 29, 1887.

2d, Arthur Ludlow, s. John and Charity (Homan) Ludlow.
     b.   1845.

4 ch.   *Mary King, b. June 24, 1867; m. Oct. 16, 1889, °Carl Frederick Glaessner.
     †*Emma Charlotte*, b. Aug. 7, 1871; m. Nov. 12, 1890, ‖Herbert Sterling Overton.
     Clarence King. b. Mar. 1873, d. ae. 7 mo.   *Louise Berry*, b. Apr. 21, 1878.
(*) Has 1 ch., Eleanor, b. Jan. 3, 1891.   (°) s. of Carl F. and Caroline Glaessner, b. Feb. 24, 1862.
(†) Has 1 ch., Helene, b. Sep. 3, 1893.   (‖) s. of John and Anna (Simons) Overton, b. Dec. 9, 1867.

13.

FANNY PELL BURKE, da. Edward and Anna B. (Parker) Burke.
     b. Oct. 25, 1862.   m.   1881.

Harry Bisgood, s. Thomas F.   Bisgood.
     b.   1857.

4 ch.   *Thomas*, b. Feb. 6, 1882.   *Arthur*, b June 12, 1884.
     Aimee, b. Dec. 16, 1885.   *Harry*, b. Oct. 18, 1890.

1.

DANIEL BROWN, s. Daniel and Frances (Watson) Brown.
    b. Nov. 15, 1710.   m. 1st,   m. 2d. Dec. 21, 1735.   d. July 12, 1786.

1st, Hannah (?) Hook,
    b. in 1709.   d Sep. 8, 1731.

2d, Mary Havens, da. (?) John and Sarah ( ) Havens.
    b. Dec. 12, 1715.   d. Sep. 5, 1796.

11 ch. *Hannah*, b. Sep. 8, 1731, d. Feb. 26, 1732.   *Ebenezer*, b. Aug. 10, 1737, d. Apr. 25, 1741.
    2. *Hannah*, b. Aug. 27, 1739, m.   Ephraim Fordham
    John, b. Mar. 20, 1741, lost at sea.   *James*, b. Mar. 31, 1743. d. Jan. 14, 1745-6.
    *Desire, b. Sep. 24, 1744; m. Mar. 29, 1770, Nicoll Havens.
    Mary, b. Nov. 4, 1746, d. unm.   *Frances*, b. Jan. 21, 1749-50.
    Abigail, b. June 12, 1752.   *William*, b. July 31, 1754; m. about 1775,   Allen.
    3. *Daniel*, b. July 31, 1756; m. Dec. 17, 1775, Esther Fanning.
(*) See Jonathan Havens genealogy, No. 10.

2.

HANNAH BROWN, s. Daniel and Mary (Havens) Brown.
    b. Aug. 27, 1739.   m.   d.

Ephraim Fordham, s. Nathan and Abigail (Bowditch) Fordham.
    b. Mar. 12, 1737.   d. May   1832.

ch. **James*, b.   m.   °*William B.*, b.   1780; m. } 1st,   +Mary
    { d,
(*) Had Roxanna who m. Nathan Stewart, Frances who m. James Bassett, and John.
(°) d. June 14, 1866; had 1 ch, Frances, d. in infancy.   (†) b. in 1782, d. 1819.

3.

DANIEL BROWN, s. Daniel and Mary (Havens) Brown.
    b. July 31, 1756.   m. Dec. 17, 1775.   Drowned Nov. 22, 1781.

*Esther Fanning, da. Phineas and Mehitable (Wells) Fanning.
    b.   d. Aug. 1817.

4 ch. *William*, b.   *Gilbert*, b.
    4. *Mary*, b   1781; m.   1798, William Corwin.
    5. *Desire*, b. Dec. 6, 1782; m. June 6, 1803, Rev. Whitfield Cowles.
(*) m. twice, her 2d husband being Henry Hudson. See Hudson genealogy, No. 2.

4.

MARY BROWN, da. Daniel and Esther (Fanning) Brown.
    b.   1781.   m. in 1798.   d.

William Corwin, s. Joseph and Anna (Wells) Corwin.
    b. Dec. 12, 1779.   d. Apr. 17, 1852.

10 ch. *Abner*, b. Jan. 13, 1800; m. Jan. 18, 1818, *Mary Corwin; no issue.
    6. *Anson*, b. Feb. 14, 1802; m. Aug. 23, 1817, Elizabeth Halleck.
    Epenetus, b. May 7, 1803. d. in 1806.
    7. *Epenetus H.*, b. July 8, 1807. m.   Mary B. Corwin.
    °*Elma*, b. July 5, 1810; m. Mar. 7, 1825, †Patrick McGown.
    8. *Joseph W.*, b. June 8, 1816; m. Jan. 4, 1841, Ann Maria Wells.
    Maria, b. Aug. 18, 1818.   *Arletta*, b.   m.   Israel Howell.
    Sylvester B., b. Jan. 12, 1825, d. in 1837.   *Polly A.*, b. in 1827, d. in 1828.
    Gilbert, b. Oct. 25, 1830; m.   Ann M. Carpenter.
(*) da. of Jeremiah and Jerusha (Edwards) Corwin, b. Mar. 31, 1790, d.   (°) Is dead; had 2 ch., John,
b. Mar. 1839, d. Dec. 4, 1858, and Margaret A., b. Aug. 20, 1843, d. Aug. 29, 1860.   (†) d. 1875, ae. 80.

5.

DESIRE BROWN, da. Daniel and Esther (Fanning) Brown.
    b. Dec. 6, 1782.   *m. June 6, 1803.   d. Dec. 10, 1850.

Rev. Whitfield Cowles, s. Josiah Cowles of Southington, Conn.
    b. June 3, 1764.   d. Nov. 19, 1840.

9 ch. *Madison*, b. July 22, 1804, d. Sep. 19, 1836.
    Gilbert, b. Jan. 2, 1807; m. May 12, 1869, Orpha Winchell.
    °*Sylvester D.*, b. Dec. 8, 1808; m.   Sarah Ostrander.
    Glorianna, b. Dec. 3, 1810; m. } 1st,   Dorance Mathews.
    { 2d,   Cowles.
    9. *William B.*, b. May 13, 1813; m. Dec. 24, 1834, Esther M. Harger.
    Henry Whitfield, b. May 21, 1815, d. Jan 25, 1816.   *Henry Whitfield*, b. Mar. 12, 1817; m.
    Ezra L'Hommidieu, b. Dec. 18, 1820, d. Feb. 28, 1822.
    10. *Ezra L'Hommedieu*, b. Oct. 9, 1822; m.   Wid. Eliza J.   (*nee* Wilcox).
(*) As his 2d wife. For 1st wife see Jonathan Havens genealogy, No. 31.
(°) Had 3 ch., Charles, Sarah who m. John Fleming, and Whitfield who d. in Civil War.

6.

ANSON CORWIN, s. William and Mary (Brown) Corwin.
    b. Feb. 14, 1802.   m. Aug 23, 1817.   d. Oct. 4, 1861.

Elizabeth Halleck, da. William and Lucretia (Overton) Halleck
    b.   1797   d. Mar.   1874.

7 ch. **11.** *Deborah A.,* b. May 14, 1818; m.   1836, James Downs.
  12. *George W.,* b. Jan 18, 1820; m. Feb. 11, 1846, Mary O. Howell.
  13. *Daniel A.,* b. May 20, 1822; m. { 1st, Nov. 26, 1845, Mary F. Corwin.
                { 2d, Nov. 11, 1851, Sarah M. Hallock.
    Lucretia, b. Oct. 9. 1824, d. Nov. 24, 1824.
  14. *Lucretia R. J.,* b. Feb. 7, 1827; m. about 1841, Ira W. Conklin.
  15. *Anson L.,* b. May 16, 1833; m. Jan. 26, 1856, Sarepta Edwards.
    Grotius S., b. May 30, 1838; m. Emma B. Strong.

7.

EPENETUS HAVENS CORWIN, s. William and Mary (Brown) Corwin.
  b. July 8, 1807. m. about 1830. d. Apr. 1, 1843.
 Mary B. Corwin, da. Benjamin and Sarah (Vail) Corwin.
  b. about 1805.
4 ch. *Oliver Havens,* b. m. Mar. 24, 1870, Eliza J. Tosick. *William Henry,* b.
   Benjamin Franklin, b. 1833, d. Aug. 11, 1834. *Mary Antoinette,* b. m. D. S. DeVinne.

8.

JOSEPH W. CORWIN, s. William and Mary (Brown) Corwin.
  b. June 8, 1816. m. Jan. 4, 1841.
 Ann Maria Wells, da. Thomas and Anne (Wells) Wells.
  b. Apr. 7, 1818
5 ch. *Epenetus Lester,* b. Nov. 2, 1841, d. Feb. 27, 1842. *James Barrett,* b. Oct. 22, 1842; m.
   Rose, b. Aug. 25, 1847, d. Sep. 15, 1847. *Frances Althea,* b. Feb. 9, 1850.
   William Melville, b. 185-.

9.

WILLIAM BROWN COWLES, s. Rev. Whitfield and Desire (Brown) Cowles.
  b. May 13, 1813. m. Dec. 24, 1834. d. Oct. 31, 1887.
 Esther M. Harger, da. Benjamin and Chloe (Case) Harger.
  b. Dec. 11, 1815. d. Sep. 30, 1852.
3 ch. *William Rollin,* b. Feb. 19, 1836, d. Dec. 2, 1862.
  16. *Benjamin W.,* b. July 5, 1841; m. Jan. 20, 1864, Jane Ely.
  17. *Caroline M.,* b. Nov. 13, 1843; m. Sep. 15, 1869, Charles V. Hillyer.

10.

EZRA L'HOMMEDIEU COWLES, s. Rev. Whitfield and Desire (Brown) Cowles.
  b. Oct. 9, 1822. m. d. Feb. 15, 1891.
 Wid. Eliza Jane (*nee* Wilcox), da. John and Eliza ( ) Wilcox.
  b. June 29, 1831.
3 ch. *Robert L.,* b. Apr. 3, 1863.
  18. *Charles W.,* b. Aug. 17, 1866; m. Feb. 22, 1892. Nellie A. Conklin.
   Helen M., b. Oct. 17, 1874.

11.

DEBORAH ANN CORWIN, da Anson and Elizabeth (Halleck) Corwin.
  b. May 14, 1818. m. 1836. d. Nov. 28, 1882.
 James Downs, s. David and Mehitable (Wells) Downs.
  b. d. May 1883.
1 ch. **19.** *Elizabeth Mehitable,* b. Feb. 20, 1845; m. Oct. 20, 1864, James D. Hallock.

12.

GEORGE WASHINGTON CORWIN, s. Anson and Elizabeth (Halleck) Corwin.
  b. Jan. 18, 1820. m. Feb. 11, 1846.
 Mary Ophelia Howell, da.
  b.
7 ch. *Mary E.,* b. July 30, 1847, d. Sep. 4, 1849. *Theodore F.,* b. Oct. 9, 1850.
   Rose Adel, b. Apr. 16, 1853. *Gertrude,* b. Nov. 22, 1856.
   Everett E., b. Sep. 2, 1859, d. Jan. 19, 1862. *Evelina,* b. Apr. 7, 1862. *Fanny,* b. Aug. 6, 1864.

13.

DANIEL ARDEN CORWIN, s. Anson and Elizabeth (Halleck) Corwin.
  b. May 20, 1822. m. 1st, Nov. 26, 1845. 2d, Nov. 11, 1851. d.
 1st, Mary Frances Corwin, da. Mathias and Julia A. (Corwin) Corwin.
  b. Dec. 2, 1827. d. Apr. 20, 1850.
 2d, Sarah M. Hallock, da. Madison and Harriet ( ) Hallock.
  b. May 13, 1832. d. May 24, 1897.
6 ch. *Charles M.,* b. Aug. 2, 1846; m. Dec. 14, 1872, *Henrietta Howell.
   Emma F., b. Apr. 3, 1848; m. °John C. Youngs.
   Willis M, b. Sep. 10, 1853; m. Apr. 1879, Carrie Downs. *Edwin F.,* b. Dec. 2, 1856.
   Daniel A., b. Feb. 6, 1862; m. Apr. 8, 1891, †Lizzie Brown.
   Frank, b. July 10, 1865; m. Mar. 4, 1890, ‖Annie M. Talmadge.
(*) da. of Josiah Howell. (°) s. of James W. and Ann E (Glover) Youngs, b. July 4, 1847.
(†) da. of J. Ira Brown. (‖) da. of Nathaniel and Mary F. Talmadge.

14.

LUCRETIA R. J. CORWIN, da. Anson and Elizabeth (Halleck) Corwin.
  b. Feb. 7, 1827. m. about 1841. d.
 Ira W. Conklin, s. Rodney and Sally (Wells) Conklin.
  b. May 15, 1819, d. 1887.

10 ch. **20.** *Elizabeth Jane*, b. Nov. 25, 1843; m. Jan. 5, 1863, James Deale.
   *Charles Ira, b. Jan. 3, 1846; m.   Anna Sinclair.
   21. *Mary M.*, b. Mar. 19, 1848; m.   Gilbert N. Squires.
   °Lucretia, b. Feb. 7, 1850; m.   Harland Page Fanning.
   +Melissa S. b. Dec. 7, 1853; m.   Lorenzo D. Hubbard.
   ‖Edgar A., b. Mar.   1856; m.   Belle Van Nort.
   ‡Ida, b. June 2, 1858; m.   Benjamin Brush.
   Sylvester D, b. Oct. 18. 1861; m.   Nellie Reeve.
(*) Had 7 ch., Leverett, Lilian, d., Elizabeth, Rufus, Lilian, Lucretia, Charles, d.   (°) d. 1888.   Had 4. ch., Nellie M., William P., Lina A., Elwood.   (+) d. 1896.   Had 3 ch., Leroy, d., Hessie M., Seymour, d.   (‖) Has 4 ch., Wilson, Edgar S., Ida, Hannah.   (‡) Has 2 ch., Carrie, Lora.

15.

ANSON LEANDER CORWIN, s. Anson and Elizabeth (Halleck) Corwin.
   b. May 16. 1833.   m. Jan. 26, 1856.
   Sarepta Edwards. da. Samuel and Fannie (Overton) Edwards.
   b. July 4, 1833.   d. June 5, 1885.
3 ch.   *Edward L.*, b. Feb. 15. 1858.   *Henrietta*, b. May 12, 1861.   *Jesse G.*, b. June 22, 1866.

16.

BENJAMIN WHITFIELD COWLES, s. William B. and Esther M. (Harger) Cowles.
   b. July 5, 1841.   m. Jan. 20, 1864.
   Jane Ely, da. Henry and Caroline (St. John) Ely.
   b. Aug. 16. 1841.
1 ch.   *Rollin W.*, b. May 22, 1865; m. Apr. 26, 1892, *Grace D. Perkins.
(*) da. of George and Harriett (Granger) Perkins, b. Aug. 10. 1865.

17.

CAROLINE MAY COWLES, da. William B. and Esther M. (Harger) Cowles.
   b. Nov. 13. 1843.   m. Sep. 15, 1869.
   Charles V. Hillyer, of Fernandina, Florida.
   b. Aug.   1841.
3 ch.   *Whitfield Cowles*, b. Feb. 20, 1873, d. May 4. 1897.
      Clair Richards, b. Jan.   1875.   *Charles Sherman*, b. Dec.   1879.

18.

CHARLES W. COWLES, s. Ezra L'H. and Eliza J. (   ) Cowles.
   b. Aug. 17, 1866.   m. Feb. 22, 1892.
   Nellie A. Conklin, da. John and Bridget (   ) Conklin.
   b. Mar. 22, 1868.
5 ch.   *Robert L.*, b. Jan. 17, 1893.   *Nellie*, b. Dec. 27. 1893, d. Jan. 16. 1895.
      Charles J., b. June 13. 1895, d. Sep. 16, 1895.
      Jerome W., b. Feb. 7, 1897, d. Mar. 2. 1898.   *Ruth Marion*, b. June 30, 1898.

19.

ELIZABETH MEHITABLE DOWNS, da. James and Deborah A. (Corwin) Downs.
   b. Feb. 20, 1845.   m. Oct. 20, 1864.
   James Decker Hallock, s. James and Harriet (Decker) Hallock.
   b. Feb. 16, 1842.
4 ch   *Harriet Decker*, b. Dec. 13, 1865.
      James Winfield, b. Mar. 1, 1868; m. Feb. 8, 1898, Grace A. Booth.
      Harry Downs, b. May 7. 1876.   *Deborah Elizabeth*, b. Aug. 27, 1884.

20.

ELIZABETH JANE CONKLIN, da. Ira W. and Lucretia R. J. (Corwin) Conklin.
   b. Nov. 25, 1843.   m. Jan. 5, 1863.
   James Deale, s. William   Deale.
   b. Nov. 14, 1839.
7 ch.   **22.** *William Herbert*, b. Mar. 2, 1864; m. June 28, 1893, Edith M. Corey.
      Elizabeth L., b. Oct. 7, 1866.   *Margaret M.*, b. Mar. 26, 1869.
      Caroline B., b. May 10, 1873, d. July 20, 1876.   *Leroy F.*, b. Sep. 5, 1875.
      Edith M., b. Aug. 12. 1881.   *James W.*, b. July 21. 1885.

21.

MARY M. CONKLIN, da. Ira W. and Lucretia R. J. (Corwin) Conklin.
   b. Mar 19, 1848   m.
   Gilbert N. Squires, s. Rogers and Jemima (Foster) Squires.
   b. Mar. 19, 1834.   d. Mar. 24, 1895.
2 ch.   *Erlie B.*. b. Nov. 27, 1867; m.   1895, *Susie Burr.   *Harry L.*. b. Nov. 25, 1873.
(*) da. George and Lucretia Burr, b. Apr. 19. 1876.

22.

WILLIAM HERBERT DEALE, s. James and Elizabeth J. (Conklin) Deale.
   b. Mar. 2, 1864.   m. June 28, 1893.
   Edith M. Corey, da. Robert and Harriet (Rackett) Corey.
   b. May   1865.
2 ch.   *Robert Corey*, b.   1894.   *Elizabeth*, b. Nov. 16, 1898.

ANCESTOR.

A.

BENJAMIN L'HOMMEDIEU.
  b.   1657.   m.   1694.   d. Jan. 4. 1749.

Patience Sylvester. da. Nathaniel and Grissel (Brinley) Sylvester.
  b.   1664.   d. Nov.   1719.
6 ch.   *Benjamin. b.   ·   m. { 1st,   1716, ⁰Mary Conklyn.
                                        { 2d, July 1, 1731, Martha Brown.
        †Hosea, b.   m.   1718, Freelove Howell.
        1. Sylvester, b. Jan. 5, 1703; m.   1737, Elizabeth More.   Patience, b.
        Peter, b.   m. Feb. 13, 1722, Sarah Corwin.
        |Susannah, b.   m. Feb. 22. 1722, Jonathan Tuthill.
(*) d. Sep. 17, 1755. (⁰) d. June 19. 1730. (†) d. Nov. 6, 1752. (||) Buried at Orient, also her husband.

1.

SYLVESTER L'HOMMEDIEU. s. Benjamin and Patience (Sylvester) L'Hommedieu.
  b. Jan. 5, 1703.   m.   1737.   d. Mar. 9. 1788.

Elizabeth More, da.
  b.   1704.   d. Nov. 6, 1798.
4 ch.   Elizabeth. b.   d. Sep. 6, 1754.   Giles, b.   d. Sep. 7, 1754.
        Grover, b.   m. Dec. 27, 1763, Esther Vail.
        2. Samuel, b. Feb. 20, 1744; m.   1774. Sarah White.

2.

SAMUEL L'HOMMEDIEU. s. Sylvester and Elizabeth (More) L'Hommedieu.
  b. Feb. 20, 1744.   m.   1774.   d. Mar. 7, 1834.

Sarah White, da. Charles White.
  b.   1744.   d. Nov. 18, 1822.
9 ch.   Sylvester. b.   d. unm.   Ezra, b.   d. unm.
        *Charles, b.   m. Apr. 24, 1800, Sarah Satterlee.
        ⁰Phebe, b. July 3. 1776; m. Sep. 20, 17 6, Richard Fosdick.
        Charity, b.   1780. d. Oct. 25, 1788.   Elizabeth, b. July 12. 1783, d. unm. May 27, 1861.
        Samuel, b. June 25, 1785; m. { 1st, Apr. 25, 1815, Maria C. Hildreth; } no issue.
                                      { 2d, Nov. 29, 1830, Mary B. Sayre;   }
        Sarah, b.   1789; m.   Joseph Crowell; no issue.
        3. Mary, b. Apr. 8, 1791; m. { 1st,   Nathan Cook.
                                      { 2d, Nov. 20, 1814. Rev. John D. Gardiner.
(*) Had ch., Charles W. who m. Wid. Elmira Howell, Stephen S. who m. Alma Hammond, and Richard F. who d. unm.   (⁰) See Jonathan Havens genealogy, No. 27.

3.

MARY L'HOMMEDIEU, da. Samuel and Sarah (White) L'Hommedieu.
  b. Apr. 8, 1791.   m. 1st,   as his 2d wife.   2d, Nov. 20. 1814. as his 2d wife.

1st, Nathan Cook, s. T. and P. Cook.
  b.   1790.   d. Nov. 7, 1811.

2d, Rev. John D. Gardiner, s. John and Elizabeth (   ) Gardiner.
  b. Jan. 2, 1781.   d. Sep. 13, 1849.
11 ch.   Samuel L'H., b. Sep. 3, 1815, d. Sep. 25, 1815.
        4. Samuel L'H., b. Aug. 30, 1816; m. Oct. 1, 1842, Annie Shaler.
        *John D., b. July 23, 1818; m. Aug. 17, 1846, Mary Starr.
        5. Frances M., b. June 25, 1820; m.   Henry L. Gardiner.
        6. Ezra L'H., b. Sep. 4, 1822; m. Oct. 7, 1846, Ruth Terry.
        7. Abraham S., b. July 19, 1824; m. Dec. 18, 1851, Caroline Frances Williams.
        8. Howard C., b. Sep. 17, 1826; m. { 1st, Aug. 22, 1866, Sarah Louise Crosby.
                                            { 2d, Sep. 5, 1871. Sarah Frances Urquhart.
        ⁰Sarah E., b. Oct. 11, 1828; m.   1857, Charles J. Carey; no issue.
        Henry Martin, Thomas Spencer, twins, b. Nov. 7, 1830; 1st d. May 9, 1832. 2d, d. July 30, 1831.
        Emily M., b. Apr. 18, 1833, d. Aug. 22. 1834.
(*) d. Feb. 14, 1875; had 1 ch., Charles Starr, b. June 2, 1847.   (⁰) d. Sep. 13, 1857.

4.

SAMUEL L'H. GARDINER, s. Rev. John D. and Mary (L'Hommedieu) Gardiner.
  b. Aug. 30, 1816.   m. Oct. 1, 1842.   d. Aug. 2, 1885.

Annie Shaler, da. Nathaniel and Annie (Stillwell) Shaler.
  b.   d. May 3, 1886.
5 ch. *Geraldine, b.   m.   Henry Kip.   William S., b. Dec. 27. 1843. d. Aug. 17, 1844.
        Josephine L'H., b.   d. ae. 15.   William S., b.
        John H. C., b.   m.   Hattie Burke; no issue.
(*) See Jonathan Havens genealogy, No. 91.

5.

FRANCES M. GARDINER, da. Rev. John D. and Mary (L'Hommedieu) Gardiner.
  b. June 25, 1820.   m. Mar. 1, 1843.

Henry L. Gardiner, s. Abraham H. and Hannah M. (Mulford) Gardiner.
  b. July 20, 1819.   d. Jan. 24, 1870.

2 ch.   *Marcia Bell*, b.   m.   Charles Stockweather; no issue.
     *Elizabeth, b.   m.   Arthur S. Ronkins.
(*) Has 3 ch., Florence, Gardiner and Isabel.

6.

EZRA L'H. GARDINER, s. Rev. John D. and Mary (L'Hommedieu) Gardiner.
    b. Sep. 4, 1822.   m. Oct. 7, 1846.   d. Aug. 22, 1893.
  Ruth Terry, da. Elijah and Lydia M. (Howell) Terry.
    b. Nov. 25, 1825.   d. Apr. 28, 1895.
4 ch.   *Mary L'H.*, b. May 10, 1848.   *Frank H.*, b. Sep. 11. 1850, d. Aug. 30, 1851.
    9. *Frank H.*, b. Jan 7, 1852; June 13. 1883, Helen R. Root.
    10. *Cornelius S.*, b. Dec. 28, 1863; m. Nov. 16, 1892, Ruth Kimball.

7.

REV. ABRAHAM S. GARDINER, s. Rev. John D. and Mary (L'Hommedieu) Gardiner.
    b. July 19, 1824.   m. Dec. 18, 1851.   d.   1892.
  Caroline Frances Williams, da. Roger and Maria (   ) Williams.
    b. Dec. 18, 1827.
3 ch. **11.** *Maria L'H.*, b. Nov. 29, 1852; m. Oct. 18, 1874, Charles H. Griffin.
    Julia E., b. Oct. 18, 1860, d. Aug. 26, 1882. *Irving L'H.*, b. Nov. 29, 1863, d. Jan. 5, 1888.

8.

HOWARD C. GARDINER, s. Rev. John D. and Mary (L'Hommedieu) Gardiner.
    b. Sep 17, 1826.   m. 1st, Aug. 22, 1866.   2d, Sep. 5, 1871.
  1st, Sarah Louise Crosby, da. Franklin and Ann M. (Post) Crosby.
    b. May 1843.   d. Aug. 4, 1869.
  2d, Sarah Frances Urquhart, da John and Anne F. (Carr) Urquhart.
    b. Oct. 11 1841.
3 ch.   *Adelaide L. G.*, b. Nov. 20. 1867.
    12. *Ethel*, b. Aug. 1. 1869; m. Oct. 17, 1894, Albert L. Judd. *John Urquhart*, b. Sep. 11, 1873.

9.

DR. FRANK H. GARDINER, s. Ezra L'H. and Ruth (Terry) Gardiner.
    b. Jan. 7, 1852.   m. June 13, 1883.
  Helen R. Root, da. George F. and Mary O. (Woodman) Root.
    b. Apr. 30, 1856.
5 ch.   *Lion*, b. Nov. 19, 1884.   *Alexander*, b. Dec. 9, 1886.
    Frank T., b. Jan. 19, 1889, d. Mar. 2, 1889.   *Clarence S.*, b. June 20, 1893.
    Ruth T., b. Oct. 16, 1894.

10.

CORNELIUS S. GARDINER, s. Ezra L'H. and Ruth (Terry) Gardiner.
    b. Dec. 28, 1863.   m. Nov. 16, 1892.
  Ruth Kimball, da. Henry M. and Mary F. (Palmer) Kimball.
    b. Feb. 18, 1872.
1 ch.   *Elizabeth*, b. Jan. 8, 1894.

11.

MARIA L'H. GARDINER, da. Rev. Abraham S. and Caroline F. (Williams) Gardiner.
    b. Nov. 29, 1852.   m. Oct. 18, 1874.
  Charles H. Griffin, of New York.
    b. Feb. 12, 1835.
5 ch.   *Nellie*, b. Jan. 20, 1877.   *Mabel*, b. Dec. 23, 1879.
    Edith D., b. Mar. 7, 1882. d. July 21, 1883.   *Gertrude F.*, b. July 22, 1885.
    A daughter, b. Feb. 4, 1888.

12.

ETHEL GARDINER, da. Howard C. and Sarah L. (Crosby) Gardiner.
    b. Aug 1, 1869.   m. Oct. 17, 1894.
  Albert L. Judd, s. Albert and Lucillia (Wells) Judd.
    b.   1864.
2 ch.   *Gardiner Wells*, b. Oct. 17, 1896.   *Howard Stanley*, b. June 26, 1898.

HALL.

1.

REV. DANIEL HALL, s. Jonathan and Alice (   ) Hall.
    b. Sep. 19, 1747.   m.   d. Jan. 20, 1812.
  Lucretia   da.
    b.   1749.   d. Sep. 4, 1825.
5 ch.   *Jonathan*, b. 1775-6, d. Aug. 12, 1837.
    *Lucretia, b.   m. Feb. 21, 1822, °David Brown; no issue.
    2. *Sophronia*, b. May 17, 1783; m. July 21, 1822, Charles Douglas.
    Mary, b. 1785-6, d. unm. Feb. 10, 1831.   *William*, b.   d. (?) unm.   1860-1.
(*) m. as his 2d wife.   (°) d. Mar. 21, 1835, ae. 51.

2.

SOPHRONIA HALL, da. Rev. Daniel and Lucretia (   ) Hall.
b. May 17, 1783.   m. July 21, 1822.   d. Jan. 5, 1852.
Charles Douglas, s. Nathan and Anna (Dennis) Douglas.
b. Dec. 13, 1768.   d. Jan. 14, 1850

2 ch.   **3.** *Daniel Hall.* b. Jan. 12. 1824; m. Dec. 26, 1844, Frances M. Latham.
    4. *Charles Carroll.* b. May 8, 1826; m. May 23, 1853, Henrietta Edwards.

3.

DANIEL HALL DOUGLAS. s. Charles and Sophronia (Hall) Douglas.
b. Jan. 12, 1824.   m. Dec. 26, 1844.   d. Mar. 4, 1867.
Frances Mary Latham, da. Peleg and Sarah (Crowell) Latham.
b. Dec. 30, 1823.   d. May 25, 1893.

4 ch.   **5.** *William Hall,* b. June 19, 1846; m. Oct. 27, 1880, Fannie Maria Griffin.
    Alden Spooner, b. Jan. 6, 1849.
    6. *Helen Latham.* b. June 21, 1851; m. Oct 23. 1878, William H. Stevenson.
    Sophronia, b. Dec. 5, 1853; m. Jan 12, 1893, *Hiram Sherrill.
(*) s. of Hiram L. and Mary A. (Miller) Sherrill, b Apr. 16, 1853.

4.

CHARLES CARROL DOUGLAS. s. Charles and Sophronia (Hall) Douglas.
b. May 8, 1826.   m. May 23. 1853.   d. June   1884.
Henrietta Edwards, da. John and Deborah (Penny) Edwards.
b. July 16, 1833.

4 ch.   **7.** *Henrietta Huntington,* b. June 22, 1854; m. July 5, 1876, Ezra N. Seeley.
    Isabelle Hall, b. Nov. 5, 1855; m. Aug. 29, 1853, *Henry Hoyt Perry.
    Fannie. b. Dec. 6, 1863.
    8. *Arthur Edwards,* b. July 11, 1868; m. June 22. 1897, Effie Belle Curtis.
(*) s. of Oliver H. and Harriet (Hoyt) Perry, b. 1848.

5.

WILLIAM HALL DOUGLAS, s. Daniel H. and Frances M. (Latham) Douglas.
b. June 19, 1846.   m. Oct. 27. 1880.
Fanny Maria Griffin, da. Jesse and Leah (Williams) Griffin.
b. Jan. 23, 1853.

3 ch.   *Helen L.,* b. July 28, 1881.   *Jesse L.,* b. Apr. 11, 1885.
    William H., b. June 25. 1889, d. Mar. 30, 1893.

6.

HELEN LATHAM DOUGLAS, da. Daniel H. and Frances M. (Latham) Douglas.
b. June 21, 1851.   m. Oct. 23, 1878.
William Henry Stevenson, s. Dr. William and Sarah (Coulter) Stephenson.
b. May 29, 1848.

4 ch.   *William Douglas,* b. Feb. 9, 1881.   *Alden Palmer,* b. Aug. 3, 1883.
    Henry Gordon, b. July 31. 1885.   *Helen,* b. Feb. 16, 1888.

7.

HENRIETTA HUNTINGTON DOUGLAS, da. Charles C. and Henrietta (Edwards) Douglas.
b. June 22. 1854.   m. July 5. 1876.
Ezra N. Seeley, s. Morgan and Sarah (Northup) Seeley.
b. Apr, 4, 1854.

3 ch.   *Isabelle D.,* b. May 9, 1877.   *Rheta N.,* b. May 9. 1880, d. July 31. 1898.
    Douglas S., b. Mar. 10, 1896.

8.

ARTHUR EDWARDS DOUGLAS, s. Charles and Henrietta (Edwards) Douglas.
b. July 11. 1868.   m. June 22, 1897.
Effie Belle Curtis, da. Theron S. and Kate D. (Clarke) Curtis.
b.

1 ch.   *Dorothy Katherine,* b. Aug. 11. 1898.

DOUGLASS.

1.

JONATHAN DOUGLASS, of New London, Conn.
b. Aug. 31, 1765.   m. May 31, 1795.   d. Sep. 30, 1840.
Abigail Lay, of Lyme Town, Conn.
b. Mar. 6, 1773.   d. Aug. 11, 1821.

6 ch.   **2.** *Josiah,* b. Apr. 17. 1796; m. Sep. 20, 1820, Eliza A. Williams.
    3. *Abigail Lay,* b. Oct. 20, 1798; m. May 24, 1826, Dr. William Terbell.
    4. *Hepsibah P.,* b. Sep. 8. 1801; m. Apr. 27, 1826, Caleb S. Loper.
    5. *Juliann,* b. June 12. 1805; m. Mar. 7, 1832, Jeremiah King.
    6. *Charles G.,* b. Oct. 28, 1810; m. Dec. 11, 1833, Nancy A. Tabor.   A twin, d. in infancy.

2.

JOSIAH DOUGLASS, s. Jonathan and Abigail (Lay) Douglass,
    b. Apr. 17, 1796.   m. Sep. 20, 1820.   d. Feb. 5, 1869.

Eliza Augusta Williams, of Stockbridge, Mass.
    b. June 18. 1797.   d. Jan. 25, 1872.

5 ch.   *Lafayette*, b. Dec. 20, 1823, m. Jan 1, 1850, *Jane White; no issue.
        Pulaski H., b. Oct. 25, 1825, d. unm.; a twin, d. in infancy.
        Adalinda Eliza, b. Feb. 2, 1829, d. unm. June 25. 1892. *Amelia Augusta*, b. Apr. 15, 1835.
(*) da. John and Bertha (Reeves) White.

3.

ABIGAIL LAY DOUGLASS, da. Jonathan and Abigail (Lay) Douglass.
    b. Oct. 20, 1798.   m. May 24, 1826.   d. Oct. 20, 1870.

Dr. William Terbell, s. William and Mary (Baker) Terbell.
    b. Feb. 14, 1798.   d. June 3, 1880

2 ch. **7.** *William D.*, b. Dec. 28. 1828, m. { 1st, May 1, 1851, Selina N. Robinson.
                                       { 2d, Oct. 16, 1871, Mary C West.
                                         { 3d, June 12, 1888, Irene C. King.
        Henry Stokes, b. June 19, 1838, d. Jan. 25, 1841.

4.

HEPSIBAH P. DOUGLASS, da. Jonathan and Abigail (Lay) Douglass.
    b. Sep. 8, 1801.   m. Apr. 27, 1826.   d. Aug. 16, 1855.

Caleb S. Loper, s. Caleb and Mary (Squires) Loper.
    b. Dec. 8, 1802.   d. Oct. 3, 1860.

4 ch. **8.** *Marcellus D.*, b. May 1, 1827; m. Nov. 30, 1858, Mary S. Horton.
      9. *Adeline E.*, b. Nov. 18, 1828; m. Oct. 8, 1850, David Williamson.
    10. *Fidelia G.*, b. Nov. 24, 1833; m. Jan. 1, 1857. John H. Manwaring.
        Mary Frances, b. Oct. 20, 1839; m. Jan. 6, 1867, *Danforth Beebe; no issue.
(*) s. of Isaiah and Pamelia (Kenney) Beebe, b Sep. 9, 1836.

5.

JULIANN DOUGLASS. da. Jonathan and Abigail (Lay) Douglass.
    b. June 12, 1805.   m. March 7, 1832.   d. Mar. 25, 1885.

Jeremiah King. s. Jeremiah and Mary (Sanford) King.
    b. Oct. 25, 1804.   d. Oct. 25, 1874.

3 ch. **11.** *Charles D.*, b. Aug. 25, 1833; m. { 1st, Mar. 17, 1857, Sarepta A. Moger.
                                   { 2d, Dec. 24, 1866, Margaret R. Martin.
      Cornelius, b. Aug. 18, 1836; m { 1st, Oct. 7, 1861, ‖Eliza A. Wiggins.
                                  { 2d,   Sarah F. Smith.
        Annie A., b. Feb. 3, 1843; m. Jan. 29, 1879, °Howard M. Jerome; no issue.
(*) Had 1 ch., Freddie P., b. Jan. 26, 1863, d. Aug. 12, 1879.
(‖) da. of Albert and Lydia (Youngs) Wiggins, b. Nov. 20, 1838, d. Apr. 22, 1875.
(°) s. of Augustus and Harriet (Terry) Jerome, b. July 17, 1849.

6.

CHARLES G. DOUGLASS. s. Jonathan and Abigail (Lay) Douglass.
    b. Oct. 28. 1810.   m. Dec. 11, 1833.

Nancy Ann Tabor. da. Pardon T. and Nancy A. (L'Hommedieu) Tabor.
    b. June 4, 1813.

8 ch. **12.** *Julia Ann*, b. Sep. 11, 1834; m. { 1st, Jan. 7, 1854, John W. Ripley.
                                 { 2d, Oct. 16. 1877, George B. Brown.
    13. *Maria G.*, b. Oct. 11, 1836; m. May 12, 1858, Epenetus F. Wheeler.
        Nancy L'H., b. Jan. 8. 1839.
        Charles G., b. June 1, 1842; m. Oct. 8, 1868, ‖Mary R. Brown.
    14. *Pardon T.*, b. Dec. 20, 1844; m. { 1st, Dec. 11. 1869, Georgiana Davis.
                               { 2d, Nov. 16, 1880, Annie B. Arnold.
        Mary Alice, b. Aug. 6, 1847.
    15. *Abby Lay*, b. July 10, 1851; m. June 10, 1875. Clarence L. Carter.
        Frank W., b. Aug. 22, 1855; m. { 1st, Dec. 23, 1880, +Mary E. Gilbert; } no issue.
                                 { 2d, Oct. 10, 1891, °Bertha Lyon; }
(*) d. Feb. 2. 1887, had 1 ch., George L., b. Oct. 9. 1869, d. Apr. 3, 1897.
(‖) da. Daniel and Eliza (Farr) Brown.
(+) da. of William and Rachael E. (Erwin) Gilbert, b. June 16, 1856, d. Nov. 21, 1881.
(°) da. of Bernado and Cordelia (Pratt) Lyon, b. Feb. 24. 1864. d. Mar. 18, 1893.

7.

WILLIAM D. TERBELL, s. William and Abigail L. (Douglass) Terbell.
    b. Dec 28. 1828.   m. 1st, May 1, 1851.   2d, Oct. 16, 1871.   3d, June 12, 1888.

1st, Selina North Robinson, da. Lemuel and Mary (Phelps) Robinson.
    b. Apr. 22, 1825.   d. Sep. 21, 1870.

2d, Mary Caroline West, da. Richard West.
    b.   d. Aug. 19, 1883.

3d, Irene C. King, da. W. Clinton and Mary (   ) King.
    b.

8 ch. *William Henry*, b. July 28, 1855. *George Robinson*, b. May 4, 1857, d. May 12, 1857.
    Edward Douglass, b. Nov. 27, 1858, d. Jan. 29, 1860.
    Robert Witson, b. Mar. 21, 1861; m.   Kate Osborn; no issue.
    Josephus Bodine, b. Feb. 12, 1863.
16. *Abby Douglass*, b. Mar. 30, 1865; m. Sep. 15, 1886, Edward D. Gardner.
    Charles Douglass, b. Oct. 16, 1867, d.   *Albert Niles*, b. Nov. 20, 1869.

8.

MARCELLUS D. LOPER, s. Caleb S. and Hepsibah P. (Douglass) Loper.
    b. May 1, 1827.   m. Nov. 30, 1858.   d. Dec. 11, 1895.
Mary S. Horton, da. Jonathan and Mary B. (Glover) Horton.
    b. Feb. 1, 1836.

3 ch. 17. *Ernest Caleb*, b. July 22, 1861; m. Oct. 26, 1889, Ida L. Rogers.
    18. *William D.*, b. May 22, 1866; m. { 1st, Dec. 23, 1890, Esther A. Tuthill.
                                { 2d, Dec. 30, 1896, Lillian M. Duvall.
    Arthur C., b. June 21, 1868.

9.

ADELINE E. LOPER. da. Caleb S. and Hepsibah P. (Douglass) Loper.
    b. Nov. 18, 1828.   m. Oct. 8, 1850.   d. Aug. 5, 1896.
David Williamson, s. James and Patty (Wines) Williamson.
    b.   d.

4 ch.   *Martha Wines*, b. Sep. 2, 1851.   *James*, b.
    *Julia Douglass, b. Apr. 7, 1853; m.   ║Julius Phelps.
    °*Bessie Woodhull*, b. Oct. 14. 1867; m. June 5. 1895, Frederick W. Hallock.
(*) Had 8 ch., Ruth, Bertha, Amy, Ethel, Willard and 3 others.   (║) s. of David B. Phelps.
(°) See Hudson genealogy, No. 150.

10.

FIDELIA D. LOPER. da. Caleb S. and Hepsibah P. (Douglass) Loper.
    b. Nov. 24, 1833.   m. Jan. 1, 1857.
John H. Manwaring. s. Charles D. and Elizabeth (Hughes) Manwaring.
    b. Dec. 12, 1834.

4 ch.   *Frank L.*, b. Mar. 6. 1858; m. Sep. 1. 1881, *Matilda Millard; no issue.
    19. *Charles D.*, b. Oct. 24. 1861; m Mar. 11. 1886. Mary E. Lewis.
    20. *H. Genevieve*, b. Oct. 9, 1863; m. Nov. 25. 1887. John S. Edwards.
    Addy M., b. May 3, 1871.
(*) da. of James and Eliza Millard.

11.

CHARLES D. KING, s. Jeremiah and Juliann (Douglass) King.
    b. Aug. 25, 1833.   m. 1st, Mar. 17, 1857.   2d, Dec. 24, 1866.
1st, Sarepta A. Moger, da. Henry and Catherine (Tuthill) Moger.
    b. Mar. 9, 1836.   d. Mar. 6, 1861.
2d, Margaret R. Martin, da.
    b.   1839.   d. July 30 1895.

4 ch.   *Fannie D.*, b. May 5, 1858; m. Jan. 2, 1888. *Albert C. Youngs; no issue.
    Lulu, b. Jan. 12, 1868; m. Apr. 14, 1891, °Charles F. Bevins; no issue.
    Cora A., b. Oct. 12, 1873.   *Herbert*, b. Jan. 29, 1876.
(*) s. of John B. and Amanda K. (Wines) Youngs, b. Jan. 8, 1858.
(°) s. of Silas and Louise (Freed) Bevins.

12.

JULIA ANN DOUGLASS, da. Charles G. and Nancy A. (Tabor) Douglass.
    b. Sep. 11, 1834.   m. 1st, Jan. 7, 1854.   2d, Oct. 16. 1877.
1st, John Wesley Ripley, s. Thomas and Elizabeth (Darling) Ripley.
    b. Apr. 7, 1825.   d. Aug. 7, 1876.
2d, George Beckwith Brown. s. Silas and Mary (Tooker) Brown.
    b. July 23, 1810.   d. Mar. 3, 1896.

2 ch. 21. *Elizabeth C.*, b. Jan. 6, 1856; m. Sep. 25, 1877, Gilbert A. Halsey.
    *John W. D., b. Feb. 5, 1870; m. Sep.   1896, Eleanor Orr.
(*) Has 1 ch., Eleanor Orr, b. July 19, 1897.

13.

MARIA GERTRUDE DOUGLASS, da. Charles G. and Nancy A. (Tabor) Douglass.
    b. Oct. 11, 1836.   m. May 12. 1858.
Epenetus F. Wheeler, s. Thomas and Eliza (Bunce) Wheeler.
    b. Nov. 9, 1834.   d. Mar. 21, 1894.

3 ch.   *Annie D.*, b. Dec. 2, 1859.
    Gertrude E., b. Aug. 7, 1864; m. Oct. 4, 1880, Henry H. Rogers.
    Eliza B., b. Jan. 24, 1871; m. July 3. 1893, Joseph P. Lowry.

14.

PARDON TABOR DOUGLASS, s. Charles G. and Nancy A. (Tabor) Douglass.
    b. Dec. 20, 1844.   m. 1st, Dec. 11, 1869.   2d, Nov. 16, 1880.
1st. Georgiana Davis of Rockland, Maine.
    b.   d.
2d. Annie Bell Arnold, da. John and Lydia (Havens) Arnold.
    b Sep. 30, 1861.

4 ch.   *William B.*, b. Apr. 16, 1871, d. Aug. 31, 1888.   *Rose W.*, b. Jan. 2, 1882.
    Alice F., b. Apr. 23, 1887.   *Guy Clifford*, b. Sep. 8, 1892.

15.

ABBY LAY DOUGLASS, da. Charles G. and Nancy A. (Tabor) Douglass.
    b. July 10, 1851.   m. June 10, 1875.

Clarence L. Carter, s. James and Harriet (Lenord) Carter.
    b.
2 ch.   *Harry L.*, b. Sep. 1876.   *Charles D.*, b. Aug. 1, 1878.

16.

ABBY DOUGLASS TERBELL, da. William D. and Selina N. (Robinson) Terbell.
    b. Mar. 30, 1865.   m. Sep. 15, 1886.

Edward D. Gardner, s. Horace B. and Caroline R. (Beach) Gardner.
    h. June 30, 1854.
3 ch.   *Margorie W.*, b. Apr. 24, 1887.   *Edwina D.*, b. Mar. 5, 1893.   *Alice C.*, b. July 30, 1894.

17.

ERNEST CALEB LOPER, s. Marcellus D. and Mary S. (Horton) Loper.
    b. July 22, 1861.   m. Oct. 26, 1889.

Ida L. Rogers, da William and Hannah W. (Sutton) Rogers.
    b. Dec. 31, 1862.
2 ch.   *Arthur D.*, b. Jan. 31, 1891.   *Chester E.*, b. Apr. 3, 1893.

18.

WILLIAM D. LOPER, s. Marcellus D. and Mary S. (Horton) Loper.
    b May 22, 1866.   m. 1st, Dec. 23, 1890.   2d, Dec. 30, 1896.

1st, Esther A Tuthill, da. John S. and Harmony M. (Penny) Tuthill.
    b. May 20, 1866.   d. Jan. 8, 1893.

2d, Lillian M. Duvall, da. George W. and Elmira J. (Jennings) Duvall.
    b. Aug 14, 1872.
1 ch.   *Lillian T.*, b. Nov. 24, 1892.

19.

CHARLES D. MANWARING, s. John H. and Fidelia P. (Loper) Manwaring.
    b. Oct. 24, 1861.   m. Mar. 11, 1886.

Mary Evalina Lewis, da. John and Augusta (   ) Lewis
    b.
4 ch.   *Leroy*, b. Feb. 22, 1887.   *Ethel*, b. Aug. 23, 1889.
        Edward L., b. Apr. 9, 1891, d. July 4, 1895.   *Charles D.*, b. Nov. 12, 1896.

20.

H. GENEVIEVE MANWARING, da. John H. and Fidelia P. (Loper) Manwaring.
    b. Oct. 9, 1863.   m. Nov. 25, 1887.

John S. Edwards, s. Jonathan and Emaline S. (Shepard) Edwards.
    b. in 1850.
3 ch.   *Pauline*, b. Nov. 2, 1889.   *May*, b. May 27, 1891.   *Frank H.*, b. July 28, 1893.

21.

ELIZABETH C. RIPLEY, da. John W. and Julia A. (Doughlass) Ripley.
    b. Jan. 6, 1856.   m. Sep. 25, 1877.

Gilbert A. Halsey, s. Ledyard and   Halsey.
    b.
3 ch.   *Grace R.*, b. July 2, 1878.   *Bertie*, b. Feb. 14, 1881, d.   *Henry Clay*, b. July 16, 1889.

EPHRAIM AND MEHITABLE KING.

1.

EPHRAIM KING, s.
    b.   m.   d. July 8, 1820.
Mehitable   da.
    b.   1736.   d. Feb. 2, 1809.
1 ch.   **2.** *Mehitable*, b   m.   Jonathan Reeve.

2.

MEHITABLE KING, da. Ephraim and Mehitable (   ) King.
    b.   m.
Jonathan Reeve, s.
    b.
11 ch.   **3.** *Elmira*, b. Apr. 22, 1806; m. June 2, 1829, Christian E. Myer.   *Harriet*, b.
        Parmela, b.   *Elisa Ann*, b.   *Philena*, b.   *Nancy Maria*, b.   *Watson*, b.
        Orran, b.   *Mary A.*, b.   (these were all bap. Oct. 2, 1816) and three others.

3.

ELMIRA REEVE, da. Jonathan and Mehitable (King) Reeve.
  b. Apr. 22, 1806.   m. June 2, 1829.   d. Dec. 3, 1888.
Christian E. Myer, of England.
  b. Oct. 10, 1805.   d. Oct. 12, 1876.
5 ch.   *Mary Elmira, b. Sep. 18, 1830; m. Sep. 15, 1847, Philetus Havens.
  4. Harriet Sayre, b. Nov. 15, 1833; m. Sep. 20, 1853, Elija J. Hutchinson.
  5. John Washington, b. Nov. 14, 1837; m. Feb. 26, 1869, Mary E. Howell.
    Elmira, b.   d. in infancy.   A boy, b.   d. in infancy.
(*) See Jonathan Havens genealogy, No. 61.

4.

HARRIET SAYRE MYER, da. Christian E. and Elmira (Reeve) Meyer.
  b. Nov. 15, 1833.   m. Sep. 20, 1853.
Elijah J. Hutchinson, s. Elijah J. and Arminda (Overton) Hutchinson.
  b. Oct. 13, 1830   d.
3 ch.   Frank Leslie, b. Apr. 6, 1855, d. unm. June 15, 1880.   Nettie D., b. Apr. 22, 1866.
  6. Frederick E., b. Apr. 10, 1868; m. July 3, 1895, Ella I. Horton.

5.

JOHN WASHINGTON MYER, s. Christian E. and Elmira (Reeve) Myer.
  b. Nov. 14, 1837.   m. Feb. 26, 1869.
Mary E. Howell, da.   and Marietta (Smith) Howell.
  b.
5 ch.   Bessie S., b.
    *Charlotte H., b.   m Sylvester Field.   °Marietta H., b.   m. William DeCastro.
    Herbert M., b.   d. in infancy.   Alice D., b.   d. in infancy.
(*) Has 1 ch.   (°) Has 2 ch.

6.

FREDERICK E. HUTCHINSON, s. Elijah J and Harriet S. (Myer) Hutchinson.
  b. Apr. 10, 1868.   m. July 3, 1895.
Ella I. Horton, da. Alexander B. and Jennette D. (Moore) Horton.
  b. June 18, 1860.
1 ch.   Leroy F., b. Feb.   1898.

MAYO.

1.

THOMAS MAYO, s. Josiah and   (   ) Mayo.
  b.   1756-7.   m. as his 2d wife   d. June 3, 1818.
Mary Ary, da.
  b.   1758-9.   d. Mar. 20, 1841.
7 ch.   *Mary, b.   m. Aug. 2, 1801, David Havens.
  2. Susannah, b. Aug. 23, 1785; m. Apr. 26, 1810. Daniel Talmage.
  3. Sally, b.   m. Sep. 26. 1814, Samuel Creary.
    Elizabeth, b. June 20, 1791, d. Sep. 29, 1800.
  4. Oliver, b. July 5, 1793; m. Oct. 2, 1815, Roxanna Case.
  5. Josiah, b. Aug. 30, 1795; m. May 7, 1815, Arminda Vail.
  6. Isaac, b.   m.   Keziah or Desire King.
(*) See Jonathan Havens genealogy, No. 17.

2.

SUSANNAH MAYO, da. Thomas and Mary (Ary) Mayo.
  b. Aug. 23, 1785.   m. Apr. 26, 1810.   d. Feb. 16, 1858.
Daniel Talmage, s. Stephen Talmage of Easthampton, L. I.
  b. July 22, 1784.   d. Oct. 3, 1858.
9 ch. **7.** Stephen Sanford, b. Sep. 4, 1813; m. June 12, 1838. Julia Ann Strong.
    Mary Avery, b. Oct. 13. 1815, d. Mar. 21, 1817.   Mary Ann, b. May 19, 1818, d. May 5, 1874.
    George Washington, b. July 18. 1820. d. Aug. 7. 1820.
        { 1st, June 8, 1847, Mary Frances Bill.
  8. George Washington, b. July 13, 1821; m. { 2d, Nov. 17. 1869, Wid. Mary Howard.
        { 3d, Oct.   1889, Jane Wheeler.
    Isaac Newton, b. May 7, 1823. d. May 31. 1853. John Milton, b. Apr. 5. 1825, d. Aug. 8, 1850.
  9. Betsey Susannah, b. Sep. 20, 1829; m. May 29, 1849, Charles W. Corwith.
    Phebe Sanford, b. Mar. 29. 1832; m.   George Goodale.

3.

SALLY MAYO, da. Thomas and Mary (Ary) Mayo.
  b.   m. Sep. 26, 1814.   d.
Samuel Creery, s.
  b.   d.

MAYO.

5 ch.   *Thomas*, b.   m.   *Samuel*, b.   d. at sea.   *Gardner*, b.
      °*Sarah*, b.   1819; m.   Stephen Hedges.
    10. *Elizabeth*, b.   1821; m.   Caleb Eldridge.
(*) Had 2 ch , William and Mary. (°) Had 2 ch., Samuel, b.   1849. d.   1896; and Edwin, b. 1854;
     m. Lucy Hoxie.

4.

OLIVER MAYO, s. Thomas and Mary (   ) Mayo.
    b. July 5, 1793.   m. *Oct. 2, 1815.   d. Sep.   1836.
Roxanna Case, da. Gillum and Esther (Hand) Case.
    b. Aug. 28, 1793.   d. Feb. 17, 1863.
3 ch.   *Oliver Case*, b. Jan. 14, 1817, killed by Indians in 1849.
         °*Caroline C.*, b. Jan. 26, 1819; m. June   1845, †Thomas P. Ripley; no issue.
         Thomas, b. Feb. 4, 1822, d. Feb. 24, 1824.
(*) As her 2d husband. See Johnathan Havens genealogy, No. 55. (°) d. Nov.   1852.
(†) s. of Thomas and Elizabeth (Darling) Ripley, b. Apr. 8, 1821, d. June 10, 1888.

5.

JOSIAH MAYO, s. Thomas and Mary (   ) Mayo.
    b. Aug. 30, 1795.   m. May 7, 1815.   d. Feb. 22, 1861.
Arminda Vail, of Southold, L. I.
    b. Mar. 9, 1795.   d. Dec. 28, 1860.
8 ch. 11. *Josiah R.*, b. Apr. 21, 1816; m. June 22, 1849, Phebe Benjamin.
    12. *Mary J.*, b. July 14, 1818; m. Dec. 20. 1836, Benjamin L. Hallock.
       *Thomas, b. Nov. 12, 1820; m. °Mary J. Reeves.
       Luther Osborn, b.   d. Apr. 12, 1823.   *Isaac*, b. Feb.   1824, d. March 5. 1824.
    13. *Charlotte Ann*, b. Aug. 13, 1825; m. Feb. 17. 1848, George W. Howard.
    14. *Arminda L.*, b. Sep. 10, 1833; m. Oct. 9, 1861, Ira C. Corwin.
    15. *Electa J.*, b. Jan. 11, 1836; m. Oct. 12, 1853, Cornelius Stryker.
(*) d. Feb. 23, 1881, had 2 ch., an infant who d., and Mary M., b. Apr. 5, 1847, d. Feb. 13. 1862.
(°) d. Mar. 19, 1896, ae. 70.

6.

ISAAC MAYO, s. Thomas and Mary (.   ) Mayo.
    b.   m.   d. before 1809.
*Keziah or Desire King, da.
    b. July 8, 1788.   d. May 12, 1852.
2 ch.   *Eliza*, b. Aug. 3, 1803; m.   Green.
       °*Lettice S.*, b. Aug. 14, 1805; m. Aug. 16, 1828, William Case.
(*) See Case genealogy, No. 3.   (°) d. Sep. 16, 1832.   See Case genealogy, No. 1.

7.

STEPHEN SANFORD TALMAGE, s. Daniel and Susannah (Mayo) Talmage.
    b. Sep. 4, 1813.   m. June 12, 1838.   d. May 26, 1868.
Julia Ann Strong, da. Thomas and   (Sanford) Strong.
    b.   d.
4 ch. **Edwin L.*, b. Sep. 25, 1844; m.   Sarah Black.
    16. *Charles T.*, b.   1846; m. Jan. 12, 1870, Elizabeth Edwards,
       Daniel S., b. Mar. 19, 1850, d. July 9, 1850.   *Susan D.*, b. Apr. 21, 1852, d. Apr. 26, 1852.
(*) Had 2 ch., Charles who d.. and Ada.

8.

GEORGE WASHINGTON TALMAGE, s Daniel and Susannah (Mayo) Talmage.
    b. July 31, 1821.   m. 1st, June 8, 1847. 2d, Nov. 17, 1869. 3d, Oct.   1889.   d. July 11, 1896.
1st, Mary Frances Bill, da.
    b. Aug. 26, 1829.   d. Nov. 8, 1868.
2d, Wid. Mary Howard (*nee* Rouviere), da.
    b. in 1825.   d. Sep. 9, 1888.
3d, Jane Wheeler, da. Joshua and Ann M. (Chappell) Wheeler.
    b.
5 ch. *Frances Jane, b. Sept. 6, 1849; m.   George R. Harrison.
       George Washington, b. May 27, 1857, d. Nov. 24, 1869.
    17. *Daniel Webster*, b. Nov. 10, 1854; m. Mar. 10, 1888, Ann E. Gordon.
    18. *Henry Seymour*, b. July 29, 1858; m. Oct. 19, 1888, Mary E. Ranger.
    19. *De Witt Clinton*, b. June 23, 1861; m. Oct. 18, 1888, Mary E. Hedges.
(*) Had 7 ch., Ella, Frank, George and four others.

9.

BETSEY SUSANNAH TALMAGE, da. Daniel and Susannah (Mayo) Talmage.
    b. Sep. 20, 1829.   m. May 29, 1849.   d. May 20, 1888.
Charles W. Corwith, s. James and Harmenia (Goodale) Corwith.
    b. Jan. 19, 1821.   d. Oct. 29, 1883.
2 ch. 20. *Charles B.*, b. Feb. 12, 1855; m.
    21. *Lillian M.*, b. Dec. 20, 1862; m. Oct. 3, 1882, Henry E. Phillips.

10.

ELIZABETH CREERY, da.   and Sally (Mayo) Creery.
   b. 1821. m.

Caleb Eldridge, s.   (   ) Eldridge.
   b.   1803.   d.   1880.
2 ch. *Emily G., b.   1848 m. Nov. 17, 1898, Henry E. Phillips.
    †Juliet E , b.   1849; m.   V. E. Lawrence.
(*) See No. 21.   (†) Has 2 ch.. Emily G. and Ruth E.

11.

JOSIAH R. MAYO, s. Josiah and Arminda (Vail) Mayo.
   b. Apr. 21, 1816.   m. June 22, 1839.   d. Feb. 26, 1895.

Phebe Benjamin, da. Ezra and Phebe (Terry) Benjamin.
   b. July 18. 1817   d. Mar. 1, 1895.

7 ch. **22.** Oliver A., b. Mar. 29, 1840; m. Oct. 8, 1868, Julia F. Webb.
     Addison F., b. Jan. 23. 1842, d. Dec. 4, 1856.
   23. Phebe A., b. Feb. 10, 1844; m. Dec. 18, 1862, George E. Webb.
   24. Arabella M., b. July 20, 1846; m. Feb. 7, 1866, Thomas J. Conkling.
   25. Ellen W., b. Oct. 3, 1851; m. Oct. 31, 1869. George W. Young.
     Francis R., b. Aug. 6, 1854, d. Dec. 7, 1856.
   26. Charles A., b. June 12, 1860; m. Dec. 19, 1888, Matilda M. Robinson.

12.

MARY J. MAYO, da. Josiah and Arminda (Vail) Mayo.
   b. July 14, 1818.   m. Dec. 20, 1836.   d. July 25, 1890.

Benjamin L. Hallock, s. Benjamin and Deborah (Wells) Hallock.
   b. Jan. 6, 1812.   d. Aug. 18, 1895.

10 ch. Mary F., b. June 18, 1838, d. Feb. 27, 1847.
   27. Electa M., b. July 23, 1840; m. Dec. 30, 1856, Elijah Hallock.
   *Patience A., b. Nov. 11, 1842; m. Dec. 29, 1868, Henry V. Downs.
     Lawrens S., b. June 20, 1845. d. June 25, 1845.
   28. Rosaline E., b Aug. 20, 1846; m. Nov. 14, 1865, John W. Woodhull.
     George H'., b. May 23, 1849, d. June 3, 1849.
   29. Mary F.. b. June 15, 1850; m. Nov. 28. 1871, George C. Cooper.
     °Deborah J., b. June 25. 1853; m. Dec. 8, 1880. Milford T. Benjamin.
   30. George O., b. Sep. 16, 1855; m. Dec. 25, 1882, Ella M. Benjamin.
     Lawrens O., b. Aug. 31, 1859, d. Feb. 12, 1860.
(*) Has 1 ch., John G., b. Aug. 20, 1873.   (°) See Hudson genealogy, No. 240.

13.

CHARLOTTE ANN MAYO, da. Josiah and Arminda (Vail) Mayo
   b. Aug. 13, 1825.   m. Feb. 17, 1848.   d. Sept. 13, 1893.

George W. Howard, s. George H. and Letitia (Campbell) Howard.
   b. June 2, 1821.

5 ch. **31.** George Henry, b. Nov. 7, 1848; m. Dec. 16. 1880. Eva J. Reeve.
   32. Samuel M., b. Feb. 18, 1851; m. Feb.   1873, Frances E. Cox.
     Bethual H., b. Dec. 11, 1852.   Letitia C., b. Feb. 20, 1855.
     Arminda V., b. Oct. 17, 1857, d. Mar. 2, 1884.
     Mary E., b. Feb. 17, 1860; m. Aug. 6, 1889, *Edward Clarke.
(*) s. of John M. and Elizabeth (Miller) Clark, b. June 25, 1854.

14.

ARMINDA L. MAYO, da Josiah and Arminda (Vail) Mayo.
   b. Sept. 10, 1833.   m. Oct. 9, 1861.

Ira Case Corwin, s. Jabez and Christina (Skidmore) Corwin.
   b. Aug. 6, 1827.   d. June 2, 1870.

2 ch. Ira Linwood, b. Sep. 13, 1862. d. Oct. 2, 1866.
     Thomas Mayo, b. June 17, 1866, d. Sep. 26, 1874.

15.

ELECTA J. MAYO, da. Josiah and Arminda (Vail) Mayo.
   b. Jan. 11, 1836.   m. Oct. 12, 1853.   d. July 19, 1861.

Cornelius Stryker, s. Samuel G. and Sarah A. (Hart) Stryker.
   b. July 20, 1826.   d. Sep. 22, 1863.

1 ch. **33.** Frances, b. Oct. 1, 1854; m. Nov. 15, 1882, Dr. James R. Latham.

16.

CHARLES T. TALMAGE, s. Stephen S. and Julia A. (Strong) Talmage.
   b.   1846.   m. Jan 12, 1870.

Elizabeth Edwards, da. Lewis S. and Emeline (Pierson) Edwards.
   b. Nov. 18, 1849.

1 ch. Frank M., b. Apr. 24, 1872.

17.

DANIEL WEBSTER TALMAGE, s. George W. and Mary F. (Bill) Talmage.
    b. Nov. 10. 1854.   m. Mar. 10, 1888.

Annie E. Gordon, da J. Homer and Kate (Rice) Gordon.
    b. Apr. 3. 1859.

1 ch.   *George Gordon*, b. July 9, 1889, d. Aug. 19, 1889.

18.

HENRY SEYMOUR TALMAGE, s. George W. and Mary F. (Bill) Talmage.
    b. July 29, 1858.   m Oct. 19, 1888.

Mary E. Ranger. da. Alfred D. and Charlotte (Parsons) Ranger.
    b. July 2, 1863.

1 ch.   *May Dimon*, b. Nov. 24, 1889, d. Oct. 11, 1890.

19.

DEWITT CLINTON TALMAGE, s. George W. and Mary F. (Bill) Talmage.
    b. June 23, 1861.   m. Oct. 18. 1888.

Mary E. Hedges, da. Albert L. and Mary (Edwards) Hedges.
    b.

2 ch.   *Marion*, b. June 10, 1892.   *Clara Hedges*. b. June 15, 1895.

20.

CHARLES B. CORWITH, s. Charles W. and Betsey S. (Talmage) Corwith.
    b. Feb. 12, 1855.   m.

    b.

8 ch.   **Anna B.*, b. Apr. 23, 1876; m. } 1st, 2d.   *Gracie M.*, b. Oct. 2, 1877.
    Fred Willis, b. Feb. 28, 1879.   *Lillian Mayo*, b. Dec. 30, 1880, d. Aug. 28, 1887.
    Jennie C., b. Apr. 8, 1882; m. Hildreth. *James*, b. June 5, 1884. One or two more ch
(*) Has 2 ch.

21.

LILLIAN MAYO CORWITH, da. Charles W. and Betsey S (Talmage) Corwith.
    b. Dec. 20, 1862.   m. Oct. 3, 1882.   d. Apr. 16, 1896.

Emily G. Eldridge, da. Caleb and   (   ) Eldridge.
    b.   1848.   m. Nov. 17, 1898.

Henry E. Phillips. s. Moses S. and Rosabell (Payne) Phillips.
    b. July 20, 1858.

4 ch.   *H. Eckford*, b. Apr. 25, 1888.   *Samuel H.*, b. Oct. 23, 1891.
    Lillian C., b. Aug. 16, 1893.   *Ruth Rosabell*, b. Apr. 10, 1896

22.

OLIVER A. MAYO, s. Josiah R. and Phebe (Benjamin) Mayo.
    b. Mar. 29 1840.   m. Oct. 8, 1868.

Julia F. Webb, da. Benjamin E. and Betsey A. (Dewitt) Webb.
    b. June 6, 1852.

3 ch.   *Amanda W.*, b Feb. 6, 1870, d. Mar. 24, 1870.   *Florence L.*, b. June 26, 1873.
    Oliver Emlen, b. May 26, 1880. d. June 11, 1880.

23.

PHEBE A. MAYO, da. Josiah R. and Phebe (Benjamin) Mayo.
    b. Feb. 10, 1844.   m. Dec. 18, 1862.   d. June 24, 1876.

George E. Webb, s. Benjamin E. and Betsey A. (Dewitt) Webb.
    b.

3 ch.   *George D.*, b. Oct. 9, 1863.   *Annie B.*, b. May 7, 1869.   *Edith G.*, b. Oct. 3, 1873.

24.

ARABELLA M. MAYO, da. Josiah R. and Phebe (Benjamin) Mayo.
    b. July 20, 1846.   m. Feb. 7, 1866.

Thomas J. Conklin, s. Platt and Mehitable (Moore) Conklin.
    b. June 29, 1841.

3 ch.   *Norman C.*, b. May 24, 1870; m. Dec 22, 1897 *Minnie Couch.
    George, b. July 5, 1876, d. July 6, 1876.   *Irene Mayo*, b. Mar. 12, 1890, d. July 18, 1890.
(*) da. Samuel J. and Laura (Mumford) Couch, b. Mar. 17, 1875.

25.

ELLEN W. MAYO, da. Josiah R. and Phebe (Benjamin) Mayo.
    b. Oct. 3, 1851.   m. Oct. 31, 1869.

George H. Young, s. Joshua C. and Mary A. (Jennings) Young.
    b. Mar. 8, 1847.

8 ch.   *George E.*, b. Aug. 19, 1870, d Sep. 8, 1878. *Addison T.*, b. Jan. 17, 1872, d. Nov. 24, 1882.
    34. *Ella May*, b. Apr. 3, 1874; m. Feb. 14, 1894, Robert M. Russell.
    Phebe Anna, b. July 12, 1877. *Leonard E.*, b. Aug. 19, 1879. *Mary E.*, b. Feb. 5, 1882.
    George W. and *Addison B.* (twins), b. July 21, 1886.   *Lewis L.*, b. Aug. 12, 1889.

26.

CHARLES A. MAYO, s. Josiah R. and Phebe (Benjamin) Mayo.
  b June 12, 1860.   m. Dec. 19, 1888.
  Matilda M. Robinson, da. Perry S. and Anne E. (Raynor) Robinson.
      b. June 16. 1868.
    3 ch. *Leland Ray*, b. Oct. 25, 1890.   *Phebe Benjamin*, b. Aug. 11. 1895.
           Walter Carlisle. b. May 16, 1897.
27.

ELECTA M. HALLOCK, da. Benjamin L. and Mary J. (Mayo) Hallock.
  b. July 23, 1840.   m. Dec. 30, 1856.
  Elijah Hallock, s. Micah and Puah (Brown) Hallock.
      b. Sep. 2. 1831.   d. Oct. 20. 1893.
    2 ch. *Lawrence W.*. b. June 18, 1860.
           Millicent E., b. Aug. 4, 1874; m. June 19, 1895, °William H. B. DuMont.
  (*) d. s. p. Oct. 15, 1897.   (°) s. of Andrew T. and Susan E. (Halleck) DuMont, b. Apr. 2. 1870.
28.

ROSALENE E. HALLOCK, da. Benjamin L. and Mary J. (Mayo) Hallock.
  b. Aug. 20, 1846.   m. Nov. 14, 1865.
  John W. Woodhull, s. John and Caroline (Miller) Woodhull.
      b.
    2 ch. *Ellennietta*, b. Aug. 28, 1866; m. Dec. 15, 1886, John M. Hallock.
      35. *Timothy M.* b. Apr. 6, 1872; m. Nov. 25. 1893, Maud V. Albertson.
  (*) See Hudson genealogy, 271.
29.

MARY F. HALLOCK. da. Benjamin L. and Mary J. (Mayo) Hallock.
  b. June 15, 1850.   m. Nov. 28, 1871.
  George C. Cooper, s. George W. and Martha (Corwin) Cooper.
      b. Feb. 10, 1852.
    1 ch. *Ida R.*, b. Apr. 6, 1874; m. Nov. 27, 1895, *Henry L. Fleet.
  (*) s. of Henry L. and Sarah J. (Betts) Fleet, b. Jan. 27, 1870
30.

GEORGE OMAR HALLOCK, s. Benjamin L. and Mary J. (Mayo) Hallock.
  b. Sep. 16, 1855.   m. Dec. 25, 1882.
  Ella May Benjamin, da. Simeon O. and Adelia J. (Hallock) Benjamin.
      b. Aug. 27, 1859.
    2 ch. *Leland Omar*, b. Aug. 5, 1884, d. May 31. 1885.   *Norma Vivian*, b. July 8, 1886.
31.

GEORGE H. HOWARD, s. George W. and Charlotte A. (Mayo) Howard.
  b. Nov. 7, 1848.   m. Dec. 16, 1880.
  Eva Jeanette Reeve, da. James F. and Mary E. (Wines) Reeve.
      b. July 16, 1854
    1 ch. *Clara Madison*, b. Oct. 28, 1882.
32.

SAMUEL M. HOWARD, s. George W. and Charlotte A. (Mayo) Howard.
  b. Feb. 18, 1851.   m. Feb.   1873.   d. Dec. 10, 1881.
  Frances E. Cox, da. Andrew and Sarah J. (Cox) Cox.
      b.
    2 ch. **36.** *Louis I*, b. Apr. 14. 1874; m. June 11, 1893, Lillian E. Lane.   *Helen C.*, b. Feb. 13, 1877.
33.

FRANCES STRYKER, da. Cornelius and Electa J. (Mayo) Stryker.
  b. Oct. 1, 1854.   m. Nov. 15. 1882.
  Dr. James R. Latham, s. George and Ellen (Ryder) Latham.
      b. Mar. 24, 1855.
    5 ch. *Royal F.*, b. Mar. 8, 1885.   *James R.*, b. July 1, 1886, d. Oct. 7, 1887.
           George W., b. July 2, 1888.   *Irving R*, b. Apr. 10, 1892.   *Frances*, b. Feb. 17, 1898.
34.

ELLA MAY YOUNG, da. George H. and Ellen W. (Mayo) Young.
  b. Apr. 3, 1874.   m. Feb. 14, 1894.
  Robert M. Russell, s. Alexandria and Maria (Myers) Russell.
      b. June 16, 1870.
    1 ch. *Robert E.*, b. Aug. 12, 1895.
35.

TIMOTHY M. WOODHULL, s. John W. and Rosalene E. (Hallock) Woodhull.
  b. Apr. 6, 1872.   m. Nov. 25, 1893.
  Maud V. Albertson, da. Richard and Sarepta (Aldrich) Albertson.
      b. July 20, 1873.
    2 ch. *Ellennietta*, b. Sep. 29, 1895.   *Dorothy*, b. June 29, 1897.

36.

Louis I. Howard, s. Samuel M. and Frances E. (Cox) Howard.
  b. Apr. 14, 1874. m. June 11, 1893.
Lillian E. Lane, da. Andrew B. and Martha J. (Wines) Lane.
  b. Apr. 20, 1869.
2 ch. *Agnes Mayo*, b. Apr. 5, 1894. *Hazel Cox*, b. May 10, 1896.

CASE AND BOISSEAU.

ANCESTORS.

A.

Samuel Case, s. Henry and Tabitha (   ) Case.
  b. in 1637. d. May 10, 1755.
Zeriah Horton, da. Joshua and Mary (Tuthill) Horton.
  b.
12 ch. *William*, b. in 1713; m. Oct. 31, 1734, Anna Cleveland.
  B *Samuel*, b.   m. Dec. 17, 1741, Esther Budd.
  Joshua, b.   m. Mar. 23, 1736, Deliverance Wells.
  Israel, b.   m. { 1st, Nov. 24, 1761, Eunice King.
                             { 2d, June 16, 1792, Wid. Mary Hart.
  Moses, b. in 1723; m. Feb. 23, 1749, Mary Hutchinson.
  Elizabeth, b.   m. Nov. 23, 1738, Joshua Hobert.
  Zeriah, b.   m Apr. 26, 1739, Joseph Corwin.
  Bethiah, b.   m. June 5, 1735, Joel Bowditch.
  Mary, b.   m. May 7, 1744, William Reeve,
  Rhoda, b.   m. Dec. 2, 1750. James Clark.
  Sarah, b. in 1732; m. Oct. 20, 1749, David Youngs.
  Martha, b.   m. { Dec. 10, 1758, Abner Wells, or
                             { May 4. 1762, Thomas Overton.
(*) See Bowditch genealogy, No. 2.

B.

Samuel Case, s. Samuel and Zeriah (Horton) Case.
  b.   m. Dec. 17. 1741. d. Sep. 17, 1783.
Esther Budd, da.
  b.
7 ch. *Esther*, b.   m. in 1764, David Talmage.
  1. *Samuel*, b.   m. Mar. 17, 1768, Eunice Glover.
  2. *Gillum*, b. 1751-2; m.   Esther Hand.
  Mary, b.   m.   John Bowditch.   *Sarah*, b.   m.   Samuel Stratton.
  †*Anna*, b. Aug. 6, 1759; m. June 24, 1783, ○John Boisseau.
  A child, b.   d. Apr. 3. 1772.
(*) d. Dec. 8, 1817. See Bowditch genealogy, No. 6.
(†) d. s. p. Aug. 8, 1817. (○) s. of John and Hannah Vail, b. Feb. 23, 1759, d Jan. 14, 1835.

1.

Samuel Case, s. Samuel and Esther (Budd) Case.
  b.   m. Mar. 17, 1768. d. Sep. 25, 1784.
Eunice Glover, da.
  b.   d. Feb. 23, 1819.
5 ch. *William*, bap. in 1765; m. Aug. 16, 1828, *Lettice Mayo.
  ○*Jemima*, bap. Oct. 29, 1769; m.   Ezekiel Havens.
  Esther, bap. in 1772, d. (?) unm.   *Samuel*, b.   d. Sep. 17, 1783,
  3. *Jeremiah*, b. Oct. 14, 1782; m. { 1st, May 7, 1803, Abigail Dickerson.
                                           { 2d, July 27, 1809, Wid. Keziah Mayo.
(*) See Mayo genealogy, No. 6.   (○) See Jonathan Havens genealogy, No. 20.

2.

Gillum Case, s. Samuel and Esther (Budd) Case.
  b in 1751-2. m.   d. Apr. 29, 1835.
Esther Hand, da.   and Abigail (   ) Hand.
  b. in 1754-5. d. June 21, 1831.
5 ch. 4. *Jacob*, b. June 23, 1782; m. Jan. 2, 1810, Hannah Horton.
  Samuel, b.   d. in infancy.
  5. *Samuel*, b. in 1786-7; m. { 1st, Nov. 18, 1813, Cynthia Reeve.
                                     { 2d   Lydia M. Cartwright.
  6. *Nancy*, b. Jan.   1792; m. Feb. 20, 1816, Jonathan Osborn.
  Roxanna, b. Aug. 28, 1793; m. { 1st, May 10, 1810, Ezekiel Havens.
                                       { 2d, Oct. 2, 1815, Oliver Mayo.
(*) See Jonathan Havens genealogy, No. 55. Also Mayo genealogy, No. 4.

3.

JEREMIAH CASE, s. Samuel and Eunice (Glover) Case.
     b. Oct. 14. 1782.   m. 1st, May 7, 1803.   2d, July 27, 1809.   d. Apr. 8, 1846.
1st, Abigail Dickerson, da.
     b.   d. Jan. 27, 1807.
2d, Wid. Keziah Mayo (*nee* King).
     b. July 8, 1778.   d. May 12, 1852.
4 ch.   **7.** *Abigail M.*, b. Apr. 21. 1811; m. Nov. 15. 1827, Nathaniel Case.
        **Isaac M.*, b. Jan. 13, 1813; m.   1834, Fanny Hallock.
        Jeremiah, b. Mar. 11, 1815, d. Apr. 12, 1815.
        Harriet N., b. June 14, 1818, d. unm. Oct. 18, 1842.
(*) 1 ch., Betsey.

4.

JACOB CASE, s. Gillum and Esther (Hand) Case.
     b. June 23, 1782.   m. Jan. 2, 1810.   d. Oct. 25, 1850.
Hannah Horton, da. Jonathan and Abigail (Horton) Horton.
     b. Mar. 10, 1792.   d. Jan. 1, 1876.
2 ch.   **8.** *Esther Ann*, b. Oct. 24, 1811; m. Aug. 23, 1834, Alfred H. Sanford.
        **Jonathan Horton*, b. in 1816-7; m. May   1840, °Elizabeth Dickinson; no issue.
(*) d. at sea, Apr. 11, 1841.   (°) d. in 1855.

5.

SAMUEL H. CASE, s. Gillum and Esther (Hand) Case.
     b. in 1786-7.   m. 1st, Nov. 18, 1813.   2d,   d. Apr. 17, 1864.
1st, Cynthia Reeve, da.   (   ) Reeve.
     b.   d.
2d, Lydia M. Cartwright, da. Anderson and Cynthia (Payne) Cartwright.
     b. in 1799-1800.   d. Mar. 23, 1878.
9 ch.   *George H.*, b.   d. unm.
        9. *Henry*, b. Feb. 10, 1815; m. June 10, 1843, Mary Ann Ross.
        10. *Arabella*, b. Dec. 10, 1827; m. Jan. 20, 1850, Samuel W. Sherman.
        **Mary Jane*, b. Oct. 5. 1829; m. June 21, 1853, John B. Bowditch.
        11. *Julia A.*, b. Oct. 27, 1831; m.   1854, William R. Duvall.
        °*Josephine*, b. Mar. 28. 1833; m. Apr. 28, 1856, David C. Osborn.
        ‖*Hannah*, b. Mar. 28, 1836; m. May 31, 1859, †Malby S. Payne.
        Kate Nicoll, b. May 28, 1838.   *Samuel*, b June 23. 1841, d. unm.
(*) See Bowditch genealogy. No. 20.   (°) See No. 11.   (‖) d. s. p. Aug. 6, 1888.
(†) s. of Selah and Elsie Payne, b. Mar. 1, 1820, d. Dec. 10, 1884.

6.

NANCY CASE, da. Gillum and Esther (Hand) Case.
     b. Jan.   1792.   m. Feb. 20, 1816.   d. Mar. 11, 1867.
Jonathan Osborn, s. Jonathan and Hetty (Van Scoy) Osborn.
     b. Oct. 21, 1791.   d. Jan. 9, 1872.
7 ch.   **12.** *David C.*, b. Jan. 16, 1817; m. Apr. 28, 1856, Josephine Case.
        13. *Mary*, b. July 25, 1823; m. May 12, 1840, Joel Tuthill.
        Jonathan N., b. May   1825, d. unm.
        14. *Hiram G.*, b. May   1827; m. Oct. 17, 1866, Nancy C. Tuthill.
        15. *Henry P.*, b. May 17, 1829; m. Oct. 23, 1853, Mary F. Barnes.
        16. *Esther*, b. July 25, 1831; m. July 26. 1849, William C. Pye.
        **Margaret*, b. Sep. 23, 1836; m.   William Strong.
(*) d. Oct. 3, 1859; had 2 ch., William who m. Estelle Rogers, and John who d. ae. 15.

7.

ABIGAIL MARIA CASE, da. Jeremiah and Keziah (King) Case.
     b. Apr. 21, 1811.   m. Nov. 15, 1827.   d. Sep. 14, 1848.
Nathaniel Case, s. Joseph and Hannah (   ) Case.
     b.
2 ch.   **17.** *Helen M.*, b. Mar. 7, 1831; m. June 9, 1851, S. Wells Phillips.
        18. *Nathaniel*, b.   m. Dec.   1855, Harriet Miller.

8.

ESTHER ANN CASE, da. Jacob and Hannah (Horton) Case.
     b. Oct. 24, 1811.   m. Aug. 23. 1834.   d. Nov. 12, 1885.
Alfred H. Sanford, s. Hezikiah and Prudence (Halsey) Sanford.
     b. Dec. 23, 1803.   d. Oct. 30, 1869.
4 ch.   *Annie Howell*, b. Nov. 25, 1835; m. Mar. 21, 1879, Melville B. Eggleston; no issue.
        Alfred H., b. July 4, 1842, d. 1844.   *Alfred C.*, b. June 23, 1847, d. unm. Sep. 22, 1870.
        **Ella E.*, b. Apr. 19, 1852; m. Dec. 6, 1871, Arthur S. Cartwright.
(*) See Conkling genealogy, No. 14.

9.

HENRY CASE, s. Samuel H. and Cynthia (Reeve) Case.
     b. Feb. 10, 1815.   m. June 10, 1843.   d. Jan. 14, 1887.
Mary Ann Ross, da. Henry and Nancy (Lane) Ross.
     b. Feb. 10, 1825.   d. Feb. 6, 1897.

3 ch. **19.** *Charles A.*, b. Feb. 8, 1845; m. June 1, 1871, Maria A. Sherman.
  Napoleon M., b. Mar. 3, 1850, d. Mar. 2, 1855.
  *Eva Geen, b. Jan. 12, 1853; m. Jan. 20, 1872, Charles M. Fenton.
(*) See John Havens genealogy, No. 98.

10.

ARABELLA CASE, da. Samuel H. and Lydia H. (Cartwright) Case.
 b. Dec. 10, 1827 or 8. m. Jan. 2, 1850, as his 2d wife.† d. Sep. 1, 1896.
Samuel W. Sherman, s. Livingston and   (Edwards) Sherman.
 b. June 22, 1813. d. July 6, 1866.

3 ch. **20.** *Mary Ludlum*, b. Apr. 4, 1851; m. June 25, 1873, Charles Bateman.
  **Julia C.*, b. Jan. 16, 1857; m. Sep. 1, 1880, °Louis B. Congdon.
  |*Belle Brandon*, b. Sep. 19, 1858; m. Feb. 20, 1877, Frank P. Conklin.
(*) d. s. p. Dec. 16. 1885. (°) s. of Timothy P. and Amanda (Bennet) Congdon, b. Oct. 18, 1852.
(‡) See Jonathan Havens genealogy, No. 241. (†) See Conkling genealogy No. 5.

11.

JULIA A. CASE, da. Samuel H. and Lydia H. (Cartwright) Case.
 b. Oct. 27, 1831. m. d. June 28, 1863.
William R. Duvall, of North Haven, Long Island.
 b. Mar. 26, 1826. d. Sep. 8, 1882.

1 ch. **21.** *William R.*, b. Oct. 23, 1858; m. Jan. 16, 1883. Annie M. Cooper.

12.

DAVID C. OSBORN, s. Jonathan and Nancy (Case) Osborn.
 b. Jan. 16, 1817. m. Apr. 28, 1856. d. Mar. 24, 1886.
Josephine Case, da. Samuel H. and Lydia H. (Cartwright) Case.
 b. Mar. 28, 1823. d. July 22, 1886.

3 ch. *Davis Walker*, b. Feb. 11, 1857; m. Oct. 22, 1895, *Alice Raynor.
  22. *Maggie*, b. May 15, 1870; m. Dec. 30, 1889, Frederick Dickerson.
  °*Mary J.*, b. May 10, 1873; m. in 1890, W. Cortland Wade.
(*) da. David and Maria L. (Ross) Raynor, b. Feb. 3, 1876. (°) See Tuthill genealogy, No. 54.

13.

MARY OSBORN, da. Jonathan and Nancy (Case) Osborn.
 b. July 25, 1823. m. May 12, 1840.
Joel Tuthill, s. Joshua and Hannah (Aldrich) Tuthill.
 b. Mar. 27, 1816.

4 ch. *Nancy Case, b. Apr. 10, 1842; m. Oct. 17, 1866, Hiram G. Osborn.
  23. *Mary Ellen*, b. Apr. 5, 1844; m. Apr. 27, 1868, Edgar Daniels.
  Anna Elizabeth, b. Sep. 20, 1851.
  24. *John Henry*, b. July 13. 1857; m. Nov. 29, 1881, Laura D. Norton. (*) See No. 14.

14.

HIRAM G. OSBORN, s. Jonathan and Nancy (Case) Osborn.
 b. May 1827. m. Oct. 17, 1866.
NANCY CASE TUTHILL da. Joel and Mary (Osborne) Tuthill.
 b. Apr. 10, 1842.

2 ch. *Everett*, b. Aug. 1, 1867. *Edith M.*, b. Nov. 26, 1872.

15.

HENRY P. OSBORN, s. Jonathan and Nancy (Case) Osborn.
 b. May 17, 1829. m. Oct. 23, 1853. d. Mar. 20, 1887.
Mary F. Barnes, da. David and Phebe (Schellinger) Barnes.
 b. Mar. 16, 1829.

1 ch. **25.** *Phebe E.*, b. Sep. 15, 1857; m. Mar. 30, 1880, Joseph C. Cousins.

16.

ESTHER OSBORN, da. Jonathan and Nancy (Case) Osborn.
 b. July 25, 1831. m. July 26, 1849.
William C. Pye, s. John and Catherine (Conklin) Pye.
 b. Apr. 11, 1826.

7 ch. **26.** *William H.*, b. June 4, 1850; m. Sep. 19, 1870, Fanny G. Tuthill.
  Elizabeth, b. Jan. 28, 1853; m. June 22, 1891, George Hill; no issue.
  **Mary E.*, b. Jan. 27, 1855; m. { 1st, July 4, George Bradt.
            { 2d,   David A. Brown.
  Ada, b. Feb. 23, 1857; m. Oct. 1873, Olin F. Miller; no issue.
  Edwin O., b. June 26, 1859, d. Feb. 23, 1878.
  °*Ernest L.*, b. July 28, 1862; m. Annie Stafford.
  |*Wallace V.*, b. Oct. 10, 1864; m. Apr. 26, 1896, Wynnifred Cole.
(*) Has 3 ch., Bessie, Leta and Ada, all m. (°) Has 5 ch. (|) Has 1 ch. named Arthur.

17.

HELEN M. CASE, da. Nathaniel and Abigail M. (Case) Case.
 b. Mar. 7, 1831. m. June 9, 1851.
S. Wells Phillips. s. Samuel and Jane (Chapman) Phillips.
 b. Feb. 1, 1827.

1 ch. **27.** *Frank L'H.*, b. Jan. 10, 1857; m. Nov. 18, 1879, Anna L. Tuthill.

18.

NATHANIEL CASE, s. Nathaniel and Abigail M. (Case) Case.
b.   m. Dec.   1855.   d.

Harriet Miller, da. David and Clara (Isaacs) Miller.
b. Nov. 18, 1831.   d.   1874.

2 ch. **28.** *Helen P.,* b. Oct. 12, 1863; m. Nov. 26, 1884, G. Frank Tuthill.
     29. *Louis M.,* b. Feb. 10, 1865; m. in. 1888. Bertha J. Bennett.

19.

CHARLES ALEXANDER CASE, s. Henry and Mary A. (Ross) Case.
b. Feb. 8, 1845.   m. June 1, 1871.

Maria A. Sherman, da. Joseph E. and Phebe E. (Downs) Sherman.
b. Jan. 24, 1856.

3 ch. **30.** *Mabel Lature,* b. Oct. 5, 1873; m. Jan. 29, 1895, Thomas M. Phillips.
     31. *Cora Lee,* b. July 1, 1875; m. Jan. 30, 1895, Frederick B. Hallock.
     Ernest A., b. July 27, 1886.

20.

MARY LUDLUM SHERMAN, da. Samuel W. and Arabella (Case) Sherman.
b. Apr. 4, 1851.   m. June 25, 1873.

Charles Bateman, s. Horatio and Margaret (Creighton) Bateman.
b. Feb. 22, 1848.

1 ch.   *Julia S.,* b. Apr. 25, 1887, d. May 8, 1887.

21.

WILLIAM R. DUVALL, s. William R. and Julia A. (Case) Duvall.
b. Oct. 23, 1858.   m. Jan. 16, 1883.

Annie May Cooper, da. George W. and C. Martha (Corwin) Cooper.
b. July 12, 1861.

3 ch.   *Clarence Case,* b. Feb. 11. 1887.   *Stanley Cooper,* b. Jan. 24, 1890.
        Ellis Siedel, b. Nov. 22, 1893.

22.

MAGGIE OSBORN, da. David C. and Josephine (Case) Osborn.
b. May 15, 1870.   m. Dec. 30, 1889.

Frederick Dickerson, s. Nathaniel and Louise B. (Simpson) Dickerson.
b. Sep. 4, 1864.

1 ch.   *Louise Belle,* b. June 23, 1891.

23.

MARY ELLEN TUTHILL, da. Joel and Mary (Osborn) Tuthill.
b. Apr. 5, 1844.   m. Apr. 27, 1868.

Edgar Daniels, s. William and Angeline (Robinson) Daniels.
b. Nov. 27, 1844.

2 ch.   *Mary Angeline,* b. Jan. 22, 1871.   *Grace Tuthill,* b. Sep. 27, 1878.

24.

JOHN HENRY TUTHILL, s. Joel and Mary (Osborn) Tuthill.
b. July 13, 1857.   m. Nov. 29, 1881.

Laura Davis Norton, da. Richard A. and Laura (Davis) Norton.
b.

2 ch.   *Maud Graham,* b. Apr. 7, 1883.   *Raymond Davis,* b. Oct. 17, 1885.

25.

PHEBE E. OSBORN, da. Henry P. and Mary F. (Barnes) Osborn.
b. Sep. 15, 1857.   m. Mar. 30, 1880.

Joseph C. Cousins, s. John C. and Rachel J. (Davis) Cousins.
b. Feb. 8, 1858.

1 ch.   *Mary E. O.,* b. Mar. 1, 1898.

26.

WILLIAM H. PYE, s. William C. and Esther (Osborn) Pye.
b. June 4, 1850.   m. Sep. 17, 1870.

Fanny G. Tuthill, da. Cephus and Sarah (Cooper) Tuthill.
b. Mar. 8, 1850.

2 ch.   *Elizabeth M.,* b. Feb. 18, 1873.   *Edward A.,* b. July 13, 1883.

27.

FRANK L'HOMMEDIEU PHILLIPS, s. S. Wells and Helen M. (Case)Phillips.
b. Jan. 10, 1857.   m. Nov. 18, 1879.

Anna L. Tuthill, da. George F. and Hannah (Webb) Tuthill.
b. Jan. 10, 1860.

2 ch.   *Ella L.,* b. Jan. 5, 1882.   *Georgianna W.,* b. July 24, 1890.

28.

HELEN P. CASE, da. Nathaniel and Harriet (Miller) Case.
  b. Oct. 12, 1863.   m. Nov. 26, 1884.
  G. Frank Tuthill, s. George F. and Hannah (Webb) Tuthill.
  b. Nov. 7, 1864.
  2 ch.   *Hattie M.*, b. June 16, 1887.   *Anna M.*, b. Mar. 8, 1892, d. Mar. 3, 1895.

29.

LOUIS MILLER CASE, s. Nathaniel and Harriet (Miller) Case.
  b. Feb. 10, 1865.   m. in 1888.
  Bertha J. Bennett, da. Abner and Esther F. (Conklin) Bennett.
  b. Aug. 10, 1870.
  4 ch.   *Helen Miller*, b. July 16, 1889.   *Madelene Esther*, b. Dec. 14, 1893.
          Louis Nathaniel, b. July 22, 1895.   *Marian Tuthill*, b. Jan. 31, 1897.

30.

MABEL LATURE CASE, da. Charles A. and Maria A. (Sherman) Case.
  b. Oct. 15, 1873.   m. Jan. 29, 1895.
  Thomas M. Phillips, s. Mahlon and Mary E. (Colver) Phillips.
  b. Aug. 22, 1873.
  1 ch.   *Ella Ethelyn*, b. Feb. 19, 1896.

31.

CORA LEE CASE, da. Charles A. and Maria A. (Sherman) Case.
  b. July 1, 1875.   m. Jan. 30, 1895.
  Frederick B. Hallock, s. Henry M. and Mary J. (Tuthill) Hallock.
  b. Aug. 4, 1870.
  2 ch.   *Aubrey Crawford*, b. Dec. 23, 1896.   *Oswald Roosevelt*, b. June 20. 1898.

MRS. ABIGAIL SAWYER.

1.

BENJAMIN SAWYER, s. (?) Moses and Mehitable (Horton) Sawyer.
  b.   m. Mar. 25, 1787.   d. July 18, 1794, or Sep. 8, 1802.
  Abigail King, da. John and Abigail (Brown) King.
  b.   1762.   d. July 11, 1843.
  3 ch.   Cynthia, b.   m.   David Jennings; no issue.
          James B., b.   m.
       2. *Mehitable A.*, b. Apr. 9, 1794; m. Oct. 1, 1818. Abraham Crook.
  (*) Had 1 ch., James who m. Wid. Maria Fournier (*nee* Fithian).

2.

MEHITABLE A. SAWYER, da. Benjamin and Abigail (King) Sawyer.
  b. Apr. 9, 1794.   m. Oct. 1, 1818.   d. Dec. 21, 1874.
  Abraham Crook, s. Samuel and Jemima (   ) Crook.
  b. Dec. 6, 1787.   d. Mar. 29, 1875.
  7 ch.   *Abby M.*, b. July 9, 1819, d. unm. Feb. 9, 1852.
          Gabriel B., b. Apr. 10, 1821; m. May 2, 1844, *A. E. Tryon; no issue.
       3. *John B.*, b. Sep. 17, 1823; m. Sarah Corwin.   *James S.*, b. Sep. 11, 1825, d. Nov. 1, 1826.
          Sylvester J., b. Oct. 1, 1827, d. Mar.   1852.   *Ezra*, b.   1832, d. Nov. 2, 1836.
       4. *Mary L.*, b. July 5, 1834; m. Dec. 21, 1854, Charles W. Jennings.
  (*) da. of Joel and Nancy Tryon, b. Aug. 26, 1823, d. Sep. 30, 1892.

3.

JOHN B. CROOK, s. Abraham and Mehitable A. (Sawyer) Crook.
  b. Sep. 17, 1823.   m.   d. Dec. 6, 1849.
  Sarah J. Corwin, da. Seth and Sarah (Post) Corwin.
  b. May 22, 1831.
  1 ch.   *Sarah Jane*, b.   m.   Halsey.

4.

MARY L. CROOK, da. Abraham and Mehitable A. (Sawyer) Crook.
  b. July 5, 1834.   m. Dec. 21, 1854.   d. Mar. 6, 1862.
  Charles W. Jennings, s. James and Cynthia (   ) Jennings.
  b. Apr. 21, 1835.
  1 ch.   *Gilbert S.*, b. Feb. 14, 1860; m. Apr. 21, 1886, Annie W. Preston.

5.

GILBERT SYLVESTER JENNINGS, s. Charles W. and Mary L. (Crook) Jennings.
  b. Feb. 14, 1860.   m. Apr. 21, 1886.
  Annie Wright Preston, da. Henry H. and Asenath W. (Congdon) Preston.
  b. Dec. 16, 1864.
  1 ch.   *Harold*, b. Oct. 6, 1890.